£15·00

I0945382

LABOR AND THE CONSTITUTION
1972 — 1975

The dismissal of the Whitlam Government on 11 November 1975 caused a ferment not only within Australia, but among lawyers and politicians in parliamentary systems around the world. The Australian Constitution was pored over as never before as observers strove, usually without much success, to understand how such an extraordinary event could have happened.

November 1975 was an extraordinary climax to what had been, in fact, an extraordinary three years. During the life of the Labor Government not a week seemed to pass without a constitutional crisis or controversy of some kind or other erupting: the Gair affair, the first double dissolution, the referendum campaigns, the resignation of Speaker Cope, the electoral boundaries cases, the appointment of Senator Murphy to the High Court, the loans affair, the Senate casual vacancy controversies . . . not to mention the series of major clashes between the Commonwealth and the States over the alleged trespass of Whitlam centralism into the State domain in areas like mining policy, social welfare, legal aid, the environment and human rights.

No single volume, however distinguished its contributors, or however dispassionate its marshalling of the arguments, can do complete justice to the complexity and variety of the constitutional issues raised during the Whitlam period. Certainly it cannot finally resolve the continuing dispute about the behaviour of the Senate and Governor-General in bringing down the Government. But the essays and commentaries assembled in this book, many of them written by leading participants in the dramas they describe, are indispensable reading for anyone seeking to understand the Whitlam period, and for anyone anxious to ensure that such divisive events do not occur again.

Labor and the Constitution
1972 - 1975

Essays and Commentaries on the
Constitutional Controversies
of the Whitlam Years
in Australian Government

Edited by
GARETH EVANS

HEINEMANN HEA MELBOURNE
LONDON

National Library of Australia
cataloguing-in-publication data:

Labor and the constitution 1972-1975.

 Index.
 ISBN 0 85859 146 4.
 ISBN 0 85859 147 2 Paperback.
 ISBN 0 435 83250 6 (HEB London)

 1. Australia. Constitution—Addresses, essays, lectures.
 2. Australia—Politics and government—1972-1975—
 Addresses, essays, lectures. I. Evans, Gareth J., ed.

342.9402

Published by Heinemann Educational Australia Pty Ltd, 85 Abinger Street, Richmond,
Victoria 3121. Computer photocomposed by Computer Graphics Corporation Pty Ltd,
Adelaide. Printed and bound at The Griffin Press, Adelaide.

Contents

Notes on Contributors

PETER BAYNE   Senior Lecturer in Legal Studies, La Trobe University. Formerly Legal Counsel to the House of Assembly and Constitutional Consultant to the Government of Papua New Guinea.

A.R. BLACKSHIELD   Associate Professor of Law, University of New South Wales.

PATRICK BRAZIL   First Assistant Secretary, Advisings Division, Australian Attorney-General's Department.

M.H. BYERS, Q.C.   Solicitor-General of Australia

ENID CAMPBELL   Sir Isaac Isaacs Professor of Law, Monash University. Member of the Royal Commission on Australian Government Administration. Books include *Parliamentary Privilege in Australia.*

HON. J.L. CARRICK   Minister for Education and Minister Assisting the Prime Minister in Federal Affairs. Senator for New South Wales and formerly State Secretary, N.S.W. Liberal Party.

A.C. CASTLES   Professor of Law, University of Adelaide. Member of the Australian Law Reform Commission. Books include *Introduction to Australian Legal History.*

MICHAEL COPER   Senior Lecturer in Law, University of New South Wales.

MICHAEL CROMMELIN   Senior Lecturer in Law, University of Melbourne. Secretary to the Victorian Chief Justice's Law Reform Committee.

DARYL DAWSON, Q.C.   Solicitor-General of Victoria.

SIR RICHARD EGGLESTON   Chancellor and Special Lecturer in Law, Monash University. Formerly Judge of the Australian Industrial Court and A.C.T. Supreme Court, and President of the Trade Practices Tribunal.

HON. R.J. ELLICOTT, Q.C., M.P.   Attorney-General of Australia; Liberal M.H.R. for Wentworth (N.S.W.). Commonwealth Solicitor-General 1969-73.

S. ENCEL   Professor of Sociology, University of New South Wales. Books include *Cabinet Government in Australia.*

GARETH EVANS — Barrister-at-Law. Lecturer and Senior Lecturer in Law, University of Melbourne, 1971-7. Consultant to the Australian Attorney-General's and Aboriginal Affairs Departments 1973-5. Former member of the Australian Law Reform Commission. A.L.P. Senate candidate for Victoria in 1975.

J.C. FINEMORE, Q.C. — Chief Executive Officer, Australian Constitutional Convention and First Parliamentary Counsel, Victoria.

P.J. HANKS — Senior Lecturer in Law, Monash University. Co-author of *Australian Constitutional Law.*

COLIN HOWARD — Hearn Professor of Law, University of Melbourne. General Counsel to the Attorney-General of Australia 1974-6. Books include *Australian Federal Constitutional Law.*

HON. MR JUSTICE M.D. KIRBY — Chairman, Australian Law Reform Commission, and Deputy President of the Conciliation and Arbitration Commission.

R.D. LUMB — Reader in Law, University of Queensland. Books include *The Constitutions of the Australian States* and *The Constitution of the Commonwealth of Australia Annotated.*

J.D. MERRALLS, Q.C. — Barrister-at-Law. Editor of the Commonwealth Law Reports.

G.S. REID — Professor of Politics, University of Western Australia. Formerly Serjeant-at-Arms in the House of Representatives. Co-author of *Out of the Wilderness: The Return of Labor.*

J.E. RICHARDSON — Robert Garran Professor of Law, Australian National University. Secretary to the Joint Committee of Constitutional Review 1956-9. Books include *Patterns of Australian Federalism.*

CHERYL SAUNDERS — Lecturer in Law, University of Melbourne. Secretary to the Victorian Delegation to the Australian Constitutional Convention.

GEOFFREY SAWER — Emeritus Professor of Law, Australian National University. Books include *Australian Government Today, Australian Constitutional Cases, Australian Federal Politics and Law 1901-29* and *1929-49, Australian Federalism in the Courts,* and *Modern Federalism.*

HON. E.G. WHITLAM, Q.C., M.P. — Leader of the Opposition in the Australian Parliament. Prime Minister of Australia 1972-5.

PETER WILENSKI   Secretary of the Australian Department of Labor and Immigration 1975. Principal Private Secretary to the Prime Minister 1972-4.

LESLIE ZINES   Professor of Law, Australian National University.

Preface

The Whitlam Government was elected into office on 2 December 1972, the first Australian Labor Party government to be so installed since 1949. Barely three years later, on 11 November 1975, it was dismissed from power by the Governor-General, Sir John Kerr, and then defeated at the polls in the election for both Houses which immediately followed. The three years of the Whitlam Labor Government,[1] culminating in the quite unprecedented events surrounding its dismissal, were probably the most turbulent and exciting in Australia's political and constitutional history. Certainly no other comparable period contributed so much that was new to the law and practice of the Constitution. Certainly no other period has seen the Australian Constitution itself brought so consistently and vividly to public attention. To follow with any seriousness, from week to week, the course of political events during the Whitlam administration, one simply had to have a copy of the Constitution open at hand in a way that would have been quite unnecessary for years at a time in earlier decades.

The essays and commentaries assembled in this book range over all the significant constitutional issues that came to the fore during the Whitlam years. Read together, they are intended to constitute both a chronicle and an analysis, systematic and dispassionate, of the constitutional issues of the period and their significance for the future.

Part 1, 'Labor's New Federalism', deals with Federal-State relations, the traditional heartland of Australian constitutional law and politics. Mr Whitlam's conception of federalism, while subtler than many of his critics allowed, certainly involved a substantially greater role for the central government at the expense of the States. The working out of Labor's policies here, involving sweeping use of the Commonwealth's financial powers, the testing to the limits of various little-explored heads of Commonwealth legislative and executive power, and attempts to clothe the Commonwealth with additional powers by formal amendment of the Constitution, inevitably provoked a lively reaction from the States and their defenders. This was expressed through High Court litigation, media campaigns and, on occasions, obstructive deployment by the Opposition of its Senate majority. Whether, amid all the alarums and diversions, any lasting changes were wrought in the federal balance is a question taken up in general terms in Chapter 1, and in specific contexts in the two chapters following.

Part 2, 'Institutions Under Change', picks up a miscellany of themes all related to the institutions of national government: Chapter 4 treats the judiciary, in particular the High Court: Chapter 5 the executive branch, focusing

---

[1]Technically there were *three* Whitlam Governments: the Whitlam-Barnard 'Duumvirate' of 5-19 December 1972, the full Ministry which succeeded it and the Ministry reconstituted after the May 1974 election. For reasons of stylistic convenience they are referred to throughout this book in the singular.

particularly on the machinery, both departmental and otherwise, through which ideas were generated and Labor policy implemented; and Chapter 6 the legislature, with the emphasis here on electoral representation, the recurring question of conflict of parliamentarians' interests, and the matter of casual vacancies in the Senate.

Part 3, 'Constitutional Crisis', is concerned with two particular institutions, the Senate and the Governor-General, which each achieved by the end of the Whitlam term a prominence quite unforseen at its outset. The focus here is squarely on the extraordinary events of October-November 1975: the blocking of the Budget by the Senate, the consequential dismissal of the Whitlam Government by the Governor-General, the commissioning of the minority 'caretaker' Government, and the double dissolution of the two Houses of Parliament. Chapter 7 deals with the relatively narrow, but enormously important, question as to the proper application of the Constitution's double dissolution rules, while Chapter 8 confronts the largest questions of them all: the legality, and constitutional propriety, of the Senate's behaviour in refusing supply and that of the Governor-General in dismissing the Government.

Part 4, 'A Labor Retrospect', traverses again the whole subject-matter of the book, but from a particular, and peculiarly important, perspective. It consists of a retrospective overview, written by Mr Whitlam himself, of the constitutional issues of the Whitlam years. Given the way in which the former Prime Minister's driving personality and intensely felt policy commitments shaped, dominated and indeed determined the whole course of events of the period, Mr Whitlam's own account of his stewardship is, to say the least, of unusual interest.

The book had its genesis in the proceedings of a Seminar held at the University of Melbourne on 6-8 August 1976 to commemorate the 75th Anniversary of the Australian Federation. Sponsored and organized by the Faculty of Law, the object of the Federal Anniversary Seminar was to provide the opportunity—before memories had faded, but after the dust of partisan controversy had settled a little—for a balanced and scholarly review of the Whitlam period, both its place in Australia's history and its significance for the country's constitutional future. The Seminar was attended by over 250 leading politicians, public administrators, judges, legal practitioners and academics from law, political science, history and related disciplines around Australia. It was widely described as one of the most distinguished gatherings of constitutional lawyers, and men and women of affairs, to have been brought together in this country. The essays and commentaries contained in the book are revised and edited versions of the papers and commentaries delivered at the Seminar, substantially changed in some cases in the light of the discussion which there took place. The main papers, or essays, were prepared in each instance by leading academic constitutional lawyers, while the commentaries were delivered by Ministers and Law Officers of the Crown, judges, senior public servants and others from the Universities, by no means all of them lawyers. A good many of the contributors played a leading part, in one role or another, and on one side of the fence or another, in the dramatic events they describe.

The issues dealt with in this volume are by no means merely of historical interest, although the status of many of the contributors is no doubt such as to make their reflections on the Whitlam years documents of considerable historical, and comparative, significance in their own right. What is more important is that the constitutional controversies of 1972-1975 were concerned with issues that will be of fundamental and continuing importance in the future. What may be at stake is not only the operation and survival of the federal system in Australia, but also, as many have argued, the survival of Australian democracy itself.

*   *   *

Among the scores who have helped at various stages in the production of this book, my thanks are due especially to the following: to the Vice-Chancellor and Dean of the Faculty of Law of the University of Melbourne for financial, and diplomatic, assistance in the mounting of the Federal Anniversary Seminar; to David Hambly of the Australian National University for planning ideas; to Tom Hazell and those in his various University fiefdoms, and to Liz Murphy and her fellow students, for help in Seminar organization; to Joan Naylor, Glad Ball, Gwen Williams and their girls for skilled secretarial services and cheerful indifference to editorial tantrums; to Julia Rowlands and Joan Kimm for help with the backbreaking task of reference-checking; to my twenty-six fellow contributors for their quite remarkable punctiliousness in meeting unreasonable writing, rewrite and proof-reading deadlines; to Tim Bass of Heinemann for dedication beyond the normal bounds; to my wife Merran for fortitude of the same order; and, not least, to Muriel Bennett of the Law School, without whom the project would not have reached first base.

Gareth Evans

March 1977

PART ONE

LABOR'S NEW FEDERALISM

Geoffrey Sawer (Chapter 1) explores the federal-State balance of power under the Whitlam administration, comparing the centralization of decision-making actually effected with that foreshadowed by the Party and predicted by its opponents. Expressing his own preference for a form of 'organic federalism', he suggests that the difficulties of achieving co-operation between the Commonwealth and States are such that 'the A.L.P. would do well to return to a frank unificationist platform'. Senator J.L. Carrick, the architect of the Liberal Party's own 'New Federalism', delivers in reply a stinging attack on both Professor Sawer's prescriptions and the 'centralist socialist' philosophy of Mr Whitlam. Professor Castles's commentary focuses attention on some of the semantic difficulties which have continually bedevilled debate on these questions.

Michael Crommelin and Gareth Evans (Chapter 2) provide a comprehensive analytical survey of the many initiatives taken by the Labor Government to utilize the powers at the Commonwealth's disposal — especially in the areas of commercial regulation, welfare spending, resource development and human rights. In an important paper, the Solicitor-General, Mr Byers, expands upon the idea that Australia's status as a nation is sufficient in itself to confer certain powers upon the Commonwealth. The Victorian Solicitor-General, Mr Dawson, comments upon the issues from the perspective of an advocate for the States (arguing before an increasingly polarized High Court bench) in many of the major constitutional battles of the period.

J.E. Richardson (Chapter 3) usefully documents the attempts made to formally alter the terms of the Constitution in the referendum campaigns and meetings of the Constitutional Convention. J.C. Finemore, the Chief Executive Officer of the Convention, urges in his commentary a hasten-slowly approach to constitutional reform. R.D. Lumb argues that the Labor referendums — especially the Democratic Elections proposal — were fundamentally misconceived, and suggests new forms of machinery, not confined to the national Parliament, for the initiation of constitutional amendments.

1 Towards a New Federal Structure?

Geoffrey Sawer

I
THE PARTY PLATFORM

From 1918 until 1971, the platform of the Australian Labor Party explicitly required the abolition of a federal constitution in Australia and the vesting of sovereign power, in the strict sense of sovereignty, in the Australian Commonwealth Parliament.[1] Regional devolution was contemplated, in terms which have sometimes emphasised the creation of new 'provinces' or 'regions', and at others have rather suggested the retention of the existing States, or something like them, though with simplified and electorally reformed constitutional structures. Probably, for most of the time it existed, this commitment to a non-federal system of government was an electoral and parliamentary liability, since there was so little possibility of its being realised and its presence in the platform provided rhetorical ammunition for the opponents of the more modest constitutional reforms which the Party in fact pressed from time to time. Give them an inch of reform, was the cry, and they will take the ell of abolishing federalism.

At any rate, in his campaign to reform the structure of the A.L.P. itself and to update its platform, pursued as deputy leader and leader from 1965 on, Mr E.G. Whitlam included revision of the constitutional objective, and in June 1971, at the Launceston Commonwealth A.L.P. Conference, the views he advocated on this question were adopted. The 'unification' platform was removed. In its place was substituted the following much vaguer aim: 'Amendment of the Commonwealth Constitution to clothe the Parliament of Australia with such plenary powers as are necessary and desirable to achieve international co-operation[2], national planning and the Party's economic and social objectives'. Then followed a curiously worded passage referring not to constitutional change, but to 'alteration of administrative arrangements' so as to 'balance the functions and finances of the Commonwealth, the State and Local governments to ensure adequate services and development of resources'; a number of specific instrumentalities to be used for these purposes were then mentioned, and local governments and semi-government authorities were promised representation on the Loan Council; finally it was said that 'records, resolutions and recommendations of Conferences of Commonwealth and State Ministers' should be 'tabled in their parliaments', which seems appropriate for ensuring effective State as well as federal supervision of the co-operative process.

---

[1]L.F. Crisp, *The Australian Federal Labour Party 1901-1951* (London, 1955) Ch. XII, and for subsequent platforms, *Australian Labor Party: Platform, Constitution and Rules,* published by Federal Secretary, A.L.P. as approved by successive biennial Commonwealth (until 1971), Federal (1975) and National (since 1975) Conferences of the Party.

[2]The Parliament in fact already has ample power for this purpose: Constitution s. 51(29).

The amplification of the Party platform from 1963 on had rapidly added to the number of specific cases for achieving Party aims by co-operative Commonwealth-State action; the 1961 Platform had few such references. However, the 1969 Platform, with its long list of cases for Commonwealth-State co-operative action, had to be read in the context of the introductory, general constitutional plank requiring the vesting of sovereign powers in the Commonwealth and the reduction of the States to the role of delegates of the Commonwealth, having only such powers as might be vested in them by the Commonwealth. In that context, the references to co-operative action could be treated as intended only to cope with the immediate or transitional situation, before the unification plank was carried into law. Once, however, the unification objective was dropped, then not only the references to co-operation with the States in the substituted plank, but also the references to co-operation scattered throughout the particular planks dealing with economic affairs, industrial relations, education, health and so on took on a new significance.

To a historian of the future possessing only the Party platforms, it might well seem that in 1971 the A.L.P. underwent a sudden lurch from an anti-federal to a pro-federal stance, with a policy favouring not only the continuance of the States but an active programme of building up their financial and administrative resources within the general parameters of the existing federal system. This historian might ponder about the introductory part of the new constitutional platform — amendment of the constitution to enable the Commonwealth to give effect to the general objectives of the Party, which include the achieving of democratic socialism. But then he might reflect that not only are so many of the detailed objectives stated in terms explicitly providing for co-operation with the States but the Preamble also states that *all* the objectives 'must be attained by the constitutional utilisation of Federal, State and Local Governments', and even the socialisation objective is required to be achieved 'in accordance with the principles of action, methods and progressive reforms set out in this platform'. Thus, if words mean anything, the methods of co-operative federalism involving the existing States are explicitly incorporated into the general as well as the specific objectives of the Party. I repeat, then, that as a matter of textual analysis, the disappearance of the unification objective in 1971 had the consequence of leaving the A.L.P. with a platform which looked like endorsing the continued existence of federalism very much as it is today, with a heavy stress on co-operative federalism rather than vesting of additional powers in the Commonwealth as the method for achieving the Party's economic and social aims. It could even be contended that no additional powers for the Commonwealth were required, so long as the latter retained the financial strength to build up economic control and social services by the machinery of conditional grants under s. 96 of the Constitution, in areas not otherwise within federal power.[3]

---

[3]The theme of co-operative spending of the Commonwealth's money gained explicit recognition in further amendments made to the platform at the 1975 Terrigal National Conference: 'The Australian Labor Party will ... involve the Australian Government and the State Governments in co-operative moves to determine mutually agreed and consistent priorities for joint planning of functions for which the Australian Government provides finance'.

II
WHITLAM ON FEDERALISM

However, party platforms are not legal constitutions and their meaning and operation are likely, much more than in the case of legal constitutions, to be determined by their makers, the politicians; politicians interpret them when in opposition by their speeches and when in power by their actions. In this case we are fortunate in that Mr Whitlam was a particularly tireless and fluent exponent of the 1971 Platform which in all essentials was affirmed in 1973 and 1975, and from December 1972 until November 1975 he led a Government which in a particularly active fashion attempted to carry out, to illustrate in action, what that Platform meant and means. Other contributors will be dealing with main areas of Whitlam Government activity, and my task is to consider mainly the Whitlam theory of a new federalism and in a very broad outline some of the machinery for giving effect to it.

First, then, Mr Whitlam's personal exposition. This is contained in many documents,[4] but I do not think it necessary to go beyond his first essay of this nature — the article in the *Australian Quarterly* for September 1971,[5] which explicitly starts off as a commentary on the changes in the federalism plank of the Party platform I have outlined above. This essay displays to the full the incisiveness and wit of his advocacy of a series of specific things needed to be done to raise the welfare and quality of life of Australians — better education, better cities, better transport, better development and use of resources, better social and health services, environmental control, a more equitable distribution of financial resources and of the burden of servicing public debt, and such specifics. When one concentrates on these highly pragmatic and obviously necessary programmes, further elaborated and particularised in his 1972 and 1974 policy speeches, one is surprised not that the A.L.P. won office in 1972 and 1974, but that its majority was not greater on both occasions. Moreover, this concentration on specific needs and demands was fully in accordance with A.L.P. tradition, which has always been to go for immediate social gains and worry little, if at all, about long-term questions of constitutional machinery. I have always thought that Labor was at best lukewarm about federation in the 1890s mainly because it was a distraction from their growing success in getting immediate demands by the methods to hand — the State parliaments with all their faults, then much greater than now — and not because of any settled views about federalism as a system. As to the greater part of Whitlam's social reform proposals, what I have said about a textual interpretation of the 1971 Platform applies; the emphasis is on using the existing constitution and the methods of co-operative federalism. The principal technique suggested or implied is a Commonwealth conditional grants system in which methods already developed by the Menzies and successor governments to 1972 were to be carried much further; more conditional grants, more complex conditions reflecting Commonwealth administrative choices of policy, more supervision of the spending, more direct grants to local government, extension of the principles already inherent in the federal States Grants Commission (with local government now

---

[4]In addition to speeches subsequently mentioned in the text, see E.G. Whitlam, 'The Future of Australian Federalism', in R.L. Mathews (ed.) *Intergovernmental Relations in Australia* (1974), and his Curtin Memorial Lecture for 1975, *Government of the People, for the People — by the People,* (Australian National University).

[5]E.G. Whitlam, 'A New Federalism' *Australian Quarterly*, vol. 43, 3 (1971) pp. 6-17.

added) and Universities Commission, more decision at Commonwealth level as to the general distribution within Australia of the revenue and loan resources already overwhelmingly within Commonwealth control, and of their spending. On transport matters he stresses the possibilities of the Inter-State Commission already provided for in the Constitution. Most of the education and health proposals already lay within Commonwealth power. So far, then, platform and explanatory exposition agree.

However, the 1971 paper does not stop there. Nowhere does it set out in a separate, distinct passage any further implications for the existing constitution which may be made from the social proposals. There are scattered passages, but they are unsystematic and to some extent self-contradictory, or they begin to look like a bold programme but then there is a retreat from the bold line of thought. The first and boldest passage is as follows:

> Ideally, our continent should have neither so few State governments nor so many local government units. We should not have a federal system of overlapping parliaments and a delegated but supervised system of local government. We should have a House of Representatives for international and nation-wide matters, an assembly for the affairs of each of our dozen largest cities, and regional assemblies for the few score areas of rural production and resource development outside those cities. Vested interests and legal complexities should not discourage or deter us from attempts to modernise and rationalise our inherited structure.[6]

This looks like the 1918 Platform — unification with many new regions having delegated functions. It is not the 1971 Platform. But he soon retreats from this ideal, and after stressing the financial handicaps of the States, writes: 'The A.L.P. proposals envisage a framework of consultation and co-operation between between tiers of government'.[7] Then in the last paragraph we find an obverse order of thought. He writes:[8] 'Each of our three levels of government has functions which it is best able to perform. The key to effective performance is not domination but consultation, not centralisation but co-ordination. An Australian Schools Commission would no more deprive the States of their schools, nor an Australian Hospitals Commission deprive the States of their hospitals, than the present Universities Commission has deprived them of their universities.' Here we have the co-operative federalism theme, using the existing States and local authorities and leaving the latter as, legally speaking, the creatures of the States. But then comes the characteristic swipe at the States 'with their irrelevant State boundaries and malapportioned electoral boundaries', and the final sentence reads: 'The new federalism will rest on a national framework for the establishment of investment priorities and a regional framework for participation in all those decisions which most directly determine the quality of our lives'. Does the regional framework there mentioned include the States? The immediate context rather suggests not, but the article as a whole rather suggests that it must. Neither the 1972 nor the 1974 policy speeches contain any general proposals about constitutional structure. They dwell on three main themes consistent with the existing structure: re-direction of spending priorities; increased Commonwealth initiation of or participation in the policy making and administration required by this re-direction; action for the most part (where the matter is not directly within Commonwealth power)

---

[6] *ibid.*, p. 11.

[7] *ibid.*, p. 12.

[8] *ibid.*, p. 17.

through co-operation with States and local government, with a more active role for the latter including direct access to Commonwealth grants.

The ambiguities in Mr Whitlam's position mentioned above can be traced back, in course of evolution, through papers delivered before 1971; three of these are conveniently collected in a pamphlet published by the Victorian Fabian Society.[9] The first was dated 1957, and is firmly unificationist in tone and recommendation. The argument is linked closely to the socialist objective, discounts the possibilities of mere regulation and of social benefits in cash form, and is pessimistic about the scope of existing federal powers. It concludes that 'our parliaments work within a constitutional framework which enshrines Liberal policy and bans Labor policy'. This essay also introduced the highly defensible view that existing States are too big and local government units too small for effective decentralisation of government, and the highly disputable and in any event irrelevant view that State boundaries were foisted on us by Whitehall. The second speech, dated 1961, is still critical of federalism — a 'transitional form of government which has been devised for former colonial territories or conquered nations' — but shows much more interest in and optimism about what can be done within the confines of the present system. It includes the important statement: 'Nationalisation is now the most difficult and least important aspect of socialism for an Australian government to achieve. It is neither essential nor sufficient'; he advocates instead the initiation of government enterprise to compete with private enterprise, with the unspoken inference that the best, socialist, corporate person will win. He further urges that for such a policy, s. 96 of the Constitution — the power to make conditional financial grants to the States — can be 'the charter of public enterprise', per medium of the States. Finally the 1963 address, entitled 'Labor Policies and Commonwealth Powers', and delivered to the A.L.P. Commonwealth Conference of that year, expands in more detail on the theme of what can be done with the existing constitution, and contains no opprobrious references to the States. His separately published Victorian Fabian Society pamphlet of 1969 on urban growth[10] develops in great detail the theme, so important in Whitlam Government policy after 1972, of urban planning and re-development, and here a constitutional framework of co-operative federalism within the existing formal system is even more plainly stated. There is the occasional scornful reference to the States, and emphasis on the need for 'national planning', but so far as constitutional structure is concerned, his optimistic conclusion is that 'only the Commonwealth has the constitutional power and the financial capacity to create the conditions in which enough Australians will prefer homes in regional centres to homes in established urban areas'. I think, then, that both in the individual mind of Mr Whitlam, and in the collective mind of the A.L.P., there has always been and always will be some basic hankering after centralization, due partly to theoretical considerations and partly to bitter experience of managing relations between Centre and States even when Labor held power in Canberra and in most States. On the other hand, the prospect of office in Canberra soon concentrates the mind of federal A.L.P. leaders on immediate prospects of achieving specific ends. Even poor old Jimmy Scullin in 1929-31, with much less prospect of achieving results by legislation than Mr Whitlam

---

[9]E.G. Whitlam, *Labor and the Constitution* (Victorian Fabian Society Pamphlet 11, Melbourne, 1965).

[10]E.G. Whitlam, *An Urban Nation* (Victorian Fabian Society Pamphlet 19, Melbourne, 1969).

had in 1972 and 1974, sought to hang on to office in order to do what could be done by mere executive power. In my judgment, the Platform of 1971 and the Policy Speeches of 1972 and 1974 aimed primarily at making the most of the Constitution as it stood.

III

LABOR IN OFFICE

Legislation and Administration

When we examine the legislative and administrative record of the Whitlam Government, the story is not markedly different. During three years the Whitlam administration secured the passage of 452 statutes. After discounting the seventy per cent or so of routine tax, spending, minor administrative and minor substantive amendment measures which take up so much government time under any government, the hundred odd important Acts were for the most part just what one would expect from the Prime Minister's 1971 paper, from the Platform (if we exclude the socialisation objective), and from the 1972 policy speech. The Government's administrative activities were very largely geared to the same set of activities — preparing the policies and so far as needed the legislation, and carrying or trying to carry the legislation and the money-spending priorities into effect. Critics contended that the trouble, especially in 1973, was a tendency to throw the money around without any priorities, but in the sense of this paper there was a very definite priority programme for the nation as a whole and it was the one promised — a shift from private to public extravagance, if you like, and within the public spending the promised emphasis, increasingly enforced on the States, in favour of education, the Aboriginals, the less favoured urban areas, public transport and so on. A good deal of the important legislation was taken up with establishing the promised Commissions to investigate and recommend, but many such bodies could be and were established by executive act without legislation.[11] Further Acts were passed to expand existing administrative departments and instrumentalities or set up new ones to perform the continuing function of greater Commonwealth participation in co-operation with States, as well as to carry out activities within the Commonwealth sphere; here, too, a good deal of the administrative expansion could be and was carried out by executive act, without legislation. Finally, so far as the programme required State and local government co-operation, the main single instrument was the conditional grant by statute under s. 96 of the Constitution; about fifty of the Acts of the period were such Grants Acts.

A good deal of the promised change in emphasis as to Commonwealth pressure could be and was done under inherited legislation; it was merely a matter of changing the administrative policy. Avoiding the emphasis on the flashy and melodramatic aspects of government activity which filled the daily press, like Attorney-General Lionel Murphy's raid on ASIO and the flaming temper of the Minister for Minerals and Resources, Mr Rex Connor, the Whitlam Government did attempt in the most assiduous manner to carry out its promised social programme and to do so by the methods of co-operative federalism, within the bounds of the existing constitutional structure. The spirit of the co-operation varied a good deal from Minister to Minister, most

---

[11]Statements tabled in the House of Representatives on 13 December 1973, 5 December 1974 and 5 June 1975 identify about 121 Commissions and Committees of Inquiry appointed by the Government and some forty-eight Acts affected by their reports or recommendations.

cordially — a surprise to me — by Mr Uren, less cordially by Mr Jones and Mr Whitlam. I regard as one of the minor triumphs of the programme the degree of acceptance which the Department of Social Security and the Social Welfare Commission obtained for that very odd animal, the Australian Assistance Plan. This co-operative strategy may have been one of the reasons for that other very odd phenomenon — the dearth of important constitutional cases in the High Court, arising from Whitlam Government activity, in the three years of its existence. If you read Arthur Calwell's admirable book about the Labor Party,[12] you will notice the great emphasis which he placed on the horrors of s. 92 of the Constitution — the guarantee of free trade between the States — and how important it was for Labor to get that section repealed or amended. Well, the Whitlam government never had occasion to mention the section and not a single case arose under it during this period as a result of Commonwealth activity. There was a bank-up of constitutional cases at the very end of the period, notably those resulting from the 1974 double-dissolution and joint sitting,[13] but these were of greater importance for politics in the narrower sense than for the federal aspects of the constitutional structure.

This is not to say that the Whitlam Government did not pay attention to the constitutional structure. They were compelled to pay a good deal of attention to it, and they endeavoured to do something about it in the three ways open to Commonwealth governments — by proposing express amendments to the Constitutional text through Bills put to the people under s. 128 of the Constitution,[14] by passing legislation and engaging in administrative activities at the margin of existing Commonwealth powers so as to challenge judicial testing and create the possibility of amendment by judicial interpretation,[15] and by making appointments to the High Court of Justices who might be expected to use opportunities for fresh interpretations as they and when they arose.[16] All three of these courses of action are discussed in detail by other contributors, and I shall not pursue them further in this essay.

Government by Double Dissolution

The principal constitutional achievement of the Whitlam Government, technically though perhaps not politically, was the discovery of government by double dissolution under s. 57 of the Constitution, which provides for the overcoming of inter-House deadlocks by dissolution of both Houses (the only way of compelling all senators to face the electors at one time), followed, if deadlocks persist, by a joint sitting of the Houses at which Bills in dispute can be carried into law by majority vote of the whole; in view of the two-to-one proportion between Representatives and Senate membership (Constitution s. 24), the probabilities are that on such occasions the Representatives view will prevail. In April 1974, Mr Whitlam was faced with some sticky political and

---

[12]A.A. Calwell, *Labor's Role in Modern Society* (Melbourne, 1963), especially Ch.12.

[13]See especially *Cormack* v. *Cope* (1974) 131 C.L.R. 432, *Victoria* v. *Commonwealth* (*P.M.A. Case*) (1975) 7 A.L.R. 1 and *Western Australia* v. *Commonwealth* (*Territory Senators Case*) (1975) 7 A.L.R. 159.

[14]See J.E. Richardson, 'Reform of the Constitution: the Referendums and Constitutional Convention', below Ch.3.

[15]See Michael Crommelin and Gareth Evans, 'Explorations and Adventures with Commonwealth Powers', below Ch.2.

[16]See A.R. Blackshield, 'Judges and the Court System', below Ch.4.

constitutional problems caused by his rather over-clever attempt at getting a
Senate majority by appointing Senator Vincent Gair, until then one of his
bitterest enemies and, until shortly before, leader of the Democratic Labor
Party, but now disgruntled by the way his own party had treated him, to an
ambassadorship; this nerved the Opposition in general and particularly the
Senate Opposition to threaten refusal of supply in order to bring on an election,
and Mr Whitlam forestalled actual refusal by obtaining a double dissolution on
the basis of six Bills which in the view of his government satisfied the
requirements of s. 57. The election result disappointed him by returning him
with a Representatives majority (one seat being lost) but still no independent
majority in the Senate, and a joint sitting was duly held and the six Bills passed
into law. The cases arising out of this — *Cormack* v. *Cope*,[17] *Western Australia*
v. *Commonwealth*[18] and *Victoria* v. *Commonwealth*[19] settled many points
about the s. 57 machinery which had hitherto been unresolved, since previous
double dissolutions (in 1914 and 1951) had been on the basis of a single Bill
and had not been followed by a joint sitting.[20] The main points were that more
than one Bill could be used as the basis for a double dissolution and carried into
law at a joint sitting, that Bills could be saved up during any one parliament for
this purpose so long as the dissolution occurs earlier than six months before the
expiry of the term of office of the then House of Representatives, that the time
limits prescribed follow the natural reading of s. 57, that the High Court will
not readily intervene to prevent a joint sitting before it is held, and that it is for
the Houses in joint sitting — not the Governor-General or Government — to
determine what measures, being the basis for the dissolution, will be dealt with.
However, the experience of 1974, and also of December 1975, demonstrates the
political risks of trying to overcome Senate obstruction in this manner. The
decisions also settled (against dissents by McTiernan, Jacobs and Murphy JJ)
that the High Court will maintain a close control of the procedure, and is not
prepared to treat the various decisions of the Governor-General involved as
'political' or non-justiciable. However, in view of the events of November 1975,
the doctrine of judicial restraint advocated by the dissentients may yet become
an embarrassment to Labor; such is always the ambiguous relation between
general legal doctrines of this sort and the ever-changing practical demands of
practical politics.

State Capitalism

There may be some old-line adherents of the left or left-centre in the A.L.P.
capable of noticing that the Whitlam paper of 1971, and his subsequent papers
and policy speeches, entirely failed to mention the socialisation objective in the
Platform. This, like the former unification objective, and notwithstanding the
Blackburn amendment,[21] has also been long regarded as a political liability.

---

[17](1974) 131 C.L.R. 432.

[18](1975) 7 A.L. R. 159.

[19](1975) 7 A.L.R. 1. This decision held invalid the *Petroleum and Minerals Authority Act 1973*, one
of the six double-dissolution measures, on the sole ground that it had not failed to pass the Senate in
accordance with the time-table required by s.57.

[20]For a full account of the present law and practice of s.57, see Leslie Zines, 'The Double
Dissolutions and Joint Sitting', below Ch.7.

[21]'The Party does not seek to abolish private ownership . . . where such ownership is utilised by its
owner in a socially useful manner and without exploitation' (1921).

Oddly, one feature of the Whitlam regime was a suggestion of renewed interest in, if not socialism, at any rate state capitalism. Neither the Whitlam article of 1971 nor the 1972 policy speech gave much forewarning of this; the latter did mention, briefly, the topic of buying back the farm, but the method suggested was chiefly the existing Australian Industry Development Corporation — a Country Party creation — and similar stock-holding devices, nothing comparable with the Chifley attempt at bank nationalisation. However, in practice the Connor adventures in loan raising, and his *Pipeline Authority Act 1973* — a miracle that it got through the Senate — and *Petroleum and Minerals Authority Act 1973*, which was slain by the High Court under s. 57 of the Constitution,[22] not to mention his company for similar purposes incorporated in the A.C.T., pointed to something rather more than regulation of private enterprise. It is a pity that the Petroleum and Minerals Authority did not survive the challenge under s. 57 in order to be challenged again under more substantive grounds. It may also be a pity that the loans affair did not get far enough to test the inherent authority of the Governor-General in Council to make contracts and engage in business, though the *Black Mountain Tower Case*[23] is not without interest in this connection. There can be no question about the ability of the Commonwealth, by the path of co-operative federalism, to embark on enterprises of all kinds if it wishes and can get States to co-operate. The perils of s. 92 in this connection have been exaggerated, and there is even now a faint possibility that the High Court will return to the original intentions of s. 92, which did not include the preservation of private economic enterprise. I doubt whether this aspect of Whitlam Government activity was due to a renewed interest in socialism for its own sake. The 1972 policy speech dwelt heavily on the exponential increase in Commonwealth revenues, due to the then still very mild inflation rate, as the source from which new ventures would be financed, plus hoped-for increases in national productivity; it took the changed economic atmosphere of 1974 to turn the Government's attention to loan-raising, and that atmosphere also made an active policy of not only buying back but running the farm (at least the minerals under the farm) credible. Nevertheless, I think that the extension of government enterprise has now again become a familiar if contentious item on the agenda of political and constitutional history.

Local Government

Whitlam in action also gave some indications as to the sort of regional reorganization which might be attempted. There were three important cases — regional grouping of local government authorities for the purpose of the Grants Commission levelling-up programme begun in 1973,[24] the Regional Councils for Social Development under the Australian Assistance Plan,[25] and the New Cities programme.[26] The Grants Commission programme is at the time of

---

[22] *Victoria* v. *Commonwealth* (*P.M.A. Case*) (1975) 7 A.L.R. 1.

[23] *Johnson* v. *Kent* (1975) 132 C.L.R. 164.

[24] Australian Grants Commission, *Annual Report* 1973, 1974, 1975.

[25] Summarised in the High Court decision concerning its validity — *Victoria* v. *Commonwealth* (*A.A.P. Case*) (1975) 7 A.L.R. 277.

[26] Cities Commission, *Report* 1973. See also the debates on the Albury-Wodonga Development Bill commencing at House of Representatives, *Debates* 1973, vol. 87, p.3534, and the *Albury-Wodonga Development Act* 1973 (Aust.), the *Albury-Wodonga Agreement Act* 1973 (Vic.) and the *Albury-Wodonga Development Act* 1974 (N.S.W.).

writing being changed by the Fraser Government, so that the grouping of local authorities for the purpose of getting federal grants will become an entirely State operation. The federal Grants Commission reports for 1973-5, however, make it plain that in any event this activity had not produced 'regionalisation' with any real structural substance. The 'regions' were temporary alliances of local government units for the purpose of application to the Grants Commission; not even the distribution or payment of the grants was handled by the 'regions', the grants being recommended by the Commission in respect of the individual local authorities and paid direct to them through the State governments. The Regional Councils under the A.L.P. were a good deal more interesting, and this was assuredly a most promising adventure in the delivery of social services. However, it was structurally a fragile affair, and certainly not well calculated to produce a new, stable kind of *governmental* unit in the Australian system. The 'regions' here began as public meetings, and continued either as unincorporated associations or as companies or associations incorporated under State law — in either case a headache from the point of view of satisfactory federal control and audit of financial affairs. This precarious character was emphasized by the decision of the High Court in the *A.A.P. Case*.[27] Three Justices (Barwick CJ, Gibbs and Mason JJ) thought the Commonwealth grants to the A.A.P. Councils were beyond federal power; three (McTiernan, Jacobs and Murphy JJ) thought they were within power; the seventh (Stephen J) declined to decide that substantive question on the ground that the Commonwealth had as yet merely appropriated money for the purpose, and he thought no State had standing to object to a mere appropriation. It is likely that if there had been substantive federal legislation, Stephen J would have found it invalid. Hence the continuation of the plan depended on the Commonwealth *not* legislating to regulate the Councils, and instead leaving them to manage their legal affairs wholly under State law. The 'New Cities' programme, notably the Albury-Wodonga case, did not attempt to set up any new kind of instrumentality for the local government of the new city. Wodonga continued for all general purposes of government a Victorian city under its own local Council, and similarly Albury a New South Wales city under its own local Council, the tripartite Commission being mainly a planning and construction authority like the N.C.D.C. in Canberra. So these experiments produced three quite different and oddly structured sorts of 'regions', none capable of taking their place in a *federal* partnership with Commonwealth and States.

IV
EVALUATION

The Meaning of Federalism

It is a fashion, followed at times by myself, to deny that one can define 'federalism' or pin down the use of the word. However, I now think that this, like most fashions, is open to criticism. We need to have some degree of confidence about the meaning and use of words, if communication between people is to be possible and effective. The occasional note of exasperation in the voice of Mr Whitlam and other A.L.P. leaders when they speak of 'federalism' indicates, to my mind, that they have a fairly clear notion of the essential connotations of the word, and so does the note of unctuous approval with which

---

[27](1975) 7 A.L.R. 277. Further discussed below in Ch.2, pp. 41-5.

the word is used by non-Labor leaders such as Senator Carrick. I think the essential point is that there is more than delegation or devolution of authority from a centre to regions; there is a degree of guarantee of the area of autonomy which the centre and the regions in the system are respectively given. It is expected that a unit in the system which feels it is being trodden on retains some capacity to fight back. The methods of assuring this vary a good deal, and so does the area within which the guaranteed autonomy exists. In my own writings on the subject[28] I have drawn on German speculation when roughly classifying existing and potential federalisms as co-ordinate, co-operative and organic. Co-ordinate federalism demands, at least in theory, a degree of separation between the operations of the units, of mutual independence in both structure and activity, which in practice has never been achieved. Co-operative federalism permits a good deal of shared activity, perfectly illustrated in Australia by the wheat marketing scheme with its necessary component of State and federal laws and administrators interlocked so as to vest the storage and sale of the product in the Australian Wheat Board (subject to the grey private market created by s. 92 of the Constitution). However, the term 'co-operative federalism' is used very loosely by politicians; their usage requires us to describe the victim of a hold-up as co-operating with the gunman. In a more reasonable usage, one discerns co-operation only if the assumptions of co-ordinate federalism are to some extent realised — that is, the co-operating governments have some possibility of choice, some bargaining power, some autonomy. So far, either the regions or the centre could be the more powerful and active units in the system. Organic federalism requires a dominant centre, having substantial control of the financial resources of the country and the ability to decide at least in general terms all major policy questions, including spending priorities. This can still leave a genuine area of autonomy to the regions, if only as to detailed administration, protected in the sense required by my concept of federalism. Australia is still in a very substantial sense in the stage of co-operative federalism, notwithstanding the financial domination of the Commonwealth, because the latter still has to rely in many matters upon inducing State agreement to its policies (including its spending priorities); the occasions for compromise and even for State refusal are much more numerous and important than the rhetoric of Premiers' Conferences would suggest, and the area of State activity unaffected by Commonwealth views is large.

Programme and Performance

Looking at the Whitlam programme and performance in the light of the above, there are only two criticisms I would want to make.

First, I think it was a mistake for Whitlam to promise that local government would be made a *partner* in the federal arrangements. Local government was not and could not possibly be given that status. The States have sturdily, often from a Labor centralist view stupidly and even viciously, but with a very substantial constitutional basis, asserted a claim to participation in Australian government which can reasonably be called partnership. Local government has no such status and could be given it only by what I would regard as a disastrous bit of constitutional tinkering — one giving them the same sort of opportunities for obstruction and mischief-making as the States have. Certainly no such

---

[28]Especially *Modern Federalism* (New ed., Melbourne, 1976).

status was given local government by the Whitlam legislative and administrative arrangements under which local government was given access to the Loan Council, nor would local government have been any better off from this point of view if the constitutional amendment proposed in 1974 had been carried; they would then merely have become legally, as well as *de facto* as they were becoming under Whitlam, the servants of two masters. It seems that Mr Fraser will now return them to the position of being servants of one master, their State. They should have been promised only greater consultative privileges, at the discretion of the Commonwealth, and a needs-conditioned grant, which is what they got.

Second, the platform, the articles and speeches and the election policy statements all at least glancingly indicated, and certainly implied, the creation of some overall direction of the grand plan; at least some way of asserting more particular spending (and possibly tax) priorities within the general shift of priorities required by the 1971 Platform. It may be that this was beginning to be achieved in 1975 at the Ministerial level, but it was never attempted at the level of co-operation with the States, much less the special interests such as big and small business, industry and craft unions and so on. Ad hoc arrangements for consultation existed, to a considerable extent inherited from previous governments. Perhaps in practice anything more than ad hoc arrangements are difficult to achieve in a society like ours. It would seem, however, that if the programme of co-operation under federal leadership indicated by both paper policy and actual performance is to be obtained in the future, the determination of overall policy cannot be left to the almost whimsical shifts of Ministerial responsibility and Cabinet-committee structure which occurred in 1974-5.

The examination of Mr Whitlam's writings and speeches, and of the 1971 Platform, attempted above has not been undertaken in any spirit of scoring points or nit-picking. I think that there were justifiable doubts in his mind about how he should handle constitutional issues for the purposes of public debate and electioneering, and they are certainly in my mind. My inclination as a student of Australian social and political history is to say that the A.L.P. would do well to return to a frank unificationist platform. I doubt whether the detailed programme can be achieved on a basis of co-operative federalism, even if the electoral basis of the States — not to mention the Commonwealth — is corrected to secure approximately one man one vote, and the upper Houses are abolished. I am quite certain that the socialisation programme could not be achieved or maintained in operation on such a basis. As indicated in my book *Modern Federalism*, I would sooner see a unified system with a good deal of *de facto* regional decentralisation and a tough Bill of Rights. I do not see the regional scheme as involving necessarily the disappearance of the States as we know them. One of the fallacies underlying Whitlam's frequent references to the origins of the States is a view that you can get a single set of regional divisions, smaller than the States, which is satisfactory for all or most purposes. It seems to me that the States as they are provide as good a set of boundaries as you are likely to get for many purposes of decision-making and administration, and no single set of regions is going to be satisfactory for all or even most purposes of devolution. However, given unification, this is a matter of administrative detail. The more important point is to ensure that the widespread and justified fear of irrational dictation from Canberra is allayed. One method of allaying it is to give much greater prominence to the platform demand for an effective Bill of Rights — not the pallid U.N. document with no greater status than that of a federal Act.[29] This should be stated as an essential concomitant of unification. The other possibility is to retain a federal element, not specifically incorporated in any existing federal system, although approximated by Australia and West Germany, and even India — a constitutional guarantee of decentralised administration. Onward from co-operative federalism to organic federalism, where all main policy choices are made by a central parliament, after such intermediate consultations as it chooses, but the detailed carrying into effect of those policies is vested in State-level authorities given a judicially-policed guarantee of continued existence.

However, if Mr Whitlam decided not to carry the academic constitutional speculations of his 1971 *Australian Quarterly* article into his 1972 policy speech for fear of confusing the public, then I sympathise with him. A number of political correspondents have complained to me about his preoccupation with the Constitution — the Inter-State Commission and all that. It is likely enough that the general public would find such questions even more difficult and suspicion-breeding. Probably it was not his purpose, when procuring the removal of the unification objective in 1971, to start a fresh round of constitutional dispute. From this point of view, the better course may well be to leave the explicit statement of the constitutional objective as it is, and to keep the sort of possibilities I have suggested in mind as ultimate possibilities.

The Proper Role of The Senate

Considering the Whitlam period of government soberly, I think it can be contended that most of the problems were not constitutional in a narrow sense, but political. The main constitutional problem was not the reach of federal power, but the structure of the Senate. Notwithstanding the voting patterns of that House, it must be regarded as owing its existence to federalism and in a sense appropriate for carrying out a federal objective — the representation at the federal level of the prevailing pattern of political opinion in each State separately considered. The most immediate constitutional problem is to make it possible for the Senate to influence but not frustrate a Representatives majority. As to money Bills, something could be done without constitutional change by a Labor government in control of both Houses; most of the ordinary costs of administration could be charged on Consolidated Revenue by standing appropriation. But a lasting solution requires a constitutional change to ensure that something less politically chancy and expensive than a double dissolution is sufficient to overcome obstruction — for example, a one month delay for money Bills and a three month delay for others. The introduction of proportional representation for Senate elections in 1949 was a predictable disaster. It would have been better to divide all States into five constituencies for Senate voting, which would incidentally have put an end to the still surviving possibility of Queensland doing this alone, in a suitably gerrymandered fashion, as was suggested during the course of the Gair affair in 1974. The simultaneous election of the Representatives and half of the Senate makes obvious good sense. There were many individual good and easily arguable proposals in the four Whitlam constitutional amendment Bills considered at the 1974 double dissolution, but mixed up with incomprehensible matter — for most Australians — such as the unnecessary double proposal about local government and

---

[29]See the discussion of the Human Rights Bill below in Ch.2, pp. 47-51.

the attempt to abolish the N.S.W. Legislative Council. The atmosphere of the period was wrong for such measures. So long as the Commonwealth retains its financial dominance, and given a reformed Senate, it should be possible for an A.L.P. government to carry through the sort of programme which the Whitlam Government attempted. It seems to me unlikely that the Fraser New Federalism proposals, built upon a sharing of income tax revenues and a returning of a limited measure of fiscal responsibility to the States, will in fact give the States the degree of financial autonomy which might alter this expectation. Hence it may well be that the best course in the short run is to avoid complicated arguments about this, that and the other kind of federalism, old or new, and to concentrate on specific social objectives. Dull for the constitutional lawyers, but we can still earn a guinea or two advising on the methods for getting around the Constitution as she is. The main enemy in the short run is not the federalism of the Constitution in general, nor the Governor-General, but the Senate.

COMMENTARIES

J. L. Carrick

Professor Sawer begins by analysing the content and general thrust of A.L.P. policy over the two decades prior to 1972. He studies the attitudes which the A.L.P. as a group and Gough Whitlam in particular have adopted to federalism and to the Commonwealth Constitution as it now stands. He emphasises that the A.L.P. platform, its derivative policies and consequent expressions were heavily directed against the States and towards unification. He notes that Mr Whitlam was foremost in such centralist attitudes. He argues, however, that a major turning-point in Labor thinking occurred with the amendments to the A.L.P. federal platform in 1971 and that Mr Whitlam was the architect of such attitudinal changes. He then asserts that the A.L.P. in government faithfully reflected the new platform and that it decided to work within the framework of the Constitution to achieve a form of co-operative federalism. He expresses the view that the A.L.P. 'would do well to return to a frank unificationist policy' and concludes that 'the main enemy in the short-run is not the federalism of the Constitution in general, nor the Governor-General, but the Senate'. The enemy of what? Presumably of Labor's objectives.

And yet, in neither the words nor the deeds of Labor or its leader is there any support for Professor Sawer's assertions. Certainly, by his own definition of 'co-operative federalism' he argues against himself. And, in fact, is he not really inferring throughout that Whitlam has remained a nostalgic and active unificationist, with a strong and unregenerate anti-State bias? What are the facts? Did the A.L.P. and Mr Whitlam suffer a genuine change in 1971, or was 1971 simply a massive cosmetic operation on the eve of a vital federal election? Or even more importantly, did the A.L.P. decide to work within the Constitution towards a true co-operative federalism or did it decide that within the existing powers of the Constitution it could achieve its former socialist and unificationist goals?

Professor Sawer asserts the former. Mr Whitlam in his Fabian Lecture of 25 June 1972[1] — significantly, in the year following the alteration of the A.L.P. platform and within months of a federal election — states the latter. The text of that 1972 lecture is critical to an understanding of the Whitlam philosophy. In it he argues that 'radical change' (his own words) in terms of Labor's socialist objectives can be achieved within the first three years of office. He goes on to say:

> It would be intolerable if a Labor government were to use the alibi of the Constitution to excuse failure to achieve its socialist objectives — doubly intolerable because it is just not true that it need do so.

He further argues:

> My basic proposition is this: if s. 92 is held up as the bulwark of private enterprise, then s. 96 is the charter of public enterprise and s. 51 the key to national responsibility and national regeneration.

And those who had perceived a new Whitlam and a new Labor Party eager to

---

[1]E.G. Whitlam, 'Labor at Home' in *Labor in Power — What is the Difference?* (Victorian Fabian Pamphlet 22, Melbourne, 1972), pp. 2-3.

put aside unification and to embrace co-operative federalism might well ponder at the following Whitlam passage from the 1972 lecture:

> I want you to think about this proposition: any function of our society which can be hitched to the star of the Commonwealth grows in quality and affluence. Any function or activity which is financially limited to the States will grow slowly or even decline. Further, a function will be fairly financed to the extent that the Commonwealth finds the money for it. A function will be unfairly and inadequately financed if the whole burden falls upon the States.

There, surely, speaks the old Whitlam, the man who expressed in his writing *Labor and the Constitution* his objective for the destruction of the States in these words:

> Much can be achieved by Labor members of the State Parliaments in effectuating Labor's aims of more effective powers for the national parliament and for local government. *Their role is to bring about their own dissolution.*[2]

An even clearer insight is recorded in Commonwealth Hansard of 13 October 1954 in Mr Whitlam's reply to the then member for Bradfield on the subject of uniform taxation and State powers. Mr Whitlam is recorded as replying:

> This uniform taxation system does as he (Mr Turner) said, debase politics. It does as he said debauch the States.
>
> And it does lead to the enunciation of the perfectly reasonable theory that those who spend the money should bear the odium of raising it.
>
> But the solution lies, not in abandoning the uniform taxation system, *but in taking over those functions of the States which the States at present administer, but for which the Commonwealth foots the bill.*
>
> We on this side of the House certainly believe that those who spend the money should have the odium of raising it and the corollary is that those who wish to get the credit for spending money should be those who raise it. . .
>
> The uniform taxation system is not something which the Constituion imposes on this Parliament. It is something which the Constitution enables this Parliament to impose on the States if it wishes to do so.[3]

This is the Whitlam who in his lecture 'Local Government — Structure and Finances' of 22 May 1970 decribed his aim for government structure as:

> .... a House of Representatives for nation-wide and international matters, an assembly for each of our dozen largest cities and a few score regional assemblies for the areas of rural population and resources development outside those cities.

The abolition of the Senate and of the six State Parliaments and the amalgamation of the 930 municipalities and shires into fifty or sixty regions subservient to a single, all-powerful House — these were the blueprints, described not long before the 1972 elections. The insistence on the establishment of regions for local government financing and the development of a number of Commonwealth initiatives by-passing the States were surely initial steps towards this broad structure.

In Mr Whitlam's words of 1972, 'Section 96 is the charter of public enterprise'. Professor Sawer suggests that 'tied grants' are instruments of Federal-State co-operation. They are in fact, as all the States know, the weapons of centralist coercion and the massive and continuous erosion of State sovereignty. To suggest that, in the great majority of instances, the States have

---

[2]E.G. Whitlam, 'The Constitution *versus* Labor' (1957) in *Labor and the Constitution* (Victorian Fabian Society Pamphlet 11, Melbourne, 1965), p.26. Emphasis added.

[3]House of Representatives, *Debates* 1954, vol. H of R 5, pp. 1964-5. Emphasis added.

any choice but to accept s. 96 grants is to fail to grasp the reality of politics. No State can refuse to do something which is electorally attractive. In consequence, as the s. 96 grants proliferate, so the Commonwealth widens its domination over State functions. The following table, prepared by the Commonwealth Parliamentary Library, tells the story:

COMMONWEALTH PAYMENTS TO OR FOR THE STATES
CURRENT AND CONSTANT PRICES 1970-71 TO 1974-75

	1970-1	1971-2	1972-3	1973-4	1974-5
In current values					
General Revenue Assistance	1,480	1,537	1,701	1,923	2,482
General Purpose Capital Funds	200	219	249	278	346
Specific Purpose Payments	728	708	931	1,568	2,868
Total	2,408	2,464	2,881	3,770	5,695
In constant values					
General Revenue Assistance	1,480	1,405	1,430 (59.0%)	1,403	1,431 (43.6%)
General Purpose Capital Funds	200	200	209 (8.6%)	203	199 (6.0%)
Specific Purpose Payments	728	647	783 (32.4%)	1,144	1,654 (50.3%)
Total	2,408	2,253	2,421	2,751	3,285

In 1972-3 (the last financial year for which the Federal Liberal Government was responsible), specific purpose payments represented 32.4 per cent of Commonwealth payments to the States. At the end of the first two years of the Whitlam Government those payments reached 50.3 per cent or more than one half. In the final year the percentage increased further. Professor Sawer, in seeking to define his concept of co-operative federalism, identifies the need for the States or regions to have 'a degree of guarantee of the area of autonomy which the centre and the regions in the system are respectively given'. But this is precisely what the s. 96 grants erode and destroy. The two are antipathetic when s. 96 is used as a major weapon of Commonwealth policy.

The philosophy of tax-harvesting by the Whitlam Government was itself conceived as a major centralist socialist weapon, aimed at significantly increasing the size of the public sector and the thrust of central policies. The following table tells its own story:

TOTAL INCOME TAX RECEIPTS

1970-71	(Actual)	$ 3,178.2 million
1971-72	(Actual)	$ 3,768.5 million
1972-73*	(Actual)	$ 4,089.5 million
1973-74	(Actual)	$ 5,490.3 million
1974-75	(Actual)	$ 7,714.0 million
1975-76	(Estimate)	$10,340.0 million

* Last L/CP Budget

In three years of Whitlam government, total receipts of personal income tax almost trebled, while customs tax, excise and sales tax doubled. The Commonwealth dominated the revenue-collection arena, to the absolute exclusion of any concept of co-operative federalism in that field which is critical to the test of sovereignty or subjection.

The same pattern of central domination was evident in a wide field of Whitlam Government legislation. In general, where Commonwealth legislation could be initiated, there was no attempt to achieve consensus or co-operation with the States. Functions which might naturally be regarded as predominantly State-oriented (for example, national parks and wildlife, environment and the like) were overrun by Commonwealth legislation, often asserting a head of constitutional power of very dubious substance. The external affairs power (and in particular international treaties) were relied on to assert centralist authority. A similar centralist philosophy dominated Labor's appointments to the High Court, where both appointees demonstrated in their opinions, as Professor Sawer has elsewhere acknowledged, that they were favourably inclined to expansive construction of Commonwealth powers.

Professor Sawer asserts that 'the main constitutional problem was not the reach of federal power but the structure of the Senate'. He acknowledges that 'notwithstanding the voting patterns of that House, it must be regarded as owing its existence to federalism and in a sense appropriate for carrying out a federal objective — the representation at the federal level of the prevailing pattern of political opinion in each State separately considered'. He concludes that 'the main enemy ... is the Senate'. Labor policy, traditionally, is the abolition of the Senate. All Mr Whitlam's main writings envisage that objective.

But it can be argued persuasively that the Senate is fundamental to the preservation of a true system of federalism and, indeed, that s. 53 of the Constitution, which defines the Senate's money powers, is imperative to that objective. Professor Sawer argues that 'the principal constitutional achievement of the Whitlam Government, technically though perhaps not politically, was the discovery of government by double-dissolution under s. 57 of the Constitution'. This, presumably, is seen as a virtue — a proper use of power to achieve an election and to secure vital legislation. He is silent on the use of s. 53 of the Constitution by an Opposition for a similar objective. At Federation, it was not seen as sufficient protection for the States that all States (large or small) should have an equal number of senators. Clearly, if the Senate were to be denied a reserve money power (the power in s. 53 to accept, request or reject but not to amend), then the more populous States in the Lower House (and in the Cabinet) could carve up the financial 'cake' to their own benefit and to the serious detriment of the smaller or less populous States. If s. 53 is to be emasculated, then the Senate will no longer be a truly federalist chamber. If the Senate is weakened or destroyed, then New South Wales and Victoria will dominate central decision-making. How then does federalism (co-operative or otherwise) survive?

Professor Sawer's subjective judgments sometimes intrude, as in the following curious passage:

> Local government has no such status and could be given it only by what I would regard as a disastrous bit of constitutional tinkering—one giving them the same sort of opportunities for obstruction and mischief-making as the States have.

Why, emotively or otherwise, have the States more capacity for 'obstruction and mischief-making' than the Commonwealth? Mistrust of power in the hands of the States or local government (or regions) is the very antithesis of federalism; in fact it is the mainspring of centralism and unification. The Professor's definition of 'organic federalism' is revealing. It reads as follows:

> Organic federalism requires a dominant centre, having substantial control of the financial resources of the country and the ability to decide at least in general terms all major policy questions, including spending priorities.

This, in plain words, appears to be a curious euphemism, convoluted in thought and an apologia for unification.

And after all, what Professor Sawer recommends to the Labor Party as its future path (that, in his own words 'the A.L.P. would do well to return to a frank unification platform') is not only the path which Labor has never diverted from, but is in fact the journey described in Professor Sawer's essay.

A.C. Castles

The linguistic underground tells us that a weasel word is one which can be used to cover the true processes of our thinking. A weasel word may be used also to hide the fact that we have perhaps done little or no thinking at all. As a result, when we use a weasel word we may often find different people talking of quite different things. The phrase 'common law', for example, may well be regarded as a convenient but often not a very meaningful combination of two weasel words. Certainly the phrase has meant different things at different periods in history. And today it may still be used in different senses.

Federalism is a classic weasel word. We may, for example, loosely describe the Australian and Canadian systems of government as being 'federal'. The fact is, however, that in constitutional terms the British North America Act gives a veto power to the central government over provincial legislation while in Australia no such authority is vested in the national government. Juristically, it might be said then, in the last analysis, that the Australian system retains more autonomy for the States and is therefore more 'federal' than in its Canadian counterpart. And yet there are those who might contend that in political terms there is greater autonomy vested in the Canadian provinces compared to the Australian States, making the Canadian system more federal at least in this sense. Certainly if autonomy of governmental units is one touchstone for determining the existence of a federal state, in practical terms the working of government in Canada today might be regarded as being more federal than its Australian counterpart. Clearly though, what is federalism in one context, or one person's view of it, may seem like centralism to another.

When we begin compounding the situation by using phrases like 'co-operative federalism', essential as these may be in terms of political rhetoric, the situation can become even more complex and uncertain. What Professor Sawer decribes as 'co-operative federalism' in the Whitlam mould, and as operative between 1972 and 1975, may mean something marginally, or even substantially, different from the notion of co-operative federalism in the thinking of Prime Minister Fraser and Premier Bjelke-Petersen of Queensland. The fact is that catch-phrases like this may tell us something, but not all that much, as Professor Sawer confirms. At best, all we can really say when this phrase is used is that there is a stated intent for our system of government to fit in somewhere on a graduated scale between what Professor Sawer describes as organic and co-ordinate federalism. Even then there may be dangers in attempting to refine this definition, even to this extent. Hold-up style federalism, fostered and nurtured by tied grants and centralised policy making sanctioned under s. 96 of the Constitution, is probably hallowed now in Australian usage as a form of co-operation. But there are those who would argue that this should not be regarded as an example of 'co-operation'.

With this in mind, in assessing whether the A.L.P. administration between 1972 and 1975 could be said to have been moving towards a new federal structure, and the centralisation which might go with this, we should, if we can, ignore the largely rhetorical flourish encompassed in the phrase 'co-operative federalism'. And as Professor Sawer points out, there is little purpose in using the stated policies of the Party as an important signpost to determine the essence of its approach to federalism. These contain elements of ambiguity and ambivalence. Rather, we should concentrate our attention on the Party's performance in office.

Overall, it can hardly be doubted that the main thrust of the administration was to move the working of government closer towards organic federalism and the centralism exemplified by this. If autonomy is the touchstone of federalism, as Professor Sawer suggests, then the existence of tied grants and the policy making which may go with them under s. 96 provides one reasonably objective test of the degree of autonomy existing between the central government and the States. And in this regard the statistics show substantial increases in the use of tied grants during the first two years of A.L.P. administration. In itself, of course, this was not an irreversible trend. But, importantly, the increased use of tied grants was coupled with the establishment of a number of new institutional arrangements for the distribution of funds, such as the Commissions to which Professor Sawer refers. Institutional forms like this can in time create dynamics of their own which are hard to unwind, as is well evidenced in the case of the Universities Commission. Institutions like this, appointed and controlled from the centre, can in time lead to a marked degree of public acceptance of what may be largely, although not entirely, an accretion of power for the centre.

Constitutionally, of course, what happened with respect to s. 96 grants was nothing new. Basically there was an acceleration and expansion of processes fostered and nurtured in twenty-three years of Liberal-Country Party rule. At the same time, however, we should not overlook efforts by the A.L.P. administration which might be regarded as attempts to set in train new methods for expanding national power by setting out to test the limits of Commonwealth authority beyond those which have often been accepted in the past for constitutional or political reasons or sometimes both. At least two of these efforts were seemingly frustrated by a hostile Senate.[1] A third has been the subject of High Court examination, but without a clear result.[2] But even without new

---

[1] One was the suggestion (floated in the relatively innocuous context of abolishing all appeals to the Privy Council) of employing the 'request and consent' procedure in the Statute of Westminster to have legislation affecting the States passed by the British Parliament: the long term possibilities of such an exercise did not pass unnoticed in the States. The other was the attempted employment, in the Human Rights Bill, of the s.51(29) external affairs power to make sweeping inroads into areas of existing State authority.

[2] *i.e.*, the employment of the Commonwealth's spending power to establish embryonic regional units of government, upheld—but perhaps only temporarily—in the *A.A.P. Case* (1975) 7 A.L.R. 277.

moves the Constitution, as the experience of the past twenty-five years has shown, places few major barriers in the way of creating *de facto* unification in a number of areas, despite apparent State authority. Increasingly, too, as Professor Sawer hints, and as Deakin predicted many years ago, the role of the courts is progressively becoming much less significant in determining the thrust and direction of our system of government as between the central government and the States. The directions in which the federation will go will therefore be largely based on politics and not on law. And clearly, as experience has shown in the United States, Canada and even Australia, there is a variety of means which can be established to ameliorate and accommodate many of the problems which can arise in the practical working of the system.

If history is not to be dismissed as being too much the product of individual taste, it might also be argued that some of the ambivalence and ambiguity which may seem to be encompassed in the A.L.P.'s programmes before the 1972 election itself reflects the fact that the A.L.P. is still not immune from countervailing centralist and centrifugal elements. Notions of federalism built into policy-making processes may be one reason for this. But the A.L.P. has more often had periods of sustained office in the States, and in some fields, as evidenced for example by the Lang period of office in New South Wales, this has enabled policies to be instituted, and nationally accepted, which otherwise may have gone for years without the prospect of implementation. There are many matters where national control is both necessary and desirable, even if the Constitution seems to declare otherwise, as in the case of industrial relations, but there are many others where a good deal of local autonomy, fiscal and otherwise, should be maintained.

2 Explorations and Adventures with Commonwealth Powers

Michael Crommelin and Gareth Evans

I
INTRODUCTION

Australian Labor Governments have usually been constitutionally adventurous, anxious to explore to the limits the powers which the Constitution confers upon the Commonwealth Government and Parliament. The Whitlam Government of 1972-1975 followed in this respect the most lively traditions of the Fisher and Chifley years. It is the object of this essay to review the main constitutional initiatives taken by the Whitlam Government across the whole spectrum of governmental activity, from control of the macro-economy to the protection of civil rights, and to determine whether, when the dust has settled, these explorations and adventures with Commonwealth power have wrought any lasting change to the distribution of constitutional power between Commonwealth and States.

The constitutional initiatives undertaken by the Whitlam Government covered a very wide canvas. It is perhaps remarkable that so many have survived unscathed. Certainly there was nothing comparable to the shattering s. 92 defeats of the Chifley Government in the *Airlines* and *Bank Nationalization* cases,[1] the striking down of large portions of the same Government's social welfare legislation,[2] or the constitutional defeats of the Fisher-Deakin years.[3] There were few challenges to the Whitlam Government's legislation, and no major defeats.[4] An explanation may be found in the fact that, while the Whitlam Government was certainly more sure-footed legally than it proved to be politically, its constitutional innovativeness lay not so much in any breathtaking assertion of quite new powers as in the unparalleled pace at which new applications of already familiar powers were explored. Still, one must be careful not to overstate the success or significance of its achievements. Some initiatives survived only by the skin of their teeth; others may yet be challenged; others again were never enacted, and hence the question of High Court challenge did not arise.

Whether the Whitlam Government is to be praised or blamed for its constitutional initiatives is as much a political as a legal matter, and opinions will

---

[1] *Australian National Airways Pty Ltd* v. *Commonwealth* (1945) 71 C.L.R. 29; *Bank of New South Wales* v. *Commonwealth* (1948) 76 C.L.R. 1.

[2] *Attorney-General (Vic.) (ex rel. Dale)* v. *Commonwealth (Pharmaceutical Benefits Case)* (1946) 71 C.L.R. 237; *British Medical Association* v. *Commonwealth* (1949) 79 C.L.R. 201.

[3] Especially *R.* v. *Barger* (1908) 6 C.L.R. 41 and *Huddart Parker & Co. Pty Ltd* v. *Moorehead* (1909) 8 C.L.R. 330.

[4] The *Petroleum and Minerals Authority Case* is no exception, being struck down for procedural rather than substantive reasons: *Victoria* v. *Commonwealth* (1975) 7 A.L.R.1. The *Family Law Case* (1976) 9 A.L.R.103, discussed in Part V below, did result in the loss of some provisions from that Act, but none of real importance.

differ. We do no more than express our firm view that there is nothing improper in a government's seeking to explore to the fullest its constitutional power. The point has been made succinctly by the present Attorney-General, Mr Ellicott, when he spoke in 1974 to the Whitlam Government's National Parks and Wildlife Conservation Bill:

> Uncertainty as to the extent of constitutional power should never of itself be a reason for opposing an otherwise worthwhile legislative exercise of power; nor should it prevent a government, properly advised, treading where angels of constitutional probity have formerly feared to tread. The High Court, as we know, will readily give us the answer.[5]

II
CONTROL OF THE NATIONAL ECONOMY

Modern economic problems are intractable enough without governments having to fight them one-handed. The perennial problem of the Australian Federation has been that no level of government in the system is armed with all the constitutional power necessary for systematic and effective macro-economic management. The founding fathers did not foresee or appreciate the necessity for government intervention in the working of the economy, either by governments generally or the central government in particular, and the Constitution they wrote reflects this inattention. The result has been recently well stated by Barwick CJ:

> [A]ny student of the Constitution must be acutely aware of the many topics which are now of considerable concern to Australia as a whole which have not been assigned to the Commonwealth. Perhaps the most notable instance is in relation to the national economy itself. There is but one economy of the country, not six: it could not be denied that the economy of the nation is of national concern. But no specific power over the economy is given to the Commonwealth. Such control as it exercises on that behalf must be effected by indirection through taxation, including customs and excise, banking, including the activities of the Reserve Bank and the budget, whether it be in surplus or in deficit.[6]

Fringe Banking

While the extent of the control over budget and credit policy which the Commonwealth in practice has been able to achieve through its miscellany of powers should not be understated, there are some gaps in the armoury. One of the major ones in the past has been with respect to credit policy in the fringe banking sector: blunt and indirect instruments like the bank rate and open market operations have been quite ineffective in regulating the activities of building societies, finance companies, credit unions and the like, although these institutions have had in recent years almost as significant an economic influence as the banks themselves. This gap was effectively filled by the Whitlam Government's enactment of the *Financial Corporations Act* 1974, which empowers the government to monitor the activities of the larger incorporated non-bank financial institutions and to apply, through the Reserve Bank, specific controls with regard to asset ratios, interest rates and lending

---

[5]House of Representatives, *Debates* 1974, vol. 92, p.4524.

[6]*Victoria v. Commonwealth (A.A.P. Case)* (1975) 7 A.L.R. 277, at p.298; see also the *Report from the Joint Committee on Constitutional Review*, 1959, paras 981, 1026-1030.

policies.[7] The Act is based squarely on the s.51(20) corporations power in that it applies to foreign, trading or financial corporations whose 'sole or principal business activities in Australia . . . are the borrowing of money and the provision of finance'. While the High Court has not yet pronounced upon the meaning of 'financial corporations' there can be no doubt but that the Act, viewed as a whole, is a law with respect to such corporations within the meaning of s.51(20). If a trade practices law regulating the trading activities of trading corporations is, as has been held,[8] at the very heart of the corporations power, then so too must be a law whose intention and immediate effect is to regulate the finance-providing activities of financial corporations.

Prices and Incomes

The Whitlam Government sought specific powers over prices and incomes in the referendum of 8 December 1973, but was resoundingly defeated.[9] It was obliged as a result to seek out more indirect means to the same end.

On the incomes side, one of the measures taken was manipulation of Australian Public Service pay levels, initially with the object — or at least effect — of leading off a frenzied round of wage-chasing elsewhere, and subsequently with the object of trying to rein wages back; needless to say the first endeavour was more successful than the second.[10] The Labor Government also took an actively interventionist role before the Arbitration Commission in national wage cases. Section 51(35) of the Constitution allows the Commonwealth to create arbitration machinery, but not to regulate private sector wages any more directly than that. It had been usual practice for national governments in recent years, recognising their limited constitutional role, merely to tender economic evidence to the Commission and not to appear in any sense as a party to the proceedings seeking to decisively influence the outcome.[11] The groundwork was laid for a significant change of attitude when, early in the life of the Whitlam Government, responsibility for preparing national wage case submissions was shifted from Treasury to the Department of Labour. Substantial submissions were made at the 1973 and 1974 hearings (including vigorous support for the implementation of equal pay), but the Government's activism, and influence, was at its height in the meetings and hearings which followed the Cabinet decision of July 1974 to support the introduction of wage indexation.

On the prices side, a valiant if somewhat rash attempt was made to curb price rises at a stroke by the across-the-board 25 per cent tariff cut announced in July 1973, but the Whitlam Government's major endeavours in this respect were built around the Prices Justification Tribunal. The Tribunal, established by the

---

[7]No such controls had in fact been applied by November 1975, but a register of the relevant corporations had been compiled: *Australian Government Gazette*, 17 October 1975.

[8]*Strickland* v. *Rocla Concrete Pipes Ltd (Concrete Pipes Case)* (1971) 124 C.L.R. 468 per Barwick CJ at p.489, Menzies J at p.508.

[9]See J.E. Richardson, 'Reform of the Constitution: The Referendums and Constitutional Convention', below Ch. 3.

[10]On the 'pace-setter' and 'fat cats' periods, see generally C.J. Lloyd and G.S. Reid, *Out of the Wilderness — The Return of Labor* (Melbourne, 1974) at pp.238-43, P. Kelly, *The Unmaking of Gough* (Sydney, 1976) Ch. 7, and J.O.N. Perkins, *Macro-economic Policy in Australia* (2nd ed., Melbourne, 1975) at p.76.

[11]E.I. Sykes and H.J. Glasbeek, *Labour Law in Australia* (Sydney, 1972) at p.614.

Prices Justification Act 1973,[12] has aroused considerable interest among both economists and lawyers as the first peacetime[13] excursion ever attempted by a Commonwealth government into the field of direct price control. The expression 'price control' is not strictly accurate, in that the Act does not impose any sanctions at all on companies which choose to ignore the Tribunal's findings. But what the Act does is impose quite substantial sanctions (in the form of $10,000 fines, recoverable in the Industrial Court) on companies within its scope[14] which do not *notify* their proposed price increases to the Tribunal, or which having notified them, go ahead and increase their prices before the Tribunal has had the time to hold (or, alternatively waive its right to hold) an inquiry into whether the increase is 'justified'.[15]

The Act depends for its constitutional validity in the first instance on the s.51(20) corporations power, being expressed to apply only to foreign, trading and financial corporations (i.e. the 'constitutional' corporations) rather than to companies, firms and traders at large. In this respect it is probably soundly based. After *Concrete Pipes*,[16] it would seem, as has already been stated, that whatever else the corporations power extends to, its minimum content is the power to regulate the trading activities of constitutional corporations:[17] the sale of goods and services is on any view the paradigm trading activity, and price-setting is inextricably connected with selling. Even if the Act should be narrowly, and implausibly, construed as extending in its immediate operation not to trading activities as such but rather internal matters preparatory to trade (because it does not bite directly on prices but only specifies procedures for their notification and examination), it is likely that it would still be upheld as a legitimate exercise of the corporations power.[18]

The real constitutional difficulty with the Prices Justification Act lies not in its affirmative base in the corporations power, but in the negative effect of s.92. Does the Act constitute an interference with interstate trade of the kind which is prohibited by that section? There are two early cases in which price fixing laws were challenged on s.92 grounds, but neither concludes the present issue.[19] In the present somewhat fluid state of the law, it would appear that

---

[12]As amended by the *Prices Justification Act* 1974.

[13]For wartime price control mechanisms, all conducted under the auspices of the s.51(6) defence power, see R. Scott, *Prices Justification in Australia* (Sydney, 1975) Ch. 1.

[14]The Act is confined in its operation to companies with an annual turnover of $20 million or more: s.5. There is also provision for the exemption of certain companies from the operation of the Act either generally or conditionally, and this has been much employed in the case of retailers and wholesalers dealing in a mass of small items.

[15]The Act does not contain any criteria as to what constitutes a 'justified' price. There has been a controversy, in which the Government intervened in interesting ways, as to what extent, if at all, the Tribunal should take into account in its deliberations the profits earmarked for new investment. Mr Whitlam wrote to the Tribunal 'indicating the Government's view' on this matter on 12 November 1974, and in July 1975 the Government appeared before the Tribunal as a party for the first time (as it was entitled to do like any other 'person or body' under s.20 of the Act) to argue successfully for a change of Tribunal viewpoint on the issue: see P.J. Parsons, 'Prices Justification in Australia — The First Twenty Months' (1975) 6 *Federal L.Rev.* 367, at pp. 388, 395-6.

[16](1971) 124 C.L.R. 468.

[17]Above, n. 8.

[18]Cf. Isaacs J in *Huddart Parker & Co. Pty Ltd* v. *Moorehead* (1908) 8 C.L.R. 330, at pp. 395-6.

[19]In *W. & A. McArthur* v. *Queensland* (1920) 28 C.L.R. 530, the main emphasis of the case was on eliciting which of the various types of sale in issue had an 'interstate' element: once that was clear, it was simply assumed, without discussion, that the law was a prohibited burden. The wide view taken of the operation of s.92 here must be seen to be associated with the view of the Court, subsequently overturned, that s.92 did not bind the Commonwealth. In *Wragg* v. *New South Wales* (1953) 88 C.L.R. 353 the emphasis was again on the interstateness element, which was held here to be not present;

legislation capable of applying to interstate transactions must, to be valid, surmount two hurdles: in the first place, it must not directly burden interstate trade or commerce, and secondly, if it does, it must be of a 'merely regulatory' character.[20] The question as to what constitutes a direct burden on interstate trade has been answered in a variety of ways over the years. Until quite recently, the prevailing test appeared to embody the approach of Dixon CJ and Kitto J[21] which ruled out only those legislative burdens on interstate trade which operated expressly by reference to an act forming some integral part of interstate trade. It now appears, however, that the present Chief Justice has gained support for his approach, which asks whether the obligation in question 'constitutes in a practical sense a burden upon trade, commerce or intercourse amongst the States or any part or aspect of it'.[22] Neither approach is at all easy to apply in practice, but while there may have at least been room for argument under the Dixonian test that the legal obligations created by the Prices Justification Act operated to burden acts 'antecedent' or 'ancillary' to interstate trade rather than that trade itself, it is much easier to assert that the practical consequences of the Act — involving as it does, at the very least, substantial delays in the implementation of price increases — would be to fetter the free conduct of interstate trade, and that it satisfies the 'direct burden' description for that reason.

But can the Act nonetheless survive, in its application to interstate trade, as being 'merely regulatory'? No generally accepted formula has yet emerged to describe the kinds of regulation which will be regarded as reasonable: the most often repeated nostrum is that of Barwick CJ to the effect that a 'law to be relevantly regulatory must in its nature and in the extent of its reach be concerned with the accommodation of the activities of members of the Australian community each to the other, particularly in matters of trade and commerce, so that it can properly be said that each is free to engage in such trade and commerce'.[23] The most relevant recent guides to the High Court's likely attitude to prices justification laws are the *Readers' Digest*[24] decision on trading stamp inducements and the *Mikasa*[25] decision on resale price maintenance. Both the laws there in question were held to be valid, though in the former case only over a vigorous dissent from Barwick CJ, who took the view that only laws aimed at controlling 'deceitful, fraudulent, restrictive or monopolistic practices'[26] could be regulated consistently with s.92. Generally

---

although Taylor J, in a judgment expressly agreed with by five other members of the Court, including Dixon CJ, said at p. 397 that the price restrictions here in issue were 'of a character entirely different from the imposts' which had earlier been held invalid in the Petrol Cases. In any event, it is to be noted that these cases were both concerned with direct price-fixing laws, rather than the kind of notification/justification obligations in issue under the Prices Justification Act.

[20] A good account of the most recent developments in s.92 law is G. Caine, 'Regulation: The Key to Control of Interstate Trade' (1976) 50 *Australian L.J.* 118.

[21] Articulated by Dixon J as early as *O. Gilpin Ltd* v. *Commissioner for Road Transport* (1935) 52 C.L.R. 189, at pp. 204-6, and by Kitto J in cases such as *Samuels* v. *Readers' Digest Association Pty Ltd* (1969) 120 C.L.R. 1, at p.31.

[22] *Samuels*, cited above n. 21, at p.17. In the most recent reported s.92 case, *North Eastern Dairy Co. Ltd* v. *Dairy Industry Authority of New South Wales* (1975) 7 A.L.R. 433, the Dixonian 'legal effect' or 'criterion of liability' test was clearly favoured only by Gibbs J, whereas the 'practical operation' test appears to have been adopted by Stephen, Mason and Jacobs JJ as well as Barwick CJ.

[23] *Mikasa (N.S.W.) Pty Ltd* v. *Festival Stores* (1972) 127 C.L.R. 617, at p.629.

[24] *Samuels* v. *Readers' Digest Association Pty Ltd* (1969) 120 C.L.R. 1.

[25] Cited above n. 23.

[26] (1969) 120 C.L.R. 1, at p.20.

speaking, notwithstanding the Chief Justice's particular caveats, there seems to be a willingness in the Court at large to accept the legitimacy of laws which do not amount to barriers to trade and commerce so much as set the 'framework' within which it is carried on.[27] In the result, it is likely that the Prices Justification Act, given both its general anti-inflationary rationale and the fact that it does not go so far as to actually compel the trader to set his prices at a particular level, would be regarded as a 'framework' law and valid for that reason. But it may be as well for the Whitlam Government's constitutional record that the Prices Justification Tribunal was one adventure that never came to be so tested.

III
REGULATION OF COMMERCE

Australia was until recently one of the least regulated industrial economies, standing in striking contrast, in particular, to the United States with its mass of detailed legislation administered through such agencies as the Federal Trade Commission and the Securities and Exchange Commission. It was not that there was no perceived need in this country for national company, securities and trade practices legislation: the problem rather lay with the perceived absence of the necessary constitutional power, and the unwillingness of governments for many years to do anything about either seeking new powers or exploring the limits of the ones they had. Certainly Australia's overseas and interstate commerce clause[28] has not been the same 'legislative cornucopia'[29] as its United States counterpart,[30] which has in that country been the primary means by which government regulation has been able to pervade nearly every aspect of commercial activity. The American Supreme Court has accepted, in a way the High Court has so far refused to,[31] that the necessary interdependence of modern economic activity is such that the national government ought to be able to control any local activity which is 'commingled' with, or indeed just has some 'effect' on, interstate of foreign commerce.

The great hope of Australian economic interventionists has been the s.51(20) corporations power which, although emasculated at its first outing by the High

---

[27]See the specific language of Menzies and Stephen JJ to this effect in *Mikasa* (1972) 127 C.L.R. 617, at pp. 640 and 655, and the discussion in Caine, cited above n. 20 at pp. 121-3.

[28]Constitution s. 51(1) 'Trade and commerce with other countries, and among the States'.

[29]A.I. Tonking, 'Federal Competence to Legislate for the Control of the Securities Market' (1973) 47 *Australian L.J.* 231, at p.235.

[30]Art. 1, s.8, cl. 3: 'Congress shall have power to regulate Commerce with foreign Nations, and among the several States, and with the Indian Tribes'.

[31]The major statement is that of Dixon J in *Wragg* v. *New South Wales* (1953) 88 C.L.R. 353, at p. 385-6; 'the distinction which is drawn between inter-State and the domestic trade of a State . . . by s.51(1) . . . may well be considered artificial and unsuitable to modern times. But it is a distinction adopted by the Constitution and it must be observed however much interdependence may now exist between the two divisions of trade and commerce which the Constitution thus distinguishes'.

This has not stopped the Commonwealth from trying, from time to time, to break down the barriers. Perhaps the most interesting experiment of the Labor Government in this respect was the Travel Agents Bill 1975 (another measure before the Senate at the time of the Government's dismissal). Clause 1 provided that 'this Act applies to and in relation to a person who is carrying on business in Australia in connexion with the carriage of persons for reward on prescribed journeys *but applies to such person in relation to the whole of his business as a travel agent*' [Emphasis added]. 'Prescribed journeys' are defined in cl. 5(2) as those with an interstate, overseas, or territorial character, the Bill clearly relying on ss.51(1) and 122 for its constitutionality.

Court in 1909,[32] had seemed (at least since the *Engineers Case*[33] in 1920 set the whole course of High Court constitutional interpretation on a new and pro-Commonwealth path) only to be awaiting for its resurrection the advent of a federal government with temerity or inclination enough to rely on it. It is in fact the coalition Government of the 1960s, and in particular its Attorney-General, Mr Garfield Barwick, as he then was, that deserves the credit for taking the first step towards the revival of the power by enacting the *Trade Practices Act* 1965, the inevitable challenge to which, in the *Concrete Pipes Case*,[34] resulted in the High Court's expansive definition of the scope of the power. But it is to the Labor Government of 1972-75 that there belongs the credit, if such it be, for following through the *Concrete Pipes* doctrine and relying on the corporations power to support an extraordinarily wide range of government economic regulation. The possibility of utilizing other heads of constitutional power to support particular forms of regulation was by no means overlooked, and the nature of these adventures will be noted in context below, but the corporations power was overwhelmingly the most important base for the Whitlam Government's programmes in this area. It is on the reach of this power that those programmes must primarily stand or fall.

Trade Practices[35]

The *Trade Practices Act* 1974 reaches much further than any of its predecessors. It specifically outlaws a number of new practices, including monopolization, exclusive dealing, price discrimination and 'arrangements or understandings in restraint of trade', creates a Trade Practices Commission with extensive oversight and enforcement powers, and introduces sweeping new criminally-punishable consumer protection provisions.

The Act is drafted in the first instance around the corporations power in that all its key provisions are expressed to apply to activities engaged in by foreign corporations, or trading or financial corporations formed within the limits of Australia, or by persons dealing with such corporations.[36] There are three major questions which arise with respect to the use of the corporations power in the Act. The first is the perennial one as to what kinds of corporations are in fact picked up by the s.51(20) description. Although the High Court has now announced that the fact that a corporation engages in trade does not necessarily make it a 'trading corporation',[37] it is nonetheless likely that the great majority of private sector companies engaged in buying and selling goods and services would be subsumed within one or other of the constitutional categories.[38] The second question is whether there are any limits, trespassed by the Act, as to the kinds of activities which the corporations power can reach. As with the other

---

[32] *Huddart Parker and Co. Pty Ltd* v. *Moorehead* (1909) 8 C.L.R. 330.

[33] *Amalgamated Society of Engineers* v. *Adelaide Steamship Co. Ltd* (1920) 28 C.L.R. 129.

[34] (1971) 124 C.L.R. 468.

[35] For a full account of the constitutional issues here, see G. Evans, 'The Constitutional Validity and Scope of the Trade Practices Act 1974' (1975) 49 *Australian L.J.* 654.

[36] See Part IV, ss.45-50, Part V, ss.52-54, 56-65 and 67-74, Part VIII on Resale Price Maintenance, and Part VII on Authorizations and Clearances. 'Corporations' are defined in s.4(1) basically in the language of s.51(20), but note also here the extension (repeated in the Corporations and Securities Industry Bill, discussed below) of 'financial corporations' to corporations which carry on banking (s.51(13)) or insurance (s.51(14)) business.

[37] *R.* v. *Trade Practices Tribunal; Ex parte St George County Council* (1974) 2 A.L.R. 371.

[38] See Evans, cited above n. 35, at pp. 656-60.

'person' powers in the Constitution, the outer limits of the corporations power are obscure,[39] but the High Court has made it clear that laws dealing with the *trading* activities of constitutional corporations are at the very heart of the power[40] and it seems that the *Trade Practices Act* 1974 can be characterized without too much difficulty as wholly to do with trading activities. What is less clear is whether the activities of persons who are not constitutional corporations can be caught up by the corporations power in so far as they engage in dealings with constitutional corporations: the Act is drafted on the assumption that either s.51(20) itself or the s.51(39) incidental power will carry such cases, but a successful challenge to the relevant provisions is not beyond contemplation.[41] The third question, which arises equally with the corporations power and the other possible supporting heads, is whether the Act infringes s.92: the short answer, since *Mikasa*,[42] is that the Act is almost certainly safe as being 'merely regulatory'.

The *Trade Practices Act* 1974, as did its 1965 predecessor, seeks to extend its operation beyond s.51(20) corporations to persons generally who are engaged in interstate or overseas trade (s.51(1)), territorial trade (s.122), and involved in dealings with the Commonwealth.[43] In addition, passing reliance is made on the external affairs power in one rather obscurely drawn provision,[44] but perhaps the most interesting new item is the reliance on s.51(5) to apply certain of the consumer protection provisions to conduct involving 'the use of postal, telegraphic or telephonic services or [which] takes place in a radio or television broadcast'.[45] Although this theme was not picked up, as it might have been, in other Labor legislation, it foreshadows a possibly greater use of the power by the Commonwealth in the future, following the United States example where it has long been central in the implementation of antitrust and securities legislation. There would appear to be, in Australia, little reason now to suppose that the High Court would rule out such uses of the power as 'doing indirectly what cannot be done directly'.[46]

The peril which any legislation runs which seeks to rely on a multiplicity of heads of power is that the High Court will decide, in the event of finding some part of the Act beyond power, that the Parliament's intentions as to the preservation of the remainder are (notwithstanding the salvationary role of

[39] *Cf.* ss.51(19) on aliens and 51(26) on 'the people of any race'. Is any law commencing 'No aliens shall . . .' or 'Every corporation shall . . .' necessarily a law with respect to aliens, or corporations? See Evans, cited above n. 35, at p.660.

[40] Per Barwick CJ in *Concrete Pipes* (1971) 124 C.L.R. 468, at p.489.

[41] See the discussion of ss.48, 49(4), 76, 80 and 96(2) in Evans, cited above n. 35, at pp. 665-6. The existence of these sections would not appear to militate against the overall characterization of the Act as being one with respect to corporations: see per Smithers J in *Commissioner of Trade Practices* v. *Caltex Oil* (1974) 4 A.L.R. 133, at p.160.

[42] *Mikasa (N.S.W.) Pty Ltd* v. *Festival Stores* (1972) 127 C.L.R. 617.

[43] The constitutional under-pinning for this provision is, in general terms, s.61 read together with s.51(39), together with a number of specific provisions depending on the transaction in question (e.g. s.51(6) for defence contracts).

[44] Section 55, dealing with misleading conduct to which the Industrial Property Convention applies. For a brief discussion of the present state of the external affairs power generally, see below pp. 48-51, and for its application to s.55, see Evans, cited above n. 35, at pp.668-70.

[45] Section 6(3). Broadcasting is now clearly subsumed within the s.51(5) classification of 'Postal, telegraphic, telephonic, and other like services': *R.* v. *Brislan; Ex parte Williams* (1935) 54 C.L.R. 262; *Jones* v. *Commonwealth (No. 2)* (1965) 112 C.L.R. 206.

[46] See Evans, cited above n. 35, at p.668; also C. Howard 'The Constitutional Power of the Commonwealth to Regulate the Securities Market' (1971) 45 *Australian L.J.* 388, at pp. 391-2.

s.15A of the *Acts Interpretation Act* 1901) insufficiently precise to guarantee its survival. Such a fate befell the 1965 Act in the *Concrete Pipes Case*,[47] and although the 1974 Act appears on its face to be an extremely sophisticated, streamlined piece of draftsmanship it is not beyond contemplation that it might be in trouble in this respect.[48]

Securities Industry

If the need for national regulation of the securities industry was ever in doubt, it was demonstrated dramatically and beyond dispute by the tabling of the report of the Senate Select Committee on Securities and Exchange (the Rae Report) on 18 July 1974. The Whitlam Government's attempt to deal with the problem, the 235-page 284-section Corporations and Securities Industry Bill, was introduced into the Parliament by Senator Murphy on 5 December 1974, and again by the new Attorney-General, Mr Enderby, on 13 February 1975; at the time of the Government's dismissal it was languishing before another Senate Committee. The primary focus of the Bill is, as might have been expected, on the regulation of stock markets and stock exchanges, and of persons dealing in securities, and it provides for the establishment of a Corporations and Exchange Commission with flexible rule-making powers as the main enforcement agency in this respect. The Bill goes, however, some distance further than this by providing for the registration of public companies, and their regulation in respect of such 'company law' matters as the disclosure and auditing of accounts, the issue of prospectuses and the conduct of takeovers.

The Corporations and Securities Industry Bill is drafted, for all practical purposes, solely in reliance on the corporations power. The registration requirements apply only in relation to s.51(20) corporations, as do the disclosure, prospectus, takeover and other such provisions; the regulation of dealing in securities is confined to the securities of constitutional corporations; and the regulation of stock exchanges is expressed so as to be capable of being confined to the activities of stock exchanges in their dealings with constitutional corporations.[49] Once again, then, the question as to what kinds of corporations are caught by s.51(20) assumes crucial importance. If Isaacs J's well-known list[50] of corporations 'outside the range of federal power' is even half right, clearly the Bill would be much emasculated; in particular, it is not difficult to regard domestically formed mining exploration companies (as distinct from those which sell their ore) as out of reach.

There is a real question as to whether the corporations power enables the full

---

[47](1971) 124 C.L.R. 468.

[48]See Evans, cited above n. 35, at pp. 654-5. The question is presently being litigated in the matter of *C.L.M. Holdings Pty Ltd*, heard before the High Court on 30-31 March 1976: see Transcript pp. 59-81, and especially the doubts expressed by Barwick CJ.

[49]Clause 53 draws the necessary, albeit rather tenuous, links with s.51(20) in the case of stock exchanges. The registration and other substantive provisions in relation to stock exchanges (Part IV) are drawn in the first instance without such express reliance: this may be an attempt to rely simply on the incidental power (as would be Part II, establishing the Corporations and Exchange Commission), or alternatively an exploration of the rather optimistic argument advanced by some commentators (e.g., Howard, cited above n. 46, at pp. 388-92, and Tonking, cited above n. 29, at p.238) that the s.51(1) trade and commerce power is sufficient in itself to support national stock market regulation.

[50]'. . . all those domestic corporations, for instance, which are constituted for municipal, mining, manufacturing, religious, scholastic, charitable, scientific and literary purposes, and perhaps others more nearly approximating a character of trading.' *Huddart Parker & Co. Pty Ltd* v. *Moorehead* (1909) 8 C.L.R. 330, at p.393.

range of regulation contemplated in the Bill. So far as those parts of the Bill are concerned which relate to the 'internal' affairs of corporations—accounts, prospectuses and the like—one strong view would have it that the power to regulate such matters is a necessary incident of the power to create corporations, and if the latter is lacking (which is assumed) then so too will be the former. Logically, this would not seem to follow inexorably. A more optimistic reading, from the Commonwealth point of view, might be based on Isaacs J's dictum in *Huddart Parker* that internal organizational matters which bear upon the corporation's 'relations to outsiders' are within power:[51] the argument here would be that potential shareholders are 'outsiders' influenced by the state of a company's books just as much as are potential creditors. Authority to similar effect may be found in the judgment of Higgins J, who was willing to allow laws about the conditions on which corporations carry on business, and instanced requirements as to the furnishing of returns, publicity, auditing and the like.[52] Some further assistance may be thought to be obtained from Barwick CJ's general dictum in *Concrete Pipes* that 'valid laws may cover a wide range of activities ... but in any case not necessarily limited to trading activities'.[53] So far as that part of the Bill is concerned which relates to the regulation of stock exchanges and persons dealing in the securities of s.51(20) corporations, its validity must ultimately depend on an acceptance of the notion that there is a close enough relationship between actual and potential shareholders on the one hand, and the corporation on the other, to enable the conclusion to be drawn that a law governing the go-between activities of brokers and dealers is in fact a law 'with respect to' the corporation. How the High Court would have reacted to this particular exploration of the reach of the corporations power it is almost impossible, on the present state of the law, to predict.[54]

It does not appear that the Corporations and Securities Industry Bill would have encountered any s.92 problems had it been enacted. Even assuming a direct burden on interstate trade, which is very doubtful, it can be seen as a paradigm 'framework' measure,[55] and furthermore one which would appear to satisfy very well the characteristics of a legitimate regulatory law set out by Dixon J in another context in the *Bank Nationalization Case*:[56] 'I do not, for example, desire to cast any doubt upon the validity of laws directly regulating banking in the interests of security, reliability, efficiency, uniformity of practice and so on'.

---

[51] *ibid.*, at p.395.

[52] *ibid.*, at p.412-3.

[53] (1971) 124 C.L.R. 468, at p.490.

[54] *Cf.* Barwick CJ in *Concrete Pipes* (1971) 124 C.L.R. 468, at p.491: 'The constitutional formula requires a substantial connection between the topic and the law. What will suffice in any particular instance to require an affirmative answer to the question whether it is a law with respect to the subject matter necessarily involves a matter of degree co-related to the nature of the power and to the provisions of the Act as they would operate in the area in which it is held they were intended to operate.'

[55] See discussion above, pp. 28-9.

[56] *Bank of N.S.W.* v. *Commonwealth* (1948) 76 C.L.R. 1, at 389.

National Companies Law

The precise terms of the Whitlam Government's much foreshadowed National Companies Bill never came to be known, as its scheduled introduction coincided with the week of the Government's final departure from office. But it was clearly intended to be a national substitute—at least to the limits that constitutional power allowed — for the existing multiplicity of State and territory Companies Acts. It was to have dealt with the incorporation of companies, their winding up, and a mass of detailed matters concerning their structure and internal functioning. It is understood that it was to have been drafted, once again, squarely in reliance on the s.51(20) corporations power.

The proposed legislation is most interesting, constitutionally, for its apparent head-on challenge to the received wisdom that the corporations power does not enable legislation with respect to the creation (and, by extension, dissolution) of corporations. It has long been accepted that the Commonwealth has power under a variety of specific heads, including ss.51(1), 51(13) and 122, to create corporations, specify conditions of their continued existence, and dissolve them,[57] but the orthodox view — supported by all the High Court dicta squarely on the point[58]—is that the general head of power in s.51(20)[59] enables legislation only with respect to corporations that are already in existence.

Whether the founding fathers intended this reading is a matter of continuing controversy.[60] What is clear is that there is no compelling argument in its favour based on either common sense or the grammatical construction of s.51(20). The word 'formed' can equally correctly be read either as a simple past participle (referring to corporations which have already been formed in the past) or as a contracted form of the future perfect (including corporations which may be formed in the future).[61] The whole phrase 'formed within the limits of the Commonwealth' can, and in our view should, be read as having no substantive significance in its own right, but rather as being an adjectival phrase employed to distinguish between two broad classes of corporation in relation to which the Commonwealth is to have power. The function of the phrase, on this reading, is not to limit the scope of Commonwealth power, but simply to draw a contrast between classes of corporations by reference to the criterion of locality.[62]

---

[57]Per Barwick CJ in *Concrete Pipes* (1971) 124 C.L.R. 468, at p.488.

[58]*Huddart Parker & Co. Pty Ltd* v. *Moorehead* (1908) 8 C.L.R. 330, per Griffith CJ at p.348, per Barton J at p.362, per O'Connor J at p.371, per Isaacs J at p.394, and per Higgins J at p.412; *Australian National Airways* v. *Commonwealth* (1945) 71 C.L.R. 29, per Latham CJ at p.57; *Bank of New South Wales* v. *Commonwealth* (1948) 76 C.L.R. 1, per Latham CJ at p.202, per Rich and Williams JJ at p.255, and per Starke J at p.304; and *Insurance Commissioner* v. *Associated Dominions Assurance Society* (1953) 89 C.L.R. 78, per Fullagar J at p.86.

[59]'(xx.) Foreign corporations, and trading or financial corporations formed within the limits of the Commonwealth.'

[60]The relevant materials are gathered by P.H. Lane, 'Can there by a Commonwealth Companies Act?' (1972) 46 Australian L.J. 407, at p.408, and Tonking, cited above n. 29, at pp. 241-2, both of whom accept the orthodox view of the section. For the other side of the argument, see J.L. Taylor, 'The Corporations Power: Theory and Practice' (1972) 46 *Australian L.J.* 5, and O.I. Frankel and J.L. Taylor 'A 1973 National Companies Act? The Challenge to Parochialism' (1973) 47 *Australian L.J.* 119.

[61]*Cf.* Stephen J on the use of the word 'supplied' in *Mikasa* (1972) 127 C.L.R. 617, at pp. 660-1.

[62]This interpretation gains considerable nourishment from Barwick CJ in *St. George* (1974) 2 A.L.R. 371, at p.376: 'The qualification "formed within the limits of the Commonwealth" is used, in my opinion, in contrast to the word "foreign". It serves to require local incorporation, the locality being any part of Australia'.

Competitive Public Enterprises

One time-honoured way of loosening the strangle-hold of various private sector monopolies and oligopolies, falling short of nationalisation on the one hand but going further than trade practices regulation on the other, is for the government itself to enter the market-place by establishing a competitive public enterprise. Examples of such enterprises which pre-date the Whitlam Government are Qantas Airways Ltd, Commonwealth Oil Refineries Ltd, Trans-Australia Airlines, the Australian National Line, the Commonwealth Banking Corporation and the Australian Industry Development Corporation. A number of additions were made, or attempted to be made, to the list by the Whitlam Government: examples are the Petroleum and Minerals Authority,[63] the Pipeline Authority,[64] the Australian Housing Corporation[65], and the Australian Government Insurance Corporation.[66]

Constitutionally speaking, there is no great danger associated with the establishment of such enterprises provided some caution is observed. It is well established, as has been already noted,[67] that a variety of heads of power will support the creation of statutory corporations for various purposes, but an appropriate connection with Commonwealth power must nonetheless be established in each case.[68] Constitutional problems may also arise with respect to the funding of an enterprise (is the expenditure within the spending power?) and in relation to any particular activity of a properly established enterprise (can it be linked with a head of power?). Some of the constitutional difficulties associated with the Petroleum and Minerals Authority are noted further below. Certainly there would appear to be no constitutional problem associated with the controversial Australian Government Insurance Corporation proposal, which seems to have been soundly based in the s.51(14) insurance power.

Inter-State Commission

Labor's grand plans for the revival[69] of the Inter-State Commission were designed to achieve recognition of its status under the Constitution as the fourth arm of Commonwealth government. The Inter-State Commission Bill

---

[63]Established by the *Petroleum and Minerals Authority Act* 1973, and struck down as unconstitutional—for procedural rather than substantive reasons—in *Victoria v. Commonwealth (P.M.A. Case)* (1975) 7 A.L.R. 1.

[64]*Pipeline Authority Act* 1973.

[65]*Australian Housing Corporation Act* 1975.

[66]The Australian Government Insurance Corporation Bill 1975 was introduced into the House of Representatives on 23 April 1975 and rejected in the Senate on 21 August 1975.

[67]Above, n. 57. See generally M. Sexton and L.W. Maher, 'Competitive Public Enterprises with Federal Government Participation; Legal and Constitutional Aspects' (1976) 50 *Australian L.J.* 209.

[68]Especially important in the present context is the s.51(1) trade and commerce power. This is, *inter alia*, the constitutional basis for TAA: see *Australian National Airways Pty Ltd v. Commonwealth* (1945) 71 C.L.R. 29. Note in this context the 1973 amendments to the Australian National Airlines Act which purport to allow TAA to engage (in competition with Ansett Airlines) in a wide range of pursuits, including the establishment of engineering services, hotels and resorts, and also to conduct intra-State services in certain circumstances: it is a real question (part of which is currently being litigated before the High Court in the matter of *Minister of Justice (W.A.) (Ex rel. Ansett Transport Industries) v. Australian National Airlines Commission)* whether s.51(1) together with the s.51(39) incidental power, will reach so far.

[69]The first Inter-State Commission was established in 1912, but foundered only three.years later on the rock of separation of powers: *New South Wales v. Commonwealth (Wheat Case)* (1915) 20 C.L.R. 54. The decision was curious, given the wording of s.101 of the Constitution and the intentions of the framers of the Constitution: see J. Finnis, 'Separation of Powers in the Australian Constitution'

1975 contained powers to deal with three subjects: State railways, interstate and overseas transport, and trade and commerce within the terms of the Constitution. The provisions affecting State railways adopted the wording of ss.102 and 104 of the Constitution, and were of practical rather than constitutional significance. They would have given the Commission considerable indirect influence in the administration of State railways. The clauses of the Bill dealing with interstate and overseas transport outlawed any preference or discrimination adjudged by the Commission to be undue and unreasonable. They also required that the terms and conditions on which a service was provided by way of or in relation to interstate transport should be reasonable and just. The omission of overseas transport from this edict apparently resulted from a narrow and rather strained view of s.101 of the Constitution, which allows the Commission to exercise 'such powers of adjudication and administration as the Parliament deems necessary for the execution and maintenance, within the Commonwealth, of the provisions of this Constitution relating to trade and commerce, and of all laws made thereunder'. The powers of the Commission with respect to interstate and overseas transport were bolstered by further powers to conduct investigations and make consequential orders, enforceable by substantial penalties.[70]

Would these provisions have fallen foul of s.92 of the Constitution? It is difficult to argue that they would not have imposed a burden on interstate trade. But application of the 'reasonable regulation' test is much more doubtful: again the result would seem to depend upon the willingness of the High Court to allow governments to set the 'framework' within which trade and commerce are conducted, as distinct from erecting barriers to that trade.[71]

The clauses of the Bill which dealt generally with trade and commerce followed a particular drafting pattern. The powers of the Commission were defined in terms of 'the provisions of the Constitution relating to trade and commerce', words taken directly from s.101 of the Constitution. The difficulty lies in deciding which sections of the Constitution are included in this description. Is it those sections making direct reference to 'trade and commerce'[72] or could it extend to all sections capable of characterisation as 'relating to trade and commerce'?[73] The High Court has held that 'any law of trade (or) commerce' in s.99 of the Constitution refers only to laws made under s.51(1),[74] but there are factors which favour a broader view of s.101: the word 'provisions' is plural, suggesting that more than s.51(1) was intended, and the words '*relating* to trade and commerce' are arguably more extensive than 'of trade (or) commerce'.

In the event, the Senate refused to pass the Bill with the broad powers as described above, and the Labor Government compromised. The *Inter-State Commission Act* 1975 contains none of these powers: they were replaced by

---

(1968) 3 *Adelaide L.R.* 159. Except for a Bill passed by the Senate in 1937 but not proceeded with, the Labor Government's action marked the only attempt to revive the Commission.

[70]$50,000 in the case of a corporation; $10,000 in the case of a person not being a corporation.

[71]Above pp. 28-9.

[72]Sections 51(1), 98, 101 and 102, subject to restrictions contained in ss. 92, 99 and 100.

[73]*E.g.* ss.51(2) (taxation), 51(3) (bounties), 51(13) (banking), 51(14) (insurance), 51(15) (weights and measures), 51(16) (bills of exchange and promissory notes), 51(17) (bankruptcy and insolvency), 51(18) (copyrights, patents and trademarks), and 51(20) (corporations).

[74]*Morgan* v. *Commonwealth* (1947) 74 C.L.R. 421.

provisions confining the Commission's activities to investigation, and then only upon the direction of the Minister.

IV
SOCIAL WELFARE

It was in respect to social welfare that the Labor Government sought to make its greatest and most lasting impact upon Australian society. Chifley had failed in his attempt to promote social and economic equality through nationalization of key industries in the Australian economy. Whitlam advocated an equality based upon a different ideal: equality of the services which the community provides. Implicit in this approach was not simply the objective of making available to those at the lower end of the social scale the services already enjoyed by others, but also the idea of increasing the overall significance of public services in the total welfare of individuals in society. Such an ambitious scheme called for vigorous action, but there was no frontal attack launched upon the limits of Commonwealth power in this area. In the main, reliance was placed upon the traditional heads of power in ss.51(23) and (23A), and 96. But along with this cautious approach there was an attempt to obtain recognition of an independent Commonwealth spending power, which would allow the Government to utilize its financial dominance without reliance upon the States.

Direct Powers

Although ss.51(23) and (23A) are sometimes regarded as conferring a general 'social welfare' power upon the Commonwealth Parliament it is clear both from the wording of these provisions and from the few cases in which they have been considered that the Commonwealth is not quite free to dispense largesse on whomsoever it pleases, however it pleases. For example, the words 'The provision of' in s.51(23A) indicate that the power is limited to the supply of allowances, pensions, benefits and services by the Commonwealth; it cannot be used to require others to provide them.[75] There is also the prohibition of any form of 'civil conscription', so far as the provision of medical and dental services is concerned. The High Court has taken a broad—some would say absurdly broad—view of civil conscription, including therein actions which might not unreasonably have been regarded as merely regulatory in character.[76] It has been suggested, further, that implicit in 'allowances' are monetary payments only, not the provision of goods and services.[77] What may be included in 'pensions' has not been determined. In contrast, there is authority for the proposition that 'benefits' extend beyond direct monetary payments and may include 'the supply of things or services'.[78]

Major items of the Labor Government's social welfare programme exhibit a keen awareness of these limits. The Medibank scheme provides a good

---

[75] *British Medical Association* v. *Commonwealth* (1949) 79 C.L.R. 201, at pp. 242-3 (Latham CJ), 254 (Rich J), 260 (Dixon J) 279 (McTiernan J) and 292 (Webb J).

[76] *ibid.*, per Latham CJ, Rich, Williams and Webb JJ; *contra*, Dixon and McTiernan JJ.

[77] *ibid.*, at p.259 (per Dixon J).

[78] *ibid.*, at pp. 229-30 (per Latham CJ), 259-60 (per Dixon J), 279 (per McTiernan J).

example.[79] Resort to compulsion was studiously avoided.[80] The scheme was not confined to reimbursement of medical and hospital expenses actually incurred by a claimant, in that provision was made for direct funding of 'approved health services',[81] but such payments clearly fall within the broader view of 'sickness and hospital benefits'. Similarly, initiatives in the fields of secondary and tertiary education, s.96 grants apart, took the form of payments to students.[82] More interesting from a narrowly constitutional point of view was the direct funding by the Commonwealth of the Curriculum Development Centre,[83] presumably also as a 'benefit to students'. The High Court has not had occasion to pronounce upon this phrase in s.51(23A) but, in view of the attitude expressed towards 'sickness and hospital benefits', seems unlikely to exclude 'services or things' from its scope.[84]

There are some instances of the limits placed upon the social welfare power being quietly ignored. It is not obvious where a statute such as the *Homeless Persons Assistance Act* 1974 fits within the structure of s.51(23A). However, in this regard the Labor Government was simply continuing the approach of its predecessors. Political considerations had often been allowed to overwhelm technical objections based upon the precise wording of ss.51(23) and 51(23A);[85] who, after all, was likely to shoot Santa Claus?[86]

The National Compensation Bill, on the other hand, did stimulate debate on constitutional questions. There was some doubt expressed whether personal injury came within the scope of 'sickness' in s.51(23A), so as to allow the payment of Commonwealth benefits therefor, but it is difficult to imagine the High Court taking so narrow a view of the section as to exclude personal injury.[87] It was also suggested that a number of benefits provided under the scheme, namely funeral, children's and relatives' benefits, benefits in respect of expenses and losses, and widows' pensions, went beyond the limitations inherent in s.51(23A).[88] However, these transgressions could have been redeemed by more careful drafting of the relevant provisions, without impairment of the wider scheme.[89] More important was the question of the validity of cl. 97 of the Bill which purported to abolish common law remedies giving compensation for those personal injuries which were covered by the scheme. In the opinion of

---

[79]The hospital side of Medibank is, of course, largely dependant upon s.96 grants, estimated in 1975-6 to amount to $707,000,000: *Payments to or for the States* (1975-6 Budget Paper No. 7) Table 172.

[80]*Health Insurance Act* 1973, esp. ss.5,23.

[81]*ibid.*, ss.39-46.

[82]*Student Assistance Act* 1973, providing for Senior Secondary Scholarships, Tertiary Education Assistance and Post-graduate Awards.

[83]*Curriculum Development Centre Act* 1975.

[84]There may be doubts entertained on this matter. Certainly at the time of the 1946 referendum which introduced s.51(23A) there were differences of opinion regarding the scope of the language employed: see I.K.F. Birch, *Constitutional Responsibility for Education in Australia* (Canberra, 1975).

[85]The *Aged Persons Homes Act* 1954 seems likely to go beyond the power in s.51(23) with respect to 'old-age pensions', unless 'pensions' is equated with 'benefits'; the *Delivered Meals Subsidy Act* 1970 confronts a similar difficulty.

[86]*Cf.* Geoffrey Sawer, *Australian Federal Politics and Law 1929-49* (Melbourne, 1963), at p.219.

[87]This accords with the view of the Solicitor-General of Australia in his opinion given with respect to the validity of certain clauses of the National Compensation Bill, published in the Report from the Senate Standing Committee on Constitutional and Legal Affairs, *Clauses of the National Compensation Bill 1974* (Canberra, 1975) at pp. 295-308.

[88]Senate Committee Report, cited above n.87, at pp. 32-33.

[89]Opinion of the Solicitor-General of Australia, cited above n.87.

three Queen's Counsel who advised the Senate Standing Committee on Constitutional and Legal Affairs with respect to this issue, the clause was beyond the legislative power of the Commonwealth.[90] The Solicitor-General of Australia disagreed, being of the view that the removal of common law rights was merely a condition upon which Parliament was to provide the benefits, and was thereby encompassed within s.51(23A).[91] This difference of opinion regarding the scope of s.51(23A) is highly significant because of the importance, perhaps necessity, of cl. 97 to the efficient operation of the compensation scheme. The fray is not one to be entered lightly, given the standing of the present combatants. Nevertheless, it does seem that the Solicitor-General's view involves an extension of the section beyond presently-defined limits, which emphasize the capacity of the Commonwealth to give without reference to any withdrawal of existing rights. Perhaps more promising for the Commonwealth (although also rejected by all three Queen's Counsel) is the s.51(39) incidental power. A broad view of that power may suffice if it could be shown that removal of certain common law rights was ancillary to an otherwise valid scheme.[92]

A number of Aboriginal social welfare programmes were undertaken under the auspices of the direct power in s.51(26) to legislate with respect to 'The people of any race for whom it is deemed necessary to make special laws'. Although difficult questions can arise in the interpretation and application of this provision, none of the Commonwealth legislation here in question—dealing with such matters as land purchases, funds for Aboriginal enterprises, and the transfer of general administration to the Commonwealth[93]—was constitutionally controversial.

Grants to States

Section 96 provides a means of implementing programmes in areas where direct legislative power is limited. It was of particular significance to Labor's social welfare programme in respect to education. Rather than attempt to establish the 'benefits to students' provision in s.51(23A) as a fully-fledged education power,[94] the Labor Government embraced the established system of 'tied' grants to States. True it was that such grants had never previously been

---

[90]The opinions of each of the Queen's Counsel, Mr F. G. Brennan Q.C. of Brisbane, Mr A.M. Gleeson Q.C. of Sydney and Mr R. E. McGarvie Q.C. of Melbourne, are published in the Senate Committee Report, cited above n.87, at pp. 233, 259 and 278 respectively.

[91]Opinion of the Solicitor-General of Australia, cited above n.87.

[92]Mild support for this approach may be derived from *Joyce* v. *Australasian United Steam Navigation Company Ltd* (1939) 62 C.L.R. 160, where the High Court held that a provision in the *Seamen's Compensation Act* 1911 requring an election between statutory compensation and common law rights was ancillary to a scheme which the Commonwealth could validly establish under s.51(1) of the Constitution.

[93]*Aboriginal Affairs (Arrangements with States) Act* 1973; *Aboriginal Land Fund Act* 1974; *Aboriginal Loans Commission Act* 1974. *Cf.* also the Aboriginal Land (Northern Territory) Bill, introduced on 22 October 1975, but still-born as a result of the events of 11 November.

[94]The *Curriculum Development Centre Act* 1975 may be viewed as a tentative step in this direction, but its importance in the total education programme appears minimal.

employed to this extent as instruments of Commonwealth influence,[95] but, with one unlikely exception, this involved no question of constitutional power. The generosity of the High Court regarding s.96 on earlier occasions had paved the way for such a development.[96] The one area here in which it has been suggested that the Labor Government may have been acting beyond its constitutional powers was in providing financial assistance to the States in aid of denominational schools. This view is based upon the prohibition in s.116 of the Constitution, that 'The Commonwealth shall not make any law for establishing any religion', as well as decisions of the United States Supreme Court which purport to erect an 'impenetrable wall' between church and state.[97] However, not even the American authorities are unequivocal on government aid to denominational schools on a non-discriminatory basis.[98] Furthermore, differences in the wording of the Australian and American constitutional provisions[99], together with an apparent willingness of the High Court to date to limit the operation of s.116,[100] all suggest that this argument has scant prospects of success.

---

[95]The use of s.96 grants to achieve policy objectives (not simply in the social welfare field) is demonstrated by the following comparison of some illustrative programmes:

Item	1970-71 ($'000)	1974-75 ($'000)
Universities	75,224	443,980
Colleges of Advanced Education	33,906	349,165
Technical & Further Education	12,535	44,997
Schools	50,572	433,917
Employment Grants	—	40,003
Aboriginal Advancement	7,002	37,049
Housing	141,681	392,389
Growth Centres	—	61,247
Land Acquisition	—	41,095
Sewerage	—	117,713
Roads	218,000	368,037
Urban Public Transport	—	45,259

Source: Payments to or for the States (1975-6 Budget Paper No.7) Table 172.

Overall, the relationship between general purpose ('untied') grants and specific purpose ('tied') grants altered dramatically, as seen in the following summary table:

	1960-1 (%)	1970-1 (%)	1974-5 (%)
General Purpose	77	70	49
Special Purpose	23	30	51

[96]*Victoria* v. *Commonwealth (Roads Case)* (1926) 38 C.L.R. 399; *Deputy Federal Commissioner of Taxation (N.S.W.)* v. *W. R. Moran Pty Ltd* (1939) 61 C.L.R. 735, affirmed (1940) 63 C.L.R. 338: *S.A.* v. *Commonwealth (First Uniform Tax Case)* (1942) 65 C.L.R. 373; *Victoria* v. *Commonwealth (Second Uniform Tax Case)* (1957) 99 C.L.R. 575.

[97]*E.g., Everson* v. *Board of Education* (1947) 330 U.S. 1.

[98]For a discussion of the American authorities, and the scope of s.116 generally, see C. L. Pannan, 'Travelling Section 116 with a U.S. Road Map' (1963) 4 *Melbourne Univ. L.R.* 41.

[99]Section 116 prohibits the Commonwealth from passing any law 'for establishing *any* religion' whereas the First Amendment precludes legislation 'respecting an establishment *of* religion'. This difference lends weight to the argument that s.116 goes no further than requiring neutrality among competing religions: *ibid.*, at p.81.

[100]*Krygger* v. *Williams* (1912) 15 C.L.R. 366; *Adelaide Company of Jehovah's Witnesses Inc.* v. *Commonwealth* (1943) 67 C.L.R. 116.

Spending Power

The Whitlam Government did embark upon a genuine adventure with the Constitution in relation to its so-called 'spending' power, founded upon ss.81 and 61 of the Constitution. Given the financial dominance of the Commonwealth in the Australian federal system, it was obvious that the establishment of an unlimited power to appropriate and disburse federal funds would signify a vital shift in the balance of power, relieving the Commonwealth of the necessity to involve the States in non-regulatory programmes. Surprisingly, perhaps, the first seventy years of federation had witnessed little discussion on the limits applicable to federal spending. On the one occasion on which the High Court had been invited to pronounce upon the matter, the decision of the majority in fact turned upon another issue.[101] Statements attributing limits to this power varied considerably: Latham CJ and McTiernan J suggested that Parliament alone could determine such limits[102] whilst Rich, Starke, Dixon and Williams JJ found in the Constitution limitations based broadly upon the scope of Commonwealth legislative, executive and judicial power.[103]

A number of the Labor Government's programmes in the social welfare area relied upon the acceptance of a broad view of the spending power.[104] The Australian Legal Aid Office, established upon an administrative basis without express legislative sanction other than the appropriation of the necessary funds,[105] is a case in point. A challenge to its validity is pending.[106] More significant in many respects, however, was the Australian Assistance Plan. It too was instituted upon an administrative basis, with no legislative support other than an item in the *Appropriation Act (No. 1)* 1974-1975 which provided funds for its implementation.[107] The essence of the A.A.P. lay in its creation of Regional Councils with authority to assess the social welfare needs of people in the regions, and to apply federally-provided funds towards meeting such

---

[101] *A.G. (Victoria) (Ex rel. Dale)* v. *Commonwealth (Pharmaceutical Benefits Case)* (1946) 71 C.L.R. 237; Latham CJ, Rich and Dixon JJ held that the statute in issue was not an appropriation act. For a discussion of this case and the spending power generally see E. Campbell, 'The Federal Spending Power—Constitutional Limitations' (1968) 8 *West. Aust. L.R.* 443.

[102] (1946) 71 C.L.R. 237, at pp. 256 (Latham CJ), 273-4 (McTiernan J).

[103] *ibid.*, at pp. 266 (Starke J), 271 (Dixon J, with whom Rich J agreed), 282 (Williams J).

[104] For example, the National Employment and Training (NEAT) System, for which the sum of $17,818,000 was appropriated by the *Appropriation Act (No. 1)* 1974-75, Item 300.4.02.

[105] *Appropriation Act (No. 1)* 1974-75, Div. 131.

[106] Proceedings have been instituted by the Attorney-General of Victoria, at the relation of the Law Institute of Victoria, but have not yet reached the stage of argument before the High Court. The Labor Government sought to place the A.L.A.O. upon a reasonably firm constitutional basis by directing that services be confined to Commonwealth 'clients': e.g. defence personnel (s.51(6)), immigrants (s.51(27)), pensioners and students (s.51(23) and (23A)), and Aboriginals (s.51(26)). The Commonwealth could face difficulties in placing this direction in evidence in High Court proceedings: see below at n.108.

[107] *Appropriation Act (No. 1)* 1974-75, Item 530, 4, appropriating a sum of $5,970,000 for '01. Grants to Regional Councils for Social Development' and '02. Development and evaluation expenses'.

needs.[108] The range of services administered by Councils under the Plan extended beyond the matters upon which the Commonwealth could legislate.[109]

The High Court confirmed the validity of the A.A.P. by a majority of four to three,[110] though upon a miscellany of grounds. Doubts persist regarding the Commonwealth's spending power. The case raised a number of important issues, each of which must be considered in assessing the overall result. These are: the limits upon s.81 of the Constitution (the appropriation power); the nature and effect of an appropriation statute; the extent of the Commonwealth executive power; the power of the Commonwealth to deal with 'national issues'; the meaning of the incidental power under s.51(39) of the Constitution; and the capacity of the States to challenge the validity of Commonwealth actions taken beyond power.

It was in relation to the s.81 question, involving the extent of the legislative appropriation power, that the Commonwealth recorded its clearest victory. Three members of the court, McTiernan, Mason and Murphy JJ, adopted the view previously expressed by Latham CJ and McTiernan J that the only limits inherent in s.81 were those which may be applied by Parliament.[111] As a result, the appropriation of funds for the A.A.P. was valid. They were supported in this conclusion by Stephen and Jacobs JJ although each reached his result upon a different ground. Stephen J decided that neither the State of Victoria nor its Attorney-General had the standing necessary to challenge the validity of an appropriation statute.[112] Jacobs J held that the question of validity of such a statute was non-justiciable.[113] The remaining members of the Court, Barwick CJ and Gibbs J, adopted a narrower approach to s.81 in holding that the Commonwealth Parliament could appropriate funds only for those matters upon which it could legislate.[114]

An examination of the scope of the executive power of the Commonwealth only became necessary, in strict terms, if it were decided both that the appropriation of funds for the A.A.P. was valid and that the appropriation statute provided insufficient authority for the expenditure of the funds in accordance with the terms of the Plan. Only Mason and Jacobs JJ came within this

---

[108]The manner in which details of the A.A.P. came before the High Court (in the absence of legislation establishing the Plan) is interesting. The plaintiffs, the State of Victoria and its Attorney-General, challenged the validity of the appropriation of funds for the A.A.P., and sought an injunction restraining the Commonwealth from spending any of those funds for the purposes of the Plan, which were not described at that stage. In its defence the Commonwealth made reference to the purposes of the A.A.P. as described in two documents, *Discussion Paper No. 1* and *Australian Assistance Plan—Guidelines for Pilot Programme*. In demurring to the defence, the plaintiffs incorporated both documents. In the absence of the reference to these documents by the Commonwealth in its defence, it is difficult to see how the plaintiffs could have satisfied the onus of proof upon them to establish the purposes of the Commonwealth expenditure, short of resorting to evidence from officers engaged in administering the Plan. Jacobs J made reference to this difficulty in the *A.A.P. Case* (1975) 7 A.L.R. 277, at p.335. The procedure adopted was obviously convenient, and may even represent the first steps in the direction of a 'Brandeis brief' mechanism. Generally on this question, see Patrick Brazil, 'The Ascertainment of Facts in Australian Constitutional Cases', (1970) 4 *Federal L. Rev.* 65.

[109]The Commonwealth contested this assertion in the case, but apparently succeeded in convincing only Jacobs and Murphy JJ that its legislative power was adequate.

[110]*Victoria* v. *Commonwealth (A.A.P. Case)* (1975) 7 A.L.R. 277.

[111]*ibid.*, at pp. 303-4 (McTiernan J), 326 (Mason J) and 344 (Murphy J).

[112]*ibid.*, at p.319.

[113]*ibid.*, at p.338.

[114]*ibid.*, at pp. 298 (Barwick CJ), 309 (Gibbs J).

category.[115] Nonetheless, all members of the Court made some reference to the issue. Considerable support was voiced for the proposition that the limits placed on executive power coincide with those applicable to Commonwealth legislative power.[116] Acceptance of this principle, however, did not in itself provide a solution because there were obvious differences displayed regarding the limits upon legislative power.

Mason J drew a distinction between 'pure' expenditure and direct involvement in a particular activity, which led him to find that the A.A.P. exceeded Commonwealth power. The reason was that establishment of Regional Councils under the Plan amounted to direct Commonwealth participation in an activity on which the Commonwealth had neither legislative nor executive power. The Commonwealth could have appropriated funds for the purposes of the Plan, and could thereby have authorized disbursement of such moneys to organizations engaged in such activities, but it could not itself become directly involved.[117] Much has been made of this distinction, not because it commended itself to any other members of the Court, but because it indicates the dividing line between an unlimited spending power and a restricted executive power which may be crucial to the validity of a social welfare programme. In this era of paper-thin majorities on constitutional questions, an adventurous central government can seldom afford to squander a single judicial vote.

At least three of the members of the Court ventured opinions upon an argument that had also arisen in a number of recent cases,[118] that the Commonwealth could exercise some powers, both legislative and executive, derived not from the precise wording of any provision of the Constitution, but rather from the 'very formation of the Commonwealth as a polity and its emergence as an international State'.[119] Amongst those who recognized this source of power, however, there were fundamental differences of opinion regarding its scope. A contrast between the views of Mason J and Jacobs J is illustrative. Mason J said that the power gave the Commonwealth the capacity to engage in enterprises and activities peculiarly adapted to the government of a nation which cannot otherwise be carried on for the benefit of the nation. Whilst he recognized that matters meeting this description may vary from time to time, according to social realities, he was at pains to point out that it was not sufficient that a programme might conveniently be formulated and administered by a national government. The power existed in respect of such matters which could *only* be dealt with by

---

[115]Only four members of the Court alluded directly to the question as to the nature of an appropriation statute. Stephen and Jacobs JJ took the view that it was no more than an earmarking of funds for a designated purpose, conferring no authority to disburse: (1975) 7 A.L.R. 277, at pp. 318-9,338. Barwick CJ, on the other hand, took the view that it did provide an authority for expenditure: at p.297. Mason J shared Barwick CJ's opinion when 'pure' expenditure was in issue, but took the view that an exercise of executive power was involved when the Commonwealth directly engages in an activity: see at p.326, and text below.

[116](1975) 7 A.L.R. 277, at pp. 295, 299 (Barwick CJ), 312 (Gibbs J), 326-30 (Mason J), 333 (Jacobs J); *contra*, 305 (McTiernan J) and 345 (Murphy J).

[117]*ibid.*, at pp. 326.

[118]*New South Wales* v. *Commonwealth (Offshore Sovereignty Case)* (1976) 8 A.L.R. 1; *Commonwealth* v. *Queensland (Queen of Queensland Case)* (1975) 7 A.L.R. 351. The concept can trace its origins back at least as far as the judgment of Dixon J in *The King* v. *Sharkey* (1949) 70 C.L.R. 121, esp. at p.148, but there the power in question was confined to protection of the institutions of government. Similar statements appeared in *Australian Communist Party* v. *Commonwealth* (1951) 83 C.L.R. 1 at pp. 187-8.

[119](1975) 7 A.L.R. 277, at p.298 (Barwick J). Gibbs J, leaves the question open: *ibid.*, at pp. 309, 312.

the national government.[120] In contrast, Jacobs J was more generous to the Commonwealth. In his view, the growth of national identity led to a corresponding growth in the area of activities which have an Australian rather than a local flavour. Such activities, necessarily undefined in scope, could be performed by the Commonwealth in the exercise of its legislative and executive powers. Significantly, Jacobs J was prepared to include the A.A.P. within this category, whereas it failed to satisfy the much stricter test propounded by Mason J.[121]

In dealing with the s.51(39) incidental power, some members of the Court afforded glimpses of what might later amount to major developments in Commonwealth legislative power. Especially interesting in this regard is the judgment of Jacobs J. A distinction was drawn between two different meanings of the word 'incidental'. First, the word may be used to describe a side occurrence which, though not essential to the main action, may be expected to arise in connection with the main action. Secondly, it may be used to describe a side occurrence with stress on its independence of the main action. The former was appropriate to describe the subsidiary power inherent in each of the other heads of s.51; the latter referred to the independent power contained in s.51(39). As a source of legislative power in its own right, s.51(39) may extend beyond the limits defined in respect of other powers, which include matters incidental in the former sense.[122] For example,

> Subject-matters of social welfare which fall outside those matters the subject of express power in other placita of s.51 are not incidental to those matters of express power . . . But it will be a matter incidental to the execution of a power to appropriate and expend moneys of the Commonwealth upon those subject-matters to appropriate and expend moneys upon other subjects of social welfare in subordinate conjunction with expenditure upon those subject-matters[123].

The link with the broad view of the Commonwealth's power to deal with national issues is apparent. It seems possible that s.51(39) is in fact the source of this power. A similar connection between the incidental and the national powers is discernible in the judgment of Mason J, although in his case the scope of the incidental power is defined more narrowly. With Murphy J the s.51(39) incidental power provided the means whereby Parliament may effectuate its unlimited appropriation power, although such legislation may be limited in its operation to whatever is strictly necessary to achieve the purpose of the appropriation.[124]

The *A.A.P. Case* was not entirely devoid of consolation for the States. On the question of standing, the States obtained recognition from three of the Justices of their rights to challenge any Commonwealth action claimed to lie beyond power. It is the rationale offered in support of such a right that is probably most interesting. Barwick CJ, Gibbs and Mason JJ agreed that the right devolved upon the States as entities in the Australian federation.[125] Their existence as

---

[120]*ibid.*, at pp. 327-8.

[121]*ibid.*, at pp. 340. Barwick CJ also denied the existence of such a power based simply upon the convenience of Commonwealth control: *ibid.*, at p.298. Gibbs J appeared to approach this question even more cautiously, not conceding any real content to such a power: *ibid.*, at p.309. McTiernan, Stephen and Murphy JJ did not refer to the matter at all.

[122]*ibid.*, at p.341; *cf. Le Mesurier* v. *Connor* (1929) 42 C.L.R. 481, at p.497.

[123](1975) 7 A.L.R. 277, at p.342.

[124]*ibid.*, at pp. 346, 349.

[125]*ibid.*, at pp. 300-302 (Barwick CJ), 314-6 (Gibbs J), 330-1 (Mason J); *contra* 319 (Stephen J).

such gave each of them an interest in ensuring that other entities in the federation, notably the Commonwealth, confined activities to available powers. This amounted to a new, and extensive, ground upon which the States could challenge Commonwealth actions in judicial proceedings.

The disparity of views apparent in the *A.A.P. Case* seriously impairs its predictive value. Nevertheless, some points must be emphasized. First, the prospects of a successful challenge to an item in a Commonwealth appropriation statute are considerably diminished by the result. Secondly, when it comes to expenditure of appropriated funds, the position is less clear, but may ultimately turn upon the method chosen for disbursement. In the eyes of Mason J at least, mere expenditure is to be judged differently from establishment of an administrative framework for provision of services. Thirdly, the future may hold prospects for substantial extension of Commonwealth power to deal with national issues, perhaps through reliance on the s.51(39) incidental power, or even independently of it.

V
LAW REFORM AND HUMAN RIGHTS

It would not be uncharitable to describe the Labor Government's efforts in this area, as indeed in one or two others, as resembling nothing so much as the man who flung himself upon his horse and rode madly off in all directions. There was certainly a flurry of legislative and executive activity. The major legislative reforms actually achieved were the *Family Law Act* 1975, the *Racial Discrimination Act* 1975, the *Administrative Appeals Tribunal Act* 1975, and the *Law Reform Commission Act* 1973. Other significant legislative innovations were the *Aboriginal and Torres Strait Islanders (Queensland Discriminatory Laws) Act* 1975, which in statutory language of somewhat unprecedented abruptness employed ss.51(26) and 109 of the Constitution to directly override certain unconscionable provisions of Queensland's 1971 Aborigines and Torres Strait Islanders Acts;[126] amendments to the Electoral Act aimed at greater equalisation in the value of House of Representatives votes;[127] amendments to the *Crimes Act* 1914 making it impossible for naturalised Australians to be deported thereunder;[128] and the repeal of regulations restricting public servants' freedom of speech.[129] Legislative measures introduced or foreshadowed but which did not for one reason or another see the light of day included the

---

[126]For a detailed account of the mischief being remedied see G. Nettheim, *Out Lawed: Queensland's Aborigines and Islanders and the Rule of Law* (Sydney, 1973).

[127]*Commonwealth Electoral Act (No. 2)* 1973 (No. 38 of 1974, passed at the Joint Sitting on 6 August 1974). In the result the legislation failed in its objective because of the Senate's subsequent refusal to accept the redistribution recommended by the Distribution Commissioners.

[128]*Crimes Act* 1973. This was not however accompanied by any amendment—necessary if the legislation was to close off the deportation option—of the provisions to similar effect in the *Migration Act* 1958, ss.13-14.

[129]Public Service reg. 34(b), providing that 'An officer shall not publicly comment upon any administrative action or upon the administration of any Department', was omitted by S.R. No. 98 of 1974.

proposed freedom of information legislation;[130] the Ombudsman Bill;[131] the historic Aboriginal Land (Northern Territory) Bill and Senator Murphy's highly controversial Human Rights Bill. Also in this category was the Australia Police Bill 1975,[132] a measure providing for the amalgamation of the A.C.T., Northern Territory and Commonwealth Police Forces, together with certain sections of the Customs and Immigration Departments, into a single national police force.

Executive[133] programmes undertaken with a law reform or human rights character included the establishment of the Australian Legal Aid Office and the Aboriginal Legal Aid Services, and the establishment of the network of Committees on Discrimination in Employment and Occupation (designed to meet Australia's international obligations under I.L.O. Convention No. 111, ratified in June 1973).[134] Other initiatives included the substantial relaxation in censorship standards brought about by a change of policy in the administration of customs legislation, and the Government's active intervention in the national wage hearings in December 1972 and subsequently in order to secure the acceptance of equal pay for women. There should also be mentioned some interesting individual assertions of executive power. One was Senator Murphy's spectacular demonstration—by way of a somewhat over-dramatic visit to the Organisation's Melbourne headquarters on 16 March 1973—that the Australian Security Intelligence Organisation, appearances to the contrary notwithstanding, was subject to Ministerial direction. Another was the Postmaster-General's direction that all postal and telecommunication services for the Rhodesian Information Centre in Sydney be withdrawn, an international relations initiative that was aborted by the High Court holding that, on the proper construction of the *Post and Telegraph Act* 1901, he had no such power.[135]

Notwithstanding the sweeping range and somewhat erratic character of all this activity, the serious or difficult constitutional questions raised by it fall within quite a narrow compass. The great majority of the initiatives fall clearly and squarely within heads of legislative power or legitimate spheres of executive action. The measures dealing with Commonwealth public servants and the administration of Australian Government departments and agencies are obviously so describable; so too are those dealing with Commonwealth electoral

---

[130]Promised in Mr Whitlam's 1972 policy speech, argued for in detail in J. Spigelman, *Secrecy: Political Censorship in Australia* (Sydney, 1972), but then made the subject of an Interdepartmental Committee inquiry, the report of which, recommending only limited reforms, was not tabled until December 1974. No further visible action occurred in the period up to the Government's dismissal.

[131]Ombudsman Bill 1975. Before the Senate when the Parliament was dissolved on 11 November 1975.

[132]Introduced into the House of Representatives on 30 October 1975, and not further debated before the Parliament was dissolved. A condition of its introduction was the incorporation of substantial civil liberty protections, both in the Australia Police Bill itself, and in a foreshadowed Criminal Investigation Bill: see the Law Reform Commission's first two reports, *Complaints Against Police* (Canberra, 1975) and *Criminal Investigation* (Canberra, 1975).

[133]'Executive' here in the sense that there is no explicit legislation supporting the programme apart from—occasionally—a line in an Appropriation Act.

[134]For a detailed account of the Committees' operations, see the *First Annual Report 1973-4* (Canberra, 1975) and *Second Annual Report 1974-5* (Canberra, 1976).

[135]*Bradley* v. *Commonwealth* (1973) 1 A.L.R. 241.

law, Aboriginals and migrants; the police measures are founded on a combination of the territories power and the Commonwealth's 'criminal'[136] power; and the Law Reform Commission is confined by its statute to reviewing those federal and territorial laws which it is within the constitutional competence of the Australian Parliament to amend or repeal—not State laws except in the context of proposals for their uniformity with the laws of the territories. The expenditure on the Australian Legal Aid Office does raise some constitutional problems, noted above.[137] The only remaining matters reflecting a spirit of real constitutional adventure, and requiring discussion for that reason, are the Human Rights Bill, the Racial Discrimination Act and the Family Law Act.

Human Rights, Racial Discrimination and External Affairs

The Human Rights Bill 1973, introduced into the Senate on 21 November 1973, was perhaps the most spectacular and far-reaching of all the Labor Government's legislative initiatives. In language of resounding generality, taken more or less directly from the United Nations-sponsored International Covenant on Civil and Political Rights of 1966, to which Australia had become a party on 18 December 1972, the Bill purported to guarantee for everyone in the country the right to enjoy the equal protection of the laws; to freedom of conscience and religion; to freedom of expression, association, assembly and movement; to privacy; and to safeguards against unfair treatment or the arbitrary exercise of power in the criminal justice process. The protections conferred by the Bill, which were to apply as against the States as well as at the national level, were to be enforced in a variety of ways, notably by conciliation through a Human Rights Commissioner followed if necessary by civil redress in the proposed new Superior Court.[138] Almost immediately after its introduction, the Bill ran into a storm of opposition, not least from spokesmen for the States. In the event Parliament was prorogued on 14 February 1974[139] without the Bill being further debated, and it was not subsequently reintroduced.

The Racial Discrimination Bill[140] fared rather better but its passage into law was a drawn-out affair nonetheless. First introduced together with the Human Rights Bill on 21 November 1973, it was subsequently reintroduced three times—in April 1974, October 1974 and again in February 1975—before finally passing into law, in much amended form, in June 1975. The *Racial Discrimination Act* 1975 is much narrower both in scope and expression than the Human Rights Bill, although it too is based on a multilateral human rights treaty to which Australia is a party, in this case the 1965 International Convention on the Elimination of All Forms of Racial Discrimination. The Act

---

[136]Founded on s.51(39) read with s.61 or, in appropriate contexts, other more specific heads: *R.* v. *Kidman* (1915) 20 C.L.R. 425; *Australian Communist Party* v. *Commonwealth* (1951) 83 C.L.R. 1.

[137]Above p.41.

[138]In response to a number of technical objections to the jurisdictional provisions of the Bill, Senator Murphy announced on 27 February 1974 that amendments would be made to enable actions under the Bill to be initiated in ordinary State courts as well as in the proposed new federal Superior Court, to remove any power in the Superior Court to override decisions of the State Supreme Courts, and to introduce safeguards against repetitious litigation.

[139]In order that the Queen should be able, with constitutional propriety, to open it again at the end of the month in the course of her visit to Australia!

[140]For a general account of the Bill as it stood after April 1974 see G. Evans 'New Directions in Australian Race Relations Law' (1974) 48 *Australian L.J.* 479; a critical examination of the Act as it emerged is B. Kelsey 'The Racial Discrimination Act 1975' (1975) 1 *Legal Service Bulletin* 272.

does begin with two clauses[141] couched in quite general terms prohibiting any form of discrimination on the basis of race, colour or national or ethnic origin, but its remaining provisions are all concerned with particular kinds of discriminatory behaviour—in relation to public places and facilities, land and housing, the provision of goods and services, employment and the like. There is in addition a particular provision dealing with the rights of Aboriginals and Torres Strait Islanders to manage their own property,[142] and a further general provision which extends the whole of the Act to discrimination against a person 'by reason that that person is or has been an immigrant'.[143] The primary enforcement mechanism is conciliation through a Commissioner for Community Relations, supplemented by civil redress in the courts.

The Human Rights Bill depended entirely for its constitutional validity, and the Racial Discrimination Act depends very largely, on the s.51(29) external affairs power. So far as other powers are concerned, in its application to immigrants the Racial Discrimination Act clearly seeks, and would seem to achieve, additional support from the s.51(27) immigration power.[144] But it would not seem, despite possible appearances, that any general support is to be obtained for that Act in s.51(26). Apart from the one section, noted above, dealing with Aboriginals and Torres Strait Islanders, the Act does not purport to deal with the people of any *particular* race, but rather with racial discrimination generally. Some particularity would appear to be necessary if s.51(26) is to apply.

It is now clear beyond doubt that the external affairs power, whatever else is within its reach,[145] extends to the domestic implementation of international treaty obligations.[146] It is equally clear, however, that the fact that a piece of legislation purports to implement a treaty—as do both the Human Rights Bill and the Racial Discrimination Act—by no means concludes the matter. There are a number of limitations, some much more clearly established than others, on the scope of the power.[147]

The first, which has not been doubted, although nowhere much elaborated, is that the international agreement must not be a mere 'device' to attract domestic jurisdiction.[148] Whatever this means, it is extremely unlikely that the High Court would call into question the bona fides of the executive government

---

[141]Section 9, prohibiting acts or omissions, and s.10, prohibiting laws.

[142]Section 10(3). This is another measure designed to overcome the effect of certain discriminatory laws operating in Queensland: *cf.* n. 126 above.

[143]Section 5.

[144]It is well established that the legislative power with respect to immigration, even if it does not extend (*e.g.* in the context of deportation) to individual immigrants after they have been absorbed into the community, does extend to the process of absorption into the community: *R.* v. *Forbes; Ex parte Kwok Kwan Lee* (1971) 124 C.L.R. 168; *R.* v. *Director-General of Social Welfare (Victoria); Ex parte Henry* (1976) 8 A.L.R. 233. A law prohibiting discrimination against immigrants would appear to be a paradigm example of a law with respect to the process of absorption: see *Henry,* per Jacobs J at p.246.

[145]See the discussion below, p.53, concerning the geographical reach of the power as asserted in the *Offshore Sovereignty Case.*

[146]*R.* v. *Burgess; Ex parte Henry* (1936) 55 C.L.R. 608; *R.* v. *Poole; Ex parte Henry (No. 2)* (1939) 61 C.L.R. 634; *Airlines of N.S.W.* v. *N.S.W. (No. 2)* (1965) 113 C.L.R. 54; *N.S.W.* v. *Commonwealth (Offshore Sovereignty Case)* (1976) 8 A.L.R. 1.

[147]The following account draws heavily upon an earlier paper by one of the authors: G. Evans, 'Prospects and Problems for an Australian Bill of Rights' in R.H. Miller (ed.) *Australian Yearbook of International Law 1970-73* (Melbourne: Dobbs Ferry, 1975), at pp. 9-11.

[148]*Burgess* (1936) 55 C.L.R. 608, Latham CJ at p.642, Starke J at p.663, and Evatt and McTiernan JJ at p.687. Dixon J at p.669, and Barwick CJ in *Airlines* (1965) 113 C.L.R. 54 at p.85 are less explicit but to the same effect.

in ratifying multi-lateral treaties of the nature and status of the International Covenant on Civil and Political Rights or the International Convention on the Elimination of all forms of Racial Discrimination.

The second limit which has been expressed, again without dissent, is that if a treaty is being relied upon to found the exercise of power, then the legislation must adhere to the terms of that treaty. What remains unclear is just how close that adherence must be. In *Burgess*, four judges took a narrow and literal view of this requirement; Starke J a much more relaxed one.[149] In *Airlines*, though the point was not much discussed a more liberal view narrowly prevailed.[150] In *Offshore Sovereignty* there was again a division of opinion, with four judges holding that the *Seas and Submerged Lands Act* 1973 was an effective implementation of the Territorial Sea and Continental Shelf Conventions there in issue, and three judges holding that it was not.[151] It must be said that the views of none[152] of the majority judges were very precisely formulated on this point; perhaps this owed something on this occasion to the fact that for at least three of them the Act was a valid law with respect to external affairs in any event, irrespective of its connection with any Conventions.[153] The most one can probably conclude from all this is that the trend of judicial opinion has been toward giving a relatively wide incidental reach to the power, and that strict literal adherence to the terms of the treaty may no longer be crucial. In both the Human Rights Bill and the Racial Discrimination Act the conformity is more with the spirit than the letter of their respective Conventions. In the former case the main departure is that the Bill consistently provides for less extensive derogations from basic rights than are permitted by the Covenant;[154] in the latter it lies in the legislation going into much greater detail than the Convention. Neither kind of deviation is in our view fatal, although each of course shortens the odds.

The third possible limitation is the most dangerous for the two human rights

---

[149](1936) 55 C.L.R. 608 per Latham CJ at p.646, Dixon J at p.674, Evatt and McTiernan JJ at pp. 688 and 692-3, and Starke J at 659-60.

[150]Barwick CJ, McTiernan, Menzies and Owen JJ took the more relaxed view; Kitto, Windeyer and Taylor JJ the narrower view (though Kitto and Windeyer JJ still upheld the legislation in question under s.51(1)).

[151](1976) 8 A.L.R. 1, The judges are, respectively, Barwick CJ, McTiernan, Mason and Murphy JJ; Gibbs, Stephen and Jacobs JJ.

[152]With the possible exception of McTiernan J, who takes the somewhat implausible view that 'The Parliament has legislated in this Act to incorporate [the rules of the Conventions] verbatim in the Act and the Act makes no addition to or omission from them': (1976) 8 A.L.R. 1, at p.19.

[153]*ibid.*, per Barwick CJ at pp. 5-6, Mason J at pp. 90-3, Murphy J at p.117. It may also be said that the minority judges took the view not so much that the Act did not adhere closely enough to the literal terms of the treaties as that it was on an entirely different subject matter, viz. internal sovereignty, not external sovereignty.

[154]For example, Art. 21 of the International Covenant on Civil and Political Rights provides for the right of assembly as follows:

The right of peaceful assembly shall be recognized. No restrictions may be placed on the exercise of this right other than those imposed in conformity with the law and which are necessary in a democratic society in the interests of national security or public safety, public order (*ordre public*), the protection of public health or morals or the protection of the rights and freedom of others.

This is rendered in the Human Rights Bill as:

13(1)   Everyone shall have the right to peaceful assembly, subject only to such limitations as are prescribed by law and are reasonably necessary in the interests of national security, public safety or public health or constitute reasonable regulations as to time, place and manner.

(2)   The burden of proving that a limitation referred to in sub-section (1) is reasonably necessary or constitutes a reasonable regulation as mentioned in that sub-section lies upon the person asserting that the limitation is so necessary or constitutes such a regulation.

initiatives in question. This is the suggestion that the subject matter of the international agreement has to be somehow 'external' in character. Hitherto the strongest expression of this view was by Dixon J in *Burgess*, when he said that the matter must be 'indisputably international',[155] but His Honour has now been joined, in the *Offshore Sovereignty Case*, by Gibbs J (also 'indisputably')[156] and Mason J ('truly').[157] Barwick CJ appears to have taken a similar line, but less explicitly.[158] At the opposite extreme are the views of Evatt and McTiernan JJ, Latham CJ and now Murphy J,[159] who have all asserted that any subject matter at all is potentially a proper subject for legislation under s.51(29). The ambiguities inherent in the whole question are nicely summed up in the suggested formula of Starke J, that the matter be 'of sufficient international significance to make it a legitimate subject for international co-operation and agreement'.[160] Assuming, as seems likely, that a formula somewhere within the range of expressions encompassed by the dicta of Starke and Dixon JJ will eventually emerge, it is of course by no means impossible that human rights matters of the kind dealt with by the legislation in question could be embraced by it. Countries have become increasingly preoccupied with each other's observance of human rights over the last few decades: what have previously been clearly 'domestic' matters have now become part of the currency of international diplomacy. Whether the High Court would be duly impressed by these considerations remains to be seen.

The fourth limitation on the scope of the power is the obvious one that its exercise is subject to express prohibitions contained elsewhere in the Constitution.[161] None of these would seem to throw any of the provisions in question into doubt.

The final possible limitation, canvassed by Starke J in *Burgess*[162] and Barwick CJ in *Airlines*,[163] is in terms of the doctrine of implied prohibitions, the notion that the Commonwealth cannot act so as to unwarrantably interfere with the function of, or threaten the independence of, the States. The argument here would be that any Commonwealth legislation with circumscribed State freedom to the extent of the proposed Human Rights Bill (the question does not arise with nearly the same force for the Racial Discrimination Act), even though circumscribing the Commonwealth equally, would to the extent of the interference offend against the implied constitutional prohibition. The doctrine was thought to be dead and buried with the *Engineers Case*[164] in 1920, but it enjoyed something of a recrudescence in the late 1940s,[165] and was again paid lip-service in the *Payroll Tax Case*.[166] It is perhaps now not really likely that the

---

[155](1936) 55 C.L.R. 608, at p.669.

[156](1976) 8 A.L.R. 1, at p.30.

[157]*ibid.*, at p.91.

[158]*Airlines* (1965) 113 C.L.R. 54, at p.85; also possibly *Offshore Sovereignty* (1976) 8 A.L.R. 1, at p.6.

[159]*Burgess* (1936) 55 C.L.R. 608, per Evatt and McTiernan JJ at p.681, Latham CJ at p.641 (but *cf.* 640); *Offshore Sovereignty* (1976) 8 A.L.R. 1, per Murphy J at p.117.

[160]*Burgess* (1936) 55 C.L.R. 608, at p.658.

[161]*ibid.*, per Evatt and McTiernan JJ at p.687, Latham CJ at p.642 and Starke J at p.658; *Airlines* (1965) 113 C.L.R. 54, per Barwick CJ at p.85.

[162](1936) 55 C.L.R. 608, at p.658.

[163](1965) 113 C.L.R. 54, at p.85.

[164]*Amalgamated Society of Engineers* v. *Adelaide Steamship Co. Ltd* (1920) 28 C.L.R. 129.

[165]*Melbourne Corporation* v. *Commonwealth* (1947) 74 C.L.R. 31.

[166]*Victoria* v. *Commonwealth* (1971) 122 C.L.R. 353.

prohibitions doctrine, or its extension, the implied immunity doctrine, would be directly employed to strike down Commonwealth legislation. What is rather more likely is that such considerations may be employed indirectly, by the development, for example, of a narrow Dixonian formula on the 'externality' point discussed above. There are ways other than head-on confrontation to curb what the High Court might consider to be the excesses of an over-adventurous Commonwealth.

Family Law

The *Family Law Act* 1975,[167] one of the most popular Labor Government measures although by no means the least controversial, was constitutionally adventurous in two main respects, both of which were quickly litigated. In the first place, and most importantly, the Act purported to apply not only, as had its predecessor, to proceedings for dissolution and annulment and ancillary matters arising in the course of such actions; it also extended, excluding State law in the process, to independently arising maintenance, custody and property matters. The ability to deal with such matters, otherwise than in the context of divorce proceedings, was argued to be essential to the development of a coherent new body of national family law. The existing authorities on the scope of the s.51(21) marriage power and the s.51(22) matrimonial causes power offered neither great encouragement nor great discouragement to this course.[168] In the result the key new provisions survived reasonably intact their scrutiny in the *Family Law Case*.[169] It was held, by a bare majority,[170] that maintenance and custody proceedings could be dealt with independently of proceedings for principal relief, but with the qualification that such actions could only lie as between the parties to the marriage: it was not within power to enable, for example, grandparents to make a custody application. Property matters, however, could only be dealt with in the course of a full-scale divorce or annulment proceeding.[171]

The second constitutional adventure was of more symbolic than substantive importance. As well as creating the new specialist federal Family Court of Australia, the Act vests jurisdiction in certain State courts, including the State Supreme Courts. Pursuing the policy of informality, the Act provides for closed courts and the absence of robes whenever and wherever jurisdiction under it is exercised. But is it within the marriage or matrimonial causes powers for the Commonwealth to so provide, and is it possible for the Commonwealth to interfere in this way with the conduct of State Supreme Courts? On these

---

[167]For a succinct account of the history and contents of the Act see The Hon. K. Enderby, 'The Family Law Act 1975' (1975) 49 *Australian L.J.* 477.

[168]See *Attorney-General (Vic.) v. Commonwealth (Marriage Act Case)* (1962) 107 C.L.R. 529; *Lansell v. Lansell* (1964) 110 C.L.R. 353; and for a careful but optimistic discussion of the potential of both powers, R. Sackville and C. Howard, 'The Constitutional Power of the Commonwealth to Regulate Family Relationships' (1970) 4 *Federal L. Rev.*30.

[169]*Russell v. Russell; Farrelly v. Farrelly* (1976) 9 A.L.R. 103.

[170]Mason, Stephen and Jacobs JJ: Barwick CJ and Gibbs JJ dissenting. The majority judges based their decision squarely on the s.51(21) marriage power, and were not prepared to read this down by reference to implied qualifications in s.51(22). Jacobs J endorsed the exercise of the power in the Act as it stood, without qualifications.

[171]Mason and Stephen JJ joined Barwick CJ and Gibbs J on this point, but would not appear to have totally excluded the possibility of a redrawn section surviving—i.e. one with a closer connection on its face to the marriage relationship, Jacobs J upheld the relevant section by reading in an implied qualification that property proceedings lay only 'for the purposes of the Act'.

questions the High Court was once again divided in the *Family Law Case*: in the result, wigs and gowns must stay in the cupboard[172] but the Supreme Court doors, if the trial judge so determines, must stay open.[173]

In the event, then, it is apparent that the Family Law Act survived its trial relatively unscathed. The limitations set upon maintenance and custody proceedings, and more substantially on property proceedings, will cut away only a very small area of the Act's operation, and the requirement of an open court in Supreme Court hearings will scarcely affect its viability.

VI
NATIONAL DEVELOPMENT

The Whitlam Government viewed the country as a single unit so far as resources and development were concerned, and was adamant that the Commonwealth should adopt a pre-eminent position in this vital area.[174] Features of Labor policy regarding minerals and energy were a renewed emphasis upon domestic ownership and control; increased public ownership; federal regulation of exploration, development, transportation, marketing, pricing and utilization; and maintenance of domestic self-sufficiency.[175] Formidable constitutional barriers stood in the way of complete realization of such policy with respect to onshore resources, but offshore the prospects were brighter.

Offshore Sovereignty

The *Seas and Submerged Lands Act* 1973 was declaratory in nature. It purported to vest sovereignty in respect of the territorial sea[176] and internal waters[177] in the Crown in right of the Commonwealth, and make that sovereignty exercisable by the Commonwealth Crown.[178] The same was attempted with the sovereign rights of Australia regarding exploration of the continental shelf[179] and exploitation of its natural resources.[180] Predictably, all

---

[172]Per Mason, Stephen, and Jacobs JJ; Barwick CJ and Gibbs J dissenting.

[173]Per Barwick CJ, Gibbs and Stephen JJ; Mason and Jacobs JJ dissenting. The basic issue in each case was whether the direction went to the 'constitution, structure or organization' of the Supreme Court (long held to be sacrosanct: *eg. Le Mesurier* v. *Connor* (1929) 42 C.L.R. 481; *Kotsis* v. *Kotsis* (1970) 122 C.L.R. 69) or whether, rather, merely to its 'practice and procedure'. There was little or no disagreement with the proposition that such directions were, initially, within the scope of the incidental power.

[174]Earlier examples of Commonwealth activity in this field are the Snowy Mountains Hydro-Electric Scheme and the Australian Aluminium Production Commisson. For details, see D.P.Derham, 'The Defence Power' in *Essays on the Australian Constitution* ed. Else-Mitchell (2nd ed., Sydney 1961), at pp. 170-174.

[175]*Initiatives in Minerals and Energy*, Report by The Hon. R.F.X. Connor, M.P., Minister for Minerals and Energy, March 1975.

[176]Also included were the airspace over the territorial sea and its bed and subsoil. The Governor-General was given the power to declare, not inconsistently with the provision of the Convention on the Territorial Sea and the Contiguous Zone (reproduced as Schedule 1 to the Act), the landward and seaward limits of the territorial sea (ss.6-7).

[177]Defined as any waters of the sea on the landward side of the baseline of the territorial sea. The Act contained a saving in respect of any waters which were, on 1 January 1901, and remain, within the limits of a State (s.14).

[178]*Seas and Submerged Lands Act* 1973, ss.6, 10.

[179]Again the Governor-General was empowered to declare limits, not inconsistently with the Convention on the Continental Shelf (reproduced as Schedule 2 to the Act) or any relevant international agreement to which Australia is party (s.12).

[180]*Seas and Submerged Lands Act* 1973, s.11.

of the States contested the validity of this statute in the High Court.[181] The decision in favour of the Commonwealth[182] may fairly be described as momentous.

The provision of the Constitution which was of greatest significance in the result was s.51(29), the external affairs power. The case involved a most important development in the scope of this power. For the first time, the view was accepted that the power extends to the making of laws with respect to places outside, or matters or things done outside, the boundaries of the country.[183] This geographical concept was expressly applied by Barwick CJ,[184] Mason[185] and Jacobs JJ.[186] Murphy J also appears likely to favour this approach,[187] although he did not do so explicitly. It is possible that Gibbs and Stephen JJ took a somewhat narrower view of the power, although the geographical test is certainly consistent with the conclusions reached by both of these Justices on the issue of the continental shelf.[188] McTiernan J did not deal with this matter.

The significance of this approach to the external affairs power lies in its confirmation of plenary Commonwealth legislative authority regarding off-shore areas. Whatever the limits upon Parliament's authority regarding domestic implementation of international obligations,[189] they have no application to Commonwealth activities seaward of the low-water mark. But this is not to say that the States have been excluded entirely from legislating with respect to the seas that constitute their boundaries.[190] Section 51(29) of the Constitution is, after all, a head of concurrent legislative power. Whether a State can legislate with respect to an offshore activity will depend upon two factors: first, does the statute demonstrate a 'sufficient connection' with the State to make it a law for the peace, order and good government of that State;[191] and, secondly, is the statute inconsistent with a Commonwealth law and thereby inoperative under s.109 of the Constitution. The latter consideration leads back to the Seas and Submerged Lands Act, to ascertain the extent to which its provisions exclude the States from legislating with respect to offshore activities.[192] So far as the

---

[181] *New South Wales* v. *Commonwealth (Offshore Sovereignty Case)* (1976) 8 A.L.R. 1.

[182] The seven Justices were unanimous in upholding the validity of s.11 of the Act referring to the continental shelf. With respect to ss.6 and 10 (territorial sea and internal waters), Barwick CJ, McTiernan, Mason, Jacobs and Murphy JJ favoured validity, while Gibbs and Stephen JJ dissented.

[183] This was the wording of Jacobs J (1976) 8 A.L.R. 1, at p.112.

[184] *ibid.*, at p.6.

[185] *ibid.*, at p.92.

[186] *ibid.*, at p.112.

[187] He took a broad view of the external affairs power: *ibid.*, at p. 117-8.

[188] *ibid.*, at pp. 48-9 (Gibbs J) 81-2 (Stephen J).

[189] Considered above at pp. 48-51.

[190] The location of these boundaries was the issue which divided the Court in considering the Commonwealth's claim to the territorial sea and inland waters. Gibbs and Stephen JJ, after long and scholarly research, held that these areas formed part of the territory of the States immediately prior to Federation. Accordingly, the external affairs power, at least to the extent that it allowed the Commonwealth to deal with matters arising outside of the States, could have no application: *Offshore Sovereignty Case* (1976) 8 A.L.R. 1, at pp. 30-42 (Gibbs J) 50-74 (Stephen J). Other members of the Court decided State seaward boundaries were found at the low water mark: *ibid.*, at pp.6 (Barwick CJ), 20 (McTiernan J), 82-90 (Mason J), 99-103 (Jacobs J). Murphy J did not decide the question of boundaries.

[191] *Millar* v. *Commissioner of Stamp Duties (N.S.W.)* (1932) 48 C.L.R. 618; *Broken Hill South Limited* v. *Commissioner of Taxation (N.S.W.)* (1937) 56 C.L.R. 337; *Johnson* v. *Commissioner of Stamp Duties (N.S.W.)* [1956] A.C. 331; *Welker* v. *Hewett* (1969) 120 C.L.R. 503.

[192] Inconsistency of state legislation with a Commonwealth law has been held to arise in three basic

territorial sea and inland waters are concerned, this depends upon the meaning attributed to the 'sovereignty' asserted by the Commonwealth.[193] Although there is room for some doubt, it would seem that 'sovereignty' means overriding rather than exclusive legislative power.[194]

In the *Offshore Sovereignty Case*[195] the Commonwealth also argued that its status as an international entity provided a source of power to pass the Seas and Submerged Lands Act. At least five of the members of the Court were prepared to admit that the development of nationhood in Australia had some relevance to the validity of the statute. However, differences in approach are evident. Barwick CJ and Murphy J were prepared to hold that, even if the Australian colonies had obtained proprietary rights or legislative power with respect to offshore regions prior to Federation, a consequence of the creation of the Commonwealth was the transfer of such rights or power to the Commonwealth.[196] In this respect they were at odds with Gibbs and Stephen JJ, both of whom conceded the importance of the Commonwealth's international status in dealing with rights acquired after Federation, but denied the possibility of any divestiture of rights held prior to 1901.[197] McTiernan, Mason and Jacobs JJ adopted an intermediate position, merely noting that it is consistent with the Commonwealth's character as an international person and with the States' lack of that character, that legislative power and jurisdiction over offshore areas should reside in the Commonwealth rather than the States.[198]

Minerals and Energy

Onshore, the Whitlam Government was forced to employ less direct methods of gaining control over mineral and energy resources. A number of powers were available,[199] but none would allow regulation of all aspects of resource development. Resort was therefore necessary to a variety of measures including direct government involvement[200] in several phases of the industries, and regulation of private enterprise to the extent of available powers.

The principal vehicles for direct government participation were the Pipeline Authority, the Petroleum and Minerals Authority, the Australian Atomic Energy Commission and the Australian Industry Development Corporation.

---

situations: where a state law cannot be obeyed consistently with obeying a Commonwealth law, where the State law modifies a right or privilege granted by a Commonwealth law, and—much more sweepingly—where the Commonwealth law manifests an intention to 'cover the field' (i.e., represent a complete statement of the law on the subject). The *Seas and Submerged Lands Act* 1973 evinces a clear intention *not* to cover the field, in that it contains an express saving of a wide range of State laws in force at the date of commencement of the Commonwealth Act (s.16(b)). However, this would not necessarily preclude inconsistency based upon either of the other criteria: *cf.* Evans, cited above n. 35, at p.670.

[193] *Seas and Submerged Lands Act* 1973, ss.6,10.

[194] The issue is dealt with squarely by Mason J, who reaches this conclusion: *Offshore Sovereignty Case*, (1976) 8 A.L.R. 1, at p.95. Jacobs J, implies a similar result: *ibid.*, at p.112-14. Statements of Gibbs J, to the effect that s.16 of the Act appears to assume that (apart from its provisions) the operation of all State laws might be excluded, appear contrary to this approach: *ibid.*, at p.27.

[195] (1976) 8 A.L.R. 1.

[196] *ibid.*, at pp.16 (Barwick CJ), 119 (Murphy J).

[197] *ibid.*, at pp.29 (Gibbs J), 70-3 (Stephen J).

[198] *ibid.*, at pp.23 (McTiernan J) 90 (Mason J) 113 (Jacobs J).

[199] *E.g.*, ss.51(1) (trade and commerce), 51(2) (taxation), 51(3) (bounties), 51(6) (defence), 51(13) (banking), 51(20) (corporations), 51(29) (external affairs), 51(39) (incidental power), 61 (executive), 81 (appropriation), 122 (territories).

[200] See also above at p.35.

The latter two bodies did not owe their existence to Labor[201] but were extensively employed to achieve policy ends.

The Pipeline Authority was established by statute in 1973[202] with a broad range of functions including the construction, maintenance and operation of petroleum pipelines, the buying and selling of petroleum and the establishment of Australian self-sufficiency in petroleum through the control of reserves. It was intended that the Authority should construct and operate a national pipeline grid linking the sources of supply of natural gas to all major population centres.[203] The Authority would purchase gas from producers and sell it to distributors, rather than operate simply as a common carrier.[204] In practice, of course, no more than one pipeline would be economically feasible for linking petroleum deposits with available markets, a feature of the petroleum industry recognised a century ago by John D. Rockefeller. The Authority would therefore be in a position to exert substantial control over the industry, producers and consumers alike, through its position as monopolistic carrier.[205]

In deference to constitutional constraints, the Act provided that the Authority could perform its functions only to the extent that they were not in excess of the functions capable of conferral on the Authority by virtue of any of the legislative powers of the Commonwealth. In particular, reference was made to the corporations power, the territories power, the trade and commerce power, the defence power and the incidental power. As a drafting device, this was nothing new: it had been employed by previous governments in the creation of both the Australian Atomic Energy Commission[206] and the Australian Industry Development Corporation.[207] Nevertheless, it is worthy of comment, as the High Court has not yet had occasion to pronounce upon its validity. The issue is one of characterization: is the statute a law 'with respect to' the nominated heads of power? Ultimately, this is a matter of degree, and opinions will differ from case to case. But as long as the area of activity in which the statutory corporation is to operate is not entirely closed to the Commonwealth, there would appear to be no reason why the extent of the Commonwealth's involvement should not be described by reference to the scope of its powers. The Pipeline Authority Act clearly falls within this principle. The attractiveness of the device, from the Commonwealth's point of view, is that it transfers the prospect of invalidity away from the statute establishing the Authority (and thereby the Authority itself), on to each particular action of the Authority. A

---

[201]The Australian Atomic Energy Commission was created by the *Atomic Energy Act* 1953. The A.I.D.C. owes its existence to the *Australian Industry Development Corporation Act* 1970.

[202]*Pipeline Authority Act* 1973.

[203]Second Reading speech by The Hon. R.F.X. Connor, M.P., Minister for Minerals and Energy, on the Pipeline Authority Bill 1973, 10 May 1973. House of Representatives, *Debates*, vol. 83, p.2011.

[204]*Initiatives*, cited above at n. 175.

[205]The foreclosure of private enterprise from gas transportation involves no infringement of s.92 of the Constitution, as long as it results from economic rather than legal considerations. The Pipeline Authority Act did not attempt to give the Authority a legal monopoly; it was hoped simply that the Authority would acquire this status by virtue of early entry into this field of economic endeavour.

[206]*Atomic Energy Act* 1953, s.17(4). The Commission was restricted in its functions to those capable of being carried out under the defence power and the territories power.

[207]*Australian Industry Development Corporation Act* 1970, s.6. Again not all Commonwealth powers were specified, merely trade and commerce, territories, and defence. In 1975 the corporations power was added by the *Australian Industry Development Corporation Act* 1975. The method of doing this is interesting, as it demonstrates the view that the corporations power enables the Commonwealth to *create* trading and financial corporations thereunder: *Australian Industry Development Corporation Act* 1970 (as amended), s.6(4); *cf.* above, p.34.

successful challenge will then result in an injunction to restrain the activity or perhaps a declaration that the activity lies beyond the statutory powers of the Authority.[208] There is no need to confront the problem of whether a provision in the statute is inseverable from the remainder of the Act, thereby placing the entire statute at risk.

The unsuccessful attempt to establish the Petroleum and Minerals Authority[209] provides another illustration of this drafting technique: broadly defined functions, which included direct involvement in exploration and production, could be exercised only to the extent of specified heads of Commonwealth legislative competence. In this case, however, the range of powers called in aid was less extensive than with the Pipeline Authority. There was no general reference to all the legislative powers of the Commonwealth, nor was the corporations power mentioned.[210] Perhaps this omission illustrated acceptance of the dictum of Isaacs J that mining corporations were not 'trading' corporations within s.51(20) of the Constitution.[211] In contrast with this caution, however, some of the provisions which defined the scope of the Authority's operations were notably generous. For example, the Authority could conduct exploration and production operations in the States, and ultimately acquire property in substances produced (upon payment of 'fair and reasonable compensation' to the States), merely upon a declaration that it was doing so for a particular purpose, namely, interstate or international trade and commerce, or ensuring the availability of adequate supplies of petroleum and minerals for defence in times of actual or threatened war.[212] These provisions raised difficult characterization questions: were they laws 'with respect to' trade and commerce, or defence? The former proposition seems especially doubtful: the trade and commerce power has never been regarded as purposive in the sense that the defence power has. And even the link with defence is rather tenuous. A declaration by Parliament or the executive as to the required purpose is not in itself sufficient.[213]

Prior to the declaration by the High Court[214] that the Petroleum and Minerals Authority Bill had not been validly enacted, the Labor Government incorporated the Petroleum and Minerals Company of Australia Pty Ltd in the A.C.T. After the High Court's decision was handed down it was announced that the company would take over the assets and activities of the defunct Authority. Included among these assets were interests in the Cooper Basin gas field in South Australia and an operating coal mine in New South Wales. This action

---

[208] *E.g., Commonwealth* v. *Australian Commonwealth Shipping Board* (1926) 39 C.L.R. 1. Note, however, that liability to discharge a debt owed to a statutory corporation could not be denied on the ground that the corporation acted beyond its powers; *cf. Re K.L. Tractors Ltd (In Liq.)* (1961) 106 C.L.R. 318.

[209] The Petroleum and Minerals Authority Bill 1973 received the royal assent after passage at the Joint Sitting following the 1974 double dissolution. It was declared invalid by the High Court in proceedings brought by four States, on the ground that the requirements of s.57 of the Constitution regarding enactment had not been satisfied: *Victoria* v. *Commonwealth (P.M.A. Case)* (1975) 7 A.L.R. 1. See further Leslie Zines, 'The Double Dissolutions and Joint Sitting', below Ch. 7. During argument in the *P.M.A. Case* the Solicitor-General of Western Australia intimated that his State wished to challenge the validity of the Act on substantive grounds, should the attack based on s.57 fail.

[210] Petroleum and Minerals Authority Bill, cl.9.

[211] See above at p.32.

[212] Petroleum and Minerals Authority Bill, cll. 43-45.

[213] *Australian Communist Party* v. *Commonwealth* (1951) 83 C.L.R. 1. See further Derham, cited above n. 174.

[214] Above, n. 209.

squarely raises the question of the scope of the Commonwealth's executive power under s.61 of the Constitution. On the assumption that the Commonwealth Parliament could not legislate to establish a statutory authority with power to conduct such activities,[215] was the establishment of the company by executive act beyond power? Earlier statements of the High Court regarding the scope of this power appear inconclusive,[216] but guidance is available from the *A.A.P. Case*.[217] It was suggested above that four members of the Court in that case indicated that as a matter of principle the limits upon legislative and executive powers of Commonwealth would in general coincide.[218] If that view is to be applied in future, the fate of the Petroleum and Minerals Company of Australia Pty Ltd appears bleak.[219]

In regulating the activities of private enterprise in the mineral and energy sectors, the Labor Government does not appear to have raised any new constitutional issues. The system of export controls based upon prohibition subject to the obtaining of a licence issued in the discretion of the Minister had long been established;[220] it was expanded under Labor and widely used as an effective instrument of regulation, largely without incident.[221] The foreign investment guidelines[222] issued with respect to exploration and production operations could have been enforced, if necessary, under the trade and commerce, banking and foreign corporations powers. And the widespread changes invoked in the taxation measures[223] applicable to the mining and petroleum industries clearly fell within the taxation power.

The Loans Adventure

On 13 December 1974 the Executive Council—comprising in this instance Messrs Whitlam, Cairns, Murphy and Connor—recommended for the approval of the Governor-General that 'the Minister for Minerals and Energy be authorized to borrow for temporary purposes' the sum of four thousand million United States dollars.[224] The Governor-General signed the authority the next

---

[215]There may be argument on this point. Possible sources of legislative power may be ss.51(1) (trade and commerce), 51(6) (defence) and 51(20) (corporations), not to mention the 'national issues' power, but none of these lends obvious support for involvement in mining activities in the States.

[216]There are numerous dicta in favour of restricting the scope of the executive power in accordance with limits on legislative power (however broadly defined): *Commonwealth* v. *Australian Commonwealth Shipping Board* (1926) 39 C.L.R. 1, at p.10; *Commonwealth* v. *Colonial Combing, Spinning and Weaving Co. Ltd* (1922) 31 C.L.R. 421, at pp. 431-3 (Knox CJ and Gavan Duffy J), 453-4 (Higgins J) and 461 (Starke J); *contra*, at p.441 (Isaacs J). Cf. *Bonanza Creek Gold Mining Co. Ltd* v. *The King* [1916] 1 A.C. 566, at pp. 580, 586, 587, referring to the *British North America Act* 1867.

[217](1975) 7 A.L.R. 277.

[218]Above, p.43.

[219]It is understood that proceedings have been commenced in the High Court by Victoria, contesting the validity of the formation of the company. The State will undoubtedly have to contend with procedural questions such as standing and justiciability, but these do not appear to give rise to the same problems regarding s.61 as may rise under s.81. From the *A.A.P. Case* (1975) 7 A.L.R. 277, for example, it seems clear that Barwick CJ, Gibbs and Mason JJ would entertain challenges by States to Commonwealth executive action. Jacobs J also seems likely to do so, while the attitudes of McTiernan, Stephen and Mason JJ are unstated.

[220]Customs (Prohibited Export) Regulations, made under s.112 of the *Customs Act* 1901.

[221]There was one challenge to the licensing system; this is described in detail below at pp. 62-3.

[222]See the press statements issued by the Prime Minister dated 3 November 1974 ('Foreign Equity in Mining') and 12 March 1975 ('Oil and Uranium Exploration: Government Guidelines').

[223]*E.g., Income Tax Assessment Act (No. 2)* 1973, *Income Tax Assessment Act (No. 2)* 1974.

[224]This and the other relevant Executive Council minutes are set out in Senate, *Debates* 1975, vol. 64, pp. 2723-4 (Answer to Question No. 646). The original authority was revoked on 7 January 1975

day.[225] Thus embarked the Labor Government on the biggest loan-raising enterprise in Australian history, an enterprise huge by any international standard and one which if carried through to fruition would have tripled the country's total accumulated overseas debt.[226] Although there occurred at the time, as news of the loan gradually emerged, considerable speculation as to what the 'real' object of the expenditure was to be, it is now well established that the contemplated outlays were all for major national development projects: uranium enrichment in the Northern Territory, natural gas and pipelines in Western Australia, petro-chemicals in South Australia, rail electrification in Victoria, New South Wales, Queensland and Tasmania, and coal ports in New South Wales.[227] In the event, no money proved to be forthcoming. And whatever the original merits of the project may have been, as events unfolded throughout 1975 the 'loans affair' became a growing source of electoral embarrassment to the Government. Eventually it came to be the 'reprehensible circumstance' on which, above all others, the Opposition relied in explaining its eventual decision to turn out the Government by blocking supply.

The Opposition argument throughout was not merely that the Government had mismanaged the enterprise and behaved foolishly, especially in its choice of intermediaries through whom to act, but that it had acted illegally, and indeed unconstitutionally. The claim was, in essence, that in authorizing the borrowing without seeking the prior approval of the Loan Council, the Executive Council had, on 13 December 1974,[228] acted in breach of certain key provisions of the 1927 Financial Agreement,[229] which required that loans of the kind in question be so approved. The Constitution was involved because of the peculiar, indeed unique, status of the Financial Agreement; until varied by some future unanimous agreement of the Commonwealth and States, its terms had by virtue of s.105A(5) of the Constitution a status equivalent to sections of the Constitution.[230]

The relevant provisions of the Financial Agreement are clauses 3(8), 4(4) and 6(7). Clause 3(8) requires the Commonwealth and the States to submit to the Loan Council the amount they desire to raise by loans each year. Excepted from this requirement are loans 'for temporary purposes', 'loans for Defence purposes' and 'conversion, renewal or redemption' loans. Clause 6(7) empowers the Commonwealth to borrow money for temporary purposes, subject only to such ceilings on interest and other charges as the Loan Council may from time to

---

and an authorization for the lesser sum of $2,000 million was substituted on 28 January 1975; the borrowing authority was finally revoked on 20 May 1975.

[225]It is apparently not unusual for Executive Council meetings to be held in the absence of the Governor-General: see C. Lloyd & A. Clark, *Kerr's King Hit!* (Sydney, 1976) p.150; P. Kelly, *The Unmaking of Gough* (Sydney, 1976) p.165.

[226]Kelly, cited n. 225, at p.162.

[227]See Mr Connor's speech in House of Representatives, *Debates* 1975, vol. 95, pp. 3610-12; also L. Oakes, *Crash Through or Crash: The Unmaking of A Prime Minister* (Melbourne, 1976) at p.65; Kelly, cited n. 225, at p.158.

[228]Also on 28 January 1975, when the figure of US$2,000 million was substituted: see above at n. 224.

[229]The Agreement was given legislative approval by the Commonwealth in the *Financial Agreement Act* 1928, and again in the *Financial Agreement Validation Act* 1929. A consolidated version is to be found in the Schedule to the *Financial Agreement Act* 1944. There is a recent detailed annotation of the Financial Agreement in R.S. Gilbert, *The Future of the Australian Loan Council* (Canberra, 1974).

[230]*Cf.* Starke J in *New South Wales* v. *Commonwealth [No. 1]* (1932) 46 C.L.R. 155, at p.186: 'It is part of the organic law of the Commonwealth. It can only be varied or rescinded by the parties thereto. Nothing in the Constitution or in the Constitutions of the States can affect it or prevent its operation.'

time have set. The clause is inexplicit as to whether such borrowing can be undertaken within or outside Australia, but presumably extends to both situations. 'Temporary purposes' are not defined, here or anywhere else in the Financial Agreement. Clause 4(4) declares that 'moneys shall not be borrowed by the Commonwealth or any State otherwise than in accordance with this Agreement'.

The proposed borrowing of the Labor Government, which was not submitted before authorization to any of the other members of the Loan Council,[231] would thus appear to have been in breach of the Financial Agreement unless it can be described as (a) a loan for temporary purposes, (b) a loan for defence purposes, or (c) was in some other way beyond the reach of that Agreement.[232] The justification on which the Government chose formally to rely was that the loan was for 'temporary purposes'. The object of the loan was expressed in an explanatory memorandum accompanying the Executive Council minute of 13 December 1974:

> The Australian Government needs immediate access to substantial sums of non-equity capital from abroad for temporary purposes, amongst other things to deal with exigencies arising out of the current world situation and the international energy crisis, to strengthen Australia's external financial position, to provide immediate protection for Australia in regard to supplies of minerals and energy and to deal with current and immediately foreseeable unemployment in Australia.[233]

There is no extant law as to the meaning of 'money borrowed for temporary purposes'. Treasury practice has been to treat the description as referring to loans repayable within twelve months: this construction gains some nourishment from the definition of 'public debt' in the Financial Agreement as including '(viii) Treasury Bills not repayable within twelve months from the date of issue'.[234] But this is not to say that another, more flexible, period than twelve months might well be construed as 'temporary' if the occasion for the borrowing—for example the propping-up of a temporarily ailing section of the economy—could itself be construed as 'temporary'. As Mr W. Deane Q.C. stated, and one must agree with him, in his much-relied-upon opinion for the Liberal Party in this matter,[235] 'Whether or not a particular loan is or is not "for temporary purposes" must in each case be a question of fact to be answered in the light of all the relevant circumstances'. And one must also agree with Mr

---

[231]The procedure, according to a standing Loan Council resolution of 1956, is for the terms and conditions of each proposed borrowing to be put to all the State Premiers, and to be required to have the prior concurrence of at least three State Premiers. (See the Opinion of Mr C.W. Harders, Secretary of the Australian Attorney-General's Department, 'Constitutional Amendment—Proposed section 51(ivA): Australian Loan Council Implications' App. G to the Report to the Executive Committee by Standing Committee A, Australian Constitutional Convention 1975, at p.43).

[232]It was clearly not a conversion loan of the type contemplated by cl. 3(8), and nor does it seem possible to argue (as do A.R. Blackshield & G. Caine in the *Australian* 16 July 1975) that the Executive Council minute merely authorized preliminary negotiations falling short of actual borrowing: the language of the minute expressly authorizes the Minister to 'borrow', and further, to execute 'any necessary documents for the purpose of making the said borrowing'. Mr Whitlam's statement on 20 May 1975 (House of Representatives, *Debates* vol. 95, p.2478) that he would have sought Loan Council approval after the loan was accomplished is beside the point: unless within one of the exceptional categories mentioned in the text, the loan would still have infringed both cll. 3(8) and 4(4).

[233]Quoted in House of Representatives, *Debates* 1975, vol. 95, p. 3595 (Mr Whitlam).

[234]Clause 2. See Gilbert, cited above n. 230, at p.56; also his commentaries on cll.5(9) and 6(7), at pp. 126-138, 143-6.

[235]Incorporated in Hansard by Mr Fraser: House of Representatives, *Debates* 1975, vol. 95, pp. 3604-3606.

Deane that the notion of temporary purposes does seem to clearly imply that the loan in question be sought to satisfy a 'passing or transient need'.[236] If the need happens to be neither an immediately pressing one, nor one that can be satisfied in a relatively short time by the injection of the funds in question, then it is difficult on any view to argue that the loan is one for temporary purposes. The difficulty that the Labor Government confronted in justifying its proposed borrowing was not only the twenty-year-long term of the intended loan,[237] but also the circumstances that (a) at the time it was sought Australia appeared to be less immediately and urgently threatened by the world energy crisis than almost any other industrialised nation, (b) the country's external financial position was healthy, and (c) the funds were proposed to be spent not on unemployment benefits, the purchase of fuel, or other immediate programmes, but rather upon major development projects few of which were then even at the blue-print stage.

If the proposed loan cannot be regarded as one for temporary purposes, it is not beyond credibility that it could be construed as one 'for Defence purposes', albeit not so labelled by the Executive Council.[238] There has long been a body of constitutional opinion that major resource projects aimed *inter alia* at establishing national self-sufficiency may be justified under the defence power: the Snowy Mountains scheme is the best-known example.[239] But apart from proving that all the projects envisaged could be brought somehow within the defence umbrella, the major difficulty here is that the Financial Agreement exception extends only to defence loans 'approved by the Parliament'. It may be possible to argue that such approval could properly be obtained after the loan was completed and not necessarily before, but clearly the chances of having a loan held covered by the defence exception, weak enough at best, are much weaker still in the absence of specific pre-existing legislative authority.

What of the argument that the proposed loan, even if not for temporary or defence purposes, may still have been beyond the reach of the Financial Agreement to control? It is just possible to argue that a Commonwealth loan for Commonwealth purposes, having nothing whatsoever to do with the public debts of the States, cannot in law be prohibited by the Financial Agreement. This is because, the argument goes, the Financial Agreement, to the extent that it relies for its validity as law on s.105A of the Constitution,[240] cannot provide for what s.105A does not—and s.105A allows an agreement to be made about Commonwealth borrowing only to the extent that this can be described as an agreement 'with respect to the public debts of the States'.[241] But there is a three-fold difficulty with this argument: it depends on a very constricted reading of s.105A, there are High Court dicta to the contrary,[242] and in any event the

---

[236]This is by no means to concede Mr Deane's infallibility in these matters. The opinion quite ignores the existence of cl.6(7) of the Financial Agreement, and as a result makes heavy weather of the threshold question as to whether the Australian Government can borrow overseas for temporary purposes at all.

[237]See the correspondence incorporated in Hansard: House of Representatives, *Debates* 1975, vol. 95, p.3613.

[238]*Cf.* A.R. Blackshield & G. Caine, *Australian* 16 July 1975.

[239]For a discussion of that legislation, see Derham, cited above n. 174, at p.171.

[240]*Cf.* the *Financial Agreement Validation Act* 1929, where the Agreement is expressly 'validated' by reference to the newly enacted s.105A.

[241]*Cf.* A.R. Blackshield & G. Caine, *Australian* 17 July 1975.

[242]Especially Rich & Williams JJ in *Bank of N.S.W.* v. *Commonwealth* (1948) 76 C.L.R. 1, at p.281:

limitation on Commonwealth borrowing in question would seem to be within Commonwealth competence to enact, in the absence of s.105A, under s.51(4) of the Constitution.

It appears, then, that the Labor Government's proposed loan raising without consultation with the States may indeed have been in breach of the Financial Agreement. In mitigation, it can perhaps be argued that the Loan Council has since its inception been very much the creature of the Commonwealth rather than the States,[243] and that the Labor Government's cynicism in by-passing it entirely was, while no more excusable for that, not so much a spectacular breach of the federal constitutional compact as an extension of that unilateral style of decision-making in loan raising matters which has characterized Commonwealth governments for decades past.

Cities

The promise of a better standard of living for that vast majority of Australians—some 85 per cent in fact[244]—who inhabit the major cities was an important feature of Labor's 1972 election programme, closely linked with the Party's stand on social welfare. The policy included a number of elements: federal assistance for major construction work, such as housing and sewerage; revitalisation of public transport systems; direct access for local government to federal funds; and reduction in the pressure placed upon amenities in the larger cities by promotion of 'growth' centres. Surprisingly, perhaps, in view of the novelty of federal involvement in such matters, there was obvious respect paid to the traditional limitations upon Commonwealth legislative competence. As a result, the mechanism of the conditional grant under s.96 of the Constitution was that most frequently employed.

This was generally the case with housing and sewerage works.[245] However, the *Australian Housing Corporation Act* 1975 does mark a departure. This statute establishes a corporation with powers to engage directly in the construction of housing as well as lending money for that purpose. As with other statutory authorities, however, these functions may be performed only to the extent that they relate to matters with respect to which the Commonwealth has power to legislate.[246]

The procedure to be followed by local government in obtaining direct access to federal funds illustrates a novel use of s.96. The *Grants Commission Act* 1973 paves the way for applications to the Commission not simply from States but in addition from 'approved regional organizations', representing the local governing bodies established in a region. Any financial assistance that is

---

'It necessarily follows from cl. 4(4) that the whole of the rights of the Commonwealth and of the States to borrow are included in the agreement and that no such rights exist outside the agreement'.

[243]This has followed not merely from the Commonwealth's voting power on the Council (where, with two deliberative votes and a casting vote to the States' one each it needs the support of only two of the States to carry any issue), but from its control of the domestic loan market (the source, since the 1930s of most public borrowing) through the central banking system, and the States' dependence on the Commonwealth to meet market shortfalls with grants and loans of its own: see R.J. May, 'Federal Finance: Politics and Gamesmanship' in H. Mayer & H. Nelson (eds.) *Australian Politics: A Third Reader* (Melbourne, 1973) at p.245: also R.L. Mathews & W.R.C. Jay, *Federal Finance* (Melbourne, 1972) at pp.186-7, 202-7.

[244]Australia, *Official Year Book* 1973, No. 59, p.135.

[245]For expenditures in these areas, see above n. 95.

[246]*Australian Housing Corporation Act* 1975, s.6.

forthcoming is to be paid to the relevant State for the purposes of the organization, and in this respect the procedure involves no departure from previous practice; the interest lies in the attempt to formalize requests for special purpose grants, provide for the assessment of such requests by an independent body, and to encourage the merger of local government and the formation of regional institutions. The Grants Commission, however, found this system to be administratively unworkable.[247]

The creation of the Albury-Wodonga Development Corporation as part of the growth centres programme deserves attention, not only by students of co-operative federalism. The Corporation owes its existence to the *Albury-Wodonga Development Act* 1973, a Commonwealth statute. Some of the functions vested in the Corporation under the Act have rather tenuous links with Commonwealth legislative power, for example,

> to facilitate the establishment in designated areas of places of business for use in trade and commerce with other countries or among the States.[248]

Nevertheless, the likelihood of constitutional challenge to the activities of the Corporation is diminished by the provision in the statute for the States of New South Wales and Victoria to confer additional functions, powers or duties upon the Corporation for the purposes of the agreement entered into between the Commonwealth and the States.[249]

Environment

The Whitlam Government was clearly anxious to reverse the policy of benign neglect of environmental considerations which characterized previous Commonwealth administrations. Again, of course, this implied trespassing upon the traditional preserve of the States. But where, in the absence of any direct power in relation to the environment, lay the constitutional power to do so? Three aspects of Labor's environment programme illustrate both the opportunities for, and constraints upon, Commonwealth action.

The *Environment Protection (Impact of Proposals) Act* 1974 has the stated objective of ensuring, to the greatest extent practicable, that matters affecting the environment to a significant extent are fully examined and taken into account in the full range of Commonwealth government operations (including expenditure).[250] Administrative procedures may be adopted by the government for the purpose of achieving the object of the Act, thereby allowing considerable flexibility in the conduct of environmental assessments.[251] The Act also empowers the Minister to direct that an inquiry be held regarding environmental aspects of Commonwealth government activities.[252] The validity of the Act in general, and of the provision concerning inquiries in particular, was challenged in *Murphyores Incorporated Pty Ltd* v. *Commonwealth*.[253] The plaintiffs held mining leases on Fraser Island in Queensland and intended to

---

[247]Grants Commission, *First Report 1974 on Financial Assistance for Local Government* (Canberra, 1974), paras 3.10, 3.11.

[248]*Albury-Wodonga Development Act* 1973, s.8(1)(b).

[249]*ibid.*, s.8(3), (4).

[250]*Environment Protection (Impact of Proposals) Act* 1974, s.5.

[251]*ibid.*, s.6.

[252]*ibid.*, s.11.

[253](1976) 9 A.L.R. 199.

export zircon and rutile produced therefrom. An inquiry was directed under the Act into all the environmental aspects of decisions by the Commonwealth regarding export of minerals extracted from the Island. Export without the approval of the Commonwealth Minister for Minerals and Energy was prohibited by the Customs (Prohibited Export) Regulations. The Minister intimated that he would consider the findings of the inquiry before making a decision on the plaintiffs' application for export approval. Only two members of the High Court found it necessary to rule on the validity of the Act in its entirety; both agreed that the Act was valid.[254] The other members of the Court[255] were able to dispose of the case by reference to the scope of the trade and commerce power of the Commonwealth. The plaintiffs submitted that the power did not enable the Commonwealth to regulate and control the environmental aspects of mining in Australia, even mining carried on for the purpose of export. This view was rejected by all members of the Court, who confirmed that Parliament could validly prohibit the export of goods, absolutely or conditionally. A discretion vested in a Minister to give dispensation from such a prohibition could be exercised having regard to any matter, not simply considerations of trading policy.

The *National Parks and Wildlife Conservation Act* 1975 provides for the establishment and management of parks and reserves by the Australian government. In the territories and offshore regions no questions of power arise. But to the extent that the Act applies in the States, questions of power are crucial. With this in mind, the Act describes its objective and states that its provisions regarding acquisition and management of parks and reserves shall be administered accordingly. The object is:

> to make provision for the establishment and management of parks and reserves—
>
> (a) appropriate to be established by the Australian Government, having regard to its status as a national government;
>
> . . .
>
> (e) for facilitating the carrying out by Australia of obligations under, or the exercise by Australia of rights under agreements between Australia and other countries; or
>
> (f) conducive to the encouragement of tourism between the States and between other countries and Australia.[256]

The effect of this statement is curious. It is clear that the Commonwealth Parliament cannot acquire power which is otherwise lacking simply by framing the objects of legislation in terms of heads of legislative power.[257] It remains always for the High Court to determine the operation of a statute and whether it falls within the scope of Commonwealth legislative competence. Viewed in this light, the fate of the Act is uncertain. The scope of the Commonwealth power to deal with national issues is undefined; the doubts surrounding the operation of the s.51(29) external affairs power have already been noted; and the attempt to establish a connection between national parks and interstate or overseas trade and commerce using the intermediary of tourism[258] is entirely novel.

---

[254] Barwick CJ and Murphy J.

[255] McTiernan, Gibbs, Stephen, Mason and Jacobs JJ.

[256] *National Parks and Wildlife Conservation Act* 1975, s.6.

[257] The complexities inherent in purposive powers, such as the s.51(6) defence power, do not arise here.

[258] *Cf.* Travel Agents Bill 1975, considered above n. 31.

The *Australian Heritage Commission Act* 1975 established the Australian Heritage Commission with a range of functions directed towards indentifica- tion and preservation of those places in Australia that hold special value for the nation. These functions have a distinctly advisory, educative and research flavour; coercive powers are absent.[259] A constitutional basis for this Act too may be sought in the s.51(29) external affairs power. The Convention con- cerning the Protection of the World Cultural and Natural Heritage[260] places a number of obligations upon parties thereto, including the duty of 'ensuring the identification, protection, conservation, presentation and transmission to future generations of the cultural and natural heritage'[261] referred to in the Convention. The similarities with the functions of the Commission are obvious. Nevertheless, the Act does depart from the Convention to some extent in defining what constitutes the 'cultural and natural heritage';[262] again, there may be argument upon the question of whether preservation of the national estate has an 'external' character.[263] The Act also raises in its purest form the oft-encountered issue of the scope of the Commonwealth power to deal with 'national' matters, arising in a domestic rather than an external context. On the basis of the *A.A.P. Case,*[264] one has little hesitation in predicting that Jacobs J would find the Act valid in its entirety.[265] Barwick CJ[266] and Mason J[267] may well uphold the validity of the advisory, identification and research functions, although there may be doubt regarding the education and acquisition roles. For Mason J the question would be whether these were matters which could only be performed effectively by the national government. On the other hand, Gibbs and Stephen JJ, in statements made in the *Offshore Sovereignty Case,*[268] exhibit a reluctance to allow a Commonwealth power of this description to impinge upon the activities of the States. The interference with the States under this Act, though, is of an entirely different character from that identified by these Justices in the *Offshore Sovereignty Case,* where divestiture of property rights was contemplated. McTiernan and Murphy JJ have not yet indicated their attitudes to this question, which can only be regarded as wide open at this stage.

VII
CONCLUSION

Three years of relentless pressure applied to the constraints upon Common- wealth legislative and executive power, to what avail? Certainly there is little evidence of any drastic re-shaping of the Australian federal system. But even a few months' hindsight shows that there were results, important results, of three basic types. First, there were developments of a purely constitutional nature. These were few in number, and still clouded in their final impact, though

---

[259] *Australian Heritage Commission Act* 1975, ss. 6, 7.

[260] Acceded to by Australia 22 August 1974; in force since 17 December 1975.

[261] Article 4.

[262] *Cf.* Convention, Article 1 and Act, s.4.

[263] See discussion above, p.50.

[264] (1975) 7 A.L.R. 277. See above, pp. 43-4, for an examination of the judgments in the case on this point.

[265] (1975) 7 A.L.R. 277, at p.340.

[266] *ibid.,* at p.298. The national power includes the power to 'explore'.

[267] *ibid.,* at p. 327, referring to the establishment of the C.S.I.R.O.

[268] (1976) 8 A.L.R. 1, at pp.29 (Gibbs J) and 71 (Stephen J).

charged with considerable potential for Commonwealth exploitation in the future. The common characteristic of these developments was a new, or at least expanded, source of Commonwealth power. Secondly, there were the many successful applications of established powers to fresh endeavours, less dramatic no doubt, but of greater significance in the implementation of Labor's economic and social policies. Here it was in a quantitative rather than a qualitative sense that Labor made its presence felt upon the Constitution. And thirdly, there was confirmation for the Party that the federal division of powers, however irksome it might be to Labor politicians and supporters, need not necessarily present an insurmountable barrier to the aspirations of an activist Commonwealth government.

To the forefront of the developments in Commonwealth power is the *Offshore Sovereignty Case*.[269] Already the seabed holds the key to Australia's energy policies. Yet the decision contains wider implications, inherent in the assertion by the Commonwealth of plenary legislative authority over the region. Control of the offshore constitutes a significant addition to the range of Commonwealth powers, similar in some respects to the territories power. In future the Commonwealth will be in a position to use its offshore jurisdiction to regulate that vast number of activities linked with the region. The *A.A.P. Case*[270] represents another Commonwealth victory, although perhaps of a battle rather than the war. The recognition of Parliament's unfettered discretion to decide the purposes of appropriations may well have removed all barriers to candidacy for Commonwealth largesse. It remains for speculation, though, how far (if at all) the Commonwealth can stray from mere donation in the direction of regulation. A most intriguing query arising from Labor's three years in office is encountered in both *Offshore Sovereignty* and *A.A.P.*: what is the fate of the Commonwealth power to deal directly with national questions, be it cloaked in the disguise of s.51(39) or precocious enough to stand alone? The Commonwealth under Labor argued strenuously for such a power in a number of cases, urging the High Court to exercise its capacity for judicial creativity and thereby lead the way towards a fundamental restructuring of the federation.[271] In many respects this may represent Labor's most ambitious constitutional adventure. At this stage, though, the response from the High Court remains equivocal.

In the application of already recognized powers to new fields of endeavour, the performance of the Whitlam Government is easier to evaluate. The major examples were the wide measure of control achieved over mineral and energy resources through the system of export licences, relying upon the s.51(1) trade and commerce power; the considerable (though still incomplete) regulation of the economy and private business obtained by use of the s.51(20) corporations power; Commonwealth entry to such disparate fields as race relations and environmental management by way of the s.51(29) external affairs power; and the pervasive network of indirect controls established in the social welfare and urban development areas using conditional s.96 grants to States. Some of these applications were distinctly innovative whilst others were remarkable only in the degree and frequency of their utilization. Altogether, they represented a

---

[269](1976) 8 A.L.R. 1, above at pp. 52-4.

[270](1975) 7 A.L.R. 277, above at pp. 41-5.

[271]Above at pp. 43-4, 54; see also M.H. Byers, below pp. 67-71.

marked transfer of governmental responsibility from the States to the Commonwealth, achieved not by the assertion of dramatic new powers but instead by the willingness to make full use of those already available.

For the Labor Party, the message is clear: although there may still be notable omissions from the Commonwealth's range of powers, these are not such as to preclude the implementation of the Party's major policies and programmes. Indeed, this had long been recognized; in 1961 it provided the theme of Mr Whitlam's Curtin Memorial Lecture, 'Socialism Within the Australian Constitution'. Furthermore, during the decade of the 1960s the programmes of the Party had been re-worked in accordance with a more modern view of socialism. Control of vital sectors of the economy was stressed in place of ownership, and a new importance was attached to government as the provider of essential services. These changes of approach clearly took account of Commonwealth powers and constitutional prohibitions, so that when Labor obtained office it was not a case of headlong and fruitless assault upon barriers to action, but instead a conscious effort to work vigorously within (and at the same time expand) the limits upon Commonwealth competence. Viewed in this light, the Whitlam Government achieved success.[272] So much so, in fact, that the great constitutional problem for Labor in the future would seem to be not the restrictions on what can be done in office, but rather the difficulty of getting there in the first place, and once there, the problem of staying there for a long enough time to change anything.

---

[272]See further on this theme G. Evans, 'Labor and the Constitution', *Meanjin Quarterly* 1:1976, pp. 3-19.

COMMENTARIES

M. H. Byers

The litigation between the Commonwealth and the States which Dr Crommelin and Mr Evans have examined raised constitutional questions for the solution of which previous decisions of the Court provided little, and but Delphic,
guidance. The sections of the Constitution were diverse, and the reasons for
judgment are often both conflicting and various. This latter is to be expected
from a vigorous Bench voyaging uncharted seas guided by a tradition of sturdy
and mutual independence. It is, after all, nearly seventy years ago since the
Chief Justice of the day, after observing it was common knowledge that the
decisions of the Judicial Committee in the Canadian cases had not given
widespread satisfaction, went on to say:

> It is said that such a state of things as would follow from a difference of opinion
> between the Judicial Committee and the High Court would be intolerable. It would
> not, perhaps, have been extravagant to expect that the Judicial Committee would
> recognize the intention of the Imperial legislature to make the opinion of the High
> Court final in such matters. But that is their concern, not ours.[1]

But what is important is the common approach to constitutional interpretation, not individual differences as to the extent of the precise limits of the
various heads of power. That the Commonwealth's national character has some
constitutional significance is accepted by all. Dr Crommelin and Mr Evans
have remarked upon it. I wish to discuss what that significance is and what are
some of its consequences.

I would do so because, once the reserved powers doctrine was discarded, the
Court was set free to construe the Constitution along its line of primary thrust:
the establishment of a national legislature. It was for that reason the Constitution was adopted. For that reason the Parliament was armed with legislative
power. In a real sense nationalism permeates the Constitution and renders
coherent both what it grants and what it denies. Section 92, for example, has
troubled the High Court because it is a political statement about the kind of
nation the Constitution intended which yet must be given legal effect.

The *Engineers Case*[2] established Commonwealth legislative power to bind
a State. The step it took was a momentous one. The theory that legislative
power falling within what the Constitution granted to the Parliament was
nonetheless reserved to the States and thus outside the granted powers, made
nonsense of the words of the Constitution. For example, it stood s.109 on its
head, as the *Sawmillers Case*[3] vividly illustrates. With this doctrine abolished,
the national character of the Parliament stood, for the first time, fully revealed.
The *Payroll Tax Case*[4] reaffirmed this power and with it the authority of that
decision. But the Constitution also requires a denial of State legislative capacity to bind the Commonwealth. The reason for this 'derives from the fact that

---

[1] *Baxter* v. *Commissioner of Taxation (N.S.W.)* (1907) 4 C.L.R. 1087, at p.1187 per Griffith CJ.

[2] *Amalgamated Society of Engineers* v. *Adelaide Steamship Company Ltd* (1920) 28 C.L.R. 129.

[3] *Federated Saw Mill, Timber Yard, and General Woodworkers Employees' Association of
Australasia* v. *James Moore & Sons Pty Ltd* (1909) 8 C.L.R. 465, at pp. 529-36 per Isaacs J.

[4] *Victoria* v. *Commonwealth* (1971) 122 C.L.R. 353.

the Crown has not by the Constitution submitted itself to the legislatures of the States'.[5] The constitutional relationship in areas of Commonwealth power is thus not one of equality but of disparity. There is no reciprocity. Within power the traffic is all one way. This is not to put the States in a position of disadvantage for the same is true outside Commonwealth power, the limits of which are indicated, both positively and negatively, by the Constitution.

The first preamble to the Commonwealth of Australia Constitution Act recites that 'the people of' the five named States 'have agreed to unite in one indissoluble Federal Commonwealth under the Crown of the United Kingdom of Great Britain and Ireland and under the Constitution hereby established'. Covering Clause 3 empowers the Queen with the advice of the Privy Council to proclaim that 'the people of' the six States 'shall be united in a Federal Commonwealth under the name of the Commonwealth of Australia', the laws of the Parliament of which, by Covering Clause 5, 'shall be binding on the courts judges and people of every State and of every part of the Commonwealth, notwithstanding anything in the laws of any State'. These provisions are unalterable. Unalterable also are their implications. The Commonwealth is indissoluble, that is, perpetual, and it is a Commonwealth of the people of the States: that is, it is national. It is a Federal Commonwealth, that is, there must always be States, the existence of which is as perpetual and essential as that of the Commonwealth, though their number, and limits *inter se* may change. Lastly, the laws of the Commonwealth must always, where there is conflict, prevail over the laws of the States: and prevail they must even should s.109 be deleted from the Constitution.

The Constitution is the means by which these essential and fundamental generalities are given effect; its provisions are their expression, even that conferring a power of alteration (s.128). The powers granted to the nation must be read as thus granted and to a perpetual organism or polity. The Commonwealth is now an international State. That fact is relevant, not only to the extent of its executive powers, but also to the ambit of such legislative powers as may be brought to play thereon or thereby or which may be by that fact otherwise affected. But we should remember that it is the one Commonwealth that has grown into international personality: there is no internal Commonwealth and another and different external one. Nationhood is not only an aid to the construction of explicit powers. It is also itself a source of power.

The Commonwealth's existence is owed to Covering Clauses 3 and 4. It was born armed with legislative powers over its external affairs and its relations with the islands of the Pacific. That birth implies 'the necessary power of the federal government to protect its own existence and the unhindered play of its legitimate activities'.[6] Its legitimate activities comprise those over the external affairs of the Commonwealth. They include, so ran, for example, one argument for the Commonwealth in the *Offshore Sovereignty Case*,[7] the territorial seas surrounding the Australian continent. So, had the colonies before Federation included such within their boundaries, whatever title and powers then existed in them were, by force of the enactment of the Constitution, vested in the

---

[5] *ibid.*, at p.373 per Barwick CJ. See also *Essendon Corporation* v. *Criterion Theatres Ltd* (1947) 74 C.L.R. 1, at pp. 21-2; *Melbourne Corporation* v. *Commonwealth* (1947) 74 C.L.R. 31, at pp. 82-3; *Commonwealth* v. *Cigamatic Pty Ltd* (1962) 108 C.L.R. 372.

[6] *Australian Communist Party* v. *Commonwealth* (1951) 83 C.L.R. 1, at p.108, per Dixon J, quoting *Black's American Constitutional Law.*

[7] *New South Wales* v. *Commonwealth* (1975) 8 A.L.R. 1.

Commonwealth. This argument was accepted by three Justices in that case and is consistent with the reasoning of all who formed the majority. I mention the *Offshore Sovereignty Case* only because it contains one illustration of the effect of the notion with which I am concerned. That decision was, as Dr Crommelin and Mr Evans point out, momentous. Some of its implications are now being worked out and many yet remain unresolved. I am not presently concerned with that case nor with what effects it may possess for the future. Its importance lies in its consequences for the legal relationship between the Commonwealth and the States ordained by the Constitution.

Let me turn to another example, the Commonwealth's spending power. An understanding of the ends to which the Commonwealth may devote its funds is essential to government. How it may do so is perhaps another matter. The judgments in the *A.A.P. Case*[8] disclose a majority which, in the result, favour a reading of the expression 'purposes of the Commonwealth' in s.81 committing to the Parliament the selection of what those purposes are or should be, subject to positive constitutional prohibitions. But it is impossible to read any judgment and remain unimpressed by the extent to which consideration of the Commonwealth's position as the national government influenced each conclusion. Some reach a conclusion by reading 'the Commonwealth' as used in s.81 to refer to those people who, by Covering Clause 3 of the Constitution are 'united in a Federal Commonwealth under the name of the Commonwealth of Australia', thus treating the national character of the Commonwealth as determinative of the nature of the purpose. It is sufficient if the purpose be national. Others commit the selection of purposes to the national Parliament. Some find the question non-justiciable, while yet others would treat the phrase as shorthand for topics within legislative competence.

If the extent of permissible appropriations is set by the legislative powers, a broad view of those powers is inevitable.

> Thus it may be granted that in considering what are Commonwealth purposes, attention will not be confined to ss.51 and 52. The extent of powers which are inherent in the fact of nationhood and of international personality has not been fully explored. Some of them may readily be recognized: and in furtherance of such powers money may properly be spent. One such power, for example, is the power to explore, whether it be of foreign lands or seas or in areas of scientific knowledge or technology. Again, there is power to create Departments of State, for the servicing of which as distinct from the activities in which the Departments seek to engage money may be withdrawn from Consolidated Revenue Fund.[9]

That paragraph is big with possibility. But it is so, as are the other judgments, because of nationhood.

I would now turn to another effect of the Commonwealth's national character upon constitutional interpretation. What I wish to examine is the reason for, and some effects of, the rule that each head of power in s.51 should, in the absence of compelling reason, be treated as an independent and separate grant. Its application to paragraphs (21) and (22) of s.51 was the first of two steps essential to the validity of the Family Law Act. In the result both steps in the argument were accepted by the majority in the *Family Law Case*[10]. Again, in the *Offshore Sovereignty Case*[11] an unsuccessful attempt was made by the

---

[8] *Victoria* v. *Commonwealth* (1975) 7 A.L.R. 277.
[9] *ibid.*, at p.298 per Barwick CJ.
[10] *Russell* v. *Russell; Farrelly* v. *Farrelly* (1976) 9 A.L.R. 103.
[11] (1975) 8 A.L.R. 1.

plaintiffs to read down the content of the external affairs power by references to those dealing with fisheries in Australian waters beyond territorial limits (s.51(10)) and Commonwealth relations with the islands of the Pacific (s.51(30)): see the judgment of Mason J.[12]

The reason for the rule lies, I suggest, in the perpetual and national character of the Federal Commonwealth. The Constitution, in a practical sense, speaks forever and on large topics. Sir Owen Dixon in the *Bank Nationalization Case*[13] quoted O'Connor J and Gray J. What was significant to the Supreme Court of the United States was that 'the Constitution ... by apt words of designation or general description, marks the outlines of the powers granted to the National Legislature'; and to O'Connor J, that the Constitution was 'intended to apply to the varying conditions which the development of our community must involve'. Some sixteen years later the Court employed O'Connor J's language (part only of which I have quoted) in support of the proposition that 'We must remember that it is a Constitution we are construing and it should be construed with all the generality which the words used admit'.[14] And let me now quote the words Mason J used in the *Family Law Case* to rebut the contention that the content of section 51(21) should be diminished because of what section 51(22) contained:

> The argument pays insufficient attention to the circumstance that it is a Constitution that we are construing and that the legislative powers that it confers should be construed liberally. There are substantial reasons for thinking that an individual grant of power under the Constitution should be accorded a full operation according to its terms, unrestricted by dubious implications drawn from the existence of another grant of legislative power touching an associated subject matter. There is no inherent reason for supposing that the legislative powers conferred by the Constitution are mutually exclusive; indeed, many instances may be given of overlapping operation.[15]

The rule renders s.51 at once more certain and more flexible. When one bears also in mind that 'the subjects on which the Commonwealth Parliament may legislate are generically described. Their denotation is not fixed',[16] the powers explicitly granted attain an amplitude which, with the inherent powers, may support that legislation which national growth is likely to require from both the Commonwealth and the States, but more importantly, for my present purposes, from the Commonwealth either alone or in association with the States.

What of the effect upon the States of the creation of a national Executive and Parliament? One obvious result of the union of the people of each State in a Federal Commonwealth was to foreclose to each State the possibility of a separate nationality. Another was that each State subjected its laws to the paramountcy of valid Commonwealth laws. A third was that each State became amenable to such laws of the Commonwealth as applied to it pursuant to the valid exercise of any head of Commonwealth constitutional power.[17]

The measure of the constitutional rights of the States is marked out by ss.106 to 108. State legislative power like Commonwealth legislative power is subject to the Constitution. In a real sense it is those sections which confer legislative

---

[12]*ibid.*, at pp. 90-2.

[13]*Bank of N.S.W.* v. *Commonwealth* (1948) 76 C.L.R. 1, at pp. 332-3.

[14]*R.* v. *Public Vehicles Licensing Appeals Tribunal (Tas.)* (1964) 113 C.L.R. 207, at p.225.

[15](1976) 9 A.L.R. 103, at p.138.

[16]*Payroll Tax Case* (1971) 122 C.L.R. 353, at p.399 per Windeyer J.

[17]*Engineers Case* (1920) 28 C.L.R. 129; *Payroll Tax Case* (1971) 122 C.L.R. 353; *Offshore Sovereignty Case* (1975) 8 A.L.R. 1.

power upon the States—a view which the fact of Federation seems to demand. The balance between Commonwealth and State legislative powers may often be delicate and uneasy. Its preservation calls more for political than legal skill. Legal skills have, with some exceptions, yielded in this field only cloudy answers.[18]

The general trend of the Constitution is clear. It created the nation from the people of all the States. Fundamental to it is a disparity between the polity it established and those it continued albeit in a new character. Already the Territories legally may be fully represented in both the Senate and the Representatives. The admission of a new State has been bruited. The extent of Commonwealth power to legislate externally is now seen to be vastly larger than was hitherto thought.

The decisions the essay examines would not have been possible but for the *Engineers' Case*[19]:

> [T]he nature of dominion self-government and the decisions just cited entirely preclude, in our opinion, an *a priori* contention that the grant of legislative power to the Commonwealth Parliament as representing the will of the whole of the people of all the States of Australia should not bind within the geographical area of the Commonwealth and within the limits of the enumerated powers, ascertained by the ordinary process of construction, the States and their agencies as representing separate sections of the territory.

And now it has been said, in the *A.A.P. Case*,[20] that

> The extent of powers which are inherent in the fact of nationhood and of international personality has not been fully explored.

In the first passage quoted, nationhood affects the quality of given powers. In the second, it is a source of power. The factor common to time and the Constitution is the Commonwealth's national character. It is that character which will, in legal terms, determine the constitutional future as it has shaped the past.

Daryl Dawson

Dr Crommelin and Mr Evans attempt in their essay to cover the whole range of the Labor Government's activities which raise constitutional issues. The essay is, therefore, necessarily long and covers a wide area. Within the limits which have been set for me, I can only pick up some of those issues, but perhaps I may first be permitted the indulgence of a few general observations.

A constitutional lawyer is, I think, as much or more concerned with how a government goes about doing something as with what it actually attempts to do. Whatever the social or political implications of the legislative and executive programme with which the essay deals (and I have no comments in those areas), it seems to me to be somewhat euphemistic to speak, in a legal context, of explorations and adventures with Commonwealth powers during the period

---

[18] *Cf. Payroll Tax Case* (1971) 122 L.R. 353.

[19] (1920) 28 C.L.R. 129, at p.153.

[20] (1975) 7 A.L.R. 277, at p.298 per Barwick CJ. See too *Commonwealth* v. *Queensland* (1975) 7 A.L.R. 351, at pp. 364 (Gibbs J), 381-2 (Murphy J).

between 1972 and 1975. The Government tended, I think, to proceed in disregard of its powers (or lack of powers) and to fashion its programme without concern for the federal structure imposed by the Constitution. Whatever the political achievement, there was not much legal initiative or enterprise. Indeed, it appeared almost at times to be the belief in Canberra that the best way of educating people in favour of central government was to act in disregard of any distribution of powers and functions. Furthermore, it was apparent that the principle upon which some activities were undertaken was that once they were operating they would provide their own atmosphere in which challenge would be more difficult, either because of the climate of public opinion or even because High Court judges are not entirely impervious to the practical effects of their decisions. There was also a propaganda aspect to the Labor programme, seen at its most obvious in the legally ineffective attempt to abolish the name 'Commonwealth of Australia' and to substitute by amendment of the Acts Interpretation Act the name 'Australia'.[1] If this was not entirely effective in making the States disappear it did succeed in irritating them no end.

To a politician this may be the stuff of life but to a lawyer not only does it represent no advance but in many respects it represents a backsliding. Let me illustrate what I mean by reference to the application or interpretation clauses in Commonwealth statutes which are discussed in the essay[2]. The authors refer specifically to the sections which are to be found in the *Petroleum and Minerals Authority Act* 1973 (which fell with the rest of that Act in the *P.M.A. Case*[3]), but the device in question was found by the Commonwealth to be generally useful[4].

The Petroleum and Minerals Authority was given wide functions which clearly exceeded the powers of the Commonwealth, but these functions were then required to be exercised only in relation to certain broad heads of constitutional power. To define the functions of an instrumentality in terms of broad constitutional powers is, I suggest, a failure to face up to constitutional problems. More than that, it is irresponsible when the problems are flung at the instrumentality itself, the courts and, most important of all, members of the public dealing with the instrumentality, particularly when criminal penalties are imposed for breaches of the Act. Perhaps the most extreme example of this type of provision is to be found in the *Australian Housing Corporation Act* 1975. The Australian Housing Corporation is given wide functions which are clearly beyond power by themselves but it is provided that those functions may only be exercised to the extent that they relate to matters with respect to which the Commonwealth has power to make laws. Specific mention is then made of the power to make laws 'for any purpose of Australia or an authority of Australia'![5]

It is just possible that the Courts will strike down such sections as constituting no exercise of any legislative power by the Commonwealth Parliament.[6] But whatever their fate, they hardly represent a desirable technique. They

---

[1] *Acts Interpretation Act* 1973, s.4.

[2] Above, pp. 55-6.

[3] *Victoria v. Commonwealth* (1975) 7 A.L.R. 1.

[4] See, e.g., *Pipeline Authority Act* 1973; *Australian Housing Corporation Act* 1975; Legal Aid Bill 1975.

[5] *Australian Housing Corporation Act* 1975, s.6.

[6] *Pidoto v. Victoria* (1943) 68 C.L.R. 87.

constitute an exploitation rather than exploration of constitutional powers and demonstrate no great initiative or enterprise[7]. There are, of course, the more carefully drafted provisions which speak in constitutional terms but which are drawn with an eye to the severance of those parts which are beyond power.[8] They are susceptible to the same criticism but less so because, on the whole, they do represent some real attempt to grapple with constitutional problems which the provisions to which I have been referring do not.

Allied with this tendency of the Labor Government to treat limitations upon its power somewhat off-handedly was a tendency in some areas not to want to do anything unless it could be seen to be being done from Canberra. I am thinking here particularly of the use of the spending power. Much of what the Commonwealth attempted to do during Labor's years of office could without question have been achieved by means of grants to the States under s.96 of the Constitution. The provision of welfare services such as legal aid, unemployment benefits or the scheme envisaged in the Australian Assistance Plan was constitutionally feasible by means of grants, conditional grants, under s.96 of the Constitution. I make this point simply because a great deal of the exploration which took place in these areas tended to be unnecessary and counter-productive. May I take as my example the Regional Employment Development (R.E.D.) Scheme. This was a scheme by which the Commonwealth Government sought to provide unemployment relief by providing funds to local bodies, including local government bodies, to enable them to hire labour for approved works. The scheme was, so the State of Victoria contended, beyond the legislative competence of the Commonwealth and, that being so, it was outside the spending power. But the point I wish to make here is that in 1972 a similar scheme had operated simply and efficiently by channelling Commonwealth funds through the State Treasury for disbursement to State departments and instrumentalities and local government bodies. In 1974, this would not do and a cumbersome, inefficient and expensive machinery was set up (or so it seemed to the State) merely to assert Commonwealth powers.

It is to the conclusions reached in the essay that I now turn. Here, correctly I think, the authors express the view that any real development of constitutional principles during Labor's period of office was limited. I am able also to agree that it was in a quantitative rather than a qualitative sense that Labor made its presence felt upon the Constitution. Indeed, that is part of my criticism. But what I should like to develop for a moment is the authors' conclusion that during the Labor years there was confirmation that the federal division of powers, however irksome it might be to Labor politicians and supporters, need not necessarily present an unsurmountable barrier to the aspirations of an activist Commonwealth government.

Of course, in terms of actual accretion of power the *Offshore Sovereignty Case*[9] is, as the essay points out, pre-eminent. Nevertheless, in their comments the authors may underestimate the difficulties inherent in the exercise of a sovereignty which stops at low water mark. These difficulties lie perhaps behind the Commonwealth's decision to accept the States' contention that they

---

[7]An allied practice which grew up during the Labor administration, perhaps less pernicious because it is difficult to see what effect it has, was to set out the *objects* of legislation in broad constitutional terms. See, e.g., *National Parks and Wildlife Conservation Act* 1975; *Great Barrier Reef Marine Park Act* 1975.

[8]*E.g. Trade Practices Act* 1974, s.6.

[9]*New South Wales* v. *Commonwealth* (1975) 8 A.L.R. 1.

retain legislative power (albeit extra-territorial legislative power) beyond low water mark.[10]

There were no other decisions with the same immediate, wide significance as the *Offshore Sovereignty Case*, but although not of immediate consequence, one of the most important decisions during the Labor administration may well have been, as the essay recognizes, the *A.A.P. Case*.[11] It was not of immediate consequence because it did not really decide anything. The State of Victoria and its Attorney-General challenged the Australian Assistance Plan on two bases, first, that the appropriation of moneys to provide funds was not for the purposes of the Commonwealth and was beyond power and, secondly, that in any event the implementation of the plan depended wholly on an exercise of the executive power, there being no statute to support it, and the executive power of the Commonwealth did not extend to such an exercise. Three Justices, Barwick CJ, Gibbs and Mason JJ, held that the Australian Assistance Plan was beyond the power of the Commonwealth and three Justices, McTiernan, Jacobs and Murphy JJ, held that it was within power or, at least, that it could not be challenged. The seventh Justice, Stephen J, held that the plaintiffs had no *locus standi* to challenge the appropriation but did not decide whether the implementation of the plan was a valid exercise of the executive power. The authors of the essay claim a victory for the Commonwealth in that case which might, perhaps, be thought to be over-enthusiastic. The claim is based upon the fact that there was a majority in favour of the proposition that the purposes of the Commonwealth are whatever purposes Parliament determines them to be without the limitations suggested by the majority in the *Pharmaceutical Bene-fits Case*.[12] But there was no majority for the view that the Australian Assistance Plan might be carried out by means of the executive power without legislative backing and it is not unreasonable to assume that Stephen J, had he decided this point, might have sided with Mason J.[13] An executive power which, apart from the day-to-day administration of the public service, requires legislative authority for its exercise would be, for practical purposes, as effective a restraint upon the Commonwealth Government as a limited power of appropriation.

But those arguments remain for another day. What is, I think, important about the *A.A.P. Case* is, first, the cleavage of views and, secondly, the lengths to which at least two of the Justices who upheld the Commonwealth submissions are prepared to go. In speaking of a cleavage of views, I think that it might be said that during the Labor administration a polarization of views developed not only in the political field but also upon the High Court. Other cases in addition to the *A.A.P. Case* which I have in mind are the *P.M.A. Case*,[14] the *Territory Senators Case*,[15] *McKinlay's Case*[16] and the *Family Law Case*.[17]

---

[10] *Pearce* v. *Florenca* (1976) 9 A.L.R. 289.

[11] *Victoria* v. *Commonwealth* (1975) 7 A.L.R. 277.

[12] *A.-G. (Victoria) (Ex rel. Dale)* v. *Commonwealth* (1946) 71 C.L.R. 237.

[13] See Geoffrey Sawer, *Canberra Times*, 5 November 1975.

[14] *Victoria* v. *Commonwealth* (1975) 7 A.L.R. 1.

[15] *Western Australia* v. *Commonwealth* (1975) 7 A.L.R. 159.

[16] *A.-G. (Australia) (Ex rel. McKinlay)* v. *Commonwealth* (1975) 7 A.L.R. 593.

[17] *Russell* v. *Russell; Farrelly* v. *Farrelly* (1976) 9 A.L.R. 103.

Perhaps fundamental divergences of view may even be discerned in non-constitutional areas.[18] It is not so much the fact of divergence of view which is important but the extent of the divergence. This is reflected in the comment in the essay that the view adopted by Jacobs J in the *A.A.P. Case* implies a significant shift in *residual* powers from the States to the Commonwealth. Put in that way, it is a somewhat startling comment, yet it is not an exaggeration. Moreover, in direction if not in method, Jacobs J commands the support of Murphy and McTiernan JJ.

In the light of these developments it is not surprising to see an exercise in realist jurisprudence undertaken by a select committee of the Legislative Assembly of New South Wales in relation to the appointment of judges to the High Court of Australia; nor is it surprising that the Committee concludes that it is anomalous that one party to the federal compact, the central government, has the right—without even obligation to consult—to appoint the umpires in the case of conflict between it and the State governments. For what is becoming apparent is not just a difference in the results achieved by the application of legal analysis. It is a difference in basic approach which must inevitably lead to a different result.

---

[18]See, e.g., *Paull* v. *Munday* (1976) 9 A.L.R. 245.

3 Reform of the Constitution: The Referendums and Constitutional Convention

J. E. Richardson

I
CONSTITUTION ALTERATION BILLS

The results of referendums for constitutional change are impressively conservative. Under the machinery provided in s.128 of the Constitution, federal electors have voted on fifteen occasions for a total of thirty-two separate proposed constitutional changes, but only five proposals, or 16 per cent of those submitted, have obtained the requisite approval.

Before Whitlam

The five separate proposed constitutional Bills which the electors have approved were carried in 1906[1], 1910[2], 1928[3], 1946[4], and 1967[5]. The proposals of 1906, 1910 and 1946 were submitted at the same time as the general elections. The most striking feature of the successes is that, with one exception, they were approved by majorities in every State. There was no substantial body of opposition to any of them. Apart from the social services referendum in 1946, however, the successful proposals were, and have been, of little direct concern to the general public. There was virtually no interest beyond the rural community in 1906 as to when senators' terms should begin. The changes of 1910 and 1928 were probably not even properly understood, but the electors were probably prepared to vote for them with the encouragement of both the Commonwealth and the States. The fifth change, in 1967, was of direct concern principally to a relatively small body of persons, and seemed to

---

[1] *Constitution Alteration (Senate Elections)* 1906. This was the first constitutional referendum. It altered s.13 to cause senators' terms to begin in July instead of January. All States carried the proposal; the total vote being 'Yes': 744,011, 'No': 162,470.

[2] *Constitution Alteration (State Debts)* 1909 (referendum held April 1910). This altered s.105 to extend the power of the Commonwealth to take over State debts to include State debts incurred since Federation. All States except N.S.W. carried it, the total vote being 'Yes': 715,053, 'No': 586,271. In 1910 another proposal, dealing with Commonwealth-State finances, was opposed at federal level by the Labor Party and failed.

[3] *Constitution Alteration (State Debts)* 1928. Added s.105A to implement the Financial Agreement of 1927 between the Commonwealth and all States. All States carried the proposal, the total vote being 'Yes': 2,237,391, 'No': 773,852.

[4] *Constitution Alteration (Social Services)* 1946. Added paragraph (23A) to s.51. Carried in all States with a majority of 2,297,934 to 1,927,148. Separate proposals to give the Commonwealth Parliament power to legislate over the marketing of primary products, and industrial employment, were strenuously resisted by the federal Opposition, in particular the U.A.P., and they failed.

[5] *Constitution Alteration (Aboriginals)* 1967. Altered s.51(26), and omitted s.127, with the result that the Commonwealth gained legislative power with respect to Aboriginals, who were also to be included in the census count. Carried in all States with a majority of 5,183,113 to 527,007.

be in keeping with a growing national conscience about the fate of the Aboriginals. States most directly concerned, such as Western Australia and South Australia, were only too willing to shed the costly responsibility, without accompanying political popularity, that governmental measures in relation to Aboriginals entailed. The change did not produce any apparent effect on the political power structures either within the States or as between the Commonwealth and the States. The social services referendum was, of course, of general interest, but it received strong support, and not even the Leader of the Opposition, Mr Menzies, vehemently opposed it. In any case, it offered financial benefits on a national basis, and the power is not suggestive of the imposition of governmental restraints upon the average elector.

Of the twenty-one separate failures before 1973,[6] eighteen involved a quest by the Commonwealth for increased economic powers. This means, taking into account the Whitlam prices and incomes referendums in 1973, that the Commonwealth has never gained any additional economic power by constitutional referendum. In 1937, the Lyons U.A.P.-Country Party coalition ministry sought federal power with respect to aviation and marketing. Since 1937, no U.A.P. or Liberal-Country Party government has sought any additional federal economic powers. In fact, the longest period between the submissions of any constitutional Bills to a referendum is the sixteen years of Liberal-Country Party government between 1951 and 1967.

Several of the earlier failures to gain economic powers are no longer particularly significant because of the role of the High Court. The High Court's interpretation of Commonwealth powers has been a paramount factor in enabling the Constitution to perform an adequate role during the developing and maturing stages of the Australian economy over the past half-century. Federal control over monopolies and combines in restraint of trade was sought in five separate proposed laws submitted to referendums in 1911, 1913, 1919 and 1926. In *Strickland* v. *Rocla Concrete Pipes Ltd*,[7] as is well known, the High Court stated that the legislative power with respect to corporations in s.51(20) of the Constitution was sufficient to enable the Commonwealth to legislate with respect to the restrictive trade practices of the corporations described in the power. The *Trade Practices Act* 1974 gives the Commonwealth most of the control which would have been possible had the early referendums been successful. Some early proposals also sought control of legislative power with respect to corporations, viz., in 1911, 1913 and 1926, but the interpretation of the corporations power in the *Concrete Pipes Case* covers most of what was

---

[6]Economic powers which have been rejected include the following:
  Intra-State trade and commerce: 1911, 1913, 1919;
  Industrial matters and employment: 1911, 1913, 1919, 1926, 1944, 1946;
  Essential services: 1926;
  Marketing: 1937, 1940, 1946;
  Prices: 1944, 1948;
  Production and distribution of goods: 1944.
The remaining proposals rejected were:
  Finance (specific per capita payments to States): 1910;
  Postwar reconstruction and democratic rights: 1944;
  Communists and Communism: 1951;
  Parliament (to remove s.24 nexus between size of Senate and House of Representatives): 1967.
For a fuller account of each referendum proposal, together with overall voting figures, see J. E. Richardson, *Patterns of Australian Federalism* (Canberra, 1973), Appendix F.
  [7](1971) 124 C.L.R. 468.

sought on those occasions. The power sought over aviation in 1937 would not now be required because of the decision in *Airlines of New South Wales* v. *New South Wales (No. 2)*[8] in 1965.

Different political parties in the federal Parliament have at different times submitted similar proposals for change. In 1913, the Fisher Labor Ministry submitted six separate proposals for increased economic powers, including powers to make laws with respect to trade and commerce generally, corporations, industrial matters, and combinations in restraint of trade. In 1919, the Hughes Nationalist Ministry sought powers over similar subject matters. In 1926, the Nationalist-Country Party coalition of Bruce and Page sought similar powers, with the exception of the power to legislate with respect to intra-State trade and commerce. In 1937, the Lyons Government submitted its marketing proposal, and an equivalent power was sought by the Chifley Labor Government in 1946. Nevertheless, as mentioned, the conservative parties of the federal Parliament have not sought an economic power since 1937. The proceedings of the Constitutional Convention in Sydney in 1973 did nothing to dispel the feeling that the non-Labor parties, either federal or State, were not particularly interested in increased federal legislative powers.

There are at least three early referendum failures which it is instructive to consider in a little detail, those of 1910, 1937 and 1946. In 1910, the Fusion Party led by Deakin, with the co-operation of the Labor Party led by Fisher, successfully sponsored the proposal for the Commonwealth to take over all State debts. However, the Finance proposal submitted separately at the same time to give the States the security of fixed per capita payments, following the expiration of their entitlement under the Braddon clause (Constitution, s.87), failed to carry, even though the proposal emanated from the conclusion of a financial agreement between the Commonwealth and the States in 1909. In a poll of about 1,400,000 federal electors, a comfortable majority of 129,000 for the State Debts change was reduced to a deficit of 25,000 votes in relation to the Finance proposal. Although the federal Labor Party supported State Debts, it was opposed to Finance. However, this early experience does not, as is sometimes thought, illustrate that the combined support of the major federal political parties is essential to the success of a referendum. At the time of the elections, the popularity of the Deakin Fusion Ministry (a fusion of Freetraders and ex-protectionist tariff reformers with Deakin's Protectionists) was already on the wane, and Labor won the elections held at the same time as the referendums. Moreover, the Finance Bill was not without its critics in the States. It was opposed, for example, by the then prominent Australian Natives Association and several newspapers, including the *Age* and the *Bulletin*. The Labor Party had indicated that it was prepared to carry out the policy of the proposal without being bound to do so by constitutional amendment. Nevertheless, it is plain enough that, if the Labor Party had supported the proposal, it would have received the requisite approval. It is submitted that, if the federal Opposition parties had adopted even a neutral attitude, it is likely that the results might have been different for Marketing and Industrial Employment in 1946, Prices in 1973, and the four proposals in 1974.

The defeat of Aviation in 1937 was a notorious and anachronistic event, denting various theories about constitutional change. As mentioned, the proposed alteration was the work of a non-Labor Government, but it had the

---

[8](1965) 113 C.L.R. 54.

support of the federal Labor Opposition, and widespread support in each State amongst Government and Opposition parties. The chief public opponents were the Labor Premiers of Western Australia and Tasmania, who expressed their own opposition to the proposal, claiming it threatened the stability of their State railway systems. In fact, the official 'No' case distributed to electors made the same argument, and further predicted a decline of prosperity in country towns and rural areas by restriction of railway services as a result of servicing metropolitan areas by air. Marketing, in 1937, also had federal Labor Party support, but the Government parties themselves were not wholly united behind the proposal, and the Labor governments of Western Australia and Tasmania were clearly opposed to it. Opposition also came from the Lang faction of the Labor Party, and in various quarters of commerce and industry, including the Associated Chambers of Commerce, and the Associated Chambers of Manufactures. Contemporary newspaper commentaries upon the results also suggested that the public had not understood the marketing proposal, and that, unobtrusively, individual segments of the commercial community suggested that likelihood of federal interference with the freedom of interstate trade to the detriment of private enterprise and employment. Further, newspaper opinion was that the unpopularity of the marketing proposal had caused an unwillingness to vest the Lyons Government with the aviation power. Although the voting for Aviation was 1,924,946 in favour and 1,669,062 not in favour, only two States had majorities, including the unusual figures in Victoria of 675,481 in favour, as against 362,112 not in favour. For Marketing, the votes in the three smallest States, South Australia, Western Australia and Tasmania, were unusually adverse. The total 'Yes' vote for the three States was 146,984, compared with a total 'No' vote of 484,518.

The 1944 Postwar Reconstruction and Democratic Rights referendum was held just one year after the general election of 21 August 1943, when the Curtin Labor Government, which had assumed office in Parliament following the downfall of the Fadden Ministry, was returned to office with a very substantial majority. The Party won forty-eight State seats in the House of Representatives, compared with twenty-four seats won by the U.A.P. and Country Party. Labor won more seats than the combined Opposition in all States, except Victoria. The total Labor vote, including State Labor (N.S.W.), was marginally less than 51 per cent, compared with 33 per cent for the anti-Labor parties. (Two per cent each of the votes were won by the One Parliament for Australia Party and the Communist Party, while votes for independents constituted 12 per cent.) Labor also gained more than 50 per cent of the votes in New South Wales, South Australia and Western Australia. In Queensland, it gained 48 per cent of votes, compared with 39 per cent for the non-Labor parties represented in the federal Parliament, and in Tasmania 49 per cent compared with 41 per cent for the federal Opposition Party, the U.A.P. There was a certain spirit of euphoria associated with the sweeping Labor victory. At the instigation of the Curtin Government, a Convention on proposed alterations of the Constitution was held in Canberra towards the end of 1942. The purpose of the Convention was to seek agreement with State political leaders on temporary increased Commonwealth legislative powers to deal with post-war reconstruction. The federal Attorney-General, Evatt, was the dominant Labor figure. The Convention approved a draft model Bill to refer certain matters to the Commonwealth Parliament for a period of five years after the cessation of hostilities. As had happened on other occasions, upon departure from Canberra enthusiasm waned in the States. Upon it becoming apparent that State co-operation was not forthcoming according to the tenor of the 1942 Convention, the Curtin Labor Ministry presented its proposals for increased Commonwealth powers for five years in the form of a single proposed law. It was defeated by a vote of 2,305,418 to 1,963,400. It is tentatively suggested that, had the proposed law been divided into a series of proposals and submitted very shortly after the August elections instead of a year later, some success would have been achieved. This point will be taken up further below.

Prices and Incomes 1973

The Whitlam Government's first referendum proposals were put to the electors on 18 December 1973, three months after the conclusion of the Australian Constitutional Convention in Sydney. Two separate proposals were submitted, one to give the Australian government control over prices,[9] and the other to grant control over incomes.[10] Electors in all States rejected both. Details of the voting were as follows:

PRICES[11]

State	In favour	Against
New South Wales	1,257,499	1,332,485
Victoria	891,144	1,081,120
Queensland	402,506	643,770
South Australia	282,754	404,181
Western Australia	169,605	362,121
Tasmania	85,631	138,416
Total	3,089,139	3,962,093

The result of the referendum for the incomes proposal was predictably worse. In fact, it was the most unfavourable result ever incurred at a referendum for constitutional change.

INCOMES[12]

State	In favour	Against
New South Wales	1,041,429	1,542,217
Victoria	657,756	1,309,302
Queensland	331,163	713,562
South Australia	193,301	490,943
Western Australia	133,531	396,199
Tasmania	63,135	159,862
Total	2,420,315	4,612,085

[9]Constitution Alteration (Prices) 1973.
[10]Constitution Alteration (Incomes) 1973.
[11]*Source*: Australia, *Official Year Book* 1974, No. 60, p. 90. There were 96,135 informal votes.
[12]*Source*: Australia, *Official Year Book* 1974, No. 60, p.90. There were 114,967 informal votes.

The Opposition Parties in the Australian Parliament, and their organizations in the States, strenuously opposed both proposals. In New South Wales, Victoria and Queensland, non-Labor governments were in office. Amongst traditional Labor supporters, the unions treated the incomes proposal with suspicion, and dislike of the proposal may have rubbed off to the disadvantage of the prices proposal, since the attitude was taken by many that price control without income control would not be effective.

During the Australian Constitutional Convention in Sydney in September 1973, Mr Whitlam had urged the State leaders to agree to refer concurrent power over prices to the national government.[13] It is open to speculation whether the prices referendum would have been successful if the incomes proposal had not been submitted at the same time. The inducement to supporters of the Liberal and Country Parties to vote for prices because incomes would also be the subject of control may not have captured any substantial number of votes in favour of prices.

Democratic Government and Local Government 1974

During the first day of the proceedings of the Australian Constitutional Convention, Mr Whitlam announced[14] that, quite independently of the Convention, his Government would submit at the next federal election constitutional proposals to synchronise elections of the Senate and the House of Representatives, to secure the principle of substantial equality of electoral divisions for all Parliaments in Australia, and to require State Houses of Parliament to be elected directly by the people. True to his word, on 18 May 1974 the electors considered these proposals and others in four separate proposed laws[15] at the same time as they voted at the general election following the double dissolution of the Parliament granted by the Governor-General, Sir Paul Hasluck, under s.57 of the Constitution.[16] The substance of each of the proposals was as follows:

(a) *Simultaneous Elections.* The principal amendment to achieve the purpose was a new s.13 stating that the term of a senator should expire upon the expiration, or dissolution, of the second House of Representatives to expire, or be dissolved, after he was chosen. A new s.12 required the Governor of a State to issue the writs for elections of senators for the State within ten days from the date of the places becoming vacant. In 1959, the Report of the Joint Committee on Constitutional Review of the Commonwealth Parliament[17] had recommended, with only a single dissent, an alteration to provide that senators should hold their places for the terms of two Houses of Representatives, and that the

---

[13]*Official Record of Debates*, 4 September 1973, p.87.

[14]*Official Record of Debates*, 3 September 1973, p.17.

[15]Constitution Alteration (Simultaneous Elections) 1974; Constitution Alteration (Democratic Elections) 1974; Constitution Alteration (Mode of Altering the Constitution) 1974; Constitution Alteration (Local Government Bodies) 1974.

[16]The four constitutional Bills had not been passed by the Senate, in which the Government lacked a majority. Instead, when the Senate had not passed the four measures after an interval of three months the House of Representatives again passed the four Bills. Again the Senate did not pass them in accordance with the wishes of the Representatives. On these facts, the Governor-General accepted the Government's advice to submit the four proposed laws to the electors in the States in accordance with the procedure specified in the second paragraph of s.128.

[17]*Report*, pp. 34-37.

Governor of a State should issue the Senate writs within ten days of the expiry, or dissolution, of the House of Representatives.

(b) *Democratic Elections.* As to the Commonwealth, the proposal sought by an additional provision in s.29 to ensure that the number of votes in each federal electoral division in a State should be as nearly as practicable the same. The 1959 Report of the Constitution Review Committee had contained[18] a unanimous recommendation to amend the Constitution to provide, in effect, that the number of electors in a federal electoral division in a State should not vary either way by more than one-tenth of a basic quota of electors. An amendment to s.30 aimed to grant federal enfranchisement to every Australian citizen upon attaining the age of eighteen.

As to the States, a proposed new s.106A required every State House to be composed of members directly chosen by the people of the State on a similar basis as provided for the House of Representatives, that is, of adult suffrage at the age of 18, and almost equally-divided electoral divisions.[19]

(c) *Mode of Altering the Constitution.* This Bill proposed to amend s.128 to enable electors in the federal territories to vote on proposed laws to amend the Constitution, and to provide, further, that it be sufficient, in addition to an overall majority of federal electors voting in favour of a proposal submitted to them, that separate majorities be obtained in not less than one-half of the States (three States) instead of a majority of States (four or more).

Again, the Constitution Review Committee, with only one dissent, had recommended[20] an alteration to s.128 to provide for separate State majorities in half of the States instead of in a majority of States. In 1946, when the electors approved the social services amendment, two other proposals, dealing with organized marketing of primary products and industrial employment respectively, obtained total majorities, but separate majorities in only three States.[21]

(d) *Local Government Bodies.* It was sought to empower the Australian Parliament, by adding paragraph (iv A.) to s.51, to make laws for federal borrowing of money for local government purposes. The Bill also included s.96A in the Constitution, drafted in the language of s.96 relating to federal grants to the States, to enable the Australian Parliament to grant financial assistance to local government bodies on such terms and conditions as it thought fit. It had been on Mr Whitlam's insistence that local government representation was allowed at the 1973 Constitutional Convention. At the Convention, the Prime Minister said that his Government would consider amending s.105A of the Constitution to enable the Commonwealth to borrow moneys directly on behalf of elected local government bodies.[22] He also expressed the hope that the Convention would agree to amend the Financial Agreement to accord local government

---

[18] *Report*, pp. 44-51.

[19] Another provision in the proposed law was to give the High Court original jurisdiction in respect of matters arising out of electoral provisions of the Constitution, in particular, those which were to be amended by the constitutional proposals.

[20] *Report*, pp. 170-2.

[21] In 1937, the Aviation proposal received a majority of total votes but gained separate majorities in only two States. In 1951, the Communism referendum failed to gain an overall majority, but there were separate majorities in three States.

[22] *Official Record of Debates*, 3 September 1973, p.15; 6 September 1973, pp. 234-6.

membership of the Loan Council.[23] Later in the year at a Premiers' Conference Mr Whitlam unsuccessfully sought to give elected local government the participation in the Loan Council he had mentioned at the Convention, and an amendment to the Financial Agreement to empower the federal government to borrow on their behalf.[24]

All four proposals perished. The total majority against varied from 247,000 for simultaneous elections to 458,000 for local government bodies out of a total vote of 7,411,000 (including informal votes, which varied from 124,000 for simultaneous elections to 139,000 for local government bodies).

New South Wales electors voted in favour of each of the four proposals, but there was no other State majority for any proposal. Details of the voting were as follows:

SIMULTANEOUS ELECTIONS[25]

State	In favour	Against
New South Wales	1,359,485	1,303,117
Victoria	1,001,111	1,033,969
Queensland	481,092	604,444
South Australia	332,369	372,666
Western Australia	248,860	315,786
Tasmania	96,793	137,156
Total	3,519,710	3,767,138

DEMOCRATIC ELECTIONS[26]

State	In favour	Against
New South Wales	1,345,983	1,316,837
Victoria	970,903	1,064,023
Queensland	474,337	611,135
South Australia	310,839	393,857
Western Australia	241,946	322,587
Tasmania	95,463	138,430
Total	3,439,471	3,846,869

[23]*ibid.*

[24]Mr Whitlam's proposals were rejected by New South Wales, Victoria, Queensland and South Australia.

[25]*Source*: Australia, *Official Year Book* 1974, No. 60, p.91. There were 123,663 informal votes.

[26]*Source*: Australia, *Official Year Book* 1974, No. 60, p.91. There were 124,171 informal votes.

MODE OF ALTERING THE CONSTITUTION[27]

State	In favour	Against
New South Wales	1,367,476	1,295,621
Victoria	1,001,753	1,033,486
Queensland	480,926	604,816
South Australia	311,954	392,891
Western Australia	240,134	324,435
Tasmania	95,264	138,674
Total	3,497,507	3,789,923

LOCAL GOVERNMENT BODIES[28]

State	In favour	Against
New South Wales	1,350,274	1,308,039
Victoria	961,664	1,068,120
Queensland	473,465	610,537
South Australia	298,489	403,479
Western Australia	229,337	334,529
Tasmania	93,495	140,073
Total	3,406,724	3,864,777

The anti-Labor federal parties opposed each of the four proposals, and, as in the case of prices and incomes, Liberal and Country Party organizations and their variants or affiliates in the States also objected. My impression is that the proposals received insufficient prominence during the political campaign of the Labor Party directed to ensuring return to office.

Lessons for the Future

Referendums can be won in the teeth of federal and State political opposition, but in this respect the question of timing is very important. Past experience suggests that chances of success will be substantially improved if the proposals can be put so as to capitalize on the popularity, perhaps inevitably transient, of the government of the day. Such a case can certainly be made in respect of the 'package deal' referendum failure of 1944: had those proposals been submitted at or very shortly after the August 1943 election, when Labor was swept back into office on a wave of euphoria, the result may well have been different. Some support, though inconclusive, for the view just expressed is to be found in the election and referendum results in 1974, when the voting for the referendum proposals, though not enough to carry them, was closely comparable with the measure of electoral support which the Labor Party received in the election

[27] Source: Australia, *Official Year Book* 1974, No. 60, p.91. There were 123,081 informal votes.
[28] Source: Australia, *Official Year Book* 1974, No. 60, p.91. There were 139,010 informal votes.

held at the same time.[29] Had it been possible to submit the referendum proposals in the first months of 1973, when the Whitlam Government was apparently at the peak of its popularity, there might well have been some success.

But perhaps the most important requirements, if future referendums are ever to succeed, are better education of the electorate and more effective publicity for constitutional proposals. It is understood that Mr Whitlam, when in office, was anxious to educate the electorate to the habit of voting upon constitutional changes to allow proposals to be treated on their merits and without preconceived suspicions. It is all too easy to assemble formidable opposition to almost any proposed constitutional change which emerges from Canberra and, where the federal government alone has sponsored a proposal, it requires a 'hard sell'. Much more effort needs to be put into explaining the reasons for change than the four proposals of 1974 received. In my opinion, after addressing 'above-average intelligence' groups in the community over many years, few constitutional proposals are understood. Propaganda and exposition should be regarded possibly as being capable of equal effectiveness. In 1951, Mr Menzies said:

> The truth of the matter is that to get an affirmative vote from the Australian people on a referendum proposal is one of the labours of Hercules. For this last referendum[30] showed us, if we needed proof, the amount of sheer hard lying that goes on in the course of a referendum campaign designed to alter the Constitution. The amount of muddled thinking and speaking that can proceed from minds that are supposed to be improved by university degrees in some cases is quite baffling to me. I don't think you will recall a single instance of a 'Yes' vote on constitutional change except a change designed to increase the amount of money being paid by the Commonwealth to someone else.[31]

A serious obstacle to constitutional change is, in my opinion, constituted by s.6A of the *Referendum (Constitution Alteration) Act* 1906. Sub-section (1) provides in effect for a case of not more than two thousand words each to be put in writing by the protagonists and antagonists of the proposed law in the federal Parliament, and for the resulting document to be distributed to each elector by

---

[29]Take for example the Mode of Altering the Constitution referendum, that which represents the voting mean of the four proposals:

State	Votes for Labor in the House of Representatives*	Votes in favour of proposed law
New South Wales	1,400,255	1,367,476
Victoria	970,236	1,001,753
Queensland	476,710	480,926
South Australia	341,563	311,954
Western Australia	261,107	240,134
Tasmania	128,787	95,264
Total	3,578,658	3,497,507

*The combined anti-Labor vote in the six States for the House of Representatives was 3,191,228 (excluding the 104,974 D.L.P. votes and 168,046 votes for the Australia Party).
Source: Australia, *Official Year Book* 1974, No.60, pp. 86, 91.

[30]Constitution Alteration (Powers to deal with Communists and Communism) 1951.

[31]L.F. Crisp, *Australian National Government* (3rd revised ed., 1974), p.40. In Ch. 2, 'The People and the Constitution', Professor Crisp has produced an interesting account of the public and political reactions to constitutional change.

the Chief Electoral Officer. Sub-section (2) provides for the consolidation of arguments where referendums upon more than one proposed law will occur on the same day. A proposed law is the legal expression of the will of the federal Parliament, but s.6A does not recognize it. Once Parliament has passed the proposed law, it should be open to the government to take all reasonable steps to publicise and advocate the proposed constitutional alteration, and the opportunity to state a contrary case should not be afforded to dissidents, as provided in the section. The section should, in the interests of achieving constitutional change, be repealed.

Another suggestion relating to the education of the public is that it may be better for a few years to induce public acceptance of constitutional change by not confronting it with momentous changes which arouse political passions. There are many worthwhile amendments of the Constitution which could be put with good chances of success. Some of them may be matters which the second session of the Constitutional Convention, held in Melbourne in 1975, had before it and which are mentioned hereunder.

II
CONSTITUTIONAL CHANGE
BY COLLECTIVE ACTION

Before Whitlam

So far, this essay has addressed itself to constitutional proposals in which the initiative has stemmed from the government in office, for the most part acting alone. The three exceptions have been the proposals submitted in 1910 (twice) and 1928, dealing with Commonwealth-State financial relationships, which were put after agreement was first reached between the Commonwealth and the States. These apart, there were before 1973 four separate occasions — in 1926, 1934, 1942 and 1959 — on which serious attempts were made to evolve programmes of constitutional reform by collaboration extending beyond the ranks of the government.

In 1926, the Bruce-Page Ministry unsuccessfully submitted two proposals to a referendum of electors. The Government then attempted to set up an all-party committee to consider constitutional changes, but the Labor Party refused to support the plan, complaining of inadequate representation. Instead, in August 1927, the government appointed a Royal Commission, with J. B. Peden, K.C., as Chairman, to enquire into, and report upon, the powers of the Commonwealth under the Constitution, and the working of the Constitution since Federation. The other members of the Commission were Abbott, Ashworth, Bowden, Colebatch, Duffy and McNamara: the last two were the only Labor men. The Commission presented a report in September 1929, containing a wide range of recommendations, including some additional federal powers, but also revealing substantial differences of opinion among the members, reflecting mainly their backgrounds and political attitudes. No attempt was ever made to implement any of the Commission's recommendations, apart from an abortive proposal by the Scullin Government in 1930, when the House of Representatives passed a Bill to alter the Constitution by conferring upon Parliament full power to amend the Constitution. The Bill was rejected in the Senate, along with two other Bills containing specific proposals for the amendment of s.51. Nothing further happened.

As Australia began to emerge from the depths of economic depression, the Lyons Government proposed to each State government that there should be a constitutional convention, but all States would not agree. They accepted an alternative proposal that there should be a conference of Commonwealth and State ministers on constitutional matters which would enable questions to be raised affecting relations between the Commonwealth and the States, and between the States themselves. The conference, held in Melbourne in 1934, was confined to government representation. The States were principally concerned with finance, and various Premiers submitted proposals for increasing State revenue, but no agreement could be reached.

The Conference also had before it memoranda on constitutional questions prepared by the Commonwealth Solicitor-General, Robert Garran, suggesting increased Commonwealth legislative power over a range of subjects, including company law, aviation, marine navigation, the whole of trade and commerce, cinematography, wireless broadcasting and television, quarantine, and fisheries. The Conference resolved, however, to consider only three major subjects — finance, trade and commerce, and industrial law. In the event, there proved to be a general unwillingness on the part of the States to concede additional powers to the Commonwealth. The Conference concluded with Menzies acknowledging that not much immediate progress had occurred, but stating that in discussing changes and developments in constitutions it was foolish to look for immediate results, and that the Conference was dealing with something which might have to develop slowly over a period of years.

Towards the end of 1942, a convention of representatives of the Commonwealth and all State Parliaments met at Canberra to consider granting increased legislative powers to the Commonwealth Parliament to provide for post-war reconstruction. Each State was represented by its Premier and the Leader of the Opposition. The Commonwealth representation consisted of the Prime Minister and three other Ministers, and three senior members of the Opposition. The Convention began with Dr Evatt presenting a draft Bill to alter the Constitution to empower the Parliament to make laws for the purpose of post-war reconstruction and by guaranteeing religious freedom, and freedom of expression. It concluded by resolving unanimously that a draft Bill be enacted by State Parliaments referring specific matters in relation to post-war reconstruction under s. 51 (37) for a period of five years from the cessation of hostilities. It was also agreed that there should later be a referendum to secure the approval of the electors to alterations of the Constitution on a permanent basis. Although the State Premiers agreed to do their utmost to secure the passage of the draft model Bill into law as early as possible, only two States eventually passed the measure in the agreed form.

In May 1956, following an election undertaking by the Menzies Government, the two Houses of the federal Parliament established the Joint Committee on Constitutional Review, consisting of members of the Government parties and the Labor Opposition from both Houses, to review the working of the Constitution and to make recommendations for amendments.[32] Prime Minister Menzies and Leader of the Opposition, Evatt, were ex officio members of the Committee, but did not attend its meetings. The Committee submitted an

---

[32]The members were Senators O'Sullivan (Chairman, replacing Senator Spicer in October 1956) and Wright, and Messrs Downer, Drummond, Hamilton and Joske from the Liberal-Country Parties, and Senators Kennelly and McKenna and Messrs Calwell, Pollard, Ward and Whitlam from the Labor Party.

interim report in 1958, and a full report in 1959. In some quarters, it was believed that the Government's primary intention in setting up the Committee was to review the operation of s.57 concerning the occurrence and settlement of deadlocks between the two Houses,[33] but Government members on the Committee were in complete agreement that the Committee should seek to discharge its terms of reference in full. They also agreed with the Labor members that the Committee should first deliberate on matters which it regarded as being of major importance, and that it should then proceed to consider other desirable changes to the Constitution, such as the omission of obsolete clauses. When it reported in 1959, the Committee expressed the hope that it would have an opportunity to continue its work in these other areas of possible constitutional change, but the Government did not respond.

The opinion was widely held at the time the Committee was constituted that the main reason for the failure of most proposals for constitutional change submitted to referendum was that they were usually opposed by the Opposition parties in the federal Parliament, and their concomitant political organizations in the States. Throughout the life of the Constitution Review Committee, Labor members expressed confidence that they would be able to gain the support, or at worst the neutrality, of State Labor organizations. The Government members seemed to think that the best opportunities for success lay with selling the Committee's recommendations to their federal parliamentary colleagues.

The Committee's reports revealed agreement to a surprising extent on a wide range of subject matters dealing with Commonwealth legislative machinery and legislative powers. Part Two of the report contained a series of recommendations relating to legislative machinery, including recommendations to remove the nexus tying the size of the House of Representatives to double the number of senators, to abolish fixed terms for senators in favour of senators holding their places until the expiry or dissolution of the second House of Representatives after their election, and to divide the States into near-equal electoral divisions. These recommendations were supported by all members, with the exception of Senator Wright. In relation to economic powers, the Committee recommended, that the Commonwealth Parliament should have concurrent legislative power with respect to navigation and shipping, nuclear energy, terms and conditions of industrial employment, corporations, marketing of primary products free from s.92, capital issues, and consumer credit. Other recommendations were to authorize States, notwithstanding s.92, to impose reasonable charges in respect of the interstate carriage of persons and goods by road, to facilitate the formation of new States by the amendment of Chapter VI of the Constitution, and to alter s.128, as already discussed.[34] Wright expressed reservations as to several recommendations, in particular, those concerning the legislative machinery and s.128, and Downer had a reservation as to the extent of the recommendation on industrial relations. Otherwise, the recommendations were unanimous.

In 1959, most members of the Committee had high hopes that its report would achieve some results in the federal Parliament. Its report received very extensive publicity in the press throughout Australia, and even Menzies seemed

---

[33]Mr Playford, Premier of South Australia, expressed such an opinion when he appeared before the Committee in Adelaide on 14 December 1956.

[34]Above at n.20.

to have been impressed with the scope and depth of its work. However, before long, there were rumblings among Government members amounting to expressions of concern that their representatives could have agreed to such extensive constitutional changes as the Committee proposed. There was undoubtedly a feeling that the Opposition members as a team had overwhelmed the Government members, none of whom, of course, were Ministers, with the exception of the Chairman. In March 1958, Sir Garfield Barwick was elected to Parliament at a by-election, and he became Attorney-General shortly afterwards. Although in that capacity he moved the reconstitution of the Committee in April 1959, following a general election in November 1958, Barwick left no doubt subsequently that he viewed the Committee's work with general disfavour. As time went on, it became apparent that the Committee's report would not receive detailed debate in the federal Parliament. One by one, Government members turned to other things. Downer had already become a member of the Menzies ministry at the end of 1958, Joske became a judge of the Australian Industrial Court in 1960, and by the end of 1963 O'Sullivan, Drummond and Hamilton had retired from politics.

In retrospect, the Committee may have been wiser to have concentrated in the first instance, apart from an amendment of s.57, on possible constitutional changes with less political content than most of the major changes recommended, leaving the recommendations on major matters to a subsequent report. Nevertheless, the experience provided a lesson in what can be achieved by agreement among politicians when not immediately answerable to their parties or in public view. When shown how developments since Federation had disturbed the validity of some of the assumptions of the founders, Government members became convinced that some substantial constitutional changes should be made. For example, though at Federation each colony had its own distinctive economy, the entire Committee was impressed with the growing integration of the Australian economy in which there was interdependence not only as between the many and various economic activities making up the economy, but also as between those activities and the state of the economy as a whole. Furthermore, a detailed review of the machinery of government had not previously been undertaken. The best hopes for constitutional change may still rest with constituting a future committee along the lines of the Constitution Review Committee, but something approaching a free vote in Parliament upon its recommendations may be necessary if results are to be achieved. It would also be a good thing if Committee recommendations were to be adopted as the policy of the Commonwealth in the event of the retention of Commonwealth-State Constitutional Conventions as a means of procuring constitutional change.

Australian Constitutional Convention, Sydney 1973

The first moves to have a Constitutional Convention came from Victoria, where, in 1970, Parliament resolved that the other States should be invited to participate in constitutional discussions, and eventually to confer with the Commonwealth. The proposal came at a time of increasing State discontent with the outcome of pilgrimages to Canberra to attend Premiers' Conferences and the Loan Council. Victorian Premier Bolte had also bitterly complained about the trend of recent High Court decisions unfavourable to the States.[35] The other States accepted the Victorian invitation, but after a series of meetings in 1972 it was apparent that the States were not likely to get very far by themselves, and by the end of the year it was agreed that the States and the Commonwealth should be represented at a convention of parliamentarians. The Whitlam Labor Government decided to adhere to the agreement to participate in a convention, but it successfully insisted that local government should be directly represented. The Sydney gathering totalled 112 delegates, more than at any of the Convention Debates in the 1890s. It included sixteen Commonwealth representatives, twelve representatives from each State, and a total of twenty-two representatives of local government.

In opening the Convention, the Governor-General, Sir Paul Hasluck, remarked that out of thirteen million people in Australia he doubted whether more than 5 per cent were closely involved in any argument on constitutional questions, though they concerned everyone in every walk of life. He said it was up to the delegates to find ways in which Australia could best be guided, and national interests best advanced. Any less effort could lead to the Convention being a 'monumental flop'.[36]

The proceedings began at Parliament House, Sydney, on the afternoon of 3 September, and continued for a further four sitting days. As intended by the Steering Committee, the Convention embarked on the principal task of identifying the areas of the Constitution in need of change. Almost at once, the Convention earnt the stamp of a gathering of parliamentarians thoroughly inhibited by their party loyalties, and repetitious speeches indicated a general disinclination of each speaker to emerge beyond the dogmas of the party to which he belonged. An exception on the non-Labor side was the Premier of Victoria, Mr Hamer. He urged the Convention to see its long-term task as one of determining where political responsibilities lay as between the Commonwealth and the States, and then ascertaining what constitutional powers should be allowed to deal with them. In my view, this should have been the theme of the Convention, but most others, and they included many who seemed to be ill-prepared in spite of the material aids placed at their disposal, were content to live according to their standing as parliamentarians. Heirs to the founding fathers were not to be seen or heard.

Two major issues dominated the proceedings, namely, the quest of the non-Labor government States and, to a smaller extent, even the Labor government States, for financial security on the one hand, and on the other the desire of the Commonwealth Government, with some support from State Labor delegates, for additional economic powers to manage the Australian economy. The Premier of the host State had already made it plain at the opening ceremony in the Sydney Town Hall that he was primarily concerned with the unsatisfactory state of Commonwealth-State financial relations. He said:

> Through the passage of time the High Court, in the exercise of its judicial function, has altered the power balance between the States and the Commonwealth. Although the bulk of legislative powers and, as a corollary, responsibility for the great range of community services, still rests with the States, the bulk of financial resources required to maintain proper standards in existing services and to initiate new ones is in

---

[35] *Western Australia* v. *Hamersley Iron Pty Ltd (No. 1)* (1969) 120 C.L.R. 42; *Western Australia* v. *Chamberlain Industries Pty Ltd* (1970) 121 C.L.R. 1; *Victoria* v. *The Commonwealth (Payroll Tax Case).* (1971) 122 C.L.R. 353.

[36] *Official Record of Debates*, 3 September 1973, p.4.

Commonwealth control. Without statesmanship an impasse seems imminent. That is the main reason why the Constitutional Convention has been convened.[37]

State Premiers and others filled the conference room with repetitious homilies as to the invidious position of the States because of the limitations upon their taxation powers, the sapping of vitality by the iniquitous interpretation and application of s.96, and the general financial ascendancy of the Commonwealth, brought about by its constitutional powers as interpreted by the High Court. When challenged to state the economic powers which he considered the Commonwealth should have, Mr Whitlam referred to the recommendations of the Constitution Review Committee as providing appropriate examples. There were many deaf ears.[38] By the time everyone who wished to speak had had their say about State finances and Commonwealth economic powers, there was insufficient time left to consider several items further down on the agenda, and these were debated in a perfunctory fashion *in globo*.

The most dominant figure during the Convention was without doubt the Prime Minister, Mr Whitlam, whose solo performances, aided by the occasional announcement from Senator Murphy, had a devastating impact on the proceedings. The principal events with which Mr Whitlam was associated seemed only incidentally to be related to the Convention. On the first afternoon, for example, he stated that the Commonwealth Government was prepared to 'go it alone' and submit proposals to referendum to ensure the principle of electoral equality throughout Australia, and that all State Houses were democratically elected.[39] On the fourth day, the Convention learnt that agreement had been reached between the Prime Minister and all Premiers, with the exception of the Premier of Queensland, at a dinner at Kirribilli House on the previous evening, that the Commonwealth and the States should, with appropriate safeguards, be able to refer matters to each other for legislative action.[40] During the Convention, Mr Whitlam urged the State leaders—not the Convention—to agree to refer concurrent power over prices to the national government.[41]

The most productive aspect of the proceedings was the decision of the Convention to establish Standing Committees to investigate fifteen agreed items, covering almost every matter referred to in the proceedings, and report

---

[37] *ibid.*, p.2.

[38] For example, Sir Charles Court, Leader of the Opposition in Western Australia, began the third day of the proceedings by warning Commonwealth centralists that there was a strong ground swell of feeling in his State, to be found at grassroots level, for secession from the Commonwealth. Sir Charles's remarks ignored the fact that at the time the electors of Western Australia had chosen to vote 'Yes' at a federal referendum on no less than fourteen occasions, compared with an average of eight and a half for the electors of the other five States. If the attitude of the Western Australian electors had been matched by electors in the other States, the Commonwealth would have gained the fourteen heads of legislative power in the referendum of 1944, and the full power over marketing and conditions of industrial employment sought in 1946.

[39] *Official Record of Debates*, 3 September 1973, p.17.

[40] *Official Record of Debates*, 6 September 1973, pp. 197-9.

[41] *Official Record of Debates*, 4 September 1973, p.87. At this point the following exchange occurred between the federal D.L.P. leader, Senator Gair, and the Prime Minister:
'Senator Gair: What about the referendum in 1948?
Mr Whitlam: Things have changed since 1948. Senator Gair may not realise that.
Senator Gair: You, Mr Prime Minister, have made me realise it.
Mr Whitlam: Even Senator Gair is making way for a younger man, I believe a man aged 67. I should have thought a reasonable thing would be to let the Australian national Parliament have the economic power possessed by every national parliament in the world . . .'

back to a further Constitutional Convention which was expected to be held in 1974. The Convention set up four Standing Committees, called A, B, C and D respectively, and allocated the items between them. The formula of composition of the Standing Committees provided for two delegates from each parliamentary delegation to be members, meaning that the Committees would also represent more or less equally opposing political viewpoints. The indications are that Standing Committees B, C and D were active, and each was able to put some proposals before the Melbourne Convention in 1975. Standing Committee A, composed almost entirely of Commonwealth and State political leaders, including the Prime Minister and several Premiers, had the task of considering, amongst others, items 2 and 3, the first relating to Commonwealth economic powers, and the second to the financial provisions of the Constitution, the two thorniest items of the Convention itself. It is understood that Standing Committee A did not proceed very far with its work.

Australian Constitutional Convention, Melbourne 1975

The second Convention was scheduled to convene in Adelaide in November 1974, but there appeared to be little enthusiasm in several States. The Queensland Government unexpectedly called a general election, and an unresolved disagreement occurred between a less-than-enthusiastic federal Government and the Opposition parties relating to the composition of the Commonwealth delegation. The Convention was cancelled. Largely as a result of strenuous individual efforts and increasing interest by the Prime Minister, in June 1975 the Executive Committee agreed to hold a full meeting of the Convention in Melbourne to commence on 24 September 1975. At federal level, the Government and Opposition parties continued to disagree about the composition of the Commonwealth delegation.[42] Then Western Australia and Queensland, non-Labor States, announced that their Parliaments would not send representative delegations, ostensibly because of the nature of the agenda, which included items on which agreement had not been reached in the Standing Committees. New South Wales also declined to attend, and at the last moment the host State, Victoria, withdrew its support. In the event, only the Labor government States of South Australia and Tasmania sent complete delegations.[43] The Commonwealth was represented only by Labor delegates, and Labor Party representatives also attended from the other four States.

The Melbourne Convention had, therefore, no claim to be fully representative, but those who attended decided to go ahead, and several resolutions were carried recommending either constitutional alterations or references of matters by all States to the Commonwealth Parliament. Some of the resolutions for constitutional change involved major matters, including:

---

[42]At the Sydney Convention, Senator Gair, as leader of the D.L.P., was a delegate. Following the elimination of the D.L.P. from parliamentary representation, the Government considered that the leader of the Liberal Movement, Senator Hall, should join the delegation, and that the number of Labor delegates should be the same as the total number of Liberal-Country Party delegates plus Senator Hall.

[43]Local government, and the Northern Territory and Australian Capital Territory were also fully represented.

(a) specific changes foreshadowed by Mr Whitlam in Sydney in 1973 to enable the Commonwealth to legislate for the borrowing of money by the Commonwealth for local government bodies, and to make grants of financial assistance to local government bodies;

(b) an amendment of s.24 to fix the number of members of the House of Representatives in each State by dividing the population of the State by a uniform figure of not less than 85,000, a proposal comparable to the referendum proposal in 1974; and

(c) an alteration to s.128 to provide for the passage of a proposed law if it was approved at a referendum by a total majority of electors and a majority of electors in half of the States: in effect, this was the proposal submitted to referendum in 1974.

There were in addition several suggested alterations of a kind which ought to be capable of gaining widespread approval at a full convention. These included the following:

(d) The recommendation that new ss.108A and 108B should be included in the Constitution. Under s.108A, the Commonwealth Parliament would be able to designate matters with respect to which all States could make laws: under the provision, it would become possible, upon reference by the Commonwealth, for each State to impose excise duties. The principal purpose of s.108B was to ensure that any State reference or Commonwealth designation of a matter was revocable, and could be made subject to conditions and for a limited period of time.

(e) The exclusive power of the Commonwealth to legislate with respect to Commonwealth places should, it was recommended, become a concurrent power (or, alternatively, should be dealt with by an appropriate designation by the Commonwealth Parliament under the proposed dual-reference provisions).

(f) It was recommended that the Commonwealth Parliament should be competent to fix retiring ages for judges of federal courts, including the High Court.

(g) It was proposed that s.51(18) should be amended to embrace various modern developments in the area of industrial property, including the protection of services marks, industrial designs, and rights of breeders of plants.

(h) Other proposals dealt with a miscellany of matters, including some affecting the government of federal territories and others discarding constitutional clauses now considered to be obsolete.

A further session was to be held in Hobart in October 1976, when all items which were the subject of resolutions at Melbourne would be recommitted. The work undertaken at Melbourne encourages, rather than discourages, the possibility of obtaining agreement on a limited range of constitutional alterations flowing from the endeavours of the standing Committees. However, experience beginning with the Convention in Sydney in 1973 suggests fairly clearly that a constitutional convention is not likely to recommend substantially increased economic powers for the Commonwealth Parliament. Some quite extraordinary circumstances would be necessary to reverse the kind of atmosphere which existed in Sydney. If increased economic powers are to be gained at all through the employment of consultative processes, the better prospects, dim though they appear to be, seem to rest in establishing an all-party committee of the Commonwealth Parliament to consider proposals in the first instance.

COMMENTARIES

J. C. Finemore

It seems to me that Professor Richardson's essay reinforces the view that I have long held that the alteration of the Constitution is a matter upon which the lawyers as such have little to contribute. There are some legal problems in relation to s.128, but it will probably be many decades, if not centuries, before they become relevant to any proposed poll.[1] I think we must look to political scientists, sociologists and historians, aided by the techniques of market research, to give us information as to the mental processes and psychological and political influences which affect the results of referendums. Indeed, when we consider that a referendum held at the same time as an election will cost at least $1,000,000, it would seem to be good business sense to do some market research on any proposal for a referendum.

The next point that has struck me in reading Professor Richardson's essay and various other commentaries on the referendum procedures in Australia is that it is generally assumed that the Australian voter is wrong in saying 'No' to so many of the proposals that have been put to him in the last seventy-five years. That may be true, but I do not think it is a matter that should be assumed. Indeed I think that there can be a very strong case made out for the innate good sense of the voters who have said 'No' so often and often so loudly. The voters do not go to a referendum in a vacuum, but with some consciousness of Australian history and politics.

They have seen the Constitution in effect substantially amended by the High Court on many occasions. They have seen a constant growth in the legislative activity of the Commonwealth Parliament. They have seen the existing powers of the Commonwealth Parliament being given extraordinarily wide interpretations. They have seen the zeal with which the existing powers are exploited by Commonwealth governments and Parliaments of whatever political complexion. Perhaps they have suspected on many occasions that proposals have been put forward for short-term party political purposes rather than to make the Constitution more efficient or equitable. Perhaps they know or at least feel that there is a difference in nature between a power that may be exercised by six State Parliaments and that same power being exercised by the central Parliament. Perhaps they realise that any power conferred upon the federal Parliament can never be recalled. Perhaps they feel that whenever there is a real need for a power in the central Parliament the ingenuity of the government's advisers aided by a sympathetic High Court will find that the central Parliament has already got that power. Perhaps they realise that there are virtually no constitutional guarantees in the Australian Constitution and that the High Court would be powerless to restrain any high handed or unjust use of the power. Perhaps they believe that they can exercise more control over State Parliaments both at the ballot box and in other ways. Even if many of these matters are logically irrelevant to the question of whether the Constitution

---

[1]For those interested in such legal problems, see Professor Richardson's Opinion, 'In the matter of Section 128 of the Commonwealth Constitution': Appendix A, Standing Committee B Report, 1 August 1974, p.18.

should be amended, they are very real to the voter and perhaps if the voter feels strongly about any of these matters he is entitled to vote 'No'.

The record of the Australian voter at referendums has often been unfavourably compared with the record of Swiss voters, but I do not think enough attention has been directed to the underlying differences between the situation in Switzerland and in Australia. In Switzerland the voters can readily initiate a referendum to undo any alteration that they have agreed to. But not only can they initiate a referendum, they can take the initiative to revoke any law made under a constitutional alteration if they feel that the power is being improperly exercised by the central government. Furthermore, the central government is not aggressive in the use of the powers that it holds and has a very small federal public service. The whole process of government at all levels is by the development of a consensus position. Indeed, the present proposals to revise the Swiss Constitution have been put forward by those who believe that there is too much consensus in government in Switzerland.

It is in relation to these considerations that the Constitutional Convention process can be useful. It can identify areas in which there is substantial unanimity. It can also identify areas in which it is quite obvious that any referendum will be bitterly fought on party lines. From the record of referendums it would seem to be hard to justify the expenditure of $1,000,000 or, if the referendum is to be held independently of an election, an expenditure of $5,000,000, in putting a contentious question to the people. The Convention can also be used to revise and refine a proposal so that objections real or fanciful can be met before the question for the referendum is adopted by the Parliament. I think this is shown by the developments in relation to the proposed referendum on the Interchange of Powers. Although the precise form of the proposal has been debated and agreed by all concerned, new doubts have been expressed and it is necessary to give further consideration to the form of the proposal so that these objections will not be used to oppose the proposal if the matter is put to the people.

I would like to suggest for consideration that an analysis of the results of the referendums proposed by the Whitlam Government is likely to show that they do not fit into the pattern of the results of previous referendums. Although it has been widely suggested that it was the Labor Prime Minister's desire to familiarise the electors with the referendum process, and by a process of education and familiarization improve the chances of success with referendums, the actual choice of matters that were put to referendum hardly seems to be consistent with that supposition.

The referendum on prices seemed to be related more to the current political pressures in relation to the inflationary tendencies in the economy and the referendum in relation to incomes was the price that had to be paid to persuade the Senate to agree to the referendum on prices.

The questions considered by the electors in May 1974 would seem in retrospect to be an even more curious choice of questions, having regard to the established conservatism of the Australian electors. Simultaneous elections might have been thought to be a proposition that was likely to gain support, having regard to the strong support that had been given to the proposal by the all party Constitutional Review Committee in 1959, but to put such a referendum to the people at a time when there was a life and death battle between the House of Representatives and the Senate ensured that the question would be debated in the most partisan political fashion, and with a view to the short-term political results of such a change rather than to its intrinsic merit.

The question on democratic elections was not confined to the matters recommended by the 1959 Constitutional Committee, but was framed so as to attempt to impose on State Parliaments constitutional requirements in relation to electoral districts and Upper Houses. This I think was certainly most provocative and ensured that many people would vote against the proposed change because they felt that it was not proper for the federal Parliament to propose restrictions on the States which had no effect on the Commonwealth Parliament or government as such.

In the case of the referendum on the mode of altering the Constitution, the deliberate joining together as a single question of the right of residents of the territories to vote at referendums and the question of the number of States required to enable a referendum to be carried probably resulted in the people rejecting an amendment that they would have otherwise agreed to. I refer to the question of votes for residents of the territories.

The question relating to local government bodies was again apparently motivated as much by the desire to denigrate State governments and enhance the relevant standing and importance of local government as by any real need to amend the Constitution to enable federal funds to be given to local government.

My point is simply that there does not seem to be any point in an educational programme which selects questions which are unlikely to be successful from a point of view of timing, which are framed in a way that makes them less likely to succeed or that are deliberately provocative so far as State governments are concerned. To increase the number of negative results at referendums must surely tend to make people think that 'No' is the normal and proper response to any question.

I was interested to note Professor Richardson's conclusion that the measure of federal success which the Labor Party enjoyed in the various States was comparable with the votes in favour of the referendum on the mode of altering the Constitution. Whilst this may be broadly so, the percentage of votes in favour of the referendum was significantly lower in all States than the Labor vote for the Representatives, and the difference in the percentage of the respective votes in the different States provides much material for speculation and perhaps research. In New South Wales the percentage of votes was 1.3 per cent less for the referendum; in Victoria 1.3 per cent more; in Queensland 0.3 per cent more; in South Australia 4.4 per cent less; in Western Australia 3.8 per cent less; and in Tasmania 14.4 per cent less.

Unfortunately after three years I think it is still not possible to judge the efficacy of the Australian Constitutional Convention in relation to promoting desirable alterations to the Constitution. I think Professor Richardson might have emphasised the particular difficulties that have faced the Convention in that period. The Convention depends upon developing a consensus as a means of facilitating amendment of the Constitution. During the last three years there has been no evidence of consensus politics in any area and the polarization of political opinion and the bitterness of political debate has made it very hard to develop a consensus in relation to constitutional reform, but even so in that period it was possible in the widely representative Standing Committees to obtain unanimity on the desirability of alterations on a wide range of matters. The matters may not be those of the greatest importance but they could make a useful start on the large task of modernising the Constitution and making it more suitable for Australia in the last quarter of the twentieth century.

If the people are to be encouraged and educated to take a more liberal, perhaps I should say a more trusting, view of amendments to the Constitution which are proposed from time to time, I think they must be given a chance to vote on what are non-controversial matters which do not involve any material increase in the power of the central Parliament or government. I refer to such matters as a retiring age for federal judges, the proposal to permit an interchange of powers between the central and State governments, the removal of obsolete provisions, permitting residents of the A.C.T. and Northern Territory to vote at referendums, and perhaps in due course some other proposals to extend the powers of the Commonwealth Parliament to take account of modern developments by alterations to ss. 51(5) (post and telegraphs) and 51(18) (copyright).

I agree with Professor Richardson's suggestion that the Commonwealth Parliament's representation in Sydney in 1973 was numerically insufficient. I agree for two reasons. One because I think it is important to emphasise time and time again that numbers do not matter in relation to the work of the Convention. The cause of any proposal for reform will not be advanced by a discussion in the Convention which results in a substantial vote against the proposal. Secondly, for better or for worse it is only the Commonwealth Parliament that can propose alterations to the Constitution, and the more members of the Commonwealth Parliament that can be directly involved in the discussions with delegates from State Parliaments and representatives from local government the better the chances that the Parliament will be encouraged to propose reforms that are likely to be accepted by the people.

While it would be unreal to suggest that a federal government should not put matters to a referendum because a Constitutional Convention is in process, I think it would be just as unreal to suggest that the putting of these referendums to the people did not make the task of the Convention more difficult. The general polarization of political opinions inside and outside the Convention in the period from 1973 to 1975 and the extension of that polarization to the realm of constitutional amendment was reflected in the Standing Committees and ultimately in the boycotting of the Melbourne Convention by many delegates.

There is just one matter upon which I must disagree with Professor Richardson. That is his proposal that s.6A of the *Referendum (Constitution Alteration) Act* 1906 should be repealed. While s.6A may be an imperfect method of explaining the case for and against the proposal, it is at least an attempt to instruct the voters on the issues. The idea that because education and instruction is inadequate to ensure change that the government should establish a Ministry of Propaganda for the purpose of ensuring changes *it* desires to the Constitution is something which I personally find completely abhorrent. I would prefer to take the long view and, with the aid of improving education in constitutional conventions and hopefully a development of a consensus approach to constitutional change, hope for change to the Constitution—but not just any change—a change that will make the Constitution more efficient and responsive to the needs of the people.

R. D. Lumb

Professor Richardon's survey of the referendums of 1973 and 1974 has shown how difficult it is to secure the support of majorities in the States as required by s.128 for approval of constitutional alteration proposals. In doing so he has caused us to question not only the techniques of achieving constitutional reform in Australia but also the philosophy lying behind such reform. The main force of my comments shall be directed to the latter, though I shall have a few words to say about the former.

The philosophy of constitutional reform of course is not monolithic. It is basically dependent on whether one accepts a centre-directed or a State-oriented starting point. In using these terms I am not suggesting that the institutional expressions or structures resulting from their adoption are mutually exclusive; that they rule out, for example, forms of co-operative federalism embodying a pooling of powers, or administrative or judicial co-operation between Commonwealth and State bodies. Indeed, those who consider that a federal division of power is the most appropriate form of government for the Australian nation would not deny the need for co-ordinated Commonwealth-State action in a number of fields—for example, securities and company law administration.

The supporters of constitutional revision who adhere to the centre-directed philosophy take pains to emphasize that their programme is also devolutionary and use the catch-cries of local community participation and administrative decentralization to show their concern for the regions. The practical implementation of these ideas is to be seen in plans such as the Australian Assistance Plan, which involve not only the establishment of Regional Councils for Social Development to carry out pilot schemes for the integration of social services, but also the provision of a broad range of such services. Such an exercise of power, even though initiated in a broad fashion by means of an Appropriation Act, involves an exercise of Commonwealth legislative and executive power which is directed to the implementation of an administrative policy and framework for the pursuit of goals which may only in a peripheral manner be dependent on the legislative powers (express or implied) of the Commonwealth.

It is in this context that we can view the failure of the 1974 Constitution Alteration (Local Government Bodies) Bill relating to the so-called third tier of government. The proposals were certainly seen by a majority of the State governments as providing an open cheque to the Commonwealth Parliament to grant moneys at large and a borrowing power which would by-pass the Loan Council. While not being inconsistent with the basic provisions of Chapter IV of the Constitution which govern Commonwealth-State financial relations, the insertion of such a provision would surely have created an alternative procedure for dividing the pool of Commonwealth revenue, possibly to the grave disadvantage of the State governments. It is not that such a constitutional change would have automatically led to a decision on the part of the Commonwealth to grant financial largesse to local government or regional bodies in order to assist them in carrying out what may be described as State-type functions. But it is clear that the provisions of the Bill would have provided the basis for restricting any renewed 'Braddon claim' of the States to tax revenue sharing. This might have been accomplished under the guise of a regional decentralization programme ostensibly designed to assist the territorial sub-divisions of the States, but only at the price of compliance with priorities determined or sanctioned by the Commonwealth.

Of course, it could be argued that the effect of the decision in the *A.A.P. Case*[1] is to accomplish certain of the ends which the Constitution Alteration (Local Government bodies) Bill was designed to achieve, namely, the provision of a constitutional basis for the direct appropriation of moneys for local government purposes which are incidental to Commonwealth purposes (whether express or implied). This possibility may be a cause of concern to the States which would not wish to see any considerable siphoning-off of a revenue by means of direct appropriation to authorities within the States. The States themselves can with justification argue that their participation in revenue sharing was guaranteed in the early period of federation, although this recognition had been lost with the expiry of the Braddon clause. The *de facto* allocation of certain proportions of Commonwealth revenue following on the *Uniform Tax Cases*[2] (augmented in 1974 by grants to local authorities through the Grants Commission) has now been altered under the new personal income tax revenue sharing scheme of the Fraser Government under which a fixed proportion (approximately a third) will go to State Governments, and also a fixed proportion (between 1 and 2 per cent) to local government bodies — but by way of s.96 tied grants. Perhaps the experience gained from the operation of this new scheme will enable proposals for constitutional reform to be formulated under which a revised Braddon clause can be inserted in the Constitution or a new Financial Agreement covering tax revenue as well as loan moneys can be negotiated which would be inserted into Chapter IV of the Constitution.

The Constitution Alteration (Democratic Elections) Bill and the Constitution Alteration (Simultaneous Election) Bill deserve comment as the first major attempts to alter the institutional basis of government in the Australian federation. As to the former, the 'one man, one vote, one value' principle which subsequently was found by the High Court[3] *not* to be embodied in s.24 was proposed to be inserted in a new s.29. Such an amendment would have favoured increased representation in the closely settled urban areas as against the less settled rural areas. Its adoption would have greatly limited the discretion which the electoral Redistribution Commissioners have under the present Electoral Act in relation to distance, 'community of interest' and other listed criteria for revising boundaries, which justify the weighting of non-numerical interests. Consequently the balancing of rural and urban representation embodies in traditional redistribution practices would have been impaired if this constitutional alteration had been approved.

A more serious objection to the Constitution Alteration (Democratic Elections) Bill was the attempt to insert into the framework of the State Constitutions a similar principle of arithmetical equality in relation to electorates for State Houses. The preservation of State Constitutions by virtue of s.106 of the Commonwealth Constitution reflects the federal accommodation of two constitutional systems. Thus, in the words of Quick and Garran,

---

[1] *Victoria* v. *Commonwealth* (1975) 7 A.L.R. 277.

[2] *South Australia* v. *Commonwealth* (*First Uniform Tax Case*) (1942) 65 C.L.R. 373; *Victoria* v. *Commonwealth* (*Second Uniform Tax Case*) (1957) 99 C.L.R. 575.

[3] *A.-G.* (*Australia*) (*Ex rel. McKinlay*) v. *Commonwealth* (1975) 7 A.L.R. 593.

the States retain their Constitutions, their Parliaments, their Executive and Judicial organizations, subject only to the loss of those powers which by the Federal Constitution are withdrawn from the scope and operation of the State Constitutions and brought within the sphere of the Federal Constitution.[4]

The proposal embodied in the Constitution Alteration (Democratic Elections) Bill would have wrought a basic change in the State Constitutions which would not have been ratified according to the processes of alteration laid down in those Constitutions.

As to the Simultaneous Elections Bill, it has been argued that the electorate is faced with too many elections and that a half-Senate election should automatically take place at the same time as a House of Representatives election. This argument must be placed alongside that of several State Governments that the structural identity of the Senate as a States House is better preserved by an institutional recognition that writs for Senate elections may be issued at times separate from those for the House of Representatives. Under the Bill, the flexibility embodied in s.12 of the Constitution was to be replaced by a rigid requirement as to timing of the issue of writs derived from s.32. It is clear that a number of the States, concerned with the implications of the controversy over the issue of writs during the Gair affair, were loathe to support an amendment which would have deprived their Executive Councils of discretion in this matter.

Something should also be said as to the two unsuccessful referendums in 1973 designed to give the Commonwealth Parliament power over prices and incomes. The political motivation for these referendums was to provide the constitutional basis for the operation of a prices and incomes policy, and to invest the Commonwealth with powers to manage the economy. As to the former object, it may be that a temporary prices and economic policy embodied in a prices-wages package might have assisted in the dampening down of inflationary pressures. But to place on a constitutional basis such powers would have enabled any future government to achieve a complete restructuring of the economy by dismantling the federal system in the economic arena. The very comprehensiveness of the economic concepts of 'a price' and 'an income' would have enabled the Commonwealth to regulate the process of production, manufacture, distribution, exchange and services by direct controls, and to assume a direct wage-fixing role.

From a structural point of view the existing Commonwealth legislative powers in s.51 over trade, corporations and the like, would have been reduced to a less important status, the arbitration process in s.51 (35) by-passed, and the residuary power of the States subjected in economic matters to paramount Commonwealth legislative power. While recognizing that uniformity in wage-fixing procedures between Commonwealth and State tribunals is a desideratum, the establishment of a blanket power over 'incomes' does not appear to be an appropriate way of accomplishing this end.

The conclusion which may be drawn from the failure of the 1973 and 1974 referendums can be simply stated: institutional and economic reforms which do not reflect a consensus of Opposition and Government views will not, under the present procedure for revising the Constitution as laid down in s.128, have much chance of success. This will be so even if the proposals are presented to the people at a general election where the governing party is returned to power.

[4]*Annotated Constitution of the Australian Commonwealth* (Sydney, 1901), p.930.

I can, however, see merit in Professor Richardson's advocacy of greater electoral educational programmes in relation to alteration proposals, although I do not agree with his suggestion for altering s.6A of the *Referendum (Constitution Alteration) Act* 1906.

What I think needs to be grappled with is the mode of altering the Constitution, and in a way which is more fundamental than that proposed in the Constitution Alteration (Mode of Altering the Constitution) Bill of 1974. A more objective mode of constitutional review would be the establishment of a statutory convention consisting of representatives who would be elected by Commonwealth-wide and State-wide electoral procedures. The function of such a Convention would be to submit at regular intervals proposals for constitutional amendment to the Parliament—such proposals being agreed to by prescribed majorities—for submission to the people under s.128. Alternatively, if one considered that this involved too serious an intrusion into the rights of Parliament to initiate amendments, then the federal principle would be promoted by amending s.128 to make provision for the submission of a constitution alteration proposal to the electorate either on the initiative of the Commonwealth Parliament *or* at the request of a majority of the State Parliaments. Either proposal would eliminate the present one-sided nature of the Constitution alteration process, and the opportunity of linking constitutional referendums with the policies of the government in power would be diminished. I do not think that a return to the parliamentary committee method of initiating alteration proposals would bring with it any greater benefits or produce a better climate for electoral approval.

PART TWO

INSTITUTIONS UNDER CHANGE

A.R. Blackshield (Chapter 4) gives a sparkling account of the various Labor attempts to rearrange the federal court system . . . and the response of the judges of the High Court when confronted with 'a "larrikin government" in Heraclitean flux'. The commentators are less inclined than Associate Professor Blackshield to concede either the existence or propriety of overt policy orientation in judicial decision-making: Mr Justice Kirby defends his brethren with the admonition 'Put not your faith in scalograms', while Mr Merralls reasserts the continuing appropriateness of the Dixonian tradition of 'strict and complete legalism'.

Enid Campbell (Chapter 5) examines from the viewpoint of a constitutional lawyer the very substantial changes which occurred under Labor in the organization and machinery of executive government, in particular the reliance on extra-departmental agencies and individuals. She deals also with some fascinating questions which arose concerning the relationship between, and respective accountability of, Ministers and their officials. The commentaries of Professor Encel and Dr Wilenski stand in interesting contrast, approaching these topics as they do from the viewpoints, respectively, of a political scientist and a closely involved senior public servant.

Peter Hanks's essay (Chapter 6) traverses the extraordinarily diverse set of controversies, nearly all of them without precedent, which arose around the institution of Parliament itself: questions about the electoral system, the representation of territories, members' pecuniary interests, the status of the Speaker, and — especially significant in the light of later events — the replacement of casual vacancies in the Senate. The nature and status of constitutional conventions is analysed in some detail by Mr Hanks, and this theme is picked up by both Patrick Brazil and Michael Coper in their wide-ranging commentaries.

4 Judges and the Court System

A.R. Blackshield

I
INTRODUCTION

The films of Arthur Penn, says an English reviewer,[1] from *Bonnie and Clyde* to *Alice's Restaurant*, share a common theme. 'Two cultures confront each other—a settled, social world growing increasingly authoritarian, and a free-wheeling anarchistic community that is becoming increasingly corrupt.'

A few Australians might recognize here a scenario for the Whitlam era of 1972-1975. But, tragically, most of us are so locked in to one or other of the confronting cultures as to recognize the appropriateness of only half the picture. To those who supported the Whitlam Government, or welcomed its good intentions, the oppposition to it seemed increasingly authoritarian. To its critics, the Government seemed freewheeling, anarchistic, and even corrupt.

Such cultural divisiveness breeds ambivalences and contradictions in community and government alike. The community demanded of the Whitlam Government both a fundamental restructuring of society, and none at all—like an innately conservative but self-consciously trendy employer, who engages a staff of radical employees to gratify his own self-image, and then does not like what he gets. If Whitlam socialism outraged the Liberals, Whitlam liberalism outraged conservatives (of all parties) more.

Yet the Government was also divided within itself. Its electoral appeal had involved a morganatic marriage of new liberalism with old socialism; and like other marriages this yielded its share of tensions and discords. These were aggravated not only by external hostilities, but by further tensions and discords within 'liberalism' itself.

Liberalism has at its roots a solicitude for the personal self-fulfilment and self-expression of individual human beings. But the needs which engage this solicitude, and the assumptions which structure it, are at any given time culture-bound. Our heritage is therefore littered with period versions of liberalism, frozen in the glacier of history like ideological mammoths, yet still claiming validity and relevance. The contemporary liberal may espouse any one of these versions; or move haphazardly from one to another; or (most easily, and therefore most frequently) accept an uncritical, indiscriminate amalgam of them all. The result is not an ideology, but a randomly acquired collection of inconsistent attitudes. A reformist programme thus inspired may achieve no more than a hodge-podge: a broadside scattering of proposals reflecting no unified strategy, but only a series of *ad hoc* reactions to particular problems, often rather shallowly related to their liberal preconceptions, and not always to the same preconceptions.

The Whitlam Government's success or failure in avoiding these pitfalls in

---

[1]Philip French, Film Review, *New Statesman*, 9 July 1976, p.56.

any given policy area is perhaps an essential yardstick by which to appraise its performance. In its policies towards the judicial process as an agency of dispute settlement and social change, and the hierarchy of courts as a focus of institutional and social authority, the dangers were, I believe, avoided with remarkable success. Tensions and cross-purposes there were, rooted precisely in competing versions of liberalism; but on the whole they came together in a coherent programme. If anything, the danger was just the reverse: that the different components of policy were so rigorously integrated and interdependent that defeat on any single front would tend to erode the whole.

For present purposes the dominant version of liberalism in the Whitlam Cabinet harked back to the American New Deal of the 1930s. Primarily, it imported naive and sometimes uncritical faith in the courts as agents of social change: a dependence of legislative reform on judicial techniques of enforcement, and on judges' capacity for dynamic social engineering. Labor's choice of judicial appointees, and much of its legislation, clearly reflected this approach. So, on the international scene, did its ready resort to the International Court of Justice in the *Nuclear Tests Case*,[2] and its withdrawal of all reservations of substance to Australia's acceptance of the compulsory jurisdiction of that Court.[3]

Yet even this New Deal liberalism conceals internal cross-purposes which the Roosevelt model never resolved. The apparent faith in the *courts* is really a faith in the power of *law*: not only adjudication but, more importantly, legislation. The result is ambivalence towards the courts, requiring of them both judicial activism and judicial restraint. Moreover, precisely as to the courts' supposed activist potential, New Deal liberalism cuts across both older and newer versions. In classical liberalism the courts are indeed a vital safeguard of freedom; but the safeguard depends on the judge's adherence to a scrupulously non-activist role. Liberty, as well as law, is secreted in the interstices of procedure. Judicial institutions have an important but limited role; and only meticulous respect for their limitations can preserve their importance.

Newer versions of liberalism challenge both classical and New Deal versions by questioning the appropriateness of judicial institutions for the implementation of policy, and even for basic interpersonal conflict resolution. On their intellectual/critical side they demand, for each policy area, institutional arrangements carefully tailored to the needs of that area. Judicial institutions may be appropriate, but only if they satisfy specific functional needs. On their more radical side, these versions deny that courts, as we know them, can ever be appropriate for the easing of human situations at all. Their cumbrous and ponderous procedures; their reliance, not on communication with litigants, but on *ex cathedra* (and sometimes *in terrorem*) posturing *at* them; the distortions and lacunae of the adversary system, and its tendency to reinforce the very hostilities that a conflict-resolution system should soften[4]— these and other

---

[2]*Nuclear Tests (Australia v. France)*: Interim Protection Order of 22 June 1973, [1973] I.C.J. Reports 99; Judgment of 20 December 1974, [1974] I.C.J. Reports 253.

[3]3 *Australian Government Digest* No. 1, at p.95 (January-March 1975).

[4]*Cf.* J. Jowell, 'The Legal Control of Administrative Discretion' (1973) *Public Law* 178, at p.199: 'The adversary adjudicative situation... places the participants in what game theorists call a "zero-sum" situation. One side must win and the other must lose; the defendant is liable or not liable, guilty or not guilty. Except for the possibility of a flexible settlement out of court, the matter is placed in a clear yes-no, either-or, more-or-less setting. Matters that are suited to compromise, mediation, and accommodation, are not best pursued in the structured adversary setting of adjudication.'

characteristics of courts are perceived as leading to irrelevance, inefficiency, and ineffectiveness in the handling of human problems. Moreover, such a system is itself perceived as a problem: an authoritarian (and hence both anachronistic and illiberal) affront to human dignity and sense. Against the New Deal assumption that courts are always good for everything, this version denies that they can ever be good for anything—at least until simplified and humanized, stripped of mystification and pomp, and induced to substitute reliance on the power of persuasiveness for the persuasiveness of power.

These, then, were the building bocks of Labor's policies towards the judicial process. How (and how far) did they come together in a coherent programme?

II
THE LABOR VISION (AND REVISION) OF THE COURTS

Hierarchical Aspects

Since the Whitlam Government of 1972-1975 shared with the Gorton Government of 1968-1971 a sense of national pride in Australian independence and self-sufficiency, it was natural that both should seek to enhance the High Court's prestige—partly by abolishing appeals to the Privy Council, so as to make the High Court of Australia an ultimate court of appeal; and partly by stripping it of jurisdictional trivialities and vexations through devolution of workload to a new Superior Court. On the former matter both Governments successfully enacted legislation; on the latter, neither did.

As to Privy Council appeals, the Whitlam Government's *Privy Council (Appeals from the High Court) Act* 1975 built directly on the Gorton Government's *Privy Council (Limitation of Appeals) Act* 1968. Under the 1968 Act special leave to appeal from the High Court was confined to certain (non-federal) matters; under the 1975 Act leave shall not be sought even in those matters. Three legal issues arise.

The most obvious issue is whether the 1975 Act is valid. As to the 1968 Act, a similar question was affirmatively answered by the Privy Council itself in *Shigeo Kitano* v. *Commonwealth*.[5] Section 74 of the Constitution permits laws 'limiting' the matters[6] in which leave may be asked; and clearly the 1968 Act went no further than 'limitation'. Hence it was valid even if (as their Lordships refrained from deciding) the power of 'limitation' could not encompass 'complete abolition'. For the 1975 Act, however, the argument is less clear. It, too, restricts only some of the total universe of appeals from the High Court to which s.74 refers; but in practice this restriction extinguishes all that remains of that universe. It therefore raises the question which *Shigeo Kitano* left open: is the word 'limiting' a limiting word?[7] There is, however, ample precedent for broad construction of empowering words in a Constitution; and Mr Justice

---

[5](1975) 5 A.L.R. 440.

[6]The petitioner in *Shigeo Kitano* had also sought to make the word 'matters' a constraint on the kinds of criteria by which the Parliament could 'limit' appeals. But this submission was clearly rejected.

[7]It might also be necessary to show that the opening words of s.74, apparently preserving Her Majesty's right to grant special leave, are compatible with 'complete abolition'. A possible view is that the relevant provision says only that 'this Constitution' shall not impair the right, leaving open the possibility that a law made thereunder might do so. See G. Nettheim, 'The Power to Abolish Appeals to the Privy Council from Australian Courts' (1956) 39 *Australian L.J.* 39, at p.48.

Jacobs may have pointed the way when in *Commonwealth* v. *Queensland* (the *Queen of Queensland Case*)[8] he remarked that the constitutional provisions 'limit' certain powers 'by extinguishing the same'. If one can 'limit . . . by extinguishing', the 1975 Act is valid.

Secondly (assuming that the Act is valid), does an appeal still lie direct from a State court in a purely State matter; or has the Commonwealth legislation, by ending appeals from the High Court in both State and federal matters, impliedly sealed off all other avenues as well? Clearly appeals from the States survived the 1968 Act;[9] and clearly they were assumed to survive the 1975 Act too, since for them there was a separate Bill—the Privy Council (Appeals Abolition) Bill 1975, which the Senate twice refused to pass.[10] The doubt arises from the High Court judgments in the *Queen of Queensland Case*. The special reference machinery there reviewed was held invalid not only for federal matters, but for purely State matters as well; and at first sight only the reasoning of Mr Justice Murphy[11] seems broad enough to explain this result. Should we infer that the other judgments must also be read as applicable to purely State matters as well? In particular, when it is said[12] that Chapter III of the Constitution, as amplified by the 1968 Act, is 'incompatible' with any future recourse to the Privy Council in federal matters, does this mean that Chapter III, as amplified by the 1975 Act, is also incompatible with any such recourse in State matters?[13]

To find the 'missing link' in the *Queen of Queensland Case* we may need to resolve a third question, which Sir Garfield Barwick first adumbrated in 1974[14] and further explored in *Favelle Mort Ltd* v. *Murray*.[15] Assuming that appeals to the Privy Council have been abolished, what is the status as precedent of past Privy Council decisions? When Canada abolished Privy Council appeals, Bora Laskin—now the Chief Justice—suggested in a Bar Review article that the Supreme Court of Canada, being now the highest court in the system, would have to treat Privy Council decisions as if they were its own;[16] and despite the analytical problems, the High Court seems to be working towards a similar result. This assumes, however, that the Privy Council has no present authority

---

[8](1975) 7 A.L.R. 351, at p.374.

[9]See A.F. Mason, 'The Limitation of Appeals to the Privy Council . . .' (1968) 3 *Federal L. Rev.* 1, at p.19.

[10]On 25 February 1975, and again on 21 August that year. Along with the Superior Court Bill, it thus became one of the 'stockpile' of Bills on the basis of which the Whitlam Government would have been entitled to seek a double dissolution.

[11](1975) 7 A.L.R. at pp. 381-2, rejecting any 'attempt to compromise Australian sovereignty and independence'.

[12]*ibid.*, at pp. 363-4 (Gibbs J; Barwick CJ, Stephen and Mason JJ concurring). The passage is framed throughout in terms of 'federal jurisdiction'—as is the narrower rationale of Jacobs J at pp. 373-4. But 'federal jurisdiction' may legitimately include the High Court's appellate jurisdiction under s.73. See *Lorenzo* v. *Carey* (1921) 29 C.L.R. 243, at p.251; Z. Cowen, *Federal Jurisdiction in Australia* (Melbourne, 1959), p.171.

[13]Despite a reading-down provision similar to s.15A of the *Acts Interpretation Act* 1901, Gibbs J at p.364, 'having regard to the manifest objects' of the impugned provisions, found it 'impossible' to construe them 'in any way that would save them from total invalidity'.

[14]*R.* v. *Joske*; *Ex p. Australian Building Construction Employees and Builders Labourers Federation* (1974) 2 A.L.R. 447, foreshadowing a possible overruling of the *Boilermakers Case*, below n. 36.

[15](1976) 8 A.L.R. 649, at pp. 657-8.

[16]B. Laskin, 'The Supreme Court of Canada: A Final Court of and for Canadians' (1951) 29 *Canadian Bar Rev.* 1038, at p.1075. At that time there was doubt as to whether or not the Supreme Court was absolutely bound by its own decisions; Laskin was thus saying only that whatever answer was chosen should govern Privy Council decisions as well.

to bind Australian courts. Assume now that the 1968 Act, but not the 1975 Act, is valid. The conclusion that Privy Council precedents are no longer binding would then apply to federal law, but not State law, since appeals on State law could still reach the Privy Council, both via the High Court and direct. This dual system of precedent might be bearable, but would surely be clumsy. But now assume that both the 1968 and the 1975 Acts are valid. On this assumption, if appeals direct from the States in purely State matters remain available, we would have not only a duality of precedent systems as between State and federal law, but a duality within State law. Both the High Court and the Privy Council would be deciding State appeals, and each as the highest court in the system. If this leads to an unresolvable logical contradiction—as I think it does—then what is 'incompatible' with Chapter III of the Constitution, as amplified by the 1968 and 1975 Acts, is the survival of any Privy Council appeals at all.

In this area, therefore, the Whitlam Government may have succeeded more fully than it knew. Its corollary Superior Court proposal did not succeed at all. Yet the ghost of such a new federal court, which has haunted the legislative lobbies now since Sir Garfield Barwick as Attorney-General first beheld it in 1963, seems unlikely to go away.[17]

In the Labor version, three shifts of jurisdiction were involved—upwards from State courts invested with federal jurisdiction; sideways from existing federal courts (bankruptcy, industrial, territorial, and now matrimonial); and downwards from the original jurisdiction of the High Court. The sideways shift was partly a matter of administrative rationalization. But the practical need for such rationalization was becoming acute as reformist programmes created ever more disparate kinds of jurisdiction to be vested *somewhere*. The High Court's original jurisdiction was already hopelessly cluttered;[18] and with no other receptacle available, the Labor Government had to work by accretions to the jurisdiction of the Australian Industrial Court, which thus foreshadowed in embryo what the Superior Court might have become. But this was only a temporary makeshift receptacle: ultimately, the success of many of Labor's reformist programmes depended on the Superior Court.

The upwards and downwards shifts, as first entertained in the 1960s, were designed to relieve overburdened courts both above and below the proposed Superior level. The initial emphasis was on the relief of congestion in State courts;[19] but Sir Garfield Barwick's first legislative proposal made light of this State need. Rather, said Sir Garfield:

> My own basic objective ... was to free the High Court of Australia ... for the discharge of its fundamental duties as interpreter of the Constitution and as the national court of appeal untrammelled by some appellate and much original jurisdiction with which it need not be concerned ... The jurisdiction ... vested in the High Court ... appears now to be too great. Its exercise requires judicial time and energy which would serve Australia better if ... [directed to the] fundamental responsibilities of the Court ...[20]

---

[17]Indeed, the ghost has now assumed flesh. Since the above sentence was written the 'current proposals' discussed below have been embodied in the *Federal Court of Australia Act* 1976.

[18]In 1964 Sir Garfield Barwick listed thirty-seven statutes which, under s.76 of the Constitution, had vested large or small areas of 'original' jurisdiction in the High Court. See Barwick, 'The Australian Judicial System: 'The Proposed New Federal Superior Court' (1964-65) 1 *Federal L. Rev.* 1, at p.22.

[19]See M.H. Byers and P.B. Toose, 'The Necessity for a New Federal Court' (1963) 36 *Australian L.J.* 308.

[20]Barwick, cited above n. 18, at pp. 2-3.

Since then, as chief administrator of the High Court, Sir Garfield has continued to press this need, as have other judges. In August 1975 Mr Justice Gibbs led Justices Stephen, Mason and Jacobs in a remarkable *obiter* plea for reform:

> A court which has the ultimate responsibility for interpreting the Constitution, and for the development of the law throughout Australia, cannot afford to occupy its time with the consideration of cases which raise no questions of substantial importance. If the Court is to be deluged with appeals of no real significance, its efficiency will inevitably be impaired, since the members of the Court will be deprived of that time for depth of study and maturity of deliberation without which a final court of appeal cannot adequately perform its functions . . .[21]

Yet even here the 'efficiency' argument is mixed with assertions of the Court's new status as 'a final court of appeal', and with consistent overtones of High Court prestige and dignity. In Labor's Superior Court proposals, this last was an overriding factor: if the High Court was to be Australia's final appellate resort, its prestige must not be soured by a base and brickish skirt. As for the upward shift from State courts, 'the essential question', said Mr Enderby in 1974, was whether 'the Australian Parliament' should assert 'its constitutional power to deal authoritatively on an Australia-wide basis with questions of Federal law':[22]

> The Government believes that the areas of major Federal law should be administered by a Federal court established under legislation enacted by this Parliament, and should not be left to be administered in State courts.[23]

Labor's Superior Court proposals differed from older and newer proposals in three main respects. First, the 'upwards shift' was more comprehensive: in particular, the earlier proposals had envisaged that federal divorce jurisdiction would remain with State courts. Secondly, the 'downwards shift' was similarly more comprehensive: not only was the High Court to shed much of its single-judge jurisdiction, but a Full Court of the Superior Court would in practice handle most of the appeals in such matters as well. (The 1968 proposal had envisaged such an internal appeal only in personal injury cases.) Thirdly, the 'sideways shift' involved more extensive rationalization. The 1968 proposal had envisaged only two divisions: a specialized Industrial Division, and a catch-all General Division. In the Labor proposal the specialized divisions proliferated to six, each reflecting a broadly defined jurisdictional area. For the territories, the long-term projection was that the important parts of their Supreme Court jurisdiction should go to the Superior Court, the rest to an Intermediate Court, and the Supreme Courts would 'wither away'. The finished system would thus have resembled the elaborate yet unified structure of United States federal courts.

All this came to nothing. The 'upwards shift' is larely forgotten; and current proposals for a 'sideways shift' seem much more modest in scope. Plans to relieve the High Court now focus on a drastic 'downwards shift' of matters—including constitutional matters—into State courts.[24] It is, no doubt, a pleasing irony that ideas born thirteen years ago of a wish to relieve State courts

---

[21] *Moller* v. *Roy* (1975) 6 A.L.R. 321, at p.330.

[22] House of Representatives, *Debates*, 16 July 1974, vol. 89, at p.245.

[23] *ibid.*, at p.244.

[24] Judiciary Amendment Bill 1976. See House of Representatives, *Debates*, 3 June 1976, no. 12, at p.2945.

should end by burdening them even more. But proposals that Commonwealth and interstate Attorneys-General be notified of State constitutional hearings, and that important matters may still be removed into the High Court, seem insufficient to avert the fragmentation of constitutional law involved. After all, fragmentation of views within the High Court is nowadays quite intractable enough. Proposals to raise the financial threshold for appeals to the High Court as of right from $3,000 to $20,000 seem even less attractive. Lord Denning is said to have sought his return to the Court of Appeal because only banks and insurance companies could afford House of Lords appeals, and he wanted to deal with real issues. It would have been comforting to think that a High Court Denning thus frustrated had at least a Superior Court to retreat to.

Procedural Aspects

The Superior Court plan was crucial to hopes of procedural reform as well. Practice and procedure in the new Court were to be prescribed by the government—initially (and experimentally) by regulations, but ultimately (to preserve judicial independence from the executive) by legislation.[25] Clearly, Labor wished to simplify and humanize court procedure. But as long as most federal jurisdiction remained in State courts (with practice and procedure determined either by those courts themselves, or by the State legislatures), the Commonwealth could not interfere—or, rather, only at the risk of both affronting State courts and exceeding its own constitutional powers, as the Family Law Act showed. The Superior Court was thus a device for combining the creation of new jurisdictions with procedural reforms to make them more approachable and effective.

Wherever it *could* prescribe procedure—in courts or in tribunals—the Government consistently favoured flexible, informal models. In the Australian Capital Territory, for instance, a new simplified small claims procedure (for claims of up to one thousand dollars, and cases of nuisance by noise) was prescribed for courts of petty sessions on 26 March 1974.[26] The usual rules of pleading, procedure and evidence were discarded. Lawyers could still appear; but the losing party would not bear costs. Extracurial investigations might be conducted by magistrates or court-appointed investigators. Decisions were appealable only by leave of the Supreme Court.

For tribunals, even greater informality was sought. A good example was the new system of appeals tribunals for determinations under the *Social Services Act* 1947. The tribunals, said Mr Hayden, would operate 'as informally as possible'.[27] The Departmental instructions went further. The tribunals 'should consider the substantive merits of the case without regard to legal forms and technicalities'. Procedures were 'entirely at the discretion of the tribunals themselves'. 'The Department and the appellant may be represented ... at hearings, but not by a legal practitioner'. 'The tribunal will attempt to ensure that a "court room atmosphere" does not exist at hearings.'[28] The more

---

[25]See House of Representatives, *Debates*, 16 July 1974, vol. 89, at p.248.

[26]See 2 *Australian Government Digest* at pp. 36, 42, 1090 (1974). There was, of course, nothing distinctive to Labor about this innovation; similar experiments were proceeding more or less contemporaneously in Victoria, New South Wales and Queensland.

[27]See 3 *Australian Government Digest* No. 1, at p.226 (January-March 1975).

[28]Department of Social Services, Policy Branch, Central Office, *Social Security Appeals System: Principles and Procedures* (December 1974) Pt. 4.

ambitious *Administrative Appeals Tribunal Act* 1975 does not exclude lawyers (s.32), and envisages public hearings (s.35); but otherwise the picture is similar. Under s. 33(1), proceedings before the Tribunal shall involve 'as little formality and technicality', and 'as much expedition', as the requirements of legislation and of 'proper consideration' permit. The Tribunal 'is not bound by the rules of evidence but may inform itself on any matter in such manner as it thinks appropriate'.

But the major vehicle for procedural experiment was the Family Court of Australia. Under s.97(3) of the *Family Law Act* 1975 the court is to avoid 'undue formality', as well as 'protracted' proceedings. By sub-section (4), neither counsel nor judge shall robe; by sub-sections (1) and (2) (with exceptions for friends and relatives, lawyers, marriage counsellors and welfare officers), proceedings shall be heard in closed court. The theme is continued in the Regulations made under the Act. For undefended cases not involving children, r. 106 (foreshadowed by s.98) permits decrees on affidavit evidence in the absence of the parties, though for defended cases r. 107 requires oral evidence. As to all other applications, the court (with the parties' consent) may 'dispense with such procedures and formalities as it thinks fit', and 'inform itself on any matter in such manner as it thinks just', rules of evidence notwithstanding (r. 108(2)). Evidence taken in other courts may be recorded and transmitted 'by videotape, film, sound recording or other electronic means' (rr. 108(5) and 118); parties and counsel shall address 'in such order as the court directs' (r. 110); and the court of its own motion may call 'any person' as a witness, with 'such directions as to examination and cross-examination as it thinks fit' (r. 111).

The application of these provisions to State Supreme Court proceedings involved not merely constitutional problems (as the *Family Law Case*[29] showed) but a cultural confrontation (from which that case arose) with judges used to older, and in their eyes better, ways. Hopes of creating a simple, untraumatic divorce procedure rested ultimately not on formal provisions in Act and Regulations, but on the creation of a new court, staffed by new, hand-picked judges. (Hence the 'novel requirement'[30] in s.22(2)(b) that 'by reason of training, experience and personality', the Court's appointees must be 'suitable' to deal with family law.) The tendency for law in the books to change, but for law in action to go on as before, has been more distressingly evident in divorce than in most jurisdictions. Labor firmly intended its Family Law Act to be an exception. After the change of government, public alarums and excursions suggested that the Family Court was at risk. But its future now seems secure. The 1976 amendments are responsibly designed to fulfil the law, not to destroy it.

Obviously, some aspects of the Family Court procedures—notably the closed courts requirement—were an institutional response to the special needs of divorce. But, broadly speaking, the new procedures are a sample of what might have happened in the Superior Court.

Along with procedural reforms to make the courts more approachable went a drive to make them financially more accessible as well. The vicissitudes of the Australian Legal Aid Office are beyond the scope of this paper. But the

---

[29] *Russell* v. *Russell; Farelly* v. *Farelly* (1976) 9 A.L.R. 103. See Ch. 2 above, pp. 51-2.

[30] Hon. Kep. Enderby, 'The Family Law Act: Background to the Legislation' (1975) 1 *University of New South Wales L.J.* 10, at p.29.

abolition of court fees, first in all territorial courts[31] and then in bankruptcy,[32] seems worthy of mention.

The Problem of Institutional Design

Mixed with the question of procedural reform is that of 'institutional design'. Given a legislative policy, what is the most appropriate institutional means for its implementation, administration and enforcement? In particular, how do we choose between the judgmental/litigious model, and the various models of tribunals, commissions, agencies and the like?[33] If both judicial and administrative models seem to be needed, how do we allocate functions between them, and fix their relations *inter se*?

The relevant literature is enormous.[34] What conclusions does it yield? In the words of Jeffrey Jowell,

> The answer is surely none . . . Each [method] possesses both costs and benefits, to the administrators, affected persons and public. What is gained in uniformity may be lost in flexibility; rules to prevent the arbitrary may encourage the legalistic; case-by-case adjudication may prevent comprehensive planning; rules that are advantageous to the administrator in shielding him from pressures and allowing the efficient and speedy dispatch of cases may offend the client who desires individually tailored justice.[35]

Jowell concludes that for each proposed task, the costs and benefits must be weighed in relation to that task. The choice between individualization and rules must itself be made by individualization, not rules.

The problem arose most acutely for Labor in its unsuccessful Human Rights Bill 1973. The American precedent might have suggested enforcement through a broad jurisdiction vested in the High Court. But that Court (as we have seen) already considered itself overburdened; and in any event it might be doubted how much constructive sympathy its judges would bring to a Bill of Rights task. (In time, a Bill of Rights jurisdiction might educate the judges; but the Labor Government was seeking more immediate returns.) Moreover, the broad declaratory remedies implied by such a solution might have a large constitutional resonance, remote from mundane human problems, and might not in practice yield immediate and effective relief. They might thus appear both too high-powered, and not high-powered enough, for the working remedial situation that the Government sought. The appointment of new High Court judges, hand-picked for Bill of Rights tasks, might perhaps have reduced these problems; but in prospect as in reality, Labor's chances for such appointments were few.

To find a judicial forum less lofty, more practical and accessible, and perhaps more open to suitable tailoring by appointment policies, Labor turned to the Superior Court and (pending its creation) to the Australian Industrial Court. By clause 40(3) of the Human Rights Bill, the Court's powers were to embrace not

---

[31]See 2 *Australian Government Digest* 625 (1974).

[32]See *Australian Government Weekly Digest*, 7-13 April 1975, at p.35.

[33]Labor, of course, made enormous use of these latter kinds of models, and very often demonstrated its deeply-rooted deference towards the judiciary by appointing judges to head them.

[34]Much of it flowing from the writings of Lon Fuller: 'The Forms and Limits of Adjudication' (Association of American Law Schools, Jurisprudence Round Table Seminar, 1959); 'Adjudication and the Rule of Law' (1960) 54 *Proceedings of American Society of International Law* 1; 'Collective Bargaining and the Arbitrator' (1963) *Wisconsin L. R.* 3; *The Morality of Law* (New Haven, 1964), pp. 170-8.

[35]Jowell, cited above n. 4, at pp. 215-6. *Cf.* H. Street, *Justice in the Welfare State* (London, 1966), pp. 5-11.

only declaratory relief but a wide range of consequential remedies: injunctions against repetition of acts infringing human rights; orders requiring affirmative action to restore the *status quo ante* (with overtones both of *restitutio in integrum*, and of adjustment *cy pres*); cancellation or variation of contracts; damages (both compensatory and for 'loss of dignity, humiliation and injury to . . . feelings'); orders, in relation to 'any court', for the setting aside or variation of judgments, new trials, or quashing of convictions; and 'such other relief as the Court thinks just, including an award of costs'.

Proceedings were to be instituted by any 'person aggrieved'. But the Bill also envisaged an administrative solution: an Australian Human Rights Commissioner who might (for himself or the person aggrieved) commence judicial proceedings, but whose main task was simply to conduct an informal investigation, after which, under clause 39(1):

(a) he may endeavour to secure from the [responsible] person a satisfactory assurance against a repetition of the act;

(b) he may endeavour to secure a settlement of any difference between the person and any person aggrieved by the act;

(c) he may warn the person not to repeat the act;

(d) he may institute a proceeding in respect of the act in accordance with sub-section 40(1).

Finally, an Australian Human Rights Council was to advise on policy matters and educational programmes.

As between judicial and administrative machinery, the Government thus wisely chose both. The effectiveness of the Human Rights Commissioner may have been dubious; but as long as the alternative of direct access to the court was also available, his presence could have done no harm. In an area as important as human rights, for which no one means of institutional protection is really adequate, we should probably assume that the more different safeguards we have, the better.

The Human Rights Bill, of course, failed. The connascent *Racial Discrimination Act* 1975, succeeded; but the institutional choice here was quite different. The reliance on an investigative Commissioner for Community Relations is virtually exclusive. By s.27 of the Act, intimidatory, punitive and coercive acts (including employment practices) are justiciable offences: but only when done in retaliation for a complaint to the Commissioner. In all other respects, s. 26 expressly provides that 'nothing in this Act makes it an offence' to do or conspire to do anything that the Act declares unlawful.

The institutional choices in the *Trade Practices Act* 1974 were rather more confused—in part because of the need to cope not only with policy problems of institutional design, but with their transcription into mandates of constitutional law in the *Boilermakers Case*[36]. The basic pattern was clear. Certain practices were now illegal *per se*, and these were to be policed by the courts. (As usual, pending the messianic arrival of the Superior Court, the Australian Industrial Court was to cry in the wilderness for it.) Other practices remained open to 'authorization' or 'clearance'; and as to these the previous Government's Trade Practices Tribunal (headed by a judge) was eased upstairs to a reviewing role, substantive power being vested in a new Trade Practices Commission requiring no legal expertise. Thus, the enforcement of rules of

---

[36] *R. v. Kirby; Ex p. Boilermakers' Society of Australia* (1956) 94 C.L.R. 254, aff'd *sub nom. A.-G.* v. *The Queen* [1957] A.C. 288, (1957) 95 C.L.R. 529.

law was to be a judicial task (involving not only actions by the Attorney-General or the Commission for injunctions and fines, but private actions for damages); while the granting of clearances (for practices not effectively lessening competition) or of authorizations (for practices substantially in the public interest) was a task for the Commission.

But, first, the need to find some role for the existing Tribunal involved the pre-emption of review functions perhaps more appropriately assigned to the Court. Second, and more fundamentally, the underlying concept of the role that was assigned to the Court was ambivalent in the extreme—reflecting an orthodox legalist concept of judges as impersonal enforcers of strict rules of law,[37] yet dependent on far-reaching and resourceful judicial development of indeterminate standards.[38] When Senator Murphy (as he then was) remarked that the Act would enable the courts 'to apply the law in a realistic manner in the exercise of their traditional judicial role',[39] he encapsuled in a single sentence the dissonance, if not incompatibility, of the adjudicative ideals presupposed.

Moreover, the practices subject to authorization or clearance were also subject to scrutiny for liability to damages, injunction or fine if not authorized or cleared; and since this scrutiny involved the application of law, it was treated as a task for the Court. The potential threefold overlap of both standards and functions betwen Court, Tribunal and Commission[40] was conducive neither to institutional tidiness and efficient administration, nor to the clear development of economic policy. In terms of restrictive trade practices, the 1974 Act was a significant advance; in terms of institutional design, it was something of a mess.

But the broader picture emerging from this survey of Labor's policies for court hierarchies, court procedure, and institutional design[41] is impressive. Competing versions of liberalism, despite their potential confusions, were pulled together to yield hard-headed and detailed institutional arrangements that had the potential to work. Where, as in the trade practices field, the mixture proved too rich, it was probably the more orthodox legalist components, rather than the more radical components, that caused the trouble. Elsewhere there was a coherent programme; and if the Superior Court was a linchpin without which the rest of the structure tended to fall apart, that was not Labor's fault.

---

[37]See Senate, *Debates*, 29 May 1973, vol. 56, at p.1949, where Senator Murphy said: 'The tendency will be . . . to make the law operate directly upon transactions and the conduct of citizens. In other words, there will be a rule of law stating this is what you do or not do, rather than a bureaucratic mechanism which has to be negotiated before one knows what is permissible and what is not permissible . . . There will be an administrative method of permitting exemptions or authorizations or clearances in cases where it might be considered that the rigour of the law ought not to apply . . .'

[38]See R. Baxt and M. Brunt, 'The Murphy Trade Practices Bill' (1974) 2 *Australian Business L.R.* 3. The central thesis of those writers is that the 'uneasy tension' between the American-inspired ideal of 'court-enforced competition', and the administrative procedure for *ad hoc* authorizations and clearances, is the source of 'both the strengths and the problems of the legislation'—as well as of its complexity: at p.5.

[39]Senate, *Debates*, 27 September 1973, vol. 57, at p.1015, repeated *ibid.*, 15 November 1973, vol. 58 at p.1874. The preceding discussion (in both places) of the 'limit to the extent to which such considerations can be treated in legislation as legal concepts capable of being expressed with absolute precision' at least shows awareness of the problem.

[40]See Baxt and Brunt, cited above n. 38, at p.41ff.

[41]Discussion of areas where the problem of institutional design was solved by decision *not* to rely upon judicial techniques would be beyond the scope of this essay.

III
LABOR'S JUDICIAL APPOINTMENTS

However we handle their design, it is commonplace that institutions are only as good as the people who staff them. Without dealing exhaustively with Labor's judicial appointments, I shall mention certain areas that seem of particular interest.

Aboriginal Appointments

Perhaps the most interesting appointments occurred at the lowest hierarchical level; and not as part of any judicially-oriented policy, but as a by-product of the Government's Aboriginal policies. On 18 September 1974, Mr Silas Ngulati Roberts became the first Aboriginal to be appointed as a Special Magistrate and Justice of the Peace in the Northern Territory; and on 27 November 1974, Mr Madjawara Amagula, M.B.E., received a similar appointment. Earlier, Mr Robert Brown, a leader of the part-Aboriginal community at Wreck Bay, was appointed to Jervis Bay as a Special Magistrate of the Australian Capital Territory.

Women's Appointments

The bold symbolic acts which marked the Whitlam Government's advent included two involving women, both University gold medallists in law. Elizabeth Evatt became a Deputy President of the Commonwealth Conciliation and Arbitration Commission, and Mary Gaudron was briefed for the Commonwealth in the reopened equal pay case. Subsequently (8 April 1974) she, too, became a Deputy President of the Commission. Thereafter, Labor's appointments at the level of Commissioner (for which no legal qualifications are prescribed) included two other women: Judith Cohen, a Melbourne solicitor[42] (19 May 1975) and Pauline Griffin, personnel manager of a Sydney pharmaceutical company (4 June 1975). But further consideration of women for judicial office came only in the Government's dying days, in the context of the search for 'suitable persons' to staff the new Family Court. Regrettably, most of the projected appointments were still in the pipeline when the business of government was abruptly halted on 11 November.[43]

The willingness to recognize outstanding women lawyers by appointment to judicial office (or to the equivalent presidential level in the Arbitration Commission) was evident enough. But perceived opportunities for such recognition tended to be limited to identifiable 'women's issues', from the equal pay case to the Family Law Act. Even Justice Evatt did not wholly escape the pattern: her successive appointments as Chairman of the Royal Commission on Human Relationships, and as Chief Judge of the Family Court, seem still to reflect a focus on a certain range of issues as peculiarly appropriate to a woman's sensitivities and interests. There is, of course, nothing wrong with such issue-oriented feminism as far as it goes; the pity is that it went no further.[44]

---

[42]Widow of the late Senator S. H. Cohen, Q.C. (Labor, Victoria).

[43]Since that time Justices Kemeri Murray (5 February 1976), Margaret Lusink (25 February 1976) and Josephine Maxwell (11 June 1976) have been appointed to the Court.

[44]In his oral comments on this paper at the Federal Anniversary Seminar (University of Melbourne 7 August 1976), Mr Justice Kirby nevertheless suggested that the above appointments may have 'set in train' forces tending to 'redress the sexual balance', which are now unlikely to be 'stopped or reversed'.

Industrial Appointments

Our concern here is with appointments to the Australian Industrial Court, and with those 'presidential' appointments to the Conciliation and Arbitration Commission which, though strictly not judicial, carry the 'designation, rank, status and precedence' of judges. Since 1972 there has been in the Commission a second category of 'presidential' positions, for those not legally qualified; these appointments carry the 'rank, status and precedence' but not the designation of judges.[45] But Labor made only two such appointments; and neither is relevant here.[46] Two other appointments were routine 'promotions' from within the system. Mr Justice Moore, already a Deputy President of the Commission, became its President on the retirement of Sir Richard Kirby (30 June 1973). Dr Ian Sharp, a former Industrial Registrar (1966-1972) and Permanent Head of the Department of Labour, became a Deputy President on 9 December 1974. These, too, require no further comment.

Seven appointments remain. Mr Justice J. B. Sweeney, Q.C. was appointed first to the Commission (1 July 1973) and thence to the Industrial Court (10 December 1973); Justices Evatt and Gaudron, M.D. Kirby (9 December 1974) and J. F. Staples (10 February 1975) to the Commission; and Justices Phillip Evatt, Q.C. (2 July 1974) and R. J. B. St.John, Q.C. (24 March 1975) to the Court. All seven were from the Bar, and all were from New South Wales.[47] All had had some industrial practice, though only for Sweeney, Kirby and Staples was this practice really extensive. Many of the seven had had some personal association (though not necessarily formal affiliation) with the Australian labor Party. But their strikingly recurrent characteristic was neither industrial expertise nor political partisanship, but an energetic dedication to causes of civil liberties, and of individual and social justice. It was here, if anywhere, that the Labor Party looked after its own, using judicial appointments to reward tireless workers in the field. But the rewards went not so much to Labor loyalists as to 'liberal' activists. And even in this sense, reward seemed not to be the motive for the appointments. Rather, pending the Superior Court, Labor

---

In addition to the appointments canvassed in the text and in n.43 above, he cited the appointments in New South Wales of Leone Glynn as Conciliation Commissioner under the *Industrial Arbitration Act*, 1940-1975 (N.S.W.), and of Helen Larcombe and Sue Schreiner as Stipendiary Magistrates.

[45]Such non-legal appointments are open to persons experienced 'at a high level' in industry, commerce, industrial relations or government service; or with university or equivalent qualifications in law, economics, industrial relations or other fields of 'substantial relevance'. See *Conciliation and Arbitration Act* 1904, s. 7(1A), introduced in 1972. As to judicial designation and status see s. 7(5), as amended in 1972 and as further amended by the Whitlam Government in 1973. (The McMahon Government's 1972 version had envisaged that after the introduction of the new qualifications *no* appointments, not even of lawyers, should attract judicial designations.)

[46]Both Professor J. E. Isaac (Faculty of Economics, Monash University) and Mr R. D. Williams (Federal Secretary of the Australian Bank Officials Association) were appointed on 16 October 1973. The latter has since retired (31 January 1975). Given its sensitivity to problems of institutional design, Labor might have been expected to make greater use of the opportunities for flexibility and expertise offered by the new avenues of appointment. The explanation may be that in their 1972 context, the new avenues were perceived as merely a by-product of the McMahon Government's drive to shift the Commission's emphasis away from its traditional role to one of overall economic management. See, *e.g.*, the 1972 version of s. 31(b), envisaging wage-fixing 'on grounds predominantly related to the national economy', and 'without examination' of the needs of particular industries.

[47]Justice Elizabeth Evatt was appointed from the English rather than the New South Wales Bar; but she was a Sydney graduate and a member of a well-known Sydney legal (and Labor) family.

seemed to be using the industrial bench not only (as we have seen) to accumulate new jurisdictions, but to stockpile a cadre of judges equipped by temperament and proven ability for constructive judicial action. These were bold souls, not timorous spirits.

High Court Appointments

A similar generalization (if no other) applies to the Whitlam Government's two High Court appointments, Justices Kenneth Jacobs[48] and Lionel Murphy.[49] It had long been assumed that Labor in power would approach such appointments cautiously, choosing only 'lawyers' lawyers' who were not positively anti-Labor. The intense controversy in 1930 over the appointments of Justices Evatt and McTiernan was an ordeal which Labor presumably had no wish to repeat. The only Labor appointment since then, of Sir William Webb in 1946[50], confirmed the common assumption. Webb had never been in politics, and despite earlier imputations of pro-Labor sympathies, 'they never showed in his judgments'.[51]

Against this background, Mr Justice Jacobs was a brilliant choice. A man of Liberal political leanings and of liberal intellect, and personally of gentle, modest and unassuming demeanour, he was universally respected and liked as judge, teacher and textbook writer.[52] He had also demonstrated, both in theory[53] and as President of the New South Wales Court of Appeal, a remarkably articulate and sensitive awareness of the opportunities—and inevitabilities—of creative judicial choice. Whether one's criterion was 'activism', 'legalism', 'realism' or 'humanity', Jacobs was an outstanding appointment. Yet this appointment remained safely within the tradition of Labor caution.

In terms of that tradition the appointment of Mr Justice Murphy was a complete surprise; but from any other viewpoint it was natural enough. Murphy was Labor's leading ideologue of judicial institutions; to that extent, no one was better suited to implement by practice and exemplarship the Labor concept of judgment. The appointment of Commonwealth Attorneys-General (including Sir Garfield Barwick) was itself a kind of tradition.[54] Yet popular hostilities to Labor (based, as suggested above, on an image of freewheeling anarchism) had also tended to focus on Murphy; and the flurry of controversy surrounding his appointment was entirely predictable.

Two factors cut the controversy short. One was the moving and impressive speech, welcoming Murphy to the bench on his swearing-in (14 February 1975), delivered by Mr T. E. F. Hughes, Q.C. (himself a former Liberal

---

[48]Took office 8 February 1974 (replacing Mr Justice Walsh).

[49]Appointed 9 February 1975 (replacing Mr Justice Menzies).

[50]This was Labor's only opportunity for a High Court appointment between 1930 and 1974; and even this opportunity arose only through a confluence of the desire to restore the Court's strength to seven, with the need to assign an Australian Judge of High Court status to the International War Crimes Tribunal for the Far East.

[51]G. Sawer, *Australian Federal Politics and Law 1929-1949* (Melbourne, 1963) p.182.

[52]K. Jacobs, *The Law of Trusts in New South Wales* (Sydney, 1958).

[53]See K. Jacobs, 'Lawyers' Reasonings: Some Extra-Judicial Reflections' (1967) 5 *Sydney L.R.* 424.

[54]In addition to Barwick, Justices Higgins, Isaacs and Latham had all been Commonwealth Attorneys-General, and Powers had been Commonwealth Crown Solicitor. A more striking precedent than any of these is that of Sir Edmund Barton, who as the nation's first Prime Minister included himself among the first appointments to the High Court. The vision thereby summoned up of Mr Whitlam appointing himself, on this impeccable precedent, is something to conjure with.

Commonwealth Attorney-General) on behalf of the New South Wales Bar. Rumblings of professional discontent in New South Wales and elsewhere were quelled by Hughes's eloquent reaffirmation of the Bar's impartial tradition. That night, at a special meeting of the Victorian Bar Council, a motion to condemn the Murphy appointment was lost by a reported margin of three to one after the chairman, Mr R. E. McGarvie, Q.C. (according to one journalistic account)

> reported that before the meeting he had received a telephone call from the Chief Justice, Sir Garfield Barwick, who had phoned to advise McGarvie of the warmth of the welcome extended to Murphy that day in the High Court in Sydney. Barwick dictated to McGarvie the text of the welcoming speech made by ex-Liberal Attorney-General Tom Hughes . . . Barwick also told McGarvie that the Queensland Bar proposed to welcome Murphy.[55]

The roles of both Hughes and Barwick must unreservedly be admired.

The other factor was the New South Wales Premier's decision to fill the casual Senate vacancy arising from Murphy's appointment by a non-Labor appointee. Whatever the other effects of this move, its immediate consequence was to shift the focus of public controversy from the Murphy appointment to the question of how casual vacancies should be filled. A State Liberal Premier had conveniently let Labor off the hook.

The evolution of Mr Justice Murphy's style, as he feels his way gradually into his job, has been interesting to watch—progressing from early concurrences confined to the words 'I agree', to brief homilies on aspects of social justice appended to the Court's judgments, and ultimately to his own full-scale judgments, frequently in dissent. The elaborate legalistic style characteristic of High Court judgments is conspicuously missing; but this seems to reflect an unwillingness, rather than inability, to play traditional High Court games. The overtones of broad principle, and even political manifesto, pervading the Murphy judgments, belong to an honourable judicial style, found to some extent in all judgments of the Supreme Court of the United States, and especially in those of its more 'liberal' Justices. Murphy's conscious adoption of this style is consistent with the entire philosophy of judgment here surveyed; and if in recent decades such a style has largely been absent from the Commonwealth Law Reports, it is high time the gap was filled. Whether or not one would want all High Court judges to adopt such a style, it has, as part of the total picture, a vital contribution to make. The danger is that more traditionally minded Australian lawyers, through impatience with the Murphy style, may fail sufficiently to absorb the substantive contribution that Mr Justice Murphy offers.

As to whether, and when, a political appointee should disqualify himself (either in all 'political' cases, or at least in challenges to legislation embodying former personal commitments of the appointee),[56] discussion is difficult. Both Barwick and Murphy appear to have adopted the same technique: conspicuous self-disqualification the first time the issue arises—for Barwick in *Tasmanian Breweries*[57] but not *Concrete Pipes*,[58] for Murphy in the *P.M.A. Case*[59] but not

---

[55] *Nation Review*, 21-27 February 1975, at p.489 (capitalization restored).

[56] See Note, (1975) 49 *Australian L.J.* 110.

[57] *R. v. Trade Practices Tribunal; Ex p. Tasmanian Breweries Pty Ltd* (1970) 123 C.L.R. 361.

[58] *Strickland v. Rocla Concrete Pipes Ltd* (1971) 124 C.L.R. 468.

[59] *Victoria v. Commonwealth* (1975) 7 A.L.R. 1.

Territory Senators[60]—but thereafter unrestricted participation in judgment, rejecting (or ignoring *sub silentio*) the supposed disqualification precept. But the wise tradition of leaving the issue solely to personal discretion[61] inhibits objective appraisal. For one thing, evidence as to whether and how far a judge has considered the issue may not be available. (Did Mr Justice Murphy disqualify himself in the *Family Law Case?*[62] Did the Chief Justice advise, or even instruct, that he so decide? Or was his absence simply an accident of that month's assignment of workload?) For another thing, any outsider's comments on a matter so intimately reserved for the individual conscience must be limited to very tentative and general remarks.

The issue is one of 'bias'; but among the many different meanings which imputations of 'bias' may have, one must make two broad distinctions. The first, as to 'political' bias, is between *party* politics and what might be called *Aristotelian* politics. For party politics to influence judgment—for a judge to favour an outcome because it suits a party paltorm—would be reprehensible whichever side of politics were involved. But Aristotelian politics—in the sense of a broad philosophical vision of what is good for society, what Geoffrey Sawer[63] calls the judge's 'general social outlook'—must enter into the composition of every judicial mind. Not only is its influence on judgment inevitable, but the absence of this influence would involve a tragic moral and institutional failure of the judicial process. The highest requirement of every judge is to implement ('without fear or favour') what he believes to be right. A judge may favour litigant X for the same Aristotelian reasons as led him, when in politics, to work with Party Y; but two effects of the same cause are not themselves in any relationship of cause and effect. It follows from this that imputations of party-political bias to judges are always unprovable.

The second distinction is between specific risks of bias due to personal involvement or interest in a litigated subject-matter; and unfocused (and often unconscious) effects of general social outlook. The disqualification issue arises, by its nature, only as to *identifiable* risks of bias. But these are often trivial risks. Moreover, they are risks to which *ex hypothesi* the judge should be advertent, and which he should therefore be able to surmount. The important biases are those of which, by their nature, neither judges nor observers may be aware. To worry about trivial and manageable instances of specific bias, while ignoring the ever-present and unavoidable influence of *deep* bias, is to cast out motes while ignoring beams. The self-disqualification precept may have an important symbolic role (since justice should manifestly be seen to be done); but it leaves the real problems untouched.

---

[60] *Western Australia* v. *Commonwealth* (1975) 7 A.L.R. 159.

[61] A charming recent example is the position of McTiernan J in *Collins (Hass)* v. *R.* (1975) 8 A.L.R. 150, at p.152. The case involved interpretation of High Court Rules to which, a quarter of a century earlier, his Honour had been a signatory. His Honour stated that if the result had turned upon his opinion, he would have withdrawn it 'to clear the way' for reargument in his absence. But 'as it is clear . . . that my opinion will not be decisive, I feel at liberty to express that opinion'.

[62] (1976) 9 A.L.R. 103.

[63] Cited above n. 51, at p.34.

IV
LABOR AND THE HIGH COURT

Finally, any questions (and answers) concerning political bias must relate in the recent context not merely to Mr Justice Murphy, but to all judges of the High Court. The Whitlam era did, after all, generate an unusually heightened political atmosphere, evoking emotional commitments on every side of politics from which High Court judges, as Australian citizens, could hardly be immune. In addition, both turbulent political events and massive reformist legislation spawned an unusual number of cases which might appear to have direct party-political overtones.

Towards the end of the Whitlam era, there emerged among lawyers a crude folklore version of 'anticipated reactions' to overtly political cases. In this folklore version, in any such case, Barwick would always and automatically vote *against* the Labor Government; Murphy, just as automatically, would always vote *for* it. Gibbs (and to a lesser extent Stephen, though with evident inner conflicts) would tend to support Barwick; McTiernan (and to a lesser extent Jacobs) would tend to support Murphy. This would leave Mason as the 'swinging voter', tending (whether through unusual conflict or unusual absence of emotional leanings) sometimes one way, sometimes the other.

The first intimations of such an assessment had come as early as the *Rhodesia Information Centre Case*;[64] it had gathered impetus (despite the intractability of the judgments) with *Cormack* v. *Cope*.[65] Thereafter the thesis presumably rests on the recent cases involving the *Petroleum and Minerals Authority Act 1973*;[66] the *Senate (Representation of Territories) Act 1973*;[67] the Australian Assistance Plan;[68] the 1975 electoral boundaries;[69] the *Seas and Submerged Lands Act 1973*;[70] and the *Family Law Act 1975*.[71]

It is obviously desirable to take this thesis beyond its impressionistic folklore version into a realm amenable to precisely defined assertions; to summarize it economically; to test its validity; and to find a neutral language for discussion of such a sensitive matter. To kill these four birds with a single stone, I here offer a scalogram[72] constructed from the above eight cases. Putative 'pro-Labor' voters are assigned conventionally to the *left* of the scale; putative 'anti-Labor' voters to the *right*. Plus signs (summed as 'Pro' at the foot of the scale) indicate 'pro-Labor' votes; minus signs (summed as 'Con') indicate 'anti-Labor' votes. Blank spaces (summed as 'NP', *i.e.*, non-participation) indicate that the judge in question either did not sit, or (for Menzies in all nine instances, Jacobs and Murphy in Item 7, and Murphy in Item 5) could not have sat, since he was not a member of the court at the relevant time.

---

[64]*Bradley* v. *Commonwealth* (1973) 1 A.L.R. 241 (Item 7 in the scalogram which follows).

[65](1974) 131 C.L.R. 432; (1974) 3 A.L.R. 419 (Item 5 in the scalogram).

[66]*Victoria* v. *Commonwealth* (1975) 7 A.L.R. 1 (Item 4).

[67]*Western Australia* v. *Commonwealth* (1975) 7 A.L.R. 159 (Items 1 and 9).

[68]*Victoria* v. *Commonwealth* (1975) 7 A.L.R. 277 (Item 6).

[69]*A.-G. (Australia) (ex rel. McKinlay)* v. *Commonwealth* (1975) 7 A.L.R. 593 (Item 2).

[70]*New South Wales* v. *Commonwealth* (1975) 8 A.L.R. 1 (Item 10).

[71]*Russell* v. *Russell; Farrelly* v. *Farrelly* (1976) 9 A.L.R. 103 (Items 3, 8 and 11).

[72]For an explanation of the assumptions, procedures and conventions involved, see A.R. Blackshield, 'Quantitative Analysis: The High Court of Australia, 1964-1969' (1972) 3 *Lawasia* 1, at pp. 13-16.

Item	Scale Type	(Me)	Mu	Ja	Mc	Ma	St	Gi	Bw	A.L.R.
1	1-6		+	−	−	−	−	−	−	7.159a
2	1-6		+	−	−	−	−	−	−	7.593
3	1-4			+	−	−	−	−	−	9.103a
4	2-4			+	+	−	−	−	−	7.001
5	3-3	+			+	−	+	−	−	3.419
6	4-3		+	+	+	−	+	−	−	7.277
7	2-3	+			+	−	−	−	−	1.241
8	2-3			+		+		−	−	9.103b
9	4-3		+	+	+	+	−	−	−	7.159b
10	5-2		+	+	+	+	−	−	+	8.001
11	3-2			+		+	+	−	−	9.103c
	Pro	02	05	07	06	04	03	00	01	
	Con	00	00	02	02	06	08	11	10	
	NP	09	06	02	03	01	00	00	00	

CR = .955; CS = .750

The placement of Menzies at the extreme left is not, of course, intended to rank him as even more 'left-wing' than Murphy, but only to acknowledge that a mere two cases afford no basis for any meaningful ranking of him at all. The evidence for Murphy is also too scanty for any meaningful ranking, though its consistency seems to warrant at least a presumptive conclusion. Again, despite adequate observations, the scalogram does not allow us to distinguish between Jacobs and McTiernan; they are therefore ranked as tied. Finally, despite 100 per cent participation, one cannot discriminate between Gibbs and Barwick. If anything, Barwick's 'inconsistent' vote in Item 10 may suggest a position less extreme than that of Gibbs.[73]

In other respects, too, the scalogram is unsatisfactory. The *Territory Senators Case*[74] is treated as two separate items: Item 1 records Murphy's threshold view that in any event the matter was simply not justiciable, and Item 9 the substantial result upholding the *Senate (Representation of Territories) Act* 1973. The *Family Law Case*[75] yields three distinct items; and even these are not exhaustive. Item 3 records Jacobs' solitary view that the Commonwealth's 'marriage' power extends to proceedings as to custody and care of children, not only independently of any 'principal' relief, but also independently of the parties' marital status. Item 8 records the holding that the *in camera* requirement could not validly apply to State courts; and Item 11 the major holding, with Stephen and Mason joining Jacobs to uphold independent proceedings affecting children and property, at least between present or former spouses. (A fourth item, upholding the prohibition of robes, is merged in Item 11.) Thus, although the scalogram contains eleven items, they are drawn from only eight cases.[76] Given the rule of thumb that at least ten cases are required for a

---

[73]Indeed, it would be possible to eliminate this 'inconsistency' altogether by shifting Barwick to third-last rank, between Mason and Stephen. The third inconsistent vote would then be Stephen's in Item 11. With some reshuffling of rows as well as columns, this would yield a scalogram alternative to that set out in the text, but equally acceptable. There might even be a more attractive elegance (though no greater correctness) in a solution thus ascribing all three inconsistencies to a single judge.

[74](1975) 7 A.L.R. 159.

[75](1976) 9 A.L.R. 103.

[76]No other recent cases seem to be eligible for inclusion. *Re Senator Webster* (1975) 6 A.L.R. 65, is clearly relevant but was decided by Barwick CJ sitting alone; and *Commonwealth* v. *Queensland* (1975)

statistically significant scale, this is (at best) a barely adequate and (at worst) an inadequate result.

Moreover, at least two of the cases included should arguably have been scaled differently, or not at all. Item 6 (the *A.A.P. Case*)[77] records the actual result—that a challenge to the Australian Assistance Plan failed—by treating Murphy, Jacobs, McTiernan and Stephen as 'positive' voters for this result. But Stephen held only that the plaintiffs had no legal standing, expressing no opinion on the issue dividing his brethren. The treatment of Item 5 (*Cormack v. Cope*)[78] is even more unsatisfactory. The result (a refusal to intervene in the 1974 joint sitting of Parliament) was unanimous. Normally, therefore, despite its obvious relevance, the case would not be included. Moreover, the differences of opinion manifest in the judgments are not reducible to any single dichoto-mized representation: as in several recent cases, the judges not merely gave different answers, but did not even ask the same questions.[79] But at least on the issue of intervention in the parliamentary process, the several different opinions expressed appear to form a spectrum—ranging from Barwick's view that the Court can always intervene, to McTiernan's that it can never do so. In the end I have ascribed to McTiernan, Menzies and Stephen the 'positive' view that the inhibitions against intervention are (at least normally) a matter of law; to Barwick, Gibbs and Mason the 'negative' view that the inhibitions are a matter of discretion. The former view, in the circumstances of 1974, was the one more favourable to the Government, the latter to the Opposition.[80] The resulting treatment is inaccurate and unsatisfying; but any other dichotomous treatment would be equally so. The distortions of a two-valued logic are as much a vice of jurimetrics as of adversary litigation.

Yet, given these very intricacies, the two 'inconsistent' votes recorded for Mr Justice Stephen are immediately explicable. The third inconsistency—for Chief Justice Barwick in the *Offshore Sovereignty Case*[81] (Item 10)—is also explicable, given his position since *Bonser* v. *La Macchia*[82] on the substantive

---

7 A.L.R. 351, above n. 8, yields no scaleable information because it was unanimously decided. Of other cases which might conceivably (but not at all convincingly) be thought to raise relevant issues, *R.* v. *Humby; Ex p. Rooney* (1973) 2 A.L.R. 297, was also unanimous; and in any event the amendment to the Matrimonial Causes Act there held valid dated from 1971. *R.* v. *Trade Practices Tribunal; Ex p. St. George County Council* (1974) 2 A.L.R. 371 (as to the scope of the 'corporations' power in relation to trade practices) similarly involved the 1971-72 version of the Restrictive Trade Practices Act; and if it *were* included, its voting pattern would be almost the polar opposite of what appears in the scalogram. By contrast, in so far as a division of opinion emerged in *Barton* v. *Commonwealth* (1974) 3 A.L.R. 70, (as to prerogative and statutory powers of extraditon), that case would fit, and thus strengthen, the scale. Moreover, it would enable us to distinguish (as the present scale does not) between the positions of McTiernan and Jacobs. Barwick, Mason and Jacobs held that the *statutory* powers of extradition could not avail the government in that case; McTiernan and Menzies expressed an inclination to disagree. But this inclination did not in the end yield a firm dissent; and the actual result, based on the prerogative power, was unanimous.

[77] (1975) 7 A.L.R. 277.

[78] (1974) 131 C.L.R. 132; (1974) 3 A.L.R. 419.

[79] Perhaps the best example is *R.* v. *Director-General of Social Welfare for Victoria; Ex p. Henry* (1975) 8 A.L.R. 233 where, in the words of the headnote, 'no two justices . . . decided for precisely the same reasons'.

[80] By contrast, in the circumstances of October-November 1975, these positions would have been reversed. It would have been fascinating to see how the judges would have reacted if the issue had come before them.

[81] (1975) 8 A.L.R. 1.

[82] (1969) 122 C.L.R. 177. On the other hand, if the alternative scalogram mentioned in n. 73 above were chosen, there would seem to be no immediate explanation of the inconsistency which would then be attributed to Stephen J in the *Family Law Case*.

issues involved. To obtain a scalogram with only three inconsistent votes, especially when all three can be so readily explained, is an extremely persuasive result. This is confirmed by the formal measures of the scale's statistical significance: a 'coefficient of reproducibility' (CR) of .955 (as against a 'satisfactory' level of about .9), and a 'coefficient of scaleability' (CS) of .75 (as against a 'satisfactory' level of about .6 or .65). Despite the weaknesses here stressed, the scalogram seems to be persuasive evidence of something. The question is, of what.

I have already expressed my own preference for 'deep' rather than 'specific' explanations. Rather than ascribing the voting pattern to party-political bias, it seems better to postulate differences in general social outlook. I have elsewhere described[83] a jurimetric technique for uncovering these deeper dimensions of High Court disagreements, by manipulating all non-unanimous cases over a certain period, to find the largest consistent scales that the voting patterns will 'fit'. The first scale to emerge from the process ('the X Scale') is presumed to represent the single most important attitudinal factor in the Court's disagreements, and the next ('the Y Scale') the second most important attitudinal factor.[84] When High Court cases are thus manipulated for successive periods (whether years, triennia, or decades), the same rankings of judges tend consistently to recur on both X and Y Scales. This suggests that the X and Y Scales must genuinely represent *something*—since if they were mere meaningless statistical patterns, the rankings would vary randomly from one period to the next.

Attempts, however, to generate (by induction from the content of the cases scaled) an impressionist characterization of what the X and Y Scales stand for have been speculative in the extreme. The X Scale has been characterized as 'collectivism' versus 'individualism'; 'socialism' versus 'conservatism'; 'economic paternalism' versus 'economic *laissez-faire*'; 'sympathy for economic underdogs' versus 'the Protestant ethic and the spirit of capitalism'. The Y Scale has been characterized as 'centralism' versus 'States' rights'; 'authoritarianism' versus 'liberalism'; 'tough-mindedness' versus 'tender-mindedness'; and high versus low degrees of preoccupation with 'public image and dignity, . . . the hierarchical and the "official" '.[85]

In 1974,[86] I tried both to shift these slogans closer to the distinctive preoccupations of lawyers, and to generalize beyond the empirical High Court data to a deeper philosophical level. The X Scale, I suggested, might reflect

a spectrum of different ways of conceiving of *rights and obligations*. The *proprietary* end of this spectrum is characterized by a tendency to accord value-priority to individual 'ownership' rights; by a tendency to conceive of *all* 'rights' as 'owned' by individuals; and by a tendency to perceive all moral problems as requiring a solution framed in terms of 'rights' thus 'owned'. The *proletarian* end of the spectrum is characterized by a tendency to give value-priority to conceptions of 'social justice' and 'common good'; by a tendency to perceive *all* 'obligations' as arising from the

---

[83]Blackshield, cited above n. 72, at pp. 27-43, building on work of Glendon Schubert there cited.

[84]I remain convinced that there is also a Z Scale, reflecting attitudes to questions of judicial technique ('legalism' versus 'realism'). But the statistical methods here referred to are powerless to produce sufficient data to explore it.

[85]See Blackshield, cited above n. 72, at pp. 32-33 and at 39-41.

[86]A.R. Blackshield, 'A Typology of Legal Systems' (mimeographed, East-West Center, Hawaii, 1974).

collective interests of society, or of a group; and by a tendency to perceive all moral problems as requiring solution in terms of such 'obligations'.

Similarly, the Y Scale might reflect

a spectrum of different ways of conceiving of *order and organization*. The *structural* end of this spectrum is marked by a tendency to accord high value to 'order' and 'organization'; by a tendency to conceive of 'order' in terms of a hierarchical structure, with ... each level ... logically 'derived' from the level superior to it; and by a tendency to conceive of 'organization' as similarly hierarchical, with successive levels of authority subordinated to one another ... [so that] power devolves along lines always firmly controlled from above. The *pluralist* end of the spectrum is marked by a tendency to accord low value to conceptions of 'order' and 'organization'; by a tendency to conceive of 'order' in terms of a Heraclitean flux, in which 'unity' consists merely of the complex but unstructured interplay of heterogeneous parts; and by a tendency to conceive of 'organization' also in terms of a fluid and mobile interaction of interdependent components.

The relevance of all this is simple. If our scalogram of 'political' cases directly reflected the judges' party-political preferences, one would expect its ranking of judges to correlate closely with that of the X Scale for the same period. 'Pro-Labor' voters on the 'political' scale would tend to be 'proletarians' (or 'collectivists') on the X Scale; 'anti-Labor' voters on the 'political' scale would tend to be 'proprietarians' (or 'individualists') on the X Scale. In fact, however, this correlation turns out to be low.[87]

To test it, I have generated X and Y Scales from a body of data comprising all non-unanimous cases decided since the appointment of Mr Justice Mason (7 August 1972), and reported up to 30 June 1976—thus covering Labor's three years in office, with a few months at each end for good measure. The total number of cases involved is 99; the total number of items used in the scaling is 110.[88]

For the seven Justices relevant here,[89] the X Scale thus generated gives the sequence (reading from the 'proletarian' or 'collectivist' end): Murphy, McTiernan, Jacobs, Barwick,[90] Mason, Gibbs and Stephen. The Y Scale sequence (reading from the 'pluralist' or 'anti-authoritarian' end) is Murphy, Jacobs, Mason, McTiernan, Stephen, Gibbs and Barwick. Our 'political' ranking, while roughly correlating with that of the X Scale, also differs significantly from it; but (apart from a trivial change of places for McTiernan and Mason) the correlation between the 'political' scale and the Y Scale is exact.

Thus we have travelled in a circle. I began by ascribing the trauma of the Whitlam years to a 'cultural confrontation': to differing degrees of willingness

---

[87]The correlation would be higher for the alternative 'political' scalogram referred to in n. 73 above. Indeed, a further legitimate reshuffling of rows and columns in that solution would give the 'political' rank order: Murphy, McTiernan, Jacobs, Mason, Barwick, Gibbs, Stephen. This would correlate with the X Scale given below just as well as the version actually chosen correlates with the Y Scale. (The only variation would be as to the ranking of Mason and Barwick *inter se*.) This solution, however, would require us both to treat all three of Stephen's 'positive' votes as inconsistencies, and to ignore their significance by assigning him nevertheless to an ideologically extreme position. The solution described in the text is therefore preferred. But the fact that there exists an alternative possible solution, which would tend to support precisely the 'political' interpretation that my main argument is concerned to reject, neatly emphasizes the inconclusiveness of all such interpretations.

[88]Due to the treatment of some cases as comprising more than one item, as with my reading of *Territory Senators* and the *Family Law Case* above.

[89]Before their deaths Menzies and Walsh (in that order) ranked on the X Scale between Mason and Gibbs. On the Y Scale Menzies ranked between Jacobs and Mason, Walsh between Stephen and Gibbs.

[90]This accords with his position in the X Scale for 1964-1969 (McTiernan, Windeyer, Barwick, Menzies, Taylor, Kitto, Owen). See Blackshield, cited above n. 72, at p.26.

to welcome, or at least tolerate, a perceived freewheeling turbulence, a Heraclitean flux. I end by suggesting that, in so far as High Court voting in 'political' cases reflected attitudinal factors, what counted, here too, was not the conventional ideological spectrum, but differing degrees of tolerance of what some perceived as a 'larrikin government' in Heraclitean flux.

Whatever the explanation may be, a divergence of attitudes in the High Court is surely no cause for concern. Julius Stone has observed that, with 'tensions and dissatisfactions' unavoidable in any society's ongoing search for justice, the ability to reflect these tensions and dissatisfactions may be 'a main role of judges in any tolerable legal order':

> The Supreme Court of the United States, in those very aspects at which British lawyers sometimes look askance, offers a supreme example ... The very varied outlooks and talents and capacities of its members, often spell discord. Yet this very discord may symbolise the will of so richly complex a people to live under broadly agreed principles, and also to sublimate the bitter disagreements which broad principles so often yield in application.[91]

This is a deeper version of the obvious point that, given the varied outlooks that exist in any society, it is better that a wide spectrum of those outlooks be reflected in the country's highest court—especially a constitutional court—than that the court should come to be seen as identified with the outlook of a single sub-society. In a High Court long perceived as conservative, Labor's appointments may have produced a 'balance' for the first time in years. If so, that may be Labor's most important contribution to the Australian judicial process.

---

[91]J. Stone, *Social Dimensions of Law and Justice* (Sydney, 1966), p.795.

COMMENTARIES

M. D. Kirby

I face an impossible task. My comment upon Associate Professor Blackshield's interesting essay must be at once relevant, useful, stimulating and above all thoroughly innocuous. How can I deal with the 'big themes' of this essay? How can I comment upon High Court or other appointments? It is simply not possible for me to deal with party political issues that are at the heart of the essay. The strength of the judiciary in the British tradition rests, in part at least, upon its plain remove from ephemeral political controversies. I retreat to less heady stuff, leaving it to other controversialists who are under no disabilities to lead the *real* debate.

This is not to say that I necessarily agree with everything in the Blackshield essay. My reservations illustrate his major conclusion. A distinction of some sort must be drawn between judicial attitudes and predilections, on the one hand and what judges actually do as judges, on the other. Forgive us, but as citizens and mortal creatures judges obviously have attitudes. These include political attitudes. Indeed in our democracy, the compulsory vote forbids judges the luxury of a total retreat from party political evaluation. Clearly, such attitudes and predispositions will affect, in a general way, some judicial decisions. It does not say very much, I am afraid, to reveal that judges have their biases. It would be curious, indeed a case for scientific wonderment, if they did not. The real issue for governments and for the community is how judges handle their attitudes.

Judges and Prejudices

Because the common law system reposes such unique importance in its judges, debate and speculation about judicial attitudes will inevitably agitate the community. It will especially fire the legal community because it feeds extensively on its own myths. When two or more lawyers are gathered together in this country, we all know that only a short interval expires before discussion turns from the qualities and attributes of the participants, to the biases and defects of the judges. The Blackshield essay has tried to reduce this timeless, fascinating exercise in gossip to the dignity of a science. It is an interesting yet unsatisfying effort. We may live under a government of laws not of men. But the laws are stated, interpreted and enforced by men. Indeed, by a few, identifiable men. Scrutiny of these few should flourish and be informed.

Is it not strange that the legal fraternity which asserts most vehemently, the absolute removal of judges from political issues, nevertheless spends so much time and mental energy examining the prejudices and attitudes of judges? Therein lies the germ of confusion. But, when quantitative analysis is finished and the scalograms are before us, what precisely does the voting pattern that emerges tell us that we did not know from common gossip or our own intuition? A scientific demonstration that Mr Justice X is, on his 'votes', at the extreme left of a scalogram and that Mr Justice Y is at the extreme right is all very interesting. But which of us learns anything really new from the scalogram appearing in the essay? Unless it is the bizarre appearance of Menzies J at the extreme left of the scale, the only thing this scalogram does is to organize knowledge which most of us who have been reading the cases had anyway. Perhaps no more should be claimed for quantitative analysis than this.

But if we are to indulge ourselves in this fascinating American[1] import, we should be aware of the need for caution. In the first place, in the United States, it is usual to find all (or almost all) judges of the Supreme Court participating in every decision. The number of cases where judges do not sit is rare. This is not the case in the High Court, even in matters involving issues under the Constitution. Secondly, although there has been an increase in individual opinion-writing, to the point indeed of provoking criticism,[2] analysis of this kind is prone to display a bias in favour of individualists and against those who concur in opinions. Thirdly, the analysis inevitably concentrates on how judges 'vote'. It makes no allowance for the reasons expressed by them. Quite different reasons may bring one judge to the same conclusion as another. The analysis has a tendency to reduce the intellectual processes of reasoned judgment to the banality of an opinion poll. Fourthly, these points assume greater importance where the sample is small. Inevitably the U.S. Supreme Court must dispatch a great deal more business than the High Court. But where, as here, we are not dealing in hundreds but only eleven issues in eight cases, the chances of really worthwhile conclusions are diminished. I say this even bearing in mind the limitations that are inherent in the endeavour to analyse a stable group of judges when time inevitably and unhappily erodes the stability of the group.

The point of this is that in constitutional as in other cases we must be alive to the unpredictable, as well as to the predictable. Governments, which appoint judges must temper the comfort and self-assurance that arises from quantum analysis with a healthy regard for the eccentricities of judicial independence. When you compare the scalogram in this essay with those appearing in Professor Blackshield's *Lawasia* article,[3] the lessons that emerge are, I would suggest, three. One is that the ranking of judges varies according to fairly specific subject matters. To lump 'constitutional' cases together may be quite unhelpful. Attitudes focus much more specifically (as does the law). Another is that the ranking of judges varies. The composite picture emerging from all votes varies significantly from the votes on particular issues. And the third is that the picture varies with the passage of time.

Judicial Patronage

There is absolutely no doubt that governments everywhere recognize the importance of judicial patronage. This is a sensitive issue. I am happy to say it is an international one. The latest part of the Congressional Quarterly to cross my desk discloses that the United States Senate has now passed a Bill which creates forty-five additional federal judgeships in twenty-eight States.[4] This Bill was delayed by the Senate leadership for six months. The United States Chief Justice blamed the Senate inaction on 'the political considerations of a presidential year'.[5] The Chief Justice and a subsequent editorial in the

[1]For a recent American analysis see W.B. Schultz and P.K. Howard 'The Myth of Swing Voting: An Analysis of Voting Patterns on the Supreme Court' (1975) 50 *New York Univ. L. R.* 798.

[2]*E.g.* Note, (1975) 49 *Australian L.J.* 156.

[3]A.R. Blackshield, 'Quantitative Analysis: the High Court of Australia, 1964-1969' (1972) 3 *Lawasia* 1, at pp. 14, 24.

[4]*Congressional Quarterly Weekly Report* vol. 34, no. 15 (10 April 1976), at p.841.

[5]*ibid.*

Washington Post put these manoeuvres into an historical perspective worthy of the Bicentennial:

> [this is] the old political tradition of delaying judgeships when the Party controlling Congress hopes to win the White House and the right to appoint any new judges . . . since 1801 new judgeships have been political footballs . . . [statistics show] that none of the major additions to the Federal Bench since World War II came later than midway in a Presidential term.[6]

It should perhaps be noted that the Bill has now passed. Perhaps agreements were reached that removed the impediment.

Lord Hailsham, the former Conservative Lord Chancellor, recently published his autobiography.[7] One chapter is titled 'Judges and Judge Making'. It deals with the question of judicial patronage in England. After lamenting the fact that none of his appointments had been made from the House of Commons,[8] Lord Hailsham said this about one of the themes presently before us:

> It is a great mistake to suppose that the possession of definite political ideas or the experience of having contested elections constitutes a slur on a judge's impartiality. Indeed, it is arguable that the opposite may be the case. Simonds, Maugham and Goddard were far to the right of the most Conservative Members of Parliament and unless I have misjudged him, Lord Gardiner is politically far to the left of Roy Jenkins, Lord Elwyn Jones or the late Mr Justice Donovan. Impartiality does not consist in having no controversial opinions or even prejudices. The Bench is not made up of political, religious or social neuters. Impartiality consists in the capacity to be aware of one's subjective opinions and to place them on one side when one enters the professional field, and the ability to listen patiently to and to weigh evidence and argument and to withhold concluded judgement until the case is over.[9]

I stop short of applying these themes in Australia. However, the point must be made that governments, of whatever political complexion, should not be lulled by scalograms into a false confidence in the predictability of their appointees. Constraints are imposed on the predilections even of a maverick by the traditions of the Bench, the training of the profession and the frequent absence of room to indulge personal prejudices, however strong. Cardozo J put it well:

> In countless litigations the law is so clear the judges have no discretion. They have the right to legislate within gaps. But often there are no gaps.[10]

I do not seek to restore the myth of 'complete and absolute legalism'. But in throwing this myth overboard, we should not fall victim to an equal heresy. Party hopes and academic expectations are bound to founder uncomfortably often on the judicial rock of impartiality and independence. All that governments can do, once an appointment is made, is to hold their breath and hope for the best.

---

[6] *ibid.*

[7] *The Door Wherein I Went* (London, 1975), p.254.

[8] *ibid.*, p.256.

[9] *ibid.*, pp. 256-7.

[10] B. Cardozo, *The Nature of the Judicial Process*, (New Haven, 1921), p.129.

The Privy Council in Decline

There are a few points of a minor nature that I feel the essay may not have brought out sufficiently. The passage on the Privy Council tends, I think, to the error that the Government's moves to establish an entirely indigenous judicial hierarchy were an Antipodean aberration. They were not. They were part of a more general, international trend. Within a year, Guyana[11] and Trinidad[12] have abolished appeals.[13] Malaysia has now removed constitutional and criminal appeals. The debate has even begun in New Zealand![14] Absence of appeal to London has not, we are told, made the Canadian heart grow fonder.[15] If we must have a Privy Council for State appeals it is interesting to speculate whether the Whitlam Government endeavoured to find an indirect path around the legal problems outlined in the essay. Would it have been constitutionally possible to establish in this country on the advice of the Australian Government an Australian Judicial Committee of the Privy Council? The Queensland venture came unstuck.[16] But could not the Queen of Australia have constituted an entirely Australian Judicial Committee? We will be told, in due course, whether such an indirect means of modernizing the Australian Constitution was considered and if so the reactions of the Australian and United Kingdom Governments. If the monarchy, with the Queen's consent, can be made indigenous, can the Privy Council be repatriated too for State appeals?

Judges Outside the Court System

A matter scarcely touched upon in this essay is the use made of judges by the Whitlam Government in a large number of inquiries. The facility is not uncommon in New South Wales. Other States have different traditions.[17] During 1974, it was said in Sydney that you could not get a matter tried in the Supreme Court of New South Wales because so many judges were involved in federal inquiries or investigations or had otherwise received a federal Commission. The list is a long one: Kerr CJ (Governor-General), Hope JA (Royal Commission on Intelligence and Security), Collins J (Royal Commission on Petroleum), Else-Mitchell J (Commission of Inquiry into Land Tenures), Meares J (Commission of Inquiry into Rehabilitation and Compensation), and Toose J (Royal Commission on Repatriation). The use of judges, including State judges, does not end there. When the Prices Justification Tribunal was set up, a Deputy President of the Arbitration Commission, Williams J, was selected to head the Tribunal. Else-Mitchell J was appointed Chairman of the Grants Commission. W.B. Campbell J had been appointed by the previous Government to be Chairman of the Remuneration Tribunal and the Academic Salaries Tribunal. Nimmo J was commissioned to inquire into

[11] *Constitution (Amendment) Act* 1973 (Guyana), (1975) 2 *Commonwealth Law Bulletin* 9.

[12] *Constitutional Commission Report* (Trinidad), (1975) 2 *Commonwealth Law Bulletin* 57.

[13] *Courts of Judicature (Amendment) Act* 1976 (Malaysia), (1976) 2 *Commonwealth Law Bulletin* 85.

[14] See (1975) 49 *Australian L.J.* 449. *Cf.* F.M. Brookfield, 'New Zealand (Appeals to the Privy Council) (Amendment) Order 1972: Another View' (1975) 6 *New Zealand Univs., L.R.* 408.

[15] D.H. Clark, 'The Supreme Court of Canada, the House of Lords, the Judicial Committee of the Privy Council and Administrative Law' (1976) 14 *Alberta L. R.* 5.

[16] *Commonwealth* v. *Queensland (Queen of Queensland Case)* (1975) 7 *A.L.R.* 351.

[17] M.V. McInerney 'The Appointment of Judges to Commissions of Enquiry and Other Extra-Judicial Activities' in *Judicial Essays* (Law Foundation of N.S.W. & Victorian Law Foundation, 1974), p.35; *Cf.* P.B. Toose, *ibid.*, p.55.

the constitutional future of Norfolk Island. Elizabeth Evatt J, whilst a member of the Arbitration Commission, received a further Commission to be Chairman of the Royal Commission on Human Relationships. J.B. Sweeney J, initially appointed to the Arbitration Commission and later to the Industrial Court, was then appointed Royal Commissioner on Certain Allegations of Payments to Maritime Unions. He also headed the Commission of Inquiry set up to report on Co-ordinated Industrial Organizations. Although the legislation was passed during the life of the present Parliament, it was the Whitlam Government which announced the intention to appoint a judge, Woodward J, as Director-General of the Australian Security Intelligence Organization. Franki J is Chairman of the Committee on Reprographic Reproduction and was sent by the Government to represent Australia at an International Conference on Copyright Law. The Law Reform Commission Act, the Administrative Appeals Tribunal Act and the Australia Police Bill all envisage a role for federal judges outside the purely curial. There are no doubt very many other examples. The tradition of using judges is not, of course, a new one in Australia. It certainly received a fillip from the Whitlam Government. It is a phenomenon that surprises overseas lawyers. Indeed I am told it surprises Victorian lawyers. Its motivation can no doubt be traced to the desire of governments for advice of a somewhat different kind than could be expected from the more orthodox sources in the Public Service. Is it the independence of the judicial mind and tradition which motivated such a use of judges?

To sum up, I would say this. The last few years have demonstrated that judges in the future are likely to have increasingly important functions outside court rooms. Within court rooms, important social and political issues must be resolved, sometimes without the benefit of 'pure legal' principle. In these circumstances, it is inevitable and healthy that the governments who appoint them and the community served should be aware of the attitudes and predilections of judges. Associate Professor Blackshield's fascinating techniques assist in this knowledge. But, given our traditions, the watch-word for governments is and should be 'Put not your faith in scalograms'.

J.D. Merralls

The main theme of Associate Professor Blackshield's essay is found in the relationship of what the essay calls 'judicial activism' with the legislative reform of the law upon a Benthamite basis. The essay is concerned with two aspects of judicial activism. One is the possibility that a court may act upon its own conception of justice and reject an accepted principle or rule in the name of social utility or convenience; the other, the ability that positive law itself may concede to adapt and apply general precepts to particular cases.

The essay touches the first aspect only obliquely, in its reference to the general social outlook which is said to be part of the composition of every judicial mind. It finds expression in a parody of the judicial oath that the highest requirement of a judge is that he should decide according to what he believes to be right.[1] Small purpose would be gained by examining the implications of that statement now. Sir Owen Dixon did that at Yale twenty years ago in his paper 'Concerning Judicial Method'.[2] But if a government were to select men as judges whose actions it believed would not be constrained by the body of acquired positive knowledge known as the *corpus juris*, it must refute the concluding opinion in Sir Owen Dixon's paper that, by abandoning the judicial administration of the law according to a received technique and the use of logical faculties for a process which accepts or condones the conscious rejection of conceptions according to personal standards or theories of justice which the judge sets up, the courts would come to exercise an unregulated authority over men and affairs which would leave our system indistinguishable from others least admired. The answer the essay offers to this charge seems to rest upon a statement that there is brought to the role of judgment willy nilly the judge's 'broad philosophical vision of what is good for society' and a contention that however much it may be concealed from sight and even from awareness by the way in which courts proceed it inevitably affects the judicial process. If that philosophical vision were not involved, it is said that a serious moral failure would occur in the process. The thesis tends to reject the charge sometimes made that the accepted common law convention of justice according to law involves a mere playing with concepts which are not easily adjusted to changing needs. Instead it suggests that at best the process is self-deceptive. But it may be thought that the thesis of the essay pays too little regard on the one hand to the actual desire of judges to apply an external standard and on the other to the way in which the living law is in fact adapted to serve the changing needs of society and the better instincts of man. Sir Owen Dixon's paper was addressed to explaining that paradox.

Before parting from this aspect of judicial activism it may be useful to recall a passing remark in Professor Shatwell's paper about the problems of law reform at the Tenth Australian Legal Convention, that the institutional role of courts is to declare established custom and to protect interests already recognized by positive morality and that even in their creative role, which appears to be more prominent at certain periods in history, their activity usually reflects a demand that positive law should give effect to a claim already recognized by custom.[3] To this comment may I add the suggestion that the courts that have been seen to exercise most effectively the art of developing and adapting the law, so as to tie a knot in the strands, were courts which worked in banc and had a sense of collegiate function? It is doubtful whether the assumption in the paper that balance is attained through discord is one which legal history or recent experience supports.

The other aspect of judicial activism is perhaps more pertinent to the period under review. Freedom of action is conferred by positive law itself. Here the new Benthamism recognizes the inadequacy of the conventional process of the law as a procedure for radical change without serious social dislocation. It

---

[1] *Cf.* Lord Denning, 'Justice is what the right-thinking members of the community think to be fair. We must try to do what is fair. I will do right—that means I will do justice not I will do law.' (A.B.C. Broadcast 1974).

[2] (1956) 29 *Australian L.J.* 468; *Jesting Pilate* (Sydney, 1965), pp. 152-65. The proceedings of the Federal Anniversary Seminar (University of Melbourne, 6-8 August 1976) showed how Sir Owen Dixon's name is revered, but his words are not read.

[3] K.O. Shatwell, 'Some Reflections on the Problems of Law Reform', (1957) 31 *Australian L. J.*, 325, at p.330.

accepts the limitations upon the reform of the law by statute that the regulation of persons and actions by words impose. It seeks to surmount them not by vain attempts to deal with every conceivable case, like some cancer-ridden tax act, but by inviting judges to approach individual cases with a legislative mind. In doing this it draws upon the drafting techniques and judicial methods, and upon the laws themselves, of the United States. And in putting its trust in judges, it calls on them to interpret reformist legislation not strictly according to the plain meaning of the words used, for they are intended only as guides, but imaginatively so that what the court deems to be the statutory purpose will be fulfilled. The new Benthamism speaks with the voice of Holmes:

> The legislature has the power to decide what the policy of the law shall be, and if it has intimated its will, however indirectly, that will should be recognized and obeyed . . . It is not an adequate discharge of duty for the courts to say: We see what you are driving at, but you have not said it, and therefore we shall go on as before.[4]

New Benthamism appears to doubt the willingness or ability of judges schooled in other techniques of statutory interpretation and unaccustomed to the drafting style and assumptions of the new laws to accept the role that is thrust upon them. Hence the judicial administration of the new statutes is intended to be removed as far as possible from the existing courts and given to 'a cadre of judges whose temperament and proven abilities would fit them for a constructive and creative judicial role'. The creation of a federal court is required if the wheels of the new legislation are not to be parted from the vehicle for want of a linchpin.

Thus the new laws are intended to be set apart from the general body of laws, and the power to enforce them to be confined by and large to courts which exercise a special jurisdiction defined by source. In some instances the new laws regulate activities concurrently with the general law. The Trade Practices Act is such a law. The precepts of the Act are general, yet they are intended to be administered apart from the general body of laws, written and unwritten, by means of special remedies in proceedings brought in courts which do not have universal jurisdiction. The fallacy from which the founding fathers proceeded in providing for a division of power between State and federal courts is followed into substantive law. The smouldering fires of originality in the creation of Australian law have not been so efficiently extinguished by fascination for an inapt foreign model since the Sherman Act was received into Australian law seventy years ago.

The paper cites Mr Enderby's statement that the Labor Government believed that the areas of major federal law should be administered by a federal court and should not be left to be administered in State courts. At the Thirteenth Australian Legal Convention Mr Whitlam asserted as a 'basic principle' the proposition that judges who are called on to interpret and apply statutes should be appointed by governments responsible to the parliaments which passed those statutes.[5] The validity of the proposition is not demonstrated by its axiomatic form. We have it from other high authority that the division of courts into State and federal can be regarded as sound neither from the point of view of juristic principle nor from that of the practical and efficient administration of justice.[6]

---

[4] *Johnson* v. *United States* (1908) 163 F. 30, at p.32. See further *Dillingham Constructions Pty Ltd* v. *Steel Mains Pty Ltd* (1975) 132 C.L.R. 323, at pp. 330-5.

[5] (1963) 36 *Australian L.J.* at p.327; *cf.* F.T.P. Burt, *ibid.*, at pp. 323-4.

[6] Sir Owen Dixon, 'The Law and the Constitution' in *Jesting Pilate*, at p.53.

A federal system of government shows some of the fundamental tenets of the Austinian faith to be unsoundly based. Life is seldom so accommodating as to regulate its activities according to the source of command, and it is hard to avoid the conclusion that there are intractable problems in defining the extent to which the jurisdiction of a federal court is to be exclusive of the jurisdiction belonging to State courts or invested in them, and that an attempt at definition may produce a division of judicial power between the two systems in which neither is competent to administer the whole body of law. Was this too high a price to be exacted in the cause of new Benthamism? The question is not adequately answered by appeals to symmetry. One wonders whether it was squarely faced.

The Human Rights Bill went further in its proposal to remove the administration of federal law from the ordinary courts. It proposed a dispensing power over the application of positive law to another standard expressed in terms of legal or moral absolutes. The ability that it conferred to set at nought positive law appeared to be limited only by the willingness of the judges to work within an orthodox frame of reference when the bones acquired flesh and by the ability of Parliament to change the law. The first limitation would depend upon the assumption after an initial phase of creative enthusiasm of constraints from which new Benthamism was committed to escape. The second would depend upon the scope of the Commonwealth Parliament's power to alter a law enacted in the furtherance of obligations undertaken by international convention.

There is a more fundamental objection to the imposition of superior standards on the general body of law. It is aptly expressed in a comment upon the conceptual basis of the conflict between law and equity in the sixteenth century:

> When the legal process is seen as procuring a result which reflects a single absolute justice, it is hard to admit that a result can be properly procured and yet be wrong. And when the legal process is seen as the application of substantive rules, it is equally hard to admit that the substantive rules, properly applied, are somehow wrong.[7]

The basic question remains—is it wise that positive law should confer upon judges power which would be denied by the conventions within which they would otherwise act? The words of an American judge provide an answer based upon the experience of a lifetime in the system from which so many of the legal innovations of the Labor years were drawn, and also an epitaph for them. They refer to guarantees of individual rights and interests entrenched by law:

> Nor need it surprise us that these stately admonitions refuse to subject themselves to analysis. They are the precipitates of 'old, unhappy, far-off things, and battles long ago', originally cast as universals to enlarge the scope of the victory, to give it authority, to reassure the very victors themselves that they have been champions in something more momentous than a passing struggle. Thrown large upon the screen of the future as eternal verities, they are emptied of the vital occasions which gave them birth, and become moral adjurations, the more imperious because inscrutable, but with only that content which each generation must pour into them anew in the light of its own experience. If an independent judiciary seeks to fill them from its own bosom, in the end it will cease to be independent. And its independence will be well lost, for that bosom is not ample enough for the hopes and fears of all sorts and conditions of men, nor will its answers be theirs; it must be content to stand aside from these fateful battles. There are two ways in which the judges may forfeit their

---

[7]S.F.C. Milsom, *Historical Foundations of the Common Law* (London, 1969), at p.84. *Cf.* Sir Leslie Scarman, *English Law—the New Dimension* (Hamlyn Lectures, London, 1974), pp. 10-21; S.A. de Smith, *Constitutional and Administrative Law* (2nd ed., Harmondsworth, 1973), Ch. 20.

independence, if they do not abstain. If they are intransigent but honest, they will be curbed; but a worse fate will befall them if they learn to trim their sails to the prevailing winds... I believe that for by far the greater part of their work it is a condition upon the success of our system that the judges should be independent; and I do not believe that their independence should be impaired because of their constitutional function. But the price of this immunity, I insist, is that they should not have the last word in those basic conflicts of 'right and wrong—between whose endless jar justice resides'.... [T]his much I think I do know—that a society so riven that the spirit of moderation is gone, no court *can* save; that a society where that spirit flourishes no court *need* save; that in a society which evades its responsibility by thrusting upon the courts the nurture of that spirit, that spirit in the end will perish.[8]

---

[8]Learned Hand, 'The Contribution of an Independent Judiciary to Civilization' (1942) in *The Spirit of Liberty* (ed. Irving Dilliard, New York, 1954), pp. 163-5. *Cf.* E.V. Rostow, *The Sovereign Prerogative* (New Haven, 1962), at pp. 130-7, 161-70.

5 Ministers, Public Servants and the Executive Branch

Enid Campbell

I
INTRODUCTION

The matters with which this essay deals are, in the main, matters on which the Constitution of the Commonwealth is either silent or its provisions meagre. The principal provisions are to be found in Chapter II of the Constitution, entitled The Executive Government. Together with the so-called 'covering clauses' of the Imperial Act of which the Constitution is part, they establish the Commonwealth of Australia as a constitutional monarchy, absorb into the fabric of Commonwealth constitutional law much of the common law of England pertaining to the Crown, and entrench some of the basic features of what is styled the Westminster system of government.

The particular concerns of the essay are with the organization and machinery of the Executive Government; relationships between Ministers and officials; and issues relating to the accountability of both Ministers and officials. I have excluded from consideration questions concerning the reserve powers of the Governor-General and his relationship with Ministers.

II
MACHINERY OF GOVERNMENT

Departments of State

The authority of the Executive Government of the Commonwealth to order and re-order the administrative machinery of the national government, while not unlimited, remains very much at large and free from legislative constraints. This authority rests on s.61 of the Constitution, which provides that the executive power of the Commonwealth is vested in the Queen and is exercisable by the Governor-General as her representative, on s.64 which by necessary implication empowers the Governor-General in Council to create departments of state, and on s.67 which provides for the appointment of non-Ministerial offices by the Governor-General in Council or other delegated authority.

Today the number of statutory, non-departmental agencies of the Commonwealth government far exceeds the number of departments of state. Excluding the federal courts and the authorities established for the Commonwealth territories, the public authorities established by or under the laws of the Commonwealth as of 1975 numbered something in excess of two hundred. Even so, the department of state has held its place at the centre of the stage of government administration. Fluid both in form and function, the department of state is the unit of public administration most adaptable to the needs and purposes of an elected political executive. Departments may be created and abolished at will, likewise the allocation of functions among them and portfolios of statutes assigned to the administration of their Ministers. Departmental personnel being part of a unified public service may be redeployed not only to carry through changes pursuant to Administrative Arrangements Orders but according to the priorities of the government of the day.

Although the Constitution reposes the power of establishing departments of state in the Governor-General in Council, there appears to be no constitutional impediment to the Parliament itself legislating for the establishment of such departments or of particular ministries. Parliamentary authority in this regard is implicit in s.65 of the Constitution. In fact the Parliament has not chosen to inhibit the executive's discretion to form and reform departments. It is true that some Commonwealth statutes seem to presuppose the continued existence of certain ministries and departments,[1] but the effect of ss. 19, 19A and 19B of the *Acts Interpretation Act* 1901 is to preserve intact the power not only to create and abolish departments, but to reassign ministerial portfolios.

The Whitlam Government utilised this power to the full. By an Administrative Arrangements Order of 19 December 1972, fourteen existing departments were abolished, and a number of new departments created, producing a total of thirty-seven departments,[2] the administration of which was divided among twenty-seven Ministers. During the ensuing three years the number of departments was by degrees reduced to twenty-eight.

One of the side-effects of the changes in the administrative arrangements was the displacement of a number of the permanent heads of departments. Under s.54 of the *Public Service Act* 1922, the power of appointing permanent heads is vested in the Governor-General. Persons so appointed become, if they are not so already, officers of the Australian Public Service, and are included in the First Division of that Service.[3] Although appointments are to specific offices, permanent heads have no secured tenure in those offices as distinct from membership of the Service. The offices are as specified in the Third Schedule to the Act, though s.25(1) of the Act affirms the power of the Governor-General to abolish any of those offices, prescribe others in addition to or in lieu thereof, or alter their names. Upon notification of the fact in the Gazette, an exercise of this power amends the Third Schedule. Probably the mere alteration of the name of the office held by a permanent head does not affect his incumbency of it. The same cannot be said where the office held by him is abolished or another office prescribed in its place. There is not, it should be noted, any express power in the Act to require the transfer of a permanent head from one such office to another.

The administrative re-arrangements that were introduced following the change of government in December 1972 necessarily entailed relocation of a number of permanent heads. In the beginning only two of those appointed before December 1972 were displaced entirely from the ranks of the permanent heads, the remaining twenty-five either continuing in their current offices or transferring to other departments. However, in succeeding years fourteen of the twenty-five either retired (four) or were appointed to other positions. Yet another four permanent heads, all appointed as permanent heads for the first

---

[1] *E.g., Supply and Development Act* 1939; *Post and Telegraph Act* 1901.

[2] On the background to the Order see C. J. Lloyd & G. S. Reid, *Out of the Wilderness: The Return of Labor* (Melbourne, 1974), Ch. 4.

[3] Section 24(1).

time after December 1972, were to be displaced and not re-appointed as department heads. All of those who were displaced otherwise than by retirement were appointed to other Commonwealth government posts: posts overseas, statutory offices, special deputy secretary positions, commissioners of inquiry, the chairmanship of Qantas. Of the total number of appointments made to the office of permanent head between December 1972 and December 1975, twenty-one were first appointments to that office, seven of them from outside the Australian Public Service.[4]

The creation and abolition of departments and variation of their functions do not create any great constitutional problems. Administrative Arrangements Orders have legal consequences though they do not in themselves enlarge the total range of legal powers available either to Ministers or their departmental officials.[5] What functions are assigned to what departments and Ministers is a political question *par excellence*, and ordinarily of no concern to the courts of law. I say ordinarily because in considering whether or not legal officers employed in the Australian Legal Aid Office were capable of acting as solicitors to members of the public, the Supreme Court of the Australian Capital Territory clearly attached importance to the fact that these officers were also officers of the Attorney-General's Department, a department responsible amongst other things for criminal prosecutions and police. One of the judges, Fox J, ventured the comment: 'That the concentration of power involved is constitutionally unsound, and inimical to the proper administration of justice' was 'beyond question'.[6]

Although the number and arrangement of departments has been accepted as the 'prerogative' of the executive branch, to the extent that annual parliamentary appropriations vote funds department by department, administrative re-arrangements during the course of a financial year can have an important bearing on the effectiveness of parliamentary control over the purse strings. When presented in March 1973 with Appropriation Bills (Nos. 3 & 4) 1972-1973 for the appropriation of moneys for new and reconstituted departments, and for the validation of expenditure charged to existing appropriations, the Senate took the opportunity to express its displeasure. While agreeing to pass the Bills, it did so under protest that 'new Government departments were created prior to consulting with the Parliament and ensuring that sufficient moneys would be made available by the Parliament to service such departments'. In so resolving the Senate warned 'that should such a procedure be adopted in the future, then the Senate ought to reject such appropriation Bills'.[7]

Non-Departmental Agencies

The reconstruction by the Whitlam Government of the administrative machinery of the Commonwealth was not confined to the departments of state. Of no less significance was the increased use made of non-departmental agencies, both statutory and non-statutory, and the opportunities it fostered for employment of personnel from outside the Australian Public Service. The

---

[4]But two were recruited from Commonwealth statutory authorities.

[5]Joint Committee of Public Accounts, *Third Report.*

[6]*Re Bannister & Legal Practitioners Ordinance 1970-1975; Ex p. Hartstein* (1975) 5 A.C.T.R. 100, at p.108.

[7]Senate, *Debates*, 29 March 1973, vol. 55, p.704.

philosophy underlying the diversification of the sources and bases of the administrative and advisory support for the government was explained by the Prime Minister in the Sir Robert Garran Memorial Oration given on 12 November 1973. The system of support developed during the first year of office he described as 'a blending of five elements': 'the Public Service, impartial, responsible and professional; task forces and committees of inquiry, with all or a large part of the membership consisting of outside experts, highly competent in their particular fields; commissions and other continuing authorities, drawing staff from inside and outside the Service investigating and managing new areas of government initiatives; a new force of long term priorities advisers—a 'think-tank'—named the Priorities Review Staff; consultants and outside advisers for Ministers'.[8]

It is not difficult to understand why a government coming to office after twenty-three years in Opposition and with such an ambitious programme for change and expansion of Commonwealth government activity should not have been content to rely upon the administrative support and advice of the career Public Service. Quite apart from uncertain confidence in the ability of the Public Service to respond readily and sympathetically to the aspirations and requirements of the new government, there was the further consideration that the skills, experience and expertise needed for the development and implementation of a number of new programmes were not always to be found within the ranks of the Service (or in sufficient strength) and in addition a felt need to move quickly both in planning and execution.

During the Labor Government's term of office more than fifty statutory authorities were brought into being or reconstituted. This figure is, however, inflated by the inclusion of a number of agencies which existed in one form or another before December 1972, but which had not at the time been underwritten by statute. The new authorities included:

(a) commercial and semi-commercial corporations such as the Pipeline Authority, the abortive Petroleum and Minerals Authority,[9] the Australian Housing Corporation, the Postal Commission and the Telecommunications Commission, the last two being hived-off from the Postmaster-General's Department;

(b) special project agencies such as the Albury-Wodonga Corporation and the Darwin Reconstruction Commission;

(c) educational institutions such as the Legislative Drafting Institute, the Trade Union Training Authority and the Film and Television School;

(d) cultural institutions and agencies for the promotion of the arts such as the National Gallery, the Australia Council and the Film Commission;

(e) regulatory agencies such as the Prices Justification Tribunal and the Trade Practices Commission;

(f) a variety of advisory bodies concerned with planning, the development of new programmes, assistance to industry and special purposes grants to the States, e.g. the Hospitals and Health Services Commission, the Social Welfare Commission, the Children's Commission, the Schools Commission, the Law Reform Commission, and the Industries Assistance Commission (which replaced the Tariff Board);

---

[8](1973) 1 *Australian Government Digest* 1600, at p.1602.
[9]See *Victoria* v. *Commonwealth* (*P.M.A. Case*) (1975) 7 A.L.R. 1.

(g) executive agencies to manage new programmes, e.g. the Health Insurance Commission;

(h) appellate tribunals such as the Administrative Appeals Tribunal and the Student Assistance Tribunals.

Doubtless there were various considerations which moved the Government to prefer statutory authorities to departments: in some instances a desire to ensure freedom from direct political control, in others to facilitate the conduct of an activity which did not lend itself to the normal system of departmental management and financing, to allow for staffing outside the Public Service Act, engagement of the services of persons from outside the Australian Public Service, full-time or part-time, and to provide for the representation of different interests on governing bodies. There could also have been some feeling that the creation of a statutory authority made political initiatives not only more visible but less easy to undo.

Statutory authorities are not newcomers to Commonwealth government administration, but their proliferation does present problems, particularly when the functions committed to them are not materially different from those traditionally performed by departments. One of the perennial problems of constitutional significance has been how to accommodate the desired measure of independence from political control with the central principles of the Westminster system which require, *inter alia,* accountability to the Parliament for the exercise of public powers which Parliament has conferred. That system tends to be associated with the practice of appointing Ministers administering departments of state from among members of Parliament and of holding those Ministers answerable to the Parliament for the actions of their subordinates. While in one sense the Minister administering the Act from which a statutory agency derives its authority may be held answerable to Parliament for the actions of that agency, he cannot be regarded as being responsible in the sense of being held culpable for actions which legally he had no authority to control or direct.

The statutory authorities of the Commonwealth differ markedly in the degree to which they are formally and actually independent of ministerial control and direction. In some instance the statute is silent on the Minister's role and powers; in others there is express power given to the Minister to give directions, generally, or in relation to policy, or in relation to the exercise of particular functions.[10] There are also some cases in which, although the agency is not subject to ministerial direction, it is obliged by its statute to have regard to government policy or principles enunciated in the statute itself.[11]

Australian constitutional theory offers less than certain guidance on ministerial authority to control, direct and influence the actions of statutory officers and agencies, at least when the statute itself does not advert to the question.[12] Certainly there was no fund of settled doctrine to which appeal might have been made when a question arose in March 1973 about the Attorney-General's authority to intervene in the affairs of the Australian Security Intelligence

[10]See, *e.g., Industrial Research and Development Grants Act* 1967, s.17; *Reserve Bank Act* 1959, s.11; *Postal Services Act* 1975, s.8; *Housing Loans Insurance Act* 1965; *Australian Industry Development Corporation Act* 1970, ss. 8A, 9.

[11]*E.g. Australian Industry Development Corporation Act* 1970, s.8; *Industries Assistance Commission Act* 1973, s.22.

[12]See *R.* v. *Anderson; Ex parte Ipec-Air Pty Ltd* (1965) 113 C.L.R. 177.

Organization. The *Australian Security Intelligence Organization Act* 1956 provides, *inter alia*, that the Organization 'shall bc under the control of the Director-General' of Security, but on the Minister's powers is silent. In the Senate on 27 March 1973, Senator Carrick asked the Attorney-General whether he agreed with the statement by a former Attorney-General, Dr H. V. Evatt, on 20 September 1949 that

> To all intents and purposes the Director-General of Security is free from ministerial direction. That arrangement is essential in order to maintain maximum internal security which, I have no doubt, all honourable members wish to have preserved.[13]

The Attorney-General replied that in his view the Director-General was subject to the directions of himself, as were other officers of the Organization. That view was based on s.6 of the Act which provides that the Director-General holds office on such terms and conditions as the Governor-General determines.[14]

Later in 1973 an opportunity was to arise for judicial testing of the effectiveness of statutory provisions which expressly limited ministerial authority to override decisions taken by an otherwise autonomous agency. That opportunity was provided by the institution of relator proceedings in the Supreme Court of the Australian Capital Territory to restrain the Postmaster-General and the Minister for Works from proceeding with the erection of a Post Office tower on Black Mountain. The National Capital Development Commission, which, under its Act, has the functions of undertaking and carrying out the planning, development and construction of Canberra as the national capital,[15] did not approve of the development. Smithers J agreed with the relators' contention that in erecting the tower against the will of the Commission the defendants were exercising functions committed by statute exclusively to the Commission.[16] He noted that under s.12 of the National Capital Development Commission Act, the Governor-General had power, in the event of the Minister and the Commission being unable to reach agreement as to the policy which the Commission should follow in relation to any matter, to make an order determining the policy to be adopted by the Commission. But at the time no such order had been made and it was not clear whether an order would be made. Accordingly, he granted an injunction. Subsequently an order was made under s.12, thereby paving the way for a successful appeal to the High Court on other grounds.[17] Seemingly both the Supreme Court and the High Court were satisfied that an order overriding the Commission on a particular planning decision was capable of being regarded as a determination of policy to be adopted.

When it is envisaged that a statutory authority should be subject to ministerial direction generally, on policy or on specific matters, it is, in my view, desirable that the power of direction be made explicit in the enabling statute, and that in order to fix responsibility where it clearly lies, there be a requirement that directions given be publicly notified by gazettal, recording in the

---

[13]Senate, *Debates*, 27 March 1973, vol. 55, p.560.

[14]*ibid.*

[15]*National Capital Development Commission Act* 1957, s.11(1).

[16]*Kent* v. *Johnson* (1973) 21 F.L.R. 177.

[17]*Johnson* v. *Kent* (*Black Mountain Tower Case*) (1975) 132 C.L.R. 164.

authority's annual report or tabling in Parliament. Practice in this regard has not been consistent.[18]

How much independence a statutory authority actually enjoys depends on a number of factors, including the terms of appointment of its governing members. The practice of reserving the power of appointment to the political executive enlarges the scope for patronage but does not of itself ensure compliance with the executive's will, especially if security of tenure is afforded during the currency of office. In a memorandum to the Joint Committee of Public Accounts in 1955 the then Chairman of the Australian Broadcasting Commission defended the appointment of part-time members as providing an essential balance between independence and public accountability. He reasoned thus:

> If an adequate measure of independence of operation and public accountability is to lie with the members of a corporation, it is essential that Parliament through its Minister should be in a position to change the personnel of its corporations at short term. The right to dispense with members at the end of statutory terms without reason given or required is the most vital of the reserved powers and the one most easily and properly exercised. Such a power cannot with equity be exercised if the members of the corporation are required to abandon their other means of livelihood, and the appropriate reserve powers of Parliament are to that extent unduly abridged.[19]

There are nonetheless some part-time appointments which potentially may compromise the independence of statutory agencies. These include the appointment of senior departmental officers and nominees or representatives of the employees of the agency. The statutory charters of a number of statutory bodies—among them the Australian Industry Development Corporation, the Australian Heritage Commission, the Australian Housing Corporation, the Australian Postal Commission, the Australian Telecommunications Commission and the Reserve Bank—provide for ex officio membership of permanent heads of designated departments or of departmental officers. Such provisions may facilitate liaison between the agency and the department administering the relevant Act, but there is always a danger that the departmental member will see his function as being primarily to represent and prosecute the point of view of the department and perhaps its Minister.[20] Similarly conflicts of interest and duty may arise when members include nominees of staff.[21] In the Supreme Court of New South Wales, Street J has stressed that even though the members of a statutory board have been elected by interest groups they are not 'a mere channel of communication or listening post'. 'The consideration which must in board affairs govern each individual member is the advancement of the public purpose for which parliament has set up the board.'[22] The same must hold true for appointed members.

---

[18]See, *e.g., Broadcasting and Television Act* 1942, s.78A; *Australian Coastal Shipping Commission Act* 1956, s.17; *Reserve Bank Act* 1959, s.11; *Postal Services Act* 1975, s.8; *Australian Housing Corporation Act* 1975, s.48; *Australian Apple and Pear Corporation Act* 1973, s.37; *Hospitals and Health Services Commission Act* 1973, s.32.

[19]*Twenty-Second Report*, p.94.

[20]See the opinion of Sir Kenneth Bailey in Joint Committee of Public Accounts, *Twenty-Second Report*.

[21]The appointment of staff members was provided for in the *Postal Services Act* 1975 and the *Telecommunications Act* 1975. A staff member has been appointed to the Australian Broadcasting Commission after election, but without amendment of the Broadcasting and Television Act.

[22]*Bennetts* v. *Board of Fire Commissioners of New South Wales* (1967) 87 W.N. (N.S.W.) 307, at p.310.

Public Servants and Statutory Officers

Not all of the statutory authorities established under the Labor Government were to survive. The Cities Commission which in 1973 succeeded the National Urban and Regional Development Authority established in October 1972 was abolished by statute in 1975 and in the same year the Government announced its intention to introduce legislation to repeal the *Social Welfare Commission Act* 1973. These moves underlined the insecurity of the tenure of those statutory office-holders who are appointed from outside the Australian Public Service, who are not covered by the *Officers' Rights Declaration Act* 1928 and who are not thereby qualified for re-instatement in the Service. The Judicial Committee of the Privy Council has held[23] that the abolition by statute of a public office has the effect of discharging any contractual rights of the office-holder, and terminating authority for payment of salary, without creating any legally enforceable right to compensation for premature loss of office. This is an unsatisfactory state of affairs which ideally should be cured by legislation.

From a constitutional point of view one of the most interesting aspects of the Whitlam Government's moves to diversify the sources of administrative support and advice was the extent to which it was prepared to act independently of legislation. There is nothing in the Constitution which compels the Executive Government to work through departments of state,[24] and it has never been disputed that the executive power of the Commonwealth extends to the appointment by Letters Patent of royal commissions of inquiry—though not, of course, the grant to commissioners so appointed of coercive authority.[25] What is not entirely clear is what scope is now left for the operation of s.67 of the Constitution.

The section gives to the Governor-General in Council power to appoint officers of the Executive Government (other than Ministers) until the Parliament otherwise provides. The *Public Service Act* 1922, enacted partly pursuant to ss. 51(36) and 67, exhaustively regulates employment of personnel in departments of state as servants of the Crown in right of the Commonwealth, whether as officers, temporary employees or as exempt officers or employees.[26] Although the creation and abolition of offices in departments in ultimately the function of the Governor-General in Council, establishment proposals cannot be approved except on the recommendation of the Public Service Board after having received a report from the relevant departmental head.[27] Under the Act appointments, promotions and transfers to positions in departments are matters in which Ministers have no part whatsoever.[28]

Presumably an office is an office in a department of state simply by virtue of its having been created as such pursuant to the Public Service Act. But there is probably no constitutional or legal inhibition on the creation by the

---

[23] *C. B. Reilly* v. *The King* [1934] A.C. 176.

[24] See *R.* v. *Macfarlane; Ex p. O'Flanagan and O'Kelly* (1923) 32 C.L.R. 518, at p.533; *New South Wales* v. *Commonwealth* (1915) 20 C.L.R. 54, at p.89 (the Inter-State Commission 'is to be a department of the Crown to assist in executing and maintaining trade and commercial law in Australia').

[25] *Colonial Sugar Refining Co. Ltd* v. *A.-G. (Commonwealth)* (1912) 15 C.L.R. 182; *McGuiness* v. *A.-G. (Victoria)* (1940) 63 C.L.R. 73.

[26] See ss. 8A, 82. Exempt officers and employees are those exempted by order of the Governor-General from the operation of specified provisions of the Act.

[27] Section 29.

[28] The power of appointment resides with the Public Service Board. Promotions and transfers are primarily the responsibility of permanent heads, but the Board also has a role.

Governor-General in Council or his delegates of non-departmental offices of the Executive Government and the appointment of persons to occupy those offices. The non-departmental character of the office would, I suppose, depend entirely on the duties attaching to the office: whether, for example, the office-holder was or was not subject to direction by a permanent head, whether he was charged with the performance of functions or the administration of legislation already committed to a department. While there can be little doubt about the sufficiency of s.67 of the Constitution to support the appointment of diplomatic representatives and royal commissioners, there are bound to be borderline cases where reliance on the section would be unsafe and where the prudent course would be to take advantage of the provision that already exists in s.8A of the Public Service Act for the engagement of 'irregulars' on special terms.

Persons engaged in the service of the Executive Government under s.67 of the Constitution do not of course become members of the Australian Public Service, and subject to any contractual arrangements that might have been made, they are liable to dismissal at pleasure, without right to compensation.[29]

Section 67 clearly has no relevance at all to the engagement by the Commonwealth of independent contractors for the supply of services, e.g. consultants. The making of contracts of this kind is regulated by the Treasury Regulations, which require approval of the proposed contract by the Minister or his delegate.[30] The Regulations permit the Secretary to the Treasury to grant dispensation in certain cases from the normal requirement that contracts in excess of a prescribed sum for the procurement of supplies (which include services) be not entered into unless tenders have been invited[31] and such a dispensation has been made in respect of a variety of professional services and management consultancy services.[32]

Following the imposition in June 1974 of a 2.6 per cent ceiling on the annual growth of full-time staff employed under the Public Service Act, the Prime Minister, acting on advice from the Public Service Board, took steps to ensure that the ceiling was not evaded by the expedient of hiring of consultants and staff on contract. On 16 September 1974 all Ministers were informed that henceforth departments and statutory authorities staffed under the Public Service Act would be required to obtain the approval of the Board before engaging either consultants or staff on contract.[33] This instruction was supplemented and amplified by a series of Board memoranda.

The control thus sought to be imposed represents an interesting example of quasi-legislation by Prime Ministerial decree. The direction given by the Prime Minister and the subsequent circulars from the Public Service Board were clearly intended to fetter the discretion given to individual Ministers under the Treasury Regulations and to operate in the same way as Treasury Directions given under reg. 127A of the Treasury Regulations.[34] Whether or not the action taken legally had the effect of limiting the scope of ministerial authority to make contracts for the procurement of services, so that the Commonwealth

---

[29]For a useful survey see P. W. Hogg, *Liability of the Crown* (Melbourne, 1971) pp. 150-8; see also G. Nettheim, '*Dunn* v. *The Queen* Revisited' [1975] *Cambridge L. J.* 253.

[30]Regs. 4(1), 49.

[31]Reg. 52AA.

[32]*Treasury Directions* 31/23, 31/55.

[33]A slightly different arrangement was made in relation to situations in which consultants and contract staff had customarily been engaged for certain departmental work.

[34]See *Audit Act* 1901, s.71(2).

would not be contractually bound by agreements made without the Board's approval, is debatable.

Ministerial Staffs

One of the administrative innovations of the Labor Government which was to provoke controversy was the upgrading and enlargement of the personal staffs of Ministers. As of 20 April 1972, the total of ministerial staff was 155; by 25 November 1974 the number had grown to 209; and by 10 November 1975 to 219.[35] Over this period there was also an increase in the proportion of staff engaged in more senior advisory positions. This reflected an altered conception of the role of a Minister's private office. At a press conference on 5 December 1972, the Prime Minister explained that the intention was 'to de-politicize the public service so that persons who are responsible for carrying out political decisions will be known to be appointed by a Minister at his whim and disposable at his whim. The public service, of course, will be less political if these are such personal advisers known to be appointed'. On a later occasion he justified the reinforcement of ministerial private offices partly on the ground that the assistance to be provided by those offices would help Ministers 'to exercise their proper constitutional authority' over departments in accordance with the spirit of the Westminster system.[36]

Appointments as personal staff were effected either by secondment from the Australian Public Service[37] or by the use of the provisions in the Public Service Act regarding employment in a temporary capacity or as exempt employees. While they were truly personal appointments, the Public Service Board played an important part in developing staffing structures, and general oversight of appointments was exercised by the Prime Minister.

Inevitably there were teething pains generated in part by uncertainty about the functions to be performed by ministerial staff, their relationship with departmental officers, their authority and responsibilities. Some clarification was achieved by Prime Ministerial directive. In a letter to Ministers and permanent heads on 29 March 1974 the Prime Minister stated that 'each member of a Minister's staff, including seconded departmental officers, is subject to direction by the Minister alone and is likewise responsible to the Minister alone'. Previously in the Sir Robert Garran Memorial Oration the Prime Minister had stressed that ministerial staff should be regarded as an extension of the Minister. 'They are', he said, 'part of the government in its political and personal sense, and in that sense, they are responsible to the people, their paymasters and political masters in the same way as Ministers.'[38]

Reactions to the new version of the ministerial private office were, not surprisingly, mixed, and not the least within the Public Service itself. Some senior officers in the Service expressed satisfaction at the prospect of being relieved of pressures to lend assistance to Ministers in purely party political matters. There was acknowledgment, too, of the value of the stimulus that might come from Ministers having alternative sources of advice and of the desirability of providing Ministers with assistance on aspects of their work

---

[35]The figures were compiled for the Royal Commission on Australian Government Administration.

[36](1973) 1 *Australian Government Digest* 1600, at p.1607.

[37]It has been estimated that at least half were in this category.

[38](1973) 1 *Australian Government Digest*, 1600, at p.1607.

which fell outside the domain of the particular department, e.g. work associated with the Minister's role as a party leader, and with Cabinet business arising from submissions of other Ministers and departments, and public relations generally. On the other hand, fears were expressed lest the ministerial private office should drive a wedge between the Minister and his department and isolate Ministers even further from the departments they administer, which they do mostly from the distance of their rooms in Parliament House. There were some complaints about what was felt to be improper intrusion by ministerial advisers in departmental affairs. But equally there were those who considered that there would be merit in associating ministerial advisers more closely with departmental operations, both for the sake of ensuring that the work of the department was more closely attuned to the Minister's thinking and of guarding against the risk of policies being formulated in the abstract without sufficient regard to the practicalities of administration and the collected experience of professional administrators. Doubtless different reactions were prompted in part by varying experiences and encounters with the private offices.

The Labor Government's development of the Ministerial private office over a little less than three years was probably not long enough to allow for the establishment of what could be recognised as constitutional conventions concerning the roles and responsibilities of those offices. Some academics speculated that what was emerging was something akin to the French cabinet system. More pragmatically, the Public Service Board submitted to the Royal Commission on Australian Government Administration that the whole concept of the ministerial private office being different from that of departments of state staffed by career public servants, the time was ripe for the employment of ministerial staff to be regulated specifically and outside the Public Service Act.

The strengthening of ministerial private offices during the Labor Government's term of office threw into relief a feature of the ministerial system at the federal level which distinguishes it from the ministerial system operating in the United Kingdom. The difference, which was adverted to by Mr Whitlam in his Sir Robert Garran Memorial Oration, is that in the United Kingdom principal Ministers receive assistance from various grades of junior office bearers who are also members of Parliament. The membership of the United Kingdom Parliament, being so much greater than that of the Commonwealth Parliament, provides a much larger pool from which to draw ministerial understudies and aides. But the chief difficulty in Australia is constitutional in origin. While s.64 may not prevent the appointment of more than one salaried Minister to administer a department of state, or even the appointment of 'overlord' Ministers superintending clusters of departments, it is generally understood to require that salaried office bearers of the Executive Government who are appointed from the ranks of parliamentarians must be appointed to administer a department, so that neither a senator nor a member of the House of Representatives can be appointed to, and remunerated for the occupancy of, the office of Assistant Minister or Parliamentary Under-Secretary—at least without risking disqualification from his parliamentary office. This inhibition does not preclude the appointment of Assistant Ministers. It means merely that an Assistant Minister needs to be appointed to administer a department of state in his own right, albeit a small and unimportant department which may have been created solely for the purpose of avoiding the constitutional hazards.[39]

This is one aspect of the Constitution which merits attention in any future re-examination of the provisions which affect the makeup and organisation of the Executive Branch.

III
MINISTERS AND OFFICIALS

Events were to occur during the Labor Government's administration which raised critical issues concerning the respective roles and responsibilities of Ministers and their departmental officers. Of these the most important were undoubtedly the issues presented by the Government's moves to raise loans overseas and the subsequent questioning of the Government's actions in the Parliament.

The Responsibility of Permanent Heads

One question of principle which arose for consideration was the division of authority and responsibility between Ministers and the permanent heads of their departments. This was a matter on which the Prime Minister sought the opinion of the Solicitor-General in relation to the action of the Secretary to the Treasury in seeking advice from the permanent head of the Attorney-General's Department, without the Treasurer's knowledge and consent on the legal effect of a letter written by the Treasurer. The particular letter had been prepared within the Minister's private office without reference to the Department.[40]

In the course of his opinion the Solicitor-General considered the effect of s.25(2) of the Public Service Act and its relationship to s.64 of the Constitution. The sub-section, which has in the past been regarded by some permanent heads as a basis for resisting ministerial intrusion into the day to day management of departments, provides that

> The Permanent Head of a Department shall be responsible for its general working, and for all the business thereof, and shall advise the Minister in all matters relating to the Department.

The material part of s.64 of the Constitution provides that

> The Governor-General may appoint officers to administer such departments of State of the Commonwealth as the Governor-General in Council may establish.

According to the Solicitor-General, s.25(2) must be read subject to s.64 such that in exercise of his responsibilities under the sub-section the permanent head is subordinate to his Minister.[41] In support he quoted from an opinion given in January 1944 by the then Attorney-General, Dr H. V. Evatt, in which the following views were expressed:[42]

> The true position is that section 25(2) is intended as a general definition of the responsibility of a Permanent Head, but it must be read with the qualification that the

---

[39]See E. Campbell, 'Ministerial Arrangements under the Constitution', *Report of Royal Commission on Australian Government Administration* (1976), App 1.G: vol. 1, pp. 191-210.

[40]House of Representatives, *Debates*, 9 July 1975, vol. 95, pp. 3582-9.

[41]*ibid.*, at p.3587.

[42]*ibid.*, at pp. 3587-8.

responsibility is subject to the higher responsibility of the Minister and must be exercised subject to the Minister's direction and control. So construed, section 25(2) conforms to the undoubted constitutional position, and subject to that qualification it stands as part of the statute law of the Commonwealth . . . The section must be read so as to harmonise with the practical working of our system of Government. Therefore, although the section has the force of law as regards the internal organization of Departments of the Public Service, it is, in relation to the Government, really an administrative provision and does not operate as a legal limitation on the Minister in the execution of his responsibility as head of the department.

. . .

Precise definition of the responsibilities and powers of the Permanent Head . . . or adjustments of those responsibilities and powers relatively to other persons . . . are, in my opinion, matters for the decision of the Minister of the Department, subject, of course, to the concurrence of other Ministers who may be concerned, or the approval of the Cabinet, where circumstances make such concurrence or approval advisable. In my opinion, section 25(2) of the Commonwealth Public Service Act is no bar to exercise by the Minister of his authority in this matter.

As a general statement of the responsibilities of permanent heads, these opinions would probably command general support. Also, they conform with the thinking behind s.25(2) which was not to insulate departmental heads from ministerial control but to make it clear that the statutory functions of the central personnel authority did not extend to management of departments. Commenting on the clause in the original Public Service Bill of 1902 from which s.25(2) is taken, the Minister for Home Affairs, Sir William Lyne, said this:[43]

Now I come to the internal administration of the different departments. The administration is to be conferred upon the permanent head . . . The clause does not mean that the permanent head is allowed to do exactly as he likes. The Minister must look to see that the work of the permanent head is properly done. I have inserted the clause after the experience I have had of the public service of New South Wales. We have sometimes had the head of the department fighting with the [Public Service] Commissioners and feeling that he has been oppressed by them. We could not have the work done as it should be done under such conditions.

The subordination of the permanent head's responsibilities under s.25(2) to those of the Minister is reinforced by s.17 of the Public Service Act, sub-section (2) of which requires that proposals and suggestions made by the Public Service Board in exercise of its functions under sub-section (1)[44] be communicated first to the permanent head for consideration and action. Sub-section (3), which provides for communication with the Minister in the event of the permanent head not concurring with the Board's proposals or not acting on them within a reasonable time, presupposes that the Minister may give directions to his Permanent Head on the matters to which the Board's recommendations relate.

To say that constitutionally the responsibilities of a permanent head under s.25(2) are subject to the higher authority of the Minister under s.64 of the Constitution does not, however, take us very far in settling the scope of the Minister's authority and correspondingly the permanent head's obligations. Section 64 cannot, I suggest, be regarded as an independent source of legal authority enabling Ministers to take action not permitted by common law. Its paramount purpose was simply to entrench the Westminster convention that

[43]House of Representatives, *Debates*, 13 June 1901, vol. 1, p.1083.

[44]Generally these functions relate to promotion and review of efficiency and economy in the management and operation of departments.

Ministers should be members of Parliament and thereby on hand to answer for the actions of the departments under their charge. While it may be invoked in aid of general assertions of power to command departmental activities, it cannot in my view stand in the way of a clear statutory enactment vesting specific legal powers in departmental officers or others. Certainly it has never been suggested that s.64 constrains the Parliament's power to repose authority directly in departmental officers and to require that such authority be exercised independently. While it may be that a statute which vests authority directly in such an officer may in some cases be read as being subject to the implied qualification that the officer shall exercise his power in accordance with ministerial policy,[45] there can certainly be no universal rule that because the repository of a statutory power happens to be an officer of a department of state, he is subordinate in the exercise of that power to the political head of the department. Were there such a general rule, there would be no scope at all for the operation of what is termed the 'independent discretion' rule according to which the Crown escapes vicarious liability for the wrongs of its servants when they are exercising powers in an independent capacity. That rule has been applied without question to departmental officers in the exercise of authority directly conferred upon them by statute.[46]

Unfortunately judicial precedents offer little guidance on the circumstances in which a departmental officer may properly be directed by the Minister in exercising discretions granted to him directly by legislation rather than by delegation. In the leading Australian case *R. v. Anderson; Ex p. Ipec-Air Pty Ltd*,[47] which concerned the exercise of the power granted to the Director-General of Civil Aviation under the Customs (Prohibited Imports) Regulations to issue licences for the import of aircraft, the judges were divided not merely on the question of whether the Director-General had in the particular instance decided under ministerial dictation, but also on the weight that the Director-General might properly give to ministerial policy. Windeyer J, at one extreme, took the view 'that the only consideration to which the Director-General could properly have been guided was the policy of the Government'.[48] In so concluding he was influenced by the fact that the Director-General was the permanent head of a department, the fact that the legislation did not lay down any criteria according to which the discretion to grant import licences was to be exercised, and the fact that the constitutional validity of the regulations depended on ultimate ministerial responsibility for decisions taken under them.[49]

Menzies J, in contrast, thought that although the Director-General could, by reason of the position he occupied, take government policy into consideration,

> There is, nevertheless, a significant difference between a discretion given to a minister and one given to a departmental head. When the latter is nominated, he must arrive at his own decision upon the merits of the application and must not merely express a decision made by the government. The position in which such an officer is put is not an easy one, but the sound theory behind conferring a discretion upon a departmental head rather than his minister is that government policy should not outweigh every other consideration. A sound governmental tradition of respect for those who shoulder

---

[45] *R. v. Anderson; Ex parte Ipec-Air Pty Ltd* (1965) 113 C.L.R. 177.
[46] *Baume v. Commonwealth* (1906) 4 C.L.R. 97.
[47] (1965) 113 C.L.R. 177.
[48] *ibid.*, at p.204.
[49] *ibid.*, at pp. 204-6.

the responsibilities of their office in making unwelcome decisions makes the choice of a departmental head, rather than his minister, as the one to exercise a discretion conferred by the legislature a real and important distinction. There are, it seems to me, sound grounds for treating a decision to be made at departmental level as something substantially different from a decision to be made at the political level.[50]

The duty to defer to and carry out ministerial instructions, where it exists, is, of course, limited to lawful directions,[51] and in this context, an unlawful direction would presumably include not only a direction compliance with which would result in the commission of a civil or criminal wrong, but a direction which if carried out would result in an excess or abuse of power. Precisely what an official should do when he has reason to question the legality of the action required of him by the Minister (or for that matter a superior officer) or the legality of action already taken by the Minister and with which he is about to be involved, is a matter of difficulty and delicacy. There is no officially endorsed code of ethics for the Australian Public Service which would provide guidance in this regard, though there are unofficial prescriptions suggesting procedures that ought to be followed.[52]

These unofficial prescriptions suggest that where there are grounds for disquiet the matter ought first be discussed directly with the Minister and that only where this step has been taken should advice be sought from the Solicitor-General or Public Service Board, or complaint made to the Prime Minister.

It is worth noting that in the United Kingdom there is a well understood practice that if the permanent head of a department, in his capacity as chief accounting officer, has reason to question the regularity of ministerial directions on financial matters, he may state his objections in writing and decline to carry out the Minister's decision unless the Minister instructs him in writing to do so. The Commonwealth Treasury Regulations, which govern the financial administration of departments, apply equally to Ministers and departmental officers. Given the responsibilities of permanent heads under s. 25(2) of the Public Service Act, the potential liability of officers to surcharge under the Audit Act, and the fact that difficulties have already arisen between departments and Ministers in the administration of departmental finances,[53] there would seem to be merit in the adoption of a similar practice in Australia.

Executive Privilege

The circumstance which presented the most acute problems concerning the relationship between Ministers and officials was the decision by the Senate in July 1975[54] to summon before it eleven senior departmental officers and the Solicitor-General to answer questions, produce all documents, files and papers in their possession, custody or control (not as yet tabled) which were relevant to dealings of the Government's Ministers, servants and agents prior to and subsequent to the Executive Council meeting on 13 December 1974, at which

[50]*ibid.*, at p.202.

[51]*ibid.*, at p.206. See also Maurice Wright, 'The Professional Conduct of Public Servants' (1973) 51 *Pub. Admin.* 1.

[52]'Draft of a Code of Ethics for Public Servants' (1965) 24 *Pub. Admin. (Syd.)* 195; R.S. Parker in *Decisions*, ed. B.B. Schaffer & D.C. Corbett (Melbourne, 1965), pp. 201-22.

[53]See *Report of the Auditor-General upon the Department of Aboriginal Affairs* (Parliamentary Paper 13 of 1974).

[54]Senate, *Debates*, 9 July 1975, vol. 64, pp. 2693-4, 2710.

meeting authority had been given to the Minister for Minerals and Energy to borrow US$4,000 million for temporary purposes. Following the issue and service of the summonses, the Prime Minister, on 15 July 1975, wrote to the President of the Senate informing him that while the public servants summoned would attend before the Senate, each would 'be instructed by his Minister to claim privilege in respect of answers to all questions upon the matters contained in the Resolution of the Senate and in respect of the production of all documents ... relevant to those matters'.[55] The Prime Minister went on to explain why privilege would be claimed:

> The inquiry is plainly an inquiry into Government policy and decisions of Government. The principle of ministerial responsibility is, and must remain, the keystone of our Parliamentary system. In keeping with that principle, officers do not decide, and are not responsible for, Government policy or Government action.
>
> What I have just said reflects a time-honoured constitutional principle of the greatest importance. It is a principle that has been frequently stated and has been endorsed by, among others, Sir Robert Menzies, who has written ... 'it would be curious and alarming if an anti-Government Senate could undermine the objectivity and non-political integrity of the Public Service by exposing its senior and most responsible officers to a Parliamentary inquisition from which they had a right to be immune and compelling their entry into a field of political debate'.
>
> In the Government's view, the real intention of the non-Government parties in the Senate is to seek to avoid the normal and proper procedures of the Parliament.

Then, after reviewing the responses already made to questioning in both the House of Representatives and the Senate, the Prime Minister concluded:

> It is clear that the non-Government parties in the Senate have by no means fully tested this matter through the normal and proper Parliamentary procedures available to them—in debate, in questions and, if necessary, in urgency motions or even no confidence motions. The House of Representatives was recalled so that the normal and proper Parliamentary procedures could apply. What the Opposition proposes is a procedure essentially foreign and contrary to established Parliamentary principles and practice.
>
> I make plain the Government's view that what the Senate is seeking to do is to obtain through officers of the Public Service information and documents which should be sought from Ministers by the normal and proper procedures of the Parliament. In taking this course, the fundamental character of Ministerial responsibility is challenged. It is the Government—not the Public Service—that will answer in the Parliament any request, any challenge put to it. It is the Government—not the Public Service—that is responsible to the people. This is in accord with the principles on which our democracy is based. If these principles are successfully challenged, Government would become unworkable.

As foreshadowed by the Prime Minister, claims of privilege were made by all the Ministers concerned[56] and separately by the Solicitor-General in respect of the summons served upon him.[57] Each Minister certified that the answering of any questions on the matters contained in the Resolution and the production of documents, files or papers relevant to those matters by officers of his department 'would be detrimental to the proper functioning of the Public Service and its relationship to government and would be injurious to the public interest'. Subsequently, each of the Ministers concerned took the precaution of instructing the witness that 'if the Senate rejects the general claim of privilege

---

[55]Senate, *Debates*, 15 July 1975, vol. 64, pp. 2729.

[56]Senate, *Debates*, 15 July 1975, vol. 64, pp. 2729-30.

[57]*ibid.*, at pp. 2730-1.

made by you, you are to decline to answer any questions addressed to you upon the matters contained in the Resolution of the Senate and to decline to produce any documents, files or papers relevant to those matters'.[58] The President of the Senate was advised accordingly. Before the witnesses were called to the Bar of the Senate, a motion was moved and passed on the procedure to be followed in the examination of witnesses, which procedure was to operate notwithstanding anything in the Standing Orders. The procedure agreed upon anticipated and made provision for claims of Crown privilege.[59] Rules 10 and 12 provided:

(10) A witness who is a departmental officer may be asked to state facts and explain any aspect of Government policy relevant to the inquiry and how it was arrived at, but may object to giving answers to questions which require him to express a personal opinion.
(12) A witness asked a question, or asked to produce documents, which in his opinion could be contrary to the public interest to answer or produce, shall have an opportunity to consult with his Minister on the matter; whereupon a motion may be moved forthwith by any Senator that further examination of the witness be deferred to a later hour or to the next day of sitting or that the sitting of the Senate be suspended to a later hour or adjourned to the next day of sitting. . .

On their appearance before the Senate, each of the public servant witnesses indicated that he regarded himself as bound by his Minister's instruction not to answer questions, and each in turn was, after unproductive questioning, excused from attendance. The Solicitor-General likewise declined to answer questions on the matters contained in the Senate resolution, not because he had received a ministerial direction, but because, he said, in law the counsels of the Crown are secret, and as Solicitor-General, he could not do anything inconsistent with the privilege asserted by the Crown.[60] He, in turn, was excused from attendance. On the following day (17 July), the Senate resolved, *inter alia*, that the ministerial directions regarding privilege and the claim of privilege by the Solicitor-General be referred to the Committee of Privileges for report by 30 September 1975, and that for the purposes of this inquiry and report, the Committee should have power to send for persons, papers and records.[61]

The Senate Committee of Privileges presented their report on the matters referred by the Senate on 17 July 1975, in October 1975. The report was agreed to by only four of the members, Labor Senators Button, Devitt, Everett and Mulvihill. The remaining three members of the Committee, Opposition Senators Greenwood, Webster and Wright, presented a dissenting report.

Serious reservations were expressed by the majority about the way in which the Committee's terms of reference had been framed. Not only did they contain 'a highly political allegation', namely that 'the action of the Government in directing public servants called to the Bar of the Senate not to answer any questions is a massive cover-up', but they were misconceived. They failed to indicate precisely what it was on which report was desired. There had been no specific allegation of breach of parliamentary privilege. Moreover the resolution of 17 July referring the Ministers' actions to the Committee was, in their view, inconsistent with the resolution of the previous day which had 'proceeded

[58]Senate, *Debates,* 16 July 1975, vol. 64, pp. 2762-3.
[59]*ibid.,* at p.2764.
[60]*ibid.,* at p.2781; see also p.2730.
[61]Senate, *Debates,* vol. 64, 17 July 1975, pp. 2806-7, 2831.

on the assumption that claims of privilege would be made by the witnesses, and that these claims would be adjudicated by the Senate'.

The majority noted that the Committee had given consideration to whether they should request the Senate to discharge its reference of 17 July and replace it by another reference requiring examination of 'the powers asserted by the Senate and the concept of 'Crown Privilege' as a question of principle'. But this suggested course had not been acceptable to the minority.

The majority seemed to accept that while there was no formal limitation on the power of the Senate to require the production of documents or the giving of oral evidence by officers of the Executive, the Senate ought to exercise self-restraint in the use it made of that power. In particular they thought that the Senate should defer to a Minister's claim of Crown privilege in respect of deliberations of the Crown if the Minister certified that disclosure was not in the public interest. Thus in the present instance the Ministers were 'entitled to certify as they did, that the undisclosed documents (if any) fell within a class of documents which were properly regarded as confidential communications' and also to claim 'immunity from exposure of public servants to parliamentary interrogation'. They doubted whether in the circumstances a court would have 'taken the view that it should go behind the Minister's certificate. In the parliamentary context of party government and Ministerial responsibility, it would be improper to do so'.

The minority summarized their conclusion as follows:

1. That a Minister's certificate of privilege for evidence, oral or documentary, sought from public servants has evidentiary value but is not conclusive.

2. That a Minister's certificate as to *all* documents and *all* questions relating to the matter of overseas loan activities of the Government was clearly unsupportable—and was not acceptable as a claim of privilege unless restricted to particular documents or particular questions or a particular class of documents or questions.

3. That the directions of the Australian Ministers to claim privilege in respect of investigations by the Senate were misconceived. Such a claim is a claim for a Senate not to require an answer or a document in appropriate cases.

4. That in practice the Senate would ordinarily refrain from requiring answers to questions as to confidential advisings by public servants.

5. That there is no practice, nor is it the law, that the simple fact that a witness is a public servant or a file a departmental file gives any privilege. The question is whether a question invades the confidentiality basic to the proper performance by the public service of its duty—and if the detriment to the public interest of disclosure by the public servant outweighs the public interest of revealing the facts to the legislature, the legislature ordinarily will not require the question to be answered or a file to be produced.

6. The ultimate decision as to whether a question must be answered or a document produced is for the Senate and not for the Executive.

7. That the Solicitor-General—not claiming any privilege on professional grounds or self-incrimination—was wrong in claiming that he should join a claim for privilege to the Ministers' claim of privilege, simply because such a claim was made and he was an officer appointed by an Executive. He erred in not discharging his higher duty to give evidence before a House of Parliament when lawfully required—subject to all proper privilege in respect of any particular question or class of questions—e.g. questions which impaired the confidentiality on which his relationship with an executive was based.

8. We do not consider it appropriate that we recommend what action should be taken by the Senate in this case. The Committee has not summoned or heard any of the witnesses concerned. The matter, therefore, is reserved for the judgment of the Senate.

Since both the majority and the minority were not in dispute on the constitutional authority of the Senate to require the giving of evidence by public servants, the differences between them were essentially on the weight and effect that ought to be accorded to ministerial claims and the sufficiency of the reasons given by the Ministers in support of their claims. Unlike the majority the minority were not prepared to regard the Minister's certificate as conclusive, though they acknowledged that production of certain classes of documents ought not normally be insisted upon. These included 'documents containing state secrets such as Cabinet discussion, defence matters, or diplomatic exchanges', Executive Council minutes and the confidential advisings of public servants to Ministers. But even in these cases the public interest might sometimes justify departure from the normal practice of not requiring disclosure. Thus 'investigation into the blunders of the Crimean War, the Dardenelles campaign, or some aspects of the Singapore surrender might be more in the national interest, even during war, than a continuance of crass incompetence and error'. So, too, there could be exceptional circumstances justifying departure from the practice of not requiring evidence of confidential advice to Ministers, for example, 'where a Minister blamed his departmental Head for erroneous advice' or where the legality of a particular transaction was called into question.

The report of the Committee has yet to be considered by the Senate, though on 30 March 1976, Senator Wright gave notice of motion that the dissenting report of Senators Greenwood, Webster and himself be adopted.

Hopefully the general issue of the operation of Crown privilege in the Houses of Parliament and before their committees will not be permitted to remain unresolved indefinitely. The issue is not a new one, and inasmuch as it concerns both Houses, it is one on which ideally the Parliament as a whole should express a view, if not by legislation, by the adoption by both Houses of common principles and procedures. The need for settlement of the governing principles and procedures will become even greater if the promise of improved and effective parliamentary scrutiny held out by the recent report of the Joint Committee on the Parliamentary Committee System[62] is realised.

The extent to which intra-departmental communications and communications between departmental officials and Ministers ought to be shielded from public view and even from the view of the Houses of Parliament and their committees, is not a question which lends itself to easy solution. Clearly there are many classes of official documents and communications the public disclosure of which would not materially impair the efficiency of the workings of the executive, candour in communication, and ministerial responsibility for the actions of departmental officers.[63] One may wonder, too, whether the justifications commonly advanced for preserving the confidentiality of documents revealing opinions and recommendations involved in deliberative and policy-making processes are as strong and compelling as those offering them maintain. It is, for example, questionable whether the reason given by Lord Reid in *Conway* v. *Rimmer*[64] for treating documents of this type as confidential has a great deal of relevance to parliamentary inquiries. Lord Reid was concerned

---

[62]Tabled on 26 May 1976.

[63]See Attorney-General's Department, 'Proposed Freedom of Information Legislation: Report of Interdepartmental Committee' (September 1974).

[64][1968] A.C. 910. See also *Lanyon* v. *Commonwealth* (1974) 3 A.L.R. 58, at p.60.

that 'disclosure would create or fan ill-informed or captious criticism'. And, he continued, 'the business of government is difficult enough as it is, and no government could contemplate with equanimity the inner workings of the government machine being exposed to the gaze of those ready to criticise without adequate knowledge of the background and perhaps with some axe to grind'.[65]

Perhaps a better reason why the Houses of Parliament and their committees should not normally press for disclosure of public servants' advice to Ministers is that if Ministers take full responsibility for the decisions which are ultimately taken or policies which are adopted, and Parliament itself holds the Minister responsible in the sense that he should bear the blame where blame is due, the advice given to the Minister, whether acted on or not, is irrelevant. Actually Ministers have on occasions sought to avoid being held culpable by volunteering information disclosing fault on the part of their departmental advisers. For example, when in 1972 the Government's decision to purchase second-hand aircraft from Jetair was questioned, Prime Minister McMahon tabled documentation which included faulty advice tendered to him, in his former capacity as Minister for Foreign Affairs, by the permanent head of the department, and advice given, at his request, by the Special Adviser on International Law on the legal effect of a letter sent by the permanent head to Jetair.[66]

It could be argued that rather than undermining ministerial responsibility, the revelation of departmental advisings reinforces it by providing an essential basis for the Parliament to make a judgment on the Minister's culpability and liability to censure. This argument does however involve a significant departure from orthodox notions of ministerial responsibility according to which Ministers must accept responsibility for the mistakes and shortcomings of their departmental officers, irrespective of whether they are personally at fault. It should be borne in mind, too, that if examination of departmental advisings was to become a regular feature of parliamentary scrutiny of governmental activities, the relationship between Ministers and public servants would inevitably undergo radical change. It is likely that officials would be far less disposed to give advice frankly, fearlessly and impartially—at least in writing—and a grave risk that Ministers would find their own freedom, and the responsibility that goes with it, diminished by the knowledge that political capital could always be made of advisings which they had chosen to ignore or reject.

The constitutional conventions that underpin the ministerial system are not static, so that at any moment of time it may be difficult to recognise what the current conventions are. And by their very nature the conventions are liable to vary from one system to another. Mutations may occur as an indirect result of legislation. Parliament may, for example, by its legislative acts, remove from the sphere of ministerial authority and responsibility areas of administration which it considers ought to be taken outside the political domain, or be supervised by persons or bodies other than Ministers. In this connection it is worth reflecting on the possible consequences of enlargement of the opportunities for independent review of administrative decisions, whether by an Ombudsman or by the Administrative Appeals Tribunal.

---

[65][1968] A.C. 910, at p.952.

[66]Senate, *Debates*, 27 September 1972, vol. 54, pp. 1205-9; House of Representatives, *Debates*, 17 October 1972, vol. 81, pp. 2687-90; 19 October 1972, pp. 2869-78.

The *Administrative Appeals Tribunal Act* 1975 provides a broad framework for the hearing and determination of appeals against administrative decisions made pursuant to legislation. At present the jurisdiction of the Tribunal is limited, but it is capable of being extended. In some instances the right of appeal to the Tribunal supersedes or is an alternative to appeal to a Minister; in others appeal may be made against ministerial decisions. Where there is a right of appeal to the Tribunal, there may be an even greater tendency to treat the decisions against which appeal may be made as decisions taken in exercise of powers which ought properly to be exercised independently of political considerations or of government policy. And inasmuch as the Tribunal establishes, over time, its own overriding standards of administrative behaviour, officials whose decisions are subject to its review could well come to regard themselves as being primarily accountable to that body, at least in respect of those of their activities which are appealable.

Similar developments could occur on the establishment of the office of Commonwealth Ombudsman, as was envisaged by the Ombudsman Bill 1975 and is envisaged by the Ombudsman Bill 1976. It is true that under the Bills the Ombudsman's jurisdiction to investigate and report was not to extend to the administrative actions of Ministers or to the actions of officials which were certified by a Minister to have been taken in accordance with a decision of a Minister or Ministers. But recommendations to Ministers were not excluded from review. And, by inference, the primary obligation to take remedial action consequent upon an adverse report lay with the department or authority concerned. While the Ombudsman review system does not encroach upon the domain of policy making, it does, within the sphere of administration upon which it operates, interpose between officials and Ministers an outside source of influence and control. Moreover, to the extent that it involves judgments being made about the acts and omissions of officials, it provides impetus to the idea that officials should be held individually and publicly accountable for their actions. In the process orthodox notions about ministerial responsibility will inevitably need to undergo modifiction. If the Ombudsman has levelled criticism against departmental officers, it would be ridiculous to suppose that the Minister should carry ministerial responsibility to the extreme of supporting his officials against the judgment of the Ombudsman.[67]

It is doubtful whether the fostering of direct and public accountability on the part of officials does any great violence to the principles underlying the Westminster system. After all, the precepts of ministerial responsibility represent just one of a variety of possible expedients for subjecting the exercise of public power to the superintendence and judgment of the people for whose benefit that power is meant to be employed.[68]

---

[67]See G.K. Fry, 'The Sachsenhausen Concentration Camp Case and the Convention of Ministerial Responsibility' [1970] *Public Law* 336.

[68]See Henry Parris, *Constitutional Bureaucracy* (London, 1969) Ch. 3.

COMMENTARIES

S. Encel

It is strange for a political scientist to see politics being discussed behind a screen of constitutional law. In this short commentary, I shall leave the legal issues to the lawyers and try to inject a certain amount of straightforward politics.

A number of sharp remarks have been made about the appropriateness, or lack of appropriateness, of British precedents and practices. No discussion of cabinet government can avoid the need to refer to British precedents. Cabinet government is very much a British invention, and its development continues to provide models for Australian practice, especially in relation to administration. Also, the British literature is rich, whereas Australian political scientists, with a few notable exceptions, have largely ignored the topic and devoted themselves to the study of political parties, psephology, and pressure groups.

The development of urban-industrial societies like Australia has, as we all know, been accompanied by an enormous increase in the size, complexity, and scope of central government. This growth has, in most cases, taken place through the grafting of new functions and new organizational systems on to political structures which, in many cases, originated in the nineteenth century and still retain much of their original character. If the grafts have not always taken, we should not be particularly surprised.

The division of functions between ministers and permanent officials is one of the important areas displaying a high level of incompatibility between nineteenth-century conventions and twentieth-century exigencies. Most of us were brought up on a constitutional theory which distinguishes between ministerial responsibility for policy and departmental responsibility for administration. When this distinction failed to operate effectively, another recourse was at hand—the idea of 'political' as contrasted with 'policy' considerations. The distinction between 'policy' and 'politics' exists, so far as I know, only in the English language, and seems to reflect a particularly Anglo-Saxon form of obfuscation.

Given the reality, familiar both to students of politics and to its practitioners, that politics, policy and administration are inextricably mingled in practice, why do these distinctions persist? I would suggest two main reasons. One is that constitutional theory would collapse without them. Constitutions cannot be devised without legal fictions, like the lack of reference to the Cabinet in the various Australian Constitution Acts, or in any British constitutional document apart from the Ministers of the Crown Acts, which are concerned with payment and not with powers or responsibilities. Cabinet is a perfect illustration of the problem, since it combines politics, policy-making and administration in the most intimate fashion. Another set of fictions surrounds the office of Governor-General, and these too involve the relations between politics, policy, and administration.

Perhaps a more powerful reason for the continued strength of these distinctions is the nature of popular discourse concerning politics. That fabled creature, the man in the street, derives most of his information about politics from the doings of elected members of parliament, and by a natural extension tends to identify this behaviour with the political process at large. We sophisticated persons know better, but the man in the street is not particularly anxious to partake of our special knowledge. It is easier to believe that the M.P.s are up there running the government, or at any rate that they should be. Australian voters would not be happy with the situation which existed under the Eisenhower regime in the 1950s, when Ike seemed to spend most of his time on the golf course and the administration was run by super-bureaucrats like Sherman Adams. American comedian Mort Sahl summed up a popular view of the Eisenhower administration when he remarked, 'They wouldn't be in Washington if they didn't know their business—and anyway they aren't there'.

The administrative class of the British civil service, a particularly sophisticated group, have never been under illusions about the links between policy and administration. This is made clear in their well-known memorandum addressed to the Royal Commission on the Civil Service in 1929:

> The business of government . . . calls for the application of wide and long views to complex problems, for the pursuit, as regards each and every subject-matter, of definite lines of action, mutually consistent, conformed to public opinion and capable of being followed continuously while conditions permit . . . it is the special duty of the administrative class of the civil service to set these wider and more enduring considerations against the exigencies of the moment.[1]

This is a political statement, which asserts the right of the officials to make political decisions even, or perhaps especially, in opposition to the immediate political aims of their ministerial superiors. Very few British politicians have been willing to face this reality, or at any rate to publish their recognition of it. A recent outstanding exception is that of Richard Crossman. In his Godkin lectures of 1970, he attacked the influence of the 'permanent politicians' of Whitehall, and their ascendency over the fleeting succession of ministers who confront them in their departments.[2] In his more recently published diaries, Crossman adds chapter and verse to these general remarks. Permanent secretaries, he notes, have no scruples about conducting intrigues against their political superiors, and they can be indiscreet, reckless, prejudiced and prone to malicious gossip. He describes the tussle he had with his own department over housing subsidies to local authorities. It was four months, he records, before the departmental officials abandoned their own policy, which would have increased rents, in the face of Crossman's determination to implement Labour Party policy of reducing rents and interest payments; and it was many more months before they actually agreed to carry out government policy.[3]

There is no doubt that such incidents occur much more frequently than they are reported, nor is it easy to decide which party has been on the side of the angels in any particular case. Professor Crisp has given us several accounts of the direct and acknowledged influence of senior public servants on policy and on political decisions, and his picture of the relationship between ministers and permanent heads is by far the best available.[4] But, like most such accounts, it is rather bland and discreetly avoids the possibility of basic conflict between ministers and officials.

---

[1] *Memorandum by Association of First Division Civil Servants*, presented to the Royal Commission on the Civil Service, 1929-31.

[2] Richard Crossman, *Inside View* (London, 1972), pp. 23-4.

[3] Richard Crossman, *The Diaries of a Cabinet Minister*, vol. 1 (London, 1975), pp. 619-20.

[4] L.F. Crisp, *Australian National Government*, (3rd ed., Melbourne, 1973), pp. 455-61.

Such conflicts were endemic during the whole period between 1949 and 1972, sometimes known as the 'Ming dynasty', which was marked by an underlying political conflict between the *laissez-faire* ideology of the Liberal Government and the Keynesian activism of many senior public servants. An instance of veiled but obvious conflict occurred during the legislative struggle over the restructuring of the Commonwealth Bank in 1957-58, when the Treasury was clearly opposed to a reduction in the powers of the central bank, demanded by the private trading banks and supported by Sir Robert Menzies against the resistance of the Treasurer, Sir Arthur Fadden, who carried the Treasury banner in Cabinet. Foreign affairs is another area where there is recurrent tension between ministers and officials. A notable case was the Suez crisis of 1956, where Sir Robert Menzies took over the control of foreign affairs from the responsible Ministers, Mr R.G. (later Lord) Casey and Sir Philip McBride (acting-minister during part of this period), both of whom espoused the departmental view which was opposed to Australian involvement in support of Sir Anthony Eden's Government.

Close to the present day, we have the complicated sequence of the 'overseas loans affair', in which officials were playing politics, both against one another and against Government policy; at the same time, ministers were trying to take over direct control of financial administration.

During the past fifteen years or so, two basic strategies for dealing with the problem have been in evidence in both Britain and Australia. Since the advent of the first Wilson Government in 1964, both Wilson and Heath have experimented with the appointment of outsiders as personal advisers, trouble-shooters and watchdogs. Crossman describes how he used the advice of his friend Lord Goodman to push through the Rent Act of 1965 against the wishes of his department, although they finally admitted they did not have the resources to frame such legislation.[5] Heath, following the recommendations of the Fulton Committee on the Civil Service in 1968, set up the Central Policy Review Staff under Lord Rothschild, who described its function as that of 'looking where you are going'.[6] During Rothschild's four-year tenure, the membership of the C.P.R.S. averaged fifteen, of whom two-thirds were economists, one-third were seconded civil servants, and the rest came from industry, politics and the universities.[7] All were young (below forty-five) as recommended in the Fulton report. Under Rothschild's successor, Kenneth Berrill, the C.P.R.S. has retained similar features, but with fewer economists. According to Berrill, the C.P.R.S. works in four areas: inter-departmental committees; original papers for Cabinet committees; the so-called 'Red Papers' on specific topics like energy, transport, and social welfare; and continuing review of governmental strategy and performance.[8]

These areas all involve a fusion of policy, politics, and administration, and it is perhaps inevitable, given the constitutional traditions already mentioned, that a special class of person had to be created to work at this level. The second Wilson administration recognized this and took the experiment further by appointing a number of 'political assistants' to ministers, most of them with an academic background. They were soon dubbed 'Labour's private army', and the

[5]Crossman, *Diaries*, p.619.

[3]Angela Croome, 'On Being a Grand Vizier', *New Scientist*, 27 April 1972, pp. 214-6.

[7]'The Brains Behind the Throne', *Sunday Times*, 25 March 1973.

[8]Angela Croome, 'Damn Hard Science', *New Scientist*, 8 January 1976, pp. 60-2.

additional label of 'chocolate soldier' was attached because some of them had worked as assistants to shadow ministers under a fellowship scheme funded by the Rowntree Trust. (In the circumstances, a better title might have been 'Smarties'.) In addition, Mr Wilson set up his own personal advisory team of eight people under the leadership of Dr Bernard Donoughue, a lecturer in politics at the London School of Economics and Political Science. These devices are a small-scale adaptation of French and American practices—the French ministerial *cabinet*, staffed by civil servants who assume a political role, and the American 'political overhead' of political appointees who carry out a mixture of political and administrative duties. Whether they can be successfully grafted on to British stock remains to be seen. In some form or other, however, they are likely to remain and to grow in importance.

The Whitlam Government also used similar devices, some of which had been mooted while Mr Whitlam was Leader of the Opposition in the 1960s. Ministerial advisers were appointed under circumstances spelt out for us in Professor Campbell's essay. The Priorities Review Staff, modelled on the C.P.R.S., was created towards the end of 1973. A large number of non-departmental agencies including task forces, commissions, and consultancies were set up. The Whitlam Goverment also used another strategy which the British have not used and show no sign of using, i.e. a general post of permanent heads. Professor Campbell has enumerated this for us: twenty-one new permanent heads appointed between 1972 and 1975, seven of them from outside the service. This kind of turnover was quite without precedent in Australian political history, although it has some affinities with Canada (where the political role of permanent heads is signalized by calling them 'deputy ministers'). The precedent appears, however, to have become established. The Fraser Government undertook a further, though less drastic rotation of departmental heads. According to recent press reports, the Government proposes to consolidate these moves by amending the Public Service Act to give permanent heads limited tenure.

Professor Campbell foresees an increase in the direct public accountability of permanent officials, and does not consider that it will do great violence to the principles underlying the Westminster system. Her insight into this question is presumably influenced by her recent experiences as a member of the Royal Commission on Australian Government Administration. However, I must respectfully disagree with her conclusion. It may be true that public accountability would not undermine ministerial responsibility, but I suspect that most ministers will insist on retaining the appearance of responsibility, especially because they value their exposure in the mass media. Politicians can hardly be expected to behave otherwise. The power of permanent officials may, however, be modified by other methods, such as those suggested by the Royal Commission, including greater public access to policy-making, decentralization of administrative responsibility, and a reduction in the hierarchical character of departments. It appears that the apparently ineluctable growth of bureaucracy has at last generated powerful counter-tendencies, not least among politicians who realize how little control they have over the machine. It is here that we may expect continuing developments, and one of the historic functions of the Whitlam Government may be that it broke the ground for them, as it broke new ground in so many other fields.

The Whitlam Government, however, made no attempt to deal with one other issue, mentioned by Professor Campbell, which is relevant to the problem of ministerial control over administration. This relates to the appointment of assistant ministers and parliamentary under-secretaries. As I have pointed out elsewhere[9], all governments have tried to dodge the fact that such appointments cannot be made without a constitutional amendment legalizing payment for this purpose. The appointment of junior ministers would alleviate some of the problems of political oversight of administration. It does, however, raise a further problem that the government benches would be dominated even more by members of the ministry than they now are. The solution to this difficulty is, of course, to enlarge the Federal Parliament, but it is unlikely that any government will now do this unless the Constitution is also amended to permit the enlargement of the House of Representatives without changing the size of the Senate. Whichever way we turn, the necessity for constitutional change is inescapable.

Peter Wilenski

Professor Encel, in his comments on Professor Campbell's essay, has taken up the unreality of the constitutional theory which distinguishes between ministerial responsibility for policy and departmental responsibility for administration. The distinction between politics, policy and administration is not even an Anglo-Saxon obfuscation. It is more narrowly a British and Antipodean one, since it disappeared from the U.S. literature some years ago with the demise of the Wilsonian 'instrumental' theory of administration. And it is important to note that the theory is unrealistic not only because public servants take part in policy formulation, but also because the decisions made by public servants in the implementation of policy are highly political ones.

Associated with this piece of constitutional mythology are a number of conventions relating to the public service, such as secrecy, anonymity, security of tenure, impartiality and objectivity. During the period of the Labor Government the credibility gap between these conventions on the one hand and political and bureaucratic reality on the other became evident as never before. Professor Campbell's essay includes reference to these issues from a legal viewpoint; for my part I should like to look at them from the viewpoint of a practising bureaucrat.

Both for the practising bureaucrat and for his minister, Labor's opening up to public scrutiny of the process of policy formulation and of programme implementation—loosely 'open government'—was a change of profound significance for these conventions. There is clearly a relationship between open government and the constitutional theory of responsible government. It was in the mid-nineteenth century that the phrase 'responsible government' came into common use. The role of the government was then relatively limited and during this short phase political parties did not yet dominate the Parliament. As a result it was relatively easy to see what acts governments were responsible for, and it had political meaning to say that Parliament was the body to which governments were responsible, as votes in Parliament could still bring down the government. To oversimplify somewhat, now that governments control parliaments through the party system they are 'responsible' in the sense that they are

---

[9]S. Encel, *Cabinet Government in Australia* (2nd ed., Melbourne, 1974), pp. 176-85.

accountable to the public at general elections. However, if this accountability is to mean anything, then the public must have the information available to it to be able to judge the performance of the government. The decision of the Senate, discussed by Professor Campbell, to call public servants before it in July 1975 highlighted the dilemma of how ministers can truly be held responsible for administrative actions when they also control access to all the information as to what actions really took place.

Labor made two major contributions to open and accountable government, one intentionally and one at least in part unintentionally. The first was the public examination by task forces, inquiries, commissions and the like of a wide range of social, economic and administrative issues, and the publication of their reports and their recommendations for public scrutiny prior to government decision. We should not underestimate the revolutionary change in government policy-making that this constituted.

It is curious, however, that side by side with this process conventional wisdom continued to stress the need for absolute secrecy and anonymity insofar as similar advice from the Public Service was concerned. The doctrine of ministerial government in no way crumbled because advice to ministers in a wide range of fields became publicly known. However it was still argued that it would in some mysterious way collapse if advice on similar matters coming from the Public Service became known. The doctrine of ministerial responsibility became no shakier than it had been before because the identity of those giving advice became public, but it was still argued that this doctrine would be seriously undermined if the views of individual public servants became known. One reason put forward was that incoming governments would not be able to work with public servants who had become publicly identified with particular views. This view was steadfastly held to by the Public Service Board and others in submissions to the Royal Commission on Australian Government Administration. It was especially curious because the media throughout the period had no trouble in identifying prominent public servants as the originators or protagonists of particular policy lines, and within the inbred Canberra community the grapevine had always kept politicians on either side well informed of the views of senior public servants. The dominance of this particular attachment to secrecy was nowhere more evident than in the deliberations of the Interdepartmental Committee studying Labor's proposed Freedom of Information Act which 'saw itself charged with bringing down a scheme consistent with the traditional view of the legal and conventional relationships involved in the Westminster system of government'.[1] It produced a report little related to the realities of government, leading to the failure of the Government to introduce Freedom of Information legislation to institutionalise open government and reduce the likelihood of its reversal.

What we had, therefore, in terms of the Westminster conventions was an extraordinary situation. On the one hand more and more policy advice was becoming known and its sources identified on the basis that the Westminster system of government would be strengthened if ministers were judged on their ability to choose which advice to follow. On the other hand the conflicting and

---

[1]L.J. Curtis, 'Freedom of Information Legislation', in *Report of the Royal Commission on Australian Government Administration* (1976), App. 2.B.: vol. 2, p.9. (Mr Curtis was a member of the IDC in question.)

clearly inoperative Westminster convention of secrecy and anonymity in the Public Service remained conventional wisdom.

I stated earlier that there were two aspects of open government, one of them partly unintentional. This latter aspect was the number of leaks to the press, often from ministers, the number of statements by ministers prior to Cabinet consideration or in defiance of Cabinet decision, and the well publicised disputes within Caucus over the endorsement or rejection of Cabinet recommendations. This process might well also have been regarded by those concerned with constitutional government as a desirable trend. First it added to public knowledge and debate. Second it downgraded somewhat the role of Cabinet, and restored to some extent the influence of the parliamentary party and gave to it some of the legislative role which Parliament itself had long ago lost when Cabinet became in functional terms the legislative as well as the executive body in the Australian Constitution. But we know that this trend was not in fact seen as a bolstering of democratic government; rather it was seen as chaos in decision-making.

That this was so may be an indication that in Australia at least secrecy is a more desired convention in relation to government than accountability. After all, a Canadian taskforce was able to comment on Australian political life in 1969 that 'totalitarian capitals apart, only official Canberra comes close to matching that special air of furtive reticence which marks the Ottawa Mandarins off from other men'.[2]

The increasing openness of government also brought under scrutiny the need for security of tenure and a career service for policy advisers. Professor Campbell has pointed to the desire for widening the range of advice as being the driving force behind the establishment of ministerial staffs and one of the motives for the establishment of statutory bodies outside the departmental system, and this implicitly challenged the claimed convention of the Westminster system that advice is best given by officials with security of tenure. The argument has always been put that security of tenure is required so that advice given will be frank, fearless, and forthright. In the words of the Fulton Committee 'Civil servants must be able to give forthright advice to their superiors and to ministers without feeling that a clash of views might lead to dismissal from the Service.[3] It is a somewhat dishonourable reflection on the men who are at the top of the civil service that if they were liable to removal they would give less than honest views. The fact is that even with tenure there are many temptations to be less than honest in advising a minister, ranging from an ambition for advancement to a desire for an easy life, or fear of the minister's temper. On the other hand, it may well be that someone whose career is largely outside the Public Service and who is merely a temporary within it, may well be more ready to give unpalatable advice. The years 1972 to 1975 provide many examples of both temporary and permanent public servants pushing views that were unpopular with ministers, or on the other hand failing to impress upon ministers arguments that should have been forcefully made. The experience should have cast doubt upon the very facile assumption that security of tenure is a necessary and sufficient condition for fearless policy advice, and yet somehow that convention remains substantially unchallenged.

Given the active and indeed valuable participation of public servants in the

[2] *'To Know and be Known,* vol. 2, (Ottawa, 1969), p.25.

[3] *The Civil Service,* vol. I, (London, 1968), p.46.

political life of the country (Barbara Castle once said 'The danger of the British Civil Service to our democracy lies in its excellence'[4]), perhaps the oddest of the conventional phrases heard about the Service is the reference to its impartiality and objectivity both in the tendering of advice and in the implementation of decisions. It is not so much that public servants have the same human failings as others and thus have their prejudices, their hidden assumptions and their unrecognised preferences, which influence not only the range of options which they can present ministers but even the selection of the facts which they consider to be relevant. It is more that the subjects on which senior public servants need to advise, or need to make administrative decisions are subjects about the distribution of wealth and power in the community, questions of value about which the words 'impartiality' or 'objectivity' have little meaning.

A recommendation to ministers from an interdepartmental committee as to whether to spend $10 million on the education of the disadvantaged or to spend it on hospital facilities, or not to spend it at all and reduce the budget deficit, can be validly or invalidly, competently or incompetently, interestedly or disinterestedly, argued; but it is not at all clear in what sense such a recommendation can be regarded as objective, since it rests entirely upon values to be attached to each of the possible ends. The fact is, of course, that public servants in different departments, all of them presumably impartial and objective, arrive at, on the basis of the same facts, quite contrary recommendations. Once a ministerial decision has been taken, similar differences in departmental 'lines' exist as to how that decision should be implemented, e.g. differences as to how the public is to be given access to a new expenditure programme. Once again the differences arise because the administrative questions to be decided are not questions of objective fact but of political value. Legal discussion of the relative standing of s. 64 of the Constitution and s. 25(2) of the Public Service Act may be important in the exceptional case, but in general obscures the fact that the system works only because there is a sharing between ministers and officials of administrative authority.

Impartiality and objectivity might perhaps be reduced to a question of political neutrality, but even here we mean political neutrality in a very narrow sense which certainly does not mean that public servants should not have political views. Sir Robert Menzies said of his experience in 1949,

> At the very outset I was told by people in my party organization that certain men in the Prime Minister's Department were or had been officers or members of the Labor Party. I recall my reply with some satisfaction. 'So long as they are competent and honest men, what of it? Kissing will not go by political favour in my department!'[5]

Menzies, it must be said, also made reference to that word 'objectivity' but once all these words are analysed we are always reduced simply to the expectation that civil servants will act honestly and competently, an expectation no different to that expected from any other sector of the community.

Professor Campbell suggests that the fostering of direct and public accountability by public servants, a process greatly accelerated by the Labor Government, will not do any great violence to the principles underlying the Westminster system. I agree with this view. However as the actions of officials become more public, their political nature will be increasingly evident and it will be

---

[4]'Mandarin Power: An attack on Civil Service Methods and How They Stifle True Political Decision'. *Sunday Times*, 10 June 1973.

[5]Sir Robert Menzies, *The Measure of the Years* (London, 1970), p. 149.

increasingly difficult to maintain some of the conventions about official behaviour I have discussed. The senior Australian official, despite his self-perception, is in no traditional sense a servant either of the public or of those whom he likes to describe as his political masters, but is a full participant in the political process. Recognition of this fact will in my view strengthen, not weaken, responsible government in Australia.

6 Parliamentarians and the Electorate

P. J. Hanks

I
INTRODUCTION

The three years of the Whitlam Labor Government revealed the truly social democratic nature of the Australian Labor Party. The Government was clearly committed to effecting structural change within Australian society but just as clearly committed to working through the established institutions of government. In particular, the Government was committed to working through Parliament to achieve its objectives.

But the Government also had a commitment to changing or restructuring the institution of Parliament: the representative character of Parliament was to be enhanced through changes to the system of distributing seats for the House of Representatives, through increasing the representation of territorial voters in the House, and introducing representation for those voters in the Senate. These changes were pursued by the Government with considerable vigour, and in formal terms the changes were achieved; but in real terms it is doubtful whether those changes will have any significant impact on the institution or its function.

Apart from those attempts at fundamental institutional change, the three years of Labor government also saw a series of issues raised in the nature of individual crises, such as the debate over private or conflicting interests of parliamentarians, the dispute over the filling of casual vacancies in the Senate, and the question of the status of the Speaker of the House of Representatives. These highlighted some critical questions about the nature of the parliamentary institution and its relationship to the community at large. My purpose is to examine both the attempts to change the institution and those individual debates and crises.

II
VOTES FOR PEOPLE

There were three separate attempts to restructure the system according to which House of Representatives electorates were distributed. First, the introduction (and ultimate passage through the Joint Sitting of 6 August 1974) of amendments to the *Commonwealth Electoral Act* 1918; secondly, the proposal submitted to referendum on 18 May 1974 entitled the Constitution Alteration (Democratic Elections) Bill 1974; and thirdly, the High Court challenge by several litigants, who appeared to receive some encouragement from the Labor Government, to the constitutional validity of the system of distribution established under the Commonwealth Electoral Act and the *Representation Act*

1905.[1] None of these attempts achieved any immediate change to the distribution of House of Representatives seats. Perhaps the only significant change in the long term will flow from the High Court's decision on aspects of the Representation Act—an issue presented to the Court for decision as something of an afterthought.

The Electoral Bills

When Labor came to government in December 1972 the 125 seats in the House of Representatives were distributed between the States as follows: New South Wales, forty-five; Victoria, thirty-four; Queensland, eighteen; South Australia, twelve; Western Australia, nine; and Tasmania, five. The Northern Territory and the Australian Capital Territory had one seat each. This allocation of seats was based on census returns (primarily the 1966 Census, with a minor adjustment, the allocation of one extra seat to Western Australia, after the 1971 Census), as prescribed by the Representation Act.[2] Within five of the States, the seats had last been distributed by the Commonwealth Distribution Commissioners during 1968, and those distributions had been proclaimed after approval by both the House of Representatives and the Senate in November 1968 and February 1969. Distribution of electoral boundaries within Western Australia had been approved and proclaimed in April 1974.

Those redistributions had been based on the *Commonwealth Electoral Act 1918* and, in particular, on the criteria for distribution laid down in s.19. That section provided that the number of electors in each electorate should neither exceed nor fall short of the quota (that is, the total number of electors in the State divided by the number of members of the House to be elected for the State) by more than 20 per cent and that in making a proposed distribution the Commissioners should consider several factors including 'disabilities arising out of remoteness or distance'[3] 'density and sparsity of population'[4] and the 'area' of any proposed electorate.[5]

It had been a regular complaint of the Australian Labor Party that these criteria for distributing seats operated to the Party's disadvantage. While the situation is complex (it is not enough, for example, to compare a party's share of the national vote with its share of the seats in Parliament), the guarded judgment of Professor C.A. Hughes on the results of the 1972 election supports the Labor Party's complaint: 'It might be reasonable to say that once again some inbuilt factor in the electoral system had disadvantaged the Labor Party.'[6] That factor was identified by Hughes as the uneven size of electorates: 'The A.L.P. has a disproportionate share of the larger divisions, 21 of the 32 with enrolments in excess of 60,000 . . .'[7]

The Labor Government moved in the first few months of office to alter the distribution system. A Bill was introduced (and passed by the House of Representatives on 4 April 1973) to amend the Commonwealth Electoral Act.

---

[1] *A.-G. (Australia) (Ex rel. McKinlay)* v. *Commonwealth* (1975) 7 A.L.R. 593.

[2] *Representation Act* 1905, s.4(1)(a).

[3] *Commonwealth Electoral Act* 1918, s.19(2)(b).

[4] *ibid.*, s.19(2)(d).

[5] *ibid.*, s.19(2)(e).

[6] C. A. Hughes 'The 1972 Australian Federal Election', *Aust.J.Pol.Hist.* 19 (1973), at p.22.

[7] *ibid.*, at p.23.

The amendments were to reduce the permissible margin for departure from the quota for an electorate to 10 per cent, and to delete from the criteria listed in s.19(2) those factors which supported smaller rural electorates: the Distribution Commissioners would no longer be charged to take account of such factors as disabilities arising out of remoteness or distance, and the sparsity or density of population within an electorate. This Bill was opposed by the Senate and was one of the six Bills on which the Governor-General based his proclamation of 11 April 1974 dissolving both Houses of Parliament.[8] It was ultimately given the royal assent after being approved at the Joint Sitting on 6 August 1974.

The amendments to the Commonwealth Electoral Act were confined to altering the criteria and the permissible deviation to be applied by the Distribution Commissioners. No change was made to the procedure of redistribution: in particular, any proposal for redistribution of electorates within a State would continue to require approval by the House of Representatives and the Senate.[9] The Government soon had cause to regret the omission. Redistribution proposals for five States, based on the new criteria in s.19 of the Commonwealth Electoral Act, were approved by the House of Representatives on 21 and 22 May 1975 and rejected by the Senate on 22 and 27 May 1975.

There seems little case for having allowed the Senate to retain its veto over the distribution of electorates for the House of Representatives. Odgers argues[10] (with his usual tenacity) that 'the Senate is the States House and it is the Senate's business to ensure that a distribution is in the best interests of a State or States'. But this assertion ignores the reality that senators do not vote as representatives of any State: when they divide it is along party lines.[11] Certainly the divisions on the motions[12] to approve the redistribution proposals reflected party, rather than geographical, interests. Nor does the assertion explain what interest senators from (say) New South Wales might have in the distribution of House of Representatives seats within South Australia. The proposed re-distribution for the latter State was, in fact, supported by six of the State's ten senators; but the combined votes of senators from other States (dividing on party lines) defeated the proposal![13]

As soon as it became apparent that the distribution proposals would be defeated in the Senate, the Government arranged for each of the proposals to be embodied in a separate Bill. These Bills were passed by the House of Representatives on 28 May 1975 and rejected by the Senate on 10 June 1975. The way was then prepared for their passage through the double dissolution procedure when the Bills were passed a second time by the House (on 11 September 1975) and again rejected by the Senate (on 8 October 1975). Indeed, the double dissolution of 11 November 1975[14] was premised on these five Bills, along with sixteen other Bills which had fulfilled the requirements of the first paragraph of s.57 of the Constitution. The consequential elections for the

[8] *Australian Government Gazette,* 11 April 1974, No. 31B.

[9] *Commonwealth Electoral Act* 1918, s.24(1).

[10] J. R. Odgers, *Australian Senate Practice* (4th ed., Canberra, 1972), p.72.

[11] *Cf. Report from the Joint Committee on Constitutional Review:* (Parliamentary Paper No. 108 of 1959-1960), paras. 82-90.

[12] Senate, *Debates,* 22 and 27 May 1975, vol. 64, pp. 1744, 1753, 1851-2, 1856, 1872-3.

[13] Senate, *Debates,* 22 May 1975, vol. 64, p.1744.

[14] *Australian Government Gazette,* 11 November 1975, No. S229.

House of Representatives were, of course, conducted on the boundaries fixed in accordance with the old criteria, which had been repealed in August 1974.

The 'Democratic Elections' Referendum

At much the same time as the Labor Government was promoting these amendments to the Commonwealth Electoral Act, it was mounting a more ambitious (indeed radical) attack on the distribution system: on 8 November 1973 it introduced into the House of Representatives several Bills to alter the Constitution. Among them was the Constitution Alteration (Democratic Elections) Bill 1974, which provided, *inter alia*, that House of Representatives electorates within each State would, as far as practicable, contain the same number of people,[15] as would electorates within each State for the election of the Houses of the State parliaments.[16] The Senate rejected the Bill on 4 December 1973. Despite the Senate's continued opposition, the proposed Bill was put to a referendum on 18 May 1974.

The Bill was vigorously (and, in the end, successfully) opposed as 'a giant Labor gerrymander' by the Government's political opponents. Their substantial point was that the proposal would give the Labor Party an advantage over other parties at elections. Given that many inner urban working-class areas contained a large proportion of non-voting people (principally immigrants) the number of voters in electorates formed from those areas would certainly be smaller than the numbers of voters in electorates formed from suburban middle-class and rural areas. That is, a distribution of seats conducted on the basis of equality of *population* would inflate the value of votes in traditional Labor seats to at least the same degree as the existing system inflated the value of votes in rural (usually anti-Labor) electorates. That argument was raised[17] during the referendum campaign of April-May 1974. In the result, the proposed alteration was decisively defeated.[18] We can only speculate on the result of that referendum had the Alteration Bill been less radical in its proposals: if, for instance, it had proposed that House of Representatives electorates within each State should have equal numbers of voters.

It seems to me that these first two attempts to alter the distribution system demonstrated a lack of serious application on the part of the Government: the first attempt (the amendment of s.19 of the Commonwealth Electoral Act) did not go far enough in that it left any redistribution, based on the new criteria, to the mercy of the Senate's veto. And the second attempt (the proposed alteration of the Constitution) went far beyond what was politically feasible—by reaching for a system which could be presented by its opponents as unduly favouring the Labor Party, the Government passed up the chance to establish a constitutional principle of one vote, one value.

---

[15]Constitution Alteration (Democratic Elections) Bill 1974, cl. 4.

[16]*ibid.*, cl. 7.

[17]Australian Electoral Office, *Arguments in Favour of and Against the Proposed Laws* (Canberra, 1974), p.12.

[18]See J. E. Richardson, 'The Referendums and Constitutional Conventions,' above at p.83.

Electoral Boundaries and the High Court

The third attempt to upset the current distribution of electorates was an attempt to use the curial rather than the legislative or political processes, and involved an attack on the validity of the recently amended Commonwealth Electoral Act. This attack was mounted in the High Court of Australia in three separate suits, which were heard and decided together.[19] As the result of an afterthought (a last minute amendment of the statement of claim so as to include an attack on the validity of the Representation Act), this assault achieved one result which is likely to have a long term effect on redistribution procedures—the invalidation of those provisions of the Representation Act which prescribed the procedures to be followed for allocating seats between the several States.

The critical issue in *McKinlay's Case* was the meaning and effect of s.24 of the Constitution. Two distinct questions were raised:

(a) Whether the system established by the *Commonwealth Electoral Act* 1918 for the distribution of House of Representatives seats *within* each of the States was valid. The plaintiffs argued that the first paragraph of s.24 demanded that, within each State, the votes of electors should be, as nearly as practicable, of equal value—that is, that if a State were divided into separate electorates, those electorates should, as nearly as practicable, be composed of equal numbers of people. (It can be seen that this argument was characterized by ambiguity: the terms 'people' and 'electors' are not synonymous.)

(b) Whether the system established by the *Representation Act* 1905 for allocating House of Representatives seats *between* the States was valid. The plaintiff argued that the second paragraph of s.24 demanded regular readjustment of the number of House of Representatives seats allocated to each of the States: sufficiently regular, that is, to ensure that whenever elections for the House were held on a regular basis (that is, approximately once every three years), the number of seats allocated to each State would be in proportion to its population at the time of that election.

As to the first question before the Court, the relevant provisions of the Commonwealth Electoral Act were enacted by the Parliament in pursuance of its power under Constitution s.51(36), read with s.29. This power to legislate is expressed by s.51 to be 'subject to this Constitution': in particular, the plaintiffs argued, it was subject to a mandate contained in s.24, that 'The House of Representatives shall be composed of members directly chosen by the people of the Commonwealth'. That provision insisted (so the plaintiffs argued) that, as nearly as practicable, the votes of electors for the House of Representatives should carry equal weight. Clearly the last paragraph of s.24, guaranteeing each original State at least five members in the House, would qualify that insistence. But, the plaintiffs argued, in order for the House to be 'chosen by the people of the Commonwealth', electorates established within each of the States should, as nearly as practicable, be of equal size—measured by population or electors. This construction of the first paragraph of s.24 was supported by a series of decisions[20] of the United States Supreme Court which had struck down the distribution of Congressional electorates within several States, on the ground

---

[19]The decision of the Court is reported as *A.-G. (Australia) (Ex rel. McKinlay)* v. *Commonwealth (McKinlay's Case)* (1975) 7 A.L.R. 593.

[20]The principal decision is *Wesberry* v. *Sanders* 376 U.S. 1(1964).

that the electorates did not contain equal, or as nearly as practicable equal, numbers of people. The cases established that Art. 1, s.2 of the United States Constitution demanded practical equality of population in Congressional electoral districts within each State. That section was in terms similar to s.24 of the Commonwealth Constitution:

> The House of Representatives shall be composed of Members chosen every second Year by the People of the Several States ...

Just as the draftsmen of our Constitution had modelled s.24 on the United States Constitution, Art. 1, s.2, so now, it was argued, the High Court should follow the United States Supreme Court in its interpretation and application of s.24.

If this argument were accepted then inevitably the relevant provisions of the Commonwealth Electoral Act (even as amended in 1974) would be invalid. Section 19, for example, declared that in fixing the boundaries for electorates, the Distribution Commissioners should consider certain specified matters and might determine upon electorates whose voting population was below or above the average voting population of the State's electorates by as much as 10 per cent. It would also follow that the current distribution, at least in the States of Victoria, Queensland and South Australia (as to which evidence was presented to the Court) would be inconsistent with s.24, and so invalid. In Victoria the largest electorate had 1.8 times as many voters as the smallest; in Queensland the ratio between the largest and smallest was almost 2:1; and in South Australia the disparity was 1.7:1.

The argument that s.24 demanded equality of electorates was not free from ambiguity. In the statements of claim filed in two of the three suits which were heard together, the plaintiffs claimed that s.24 of the Constitution demanded that electorates within any one State be composed of equal numbers of people *or* of equal numbers of voters. The two demands could not, of course, be mutually consistent. To demand equality of numbers of people in electorates is not to demand equal votes of equal value. A similar conflict or ambiguity runs through the decision of the United States Supreme Court on which the plaintiffs relied in *McKinlay's Case*. In *Wesberry* v. *Sanders*,[21] for example, the Supreme Court insisted that Art. 1, s.2 of the United States Constitution meant that 'one man's vote in a congressional election is to be worth as much as another's'. In the same case, the Court observed[22] that the framers of the Constitution intended that 'population ... was to be the basis of the House of Representatives.' In *White* v. *Regester*, Brennan J declared

> Our paramount concern has remained on individual and personal right—the right to an equal vote ... We have demanded equality in district population precisely to insure that the weight of a person's vote will not depend on the district in which he lives.[23]

The members of the High Court were clearly conscious of this internal conflict in the plaintiff's argument;[24] but only McTiernan and Jacobs JJ in their joint judgment, and Murphy J, made any attempt to resolve the conflict. For the majority of the court (including McTiernan and Jacobs JJ) the resolution of the conflict was not necessary to the decision. Six of the judges (Barwick

---

[21]376 U.S. 1, at p.7.

[22]376 U.S. 1, at p.9.

[23]412 U.S. 755 (1973), at p.781.

[24]See, for example, the comments of Barwick CJ, (1975) 7 A.L.R. 593, at p.605.

CJ, McTiernan, Gibbs, Stephen, Mason and Jacobs JJ) rejected the plaintiff's argument that s.24 established a principle of equality of electorates within States, whether measured by population or number of electors. Indeed Barwick CJ and Gibbs J could discover no minimum constitutional standards in s.24 controlling the distribution of electorates within States. They argued that the first paragraph of s.24 demanded only direct election of members of the House of Representatives rather than indirect election as by an electoral college:[25] 'The words [of s.24] appear to have nothing whatever to do with the determination of electoral divisions within a State'.[26] The American cases upon which the plaintiffs had relied were irrelevant: they were influenced by the Supreme Court's (questionable) 'view ... of American history and ... the statements made in the American conventions'; they 'were a response to the particular needs of the United States'. The historical bases of those decisions 'had no counterparts in Australia'.[27]

Two other members of the Court, Stephen and Mason JJ, also discounted the American decisions. However, each was prepared to find some minimum standards prescribed by the first paragraph of s.24. Stephen J declared that s.24 embodied the principle of 'representative democracy [which] is descriptive of a whole spectrum of political institutions', a spectrum which had finite limits: a particular electoral system might lack 'some quality which is regarded as essential to representative democracy' and so contravene s.24.[28] The application of this cryptic minimum standard can only be left to speculation: certainly, Stephen J did not elaborate or provide any examples of the type of electoral system which he would regard as inconsistent with 'representative democracy'. Mason J framed his minimum standards rather less cryptically, but just as tentatively. Before concluding that 'equality or practical equality in the value of a vote ... is not a constitutional requirement,' he remarked:

> It is perhaps conceivable that variations in the numbers of electors, or people in single member electorates, could become so grossly disproportionate as to raise a question whether an election held on boundaries so drawn would produce a House of Representatives composed of members directly chosen by the people of the Commonwealth ...[29]

Of the majority judges, McTiernan and Jacobs JJ, in their joint judgment, gave the least equivocal account of the minimum standards which, they believed, s.24 imposed. It seems that they regarded the words 'chosen by the people of the Commonwealth' as imposing some standards which were not fixed as at 1901, but respond to changing circumstances and attitudes. Adult suffrage is one such standard: it 'may now be recognized as a fact, and as a result it is doubtful whether, ... anything less [would be] a choice by the people,[30] Nothing in the history and development of the Commonwealth demanded equality of population in electorates within a State. But 'the notion of equality is present': it 'remains one of degree'.[31] In their view the degree of inequality permitted by s.19 of the Commonwealth Electoral Act (10 per cent above or

---

[25](1975) 7 A.L.R. 593, per Barwick CJ at p.603, Gibbs J at p.622.

[26](1975) 7 A.L.R. 593, per Gibbs J at p.621.

[27](1975) 7 A.L.R. 593, per Barwick CJ at p.605; see also per Gibbs J at p.624.

[28](1975) 7 A.L.R. 593, at p.632.

[29](1975) 7 A.L.R. 593, at p.636.

[30](1975) 7 A.L.R. 593, at p.616.

[31]*ibid.*

below the quota) was consistent with that notion. However, if electoral divisions contained large inequalities, 'an election conducted by these divisions would not be a choosing of members by the people'.[32] Turning to the evidence presented in these cases, they noted that the ratio between the largest and smallest electorates in the three States ranged (as at 18 May 1974) from 1.7:1 (South Australia) to almost 2:1 (Queensland). But those variations were not so great that they contravened the demand of s.24 that the members of the House of Representatives be chosen by the people.

What, for McTiernan and Jacobs JJ, *would* be too great a variation? Commenting on the landmark decision of the United States Supreme Court, *Wesberry* v. *Sanders*,[33] they said:

the actual result in [that case] may well be the result which would follow from the application to those facts of the principle which we have earlier suggested.[34]

Under the distribution struck down by the Supreme Court, the largest district had a population of 823,680, the smallest a population of 272,254. The average population of the Congressional districts in the State in question was 394,312. If we assume that this observation was intended to indicate the type of maldistribution which their Honours would disallow as inconsistent with s.24 (and that seems a reasonable assumption), we can say that a ratio of 2:1 between the largest and the smallest electorate in a State is not objectionable, but a ratio of 3:1 would be. Alternatively, a deviation of 91.5 per cent from the quota (the deviation of the largest electorate in Queensland, as at 18 May 1974) would be consistent, but a deviation of 108.9 per cent (the deviation of the largest Congressional district in Georgia) would be invalid.

The seventh (and the dissenting) member of the Court, Murphy J, found a stricter minimum standard in s.24. Essentially, he declared that the provision demanded the practical equality of electorates within each State, measured by the number of voters in each electorate. The growth of 'constitutional principles' had established as constitutionally inviolable a franchise free of property tests or sex discrimination.[35] It had also established 'the democratic theme of equal sharing of political power which pervades the Constitution'.[36] Further, the U.S. Supreme Court's construction of Art. 1, s.2 was 'compelling in its reasoning and applicable to our Constitution'.[37] Finally, His Honour found support for his interpretation in the text of the Constitution:[38] in the terms of s.30 which declared that 'in the choosing of members each elector shall vote only once'; in the fall-back provision in s.29, 'In the absence of other provision, each State shall be one electorate'; and in the subjection of the Parliament's power to prescribe an electoral system (s.51(36) with s.29) 'to this Constitution', that is, its subjection to the command in s.24.

In the result, then, of the seven judges who participated in *McKinlay's Case*, only one was prepared to find and to apply a clear mandate from s.24. But five of the seven judges acknowledged the possibility that a particular distribution

---

[32](1975) 7 A.L.R. 593, at p.618.
[33]376 U.S. 1 (1964).
[34](1975) 7 A.L.R. 593, at p.618.
[35](1975) 7 A.L.R. 593, at p.642.
[36](1975) 7 A.L.R. 593, at p.644.
[37](1975) 7 A.L.R. 593, at pp. 644-5.
[38](1975) 7 A.L.R. 593, at pp. 645, 646.

of electorates could be invalidated by the High Court's application of s.24. *McKinlay's Case* does not eliminate the possibility that the Court will at some future time, declare the distribution of electorates within a State to be unconstitutional.

On the second issue before the Court, the majority (Barwick CJ, Gibbs, Stephen and Mason JJ) held that the delaying potential of ss. 24 and 25 of the Commonwealth Electoral Act spelt the invalidity of s. 3, s. 4 and (here Murphy J joined the other four judges) s.12(a) of the Representation Act.

The relevant provisions of the Representation Act were enacted by the Parliament under s.51(36) of the Constitution, read with the second paragraph of s.24. Reading the Representation Act with s.8 of the *Census and Statistics Act* 1905, and ss. 24 and 25 of the Commonwealth Electoral Act, there is established the following procedure for the allocation of seats between the several States:

(a) The Chief Electoral Officer is directed to 'ascertain the numbers of the people of the Commonwealth, and the numbers of the people of the several States'.[39]

(b) For this purpose the Chief Electoral Officer is to take 'the numbers of the people of each State as shown by any Commonwealth census'.[40] Such censuses are to be held 'in every tenth year . . . or at such other time as is prescribed'.[41]

(c) This information is to be embodied in a Certificate, forwarded to the Minister,[42] published in the Gazette and laid before both Houses of Parliament[43] and shall 'be evidence of the numbers of the people of the Commonwealth and of the several States'.[44]

(d) Immediately after the issue of the certificate, the Chief Electoral Officer is to allocate to each State the number of members to be returned to the House[45] by dividing the number of people of the Commonwealth by twice the number of senators (thus producing a 'quota') and by dividing the number of people in each State by the quota—and allowing an extra member for any remainder.[46]

(e) The Chief Electoral Officer is forthwith to notify the Minister of the number of members to be chosen for each State.[47]

(f) However, any alteration in the number of members to be chosen from a State shall not take effect until the government, the Distribution Commissioners and the Houses of Parliament have initiated, conducted and endorsed a redistribution of electorates for that State,[48] nor shall it affect any by-election for a House of Representatives elected before such redistribution.[49]

---

[39] *Representation Act* 1905, s.2.
[40] *ibid.*, ss. 3(1) and 4(1).
[41] *Census and Statistics Act* 1905, s.8.
[42] *Representation Act* 1905, s.6.
[43] *ibid.*, s.7.
[44] *ibid.*, s.8.
[45] *ibid.*, s.9.
[46] *ibid.*, s.10.
[47] *ibid.*, s.11.
[48] *ibid.*, s.12(a), read with the *Commonwealth Electoral Act* 1918, ss. 24 and 25.
[49] *Representation Act* 1905, s.12(b).

The plaintiffs argued, and the majority of the Court agreed, that some of the critical sections of the Representation Act were invalid: in particular, ss. 3 and 4, which provided that the re-allocation process could not be started until there was a Commonwealth census (which might, under s.8 of the Census and Statistics Act, be delayed indefinitely by the Government); and s.12(a) which delayed the conclusion of the re-allocation process until the government, the Distribution Commissioners and the Houses of Parliament had carried out a redistribution (which might, under ss. 24 and 25 of the Commonwealth Electoral Act be delayed indefinitely by the government and either House of Parliament). Gibbs J, with whose reasons Stephen and Mason agreed, declared that s.24 demanded that when the House continued for its normal term of three years a re-allocation must be made before its expiry or dissolution.[50] Accordingly, ss. 3 and 4 of the Representation Act, which tied the re-allocation to the Commonwealth census, were invalid. Re-allocations must be made every three years, not every ten years (the period mentioned in s.8 of the Census and Statistics Act) or every five years (the period which the government has currently prescribed under s.8 of that Act). It did not follow that the Commonwealth was obliged to hold a triennial census. Section 24 of the Constitution does not tie the representation of the States to population figures as established by the census:

> the Constitution requires that the number of members chosen should be in the correct proportion, and it does not require that census figures should be used . . . [O]n some occasions statistics other than those provided by the census may have to be used in ascertaining the numbers.[51]

Similarly Barwick CJ declared that the allocation 'of members to be chosen in the States must be determined for each regular election for the House of Representatives'.[52] And, in the regular re-allocation, 'it will be the latest available statistics which will have to be employed . . . perhaps even if they are not statutorily compiled'.[53] On the other hand, McTiernan and Jacobs JJ, who dissented on this point, declared that the constitutional requirement (that the number of members to be returned for each State should be in proportion to its population) 'must be given a practical operation' and the current system which linked the determination of the number of members for each State to a five-yearly census was valid.[54]

Murphy J did not refer to the question of the validity of ss. 3 and 4 of the Representation Act. But he concluded, as did Barwick CJ, Gibbs, Stephen and Mason JJ, that s.12(a) of the Act was invalid because it made the allocation of seats among the several States dependent on the conclusion of redistribution of electorates within those States whose representation was reduced or increased, and that process of redistribution could be delayed indefinitely. As Murphy J expressed it,

> Under the legislative scheme the redistribution need never occur. This plainly enables the command in s.24 of the Constitution to be circumvented.[55]

[50](1975) 7 A.L.R. 593, at p.628.
[51]*ibid.*
[52](1975) 7 A.L.R. 593, at p.609.
[53](1975) 7 A.L.R. 593, at pp. 608-9.
[54](1975) 7 A.L.R. 593, at p.619.
[55](1975) 7 A.L.R. 593, at p.650.

Gibbs J (whose reasons were adopted by Stephen and Mason JJ) observed that Parliament could, consistent with s.24 of the Constitution, enact that a re-allocation of seats between the States should not take effect until there had been a redistribution of seats within the affected States: but it must be ensured 'that the redistribution would follow directly upon the determination' under s.24; it must be ensured that it 'would take place with all due diligence'.[56] As the legislation currently stood 'no redistribution need ever be made and ... the determination might never take effect'.[57] Accordingly, s.12(a) was invalid. Similarly, Barwick CJ believed that s.12(a) was invalid because it tied the re-allocation of seats to a redistribution which need not 'occur in time for the holding of an ordinary general election or, for that matter, at all'.[58] McTiernan and Jacobs JJ were not prepared to declare s.12(a) invalid but did declare that it could not validly operate so as to prevent the number of members chosen in the several States being in proportion to their respective populations.[59]

The Court's decision on the Representation Act has left the current Government with two problems. The first of these should pose no real difficulties—it arises out of the invalidation of ss. 3 and 4. The Government must now establish a procedure for counting the population of the Commonwealth and of the States approximately once every three years, that is, in time to enable a re-allocation of seats between the States for each regular general election. The second problem left by this aspect of *McKinlay's Case* is more intractable: the Government must alter the process for redistributing electorates within States, at least where that redistribution is necessary to give effect to a re-allocation of seats between the States. In particular, that redistribution process must cease to be absolutely dependent upon the discretion of the government, the House of Representatives and the Senate. There is nothing in this aspect of *McKinlay's Case* which insists that such redistribution be depoliticized: indeed, it would be quite consistent with the decision if such redistributions were to be committed to a minister of the Crown, or to the House of Representatives, rather than to Distribution Commissioners. The constitutional considerations demand only that the redistribution process be begun promptly and that its conclusion not be delayed or obstructed for an indefinite period.

Could the Government, while instituting a new, less discretionary and potentially dilatory, system for redistribution consequential upon re-allocations, retain the existing system for redistribution consequential upon shifts in population within a State? Or is there anything in *McKinlay's Case* which casts a shadow on that system, particularly on the degree of discretion and the power of obstruction and delay vested in the government and the Houses of Parliament by ss. 24 and 25 of the Commonwealth Electoral Act?

The validity of those sections was challenged in the suit brought by South Australia against the Commonwealth, heard and disposed of at the same time as *McKinlay's Case*. And the challenge was rejected by the majority of the Court. However, if one accepts that the first paragraph of s.24 of the Constitution imposes some minimum standard of representativeness (and three of the judges, McTiernan, Jacobs and Murphy JJ were committed to such a proposition, while two judges, Stephen and Mason JJ, appeared to regard such a

---

[56](1975) 7 A.L.R. 593, at p.629.
[57]*ibid.*
[58](1975) 7 A.L.R. 593, at p.612.
[59](1975) 7 A.L.R. 593, at p.620.

proposition as arguable), then, I believe, ss. 24 and 25 of the Commonwealth Electoral Act could be exposed to an attack similar to that mounted (successfully) on s.12(a) of the Representation Act in *McKinlay's Case*. Just as, according to Gibbs J, s.12(a) was invalid because it provided (when read with ss. 24 and 25 of the Commonwealth Electoral Act) 'that the determination [required by the second paragraph of s.24] might never take effect'[60] so, it could be argued, ss. 24 and 25 of the Commonwealth Electoral Act are invalid because the minimum standards demanded by the first paragraph of s.24 of the Constitution (whatever those standards are) might cease to have effect. If s.12(a) of the Representation Act were struck down because it had the potential to frustrate and defeat the second paragraph of s.24 of the Constitution, so ss. 24 and 25 of the Commonwealth Electoral Act should be struck down because they have the potential to frustrate and defeat the first paragraph of s.24 of the Constitution. There does appear to be considerable consistency and symmetry in this argument. So much was recognized by McTiernan and Jacobs JJ who declared that ss. 24 and 25 of the Commonwealth Electoral Act could not validly operate so as to defeat the requirement that members of the House of Representatives should be chosen by the people of the Commonwealth and that s.12(a) of the Representation Act could not validly operate so as to defeat the requirement that the number of members chosen in the several States should be in proportion to their respective populations.[61] Again, Murphy J said: 'As ss. 24 and 25 would allow the Constitution to be contravened, I would declare each invalid.'[62] And, later, his Honour said '[The legislative scheme] plainly enables the command in s.24 of the Constitution to be circumvented. I would declare s.12(a) invalid'.[63]

On the other hand, Stephen J (who believed that the opening words of s.24 embodied the principle of 'representative democracy',[64] though not 'any rigid rule of numerical equality'[65]) dismissed the challenge to ss. 24 and 25 of the Commonwealth Electoral Act on the basis that those sections had 'not been shown, upon the material before this court, to operate inconsistently with accepted principles of representative democracy . . .'[66] That is, the evidence before the court on the past and current operation of the distribution system did not establish that ss. 24 and 25 of the Act had (so far) produced a situation inconsistent with s.24 of the Constitution. But his Honour went on immediately to endorse the reasons of Gibbs J for striking down s.12(a) of the Representation Act: it was struck down, not because it had produced a situation inconsistent with s.24 of the Constitution (Gibbs J said 'there is no evidence to that effect'[67]) but because the legislation had the *potential* to defeat s.24.

---

[60](1975) 7 A.L.R. 593, at p.629.
[61](1975) 7 A.L.R. 593, at p.621.
[62](1975) 7 A.L.R. 593, at p.649.
[63](1975) 7 A.L.R. 593, at p.650.
[64](1975) 7 A.L.R. 593, at p.632.
[65](1975) 7 A.L.R. 593, at p.634.
[66](1975) 7 A.L.R. 593, at p.635.
[67](1975) 7 A.L.R. 593, at p.629.

III
THE SENATE: WHOSE HOUSE?

The addition of territorial senators to the Senate was the most radical change in the formal structure of the Commonwealth Parliament during the three years of the Whitlam Government. But it could be described as a substantial change only if we accepted the notion that the Senate was the States House. But reality does not reflect that notion. Power in the Senate is distributed not according to State interests and alliances but according to party allegiance. The addition of territory senators and their election on 13 December 1975 did not disturb the distribution of political power in that chamber.

The *Senate (Representation of Territories) Act* 1973 was (despite its title) passed into law on 7 August 1974. It had been one of the Bills on which the Governor-General had premised the double dissolution proclamation of 11 April 1974[68] and was passed at the Joint Sitting of the two Houses on 6 August 1974. The Act provided that (a) the Australian Capital Territory and the Northern Territory should each be represented in the Senate by two senators chosen by the people of the territory voting as one electorate;[69] (b) each such senator was to have all the powers, immunities and privileges of a senator for a State: in particular he might vote on all questions arising in the Senate;[70] and (c) each such senator was to serve only until the next general election of members for the House of Representatives—a maximum term of three years.[71]

So, apart from term of service, a senator for a territory was to be in all respects equal to a senator for a State. And that equality, it was claimed by a number of the States, spelt the invalidity of the legislation. In the *Territory Senators Case*,[72] the States of Queensland, Western Australia and New South Wales commenced proceedings before the High Court asserting the substantive invalidity of the Act. The last two States also asserted that there were fatal defects in the procedure by which the Act had been passed. The State of Victoria was given leave to intervene in support of the other States. In this essay, I shall confine my attention to the question of substantive validity of the Act.

The plaintiffs claimed, against the defendant Commonwealth, a declaration that the Senate (Representation of Territories) Act was invalid on the ground that it conflicted with s.7 of the Constitution which provided (in its first paragraph):

> 7.   The Senate shall be composed of senators for each State, directly chosen by the people of the State, voting, until the Parliament otherwise provides, as one electorate.

In response, the Commonwealth raised s.122 of the Constitution which, it argued, supported the Act:

> 122.   The Parliament may make laws for the government of any territory . . . and may allow the representation of such territory in either House of the Parliament to the extent and on the terms which it thinks fit.

---

[68] *Australian Government Gazette*, 11 April 1974, No. 31B.

[69] *Senate (Representation of Territories) Act* 1973, s.4.

[70] *ibid.*, s.5.

[71] *ibid.*, s.7(2).

[72] *Western Australia* v. *Commonwealth* (1975) 7 A.L.R. 159.

There does appear to be some conflict in the provisions of these two sections. Neither of them is expressed to be 'subject to this Constitution', so one cannot find textual support for reading one or the other as the dominant section. But the plaintiff States argued that s.7 should be read as the dominant provision, because of the federal nature of the Constitution and of the role of the Senate in the preservation of that federal nature. Three members of the High Court, Barwick CJ, Gibbs and Stephen JJ, accepted this argument, but the majority of the Court, McTiernan, Mason, Jacobs and Murphy JJ, held that s.122 must be given full effect, unfettered by any implication which might be drawn from s.7 or from the special status of the Senate as a States House (or guardian of the federal compact).

The States' arguments depended upon the Court reading s.7 of the Constitution as containing an exhaustive statement of the membership of the Senate—it was to 'be composed of senators for each State'. A number of other constitutional provisions (such as ss. 11, 15 and 21) confirmed the notion that the Senate was conceived as consisting only of senators from the States. The power given to the Parliament in s.122, to allow representation in the Senate to territories, should be construed (so the argument went) as allowing something less than full representation, such as non-voting representation. However, Mason J (with whose opinion McTiernan J concurred) pointed out that this method of constructing, out of s.7 and associated sections, a proposition about the exclusively State membership of the Senate, ignored the presence of s.122 in the Constitution.

The apparent conflict could be reconciled if one did not read s.7 (and s.24 dealing with the House of Representatives) as speaking for all time. Rather, the sections should be regarded as providing for the composition of each House, while taking account of the prospective possibility that territorial members might be added at a later date when Parliament deemed that their development warranted such membership:

> Understood in this light, ss. 7 and 24 make exhaustive provision for the composition of each House until such time as Parliament might see fit to allow representation to a territory under s.122.[73]

Similarly, Jacobs J concluded that s.122 contained 'a provision which operates by way of proviso or exception to and by way of extension of s.7'.[74] His Honour travelled well outside the terms of the Constitution to support this conclusion, and reviewed aspects of the historical context in which the Constitution was drafted, in particular the anticipated accession to the Commonwealth, as territories, of the various British colonies in the Pacific.

Further, there was no suggestion in the Constitution that the inhabitants of the Australian Capital Territory ('of no mean size') should be disenfranchised.[75] Jacobs J appears to have proceeded on the assumption, strongly articulated in the judgment of Murphy J, that the Constitution was intended to introduce and maintain a *democratic* political system.

Murphy J asserted, as he was to assert in the later decision on the distribution of electorates in the House of Representatives (*McKinlay's Case*,[76] discussed

---

[73] (1975) 7 A.L.R. 159, at p.207.
[74] (1975) 7 A.L.R. 159, at p.208.
[75] (1975) 7 A.L.R. 159, at p.210.
[76] (1975) 7 A.L.R. 593.

above), that in interpreting the Constitution the Court should keep in mind 'the purpose of the Constitution and the fundamental constitutional doctrines which were its background'.[77] Amongst those doctrines was the concept of democracy: 'The Constitution is designed for a democratic society'.[78] His Honour explained the nature of this concept by referring to (amongst other sources) Mill's *Representative Government*. One of the passages from Mill, quoted by Murphy J, included the following proposition: 'In a really equal democracy every or any section will be represented, not disproportionately but proportionately'.[79] The inappropriateness of such a principle to the Australian Senate[80] does not appear to have deterred the judge, for he concluded:

> The permanent deprivation of representation by membership in the Senate or the House of Representatives is a serious exclusion from the democratic process . . . It is contrary to the democratic theme of the Constitution that Parliament should not be able to allow representation by membership in either House to territories at the time and on the terms which the Parliament considers appropriate.[81]

His Honour referred to a number of other considerations which supported the plenary nature of s.122: the section used the word 'representation', which was also used in ss. 7, 21, 121 and 128. In each of those provisions the word clearly referred to membership. Looking to those other provisions for guidance, and taking account of the ordinary meaning of the word, his Honour concluded that ' "representation" in s.122 plainly means "membership" '.[82] Further, the analogous position under the United States Constitution could be used to support this interpretation of s.122: by the end of the nineteenth century it was well established that U.S. territories could not send members, only non-voting delegates, to Congress. There was no provision in the U.S. Constitution dealing with such representation. Section 122 could be regarded as a deliberate attempt to ensure that the privilege of returning members to 'each House should not be denied forever to the people of the territories.'[83]

All three of the dissenting justices (Barwick CJ, Gibbs and Stephen JJ) recognized the apparent conflict between s.7 and s.122; but that conflict was to be resolved by allowing the proposition expressed in s.7 to dominate or control the interpretation of s.122. Each of the justices made some reference to the wide range of participation which the word 'representation' could denote: that word, according to Stephen J, was 'not a term of art and the meaning to be given to it must be consistent with the whole structure which the Constitution has created'.[84] Barwick CJ argued that the nature of the representation contemplated by s.122 should be determined by considering the federal nature of the Constitution and the various sections dealing with the composition of Parliament.[85] The Chief Justice placed considerable emphasis on 'the central and dominant purpose of the Constitution', which had been to create 'an

[77](1975) 7 A.L.R. 159, at p.217.

[78]*ibid.*

[79]J.S. Mill, *Considerations on Representative Government* (World's Classics ed., London, 1912), p.248.

[80]Section 7 of the Constitution guarantees the smallest original State the same representation in the Senate as the largest original State.

[81](1975) 7 A.L.R. 159, at p.219.

[82](1975) 7 A.L.R. 159, at p.217.

[83](1975) 7 A.L.R. 159, at p.218.

[84](1975) 7 A.L.R. 159, at p.195.

[85](1975) 7 A.L.R. 159, at p.174; and see Gibbs J at pp. 186-7.

indissoluble federal Commonwealth' in which the States were to play a crucial role.[86] Clearly His Honour believed[87] that to allow full representation for the territories in the Senate would be to undermine that federal character of the Constitution. All three dissenting justices turned to the terms of s.7 (and its associated sections) to establish the proposition that the Senate was intended to be and to remain a States House. The proposition, expressed in s.7, that 'The Senate shall be composed of senators for each State', was read as an exhaustive and exclusive proposition. That meaning was reinforced by such other provisions as ss. 8, 9, 10, 11, 12, 13 and 14. These were the provisions dealing with the election of senators: voting qualifications, voting systems, the issue of writs and the rotation of senators; each section was framed in terms which could apply only to State senators. The indication that there were intended to be no other senators was strong.[88] And ss. 15 and 21, dealing with casual vacancies in the Senate, were, in the words of Gibbs J, 'consistent with no other conclusion',[89] for those sections clearly proceeded on the assumption that every senator should be a representative of the people of a State.[90] Finally, each of the dissenting justices referred to the fact that, in 1900, the United States Constitution was interpreted as denying membership of Congress to U.S. territories. The principle of non-voting representation for territories was, therefore, 'hardly . . . unfamiliar to some at least of those responsible for the framing of our Constitution.'[91] That is, it was to be supposed that the draftsmen of our Constitution adopted that principle, despite their deliberate insertion in s.122 of a clause allowing Parliament to confer representation on these territories, a clause which had no counterpart in the United States Constitution. It may be true that that document was 'in large part a model for the Constitution of Australia', as Barwick CJ maintained;[92] but it is difficult to accept that the founders of our Constitution followed the model faithfully in this area. The conclusion expressed by Quick and Garran was that, in this respect, the Australian Constitution did not follow the United States model.[93]

Whatever the long-term implications of the High Court's decision in the *Territory Senators Case,* the immediate, short-term implications were almost certainly critical. The Court's decision was handed down on 10 October 1975, while the federal executive of the Liberal Party was meeting in Canberra. The executive was debating whether the Opposition parties should move in the Senate to delay passage of the Government's Appropriation Bills and so force the Government to an early election. The Court's decision opened up the prospect (possibly remote but nevertheless real) that the Government might win brief control of the Senate: the four new territorial senators were to be elected at the next half-Senate election[94] which (with the co-operation of at least one of the State Governments under s.12 of the Constitution) could according to the Constitution, s.13, be called on immediately. The newly elected territorial

---

[86](1975) 7 A.L.R. 159, at pp. 171-2.

[87](1975) 7 A.L.R. 159, at p.174.

[88](1975) 7 A.L.R. 159, per Gibbs J at p.185, Stephen J at pp. 195-6.

[89](1975) 7 A.L.R. 159, at p.185.

[90](1975) 7 A.L.R. 159, at p.186.

[91](1975) 7 A.L.R. 159, per Stephen J at p.197; and see Barwick CJ at p.175, Gibbs J at pp. 189-90.

[92](1975) 7 A.L.R. 159, at p.175.

[93]J. Quick and R. Garran, *Annotated Constitution of the Australian Commonwealth* (Sydney, 1901), p.973.

[94]*Senate (Representation of Territories) Act* 1973, s.7(1).

senators would take their places on the declaration of the polls,[95] while any newly elected State senators would take their places only from 1 July 1976.[96] Therefore, if the Government, or candidates sympathetic to the Government, could win three of the four places for territorial senators, the balance of power in the Senate could be altered, to allow passage of the legislation implementing the proposals of the Distribution Commissioners—to allow a substantial redistribution of electorates for all States except Western Australia, to the political cost of one of the Opposition parties, the National Country Party. The prospects of the Government gaining control of the Senate in this way were not strong: they depended upon the independent 'casual vacancy' Senators Bunton and Field being replaced by A.L.P. candidates, upon the independent Senator Hall voting with the Government, upon an 'independent' supporter of the Government (Gorton) winning one of the two Australian Capital Territory places and upon Government candidates winning the other A.C.T. place and one of the two Northern Territory places. It was, to put it mildly, a complicated strategy. Nevertheless it has been reported that members of the Opposition were strongly influenced by the prospects of possible advantage for the Labor Government in the Court's decision to move almost immediately to delay the passing of the Appropriation Bills. Kelly describes[97] the High Court's decision as 'the single most important event . . . shaping Fraser's decision to block the budget'. He also asserts that 'a large number of Liberals changed their attitude' on the issue of blocking supply because of the decision. The move to force a general election by delaying passage of the Appropriation Bills was, essentially, a device to forestall an early half-Senate election with its consequent risks for the Opposition's continued control of the Senate.

What of the decision's long-term implications? It is difficult to regard it as portending any fundamental changes: the decision did allow, at the elections of 13 December 1975, the size of the Senate to grow from sixty senators to sixty-four senators; but of the four newly created places, two were won by the new Government and two by the Opposition. So the real balance of power remained unaffected. On the other hand, the addition of these four senators may reinforce the case made by the Senate during October and November 1975 to exercise the power to turn out a government: before the addition, the Senate's claim to be a truly representative chamber suffered from a number of defects, among them the absence of any representation in that chamber for the people resident in the Australian Capital Territory and the Northern Territory. That defect, at least, was removed on 13 December, 1975.

The decision also opened up the possibility that a future Parliament might enact legislation enlarging the representation of one or both territories to such an extent that the current character and political complexion of the Senate could be radically altered. For example, a government which was in the minority in the Senate might conceivably obtain the enactment of legislation which added 100 senators from the Australian Capital Territory; and might court the voters of that Territory through generous salary and leave concessions to Commonwealth Public Servants; and might in this way gain control of the Senate. This is a rather elaborate scenario, and it suffers from one flaw: such legislation would need to be enacted by Parliament, including the Senate.

---

[95] *ibid.*, s.6.
[96] Constitution, s.13.
[97] P. Kelly, *The Unmaking of Gough* (Sydney, 1976), pp. 258-9.

Either the Senate's assent to the legislation (the senators' 'willing participation' in hastening their journey into political oblivion, as Mason J expressed it)[98] or the approval of a joint sitting of both Houses after a double dissolution, would be essential. The political constraints which would inhibit a government from effecting such a strategy are indeed substantial. The assumption ought to be, as Mason J said, that 'Parliament will act responsibly' or as Jacobs J expressed it, 'Parliament itself [is] the safeguard against the absurd possibility'.

However, the real effect of the Senate (Representation of Territories) Act, and of the High Court's decision on its validity, is to destroy the credibility of the claim that the Senate is the States House, representing the interests of the States and guarding against the passage of legislation inimical to the interests of the States. The claim was hardly credible before the passage of this Act: seventy-odd years of party politics in the Senate had undermined it. But the claim was still advanced by those who thought that the Senate had a unique position which should at least be defended or by those who wished to stake a claim for the Senate possessing the extraordinary power of life and death over a government formed from the House of Representatives. But now the presence of four territorial senators divided, like their State colleagues, along party political lines, must destroy this shibboleth. Or will it?

IV
THE SENATE: CASUAL VACANCIES

Clearly the function of filling a casual vacancy in the Senate, such as that caused by the resignation of Lionel Murphy on 9 February 1975, is committed to the Houses of Parliament of the State or, if the Parliament is not in session, to the government of the State, from which the former senator was elected. Section 15 of the Constitution is quite explicit on this. The width of the power conferred by s.15 was amply demonstrated when the New South Wales Houses of Parliament at a joint sitting chose an independent local government politician, Cleaver Bunton, to fill the place vacated by Murphy, and when Bunton subsequently took his place in the Senate without challenge.[99] But the question whether the Houses of Parliament in New South Wales had acted properly or within the spirit of the Constitution (as opposed to legally or according to the letter of the Constitution) was strongly disputed.

On 12 February 1975, in anticipation of the action of the Houses of the New South Wales Parliament, the Leader of the Government in the Senate moved that the Senate declare its support for the replacement of vacating senators by the appointment of senators belonging to the same political parties, a 'long-established convention [which] may not be followed in relation to the filling of the vacancy now existing in the representation of the State of New South Wales'.[100] The substance of the motion was substantially diluted by an Opposition amendment which was accepted by the Government and carried without division.[101] The amended motion recognized that the filling of a casual vacancy was 'the sole responsibility of the Houses of Parliament of the State' or the State government and 'commended' to those bodies 'the practice which has

---

[98](1975) 7 A.L.R. 159, at p.207.

[99]Senate, *Debates,* 4 March 1975, vol. 63, p.561.

[100]Senate, *Debates,* 12 February 1975, vol. 63, p.111.

[101]Senate, *Debates,* 13 February 1975, vol. 63, p.173.

prevailed since 1949', of appointing or choosing a senator from the same political party as the vacating senator.[102]

Clearly the Opposition regarded the reference to a 'practice' rather than a 'convention' as significant: Senator Wright, speaking on the motion, made it clear that this was a deliberate substitution: 'this so-called convention—I call it a practice',[103] he declared. Earlier, he had said that 'The Senate . . . ought to be quite careful and most cautious about its language in this respect'.[104] On the other hand, while the Government accepted the Opposition's amendment, Government senators continually referred[105] to the 'convention' that State Parliaments or governments appoint or choose senators from the same political party as those whose resignation, death or disqualification have created vacancies in the Senate, as did the Liberal Movement Senator Hall.[106]

The Government returned to this issue later in the same year. When it became clear that the Queensland Legislative Assembly intended to vote to fill the vacancy created by the death of Senator Milliner by choosing a candidate who did not have the support of the late Senator Milliner's party (the Australian Labor Party) the Government moved,[107] in the House of Representatives, that the House commend 'to the Parliaments of all the States the practice which has prevailed since 1949' and that the House express its great concern over 'reports that the long-established convention may not be followed' by the Queensland House. That motion was carried,[108] without division, by the House of Representatives on 3 September 1975.

The view that there is a distinction between a 'constitutional convention' and a 'desirable political practice', argued forcefully by Senator Wright during the Senate debate, was reiterated in a comment appearing in the *Australian Law Journal* of April 1975.[109] A convention, according to the *Journal*, was best defined negatively, by listing those 'qualities it does not have'. It is not a rule of law, in the sense that the courts do not check breaches of a convention; it is not a practice, nor is it merely 'a desirable political understanding—a kind of "gentlemen's agreement" '.[110] Even as a negative definition, this is hardly illuminating, for the concepts which, it is said, a convention does *not* resemble, can hardly be said to be clearly defined and unequivocally identifiable. Are all rules of law within the jurisdiction of the courts to control?[111] What is a 'practice'? What is an 'understanding'? In whose mind are these terms to be defined? By what criteria are we to allocate some things which public people do to a box marked 'conventions' and others to a box marked 'practices'? The *Australian Law Journal* suggested that conventions were to be distinguished by one essential criterion:[112]

---

[102]Senate, *Debates,* 12 February 1975, vol. 63, p.116.

[103]Senate, *Debates,* 13 February 1975, vol. 63, p.164.

[104]Senate, *Debates,* 13 February 1975, vol. 63, p.162.

[105]See, e.g., Senate, *Debates,* 12 February 1975, vol. 63, at p.111 (Wriedt), pp. 117, 118 (D. McClelland); 13 February 1975, at pp. 150, 152 (Everett), pp. 159, 160 (Button), pp. 152, 168 (Wheeldon).

[106]Senate, *Debates,* 12 February 1975, vol. 63, pp. 127, 128.

[107]House of Representatives, *Debates,* 3 September 1975, vol. 96, p.924.

[108]House of Representatives, *Debates,* 3 September 1975, vol. 96, p.941.

[109]Note, (1975) 49 *Australian L. J.* 153.

[110]*ibid.,* at p.156.

[111]See S.A. de Smith, *Constitutional and Administrative Law* (2nd ed., London, 1973) pp. 50-3.

[112](1975) 49 *Australian L.J.* 153, at p.156.

Underlying a convention, there must be some element of recognition of an obligation that it should be followed as a matter of course ... The more important true constitutional conventions are those which concern the relations between the royal prerogative and Parliament, and these best illustrate the characteristics referred to above.

But neither the criterion offered by the *Journal* ('recognition of an obligation') nor the example referred to (the relations between Crown and Parliament) bring us any closer to understanding the nature of conventions, nor to a capacity to recognize or identify specific conventions. By whom is the 'obligation' to be recognized? By all participants in the political process? By the majority of participants? By the participant whose conduct is sought to be checked or controlled? And what are we to make of 'the more important true constitutional conventions' since 11 November 1975?

The term 'conventions of the constitution' is a familiar, if somewhat elusive, term to most students of government and politics. Professor Dicey is generally credited with developing the notion of constitutional conventions. He observed that the rules which make up constitutional law are of two types.[113] The first are those rules which are enforced by the courts;

The other set of rules consist of conventions, understandings, habits, or practices which, though they may regulate the conduct of ... officials, are not in reality laws at all since they are not enforced by the courts. This portion of constitutional law may, for the sake of distinction, be termed the 'conventions of the constitution', or constitutional morality.

Mill had already referred to the 'unwritten maxims of the constitution'[114] and Anson was to describe these precepts as 'the custom of the constitution'.[115] Jennings explained that these conventions 'provide the flesh which clothes the dry bones of the law; they make the legal constitution work; they keep it in touch with the growth of ideas'.[116] De Smith argues that the rules of strict law (the justiciable rules) can 'give a grotesquely misleading picture of the rules actually observed' by the participants in government; accordingly the conventions which those participants observe ought to be treated as part of constitutional law.[117] Perhaps the clearest description of the function of these conventional rules is that provided by Marshall and Moodie. They point out that these conventions will be found in all constitutions, even the recently established. No rule of law is self-applying and conventions are quickly developed to govern the application of the rules—to interpret the rules or to prescribe the circumstances of their application. No matter how detailed the formal rules may be, in a changing world it is rarely possible in advance to eliminate doubts by legislation:

The result is often to leave a significant degree of discretion to those exercising the rights or wielding the powers legally conferred, defined, or permitted. As Dicey pointed out, it is to regulate the use of such discretionary power that conventions develop.[118]

Recently it has been suggested that conventions play a larger role in countries which, like Australia, have written constitutions: 'the greater the degree of

---

[113]A.V. Dicey, *Law of the Constitution* (10th ed., London, 1959), p.24.

[114]Mill, cited above n. 79, p.148.

[115]W.R. Anson, *Law and Custom of the Constitution,* vol. I (Oxford, 1886), p.23.

[116]W. Ivor Jennings, *The Law of the Constitution* (5th ed., London, 1959), pp. 81-2.

[117]de Smith, cited above n. 111, p.48.

[118]G. Marshall and G.C. Moodie, *Some Problems of the Constitution* (4th ed., London, 1967), p.26.

constitutional rigidity, the greater is the need for the benefits of informal adaptation which conventions bring'.[119]

It is clear that there are a series of propositions (which we might label as conventions or practices of the Constitution), distinct from the propositions recognized and enforced by the courts, which appear, at least, strongly to influence or control the actions of people in public life. To assert that these conventions are non-justiciable is not to deny that occasionally the existence of a convention is recognized by a court of law, and allowed to influence the court's decision. For example, the majority of the High Court referred in the *Engineers Case*[120] to the convention of responsible government which, the judges argued, rendered United States decisions on intergovernmental immunities peculiarly inappropriate to the Australian federation.[121] In the *Copyright Owners Case*,[122] Dixon CJ referred to the convention, which had evolved between 1911 and 1928, that the United Kingdom Parliament would only legislate for Australia at Australia's request, and held that legislation passed by the Parliament in 1928 must be presumed to have been intended not to apply to Australia. But these are unusual cases: many of the propositions which are alleged to be firmly established as conventions have not received the *imprimatur* of the courts, nor have the courts provided any authoritative statement of the criteria by which conventions are to be recognized. As de Smith wrote,[123] 'the tests for the ascertainment of conventions are neither universally agreed nor, when agreed, easily applied in a large number of marginal cases'. De Smith went on to recognize that 'divided counsel' might be heard in the course of many debates over the existence and nature of conventions; and that a critical part might be played by 'personal inclination and political expedience [and] partisan sentiment'.[124]

Indeed, the lack of certainty, the high degree of subjectivity (and, perhaps, hypocrisy) which surrounds this question of conventions has prompted some writers to suggest that we should 'delete those pages in constitutional textbooks headed Conventions, with their unreal distinctions and their word puzzles'.[125] We should, rather, recognize that the formal justiciable rules of the Constitution are reinforced or filled out by political rules and practices of varying strengths, which operate as reasonably accurate descriptions and predictions of political behaviour. But they are not prescriptions or rules of obligation. We might, of course, continue to label these political rules as conventions. But we should abandon the notion that conventions are clearly identifiable by weighing up historical precedents or that the legitimacy of conventions depends upon feelings of 'obligation'. The most that one can say is that there is a series of political rules which, from our observation and from our understanding of the function of our political system, we can identify. These rules describe the way

---

[119]C.R. Munro, 'Laws and Conventions Distinguished' (1975) 91 *L. Quarterly Rev.* 218, at p.219.

[120]*Amalgamated Society of Engineers* v. *Adelaide Steamship Co. Ltd* (1920) 28 C.L.R. 129, pp. 146-8.

[121]For a recognition and application of the convention in a different context see *Liversidge* v. *Anderson* [1942] A.C. 206.

[122]*Copyright Owners Reproduction Society Ltd* v. *E.M.I. (Australia) Pty Ltd* (1958) 100 C.L.R. 597, p.612.

[123]de Smith, cited above n. 111, p.58.

[124]*ibid.*, p.60.

[125]Comment, [1963] *Public Law*, p.402; Munro, cited above n. 119, p.235. See also the commentary by Professor Reid, below Ch. 7.

the system works and enable us to predict how the system will operate in future. They are not constant: the system will need to adapt to changed circumstances and that adaptation is most likely to be accomplished through changes to these informal political rules. Recognizing that constitutions are concerned with political power and its distribution and that their primary function is to fix or stabilise a particular, selected, distribution of power while allowing for gradual, evolutionary shifts in power, a critical function of the political rules or conventions is to express or describe the current distribution of power. And in a society which professes and practises (with some pragmatic modifications) democracy, the political rules or conventions have another critical function: they connect or link the political system with the general view or consensus of what may or may not legitimately be done within the political process: an action that is likely to destroy public respect for the existing distribution of power could not be described (in a democratic society) as conforming to the political rules or conventions. Marshall and Moodie assert 'that the conventions describe the way in which certain legal powers must be exercised if the powers are to be tolerated by those affected'.[126]

What, then, can we say of the power conferred by s.15 of the Constitution on State Houses of Parliament and governments, to choose a senator to fill a casual vacancy? Is it possible (or was it possible, before the choice of Senator Bunton) to induce any general proposition about the way in which that power was exercised? Is it possible to support the contention of the Labor Government that a convention had evolved, in accordance with which the choice would be confined to a number of the same political party as the vacating senator?

Between 1901 and 1974, there were sixty-three places vacated in the Senate before the expiry of the senators' terms. On three occasions, in 1928, 1931 and 1946, State Houses of Parliament chose a new senator from a different political party.[127] However, it is misleading to treat those seventy-four years as a single period. The introduction in 1949 of proportional representation (through the single transferable vote method) dramatically changed the nature of political representation in the Senate. Whereas, before 1949, large, even grotesque, party majorities had been common, after 1949 the voting system ensured a closely divided chamber.[128] Since 1949 there had been (until Murphy's vacancy) twenty-five casual vacancies. Each of those vacancies was filled by the State Houses or government 'choosing' a senator from the same political party as the vacating senator.[129] Ten of the new senators were chosen by State Houses or governments controlled by political parties professing opposition to the new senators' parties. On each occasion the new senator had been nominated to the State Houses or government by the political party to which the vacating senator had belonged. The available evidence suggests that the consistent filling of the vacancies in this way, on twenty-five separate occasions, was more than a coincidence. In 1951, when the Western Australian Government was called on

---

[126]Marshall and Moodie, cited above n. 118, p.35.

[127]Odgers, cited above n. 10, p.58.

[128]During the first forty-eight years of the Commonwealth Parliament the closest distribution of the thirty-six senators was nineteen non-Labor to seventeen Labor (between 1940 and 1943). For forty-five years of that period the stronger political group in the Senate had a majority of at least six senators. For twenty-four years the margin between the parties was at least twenty senators. After the introduction of proportional representation and the increase of the Senate to sixty members, the margin between the parties became much narrower. From 1964 to 1975, no political party had a majority in the Senate, and votes of independent and D.L.P. senators were critical. See table in Odgers, cited above n. 10, p.6.

[129]Senate, *Debates*, 4 May 1976, no. 9, p.1475.

to fill a vacancy, the Premier of that State expressed the following view (in accordance with which the Government acted):[130]

> [I]n view of the fact that proportional representation is now the method of election to the Senate, a member of the same party, nominated by the executive of the party, should be appointed when future vacancies arise through death or other causes.

In 1958 the Joint Committee on Constitutional Review declared that all its members (from different political parties) 'were strongly of the view that the principle [of choosing a new senator from the same political party as the vacating senator] should be observed without exception'.[131] The Committee noted that it had not been able to draft a constitutional amendment to make this choice obligatory, but it thought such an amendment desirable, as had a Senate Select Committee which had considered the question in 1951.[132] In its final 1959 Report, the Joint Committee on Constitutional Review referred to the difficulties of constitutional amendment, pointed out that the pre-1949 appointments of senators from opposing political parties had been 'the exceptions and not the rule' and repeated its unanimous support of the principle emphasized in its 1958 Report—'so that the matter may become the subject of a constitutional convention or understanding, which political parties will always observe'.[133] In 1966, the Premier of Victoria, Mr Bolte, declared that the 'rules and practice' established during his government required 'that if a vacancy should arise in the Senate affecting this State, the Party to which the late Senator belonged . . . would nominate the successor'.[134] In 1971, the Premier of Queensland, Mr Bjelke-Petersen, referred to the resignation of a Liberal Party senator for Queensland, Senator Rankin, and advised the Leader of the Opposition in the Queensland Parliament that:

> the accepted practice when a casual vacancy of this nature occurs is for the new Senator to be of the same political party as his predecessor and I have asked the Queensland division of the Liberal Party of Australia to advise me, as quickly as possible, of the name of the person they wish to nominate on this particular occasion.[135]

The Clerk to the Senate has explained[136] that since 1949, 'the States have demonstrated their readiness to choose a new Senator of the same political party as was the Senator he replaces . . . A convention has been so established . . .' Lumb and Ryan also refer[137] to 'the growth of a convention that a person belonging to the same political party as that to which the late senator belonged should be chosen'. This, they maintain, 'would give expression to the popular will expressed' in the former senator's election.

It is clear that there were twenty-odd years of consistent practice, clearly deliberate, not attributable to collective absence of mind. There is no reason to suppose that twenty years' experience provides insufficient evidence from

---

[130]Senate, *Debates*, 12 February 1975, vol. 63, p.112.

[131]*Report*, cited above n. 11, App. C, p.197.

[132]Senate, *Select Committee on Constitution Alteration (Avoidance of Double Dissolution Deadlocks) Bill 1950: Report*, Parliamentary Paper S.1 of 1950-51.

[133]*Report*, cited above n. 11, para. 291.

[134]Victoria. Legislative Assembly, *Debates*, 26 October 1966, pp. 1332-3.

[135]Senate, *Debates*, 4 May 1976, no. 9, p.1477.

[136]Odgers, cited above n. 10, p.65.

[137]R.D. Lumb and K.W. Ryan, *Constitution of the Commonwealth of Australia Annotated* (Sydney, 1974), p.44.

which to induce a general proposition. De Smith refers[138] to the evolution, over periods of this length, of the convention that the Crown is obliged to assent to a Bill passed by the Houses of Parliament, and the convention that the Prime Minister of the United Kingdom be chosen from the House of Commons.

So much for experience. But what of reason: is it possible to argue that a political rule or convention, controlling appointments under s.15 of the Constitution, is necessary for the proper working of the constitution, or critical to the acceptance and tolerance of the political system (the distribution of power) by the people? To what extent would such a rule advance or inhibit democracy, as Australians know it? On this level, the case for a political rule or convention of the nature described by the Joint Committee on Constitutional Review is strong. The system of electing senators ensures that the membership of that chamber will not be dominated by any single political group: a party or a coalition of parties may have a majority but that majority is unlikely to be large. Frequently a party which holds a majority of the seats in the House of Representatives will not control the Senate. It will often be the case, therefore, that the change in political allegiance of one senator will swing control of the Senate from one party to the other. Even the absence of a senator from one party may be enough to give the other party temporary control of the Senate.[139] Of course it is quite consistent with a system of parliamentary democracy for party strength to change consequent upon a general election or a by-election. But it is hardly consistent with any democratic system of government for control of an elected chamber to pass from one group to another at the whim of one individual (a State Premier) or a small group of politicians (the majority members of a State's Houses of Parliament or a State government). For an individual or a small group of people to use the power conferred by s.15 of the Constitution as a means of distorting the balance of political power in the Senate is to debase our political system and to bring that system into contempt. The unlimited discretion conferred by s.15 should be viewed in the context of the growth and evolution of our political system. The power remains unfettered, so far as the formal, justiciable rules of law are concerned, but, as Dicey pointed out,[140] conventions develop to regulate the use of discretionary powers. There is no question of a restrictive convention (of the nature argued for by the Joint Committee in 1959) being 'in clear conflict with the unambiguous terms of a provision [s.15] in a written constitution', as the *Australian Law Journal* apparently believed.[141] The power conferred by s.15 remains intact: but the convention tells us how it has been exercised in the past and how, so long as our political system remains unchanged, we can expect the power to be exercised in the future. Conventions keep the legal rules in contact with political developments: while we might have expected a wide range of discretion to be exercised in the choice of senators under s.15 up to 1949, once the Senate underwent the critical political change which came with proportional representation, the application of the power also required change.

The real vice in an unfettered and partisan exercise of the power conferred by s.15 is that it places the stability of our political system at substantial risk. It

[138]de Smith, cited above n. 111, pp. 58, 59.

[139]As the absence of the late Senator Milliner (or a Labor Party replacement) gave the Opposition sufficient control of the Senate to defer consideration of the Appropriation Bills in October and November 1975, thus precipitating the crisis of 11 November 1975.

[140]Dicey, cited above n. 113, pp. 426-9.

[141](1975) 49 *Australian L.J.* 153, at p.155.

also threatens to undermine public confidence in our political system: and that confidence is essential to the continuance of parliamentary democracy. For voters to see that their deliberately expressed choice can be subverted by a small group of politicians is for those voters to see that political power lies not with them but with an oligarchy. It is hardly conceivable that such an unequivocal assertion of oligarchical power will enhance public respect for the established distribution of authority.[142]

Both subversion of democratic principle and the creation of instability were graphically evident in the 1975 casual vacancy replacements. The members of the New South Wales Parliament chose, in February 1975, as a senator for that State, a man who was a member of no political party, and left those New South Wales voters who had supported the Australian Labor Party on 18 May 1974 under-represented in the Senate. While the new senator supported the Government on some vital issues, such as the passage of supply, he voted against the Government on other important issues such as the re-distribution proposals of the Distribution Commissioners, for which, given the results of the double dissolution election of 18 May 1974, the Government appeared to have a mandate. If the choice of Senator Bunton demonstrated the threat to democracy inherent in an untramelled exercise of the s.15 power, that of Senator Field showed that the stability of our system of Parliamentary government could be undermined through a capricious use of the power. The choice of Field, a former member of the Labor Party, committed to the destruction of the Whitlam Labor Government, had a critical impact on party strength in the Senate: the Labor Party was reduced to twenty-seven senators and could hope for the support of two independent senators (Hall and Bunton) on the approaching supply legislation. The Liberal and National Country Parties had thirty senators and could expect that the third independent senator (Field) would support any move to reject or defer the supply legislation. In the event, Field took no part in the votes for the deferral of supply: he was granted leave of absence from the Senate on 1 October 1975, to defend a High Court challenge to his qualifications. But his presence or absence was irrelevant: the action of the Queensland House of Parliament had reduced the Labor Party's representation to a point when it could not defeat (with the aid of Hall and Bunton) the Opposition's motions to defer supply. Party strength in the Senate was distorted not so much through the appointment of an anti-Labor Party senator as through the failure to appoint an endorsed Labor Party senator. And that distortion allowed the Senate to vote to defer supply (a motion which could not have been passed if the late Senator Milliner had been replaced by a Labor Party Senator) and to bring on the instability and crises of October, November and December, 1975.

V
CONFLICTS OF INTEREST

The Australian Constitution makes a superficial attempt to deal with conflict of interest problems. The relevant provisions are s.44 (iv) and (v), and s.45 (i) and (iii). These provisions appear to have, as their primary objective, the avoidance of conflicts generated by Crown patronage (a curious concern when the executive government can, through the mechanism of party discipline, so effectively

---

[142]Marshall and Moodie, cited above n. 118, p.35.

control parliamentarians' votes and articulated political views). The provisions say nothing of conflicts between private, commercial, familial, industrial or professional interests and public obligations. They say nothing of the possible conflicts generated through the energetic activities of lobbyists or through the pressures of trade unions. Nevertheless, the provisions do establish a primitive code which, given a not too restrictive reading, could avoid a considerable number of situations of potential conflict. But, naturally, here is a nettle which few politicians have ever been eager to grasp: the fundamental question of the incompatibility of private interests of parliamentarians and their public duties has been little debated; nor has the more technical problem of identification and removal of potential conflicts; nor the critical question of which institution should be entrusted with the function of checking and controlling conflicts of interest.

After a long period of discreet neglect of these questions, the Commonwealth Parliament and the Australian community were obliged to confront them on several occasions during the three years of Labor Government. Twice attention was focused on the question as a result of attempts (by one party or another) to gain increased representation in the Senate. On another occasion the issue of what appeared to be an inadvertent technical conflict of interests was raised. And running through most of the last year of the Labor Government an attempt was made to review the whole question of conflicting financial interests and to institute new supervision and control procedures.

Vincent Gair: Senator or Ambassador?

The conflict of interest issue was first raised during the political manoeuvres which preceded the double dissolution of 11 April 1974; and it was, consequently, debated as a politically-charged question. The Government had planned to create a casual vacancy in the Senate (for Queensland) by appointing Senator Gair as Ambassador to Ireland, so that Queensland electors would return six rather than five senators at the half-Senate elections due in May 1974. The Queensland Government, in an attempt to frustrate the Government's plan, issued writs for that election on the evening of 2 April 1974. The Queensland Government maintained that the sixth vacancy could not be filled at the half-Senate election because that election had begun on 2 April,[143] before Gair (whose place had been intended by the Australian Government as the sixth vacancy) had resigned his place in the Senate (under s.19 of the Constitution). As the Leader of the Opposition in the Senate put it on 4 April 1974, 'The Premier of Queensland trumped the ace'.[144]

To this, the Australian Government replied by arguing that Gair's place in the Senate had become vacant several days before 2 April, by the operation of ss.44 and 45 of the Constitution. Ultimately, this dispute was submerged by the threat of the Opposition parties to block the Supply Bill in the Senate, and the subsequent double dissolution of Parliament on 11 April 1974. But the Senate debate on Gair's disqualification raised some important issues which merit discussion. Those issues are, first, whether Gair had been disqualified from

---

[143]See *Vardon* v. *O'Loghlin* (1907) 5 C.L.R. 201.
[144]Senate, *Debates*, 4 April 1974, vol. 59, p.688.

sitting in the Senate and his place made vacant by ss.44 and 45 of the Constitution; and, secondly, whether a House of Parliament is the appropriate forum
for the resolution of disputes over members' qualifications.

The Government's argument on the disqualification question, developed
during Senate debates on and after 3 April, was that Gair had held 'an office of
profit under the Crown' (the ambassadorship) upon either 14 March or 21
March. On the former day the Prime Minister wrote to the Governor-General,
recommending that the Governor-General approve of Gair's appointment as
Ambassador. The Governor-General's approval was given that day. On 21
March the Governor-General, sitting in the Executive Council, approved a
Minute Paper 'in relation to the appointment of Senator the Honourable
Vincent Clair Gair as Ambassador Extraordinary and Plenipotentiary of Aus-
tralia to the Republic of Ireland'.[145] The Minute provided that the Minister of
State for Foreign Affairs should fix Gair's salary and allowances, the other
terms and conditions of his appointment and the date of the commencement of
his appointment. On the basis of these documents the Australian Solicitor-
General advised the Government 'that as from 14 March the former Senator
became a person who then held an office of profit under the Crown'. The
Solicitor-General cautioned that 'the matter is not totally free of doubt', but he
asserted that Gair became Ambassador to the Republic of Ireland on 14 March,
and 'The office is clearly an office of profit and is clearly held under the
Crown'.[146] The General Counsel to the Attorney-General expressed a more
equivocal opinion that Gair had 'at the latest by 21 March 1974 held an office of
profit under the Crown'.[147]

There are some difficulties in the way of concluding, as did the Solicitor-
General and the General Counsel, that Gair 'held' any office (in particular that
of Ambassador to Ireland) on March 14 or March 21. For on both these dates
and, indeed, up to 30 April 1974, another person occupied the office of Ambassador to Ireland, Mr K. Brennan. The editor of the *Australian Law Journal* has
drawn attention to this difficulty.[148] He suggests that diplomatic practice
('which seems implicitly to recognize only the possibility of one single Head of
Mission to represent a sending country')[149] made it doubtful that Gair held an
office of profit under the Crown (the ambassadorship) at the relevant time.
However, that seems a rather narrow and technical approach to the problem,
which involves the application of the prohibition against office-holders sitting
in Parliament. A more functional approach to the specific problem which arose
around Gair's appointment would take into account the fundamental purpose
of that prohibition. At the very least, s.44 (iv) was intended to prevent any
revival of the practice (forbidden in Great Britain by the Act of Settlement of
1701[150]) of the executive government suborning votes in the Houses of Parliament through purchase—that is through the grant of offices of profit under the
Crown. If that purpose is to be served by s.44 (iv) then diplomatic practice
cannot be decisive of the question whether a member has been disqualified.
Whether or not Gair was entitled to exercise the office of Ambassador to Ireland

[145]Senate, *Debates*, 3 April 1974, vol. 59, p.664.
[146]Senate, *Debates*, 3 April 1974, vol. 59, pp. 638-9.
[147]Senate, *Debates*, 4 April 1974, vol. 59, p.683.
[148]Note, (1974) 48 *Australian L.J.*, p.222.
[149]*ibid.*, at p.223.
[150]12 & 13 Will. III, c. 2, s. 3.

would not be relevant; but it would be relevant to ask whether the appointment of Gair to that office had proceeded so far that his independence and integrity as a 'Parliament man' was compromised. The acceptance of the offer of the post by Gair, the approval of his appointment by the Governor-General, the *agrément* of the receiving government, and the formal delegation to a Minister of State of the authority to fix the date of commencement of his appointment and his remuneration are, I submit, substantial and significant steps along that path.

The second part of the Government's argument rested on s.45 (iii) of the Constitution and on the opinions of the Solicitor-General and the General Counsel to the Attorney-General. The Solicitor-General advised the Government that as from 14 March 1974, Gair must be regarded as having agreed ' "to take a fee or honorarium for services rendered to the Commonwealth" [by agreeing] to accept the emoluments which the post of Ambassador confers on him'.[151] While the Government also sought to rely on the General Counsel's opinion on this point, I doubt that it added very much to their case. For example, the General Counsel observed that ss.44 (iv) and 45 (iii) were 'probably intended to be complementary to each other', the former dealing with a continuous employment, the latter with some limited or short term services.[152] But if s.45 (iii) is limited in its application to 'short-term services' how could it cover Gair's case? Even the abrupt recall of our Ambassador to Ireland after eighteen months of service in Dublin could not convert Gair's commission into one for 'short-term services'.

In the event, the interpretation and effect of ss.44 and 45 received a rather one-sided debate in the Senate on 3, 4 and 8 April 1974. On 4 April, the Leader of the Government (Senator Murphy) moved that the question of the alleged vacating of Gair's place in the Senate be referred to the High Court of Australia sitting as the Court of Disputed Returns.[153] During the debate which followed, the arguments based on ss.44 and 45 were repeated by Government senators but ignored by the Opposition. Finally, the Senate carried a severely amended version of the Government's motion, the amendment having been moved by Senator Withers. The amended motion declared that as at '3 April 1974 Senator Gair had not resigned his place . . . and he was therefore, at the time . . . a senator for Queensland . . .' The motion went on to censure the Government's actions and called on it to resign.

In passing this motion, the Senate had purported to exercise the power originally conferred on it by s.47 of the Constitution to determine '[u]ntil the Parliament otherwise provides, any question respecting the qualification of a senator . . . or respecting a vacancy'. Senator Murphy sought, during the debate, to convince the Senate that the power of determination had lapsed, because the Parliament had otherwise provided. Speaking in support of his motion to refer the Gair question to the High Court, Murphy pointed out that in 1907 Parliament had enacted s.203 of the Commonwealth Electoral Act in the following terms:

> Any question respecting the qualifications of a Senator or of a Member of the House of Representatives or respecting a vacancy in either House of the Parliament may be referred by resolution to the Court of Disputed Returns [which] shall thereupon have jurisdiction to hear and determine the question.

---

[151]Senate, *Debates*, 3 April 1974, vol. 59, p.638.

[152]Senate, *Debates*, 4 April 1974, vol. 59, p.683.

[153]Senate, *Debates*, 4 April 1974, vol. 59, p.681.

Murphy then argued that the procedure outlined in s.203 was the proper means of ensuring that the complex issues involved in Gair's case be finally and impartially resolved and, moreover, it was the *only* available procedure for that resolution. Section 203 should be regarded as exhausting the power of the Houses of Parliament to deal with questions of disqualification or of vacancy; the Houses might have a discretion to refer or not refer such a question to the High Court, but if one of the Houses declined to refer such a question, the House could not determine the question itself. This view had been supported, according to the senator, by Garfield Barwick, in an opinion 'given on 2 February 1952'.[154] Presumably the opinion was given to the Commonwealth Attorney-General's Department: Murphy's account of the opinion was not exhaustive; he did not, for instance, purport to quote from it *verbatim*. But he did offer this summary of the opinion:[155]

> [E]ven though the matter may not be one to be expressed dogmatically, nevertheless the provision in s.203 displaced the former provisions and the use of the word 'may' is not in the circumstances strong enough to amount to a reservation of the former jurisdiction of the House.

An Opposition senator, Senator Wright, raised a powerful objection to Murphy's argument:[156]

> When Parliament was dealing with disputed elections it provided in s.183 that the validity of any election may be disputed by petition addressed to the Court of Disputed Returns and not otherwise. This is a clear and specific direction that any question as to a disputed election has to go before the High Court. But when it came to a question of a vacancy other than a disputed election, Parliament carefully chose the word 'may' without saying that it should not be determined otherwise.

Murphy's argument must be regarded as having been rejected by the majority of the Senate when it voted for the amended motion sponsored by Senator Withers. It is an argument which attracts little support from commentators. Enid Campbell, for example, writes that s.203, while authorising the Houses to refer questions to the High Court, 'does not divest them of authority to determine these questions for themselves if they so choose'.[157] Lumb and Ryan declare that 'each House retains the power to decide whether to deal with the matter itself or to refer it to the court'.[158] Gareth Evans observes that the practice of the Houses has been 'to deal with qualifications questions themselves, ignoring pleas—genuine or not—that such matters are better dealt with in the politically neutral atmosphere of the courtroom'.[159]

Nor did Senator Murphy's argument come to be tested in any other arena. The Senate and the House of Representatives were dissolved on 11 April 1974, three days after the Senate carried its motion determining that Gair had remained a senator until (at least) 3 April 1974. Consequently the question whether five or six senators should be returned from Queensland was no longer a practical question, for each of the six States was to return ten senators.

[154]Senate, *Debates*, 4 April, 1974, vol. 59, p.686.

[155]Senate, *Debates*, 4 April, 1974, vol. 59, pp. 682-3.

[156]Senate, *Debates*, 8 April 1974, vol. 59, p.725.

[157]E. Campbell, *Parliamentary Privilege in Australia* (Melbourne, 1966), p.98.

[158]Lumb and Ryan, cited above n. 137, p.62.

[159]G. Evans, 'Pecuniary Interests of Members of Parliament under the Australian Constitution', (1975) 49 *Australian L.J.* 464, at p.471.

Senator Webster

In April 1975, the Joint Committee on Pecuniary Interests of Members of Parliament heard evidence from a professional journalist on the staff of the *Age* newspaper to the effect that Senator Webster was a shareholder in, and a director of, a proprietary company with which some departments of the Commonwealth Government had had commercial dealings. The chairman of the Committee referred the journalist's statements to the Senate,[160] as it appeared that the senator might be disqualified from sitting in the Senate or might, at the time of his election in May 1974, have been disqualified from being elected to the Senate under s.44(v) of the Constitution. The Senate resolved that two questions be referred to the High Court as the Court of Disputed Returns:[161] first, whether Senator Webster was incapable of being chosen or of sitting as a senator; and secondly, whether Senator Webster had become incapable of sitting as a senator. The matter was heard before the Chief Justice on 2 and 3 June 1975, His Honour having decided that the questions raised by the reference were not of sufficient constitutional importance to warrant a hearing by a full bench.[162]

Evidence produced before the Chief Justice established that at the time of the Senate poll on 18 May 1974, Webster was one of nine shareholders in J.J. Webster Pty Ltd. As at 18 May 1974, Webster was also managing director, secretary and manager of the company. He left those positions in April 1975. His only reward from the company was a fixed salary and use of a company car. The company sold timber and hardware to the Commonwealth Department of Housing and Construction. Most of these goods had been the subject of quotations made by the company to the Department, in which the former agreed to supply certain goods at specified prices over a limited period. The Department 'accepted' these quotations but made no promise to buy any of the goods. From time to time the Department placed orders with the company for certain goods at the prices quoted, and the company supplied the goods at those prices. Occasionally, too, the Department ordered goods from the company without any prior quotation.

There seemed to be two issues for Barwick CJ to determine. First, did the company have, during the relevant period, 'any agreement with the Public Service of the Commonwealth'? Secondly, if so, could Webster be said to have a 'direct or indirect pecuniary interest' in that agreement? If he did, he could hardly take advantage of the exemption in s.44(v); J.J. Webster Pty Ltd did not consist of more than twenty-five persons.

As to the primary issue, the Chief Justice decided that the company had made no 'agreement', within s.44(v), with the Public Service of the Commonwealth. To come to this conclusion Barwick CJ applied what seem to be conflicting principles of statutory interpretation. At one point his Honour asserted of s.44(v) that 'There being penal consequences of its breach, the paragraph should receive a strict construction'.[163] (It is not clear to me why Barwick CJ described disqualification from election or sitting as a penal consequence: I believe the provision is more a protective than a penal provision—its function is to protect either the institution of Parliament or the community, not to

---

[160]See Senate, *Debates*, 15 April 1975, vol. 63, p.981.
[161]Senate, *Debates*, 22 April 1975, vol. 63, p.1223.
[162]High Court, Transcript of Proceedings, Sydney, 2 June 1975, p.53.
[163]*Re Senator Webster* (1975) 6 A.L.R. 65, at p.71.

punish malefactors.[164]) Apparently this strict construction led to the line of reasoning that s.44(v) dealt with only those arrangements which the law courts would classify as contracts. However, at another point his Honour turned to the purpose which s.44(v) was designed to achieve: this was 'fundamental to the decision of the questions posed by the Senate'. That purpose was 'to secure the freedom and independence of the Parliament from the Crown and its influence'.[165]

That purpose was to be deduced from the purpose of what Barwick CJ described as 'the precise progenitor of s.44(v)', s.1 of the *House of Commons Disqualification Act* 1782, described by Lord Haldane LC in *Re Sir Stuart Samuel* in the following terms:[166]

> [T]he mischief guarded against is the sapping of [Parliament's] freedom and independence by members being admitted to profitable contracts.

Apparently that purpose demanded that s.44(v) be applied only to certain types of contract with the Crown: 'executory contracts, that is to say, to contracts under which at the relevant time something remains to be done by the contractor in performance of the contract . . .'.[167] And the contract must be one to be performed over a substantial period, it must be more than a 'casual or transient' contract.

His Honour then pointed out that the company's quotation for (or offer to supply) goods at a specified price was a standing offer to supply: but it could not be said to be accepted until the Department placed a specific order. Only then did a contract arise, but each of these contracts was a separate and distinct agreement. Therefore, assuming that the purpose of s.44(v) was to protect the independence and integrity of Parliament from purchase by the Crown, and assuming that this independence and integrity would only be compromised if a member entered into a long-term, standing contract with the Crown, rather than a series of short-term contracts, the company could not be said to have any agreement with the Public Service of the Commonwealth during the relevant period. In Barwick CJ's view, the mere existence of a supply contract would have disqualified a member when the House of Commons Disqualification Act was first passed in 1782, but times had changed: 'in modern business and departmental conditions the possibility of influence by the Crown is not so apparent'.[168]

It seems to me that two points of criticism could be offered at this stage: an interpretation which confines s.44(v) to long-term agreements for the supply of commodities to the Crown, but which omits a series of short-term agreements of a similar nature from the grasp of s.44(v), seems an imperfect way of securing the independence and integrity of Parliament. Secondly, I am not sure that it is as obvious as the Chief Justice maintained that the purpose of s.44(v) is confined to protecting the integrity of Parliament. That may have been the concern of the parliament which passed the Act of 1782 but it may be that the draftsmen of s.44(v) were also seeking 'to protect the public against fraudulent

---

[164]See *Kariapper* v. *Wijesinha* [1968] A.C. 717, at pp. 737-8.
[165](1975) 6 A.L.R., 65, at p.69.
[166][1913] A.C. 514, at p.524.
[167](1975) 6 A.L.R., 65, at p.71.
[168]*ibid.*

conduct of members of the House'.[169] It is certainly worth observing that there is some difference in the wording of the Act of 1782 and s.44(v) of our Constitution. While the British legislation disqualifies any person who holds or enjoys any contract agreement or commission made with the Crown, s.44(v) disqualifies a person who has a direct or indirect pecuniary interest in any such agreement. This emphasis on 'pecuniary interest' is peculiar to s.44(v), in that none of the earlier British or Australian colonial legislation contains such a qualification.[170] Indeed that reference to 'pecuniary interest' as a disqualification was apparently inserted in s.44(v) between the 1897 Sydney Convention and the 1898 Melbourne Convention;[171] and during the Sydney debate on what was later to be s.44(v) the thrust of the debate was towards the need to prevent members of the national Parliament from using their elected office for personal gain.[172] It is permissible, and not altogether unrealistic, to infer that the drafting amendment[173] to s.44(v) (emphasising the notion of 'pecuniary interest') was made as a response to the Sydney delegates' preoccupation with the corrupt use of office rather than with the suborning of parliamentarians by the Crown.

If that purpose were accepted as one of the purposes of s.44(v) then an interpretation which confined its application to long-term agreements with the Crown would not be compelling. One other consideration supports the argument that the purposes of s.44(v) might be wider than those supposed by Barwick CJ. Some criticism had been levelled, as early as 1869, at the relevance of the Act of 1782 'to the present state of commerce'.[174] If, almost forty years later, the founders of the Australian Constitution included a clause in their Constitution in somewhat similar terms to the Act of 1782, but containing some textual differences, should we automatically assume, as Barwick CJ did, that the founders intended to adopt the purposes of the British Parliament of 1782?

Having found that s.44(v) could have no appplication to Senator Webster on the very basic ground that at no relevant time had there been any 'agreement' (within the provision) between J.J. Webster Pty Ltd and the Public Service of the Commonwealth, the Chief Justice then expressed an opinion on the second issue (although that issue was no longer necessary to the case), namely, whether the senator could be said to have a pecuniary interest, direct or indirect, in any agreement. While his Honour's reasons are not free from equivocation on this point, it seems that Barwick CJ believed that Senator Webster did not have any such interest. Indeed, the Chief Justice suggested that a shareholder in a company (no matter what its size) could not be said to have, as a shareholder, any pecuniary interest in the company's agreements. A shareholder may possibly have such an interest in a particular agreement 'due to particular circumstances'.[175] But the general legal rule that a shareholder (even one owning 'almost all the shares of a company') has 'no legal or equitable right or

---

[169](1975) 6 A.L.R., 65, at p.70.

[170]My attention was drawn to this argument by J.D. Hammond, whose comment on *Re Senator Webster* appears in (1976) 3 *Monash L. Rev.* 91.

[171]Australian Constitutional Convention, *Official Record of Debates*, Melbourne, 1898, pp. 1931-2.

[172]*Official Record of Debates*, Sydney, 1897, p.1022 ff.; Evans, cited above n. 159, p.467.

[173]See Barton J on the relevance of drafting changes in *Tasmania* v. *Commonwealth and Victoria* (1904) 1 C.L.R. 329, at p.351.

[174]*Royse* v. *Birley* (1869) L.R. 4 C.P. 296, at p.319.

[175](1975) 6 A.L.R., 65, at p.77.

interest in the company's assets',[176] were not amended by 'the terms of the paragraph'.[177]

I find that argument and conclusion difficult to accept. It seems to me that the draftsman of s.44(v) went to some pains to ensure that people did not evade the prohibition or disqualification in that paragraph by making their dealings with the Crown behind a corporate veil. First there is the reference to 'direct *or* *indirect* pecuniary interest'. Secondly, there is the exempting clause which excuses (perhaps quite illogically, but nevertheless unequivocally) from the disqualifications of s.44(v) persons who are members of incorporated companies with more than twenty-five members. As Gareth Evans puts it:[178]

> It is clear from the specific exclusion of companies with over twenty-five members, that the interests of a shareholder—indirect as they may be—in the government contracts into which smaller companies enter are manifestly within the ambit of the section.

But in the opinion of Barwick CJ the shareholder 'under the general law, plainly . . . does not' have a pecuniary interest in the transactions of the company, and there is 'good reason to conclude that the same is true in relation to s.44(v)'.[179]

Patrick Field: Senator or Public Servant?

As has been described above, in September 1975 the Legislative Assembly of Queensland chose Patrick Field to hold the place made vacant by the death of the late Senator Milliner, the Assembly exercising the power given to it by s.15 of the Constitution. Field had apparently been a member of the Australian Labor Party, but his acceptance of the place conferred on him by the Assembly terminated that membership; he was also on record as declaring that he would vote to bring down the Whitlam Government, if given the opportunity.

It was, therefore, hardly surprising that Government senators sought to prevent Field being sworn as a senator. When the President of the Senate announced that he had received from the Governor of Queensland a certificate certifying (under s.15 of the Constitution) the choice of Field as a senator, Senator Georges alleged that at the time of Field's choice by the Queensland Legislative Assembly, he was still a member of the Queensland Public Service.[180] The leader of the Government in the Senate, Senator Wriedt, then moved[181]

> That the eligibility of Senator-elect Field be referred to the Committee of Disputed Returns and Qualifications.

This Committee, whose members are appointed at the commencement of every Parliament, had not functioned since 1907. In the event, Senator Wriedt's motion was resolved in the negative—twenty-six votes for, twenty-six votes against, with the Opposition granting the Government a pair, 'to compensate

---

[176]*ibid.*, citing *Macaura* v. *Northern Assurance Co. Ltd* [1925] A.C. 619, at p.626.

[177](1975) 6 A.L.R., 65, at p.78.

[178]Evans, cited above n. 159, p.469.

[179](1975) 6 A.L.R. 65, at p.78.

[180]Senate, *Debates*, 9 September 1975, vol. 65, p.603.

[181]*ibid.*

for the vacancy caused by the death of Senator Milliner'.[182] Field was then sworn in as a senator.

The Government, having failed to prevent the arrival and establishment of Field in the Senate-chamber, then sought to effect his departure by moving that his eligibility be referred to the Standing Committee. Debate on this motion was adjourned and, on 1 October 1975, Senator Wriedt announced that the Government did not intend to proceed with the motion. It seems that proceedings had been issued in the High Court of Australia against Field challenging the validity of his election. It is not known whether these proceedings took the form of a petition filed under s.185 of the Commonwealth Electoral Act, or of a writ issued out of the High Court under the *Common Informer (Parliamentary Disqualfications) Act* 1975, though the latter seems more likely. This legislation was enacted by the Parliament in April 1975 immediately after the question of Senator Webster's qualifications to sit in the Senate had been raised. Its purpose was to limit the amount which a common informer might recover from a person who, while disqualified, sat in Parliament, and to confine proceedings for the recovery of such amount to the High Court of Australia.

The Act clearly varied the effect of s.46 of the Constitution which had allowed ('until the Parliament otherwise provides') a common informer to sue, in any court of competent jurisdiction for the sum of £100 for every day on which a disqualified person sat in the Parliament. Under the Act the common informer is limited to recovering $200 for the whole period during which the disqualified member sat in Parliament before the service of originating process on him and $200 for each day on which the disqualified member sat in Parliament after the service of that process. It is hardly surprising, therefore, that the Senate resolved on 1 October 1975 to give Field leave of absence from the Senate, which leave was extended for a further month on 5 November 1975.[183] In the result, therefore, it seems that those who were politically opposed to the presence of Patrick Field in the Senate were able at least to discourage him from participating in its proceedings; but there seems little chance, since the events of 11 November and 13 December 1975, that the suit against Field will ever come on for hearing.

Postscript—The Joint Committee

During the last year of the Whitlam Labor Government, the adequacy of ss.44 and 45 in dealing with contemporary conflicts of interests situations came under consideration by a Parliamentary Committee, the Joint Committee on Pecuniary Interest of Members of Parliament, formed on 31 October 1974. The Committee had been asked to consider and report upon a much broader issue: whether a register of the pecuniary or other interests of parliamentarians should be established. In the course of its report,[184] tabled in the House of Representatives and the Senate on 30 September 1975, the Committee observed that 'the apparent prevention of conflict of interest situations to be derived from [s.44(v)] may prove to be illusory'.[185] After considering the judgment of Barwick CJ in

---

[182]Senate, *Debates*, 9 September 1975, vol. 65, p.605.

[183]Senate, *Debates*, 1 October 1975, vol. 65, p.823; 5 November 1975, p.1753.

[184]*Report of the Joint Committee on Pecuniary Interests of Members of Parliament*, Parliamentary Paper No. 182 of 1975, p.7.

[185]*ibid.*, p.8.

Re Senator Webster, the Committee concluded that s.44(v) could not 'be considered as a safeguard against conflicts of interest and duty'.[186]

The Committee was also sceptical about the value of s.45(iii) as affording any greater safeguards. The Commitee emphasized that these constitutional provisions were concerned with avoiding conflict of interest situations by encouraging Parliamentarians to divest themselves of, or to avoid acquiring, potentially competing interests. Such an approach could not succeed in avoiding conflicts of interest unless Parliamentarians divested themselves of all private interests. It would be more realistic, the Committee considered, to 'require not divestment of potentially conflicting pecuniary interest but *disclosure* of those interests'.[187]

The Committee did not recommend any change to the disqualification provisions in s.44 or the vacating provisions in s.45, but it recommended the establishment of a register of the pecuniary interests of members of Parliament, to which register members of the public would, under certain conditions, have access.[188]

Given the relatively primitive nature of the conflict of interests provisions in ss.44 and 45, and the rather narrow interpretation which s.44(v) received in *Webster's Case*, and which s.44(iv) and 45 (iii) appear to have received at the hands of the Senate in the case of former Senator Gair, there is a strong case to be made for developing other controls to deal with conflict of interest situations. Indeed the flurry of activity around these provisions of the Constitution can only lead to the impression that their current function is not so much to protect the institution of Parliament or the community from the harm which might flow from conflicts of interest but rather to provide the material for political debate and the temporary advancement or retardation of one or other side in that debate. This impression is confirmed by the apparent unwillingness of the Senate to refer the Gair and Field disputes to either the Court of Disputed Returns or to its own Standing Committee on Disputed Returns and Disqualifications, and by the apparent eagerness of Government senators to use the provisions as a means of obtaining immediate political advantage. It seems that few members of the Senate were (during the 1974 and 1975 debates and controversies) conscious of the fundamental purposes of ss.44 and 45—the rather antiquarian concern for the preservation of the independence of Parliament from the Crown, and the more contemporary concern that Parliamentarians not place their duty to the community behind their self-advancement. Rather, their appeals to those sections, or their denial of the relevance of those sections, reflected a concern for political advantage. It is probable that the constitutional provisions, with their rather primitive drafting and their heavy-handed penalties, encourage this political manoeuvring: if the community is concerned to deal with conflicts of interests within the national Parliament, then alternative controls are needed.

However, the case for alternative controls which is developed at length in the Report on Declaration of Interests is clearly not one which carries overwhelming conviction, for the recommendations of the Joint Committee are yet to be adopted by either House of Parliament.

---

[186] *ibid.*, p.9.

[187] *ibid.*, pp. 22-7.

[188] *ibid.*, p.26.

VI
THE OFFICE OF SPEAKER:
CONVENTION CONFRONTS REALITY

The Speaker of the House of Representatives occupies one of the few political offices which receives specific recognition in the Australian Constitution.[189] Provision is made for the election, resignation or removal of the Speaker,[190] for the choice of a Deputy-Speaker,[191] for the issue by the Speaker of writs for by-elections,[192] the receipt by him of a member's resignation[193] and for his voting rights in the House.[194]

Yet clearly the office of Speaker is not one of critical importance to the functioning of our polity: very few constitutional lawyers or political scientists have paid it any attention and even such an official government publication as the Year Book of Australia is able to describe the 'Parliamentary Government' of Australia without mentioning the office, let alone describing its function.[195] And the Australia Handbook does no more than paraphrase two of the provisions of the Constitution,[196] in its account of the office.

However, we must recognize that the office of Speaker of the House of Representatives has a considerable lineage—it derives from the Speakership of the House of Commons established at least as early as 1376.[197] Clearly, the original functions of the Speaker (to act as a bridge between the House and the Crown, nominally speaking on behalf of the House to the Crown, but in reality controlling the proceedings of the House in the interests of the Crown, of the executive government) have been submerged by the growth of cabinet government. A rather more sophisticated device has been developed to link the executive government and the representative legislative assembly. (We know, now, that an attempt on 11 November 1975 to revive that original and fundamental function of the Speaker—to convey the House's views to the Crown—met with little success.[198])

But one important aspect of the Speaker's original function remains. It is he who is responsible for controlling debate and maintaining order and decorum within the House: in large part it is the Speaker's responsibility to create and retain an atmosphere in which rational debate is feasible. Clearly the Speaker must rely, in the discharge of this duty, on the support of the House, that is, on the support of the government party. Under the Standing Orders[199] of the House, dissent may be moved from any ruling of the Speaker; and, unless the Speaker is supported by the majority of the House, his authority is ephemeral. The sanctions for breach of the rules of parliamentary etiquette and debate (suspension or, exceptionally, expulsion) lie in the power of the House, rather

---

[189]Contrast the positions of the Prime Minister and Leader of the Opposition, and the institution of Cabinet, none of which are referred to in the Constitution.

[190]Constitution, s.35.

[191]Constitution, s.36.

[192]Constitution, s.33.

[193]Constitution, s.37.

[194]Constitution, s.40.

[195]Australia, *Official Year Book* 1974, No. 60, pp. 77-86.

[196]Australian News and Information Bureau, *Handbook Australia* (Canberra, 1970), p.77.

[197]C.R. Lovell, *English Constitutional and Legal History* (New York, 1962), p.186.

[198]See below, p.203.

[199]House of Representatives, *Standing Orders*, Order 100.

than the Speaker. Consequently, a Speaker who is not supported by the government party could have little chance of controlling the affairs of the House and the behaviour of individual members.

Of course, in the Australian context, the government's obligation to support the Speaker and his rulings could hardly be described as unduly onerous, for the Speaker can be expected to carry out his functions in a relatively partisan fashion. As Bolton[200] points out 'it has been usual both in Federal and State politics, for the Speaker to change with the party in power'. There are conventions established in the United Kingdom that the Speaker of the House of Commons, once elected, severs his ties with his party, that he is not opposed at any subsequent general election, nor at any subsequent election for the Speakership, and that he does not vote in any division (whether a casting vote on a matter before the Houses or a deliberative vote in Committee). These conventions are, in Australia, 'noticeable by their absence', as Enid Campbell[201] put it. Another understated proposition is provided by Bolton:[202] '[T]he figure of Mr Speaker is less ... detached in Australian politics than in British'.

Despite the none too heavy nature of this obligation to support the Speaker, the Labor Government found itself, in February 1975, unable to continue to carry the burden. Effectively, the Government withdrew its support from the Speaker in an open and spectacular fashion. A Minister of State, encouraged by the Prime Minister, refused to withdraw objectionable words which challenged the authority of the Speaker, the Leader of the House failed to move the suspension of a member named by the Speaker, and the Government voted against the suspension of that member: a series of direct challenges to the Speaker's authority. Speaker Cope immediately announced his intention to tender his resignation to the Governor-General (according to s.35 of the Constitution), and handed over the chair to the Deputy Speaker.

This was not the first occasion on which a Speaker's authority had been challenged in the House of Representatives by a government. In December 1953, the Government had moved, and carried on division, dissent from Speaker Cameron's ruling that a statement by Prime Minister Menzies was unparliamentary. However, a reading of the debate as recorded in Hansard suggests that the Speaker's original ruling had been made in haste and almost immediately regretted[203] by him. Certainly the Speaker had declared, after a series of points of order taken on his ruling, that he 'should be pleased if some honorable member would move that my ruling be dissented from',[204] an invitation which the Government had accepted. Further, Cameron had not left the chair during the debate on the dissent motion and had not, of course, spoken against the motion. And, once the motion had been carried, he had given no indication of even thinking about resignation. Clearly there is only a superficial analogy between that occurrence and the events of 27 February 1975, and those events must be regarded as diminishing the authority and status of the Speaker.

[200]G. Bolton, 'The Choice of the Speaker in Australian Parliaments' in *Readings in Australian Government*, ed. C.A. Hughes (Brisbane, 1968), p.158.

[201]Campbell, cited above n. 157, p.11.

[202]Bolton, cited above n. 200, p.155. See also J.D.B. Miller and B. Jinks, *Australian Government and Politics* (4th ed., London, 1971), p.94.

[203]Speaker Cameron was notorious for his impetuosity: see F.C. Green, *Servant of the House* (Melbourne, 1969), pp. 136-7.

[204]House of Representatives, *Debates*, 2 December 1953, vol. 2, p.769.

We might explain the extraordinary events of that day by placing them in their immediate political context: in the context of the recent appointment by the New South Wales Houses of Parliament of a non-Labor senator to replace former Senator Murphy; of serious speculation that this replacement might combine with the Opposition in the Senate to block the Supply Bill in April; of the increasingly insecure position of the Leader of the Opposition, Snedden, who was to be replaced on 21 March. Given those tensions, it was not surprising that proceedings in Parliament were characterized by hostility, accusations, interruptions, points of order and personal explanations. The proceedings on the morning of 27 February 1975 were not (apart from the confrontation between the Government and the Speaker) atypical. During question time, only two questions without notice were asked: one to the Prime Minister (answered in seven lines of Hansard) and one to the Treasurer, Mr Hayden. The answer to this second question spread over almost five pages of Hansard: but much of that space was occupied with points of order (ten of which were raised by the Opposition), interjections (Hansard records twenty interjections from Opposition members during Hayden's reply), calls to order (Hansard records twenty such calls from the Speaker) and a division (on a motion that the Minister be no longer heard—lost, of course). It is clear that, on the Government benches at least, there was dissatisfaction with the Speaker's failure to control parliamentary proceedings—expressed by the Minister for the Capital Territory, Bryant, in rather oblique terms:[205]

For two years we have watched [the Opposition] destroying this institution, making it impossible for the Speaker to handle question time and turning the place into a rabble.

But, all those factors taken into account, the Government's open defiance and desertion of the Speaker could only be described as a serious assault on the status and authority of the office. It may be true, as Bolton has argued, that the Speaker's office has always been regarded as a political and partisan office in Australia. The Speaker almost always belongs to the party in government, and he is expected to support that party in a close division with his casting vote. He is 'the creature of his party'.[206] The events of 27 February 1975 confirmed, in an open and, indeed, brutal fashion, this hard reality.

The clearly diminished status of the Speaker was further confirmed in a rather more subtle fashion by the Governor-General, Sir John Kerr, on 11 November 1975. At 3.15 p.m. on that day the House of Representatives resolved that it had no confidence in Prime Minister Fraser, who had been commissioned by Kerr less than two hours earlier. The House directed the Speaker to convey the terms of the motion to the Governor-General, who was unwilling to receive the Speaker until 4.45 p.m. In the meantime, the Governor-General prorogued and dissolved the Parliament. On 17 February 1976 the former Prime Minister and current Leader of the Opposition, Mr Whitlam, declared that the Governor-General had insulted the Speaker, 'and that the office of Speaker and all the rights and privileges it embodies were treated with contempt'.[207] I believe there is substantial truth in that charge: but a similar charge can be levied against the former Prime Minister and the supporters of his Government. Their actions on 27 February 1975 can only be regarded as

[205]House of Representatives, *Debates*, 27 February 1975, vol. 93, p.881.
[206]Bolton, cited above n. 200, p.161.
[207]House of Representatives, *Debates*, 17 February 1976, no. 1, p.5.

diminishing the authority of the Speaker within the House, while the action (or inaction) of the Governor-General on the afternoon of 11 November 1975, seriously undermined the authority of the Speaker and the constitutional position of the House within the broader governmental framework.

COMMENTARIES

Patrick Brazil

> Democracy is like a raft. It never sinks but, damn it, your feet
> are always in the water.[1]

Mr Hanks's essay thoroughly and perceptively charts part of the lurching course of the raft of democracy in the era under survey. I want to comment briefly on a number of disparate matters, namely a democratic principle; a federal principle; the citizen's right to enforce voting requirements; disqualification; and conventions in a democracy.

A Democratic Principle?

In statutory enactments, in constitutional proposals and challenges and in High Court judgments, some major issues were, for the first time, fairly and squarely faced. For example, does the Constitution embody a concept of representative democracy, or are such matters relegated to political philosophy and the partisan debates of politics? Alternatively, can at least certain minimum democratic requirements be identified in the Constitution, and can these be enforced and by whom?

What are the answers that have been given? Four, or possibly five, of the seven judges in *McKinlay's Case*[2] were prepared to find some minimum standards prescribed by the first paragraph of s.24 of the Constitution. If I have read the essay right, its author would agree with me in thinking that the consequences are not likely to be of great practical significance in the immediate future. Yet the development is of interest and some importance, and we should be grateful for Mr Hanks's exposition. It shows that a concept of representative democracy may be discerned in s.24 of the Constitution in the words 'chosen by the people of the Commonwealth'.

It is not easy however to say what those minimum requirements are. The background is that when the Constitution came into operation in 1901, it expressly adopted, until the Commonwealth Parliament should otherwise provide, the franchises in force for State lower Houses in 1901. Adult suffrage was unknown in the majority of the States. In all but two of the States, women had no vote. A property qualification was applicable in at least one of the States. In one State people of certain races were debarred.[3]

One may test the matter, then, by asking some questions. Could a property qualification be reintroduced today? Could women today be deprived of the franchise? I myself would agree with McTiernan and Jacobs JJ, and Murphy J,

---

[1]Fisher Ames, quoted in D.W. Brogan, *The Free State: Some Considerations on its Practical Value* (London, 1945), p.7.

[2]*Attorney-General for Australia (Ex rel. McKinlay)* v. *Commonwealth* (1975) 7 A.L.R. 593.

[3]*ibid.*, at pp. 601, 633.

that these questions should now be answered 'no'.[4] The content of the words 'chosen by the people' has not been frozen as at 1901. The now long established universal adult suffrage may be taken as establishing a common understanding that anything less than it could not now be described as a choice by the people.

The decision in *McKinlay's Case* makes it clear, however, that 'chosen by the people' cannot be taken to require arithmetical equality in relation to the value of votes—whether equality is regarded as meaning that electoral divisions should be composed of equal numbers of *people* or of equal numbers of *voters*. We only have the possibility that if, say, redistribution were postponed until the ratio between the largest and the smallest electorate were three to one or more, an election on that basis may be held not to be a choosing by the people. That, I suppose, sets some sort of benchmark.

Sections 24 and 25 of the Commonwealth Electoral Act were nevertheless held valid, even though they might conceivably operate to produce such an invalid effect. On the other hand, ss.3, 4 and 12(a) of the Representation Act were held invalid. Such distinctions are not easy to explain to laymen.

A Federal Principle

The provisions of the Representation Act were of course held invalid because of conflict with the second paragraph of s.24 of the Constitution, not the first paragraph. That second paragraph embodies a *federal* principle—that the number of members for the several States shall be in proportion to their respective populations—and we find that the majority of the High Court was alert to ensure complete respect for that principle.

I shall say no more on this aspect, except to agree with Mr Hanks that a clear consequence of the invalidity of the provisions of the Representation Act is that the Commonwealth Electoral Act will have to be reviewed even though it was not held invalid. Under the present Electoral Act a redistribution to give effect to the requirements of the second paragraph of s.24 may be delayed because the positive approval of both Houses is required, and that approval may not be forthcoming. Some means will have to be devised to ensure that redistribution to give effect to the second paragraph of s.24 takes place before the next regular general election due in 1978. For obvious reasons, however, I shall not myself canvass the possibilities in that regard.

Enforceability

Constitutional rights, to be really rights, must be enforceable. In our present area of discourse, constitutional electoral rights, there are two potential road blocks—lack of justiciability and lack of standing to sue. The judgments in *McKinlay's Case* represent some advance in removing those road blocks. Constitutional requirements relating to voting were accepted as being justiciable matters that can be entertained by the Courts.

The individual voter's standing to enforce those requirements is less clear. However, in this regard, the proceedings in *McKinlay* have significance for a reason that may not be so apparent on the face of the record. The proceedings were the first in which a Commonwealth Attorney-General granted his fiat to an individual for a suit for a declaration that Commonwealth legislation is *ultra*

---

[4]*ibid.*, at pp. 616, 642.

vires the Constitution. If anything, the previous practice had been the other way. It is true that in the *Commonwealth Shipping Board Case*[5] the Commonwealth Attorney-General's fiat had been granted, and it is also true that the Court in that case went into constitutional matters. However, it appears that the then Attorney-General, Sir John Latham, in granting his fiat, did not envisage that constitutional questions, as distinct from other questions of *ultra vires*, would be raised. He thought that, as a general rule, the Commonwealth Attorney-General should not allow his name to be used in an action challenging the validity of a Commonwealth statute.

The case for saying that the Commonwealth Attorney-General's fiat should be issued in appropriate cases to enforce constitutional requirements is a very strong one. The relevant principle is that the Attorney-General, in granting his fiat, is representing the public interest in having the law observed. It may well be asked whether that interest is any less where the law in question has the status of the Constitution than where it consists of an Act of Parliament or something of even lower status. Of course the issue of a fiat can never be an automatic or a mechanical matter; a discretion is involved and an Attorney-General would want to be convinced that a real and substantial question is involved and that there is no other remedy open to the applicant for the fiat.

Disqualifications of Parliamentarians

On disqualifications, let me first fill in the record on some points. I understand that the common informer proceedings against Mr Patrick Field, which are referred to in the essay, have been abandoned. For the sake of completeness, one should also refer to the common informer proceedings (apparently also now lapsed) that were brought against Dr Jim Cairns because of his tenancy of a government flat in Canberra, it seems upon terms that were no different from other comparable government tenancies.

In *Re Senator Webster*[6] we have, of course, the only judgment given to date upon the 'pecuniary interests' provisions contained in s.44(v) of the Constitution. The Court of Disputed Returns for that purpose consisted of only one judge, so that the general views expressed are not binding for future cases. It seems to me that the view of the Chief Justice that membership of a trading corporation does not in itself involve an *indirect* pecuniary interest in the trading contracts of that company is not, with respect, very persuasive. I point out that the decision did not turn on that point.

On the other hand I think that there should be agreement with the general thrust of the Chief Justice's judgment that s.44(v) is not to be read in a strict literal fashion so as to disqualify members for engaging in quite trivial or everyday transactions with government departments. It is surely right to apply the mischief rule to s.44(v). Indeed it seems to be a pre-eminent case for interpreting a provision in the light of the mischief it was intended to deal with.

What was the mischief in this case? What Professor La Nauze has called, in another context, the 'hypothetical history' of lawyers indicates that the mischief was the undermining by the executive of the independence of members by the letting of lucrative contracts. In more modern times, and specifically in the era

---

[5] *Commonwealth & Attorney-General for the Commonwealth (Ex rel. Edwards)* v. *Commonwealth Shipping Board* (1926) 39 C.L.R. 1

[6] (1975) 6 A.L.R. 65.

under survey, concern has developed to deal with 'conflict of interests' situations—situations in which members might appear to be using their position to
their own personal profit or advantage. To some extent these are overlapping
circles, but they do not overlap completely and they do provide two distinct
possible rationales for s.44(v).

The historians' history of the genesis of s.44(v) could well favour the second
rationale. Thus, the Honourable Isaac Isaacs, as he then was, said at the
Convention Debates in Sydney in 1897 that 'the object of the clause is to
prevent individuals making a personal profit out of the public positions'.[7] Mr
Hanks undoubtedly leans to this view, as a matter not only of history but also,
as I follow him, as a matter of legal interpretation. I think that history on
balance is on his side. Whether his legal interpretation alternately prevails
remains to be seen.

The real solution would be to revise the 'primitive' rules in ss.44 and 45 as Mr
Hanks has described them—in the light of present day values and concerns. But
constitutional amendments are so difficult to achieve.

A Convention in Relation to Casual Senate Vacancies?

Had a constitutional convention developed that casual Senate vacancies are to
be filled by a person of the same political party as the senator whose seat had
become vacant? As is observed in the essay, there could be no doubt at all that
the appointments to the casual vacancies in question were perfectly legal in the
sense that the State Parliaments had the legal capacity to do what they did, but
this is quite consistent with a convention having developed on the matter.

Let me quote Dicey on this point ('roll the Dicey' as Professor Sawer puts it).
Dicey said that, on examination, conventions of the constitution have all one
ultimate object:

> to secure that Parliament, or the Cabinet which is indirectly appointed by Parliament,
> shall in the long run give effect to the will of that power which . . . is the true political
> sovereign of the State—the majority of the electors or (to use popular though not quite
> accurate language) the nation.[8]

The fact that the practice about casual vacancies would have satisfied the
ultimate object of conventions discerned by Dicey—to give effect to the will of
the majority of electors—does not prove that it was in truth a convention. But
it does, at least, show that the alleged rule was eminently eligible to develop
into a convention.

It is difficult to know how the position now stands. Conventions in some ways
resemble customary rules of international law, for in their case also there is
often no tribunal that can enforce them. Sometimes they are broken, but unless
the departure from them is persistent the international rule may endure
notwithstanding those departures. On the other hand, international law also
had a doctrine of reprisal, which may be of some relevance to the future in
relation to casual vacancies.

---

[7] Australian Constitutional Convention, *Official Record of Debates*, Sydney, 1897, p.1023.
[8] A.V. Dicey, *Law of the Constitution* (10th ed., London, 1959), p.429.

Michael Coper

Mr Hanks has been given a great diversity of issues to deal with, and in the space available it is not possible for me to do more than comment selectively on a few of the more interesting questions he raises. I shall refer first to a number of aspects of the judicial process which were highlighted by the High Court's disposition of the *Territory Senators, McKinlay* and *Webster* cases; and turn secondly to the absorbing question of the role of the States[1] in determining the composition of the federal Parliament.

The Judicial Process

In the *Territory Senators Case*,[2] there was indeed, as Gibbs J put it, a 'striking inconsistency'[3] between the provisions of ss.7 and 122 of the Constitution. I would go further and say that the linguistic or textual considerations were quite inconclusive; for each argument which led to one conclusion, a respectable principle of interpretation could be invoked to point to the opposite conclusion.[4] But this inconclusiveness did not stop with the textual considerations: s.122 could be controlled by the evident historical purpose of creating the Senate as the States House,[5] or it could be viewed as an anticipation of the day when Parliament might decide that a territory was sufficiently developed to warrant full representation.[6] Again, it could be said in relation to the 'swamping' threat, that Parliament should be trusted, that the possibility of abuse of a power should not restrict its interpretation,[7] and it could be countered that such a possibility indicated that an unrestricted interpretation could not have been intended.[8] Even the analogy with the United States situation was double-edged; limited territorial representation there underlined the familiarity of our founding fathers with such a concept,[9] yet s.122 could be seen as a deliberate departure from that model.[10]

The four-three split on the bench symbolises both the open texture of most constitutional questions and the very difficult task the High Court has in resolving them. Gibbs J took the opportunity to point out that the function of the Court 'is to consider not what the Constitution might best provide but what, upon its proper construction, it does provide'.[11] In the circumstances, I wonder

---

[1]This role is obvious enough in relation to the Senate, of which more below, but it is also true, to a lesser but surprising extent, in relation to the House of Representatives: *cf.* ss.24, 29, 41, 121 and 128.

[2]*Western Australia* v. *Commonwealth* (1975) 7 A.L.R. 159.

[3]*ibid.*, at p.185.

[4]For example, the minority said that the words of s.7 were capable of only one meaning, namely that the Senate shall be *composed of*, not merely include, senators from each State, whereas the word 'representation' in s.122 was capable of several meanings and should therefore be given a meaning consistent with s.7, a meaning which could not then include voting powers; on the other hand, said the majority, the same word should be given the same meaning in different sections, and the word 'representation' in every other part of the Constitution, especially in s.121, clearly included voting powers: (1975) 7 A.L.R. 159, at pp. 172-4 (Barwick CJ), 185-7 (Gibbs J), 195-8 (Stephen J); 206 (Mason J), 208 (Jacobs J), 216-7 (Murphy J).

[5](1975) 7 A.L.R. 159, at pp. 172, 176 (Barwick CJ), 187-9 (Gibbs J), 195-6 (Stephen J).

[6]*ibid.*, at pp. 206-7 (Mason J), 208-10 (Jacobs J).

[7]*ibid.*, at pp. 207 (Mason J), 210 (Jacobs J), 220 (Murphy J).

[8]*ibid.*, at p. 189 (Gibbs J).

[9]*ibid.*, at pp. 175 (Barwick CJ), 189-190 (Gibbs J), 197-8 (Stephen J).

[10]*ibid.*, at pp. 205 (Mason J), 218 (Murphy J).

[11]*ibid.*, at p.189.

if this is a fair and accurate description of the task thrown up by the *Territory Senators Case*, or doth His Honour protest too much?

In contrast with the openness of the linguistic or textual considerations in that case, the wording of Part III of Chapter I of the Constitution, in issue in *McKinlay's Case*,[12] appeared to leave little scope for implying that electoral divisions for House of Representatives elections must contain equal numbers of people or voters. Indeed, the point seemed so clear to a reviewer of Professor Sawer's book *Australian Federal Politics and Law* that he included Professor Sawer's apparently contrary view in his list of factual errors![13] But no one would deny that the need to make implications is unavoidable in interpreting the Constitution; the Constitution does not say anything explicitly about the relative size of electorates, and therefore leaves the absence of a precise equality requirement to be implied from its silence. In my view Murphy J marshalled substantial arguments, including textual ones, to support his lone dissenting opinion on this point in *McKinlay*. It must be remembered, also, that notwithstanding the weighty, if not compelling, textual arguments of the majority which denied any precise equality requirement, all of the Justices except Barwick CJ and Gibbs J found *some* limitation in the words 'chosen by the people'.

So, as with the *Territory Senators Case*, the process of drawing the correct implication from the text of the Constitution went beyond merely linguistic arguments. Again as with the *Territory Senators Case*, the broader factors which were relevant included the historical purposes of Part III of Chapter I and the degree of faith which it was appropriate to place in the institution of Parliament. Some interesting contrasts emerge here, perhaps even some judicial somersaults. In relation to the historical aspect, Mason J was unable in *McKinlay's Case* to regard the House of Representatives part of the Constitution as providing for the comparatively modern development of the precise equality idea,[14] yet in the *Territory Senators Case* he held that the Senate part should not be regarded as speaking for all time.[15] On the question of the admissibility of the Convention Debates, Barwick CJ referred in *McKinlay's Case* to the 'settled doctrine' that they will not be used as an aid to the construction of the Constitution,[16] yet in *Re Senator Webster*,[17] (where he was sitting alone as the Court of Disputed Returns), he had actually cited them in the course of his endeavour to ascertain the meaning of s.44(v).[18]

On the question of the degree of trust which should be placed in the Parliament, Barwick CJ and Murphy J each switched their opposite positions. In the *Territory Senators Case* where the issue was the potential 'swamping' of the Senate, Murphy J stressed the trust which the Constitution placed in the

---

[12]*Attorney-General for Australia (Ex rel. McKinlay)* v. *Commonwealth* (1975) 7 A.L.R. 593.

[13]J.Q. Ewens, Book Review, (1964) 1 *Federal L. Rev.* 165, at p.166.

[14](1975) 7 A.L.R. 593, at p.637.

[15](1975) 7 A.L.R. 159, at p.206. Certainly, s.122 provided a textual basis for progressive interpretation in the *Territory Senators Case*, but in *McKinlay's Case* McTiernan and Jacobs JJ saw the meaning of 'chosen by the people' as depending on 'the common understanding of the time' ((1975) 7 A.L.R. 593, at p. 616) and Mason J has himself forcefully advocated a contemporary approach in other contexts, notably in relation to s.92 (see *North Eastern Dairy Co. Ltd* v. *Dairy Industry Authority of New South Wales* (1975) 7 A.L.R. 433, at p.471).

[16](1975) 7 A.L.R. 593, at p.600.

[17](1975) 6 A.L.R. 65.

[18]*ibid.*, at pp. 70-1.

Parliament,[19] yet in *McKinlay's Case*, where the issue was the achievement of a fair distribution of electoral divisions, he characterised a similar argument as 'hollow'.[20] The Chief Justice in *McKinlay* stressed that the confidence reposed in the Parliament by the Constitution had not been misplaced, and praised Parliament's 'real endeavour' to secure equality of voting value,[21] yet in *Territory Senators* he was concerned with the potential of the power to admit territorial senators for subverting the Constitution.[22] No doubt the two questions do not raise identical considerations, but the contrasts are nonetheless striking.

The real issue on the electoral question in relation to the extent of responsibility the High Court should entrust to Parliament is whether, assuming the desirability of precisely equal electoral divisions, the Court or the Parliament is the appropriate institution to achieve that desired end. Murphy J opted for a judicial remedy, pointing to political self-interest as the obvious stumbling block to legislative action, yet *McKinlay's Case* has been the only occasion to date on which His Honour has not adopted a position of extreme judicial self-restraint in relation to legislation of the federal Parliament. Lest it be retorted that in every case it has been Labor legislation, I should mention that His Honour's radical departure from settled doctrine in relation to s.92, to the effect that the section applies only to fiscal burdens,[23] demonstrates the same deference to the legislative branch, both federal *and* State, and a stand against judicial legislation by seeking a test capable of precise application. Even his view in *McKinlay's Case* evidences the same kind of stand, as it was on this basis that he rejected the lesser limitations imported into s.24 by McTiernan, Stephen, Mason and Jacobs JJ.

However, the assumption that democracy demands precise numerical equality of electoral divisions needs to be carefully examined. McTiernan and Jacobs JJ were of the opinion that given the maximum permissible departure from the quota of 10 per cent, some of the criteria in s.19 of the Commonwealth Electoral Act may be necessary to *ensure* a choice 'by the people'.[24] Of course, the 1975 election was not held in accordance with the requirements of s.19, and the existing disproportion in the size of electoral divisions casts some doubt on the value of the limitations envisaged by McTiernan, Stephen, Mason and Jacobs JJ and correspondingly strengthens the position of Murphy J. Mr Hanks notes that with the passage of time a further claim that the envisaged limits have been transgressed could well be made out, and there is much force in the logic of his main conclusion that in any event, ss.24 and 25 of the Commonwealth Electoral Act could be declared invalid now, for analogous reasons to those which were given for the invalidation of s.12(a) of the Representation Act. McTiernan and Jacobs JJ saw the analogy,[25] but the diversity of opinion among the Justices as to whether and which parts of the legislation were totally

[19](1975) 7 A.L.R. 159, at p.220.

[20](1975) 7 A.L.R. 593, at p.644.

[21]*ibid.*, at pp. 606-7.

[22](1975) 7 A.L.R. 159, at p.176.

[23]*Buck* v. *Bavone* (1976) 9 A.L.R. 481, at p.498; *Perre* v. *Pollitt* (1976) 9 A.L.R. 387, at p.400.

[24](1975) 7 A.L.R. 593, at pp. 616-7.

[25]*ibid.*, at pp. 617,621.

or partially invalid, or were valid but could not operate unconstitutionally,[26] left the effect of the decision so obscure that the Court felt it necessary to issue a separate statement in addition to its formal orders to explain the effect of those orders![27]

For the Justices who preferred to invalidate s.12(a) of the Representation Act rather than to limit its operation, a question arose as to the validity of the imminent election and perhaps of previous ones. One answer was to hold that even if there were evidence to establish an infringement of the proportionality requirement, the duty flowing from ss.28 and 32 to hold an election would override the duty to ensure the proportionate representation of each State.[28] Another answer was to hold that the proportionality requirement was applicable only to ordinary triennial elections and therefore did not affect the pending election.[29] There is no explicit constitutional basis for drawing a distinction between ordinary elections and 'snap' elections, and the holding on this point is a good example of how commonsense and practicality is converted by the bare fact of judicial decision into legal doctrine.

The Role of the States in Relation to the Senate

Whether or not the claim that the Senate is the States House is any longer (or ever was) tenable, the fact remains that under the Constitution the States retain considerable power over aspects of the Senate's composition. The most striking example, in view of the critical role it played in the demise of the Whitlam Government, is the power of the States to fill casual vacancies,[30] and I shall comment on this below in the context of the so-called conventions of the Constitution. But each State also has the power, subject to Commonwealth law, to make laws prescribing the method of choosing the senators for that State, and also the power to determine the times and places of the election;[31] moreover, the issuing of writs is committed by s.12 to the Governor of the State. These apparently innocuous provisions achieved some prominence in 1975 when some of the States threatened to use them to thwart the Whitlam Government's half-Senate election strategy. The strategy failed for other reasons, but it is interesting to speculate on what might have happened if the half-Senate election had proceeded at the federal level and any State governments had advised their Governors not to issue writs.

It seems to me that the State Governors have a constitutional duty to issue writs for any kind of Senate election, even though s.12 makes this explicit only in the case of a dissolution of the Senate; there is a time limit in s.13 within which it is required that the election to fill ordinary vacancies occurring through rotation shall be held, and the two provisions may be taken together as dealing with the time limits attached to the exercise of the Governor's stated duty (in the case of a dissolution) or implicit duty (in other cases) to issue writs. An analogy might also be drawn with the duty to hold a House of Representatives election every three years, which is derived at least in part from wording in

---

[26] *Cf.* Note, 'Constitutional Validity of Legislation According to the Circumstances' (1976) 50 *Australian L.J.* 205.

[27] (1975) 7 A.L.R. 593, at pp. 650-1.

[28] *ibid.*, at pp. 627, 629-630 (Gibbs J).

[29] *ibid.*, at pp. 610, 613 (Barwick CJ), 628-9 (Gibbs J).

[30] Constitution, s.15.

[31] Constitution, s.9.

s.32 identical to that in s.12, and which Gibbs J regarded in *McKinlay's Case* as an 'overriding' duty.[32] On the other hand there is a distinction in that the Senate can continue to function constitutionally at half-strength.[33]

However, there is some authority to suggest that a judicial remedy is not available to compel a State Governor to issue writs for a Senate election (*R. v. Governor of South Australia*[34]), and in any event the duty could presumably be discharged at any time within the time limit. So we are again in the sphere of conventions: is there a convention that the State Governor acts in this matter on the advice of the federal government? How should he regard conflicting advice from his State government?

The High Court suggested in *R. v. Governor of South Australia* that if a State government advised the Governor not to issue writs, and refused to afford him the necessary administrative facilities, then the Governor might be able to discharge his duty to issue the writs, if he has such a duty, only by dismissing his ministers and finding others.[35] In the light of Queensland Governor Sir Colin Hannah's public remarks in October 1975 in support of the Coalition parties' moves to force a general election, such a course of action in Queensland would have been, to say the least, unlikely. Given a Governor sympathetic to his State government's wishes, and assuming the absence of a judicial remedy, the Queen might have been asked (via the Governor-General?) to sack the Governor, and appoint another Governor who would sack his ministers! After what actually happened last year, I lack the confidence to say that this scenario is far-fetched. But whatever might have happened, merely to canvass the possibilities is to demonstrate that the notion of the Senate as the States House lives on in subtle and potentially critical ways.

Let me conclude on the question of casual vacancies in the Senate. Mr Hanks convincingly demonstrates that there is a convention (or was one—more on this in a moment) to the effect that a casual vacancy should be filled with a person of the same political party as that of the vacating senator. There may be some room for arguing that the convention applies only to 'naturally occurring' and not to 'contrived' vacancies, but such a distinction is elusive; in any event, the distinction would leave untouched the breach of the convention in the case of Senator Field. The convention is said to date only from 1949 because of the increased likelihood since that date of very narrow majorities in the Senate and the consequent effect of the filling of a vacancy on the balance of power, but the fact that the Coalition parties presently have a comfortable majority does not weaken Mr Hanks's position, as the convention is based not merely on the size of the majority from time to time but on the projected and actual consequences of the new voting system which remains a constant factor in precluding the very large majorities possible before 1949.

The important question now is, what is the consequence of the two breaches of the convention in 1975? One can hardly agree with the editorial view of the *Australian Law Journal* that the first breach was conclusive evidence that the convention did not exist;[36] conventions are 'binding' in the sense that they

---

[32]Above, n. 28.

[33]Constitution, ss. 11, 22.

[34](1907) 4 C.L.R. 1497.

[35]*ibid.*, at p.1511.

[36]Note, ' "Casual" Senate Vacancies under s.15 of the Commonwealth Constitution' (1975) 49 *Australian L.J.* 153, at p.156.

ought to be followed, and if the *Australian Law Journal* were correct, it would not be meaningful to speak in terms of a breach at all. Obviously past practice is indispensable evidence of the existence of a convention, but as Mr Hanks points out, the rational basis of the practice is a further ingredient. It doesn't matter whether you label the normative rule as a convention or anything else; the fact is that it describes a practice which ought to be followed. The elevation of the term 'convention', no doubt as a result of its typical usage in describing practices which are in fact always followed, has tended to distract attention away from this simple point. That there are some rules of practice, departure from which is impossible to imagine, should not deny the usage of the term 'convention' in relation to other rules which have compelling rational value, but which may conceivably be breached in the interest of short-term political expediency.

The problem, of course, with breaches of convention is not merely that they cast doubt on the continued existence of the normative aspect of the practice concerned but that they also weaken the normative value of conventions generally. The two breaches of the casual vacancies convention in 1975 had both of these effects. So far as the continued existence of the convention is concerned, further breaches would establish that it no longer exists (but not that it never existed, as the *Australian Law Journal* would have it), because actual practice is clearly a necessary precondition for the normative content of the rule, even if it is not sufficient. The critical time for the convention will come when the next opportunity for breaching it occurs; if the rule is followed the convention will be confirmed and renewed; if the rule is breached the convention will disappear.

I see no difficulty in taking this prospective view; after all, even legal rules exhibit uncertainty and their identification often depends on prediction, the prediction of a judicial decision. But it is precisely because the next occasion is critical that the rational value of the convention needs to be emphasised now and the two breaches in 1975 condemned. The continued existence of the convention depends on the existence of a consensus of opinion to constrain the political actors in the future, and public affirmations of the convention now are ingredients in the identification of that consensus.

Public statements from university lawyers run the risk of being regarded, as were so many statements in October and November 1975, as the 'bleatings of academics'. Indeed, the public reputation and credibility of academic lawyers generally took quite a battering, for reasons which would require too great a digression to elaborate here, but which included the failure of the public and, I think, of some of the political actors, to appreciate the nature and importance of conventions. It is nonetheless important for academics to play an active educative role, despite the danger, in great political controversies, of being seen (sometimes rightly) to be manipulating the uncertainty of the law for political ends. But in the context of the casual vacancies convention the public statements of the political actors themselves are even more important. I would hope that the spokesmen of all political parties, and in particular the Labor Party—whose actions when given the chance to retaliate will be, after all, the acid test—will take the earliest opportunity to reaffirm their commitment to the convention.

PART THREE

CONSTITUTIONAL CRISIS:
THE SENATE AND THE GOVERNOR-GENERAL

Leslie Zines's essay on the operation of s.57 of the Constitution (Chapter 7) is essentially, and necessarily, technical. It deals with the complex and difficult questions which arose in the aftermath of the 1974 double dissolution, and again in 1975: precisely what preconditions have to be satisfied before a double dissolution, as distinct from a dissolving of the House of Representatives alone, becomes an available option? How much individual discretion does the Governor-General retain? To what extent, if at all, can dissolution controversies be adjudicated by the courts? Professor Zines concludes that the 1975 double dissolution, despite its extraordinary character (in that it was granted to a Party whose *opposition* to Bills had itself primed the s.57 machinery), was strictly legal: Peter Bayne, however, squarely challenges this position in his closely argued commentary. Professor Reid contributes the provocative suggestions that good government would be enhanced by the courts keeping their collective nose entirely out of Parliament's business, and rational debate enhanced by constitutional lawyers ceasing entirely to talk about constitutional conventions!

Colin Howard and Cheryl Saunders (Chapter 8) focus directly on the dramatic and unprecedented events of October and November 1975—the blocking of the Budget by the Senate culminating in the dismissal of the Labor Government by the Governor-General, Sir John Kerr. Though expressing their political impartiality, the authors do not seek to disguise their conviction, argued for with a wealth of historical and analytical material, that the actions of both the Senate and Governor-General were fundamentally wrong. Sir Richard Eggleston's commentary is the most clearly and fully articulated statement of the position which he made peculiarly his own during the course of the constitutional crisis (and which is still the subject of intense controversy), viz. that the behaviour of the Senate in blocking the Appropriation Bills was not merely improper, but illegal.

The long commentary by R.J. Ellicott, Attorney-General under the Fraser Government which succeeded Whitlam's, is the fullest statement of the case in *favour* of the Senate's and Governor-General's actions yet to appear from a Government spokesman. Mr Ellicott argues that the Senate always has had the power to block supply, that it was justified in using it against the Labor Government, that when it did so Mr Whitlam had a duty to go to the people, and that when he refused the Governor-General was entirely justified in moving as he did at the time he did.

7 The Double Dissolutions and Joint Sitting

Leslie Zines

I
THE DOUBLE DISSOLUTION OF 1974

On 4 April 1974, Mr Snedden, Leader of the Opposition, announced in the House of Representatives that the Opposition would oppose Appropriation Bills (No. 4) and (No. 5) 1973-1974 and that he expected that they would be opposed in the Senate. He added that if the Coalition members and those of the Democratic Labor Party opposed the Appropriation Bills in the Senate they would be defeated and in that event the Government must go to an election. The Prime Minister replied that if the Senate rejected any money Bill he would 'advise the Governor-General not merely to dissolve the House of Representatives but to dissolve the Senate as well'.[1] On 10 April 1974 Senator Withers, the Leader of the Opposition in the Senate, moved an amendment which, if carried, would have deferred Appropriation Bill (No. 4) until the Government agreed to a general election. The Leader of the Australian Country Party and the Leader of the D.L.P. associated themselves with Senator Withers's action.[2] The Prime Minister then advised the Governor-General to dissolve both Houses of Parliament under s. 57 of the Constitution and that advice was accepted, subject to the condition that provision would be made for carrying on of the services of government until the new Parliament assembled. The Senate, on hearing of these events, passed the Appropriation Bills on 10 April 1974 and His Excellency, Sir Paul Hasluck, dissolved the House of Representatives and the Senate by Proclamation dated 11 April 1974.

The Prime Minister's advice to the Governor-General was constitutionally based on the view that the conditions in s. 57 of the Constitution upon which the Governor-General was empowered to dissolve both Houses simultaneously had been fulfilled in respect of six Bills, namely, the Commonwealth Electoral Bill (No. 2) 1973, the Senate (Representation of Territories) Bill 1973, the Representation Bill 1973, the Health Insurance Commission Bill 1973, the Health Insurance Bill 1973 and the Petroleum and Minerals Authority Bill 1973. Accompanying the advice was an opinion of the Attorney-General, Senator Lionel Murphy, advising that each of the proposed laws had satisfied the requirements of the first paragraph of s. 57 and a joint opinion by the Attorney-General and the Solicitor-General advising that s. 57 of the Constitution was applicable in respect of more than one proposed law.

In the weeks and months that followed the proclamation of dissolution a number of different questions as to the interpretation and application of s.57 presented themselves for resolution: whether a double dissolution could be

---

[1]House of Representatives, *Debates*, 4 April 1974, vol. 88, at pp. 1048, 1054.
[2]Senate, *Debates*, 10 April 1974, vol. 59, pp. 887, 889.

based on more than one Bill (thus allowing 'stockpiling' by the Government), the problem of applying the 'after an interval of three months' formula in s.57, and the whole question as to the justiciability of dissolution controversies, including the implications—extraordinary on their face—of declaring, after the event, a dissolution invalid. These questions are treated successively below. The very first question to arise, however, was in many ways the most fundamental. Did the Governor-General have any personal discretion at all in respect of a double dissolution, or was he obliged simply to accept the advice of his ministers?

The Discretion of the Governor-General

In respect of the 1914 double dissolution, Prime Minister Cook, in advising the Governor-General, stated that the power vested in the Governor-General by s.57 was one on which he should be guided by the advice of his ministers.[3] However, Sir Samuel Griffith (whose advice had been sought with the consent of Cook) had written to the Governor-General that His Excellency had to form his own judgment as to whether a double dissolution should be granted and need not follow his ministers' advice.[4] The Governor-General, in acceding to the Prime Minister's request, said that he had done so 'having considered the parliamentary situation'.

In 1951 Mr Menzies, in his advice to Sir William McKell, stated, first, his view that the Governor-General was not bound to follow his advice as to the existence of the facts required to satisfy the provisions in s.57 and that the Governor-General had to satisfy himself on that matter. However, on the general question of whether the Governor-General should dissolve both Houses given the existence of the conditions prescribed in s. 57, he said:

> I am not to be taken as affirming that any circumstances other than those referred to in section 57 are relevant to the granting or refusal of a dissolution of both Houses. But I have not failed to notice ... that, on the one former occasion upon which, in 1914, a Double Dissolution was sought and obtained, some importance appears to have been attached to the unworkable condition of the Parliament as a whole. Possibly such considerations were given a weight 37 years ago which they would not now be given, having regard to modern constitutional developments.[5]

He then went on to deal with other cases in which the Government had been hindered or frustrated by the Senate in carrying out its policy. The Governor-General's reply was 'I have given most careful consideration to the documents referred to and have decided to adopt the advice tendered in your memorandum'.[6]

The two precedents that existed in 1974 did not therefore provide much guidance as to the conventions on this matter. Menzies's position was in fact stated in less strong terms than that of Cook, but Sir William McKell's reply did not indicate whether he followed the advice because he was so advised or because the additional reasons given by Menzies had convinced him that a double dissolution should be granted.

The question whether the Governor-General was bound to accept the advice

---

[3] *Parliamentary Papers* 1914-17, vol. 5, p.129 ff.
[4] Quoted in J.I. Fajgenbaum and P.J. Hanks, *Australian Constitutional Law*, (Sydney 1972), p. 93.
[5] *Parliamentary Papers* 1957-58, vol. 5, p. 926.
[6] *ibid.*, p. 937.

of his ministers to dissolve both Houses of Parliament if the conditions of s.57 were satisfied was examined in detail by Professor Lane in 1973.[7] He concluded on the basis of precedent that the Governor-General had such a discretion. This conclusion was further supported analogically by the consideration of precedents and authoritative works concerned with the power of Governors and Governors-General to accept or refuse advice to dissolve Parliament in situations that did not involve s.57 of the Constitution. Professor Lane, however, pointed to the difficulty of the Governor-General refusing such advice where no alternative government was possible and the ministry would not be prepared to remain in office in the face of a refusal by the Governor-General to accept advice to dissolve.

In 1974 the Prime Minister's advice did not refer at all to whether there was a duty on the Governor-General to act on the advice of his ministers. As in the earlier cases, Mr Whitlam did not merely set out the circumstances that showed that the conditions of s.57 had been met: he went on to deal generally with the state of affairs between the two Houses and to argue that the Government was unable to function adequately because of obstruction in the Senate. The Governor-General stated that he accepted the opinions of the law officers that the requirements of s.57 had been satisfied and then went on:

> As it is clear to me that grounds for granting a double dissolution are provided by the Parliamentary history of the six Bills listed above, it is not necessary for me to reach any judgment on the wider case you have presented that the policies of the Government have been obstructed by the Senate. It seems to me that this is a matter for judgment by the electors.[8]

If one looks merely at the Prime Minister's advice and the Governor-General's reply, the impression is gained that the Prime Minister thought that the general parliamentary situation was relevant in providing grounds for the dissolution. The advice does not even contain the reservation made by Sir Robert Menzies, nor is there any statement that the Governor-General is bound by the advice of his ministers. Sir Paul Hasluck's reply seems to indicate that he refused to consider the general parliamentary situation because it was irrelevant to the question of whether he should dissolve the Parliament.

Yet, public statements made by Mr Whitlam and by the Governor-General on other occasions lead to opposite conclusions. On 24 October 1972 Sir Paul Hasluck, as Governor-General, had set out in the Queale Memorial Lecture some of his views regarding the office of Governor-General.[9] On the question of the dissolution of Parliament, he said that 'A solemn responsibility rests on him [the Governor-General] to make a judgment whether a dissolution is needed to serve the purposes of good government . . .' He placed considerable emphasis on Parliament becoming 'unworkable' as a major ground for dissolving the House of Representatives and added that 'The dissolution of Parliament is an example of one of the matters in which the Constitution requires the Governor-General to act on his own'. This attitude appears inconsistent with his letter to Mr Whitlam where he seems to reject the relevance of the general parliamentary situation and to concentrate on the Bills that had satisfied the conditions in s.57. But in the Queale Lecture the Governor-General did not

---

[7] P.H. Lane, 'Double Dissolution of Federal Parliament' (1973) 47 *Australian L.J.* 290.

[8] *Documents Relating to the Simultaneous Dissolution of the Senate and the House of Representatives by His Excellency the Governor-General on 11 April 1974* (Tabled in Parliament, 29 October 1975), p.38.

[9] An edited text of the Queale Lecture appears in the *Australian,* 23 October 1975.

address himself to a double dissolution; he was concerned only with a mid-term dissolution of the House of Representatives. The action threatened in the Senate in relation to the Appropriation Bills would clearly have given the Prime Minister on any view a right to expect the Governor-General to dissolve the House of Representatives if so advised. The pragmatic answer in relation to the 1974 double dissolution is that there was no possibility of an alternative government being formed and the Whitlam Government would certainly not have accepted a refusal of the Governor-General to dissolve both Houses. The Governor-General, therefore, would have had no alternative but to accept the advice.[10]

The question of whether the Governor-General has a personal discretion in the matter was referred to by some members of the High Court. In *Victoria* v. *Commonwealth* (the *P.M.A. Case*)[11] the matter was raised in relation to the argument of the Commonwealth that s.57 should be interpreted as giving to the Governor-General the power conclusively to determine whether the conditions laid down by s.57 as prerequisites to a double dissolution and a joint sitting had been satisfied. Mason J said:

> It is no easy matter to define the role of the Governor-General under section 57. Does His Excellency make a personal judgment or does he, in accordance with English constitutional convention, act on the advice tendered to him by the Government? Although the problem was left unresolved by the argument, I am persuaded that the section does not confer on the Governor-General a power to decide conclusively whether the conditions have been satisfied.[12]

In *Western Australia* v. *Commonwealth* (the *Territory Senators Case*)[13] Barwick CJ referred to the issue[14] and similarly left the question unresolved. Jacobs J, on the other hand, clearly stated that

> Neither the Queen nor the Governor-General acts personally. This is true of the powers of the Governor-General under s.57. He in all respects exercises his powers under the section on the advice of an Australian minister.[15]

Similarly, Murphy J, referring to the decisions that the Governor-General is empowered to make under s.57, said:

> the decision whether the procedures in s.57 for a double dissolution had been observed is a political decision, confided by the Constitution not to the judiciary, but to the Governor-General. The decision is to be made by the Governor-General on the advice of the Executive Council (Constitution s.62).[16]

The matter, of course, is in the area of convention rather than law. As s.57 simply gives the power of dissolution to the Governor-General the dissolution could hardly be invalid solely because it was done without advice; if the Governor-General refused to act on advice, there would be no action to invalidate. Nevertheless, the conventions of responsible government are recognisable by the courts[17] and they can be relevant in some aspects of

---

[10]*Cf*. P. Hanks, 'Vice-Regal Initiative and Discretion' [1975] *Australian Current Law Digest* 294.

[11](1975) 7 A.L.R. 1.

[12]*ibid.*, p.63.

[13](1975) 7 A.L.R. 159.

[14]*ibid.*, p. 168.

[15]*ibid.*, p. 213.

[16]*ibid.*, p.225.

[17]*Amalgamated Society of Engineers* v. *Adelaide Steamship Co. Ltd & Ors* (*Engineers Case*) (1920) 28 C.L.R. 129.

interpreting the Constitution. A statement by the Court that a convention exists would tend to be regarded as conclusive and would have a powerful effect on its preservation. But as the matter stands the issue is judicially unresolved.

As mentioned earlier, Mr Menzies's advice in 1951 was that the Governor-General was not bound by his ministers' views as to 'the existence of the facts' required to satisfy the provisions of s.57. Of course whether the conditions laid down by s.57 have been satisfied involves not only issues of fact but of law as the later cases of *Cormack* v. *Cope*[18] and the *P.M.A. Case*[19] show. It is unlikely that there could be any dispute as to the primary facts, namely, what was said and done in the Senate. Disagreement is more likely to arise over the interpretation of those events. In 1951 and 1974 the Governor-General accepted the opinions of the law officers and, in the former case, a further opinion by Mr Barwick (as he then was) which had been commissioned by the Prime Minister. In the Queale Lecture Sir Paul Hasluck suggested that on questions of constitutionality he could obtain advice from 'the Chief Justice, the Attorney-General or eminent counsel'. Later, he said, that if the Governor-General 'wishes for guidance on any legal or constitutional points that may arise he will seek it from the Attorney-General or from eminent authorities of his choosing and not from staff of his own'. The last statement is ambiguous as it is not clear whether it is the Attorney-General or the Governor-General that does the choosing.

Mr Lindell and I argued in a letter to the *Canberra Times* on 2 August 1975 that a Governor-General should not, as a general rule, himself judge the legality of acts of the Government and that that question should be left to the courts. We said:

> The question of 'plain illegality' referred to by Sir Isaac raises difficulties. How is a Governor-General who is not a lawyer (or even one who is, but who lacks the learning of Sir Isaac or the present incumbent) to determine whether there is plain illegality? If he does not accept the advice of his advisers, to whom is he to turn for a legal opinion?
>
> If he should obtain advice from elsewhere, why should that opinion be regarded as more authoritative than that of the Attorney-General or the Solicitor-General? It seems to us, in any case, that there cannot be one rule of action for a Governor-General who is a lawyer and another for one who is not.
>
> The branch of government whose prime duty it is to authoritatively determine the law is the judiciary.

This letter was quoted by the Governor-General at the Australasian Universities Law Schools Association Conference at the University of New South Wales in August 1975 but he expressly stated he was not indicating whether he agreed with it or not. One issue on which we said we reserved our opinion was where there was no means of obtaining a judicial determination. I might now add that there is a further situation where the view propounded runs into difficulties—namely, where the damage will be done before a judicial determination can be obtained. This is, in my view, the case with a double dissolution.

Professor Sawer has argued[20] that, as the High Court in *Cormack* v. *Cope*[21] and the *P.M.A. Case*[22] decided that it would take jurisdiction to determine

[18](1974) 131 C.L.R. 432.

[19](1975) 7 A.L.R. 1.

[20](1976) 52 *Current Affairs Bulletin* No. 10, at p.27.

[21](1974) 131 C.L.R. 432.

[22](1975) 7 A.L.R. 1.

whether the legal requirements of s.57 had been complied with in a particular case, it is now unlikely that a Governor-General will ever reject ministerial advice on that score because he can leave the legal issues to be fought out in the courts. While that is so in so far as the validity of legislation passed at a joint sitting is concerned, most of the judges have indicated that they would not, or at any rate probably would not, declare a dissolution of Parliament invalid even though it was unauthorised by s.57. That issue is treated later in this essay. If, however, that is the case, a Governor-General faced with advice that he considers to be in blatant disregard of the Constitution may not be able to rely on the Court to resolve the issue in time. This is, in my view, a case where the Constitution might be amended to allow the Governor-General to obtain an advisory opinion from the High Court.

Cormack v. Cope and the Question of Stockpiling

The result of the election following the double dissolution in 1974 was that the Labor Government was returned with a majority in the House of Representatives but not in the Senate. The Bills which provided the occasion for the double dissolution were again passed by the House of Representatives and were rejected by the Senate. A Proclamation of the Governor-General dated 30 July 1974, after reciting that in respect of the six Bills the conditions upon which the Governor-General was empowered by s.57 of the Constitution to convene a joint sitting had been fulfilled, convened a joint sitting of members of the two Houses for 6 August 1974 'at which they may deliberate and shall vote together upon each of the said proposed laws as last proposed by the House of Representatives'.

After the Governor-General's Proclamation, but before the scheduled meeting of the joint sitting, two actions—reported together as *Cormack* v. *Cope*[23]—were brought in the High Court for interlocutory relief. The first action[24] was brought by two members of the Senate seeking a declaration that the Proclamation was invalid because the procedure described by s.57 was limited to a double dissolution and joint sitting in respect of one Bill only. The second action[25] was brought by Queensland which submitted that the joint sitting could not deliberate upon the Petroleum and Minerals Authority Bill because the provisions of s.57 had not, with respect to that Bill, been followed. The argument was that the requisite three months period had not expired before the House of Representatives had passed the Bill for a second time. It was held in both actions that no interlocutory relief should be granted.

All the judges, except McTiernan J, considered that after a Bill has been passed by a joint sitting, the Court could examine whether the provisions of s.57 had been satisfied and, if not, declare the measure invalid. They were divided as to whether the Court had jurisdiction to intervene beforehand;[26] but even those who thought there was jurisdiction relied on the fact that the matter could be dealt with later for refusing the interlocutory relief. All the judges,

---

[23](1974) 131 C.L.R. 432.

[24]Cormack and Another v. Cope and Others.

[25]The State of Queensland and Another v. Whitlam and Others. This question was later litigated in the *P.M.A. Case* (1975) A.L.R. 1.

[26]Barwick CJ and Gibbs J thought that the Court did have such jurisdiction, Mason J left the question open and Menzies and Stephen JJ considered that the Court did not have jurisdiction except perhaps where it would not be possible to invoke judicial review at a later stage.

except McTiernan J (who regarded the matter as non-justiciable), rejected the argument that the phrase 'any proposed law' in s.57 was confined to a single Bill and held that the provision operated distributively, so that a double dissolution could be granted or a joint sitting convened in relation to any number of Bills that met the requirements of s.57.

The main argument presented for treating s.57 as applicable only to a single proposed law was that the provision laid down an extraordinary procedure which was an exception from the bicameral principles otherwise provided for in the Constitution. In interpreting s.57 to extend beyond a single proposed law, the way would be open, it was argued, for a government to build up a storehouse of Bills which would in turn lead to 'government by double dissolution'. Most of the judges, however, were of the opinion that the restrictive interpretation would lead to even worse results. For example, Stephen J said that:

> The possibility of any abuse of s.57 by the lower House appears to me to be a less real fear than the probability that to accede to the plaintiff's contention will, for all practical purposes, deprive s. 57 of its ability to resolve disputes extending beyond the merits of a single proposed law.[27]

Barwick CJ, while agreeing with the conclusion of the other judges in this regard, expressed concern that that interpretation made a considerable inroad upon the basic concept of the Constitution which provides for a bicameral system of Parliament.[28] He then, rather surprisingly, suggested 'the formation and observance of a parliamentary convention designed to implement the spirit of parliamentary government as under the Constitution'. This statement is interesting not only because it reflects an unusual notion of the judicial role, but because of the assumption that the place of the Senate in our system of government is to be understood not only from the provisions of the Constitution but from some ethical norm to be deduced from its 'spirit'. This argument goes beyond that which suggests that s.57 be given a restrictive interpretation because it is an unusual exception from the rule of bicameralism. His Honour rejected that argument and accepted that the Constitution allowed a 'storehouse of proposed laws' to be built up during the life of a Parliament, but then suggested that to exercise that undoubted legal power could somehow be wrong. Such an approach can only be based on a view that our bicameral system has a virtue beyond the fact that it is legally required.

Barwick CJ saw one way to limit the threat to the Senate's position. In the *Territory Senators Case*[29] it was argued that the Joint Sitting in 1974 had no power to pass the *Commonwealth Electoral Act (No. 2)* 1973 because seven and a half months had elapsed between the second rejection of the Bill by the Senate and the double dissolution. The Court unanimously rejected that argument. All the judges, other than Barwick CJ, relied on the fact that s.57 did not provide for an express time limit for a double dissolution after a second rejection of the Bill by the Senate (except for that referred to at the end of the first paragraph of that provision). The Chief Justice, however, implied a time limitation and expressly relied on the 'dangers to the bicameral system'. His Honour stated that the development of conventions would take time and would depend on 'the maturity' of Parliament. (The assumption appears to be that those who do not wish to strengthen bicameralism beyond that which the

---

[27] *Cormack* v. *Cope* (1974) 131 C.L.R. 432, at p.470.
[28] *ibid.*, at p.456.
[29] (1975) 7 A.L.R. 159.

Constitution itself lays down are not as mature as those who would wish to take it further.) He held, therefore, that

> the second occasion on which the bill has not been passed must be so related in point of time to the date of the dissolution as to form part of the same current situation between the House and the Senate[30]

The advantage of this interpretation was that Bills could not be stockpiled. In the event, however, he considered that the Act here in question did meet the requirements of s.57.

The Chief Justice was also alone in the views he expressed in *Cormack* v. *Cope*[31] regarding the validity of the Proclamation convening the Joint Sitting. As explained above, the Proclamation specified the business of the Joint Sitting to be the consideration and voting on the six named proposed laws. All the judges who regarded the question as justiciable agreed that the Governor-General did not have power to direct the members upon what proposed laws they might deliberate.[32] Section 57 itself determined what might be done at the joint sitting and it was for the Court to interpret and apply that provision while Menzies, Gibbs, Stephen and Mason JJ were of the opinion that although the part of the Proclamation specifying the business of the joint sitting might be 'surplusage' or 'unnecessary material', it did not affect the validity of the Proclamation. Barwick CJ, however, expressed the view that the Proclamation was probably invalid; but as the proceedings were interlocutory he did not have to decide the question.

The *P.M.A. Case* and the Question of Time

In the *P.M.A. Case*[33] the High Court had to squarely confront the question whether the second passage of the Petroleum and Minerals Authority Bill by the House of Representatives was 'after an interval of three months' within the meaning of s.57. Subsidiary issues, involved in the resolution of that question, were the notion of certainty in the formulation of rules, the position of the Senate in our system of government and the relevance of practical problems of government to judicial interpretation.

The Petroleum and Minerals Authority Bill was first passed by the House of Representatives on 12 December 1973 and introduced into the Senate on 13 December. The Senate adjourned until February. Parliament was prorogued on 14 February 1974 until 28 February 1974. On 2 April 1974 the Senate negatived a motion that the Bill be now read a second time. The Bill was passed again by the House of Representatives on 8 April 1974, introduced into the Senate on the same day and on 10 April 1974 the Senate resolved that the Bill be deferred for six months (a traditional form of rejection).

The issue was whether the House of Representatives, in passing the proposed law for a second time, i.e. on 8 April 1974, did so 'after an interval of three months'. Barwick CJ, Gibbs, Stephen and Mason JJ held that the three months interval was measured from the Senate's rejection or failure to pass and that, in the circumstances, the Senate had not failed to pass the Bill on 13 December

---

[30]*ibid.*, p.167.

[31](1974) 131 C.L.R. 432.

[32]In the *Territory Senators Case* (1975) 7 A.L.R. 159, at p.200, Stephen J later modified his views on this issue to a considerable extent.

[33](1975) 7 A.L.R. 1.

1973 (the day it was introduced into the Senate and the last day before the Senate adjourned). Consequently, this legislation had not fulfilled the requirements of s.57 and the Act was therefore invalid. McTiernan and Jacobs JJ dissented, the former on the ground dealt with below, that the issue was non-justiciable, and the latter because he considered that the requirements of s.57 had been fulfilled.

All the judges recognised that the words 'fails to pass' were capable of a number of interpretations. The majority took their stand on what they saw as the purpose of the provision. Except in relation to certain aspects of money Bills, the Senate, they pointed out, had equal power with the House of Representatives. The object of the three months period, in their view, was to allow time for a reconciliation of differences between the Houses by reconsideration and consultation. This meant that the Senate had to be given time properly to consider the proposed legislation and to determine its attitude to it before the three months interval could be said to commence. To decide whether it had failed to pass the Bill, the Court would have regard to the actions and resolutions of the Senate (as distinct from speeches by individual senators), the usual practices and procedures of the Senate, and whether it had taken longer than a 'reasonable time' to take a stand as to the acceptance, rejection or amendment of the proposed legislation.

The difficulty and uncertainty involved in determining the date at which the Senate could be said to have failed to pass the legislation were recognised by all. The problems facing the Governor-General in deciding those questions for himself were admitted. But those consequences were regarded as being outweighed by considerations relating to what Stephen J referred to as the 'legislative model' which it was said the Constitution provided. That model was a bicameral system with the upper House having, with few exceptions, full power of initiation, rejection and amendment of Bills. This was seen as both the historic intention of the founders and the clear conclusion to be derived from the proper reading of the Constitution. Emphasis was therefore placed on the extraordinary nature of s.57 and the consequences for the Senate's power and position if it were held that the three months period commenced from when the House of Representatives passed the proposed law or if the Senate could be said to have failed to pass it on the day it was received. Such an interpretation could subject the Senate to the will of the House of Representatives.

To say that s.57 is an exception from fundamental principles relating to bicameralism or a departure from the constitutional model is, of course, to beg the question. In *Cormack* v. *Cope*[34] similar arguments were used in attempting to persuade the Court to limit s.57 to a single Bill, but those arguments were rejected. The fact is that the Constitution provides both for bicameral machinery and, in the case of s.57, for a unicameral process. To say that the first situation is the 'model', which is merely to say it is usual or normal, cannot itself provide the answer as to when and in what circumstances s.57, and therefore unicameralism, operates or which of the alternative interpretations of that provision put to the Court should be adopted. On any view s.57 would, to some extent, be 'exceptional'. The issue is, to what extent?

Thus, in *Cormack* v. *Cope*,[35] Stephen J admitted that the interpretation he gave to s.57 in that case might leave 'open the way to wholesale impairment of

---

[34](1974) 131 C.L.R. 432.
[35]*ibid.*

the legislature's bicameral character'; however, he referred, among other things, to the safeguard of 'an intervening appeal to the electorate' and to the fact that the intended effect of s.57 was to infringe the generally bicameral character of the legislature. He also stated that the nature of the solution for deadlock arrived at was 'one tending to ensure that the will of the lower House should prevail'.[36]

In the *P.M.A. Case*[37] the position of the Senate was given far greater emphasis, not only in respect of its near equal power with the House of Representatives but also as a body with a continuity of existence. The argument referred to in *Cormack* v. *Cope*[38]—that the result of a double dissolution was a general election—was met by the proposition that the continuity of existence of the Senate was 'a central feature of our legislative model'. The submission that the intention of s.57 was to secure the effectiveness of the will of the House of Representatives was denied by Barwick CJ, Gibbs and Stephen JJ. No significance was attached to the fact that the House of Representatives had the initiative in the formulation of the proposed law and its re-enactment.

The principles and value judgments involved in the judgments of the majority can best be viewed in the light of the judgment of Jacobs J who dissented. He also purported to rely on 'the purpose of the constitutional provision disclosed by its language', but found the purpose quite different. It was, in his view, to allow

> to the Senate a period of three months from the time when it was first open to it to consider a proposed law passed by the House of Representatives. So long as it does not pass the proposed law it is in a state or condition of failing to pass it.[39]

Therefore, the period of failing to pass commenced from when the House of Representatives sent the Bill to the Senate.

His Honour rejected the majority view for a variety of reasons including the role the Court should play, practical problems of government and the need for certainty of rules. On the question of certainty, he said that where great political issues were at stake, it was necessary that the Constitution speak 'unequivocally'. Under the majority approach, the determination of when the Senate had failed to pass the proposed law 'could be fraught with difficulty'.[40] Secondly, the House of Representatives before it could pass a Bill again for the purposes of s.57 would have to make an 'invidious' inquiry into the conduct of the Senate and a court (not necessarily the High Court) might also have to make that inquiry and might come to a contrary conclusion. While such a state of affairs might be inevitable in relation to private rights, 'we are dealing with public rights which lie at the heart of our constitutional democracy'. The results of error could be extraordinary in that the Senate might have been wrongly dissolved or the dissolution itself might be void. He also did not think that it was appropriate to make implications regarding what was a reasonable time in all the circumstances to allow the Senate before it could be said to have failed to pass the proposed law.

In the judgment of Jacobs J the 'constitutional model' was quite different

---

[36] *ibid.*, at p.470. In the *P.M.A. Case* (1975) 7 A.L.R. 1, at p.52, he resiled from the last mentioned consideration.

[37] (1975) 7 A.L.R. 1.

[38] (1974) 131 C.L.R. 432.

[39] *P.M.A. Case* (1975) 7 A.L.R. 1, at p.73.

[40] *ibid.*

from that seen by, for example, Stephen J. There is in the former judgment little or no mention of the great position, functions and powers of the Senate; the three months period was not, in his opinion, granted so that both Houses might try to reconcile their differences; rather,

> the object of section 57 is attained once the proposed law is passed by the Senate in a form acceptable to the House of Representatives. Accordingly, both time and recurrent opportunity are intended to be given *to the Senate*, to resolve the actual or inchoate deadlock.[41]

That view was reinforced by the practical problems involved in the opposing view.

The playing down of the position of the Senate is also obvious in Jacobs J's treatment of the alternative ground he relied upon to dismiss the action. Even if the majority view were accepted, he thought that the statement of claim did not disclose a cause of action. The facts alleged, in his opinion, did not establish that the Senate had not failed to pass the proposed law three months before 8 April 1974 (when the House of Representatives passed it for the second time). In contrast to some of the other judges, who stated that the Senate was not subject to the bidding of the House of Representatives, Jacobs J said that even if the Court took notice of the Senate practice in adjourning for the Christmas recess, 'it does not follow that in the particular circumstances it was reasonable for the Senate to adjourn leaving the business undone despite the urgings of the country's government and the lower House that the business be done'.[42] Indeed he went further and said he would conclude from the allegations in the statement of claim that the Senate, by simply adjourning on 13 December 1973 until February 1974, had failed to pass the Bill.

One argument emphasised by some of the majority judges against the view that the policy of certainty required the time to run from the passing of the Bill by the House of Representatives or its introduction into the Senate was that it might still be necessary to determine when the Senate had failed to pass the Bill for a second time. There was no way of avoiding that, they thought, unless it could be said that the Senate, in order to avoid a double dissolution, had to pass the Bill instantly—a view which they considered to be absurd. Jacobs J was required to fall back on the reserved powers of the Crown to deal with that argument. He reasoned that, after the House of Representatives had passed the proposed law a second time, the Senate may pass it and so long as it did not do so it was in a state of failing to pass it. The Governor-General might, during that time, dissolve both Houses of Parliament. But he added 'Advice to allow no time would be so extraordinary that it might require some extraordinary course on the part of the Governor-General'.[43]

The Justiciability of Dissolution Controversies

Cormack v. *Cope*[44] was decided in a hurry and there was little time for the judges to consider the matter before delivering judgment. Several issues raised in that case were to receive, as has been seen, fuller treatment in later cases

---

[41] *ibid.*, p.72. Emphasis added.

[42] *ibid.*, p.76. Yet, ironically, it was the Leader of the Government in the Senate, Senator Murphy, who ensured the adjournment. Senate, *Debates* 13 December 1973, vol. 58, p. 2861.

[43] *ibid.*, p.74.

[44] (1974) 131 C.L.R. 432. On the matter of haste see Gibbs J at p.467.

involving s.57. By then the membership of the Bench had changed: Menzies J had died and Jacobs and Murphy JJ had been appointed to the Court. One of the most important issues was that of justiciability. In *Cormack* v. *Cope*[45] only McTiernan J had been of the view that the issues were non-justiciable. In the *P.M.A. Case*[46] Murphy J did not sit and Jacobs J did not feel obliged to decide the question of justiciability. In the *Territory Senators Case* both Jacobs and Murphy JJ stated that they, like McTiernan J, considered the issues not to be justiciable.[47]

The argument of the Commonwealth relating to justiciability was put in a number of ways: (a) that the Governor-General had the constitutional function to decide whether the conditions under s. 57 had been fulfilled; (b) that the provisions were directory and not mandatory; and (c) that the matter before the Court was a proceeding in Parliament which could not be investigated by the judiciary. The majority in each case rejected these arguments, strongly asserting the right and duty of the Court to decide whether the law-making process prescribed by the Constitution had been followed. Both Barwick CJ and Mason J referred to the role of the Court as 'the guardian of the Constitution'.[48] Reliance was placed on the fact that s. 57 provided extraordinary law-making power, the conditions for the exercise of which had been delineated with some care and in detail. The argument that the matter was one to be left to the Governor-General for determination raised the issue as to whether the Governor-General determined the matter for himself or on advice, but that issue was not developed or resolved. Rather the form of s. 57 was relied upon, namely that the conditions of that section did not refer to the opinion of the Governor-General.

McTiernan J's judgment in the *P.M.A. Case*[49] referred to the issue whether the Senate had failed to pass the Petroleum and Minerals Authority Act on 13 December 1973 as 'a political question' and not within the judicial power of the Commonwealth. The question was non-justiciable, he said, because it was inappropriate for judicial consideration. Murphy J in the *Territory Senators Case*[50] said he agreed generally with McTiernan J and emphasised that the judiciary was not equipped to investigate circumstances which needed to be taken into account in determining whether the requirements of s. 57 had been met. The political aspect of the matter was, in his view, underlined by the fact that the decision to dissolve both Houses meant an immediate reference to the electorate. His Honour seemed to be of the opinion that s. 57 intended the Governor-General and his advisers to make the decision because it could only properly be made by having regard to non-justiciable considerations and to matters which could not be evidence admissible in a court.[51]

Jacobs J delivered the most elaborate statement on this question. He said:

> The procedure prescribed leads to the expression by the people of their preference in the choice of their elected representatives, a preference expressed with the knowledge that a joint sitting of those representatives may need to take place, and no court in the

[45] *ibid.*; McTiernan J's opinion is at p.461.
[46] (1975) 7 A.L.R. 1.
[47] (1975) 7 A.L.R. 159 at pp. 210-11 (Jacobs J), 225-6 (Murphy J).
[48] *P.M.A. Case* (1975) 7 A.L.R. 1, at pp. 11-12 (Barwick CJ), 61 (Mason J).
[49] (1975) 7 A.L.R. 1, at p.24.
[50] (1975) 7 A.L.R. 159, at pp. 225-6.
[51] *ibid.*

absence of a clearly conferred power has the right to thwart or interfere with the people's expression of their choice. The people's expression cures any formal defects which may have previously existed. That is democratic government within the terms of the Constitution by which the people elected to be governed. The concern of this court is with the respective limits of legislative power of the Commonwealth and the States and with the application to legislation, State or Federal, of the provisions of the Constitution in order to test the substantial validity of that legislation. There is no indication that the Court was empowered to superintend the legislative procedures, above all a legislative procedure which involves as a consequence the election by the people of their representatives and as a sequel thereto a particular form of further legislative process.[52]

He added that he could not conceive that a court 'can tell Parliament that, though it has power to pass the law, it should pass it again and next time do it properly'. His Honour, however, felt bound by the recent decision of the majority in the *P.M.A. Case*[53] to regard the issue as justiciable.

From *Cormack* v. *Cope*[54] to the *Territory Senators Case*[55] the majority of the Bench in favour of treating the issue as justiciable was thus reduced from 5:1 to 4:3. It may be therefore that the question is not settled for all time. There is little purpose to be served in arguing on the basis of authority which view regarding justiciability is 'right'. As the judgments show, the authorities can be viewed as supporting (or can be manipulated to support) either view. From the majority viewpoint s. 57 is a detailed and elaborate provision in the Constitution which we know was treated historically as a matter of great importance in the struggle between the larger and smaller colonies. To suggest it is a matter that cannot be adjudicated upon by the High Court is in effect to rely upon the bona fides and good judgment of the government of the day or perhaps (depending on which view is adopted) the independent judgment of the Governor-General. In general, the main argument in favour of the majority position is the rule of law with its emphasis on the Court as the guardian of the Constitution.

The opposing view is based partly on the difficulty or inappropriateness of the Court determining many of the questions that arise under s.57 and the right of Parliament to conduct its affairs freely and without judicial scrutiny. But the main policy consideration relied on seems to be that as the steps prescribed by s. 57 lead to a democratic election, it is either inappropriate or presumptuous for the judiciary to intervene. As the object of s.57 is that the people are to determine (admittedly in an indirect fashion) whether they wish to be governed by the proposed laws the Court should not prevent the expression of this 'democratic will'. On this issue, in which the 'rule of law' is set up against 'democratic processes', I am personally inclined in this case toward the former. If one commences with the position that, generally speaking, the provisions of the Constitution are binding on governments and Parliaments, the minority view on the justiciability of s.57 leads either to the government of the day being judge of its own cause or else encourages the Governor-General to act independently 'as the guardian of the Constitution', in the absence of the Court being able to do so. The first result I regard as wrong for obvious reasons. As far as the second result is concerned, I am opposed, for the reasons stated earlier in

---

[52] *ibid.*, at p.211.
[53] (1975) 7 A.L.R. 1.
[54] (1974) 131 C.L.R. 432.
[55] (1975) 7 A.L.R. 159.

this essay, to the Governor-General independently determining the lawfulness of the government's behaviour where it is possible to avoid putting him in such a position.

To argue that an election cures any defects might suggest that it is unimportant whether the government or the Governor-General has regard to the provisions of s.57 because of the greater good that results, that is, the expression of the democratic will. This, however, is to ignore the fact that the Constitution itself makes it clear that this particular form of democratic process is to take place only in prescribed circumstances. If conditions are prescribed before a certain form of election can be held, it is difficult to understand how an unauthorised election can be 'cured' merely by the fact that it has occurred. To say that elections are themselves good things and override all other considerations is somewhat reminiscent of the argument used to justify the Senate in 1975 deferring supply, namely, that it enabled the people to decide.

The Problem of Invalid Dissolutions

The *P.M.A. Case*[56] was heard by the High Court on 24-27 February 1975 and the decision given on 24 June 1975. Comments by Barwick CJ and Gibbs J in *Cormack* v. *Cope*[57] had made clear that the invalidity of the *Petroleum and Minerals Authority Act* 1973 was a distinct possibility. In an address to the Eighteenth Australian Legal Convention on 2 July 1975 Mr Whitlam, in apparent reference to the Petroleum and Minerals Authority Act, said:

> I hate to think that, if the double dissolution had been granted on the sole Bill which has been the subject of judicial interpretation, instead of six Bills, we might have to resuscitate a defunct Parliament of fifteen months ago. I mustn't enlarge on that; I have to be more discreet.[58]

The appalling consequences of a Governor-General or his advisers making a 'mistake' regarding whether a Bill has complied with s.57 and so wrongly dissolving Parliament was urged by the Commonwealth as a reason for regarding the requirements of s.57 either as 'non-justiciable' or as 'directory' rather than 'mandatory'. The opposing view could, it was submitted, lead to a dissolution and subsequent election being void, so that no valid laws could be made. This was one of the factors that influenced Jacobs J. In the *P.M.A. Case*[59] he said:

> The lives of the Government and the national Parliament are in such a case at stake. In particular, the life of the elected Senate is at stake. If an error be made a Senate elected by the electorate for a certain period will be wrongly dissolved or on another view the dissolution itself may be void. It would indeed be an extraordinary result. It may be that this consideration is of even greater importance on the question whether the matter is justiciable before this Court at all, but it is by no means unimportant on the issue of construction if it be assumed that the issue is justiciable.

The majority judges, however, did not feel compelled to the conclusion, that, if the provisions of s.57 were both justiciable and mandatory in relation to the convening of, and legislation passed at, a joint sitting, the same must be true if the validity of the double dissolution was the sole issue before the Court. These

---

[56](1975) 7 A.L.R. 1.
[57](1974) 131 C.L.R. 432.
[58](1975) 49 *Australian L.J.*, at p.310.
[59](1975) 7 A.L.R. 1, at pp. 73-4.

suggested consequences of the Court's decision on the validity of the Petroleum and Minerals Authority Act were rejected by Barwick CJ and Stephen J and were, it seems, also unacceptable to Gibbs and Mason JJ. It would seem, therefore, that all the judges would treat the issue as non-justiciable, at any rate where the action is challenged after a Proclamation of dissolution is made.

The reasons given by the majority judges, however, are unconvincing. It seems to be clear that outside s.57 there is no power to dissolve the Senate.[60] Yet, the Chief Justice referred to the dissolution as 'a fact which can neither be void nor undone' even though it could be shown to be unauthorised by s.57 and lead to the invalidation of legislation passed at a joint sitting. Similarly Stephen J said:

> In the case of s.57 no such consequences would, in my view, ensue; once the Governor-General has *in fact* dissolved both chambers, whether or not he is justified in doing so in terms of s.57, the existing Parliament will have been brought effectively to an end and the new Parliament which results from the issue of writs and the holding of an election following such dissolution will be quite unaffected by whatever may or may not have preceded that dissolution.[61]

The judges, however, do not explain in what way the dissolution is a 'fact'. The question whether, as a result of certain actions and the execution of certain documents, Parliament is dissolved can reasonably be described as a question of law. If the Constitution laid down a condition precedent for exercising the power to dissolve both Houses and provided that the condition was mandatory, it would hardly be illogical or a confusion of fact and law to conclude, if the Governor-General executed an instrument which stated that Parliament was dissolved when the condition precedent had not occurred, that the instrument did not validly dissolve Parliament, that it was a nullity and that, therefore, Parliament was not 'in fact' dissolved. To say that Parliament is dissolved even though the dissolution is not authorised, is surely to conclude that the provisions laying down the condition precedent to dissolution are either directory, and not mandatory, or are not justiciable. The only relevant 'fact' is a document executed by the Governor-General stating that the Houses are dissolved. To call the legal effect of that document a 'fact' is not very helpful.

Mason J seemed a little more open in suggesting that there may be some logical inconsistency in the way the Court treats s.57 for purposes of dealing with legislation passed by a joint sitting on the one hand and the dissolution of the Houses on the other:

> Even if it be thought that a logical consequence of granting relief to the plaintiffs now would be to expose a prospective dissolution of Parliament under s. 57 to judicial scrutiny, this does not demonstrate that relief cannot be granted in the present cases.[62]

This statement is reminiscent of Lord Halsbury's famous dictum in *Quinn* v. *Leathem*[63] which at least makes it clear that deductive reasoning is not always compelling in judicial decision-making.

Gibbs J's approach is complex. He was 'not persuaded' that if the Senate were

---

[60] *P.M.A. Case* (1975) 7 A.L.R. 1, at p.11 per Barwick CJ, p.40 per Gibbs J; J.L. Goldring, 'The Royal Prerogative and Dissolution of the Commonwealth Parliament' (1975) 49 *Australian L.J.* 521.

[61] (1975) 7 A.L.R. 1, at p.59. Emphasis added.

[62] *ibid.*, at p.63.

[63] [1901] A.C. 495, at p.506.

improperly dissolved, the new Parliament would be invalid. The reasons he gave were that

> the conditions which s.57 attaches to the exercise of the powers which it confers do not also attach to the powers given by ss. 12 and 32 of the Constitution to cause writs to be issued for the election of members of the Senate and of the House of Representatives. If the Senate were *in fact* dissolved, and if thereafter writs for an election were issued, the election was held and a new Parliament was summoned to meet, I can see no difficulty in holding that the new Parliament would have been validly assembled.[64]

He then went on to say, however, that the Court might intervene 'to uphold the Constitution and prevent an invalid Proclamation for the dissolution of the Senate from being given effect'.

There are several difficulties with this reasoning. To say that s.12 (authorising State Governors to cause writs to be issued for Senate elections) and s.32 (empowering the Governor-General in Council to cause writs to be issued for general elections of the House of Representatives) are not subject to the conditions of s.57 does not meet the point made by the Commonwealth. Writs cannot be issued under s.12 unless the Senate is dissolved and those under s.32 can only issue on the expiry or dissolution of the House of Representatives. Indeed each provision requires the writs to issue within ten days of those events respectively.[65] So we are back to the issue (according to the Commonwealth argument) whether the Senate, for example, was validly dissolved which in turn takes us back to s.57.

In referring to the Senate as being 'in fact dissolved', His Honour might seem to be following the views of Barwick CJ, who regards a Proclamation providing for dissolution as effective in dissolving the Houses whether or not it is authorised. But His Honour's suggestion that the Court could perhaps 'prevent an invalid Proclamation for the dissolution of the Senate from being given effect' seems inconsistent with the notion that the invalid Proclamation results 'in fact' in the dissolution of the Houses. If the Proclamation has been made, what more is required to give it effect?

It is submitted that the only satisfactory explanation of the attitudes of the judges in this matter is that logical consistency has given way to policy considerations, involving political and social consequences. In effect the provisions of s.57 are justiciable and mandatory for the purpose of testing the validity of legislation passed at a joint sitting but not for purposes of declaring invalid a dissolution or an election or legislation subsequently passed in the normal way by a Parliament so elected. The position of the Senate in our system as perceived by the majority justified the former view and the consequences to the system as a whole produced the latter view. It is suggested this is so despite the statement of Gibbs J that 'The plain words of s.57 cannot be denied their true effect for fear of what might possibly ensue if the Governor-General exceeded his constitutional powers'.[66]

There is a question whether a High Court ruling could be obtained, by for example the Attorney-General of the Commonwealth, as to the validity of a

---

[64](1975) 7 A.L.R. 1, at pp. 41-2. Emphasis added.

[65]It appears that these time limits are directory rather than mandatory: *Vardon* v. *O'Loghlin* (1907) 5 C.L.R. 201, at p.215, *Simpson* v. *Attorney-General* [1955] N.Z.L.R. 271; but that does not affect the argument.

[66](1975) 7 A.L.R. 1, at p.42.

dissolution before action is taken by the Governor-General. I mentioned earlier the difficulty of a Governor-General who is faced with advice to dissolve that he considers is not in accordance with the Constitution. The remark of Gibbs J, quoted above, indicates that he would probably regard the matter as justiciable. The emphasis given by the judges in *Cormack* v. *Cope*[67] to the fact that the issues there raised could more properly be dealt with at a later stage might indicate that they would be prepared to intervene, if it was not possible to invoke judicial review at a later date, so as to prevent an invalid executive act from taking effect. The matter, however, is very doubtful.

II
THE CONDUCT OF THE JOINT SITTING 1974

The Proclamation convening the joint sitting directed the members to deliberate and vote on six named Bills which provided the reason for the Governor-General earlier dissolving both Houses. As mentioned earlier, although most of the judges in *Cormack* v. *Cope*[68] considered that that was an error, only Barwick CJ regarded the Proclamation as invalid for that reason. Generally, the reasons given for treating the direction as at least unnecessary was that s.57 itself laid down what could be done at a joint sitting; the Governor-General's function was merely to convene it. The majority held the direction to vote on named Bills as merely unnecessary material or surplusage. For the Chief Justice it went to the heart of its validity because the expression 'shall vote upon each [proposed law]' in the Proclamation was, in his view, 'something in the nature of a direction. It is not something that is merely descriptive'.[69] Although he held that interlocutory relief should not be granted, he stated that at a hearing there was a likelihood of a finding of invalidity in relation to the Proclamation. The other judges, however, considered that as s.57 itself determined what might be done at a joint sitting the members at such a sitting could simply ignore the 'direction' in the Proclamation. It has been suggested that this decision could affect the conduct of a future joint sitting. The joint sitting in 1974 was the first in the history of the Commonwealth. The only provision in the Joint Standing Orders of the House of Representatives and the Senate was for the members present at a joint sitting to appoint a chairman by ballot provided that, until such appointment, the Clerk of the Senate should act as chairman. The two chambers agreed on special rules of procedure[70] and in matters not covered by the rules, the Senate's Standing Orders were to apply. Consistently with the requirement in s.57 for an absolute majority of the total number of members of the two Houses to affirm a motion, the rules provided that the chairman was to have one (deliberative) vote.

A number of enactments were passed to ensure that the protection and privileges available to members during normal sessions of Parliament extended to the joint sitting. These enactments were the *Evidence Act* 1974, the *Parliamentary Papers Act* 1974 and the *Parliamentary Proceedings Broadcasting*

---

[67](1974) 131 C.L.R. 432.

[68]*ibid.*

[69]*ibid.*, at p.459.

[70]House of Representatives, *Debates,* 1 August 1974, vol. 89, p.1005 ff.; Senate, *Debates,* 1 August 1974, vol. 60, p.697 ff.

Act 1974. Each House passed resolutions that at a joint sitting 'the proceedings are proceedings in Parliament and that the powers, privileges and immunities' of the members of the House or the Senate 'shall *mutatis mutandis* be those relating to a sitting of' the House of Representatives or the Senate as the case may be.[71] These resolutions were made under s.50 of the Constitution giving each House of the Parliament power to make rules and orders with respect to

(i) The mode in which its powers, privileges, and immunities may be exercised and upheld;

(ii) The order and conduct of its business and proceedings either separately or jointly with the other House.

There was doubt whether s.49, providing that the powers, privileges and immunities of the two Houses should be those of the House of Commons, would be applicable to the joint sitting as there were no provisions for such sittings in relation to the House of Commons.[72]

At the Joint Sitting the legal effect of the Governor-General's Proclamation was argued in relation to a ruling of the Chairman. Mr Wentworth M.H.R. moved that so much of the Standing Orders be suspended as would prevent him from moving a motion

> That this Joint Sitting of the Houses should not be finally adjourned until either it has adequately discussed the present economic and industrial situation in Australia or else the Government has indicated that both Houses will meet next week to discuss these matters.[73]

The Chairman, Mr Cope, ruled the motion out of order on the ground that 'Neither section 57 of the Constitution nor the Proclamation' authorised the consideration of any matters (other than the six proposed laws referred to in the Proclamation). Mr Wentworth moved that the ruling be disagreed with and the motion was lost. Mr McMahon M.H.R. then stated that the Chairman had acted on 'Proclamations which the Chief Justice said were improper'.[74] He was ruled out of order.

It is clear in the light of *Cormack* v. *Cope*[75] that a Proclamation in the future convening a joint sitting is unlikely to direct members as to the business they are to conduct. If it did, it would not be binding on the members and the chairman could not properly rely on it to rule that a motion such as Mr Wentworth's was out of order. Mr R. E. Bullock, Deputy Clerk of the Senate, has suggested that the views of the judges throw doubt on some of the procedures at a joint sitting.[76] Certainly, if the Proclamation does not specify the proposed laws to be considered, some procedure will need to be worked out to introduce the Bills to be dealt with. However, Mr Bullock goes on to say that, if the joint sitting were able 'to discuss, and presumably arrive at a decision carrying some weight on, matters other than proposed laws which fall within the scope of s.57, the writer, as a Senate officer, sees much cause for alarm'.[77]

---

[71]House of Representatives, *Debates*, 31 July 1974, vol. 89, p.908; Senate, *Debates,* 1 August 1974, vol. 60, p.685.

[72]House of Representatives, *Debates*, 31 July 1974, vol. 89, p.908 (Ellicott).

[73]Joint Sitting, Senate and House of Representatives, *Debates*, 6 August 1974, vol. H. of R.89, p.130.

[74]*ibid.*, p.132.

[75](1974) 131 C.L.R. 432.

[76]*The Table* (1975) vol. XLIII, p.22.

[77]*ibid.* It is incidentally striking that Mr Bullock should admit as a reason for his alarm the fact that he is a Senate officer. Professor Crisp has noted the general attachment Senate officers acquire towards

It seems clear from the opinions stated by the judges in *Cormack* v. *Cope*[78] and the *P.M.A. Case*[79] that the Court will not interfere with the intra-mural proceedings of the legislature. The only claim to judge the validity of such action arises where it constitutes a condition of law-making as in s.57. It seems, therefore, that if the Joint Sitting had agreed to discuss the matters raised by Mr Wentworth, no judicial order restraining such action could have been obtained.

It would, however, still be open for the chairman to hold (as did Mr Cope as an alternative ground) that s.57 confines the business of the joint sitting to dealing with the proposed Bills.[80] Mr Wentworth's argument was that the third paragraph of s.57 states what the members 'may' and 'shall' do together, but does not forbid them from discussing other matters. As the issue appears to be non-justiciable, and is certainly arguable, it will presumably in the future be dealt with either by Standing Orders or, in any particular case, by political considerations, that is according to whether the chairman's ruling is agreeable or not to the party or parties having a majority of members at the joint sitting.

III
THE DOUBLE DISSOLUTION OF 1975

The events leading to the double dissolution of 1975 are dealt with in the essay by Colin Howard and Cheryl Saunders. I am not concerned here with the legality or propriety of the Governor-General terminating the commission of Mr Whitlam. Assuming that the events of the time justified that action, then it was certainly proper to call an election for the House of Representatives, with or without a half-Senate election. But why a *double* dissolution?

The Governor-General's Proclamation of 11 November 1975 dissolving the Senate and the House of Representatives referred to twenty-one Bills which it was considered fulfilled the requirements of s.57 as conditions precedent to a double dissolution. That dissolution was performed formally on the advice of Mr Fraser as caretaker Prime Minister. It would appear appear, however, that it came about on the initiative of the Governor-General. In his public statement issued on the day of Mr Whitlam's dismissal, he said:

> The deadlock which arose was one which in the interests of the nation had to be resolved as promptly as possible and by means which are appropriate in our democratic system. In all the circumstances which have occurred the appropriate means is a dissolution of the Parliament and an election for both Houses. No other course offers a sufficient assurance of resolving the deadlock and resolving it promptly.

The deadlock to which His Excellency was referring was that over supply (which could, on any view, be his only ground for intervening in the way he did). Yet the Appropriation Bills, as he admitted, had not gone through all the stages prescribed by s.57 which would have taken many months to achieve. The solution which he considered to be the 'appropriate means' for resolving the deadlock over supply would therefore not have been available to him except for

---

the powers and status of their chamber: L. F. Crisp, *Australian National Government* (Melbourne, 1965) p.313.

[78](1974) 131 C.L.R. 432.

[79](1975) 7 A.L.R. 1.

[80]Views expressed by Stephen J in the *Territory Senators Case* (1975) 7 A.L.R. 159, at pp. 199-200, could confine the business of the sitting even further. See further below.

the fortuitous circumstance that there was a 'stockpile of Bills' which had fulfilled the requirements of the first part of s.57.

The argument as to the legality and propriety of the Governor-General dissolving both Houses relates to the fact that the dissolution was for a purpose other than that intended by s.57, and that it was granted on the formal advice of the person who had been Leader of the Opposition when the Bills failed to pass in the Senate and who had, therefore, opposed the Bills.

Legality

It can be argued (a) that the power granted by s.57 to dissolve both Houses is a statutory power which can be exercised only for a proper purpose; (b) that the only proper purpose is the resolution of a deadlock in respect of Bills that have satisfied the earlier requirements of s.57; (c) that the purpose of the 1975 double dissolution was quite different; and (d) that therefore the dissolution was illegal, even though as no joint sitting had followed, the question cannot be judicially determined.[81]

There may be some support for this argument in the reasoning of Stephen J in the *Territory Senators Case*[82]. One issue there was whether the convening of the Joint Sitting in 1974 was invalid because the Proclamation directed members to deliberate and vote on six Bills including the Petroleum and Minerals Authority Bill, which latter Bill the Court had held had not satisfied the requirements of s.57. The Court unanimously held that the reference in the Proclamation to the Petroleum and Minerals Authority Bill did not affect the validity of the Proclamation. Stephen J, however, said:

> The authority of His Excellency to perform each of these two acts is, by the terms of s.57, made to depend upon there having occurred the prior events to which the section refers; their occurrence is a condition precedent to his power. It follows not only that this condition precedent must have been satisfied but also that, in the case of each of the two acts, the act must be related to and be consequent upon the events which themselves constitute the satisfaction of the condition precedent.[83]

He went on to say that the power in s.57 to dissolve the Parliament and to convene a joint sitting was conferred only for the purpose of resolving the legislative deadlocks which by s.57 were conditions precedent to the exercise of that power:

> That power may only be employed, like other statutory powers, for the purpose for which it was conferred and where, as in the instances which I have given, it appears that it has been employed for quite other purposes its exercise will be unauthorised by section 57.[84]

Indeed, he went further and said that the Governor-General's recited purpose (if valid) was determinative of what the joint sitting could consider; so that if, for example, the Governor-General's Proclamation had recited only one of the five Bills that had satisfied the requirements of s.57, the joint sitting could not

[81]Leslie Katz's letter to the *National Times* 22-27 December 1975, p.2. In his article 'The Simultaneous Dissolution of Both Houses of the Australian Federal Parliament 1975' (1976) LIV *Canadian Bar Rev.* 392, Mr Katz has argued that the double dissolution of 1975 was invalid, but that as no challenge was made to the dissolution before the elections, the new Parliament must be considered to be validly constituted. My views, however, remain those stated in the text.

[82](1975) 7 A.L.R. 159, at pp. 199-201.

[83]*ibid.*, at p.199.

[84]*ibid.*, at p.200.

consider the others. The 'purpose' of the Governor-General was therefore relevant in two respects: if it was not a proper purpose the dissolution or the joint sitting was not authorised even though the conditions precedent in s.57 had been satisfied in respect of one or more Bills and, secondly, if the purpose of convening the joint sitting was limited to a particular measure, the joint sitting could not consider others, even though they had fulfilled the requirements of s.57. We are only concerned with the first proposition.

I do not think that the argument that the double dissolution of 1975 was not authorised by s.57 is a valid one for a number of reasons. First, the views expressed by Stephen J seem inconsistent with those of the other judges (at least in respect of a joint sitting) in the *Territory Senators Case*[85] and of all the judges in *Cormack* v. *Cope*.[86] The prevailing view is that the Governor-General cannot direct the members at a joint sitting as to what business they shall conduct and that s.57 itself determines what the joint sitting's business is or can be. Similarly, in relation to dissolution, Barwick CJ said:

> Whilst it is true that there must have been in fact the required rejection of a proposed law by the Senate before the Governor-General may lawfully dissolve both Houses, he does not dissolve the Houses in relation to or in respect of any particular law. He merely dissolves the Houses.[87]

Secondly, there is considerable authority to the effect that the principles which govern the exercise of 'discretionary powers confided to subordinate administrative officers or bodies' are not applicable to those of the Governor-General.[88]

Thirdly, it is doubtful if even Stephen J would, in determining whether a double dissolution was authorised, have regard to considerations or reasons other than those asserted in the Proclamation itself, because 'it is not open to impute *mala fides* with respect to an act of the King by himself or his representative'.[89] Stephen J, in giving examples of the application of the principles he expounded, referred to recitals in the Proclamation as indicating the purpose of the Governor-General.

Fourthly, if it is true that the Governor-General has or ever had a discretion in deciding whether or not to act on the advice of his Prime Minister to grant a dissolution, it must be because it is considered that grounds in addition to those relating to the particular Bill or Bills that provide the occasion for the double dissolution are required. The advice to the Governors-General in relation to the 1914, 1951 and 1974 double dissolutions were replete with references to the 'parliamentary situation' which went beyond the particular Bill or Bills that had fulfilled the requirements of s.57. Sir Samuel Griffith, in his advice to the Governor-General in 1914, mentioned as one of the reasons for the Governor-General acting on the advice of his ministers 'that there exists such a state of practical deadlock in legislation as can only be ended in that way'.

---

[85] (1975) 7 A.L.R. 159, at pp. 170 (Barwick CJ), 183 (Gibbs J), 222 (Murphy J).

[86] (1974) 131 C.L.R. 432.

[87] *Cormack* v. *Cope* (1974) 131 C.L.R. 432, at p.450.

[88] *Australian Communist Party* v. *Commonwealth (Communist Party Case)* (1951) 83 C.L.R. 1, pp. 178-80, 221-2, 257-8; P.W. Hogg, 'Judicial Review of Action by The Crown Representative' (1969) 43 *Australian L.J.* 215; D.G. Benjafield and H. Whitmore, *Principles of Australian Administrative Law* (4th ed., Sydney, 1971), pp. 130, 165; G. Lindell, 'Justiciability of Political Questions' (Unpublished thesis, University of Adelaide, 1972).

[89] *Communist Party Case* (1951) 83 C.L.R. 1, at pp. 257-8.

Propriety

While I have no doubt that the double dissolution was one that was authorised by s.57, the question remains whether the exercise of the power was proper in the circumstances. Section 57 was, of course, aimed at enabling the government, that is those who had the confidence of the House of Representatives, to go to the people where there was obstruction by the Senate. The section, for example, does not apply in respect of Bills initiated in the Senate. Neither the Governor-General nor Mr Fraser sought a double dissolution to resolve the deadlock between the Houses in relation to the specified twenty-one Bills. The Governor-General's only concern was with supply and Mr Fraser and his Party had in fact desired and obtained the defeat of the twenty-one Bills in the Senate. Also, the relevant Senate resolution relating to the Appropriation Bills merely resolved not to proceed with them 'until the Government agrees to submit itself to the judgment of the people'.

Having regard to the history that led to the formulation of s.57, it certainly appears paradoxical and even ironical that the dissolution was brought about against the wishes of the House of Representatives and on the formal advice of the leader of a party that was concerned to obstruct it. In the Governor-General's statements issued on 11 November 1975 it is clear that when he referred to 'a resolution of the deadlock', he was having regard only to the Senate's deferral of the Appropriation Bills that had come before it. In those circumstances it was not correct to say that only a double dissolution offered 'sufficient assurance of resolving the deadlock and resolving it promptly'. In fact a House of Representatives election with or without a half-Senate election would have satisfied the Senate's condition and resulted in the enactment of the Appropriation Bills. It seems, therefore, that he must have had regard also to the longer-term situation. While on 11 November 1975 it could not have been predicted with certainty that a double dissolution would resolve the 'parliamentary situation' that had developed, it is no doubt true that there was a greater probability of it doing so than any other form of dissolution or election. But the Governor-General's statement and his 'Detailed Statement of Decisions' are most unsatisfactory in this regard. Throughout both statements he concentrated on the particular deadlock over supply. The Governor-General, therefore, did not anywhere adequately explain the reason for his view that only a double dissolution could promptly resolve the situation.

Nevertheless, I consider, again assuming the dismissal of Mr Whitlam and the commissioning of Mr Fraser to have been justified, that the dissolving of both Houses was the appropriate action. The Senate had caused the deadlock and, if the House of Representatives was to go to the people, so should it. If only the House of Representatives had been dissolved and Labor had been returned to power, the chain of events under s.57 in respect of the twenty-one Bills might have been broken and Labor would have lost the chance of having them passed at a joint sitting. I think that the request by the Governor-General to Mr Fraser to give an undertaking that he was prepared to recommend a double dissolution was in the same spirit as his request that his Government would make no appointments or dismissals until the election was held. It recognised that the Fraser Government would take over office in unusual circumstances and that it should not, therefore, have the powers and privileges of a government that was in office because it held the confidence of the lower House. (I am not concerned here with the question whether the Governor-General has authority to impose the conditions that he did.)

It seems to me that fairness dictated that a double dissolution take place if that course were available.

From an educative point of view it might perhaps be regarded as unfortunate that any of the twenty-one Bills was available to provide the occasion for a double dissolution. If they had not been, the defects of our Constitution and the consequences to the system of the Senate deferring supply would have been even more obvious. The Senate would have forced the Government to the polls without threat to itself. However, that issue is the subject of another essay.

COMMENTARIES

G. S. Reid

Taken as a whole and despite its title Professor Zines's paper is concerned with a single subject—s.57 of the Constitution. I intend to focus attention primarily on the question of justiciability because most issues raised in his essay are subordinate to it. I will then turn to a matter central to any account of the 1974 and 1975 double dissolutions, that is, the question of 'constitutional conventions'.

Justiciability

The justiciability question in respect of s.57 arises in the High Court's majority judgments in *Cormack* v. *Cope*[1] and the *P.M.A. Case*.[2] In essence, the justiciability decisions therein led the Court to declare the *Petroleum and Minerals Authority Act* 1973 to be invalid, on the ground that its passage through Parliament did not comply with the procedural provisions of s.57. The judgments have profound implications for parliaments in Australia, both Commonwealth and State, and for the practice of politics in Australia. I am not in agreement with the majority decisions in these two cases, and I accordingly find Professor Zines's essay questionable in this respect.

Symbolically, the Petroleum and Minerals Authority Act represented the centre-piece of the Whitlam Government's statutory programme. The Court's decision, therefore, had high political significance. But, like McTiernan J, I believe that the law-making prescriptions of s.57 were outside the ordinary scope of inquiry by the Court.

The contrary viewpoint was put rhetorically by Barwick CJ in *Cormack* v. *Cope*.[3] He described a submission made by the Attorney-General:

> ... this Court could not inquire into the regularity of what the Governor-General had done or, indeed, into the regularity of any steps in the law-making process required by s.57... The Courts in the United Kingdom have traditionally refrained from any interference in the law-making activities of Parliament.

and in rebuttal offered the following:

> ... the submission, in my opinion, was basically misconceived. We are not here dealing with a Parliament whose laws and activities have the paramountcy of the Houses of Parliament in the United Kingdom. The law-making process in the Parliament in Australia is controlled by a written Constitution. This is particularly true of the special law-making process for which s.57 makes provision.

At a stroke, therefore, the Chief Justice dismissed the influence of the *Bill of Rights* of 1689, which every school-historian for centuries has had to learn by heart:

> That the Freedom of Speech, and Debates or Proceedings in Parliament ought not to be impeached or questioned in any Court or Place out of Parliament.

---

[1](1974) 131 C.L.R. 432.

[2]*Victoria* v. *Commonwealth* (1975) 7 A.L.R. 1.

[3](1974) 131 C.L.R. 432, at pp. 451-2.

And he thereby dismissed a whole string of prestigious commentaries on the laws of England (including Blackstone's)[4] together with the precedents of *Stockdale* v. *Hansard*[5] and *Bradlaugh* v. *Gossett*,[6] the spirit of which was captured in the judgment of Lord Coleridge CJ in the latter: 'What is said or done within the walls of Parliament cannot be enquired into in a court of law'.[7] Instead, the Chief Justice accepted a new precedent—the Privy Council judgment in *Bribery Commissioner* v. *Ranasinghe*[8] to the effect that 'where the law-making process of a legislature is laid down by its constating instrument, the courts have a right and duty to ensure that the law-making process is observed'.[9] On that reasoning, Barwick CJ concluded:

> Whilst it may be true the Court will not interfere in what I would call the intra-mural deliberative activities of the Parliament, it has both a right and a duty to interfere if the constitutionally required process of law-making is not properly carried out.[10]

The majority of the Court joined the Chief Justice, thereby also setting aside the frequently quoted judgment of Griffith CJ in *Osborne* v. *Commonwealth*[11] that in the case of ss.53 and 54 the expression 'proposed laws' relates to

> Bills or projects of laws still under consideration and not assented to ... Whatever obligations are imposed by these sections are directed to the Houses of Parliament whose conduct of their internal affairs is not subject to review by a Court of Law.

This was 'not acceptable as a statement of universal application'.[12] The majority set aside a succession of learned opinions published in the records of the Australian Government from Solicitors-General of the Commonwealth and their counsel. Although not necessarily acceptable to the Court, authorities such as Garran, Knowles, Bailey and Castieau had put their names to official opinions which claimed categorically:

> No court could prevent or restrain a breach [i.e. of s.54]. The whole matter is left for political action. If the Senate does not uphold its privileges there is no other remedy[13]

---

[4]Sir William Blackstone, *Commentaries on the Laws of England*, vol. 1 (18th ed., London 1929), pp. 163-4:

> The *privileges* of parliament are likewise very large and indefinite. And therefore when in 31 Hen. IV the House of Lords propounded a question to the judges concerning them, the chief justice, Sir John Fortescue, in the name of his brethren, declared: 'that they ought not to make answer to that question; for it hath not been used aforetime that the justices should in any wise determine the privileges of the high court of Parliament. For it is so high and mighty in its nature, that it may make law: and that which is law, it may make no law: and the determination and knowledge of that privilege belongs to the lords of parliament, and not to the justices'.

See also *Erskine May's Parliamentary Practice*, ed. Sir Barnett Cocks (18th ed., London, 1971), pp. 82-3.

[5](1839) 112 E.R. 1112. Extracted in W.C. Costin and J.S. Watson (eds.), *The Law and Working of the Constitution*, vol. II (London, 1952), pp. 264-273.

[6](1884) 12 Q.B.D. 271. Extracted in Costin and Watson, cited above n.5, pp. 298-307.

[7](1884) 12 Q.B.D. 271, at p.275.

[8][1965] A.C. 172.

[9]*Cormack* v. *Cope* (1974) 131 C.L.R. 432, at p.452.

[10]*ibid.*, at p.453.

[11](1911) 12 C.L.R. 321, at p.336.

[12](1974) 131 C.L.R. 432, at p.454.

[13]Opinion of Messrs Garran, Knowles, Bailey and Castieau, tabled in House of Representatives 16 March 1943: quoted in *Report from the Committee Appointed by Government Senators on Appropriation Bills and the Ordinary Annual Services of the Government*, 28 October 1964 (Parliamentary Paper No.55 of 1967), p.15.

and

> ... it seems to be clearly enough established that constitutional provisions expressed to apply only to proposed laws, as contrasted with laws which have been passed by Parliament, are to be regarded as addressed exclusively to the Houses of the Parliament in the conduct of their own internal affairs, and are not justiciable in the courts.[14]

But the Court decided otherwise. The law-making parts of s.57 are justiciable. And Professor Zines approves. His essay explains the argument for justiciability in terms of protecting the 'rule of law' against some demonic erosion by 'democratic processes'. Zines opts for the rule of law. Unless the High Court intervenes and interprets s.57, he finds that a government (albeit elected) could become 'judge of its own cause'. That, he claims, would be 'wrong for obvious reasons' (apparently it would endanger the rule of law). And another fate would be that the Governor-General could be called upon to determine 'the lawfulness of the government's behaviour' and that too would offend the rule of law, notwithstanding that s.61 of the Constitution clearly places the 'maintenance' of the Constitution in the Governor-General's, and not the High Court's, hands.

Professor Zines's thesis is infused with a suspicion, if not an intolerance, of the political processes for which the Constitution provides (and he is not alone in this). He is apparently not prepared to permit the parliamentary conflict to be pursued to its full parliamentary extent with the reassurance that if a wrong is done it will be adjudged, in due course, by an electorate. In this, he rejects the attainments and presumptions of England's Glorious Revolution, and all those who have upheld those attainments and presumptions over three centuries. He approves of the High Court becoming our new guardian of the rule of law, of the Constitution and of some of the processes of law-making. He approves of that institution of our government which adjudicates in disputes about the law, having a hand in the processes for the making of the law. I find his thesis more a threat to the rule of law than a safeguard. It threatens the status and authority of the Houses of the Parliament and their officials. For although Dicey contended that 'Englishmen are ruled by the law, and by the law alone',[15] he did not contend that the judiciary should determine how that law is to be made.

Professor Zines, and for that matter the High Court, does not appear to have considered the consequential implications of admitting those parliamentary procedural parts of s.57 as justiciable, or of Barwick CJ's claim that

> ... there is no Parliamentary privilege which can stand in the way of this Court's right and duty to ensure that the constitutionally provided methods of law-making are observed

and that

> ... the Court in point of jurisdiction is not limited to that method [s.57] of ensuring the observance of the Constitutional processes of law-making.[16]

Clearly, the question of justiciability does not end at s.57. Several sections of the Constitution refer to 'proposed laws' and to the related methods of

---

[14]Professor Bailey. See Joint Committee of Public Accounts, *Fifty-Fourth Report* (Parliamentary Paper No.70 of 1961), App.A: Opinion of Solicitor-General Dated 6 March 1961, p.20.

[15]A.V. Dicey, *Law of the Constitution* (10th ed., London, 1959), p.202.

[16]*Cormack* v. *Cope* (1974) 131 C.L.R. 432, at p.454.

law-making. If the Court should accept that those provisions are also justiciable, then the Court has established for itself a new province for adjudication. Apparently every 'constitutionally provided' method of law-making is now liable to the Court's intervention or, as Barwick CJ claims, 'the Court is able, and indeed in a proper case bound, to interfere'.

It is to be hoped that the profound difficulties experienced by the Court in interpreting the elusive 'fails to pass' in s.57, and its futile reasoning about 'legislative model(s)', 'spirit of parliamentary government', 'the maturity of parliament', 'heart of our constitutional democracy', 'proper reading' and 'reasonable time', will persuade the Court that its decision on justiciability has taken it across the threshold of, and into, a veritable political jungle—into a sphere which offers no hospitality for a prestigious judicial institution.

It is interesting, therefore, to contemplate where the justiciability decision will end. Will the Court interfere in the controversial matters relating to the law-making process in accordance with ss.53 and 54 (vital to the role of the Senate in financial affairs); for example, will it rule on what is embraced in those sections by the expression 'ordinary annual services of the government', or on the political struggles relating to 'requests' by the Senate, or the pressing of requests? Will the Court interfere in the established practice of the House of Representatives of interpreting 'shall not be passed' in s.56 to mean 'shall not be introduced', and thereby advantage Opposition members in the law-making process? Will the Court adjudicate on the meaning of the words 'passed by both Houses' in s.58, and if so, how will it keep itself out of the intra-mural processes? And how will the Court maintain the requirement of s.53 that 'Except as provided in this section, the Senate shall have equal power with the House of Representatives in respect of all proposed laws'?

Perhaps we can take heart in Professor Zines's comment that the majority of the bench on justiciability was 'reduced from 5 : 1 to 4 : 3'; and that 'it may be therefore that the question is not settled for all time'. But, be that as it may, the Court's decision enabled the symbolic centre-piece of the Whitlam Government's legislative programme to be declared invalid on a technicality. Professor Zines's essay does not make that clear.

Conventions of the Constitution

I had formed the impression, after following the extensive public prose of some constitutional oracles since October-November 1975 that they had finally and painfully found that 'conventions of the Constitution' were a chimera (a creation of the imagination, or a foolish fancy), and were bound to lead them into trouble in understanding the affairs of real government. But lo-and-behold, they are back with us in Professor Zines's essay.

The double dissolutions of 1914 and 1951, claims Professor Zines, do not 'provide much guidance as to the conventions on the matter'. And he suggests that the discretionary powers of the Governor-General are 'of course, in the area of convention rather than law'. In addition, he asserts 'the conventions of responsible government are recognisable by the courts and they can be relevant in some aspects of interpreting the Constitution'. In his opinion 'A statement by the Court that a convention exists would tend to be regarded as conclusive and would have a powerful effect on its preservation'. Granted, he implies criticism of Barwick CJ's quest for 'the formation and observance of a parliamentary convention designed to implement the spirit of parliamentary government as under the constitution',[17] and His Honour's comment that 'the emergence of such conventions . . . must depend on the passage of time and the maturity of the Parliament'.[18] But Zines's criticism was not about the notion of 'convention'.

My own interpretation of 'conventions of the Constitution', which was confirmed so conclusively in November 1975, is that the expression is little more than an article of political rhetoric and that our academic constitutional lawyers were publicly using it as such.

It is well known that Australia's written Constitution is silent on many important aspects of government. It says nothing about the Prime Minister, the Cabinet, responsible government, ministerial responsibility, electing a government, dismissing a government, parliamentary control, what is to be done if the Senate refuses to pass an appropriation Bill (or a supply Bill), and so on. In reality this void is filled-in by well established practice, methods, habits, maxims, usages, many of them of long-standing, which were inherited from colonial Parliaments, which in turn inherited them from Westminster. It is these practices, methods and usages which tend to be referred to, albeit vaguely, as 'conventions of the Constitution'. For example, it is often alleged:

(a) that the leader of that political group which has a majority in the House of Representatives must (or should) be called by the Governor-General to form a government (that is, to nominate those who will take over the ministerial offices of state);

(b) that the Prime Minister must (or should) be a member of the House of Representatives;

(c) that the government will (or should) resign if it does not possess the confidence of the House of Representatives;

(d) that major decisions of government will (or should) be taken by the Cabinet;

(e) that when there is a casual vacancy in the Senate it will (or should) be filled by a senator with the same party political allegiance as his predecessor;

(f) that the Governor-General will (or should) act on the advice of his ministers of state; and so on.

In one sense these are descriptions of what has happened in the past. But some people go beyond mere description of method and ascribe some prescriptive (or normative) quality to the practices of the past as obligatory rules for the future. Take, for example, the notorious letter of the big four (Professors Zines, Howard, Sawer and Castles) published in the nation's press on 11 October 1975.

> The unwritten rule in question . . . is the convention that control of the supply of money to the Government . . . should rest with the Lower House . . . where Governments are made.

We've come a long way since then, but we've heard many more assertions of the same general character. For example:

(a) Mr Whitlam breached constitutional convention in not resigning his commission (or not requesting an election) when faced with the Senate's refusal to pass the Appropriation Bills;

---

[17] *Cormack* v. *Cope* (1974) 131 C.L.R. 432, at p.456.

[18] *Western Australia* v. *Commonwealth (Territory Senators Case)* (1975) 7 A.L.R. 159, at p.165.

(b) the Governor-General breached constitutional convention in dismissing Mr Whitlam when he had a majority in the House of Representatives;

(c) the Governor-General breached constitutional convention in calling Mr Fraser (the minority leader) to form a caretaker government when he was in a minority in the House of Representatives;

(d) the Senate breached constitutional convention in refusing to pass the Appropriation Bills; and so on.

I submit that charges and counter-charges about conventions (in the context of November 1975 at least) are simply political rhetoric. But can we now go along with Professor Zines's confidence that they will be more meaningful in the future? I think not.

We will not get far in helping to fathom, or to understand, our system of government if we inanely chant 'convention' at every threatened or proposed change of course. Nor can we be confident that the High Court could fill in what the Constitution does not say by declaring convention, any better than the way the void has been filled in in the past. The use of 'convention' in the way of Professor Zines (and of his colleagues) and also Barwick CJ is part and parcel of the 'guardian' principle which also dominated Zines's, and the Court's, reasoning about justiciability. If the Court declares convention, then it would seem to be making justiciable what is *not* in the Constitution. However, if the Court says an established practice is a convention, then presumably (according to Zines) it will be a convention. So be it!

Every alleged convention in Australian government (that is, every established practice or method) is explicable in terms other than convention; that is, if we take the trouble to reason 'why'. My point is that academic analysts should be trying to explain why things are done, or should be done, in government, in a particular way, rather than categorically projecting the past into the future in the name of convention. It is profitable to reflect on the words of Professor H.J. Laski (as quoted by Dr Evatt):

> Theories of constitutional form [e.g. conventions] will be adjusted overnight to suit the interests of Conservatism.[19]

If we argue that this 'great penumbral area of the Constitution' should be codified in the name of conventions, then we shall invite into our constitutional disputes more of what has happened in our recent past.

I contend that we would all be better off if, in lieu of parroting convention, we reasoned why the Governor-General should (or should not) accept the advice of his ministers; why the Governor-General should (or should not) seek advice from the Chief Justice; why the Senate should (or should not) defer or reject Supply, and so on. The notion 'convention of the Constitution' forecloses reasoning and bedevils our understanding of the processes of democratic government.

---

[19]H.J. Laski, *Crisis and the Constitution*, pp. 13-14, quoted in H.V. Evatt, *The King and His Dominion Governors* (2nd ed., Melbourne, 1967), p.11.

Peter Bayne

These comments will attempt, first, to draw out of the constitution-making process in Papua New Guinea, of which I have had some experience, some lessons which may be of value in the Australian context, and, secondly, to discuss the validity of the double dissolution of 11 November 1975.

The Constitution of the Independent State of Papua New Guinea creates a unicameral, unitary system which incorporates the principle of responsible government. Although at one time a type of federal system was considered, it was never contemplated that it would be bicameral. There was, therefore, no consideration given to the problem of how to reconcile the principle of responsible government with the principle of a strong second chamber. Modern constitution makers in the British Commonwealth have been acutely aware of this problem, and have generally resolved it in favour of responsible government. For example, in the now superseded Constitution of the Federal Republic of Nigeria and the current federal Constitution of Malaysia, the upper House may delay a money Bill for no more than one month. The situation in Canada is also instructive, for although the Canadian Senate does have the power to refuse supply, the possibility that it might be exercised does not appear to have ever been seriously contemplated.[1] On this general issue, it is also worth noting the comment of the author of a modern study of federalism:

> Conceivably, a Cabinet system could be responsible to both Houses jointly, but this would raise serious practical problems when the two Houses did not agree. In such cases, dissolution would not be an effective way to solve the difficulty unless both Houses were elected by popular vote. Even then, such a system would be too complicated to be feasible without a few strong parties and strict party discipline.[2]

The question of the possible role of a Head of State in Papua New Guinea was, however, considered at great length. The Constitutional Planning Committee recommended against a Head of State, and devised a system in which the functions usually performed by such a person were distributed between the Prime Minister, the Speaker, and the Chief Justice. These proposals were not adopted for reasons largely extrinsic to their merits, and the Constitution created the office of a Governor-General possessing closely circumscribed powers. Both the report of the Committee and the Constitution deserve study by those interested in reform of the office of Governor-General under the Australian Constitution.[3]

The Papua New Guinea experience is relevant in another respect. The report of the Constitutional Planning Committee, and the whole tenor of the debates in the National Constituent Assembly, reflect a desire on the part of those who enacted the Constitution to construct a system of government based on the cognate notions of the 'rule of law' and 'constitutionalism'. The notion of constitutionalism is perhaps more appropriate to a system such as ours where there is a written constitution, and it is also the one more widely used

---

[1]P. Bayne, 'Upper Houses Outside Australia', [1975] *Australian Current Law Digest* 301, at pp. 303, 304.

[2]R.R. Bowie, 'The Federal Legislature' in *Studies in Federalism*, ed. R.R. Bowie and C.J. Friedrich (Boston, 1954), at p.28. See too K.C. Wheare, *Legislatures* (2nd ed., London, 1968), at p.135.

[3]*Final Report of the Constitutional Planning Committee* (1974) Part 1, Ch. 7; *Proposals on Constitutional Principles and Explanatory Notes* (1974); *United Party Proposals on the Constitution* (1974); *Debates of the National Constituent Assembly* (Transcript); *The Constitution of the Independent State of Papua New Guinea*, ss.82-98, 138-140.

throughout the world. Its basic thrust was well expressed by the late Professor de Smith:

> Constitutionalism in its formal sense means the principle that the exercise of political power shall be bounded by rules, rules which determine the validity of legislative and executive action by prescribing the procedure according to which it must be performed or by delimiting its permissible content . . . Constitutionalism becomes a living reality to the extent that these rules curb the arbitrariness of discretion and are in fact observed by the wielders of political power, and to the extent that within the forbidden zones upon which authority may not trespass there is significant room for the enjoyment of individual liberty.[4]

Professor de Smith went on to be more specific about the substantive content of the notion, and referred to the need for free elections, the ability to freely campaign for those elections, and an independent judiciary, but his first substantive requirement of constitutionalism was a 'government . . . genuinely accountable to an entity or organ distinct from itself'.[5] This notion of constitutionalism is particularly relevant to Professor Zines's discussion of the validity of the double dissolution of 11 November 1975.

A discussion of the legality of the double dissolution raises two questions: first, whether a court would review the exercise of the power by the Governor-General to dissolve two Houses; and, secondly, whether a court would review the legality of the dissolution. These two questions are intertwined, but, as the High Court appears to treat them separately (and indeed appears to give inconsistent answers to them), they are treated separately for the purposes of this analysis.

The scope of judicial review of the power of the Governor-General to dissolve both Houses must be considered on the basis that the only source of such power is s.57 of the Constitution. In his statement of reasons issued on 11 November 1975, the Governor-General seems to suggest that he was exercising a reserve power to dissolve, but such a suggestion is not tenable. Judicial and academic authority seem agreed on the proposition that the power to dissolve both Houses is a statutory power found only in s.57.[6] Professor Zines considers whether judicial review of an exercise of this power might include an inquiry as to whether the power to dissolve was in fact used for the resolution of the deadlock which must exist as a condition precedent to the exercise of power. It is of course a general principle of our system of public law that powers must be exercised for the purposes for which they are granted, and that any exercise of a power for another purpose renders the action invalid. There are passages in the judgment of Stephen J in the *Territory Senators Case* which support the applicability of this principle to an exercise of power under s.57. In relation to the events of 11 November 1975, the statement by the Governor-General that he was dissolving the Houses to resolve the deadlock over supply (rather than to resolve the deadlock over the twenty-one Bills mentioned in the Proclamation), appears to provide a basis for the application of the principle, (notwithstanding that there was in fact no deadlock over supply at the time the

---

[4]S.A. de Smith, 'Constitutionalism in the Commonwealth Today', (1962) 4 *Malaya L.R.* 205, at p. 205.

[5]*ibid.*

[6]See generally J. Goldring, 'The Royal Prerogative, and Dissolution of the Commonwealth Parliament' (1975) 49 *Australian L.J.* 521. Barwick CJ has been emphatic on this point: *Cormack* v. *Cope* (1974) 131 C.L.R. 432, at p. 450; *Victoria* v. *Commonwealth (P.M.A. Case)* (1975) 7 A.L.R. 1, at p.11; *Western Australia* v. *Commonwealth (Territory Senators Case)* (1975) 7 A.L.R. 159, at p. 165.

Proclamation was made). However Professor Zines concludes that the principle does not apply. It is submitted that this conclusion is not correct.

In a passage not quoted by Professor Zines, Stephen J dealt separately with the question of the validity of a double-dissolution. The relevant passage is as follows:

> Thus, to take by way of illustration one of these acts, that of dissolution, it must have been preceded by a twice repeated rejection (or its equivalent) by the Senate; this is the requisite condition precedent to the exercise of the power. The power may also only be exercised in reliance upon the fact of that twice repeated rejection and not in purported reliance upon some quite different event. If it should appear, perhaps from some recital in the dissolution proclamation, that His Excellency has purported to dissolve both chambers for some other reason, not itself involving satisfaction of the necessary condition precedent called for by s.57, the fact that there did also exist circumstances which would have provided a proper ground for dissolution will not make the dissolution one authorised by s.57.[7]

The probable incorrectness of some of Stephen J's remarks concerning the conduct of the Joint Sitting do not affect this statement, and the application of the general principle may be considered irrespective of whatever limits Stephen J may have placed upon it. It is submitted, too, that the remarks of Barwick CJ are not to be read as precluding the application of this principle of review, and, if they are to be so read, it is difficult to reconcile them with other remarks of the Chief Justice in this series of cases.[8] On the other hand, statements by McTiernan, Mason and Murphy JJ do appear to negate the possibility of review of the Governor-General's power under s.57.[9] However, these views are based on an assumption that the Governor-General would necessarily act on the advice of the Executive Council, and they are distinguishable on this ground.[10]

The reasoning of the High Court in *Australian Communist Party* v. *Commonwealth*[11] is also distinguishable. Three of the four judges in that case who addressed themselves to the scope of judicial review of the powers vested in the Governor-General by the Act in question, placed primary emphasis on the wording of that Act, and, in particular, pointed to the subjective element in the discretion conferred on the Governor-General.[12] The position under s.57 is different: '[I]t presupposes the occurrence of specified events as facts; it makes no reference to the opinion of the Governor-General, a traditional formula which could and should have been invoked had it been intended to place his decision beyond the reach of the court in a suit for a declaration of invalidity'.[13] The judgment of Dixon CJ in the *Communist Party Case* does provide support for a proposition that the powers of the Governor-General are not reviewable according to ordinary principle,[14] but the opinion does not go

---

[7] *Territory Senators Case* (1975) 7 A.L.R. 159, at p.199.

[8] *P.M.A. Case* (1975) 7 A.L.R. 1, at p.11; *Territory Senators Case* (1975) 7 A.L.R. 159, at p.165.

[9] *Territory Senators Case* (1975) 7 A.L.R. 159, at pp. 203 per Mason J (with whom McTiernan J agreed), 226 per Murphy J.

[10] L. Katz, 'The Simultaneous Dissolution of Both Houses of the Australian Federal Parliament', (1976) LIV *Canadian Bar Rev.* 392, at p.399 states that it could be argued that Mason J 'was therefore influenced by the consideration that in that situation it would be impossible as a practical matter to discover any ulterior purpose for which the dissolution could have taken place'.

[11] (1951) 83 C.L.R. 1.

[12] *ibid.*, at pp. 221-2 (Williams J), 257-8 (Fullagar J) 279-81 (Kitto J).

[13] *P.M.A. Case* (1975) 7 A.L.R. 1, at p.63 (Mason J).

[14] (1951) 83 C.L.R. 1, at p.180. There is some support for this view in other Australian cases, but in *Treasury Gate Pty Ltd* v. *Rice* [1972] V.R. 148, 163, Newton J appears to have approved the view of P. W. Hogg, 'Judicial Review of Action by the Crown Representative', (1969) 43 *Australian L.J.* 215, at

so far as to deny that Parliament may, by appropriate wording, make an action of the Governor-General reviewable. The question of review must remain ultimately one of statutory interpretation, and the language of s.57 indicates clearly enough that it did mean to put limits to the actions of the Governor-General. An argument in support of review does not need to go so far as to deny the principle that 'it is not open to impute mala fides with respect to an act of the King by himself or his representative',[15] for the principle that a power may not be exercised in bad faith is different to the principle that it may not be exercised for an improper purpose.

It is submitted, therefore, that the purpose of a double dissolution under s.57 *is* examinable by a court. If the Governor-General may take into account considerations other than whether the conditions precedent set out in s.57 have been met, the scope of review should extend to a review of these other considerations.

In accordance, therefore, with principles of our public law inherent in the notion of constitutionalism, the executive act of the Governor-General in dissolving both Houses of Parliament on 11 November 1975 was invalid and the dissolution should have been open to challenge. With the possible exception of Gibbs J, the reasons offered by the High Court Justices which suggest that such a challenge would not be possible are not convincing. However, the practical difficulties of these conclusions are obvious, and a realist might argue that in the highly charged political atmosphere which resulted from the failure of the Senate to pass supply, it would have been too much for our system to have borne the reversal of the dissolution. The situation would have been much worse if the Senate had not in fact passed supply prior to the dissolution. The argument might then proceed that in these circumstances the principle of constitutionalism must be sacrificed for the sake of the system. The force of this reasoning is obvious, and may well underlie the attitude of the High Court. There are, however, two further comments to be made.

First, the view that a dissolution is not reviewable has implications for the interpretation of s.53. In the case of an ordinary double dissolution, this view would not work great harm. In the 1914, 1951, and 1974 dissolutions the decisions were in effect made by the government of the day. In such a case, one might say that the government was estopped from denying the validity of the dissolution. Further, there is only a slim chance that a government would attempt a dissolution where there was any doubt as to its validity. However, this consideration is not at all relevant where the dissolution is forced upon a government by a hostile Senate, and it is in this situation that the injustice of precluding review is most apparent. This brings us to the question whether our system should permit this possibility. If s.53 were to be interpreted so as to preclude the Senate from blocking supply, the possibility would not arise.

Secondly, there is in all this a lesson for those of us who teach, write and read constitutional law: it is that constitutionalism has a limited usefulness as a tool for analysis. Those who accept it as an ideal will continue to evaluate behaviour according to the principle it expresses, but cannot continue to analyse actual

---

p.222, that 'the objection to the doctrine [that action by the Crown representative is unreviewable] as being contrary to the rule of law is so fundamental that it cannot be dismissed simply because the doctrine has been applied in a few decisions'.

[15] (1951) 81 C.L.R. 1, 257-8 per Fullagar J; furthermore, in the first part of the sentence quoted, His Honour referred expressly to the situation where the matter was left to the opinion of the Governor-General. His remarks may, therefore, be limited to that situation.

practice on the assumption that it is observed. Of course, to the extent that some actors in the system believe in it and attempt to behave according to it, it does have an influence on behaviour. Clearly however, many actors in the system are not motivated primarily by a desire to conform to constitutionalism, and a study of the practice of constitutional law must therefore also be a study of these motivations. Such an analysis will make history more meaningful and give us a better picture of how our system works.

8 The Blocking of the Budget and Dismissal of the Government

Colin Howard & Cheryl Saunders

I
INTRODUCTION

This essay concentrates on the two major constitutional issues raised by the political events of 1974 and 1975, the power of the Senate to refuse supply and the power of the Governor-General to dismiss a government on the ground that it cannot guarantee supply.

For the most part, knowledge of the notorious facts is taken for granted. The opening section traverses the historical background to the power of the Senate to refuse supply. This inquiry was undertaken because although many assertions were made in 1975 about what had happened at the Convention debates, it became apparent that few people actually knew what had happened. The remainder of the essay undertakes a politically impartial examination of the various legal and constitutional propositions which either were or could have been advanced on one side or the other.

The authors have not interpreted the word 'impartial' as depriving them of any right to have and express a view of their own. On the contrary, they have written from the standpoint of constitutional lawyers concerned to evaluate the arguments by reference to the usual criteria of regard for established precedent and the rational interpretation of available materials. In general they have arrived at the view that comparatively little express evaluation is necessary. For the most part the facts and the processes of reasoning involved speak for themselves.

The constitutional doctrines which have emerged from the events of 1975 cannot be viewed with enthusiasm. Their basis in precedent and rational construction of the Constitution is slight indeed. Their content is obscure and their quality doubtful. They do not in fact add up to a coherent structure at all. It is a matter for regret that the most persuasive and rigorous interpreter of the Australian Constitution that we have ever had, Sir Owen Dixon, is no longer with us to give us the benefit of his views on the arguments which went to justify the deliberate disruption of the normal processes of government in 1975 and the arbitrary removal of an elected government. Whatever view he would have taken of the matter, one can be sure, with nostalgic regret, that its presentation would have been both logically impeccable and informed by a sure instinct for the genius of our institutions. This is not the case at present.

II
THE BLOCKING OF THE BUDGET

The Convention Debates

The genesis of the constitutional provisions dealing with the composition and powers of the Senate is relevant for at least two reasons.

First, the federal nature of the Constitution was relied upon expressly by both the Governor-General[1] and the Chief Justice[2] as justification for the dismissal of a government with a majority in the House of Representatives after the Senate refused to pass supply in 1975. Two consequences were claimed to flow from the fact of federalism: the power of the Senate to reject or fail to pass an appropriation Bill and the obligation of a government to resign if it failed to obtain a vote of supply from both Houses. The principles of responsible government as understood and applied in the United Kingdom were therefore said to be modified in Australia to the extent that a government must have the confidence of both Houses of Parliament. As neither of these two incidents of federalism appeared in the first seventy-three years of Australian federal history, and the practical part now to be played by the Senate in the operation of Australian federalism is somewhat obscure, it becomes instructive to examine the intentions of those who framed the Constitution for confirmation or rebuttal of these claims as a matter of history.

Secondly, many of the provisions governing the composition and powers of the Senate appear either anomalous in the light of contemporary political circumstances, or mutually inconsistent. For example, the powers which the States retain to issue writs for Senate elections (s.12) or to fill casual Senate vacancies (s.15) are now circumscribed by conventions which require in the case of the former that the Governor of a State issue writs for a Senate election when requested to do so by the Governor-General, and in the case of the latter (if this convention still exists) that the State concerned fill a casual vacancy with a senator of the same political persuasion as the senator whose seat has been vacated.[3] A striking example of apparent inconsistency is the impracticability of using the deadlock procedure provided by s.57 to resolve a deadlock caused by the rejection of supply by the Senate acting pursuant to s.53.[4] It can be argued also that the relation between the principles of responsible government and the financial powers of the Senate is at least unresolved by the Constitution, if not impossible of resolution. In most of these cases, ambiguities in the text of the Constitution cannot be disposed of without making assumptions about the purpose of the provisions. An examination of the history of the framing of the Constitution provides a factual basis for such assumptions.

It was accepted from the outset that the federal Parliament would be a bicameral legislature comprising a lower, popularly elected House, and an upper House, with rotating membership, in which the original States would be represented equally.[5] It was accepted also that the upper House, or Senate,

---

[1] See the Governor-General's statement of reasons of 11 November 1975: (1975) 49 *Australian L.J.*, at pp. 646-7.

[2] Advice from the Chief Justice of the High Court, Sir Garfield Barwick, to the Governor-General, dated 10 November 1975: (1975) 49 *Australian L. J.*, at p.648.

[3] *Report from the Joint Committee on Constitutional Review* 1959, paras. 290-1.

[4] This is taken up below at pp. 259, 264-5 and 281.

[5] These matters were conceded by Parkes in the initial resolutions put to the Convention in 1891:

would have equal powers with the lower House, the House of Representatives, as regards all legislation except certain classes of money Bills: over these the Senate should have the power of veto, but not the power of initiation.[6] These principles were adhered to throughout the sessions of the Conventions, with only occasional wavering.[7]

Other aspects of the Senate's structure and powers were among the most divisive issues at the Conventions, and were hotly debated. Differences of opinion emerged in particular over the question whether the Senate should have the power to amend or 'veto in detail' appropriation Bills or Bills imposing taxation.[8] The compromise finally reached on this issue denied the Senate the power to initiate or amend defined classes of financial legislation[9] but empowered it to return such legislation to the House of Representatives 'requesting, by message, the omission or amendment of any items'. The terms of the compromise were negotiated originally at the 1891 Convention,[10] confirmed (not without drama) in Adelaide in 1897,[11] and retained with only minor embellishments thereafter.

As is the nature of compromise, this one was not wholly satisfactory, except insofar as it offered an immediate solution to a highly contentious problem.[12] It was made more acceptable to some by two later amendments. The first required the Senate to be chosen directly by the people (s.7), rather than by the legislatures of the States.[13] The second provided a procedure for the resolution of deadlocks (s.57).[14]

The conflict in the Conventions over the powers of the Senate is commonly ascribed to the division of interest between large and small States. There is a great deal of evidence to support this, at least on a superficial level.[15] The original concessions made on equality of State representation in a Senate of considerable powers were based on the assumption that this was the least the small States would require as an inducement to federate. Moreover, throughout the debates the representatives of the smaller States were, by and large, the

---

... my act was a very voluntary one—to offer to the smaller states just the same representation as that which the state of New South Wales would possess. I offered voluntarily ... an equal representation to Western Australia as either Victoria or New South Wales would have in the senate. But I stipulated that that power which is held by the House of Commons should be held by the house of representatives ...

Australian Constitutional Convention, *Official Record of Debates*, 1891, p.448. The text of the resolutions is on p.23.

[6] *Official Record of Debates*, 1891, p.23.

[7] See the debate on the proposal of the Parliament of New South Wales that representation in proportion to population be substituted for equal State representation in the Senate. *Official Record of Debates*, Sydney, 1897, p.258.

[8] Described by Parkes as 'a new-fangled proposition, entirely un-English, and utterly opposed to the development of constitutional government'. *Official Record of Debates*, 1891, p.320.

[9] Section 53. See also ss. 54 and 55.

[10] J. Quick and R. R. Garran, *Annotated Constitution of the Australian Commonwealth* (Sydney, 1901) pp. 131-2; J. A. La Nauze, *The Making of the Australian Constitution* (Melbourne, 1972) p.47; *Official Record of Debates*, 1891, p.706. The proposal was agreed to at p.762.

[11] Quick and Garran, cited above n. 10, p.173; La Nauze, cited above n. 10., Ch. 9.

[12] *Cf.* Deakin's closing remarks in the debate in 1891: 'I believe that the day will come when the electors of this country will demand that the powers granted by this clause shall be considerably restricted'. *Official Record of Debates*, 1891, p.761.

[13] As provided by cl.9 of the 1891 draft Bill. *Official Record of Debates*, 1891, p.588.

[14] See above n. 4.

[15] *Cf.* Quick and Garran, cited above n.10, p.189. The authors state that the principle of equal State representation was supported on the basis of 'practical compromise' not 'abstract logic'.

advocates of a powerful Senate.[16] They argued that the interests of less populous States would be disregarded in a House of Representatives elected on the basis of population but might be protected by a Senate in which the States were equally represented. Consequently most delegates expected (or said they expected) the primary function of the Senate to be that of a States House. The arguments for greater Senate power over financial legislation were based solely on this expectation.

Nevertheless, there is some evidence that the concept of a powerful Senate was supported by the more conservative delegates also, particularly those who were members of Legislative Councils, irrespective of their States of origin.[17] Whereas a division on lines of State interest alone would have placed New South Wales and Victoria on one side and the other States on the other, there were many instances of deviation from this pattern. For example, Playford (South Australia) supported Deakin, Gillies (Victoria) and Parkes (New South Wales) in the Constitutional Committee debates on the powers of the Senate in 1891.[18] Kingston (South Australia) spoke strongly, in the debate on the power of the Senate to amend money Bills in Adelaide in 1897, in support of Reid's amendment designed to deny the Senate that power.[19] On the other hand, in the formative debates on the matter in 1891 the two Victorian Legislative Councillors supported the power of the Senate to veto money Bills in detail, in opposition to the other Victorian delegates.[20]

Although proponents of a strong Senate based their arguments primarily on federal necessity, there were some who also supported it as a House of review, acting as a check on legislation of the lower House.[21] This second, subsidiary, function of the Senate was the justification for its continuous character, achieved by the rotation of senators (s.13). It was not used as justification for the power of the Senate to reject money Bills.

The constitutional scheme devised for the Senate was criticised in several fundamental respects by a minority of delegates during the sessions of the Conventions. Some delegates foresaw the development of national political parties and the inevitable defeat of the Senate's expected role as protector of State interests. Deakin, with his usual perspicacity, was among them:

---

[16]In the crucial debate in Adelaide in 1897 on the power of the Senate to amend money Bills, the division was almost precisely on big State/small State lines, with five defections from the South Australian and Tasmanian ranks to give those opposed to wider Senate power a majority of two. *Official Record of Debates*, Adelaide, 1897, p.575. But *cf.* La Nauze, cited above n.10, p.146 for the background to this decision.

[17]On another occasion Deakin classified a combination of supporters of a powerful Senate as one of 'reactionary radicals and iconoclastic conservatives'. *Official Record of Debates*, 1891, p.710.

[18]La Nauze, cited above n.10, pp. 47-8, reproduces a letter written by Deakin to C. H. Pearson containing an account of the Committee's deliberations. Deakin consistently characterizes his opponents as 'conservative'.

[19]'I do not hesitate to give expression to my views, which may perhaps be considered personal to myself, believing as I do that in this respect I stand alone and separated from my colleagues of South Australia.' *Official Record of Debates*, Adelaide, 1897, p.488. And see Quick and Garran, cited above n.10, p.173.

[20]*Official Record of Debates*, 1891, Cuthbert, p.291, Fitzgerald, p.172.

[21]'But never let it be thought that our superstructure will ever be lasting if any clause in our charter allows the people's will in its burst and flush of impetuosity at once to reach the statute-book. That is not what the sober-thinking, solid, and—I will use the word—conservative senate is for'. Fitzgerald, *Official Record of Debates*, 1891, p.171.

We shall have party government and party contests in which the alliances will be among men of similar opinions, and will be in no way influenced by their residence in one State or another.[22]

Macrossan[23] and Isaacs[24] made similar predictions. Their arguments were not accepted by the majority of delegates, who were more influenced by the immediate conflicts between large and small States in the Conventions and the passionate divisions between Protectionists and Freetraders, which also tended to run on State lines. Griffith made a prediction to the contrary, describing party government as 'a thing of which we have had some experience in Australia, but which I am afraid is becoming somewhat discredited'.[25]

Some delegates challenged the assumption that peculiarly State interests would continue to exist after federation which the Senate would be capable of protecting, however extensive its powers. Reid bluntly demanded particulars in order to 'clear the air of all these mysterious fears of brutal domination over principles which are dear to the hearts of every true-born Australian in the smaller states'.[26] Deakin made a similar point, more artistically, but with no less scepticism:

> Let them in the first instance define state rights, and then let us see how they will be impaired. I will be second to no delegate in my anxiety to preserve what I understand to be state rights. So anxious am I to preserve them, that I would never dream of intrusting them to a senate. Let us know what state rights are, and let us be careful to secure them under our constitution, so that they may never be liable to be swept away.[27]

These arguments too found little favour with the majority of delegates.[28]

Others took up the theme in a different guise. Higgins doubted that State interests could be identified but, abandoning that line of argument as fruitless suggested that the Constitution should compel senators to vote by States.[29] Kingston, more easily persuaded of the reality of State interests, but sceptical of future Senate performance, made a proposal which was not only novel but also instructive as to the part which he expected the Senate to play in the federation:

> ...within the four corners of the act which we propose to pass we should for the guidance of the senate lay down the principle which we hope and expect will direct them in the discharge of their senatorial duties. So far as I can understand that principle, it is that the will of the people as expressed in the house of representatives should prevail, and should not be interfered with by the senate in the slightest degree, except in cases where state rights and state interests are involved.[30]

---

[22] *Official Record of Debates*, Adelaide, 1897, pp. 297-8.

[23] *Official Record of Debates*, 1891, p.434.

[24] *Official Record of Debates*, Adelaide, 1897, pp. 173-5.

[25] *Official Record of Debates*, 1891, p.431.

[26] *Official Record of Debates*, Sydney, 1897, p.650. Reid was speaking in the debate on the deadlocks provision. See also pp. 658-9.

[27] *Official Record of Debates*, 1891, p.82.

[28] In answer to Deakin, Barton claimed it was State interests, rather than State rights, with which the Senate would be primarily concerned. He did not define these interests, however. *Official Record of Debates*, 1891, p.90.

[29] *Official Record of Debates*, Sydney, 1897, p.263.

[30] *Official Record of Debates*, 1891, p.737. This would have satisfied another criticism of Deakin's that even if State interests were raised before the Senate, they would form a very small proportion of its business. *Official Record of Debates*, Adelaide, 1897, pp. 293-4.

In particular, delegates questioned the assumption that the Senate could not protect State interests effectively unless it had broad financial powers. They claimed that there were no circumstances in which Senate interference with Bills imposing taxation or appropriating revenue could be justified on the grounds of protection of State interests: consequently the argument for wider Senate financial powers must be based on a false premise. They founded this claim not only on the character of financial legislation,[31] but also on the peculiar position of taxation legislation in constitutional theory.[32] In reply, supporters of a strong Senate produced specific examples of money Bills which might affect States as States and therefore justify Senate interference. One example given was that of a land tax which might be 'in several states a most just and proper thing, while in other states it might be most unfair and improper'.[33]

It should be understood that the debate on the powers of the Senate over financial legislation usually took place in the context of the power to amend or veto details of financial legislation. The attention of delegates was therefore focused on examples of taxation or appropriation Bills which might include individual clauses to which the Senate might object. There was little debate on the power of the Senate to veto an entire Bill, for it was generally accepted that it could do so.[34] Nevertheless, the expectation of delegates about the circumstances which would surround the exercise of the power of absolute veto can be gathered from the few occasions on which the matter was directly raised and, by cautious inference, from the debate on the power to amend.

Three points must be made. First, it was contemplated always that such Bills would be rejected by the Senate because of disagreement with the content of the Bills themselves.[35] It was in consequence of this understanding that supporters of the Senate sought for it a power of veto in detail, to enable legislation to be rendered less objectionable without resort to the extreme measure of absolute veto. The compromise finally accepted was the power of the Senate to return these Bills to the House 'requesting, by message, the omission or amendment of any items or provisions therein'.[36]

The second follows from this. The exercise of the Senate's power of veto of a financial Bill was usually contemplated in the context either of a Bill appropriating revenue for a particular project or of a Bill imposing taxation, for it was possible to imagine a dispute over the policy expressed in such Bills. Thus even Deakin envisaged the rejection of a major taxation measure by the Senate and assumed that the policy disagreement would be settled by an

---

[31]For example, Parkes argued that by its very nature taxation legislation must affect people as individuals, not as residents of States. *Official Record of Debates*, 1891, p.449.

[32]'You cannot allow a small section to govern the majority on a question of finance; you cannot give 250,000 persons the power to tax 2,500,000 against their will'. Munro, *Official Record of Debates*, 1891, p.53.

[33]Griffith, *Official Record of Debates*, 1891, p.40; *cf.* also Barton, p.90.

[34]*E.g.* Deakin: 'This power of veto may be exercised absolutely. I am not now disputing their right to exercise that power'. *Official Record of Debates*, Adelaide, 1897, p.507.

[35]See Playford, *Official Record of Debates*, 1891, p.58. See also Cuthbert, p.293, with reference to the comparable power of the Victorian Legislative Council:

> although the power of veto is all very well in its way, and is, I admit, a great power, still it must be very carefully exercised, and under very peculiar circumstances indeed. The Council must be perfectly satisfied in their own minds that the propositions laid down in the bill submitted to them are radically wrong ...

[36]Section 53.

immediately ensuing election.[37] But the exercise of a Senate veto over Bills appropriating money for the ordinary annual services of government was simply not taken as a serious prospect because such a Bill related to no new policy decision. The observations of two delegates are worth recording. The first are from McMillan, a conservative from New South Wales:[38]

> I do not think that hon. members who represent the smaller states would for a moment attempt to interfere with the ordinary appropriation bill of the year—that is the bill covering the salaries of clerks, and other necessaries for carrying on the government of the country.[39]

The second is an exchange between Smith and Griffith:

> Col Smith: Would the hon. member allow the senate to alter an appropriation bill?
>
> Sir Samuel Griffith: If it is the annual appropriation bill which is sought to be withdrawn from the senate, I do not think the matter is worth discussing. Nobody would want to alter it, unless the house of representatives were to attempt to coerce the senate by putting in improper or unusual items. I want to get at what we are quarrelling about. So far as the ordinary items of an appropriation bill are concerned, I do not think the subject is worth half an hour's discussion.[40]

Thirdly, the possibility was raised but dismissed that the Senate might exercise its power of veto, an inconclusive election be held, and the Senate exercise its veto again. A suggestion that the Senate's veto be limited to a single one was not adopted:

> I would leave to the Upper Chamber the absolute power of veto, and trust to the good sense of the community, and to the final fairness of public opinion, to bring it into harmony with the popular Chamber.[41]

Many delegates were concerned that the existence of a powerful second chamber would be incompatible with a system of responsible government which in its traditional form required that the ministry sit in the popularly elected House and derive its authority from the confidence of a majority of that House.[42] The different basis of composition of the Senate, and its supposedly different interests, made it likely that there would be occasions on which the views of the majority in the lower House would not be reflected by the majority in the Senate. Yet the Senate would have the power to reject or amend legislation which formed part of the policy on which the government was elected, a power which might ultimately cause the downfall of the government.

The problem was never satisfactorily solved. There were two obvious alternatives. The first was to forego responsible government and adopt some such system of executive government as in the United States or Switzerland, which had been proved compatible with federalism. This was not acceptable to most delegates, to whom responsible government was both familiar and

---

[37] *Official Record of Debates*, Adelaide, 1897, p.295.

[38] Described by La Nauze, cited above n.10, p.146, as reluctantly joining his fellow delegates from New South Wales in the crucial 1897 vote.

[39] *Official Record of Debates*, 1891, p.389.

[40] *Official Record of Debates*, 1891, pp.428-9.

[41] Deakin, *Official Record of Debates*, Adelaide, 1897, p.295.

[42] Griffith's notion of responsible government was slightly different:

> Many hon. members . . . think that the essence of responsible government is that ministers should sit in Parliament, whereas I contend that the essence is that ministers should not be dissociated from Parliament.

Official Record of Debates, 1891, p.37.

desirable.[43] The second was to modify either the powers or the composition of the Senate: an impossible alternative in practice, given the delicate balance of the existing compromise.

A third possibility, which was eventually adopted, was to devise a new system of government from a combination of responsible government and federalism. The details of this complex structure were neither resolved in the Conventions nor embodied in the Constitution. Instead, both sets of principles were incorporated in the Constitution (somewhat vaguely in the case of responsible government) in the hope that the logical inconsistency between them would work itself out in practice. In the words of Griffith: 'I propose to leave to the future the avoiding of these difficulties, and that we should not make difficulties in advance'.[44]

Nevertheless, the emphasis placed by delegates on the components of their system of government changed during the course of the Conventions. In 1891, although the inconsistency between responsible government and federalism was perceived clearly,[45] the Convention decided that the federal structure of government was of paramount importance. Accordingly, while the 1891 draft Bill spelt out in detail the powers of the Senate, it contained no compulsory requirement of responsible government. It was phrased, in Griffith's words, so 'that responsible government may—not that it must—find a place'[46] in the structure of government.

During the Convention of 1897 and 1898 delegates resolved more firmly to adopt the principles of responsible government.[47] Their primary concern was to embody its necessarily changeable and indeterminate principles in the Constitution in words flexible enough to enable them to develop and adapt to new circumstances in the future. This was done, although sketchily indeed, in ss. 61-67 of the Constitution. By this time the provisions dealing with the composition and powers of the Senate were settled except in the most minor respects. There was no attempt to deal with the possibility[48] that both sets of principles might be pushed to their logical extremes and come into direct conflict, far less with the ramifications of such a struggle if, as a few had predicted, the Senate was no longer fulfilling its federal function by the time that the principles of responsible government had developed to the point where they were an integral working part of the Australian Constitution.

Nevertheless delegates accepted the likelihood of conflict between the House of Representatives and the Senate to the extent of including a provision for the resolution of deadlocks in the Constitution (s.57). Although the matter had

---

[43]'I for one, as I do not wish my boots made in Germany, do not want my Constitution made in Switzerland.' Barton, *Official Record of Debates*, Adelaide, 1897, p.24.

[44]*Official Record of Debates*, 1891, p.48.

[45]'. . .there will be one of two alternatives—either responsible government will kill federation, or federation in the form in which we shall, I hope, be prepared to accept it, will kill responsible government'. Hackett, *Official Record of Debates*, 1891, p.280. See also Baker, p.465.

[46]Quick and Garran, cited above n.10, p.132.

[47]*ibid.*, p.169.

[48]But *cf.* Munro in 1891: '. . . how can you have responsible government if you have a governor calling in an executive as his advisers, and if after that executive has submitted financial measures to the house of representatives, and shown that they are absolutely necessary for the good of the country, the senate vetoes the measures. Where, then, does the responsibility lie?' *Official Record of Debates*, 1891, p.49.

been raised by a few delegates early in the Conventions,[49] it did not become a major issue until the Sydney session in 1897,[50] The aim was to attain an acceptable balance between the power of the Senate to protect State Interests and the responsibility of the lower House. Proposed solutions included a referendum on deadlocked Bills, a joint sitting of both Houses, a dissolution of the House of Representatives followed by a dissolution of the Senate, and a concurrent dissolution.[51] The method finally chosen, now embodied in s.57, requires a concurrent dissolution of both Houses, followed by a joint sitting. A prerequisite of the double dissolution is the attempted passage of the contentious legislation through both Houses twice, with an interval of three months between, as now held by the High Court,[52] the first rejection by the Senate and the second passage by the House of Representatives.

The three-month interval which is required in addition to the time-consuming processes of the normal parliamentary passage of legislation, plus dissolution and re-election, make s.57 an unsuitable provision for the resolution of a deadlock caused by the failure of the Senate to pass an appropriation Bill.[53] The historical explanation for this seems to depend upon a mixture of expediency, assumptions about contemporary constitutional practice and expectations of future constitutional development.

The patent inconsistency between ss. 53 and 57 is symptomatic of the generally unsatisfactory nature of the provisions relating to the powers and composition of the Senate if read literally and in isolation from the rest of the Constitution. To a considerable extent this is owing to the fact that with the exception of the (equally unsatisfactory) financial clauses, the provisions relating to the Senate were the most contentious at the Conventions. They are the direct result of a contemporary political compromise.

Some delegates looked beyond the immediate goal in an effort to envisage how the Senate would operate, what powers it would need to perform its expected functions and whether these powers would operate consistently with other constitutional provisions. Apparently none of them carried their expectations or apprehensions of the future to their logical conclusion, possibly because the immediate exercise would have been endangered had they done so.

Some were aware however that much had been left to chance and constitutional developments outside the written text. These fears were expressed by Downer in debate on the adoption of the 1891 draft Bill:[54]

> . . . there can be no doubt that the interpretation of the constitution will be governed at least as much by the general understanding of its meaning as by the precise words in which that meaning is expressed. I do not think that it is possible that the

---

[49] *E.g.*, Deakin, *Official Record of Debates*, 1891, p.385.

[50] It was discussed at some length in Adelaide in 1897, but according to Quick and Garran ['I]t was as yet by no means generally recognized that for "deadlocks" in this wider sense, any cure was necessary or desirable', cited above n.10, p.181. A deadlock in the narrow sense was understood to be one which arose when financial legislation was rejected by an upper House by virtue of the objection of that House to provisions which were tacked to it. This was met in the Australian Constitution by ss. 54 and 55, the first deadlock provisions.

[51] The main debate on this subject appears in the *Official Record of Debates*, Sydney, 1897, at pp. 541 ff. An outline of the various deadlock proposals appears in the index under 'Commonwealth of Australia Bill: cl.57'.

[52] *Victoria* v. *Commonwealth (P.M.A. Case)* (1975) 7 A.L.R. 1.

[53] As speedily became apparent in the weeks after the Senate deferred supply in 1975.

[54] Which for present purposes was sufficiently similar to the final version.

constitution is after all sufficiently elastic to enable the senate to be all that, personally, I would desire it to be ... but, unfortunately, the words used are sufficiently elastic to be interpreted by one portion of the Convention in one way, and by the other portion in another direction. I sincerely hope that no trouble may come out of this.[55]

The Senate as a States House

It is clear then, that the expected role of the Senate as the protector of State interests was the main justification advanced in the constitutional Conventions for the considerable powers with which the Senate was endowed, although a subsidiary function was expected to be that of a House of review.

In fact on nearly all occasions[56] in the past seventy-five years senators have voted according to parties rather than according to States. On the evidence it can hardly be seriously maintained that the Senate any longer operates as a States House, even if it ever did, except in the superficial sense that it is comprised of an equal number of senators from each State. It is sometimes argued that equality of State representation does have practical significance, if not in the Senate itself, then in the 'councils of parties and Ministers'.[57] This may be so, although the degree of significance is difficult for the uninitiated to evaluate. Even if it is so, it is hard to see how the Senate as an institution can be said to be effective in this way, as opposed to individual senators. Nor is it in any way comparable to the function the framers of the Constitution had in mind for the Senate when they bestowed upon it the extensive powers in s.53.

There are no doubt circumstances in which the party policy of the majority in the Senate coincides with the interests of some State governments, or even all State governments, on a particular issue. The mere fact of such a coincidence does not justify the assertion that the Senate is acting as a States House, although it is sometimes claimed to do so.[58] Furthermore such occasions are more than balanced by the more usual case in which the party policy of the majority in the Senate is diametrically opposed to the interests of the States. For example, after the invalidation of State receipt duties by the High Court in the *Hamersley Case*[59] in 1969, the Commonwealth Government and the States reached agreement to the effect that the States would continue to refrain from imposing a receipt duty on wages[60] if the Commonwealth would impose and collect for the States a receipts duty of the kind invalidated by the High Court. The Commonwealth Government duly introduced five Bills[61] to carry out the agreement which were defeated[62] by the Senate using the power

---

[55] *Official Record of Debates*, 1891, p.919.

[56] Some possible exceptions are asserted by J. R. Odgers, *Australian Senate Practice*, (4th ed., Canberra, 1972), pp. 5-12.

[57] See the evidence of H. R. Nicholas to the Royal Commission on the Constitution 1927-29, quoted (with elaboration) by Odgers, cited above n.56, p.9. See also *Report from the Joint Committee on Constitutional Review*, 1959, para. 89.

[58] See, for example, the comments of Senator Durack on the amendments made in the Senate to the National Roads Bill 1974: 'a classic case of the Senate acting properly', *Age*, 18 September 1974.

[59] *Western Australia* v. *Hamersley Iron Pty Ltd (No.1)* (1969) 120 C.L.R. 42.

[60] Which was constitutionally valid but contrary to the current Commonwealth-State financial agreement.

[61] States' Receipts Duties (Administration) Bill 1970, States' Receipts Duty Bills (Nos. 1, 2 and 3) 1970, States Grants (Receipts Duty) Bill 1970.

[62] Senate, *Debates*, 1970, vol. 44, pp. 2681-2.

to reject financial legislation which had been conceded to it originally to enable it to protect State interests effectively.[63]

It will be remembered that some of the delegates to the original Conventions questioned the separate identity of State interests in matters with respect to which the Commonwealth Parliament had power to legislate; in particular with respect to taxation measures. Their reservations are given inadvertent credence by the Clerk of the Senate, J. R. Odgers, in the fourth edition of *Australian Senate Practice*.[64] Concerned to defend the Senate's support of the Uniform Tax Scheme, he says: 'It is true that from time to time certain States have made useful political capital out of this issue, but the simple truth probably is that the people want uniform taxation'. Parkes would have been in complete agreement.

The obvious political fact that for most practical purposes a vote in the Senate is a vote on party lines, dictated by party policy, will be taken for granted in the rest of this discussion. Although this does not of course have the effect of altering the express provisions of the Constitution, it distorts the scheme of the Constitution. It should be noted that the influence of political parties in the Senate also affects its function as a House of review. This aspect of its activities was given considerable impetus by the introduction of the system of Senate standing committees in 1970,[65] but the membership of committees, and rights to chairmanship, reflect the political facts of the House itself.

Interpretation of the Present Constitution

Introduction. In an earlier section an examination was made of the intentions of the framers of the Constitution towards the powers which the Senate should have and the functions it should perform. The purpose of this section is to examine the present position: to determine whether the Senate now has the constitutional right to force from office a government with a majority in the House of Representatives. The inquiry is directed not only to the validity in constitutional law and practice of the deferral of the budget by the Senate in 1975, but also to the constitutional consequences of the deferral.

If such a right exists, it has serious implications for the relationship between the two Houses of the federal Parliament, the responsibility of ministers to the more popularly elected House (and through it, to the electors), and the standard of government during the relatively frequent periods when the party with a majority of seats in the House of Representatives does not have a majority of seats in the Senate also.

The resignation or dismissal of a government is normally followed by the dissolution of the House of Representatives.[66] It does not necessarily involve the dissolution of the Senate; in fact it cannot do so unless the particular

---

[63]La Nauze, cited above n.10, p.148, says of this episode 'The ironies of the Senate as a States' House could go no further'. *Cf.* Odgers, cited above n.56, p.12.

[64]Odgers, cited above n.56, p.10.

[65]*ibid.*, p.419 ff. Since the events of October 1975, there has been one instance of senators acting independently, in defiance of the party line. On 27 April 1976, six Liberal senators crossed the floor to vote against clauses in the Social Service Amendment Bill 1976 which abolished funeral benefits for pensioners. This may be viewed as evidence that the Senate is becoming a more effective House of review, although the functions of a House of review should involve careful contemplation of complicated legislation rather than rejection of government policy embodied in a simple Bill on the basis of disagreement with it. But such a development would not be relevant to the power of the Senate to reject supply.

[66]In such circumstances as those presently under consideration there must be a dissolution of and an election for the House of Representatives if parliamentary government is to continue.

requirements of s.57 have been fulfilled.[67] The existence of a right to deny the government supply therefore enables the Senate to force a dissolution of the House of Representatives while remaining unaffected itself. This becomes even more startling when it is remembered that in most cases the House of Representatives will have been elected more recently than at least half the Senate, and possibly more recently than the whole of the Senate. If the composition of the House represents the latest expression of the will of the people, the election may solve nothing. But the Senate may persist with its refusal to pass supply. There is no constitutional impediment to this course of action. The only restraint is the judgment of the majority[68] in the Senate as to what is politically expedient.

The possession of such a right by the Senate has implications for the conduct and standards of government. A government which controls only the lower House may have to modify its policies and activities to satisfy the Senate majority, or, in the absence of a clear majority, the few senators who hold the balance of power. The result is that at best a government chosen on a more popular basis is controlled by a majority in a House chosen on a less popular basis, and at worst, a government is directed by the decisions of a few minority senators.

The possibility that supply may be rejected undermines the ability of both the government and the administration to plan and implement a comprehensive programme during the government's term of office.[69] A government faced with such a threat will be reluctant to court mid-term unpopularity, even with measures which would, in the long run, be of greater benefit.[70] There may be occasions in which mid-term unpopularity reflects bad government. It is hardly to be maintained that the sole power to make such a judgment can be entrusted safely to an Opposition.

The Senate's Theoretical Power to Refuse Supply.   Section 53 expressly restricts the power of the Senate in relation to financial legislation in three ways.[71] First, it may not originate 'proposed laws appropriating revenue or moneys, or imposing taxation'. Secondly, it may not amend 'proposed laws imposing taxation, or proposed laws appropriating revenue or moneys for the ordinary annual services of the Government'. Thirdly, it may not amend any law 'so as to increase any proposed charge or burden on the people'. These three restrictions are imposed by the first three paragraphs of s.53 respectively. The last two paragraphs of the section deal with the powers which the Senate does have over legislation. It may return any proposed law which it may not amend to the House of Representatives requesting 'the omission or amendment of any items or provisions therein'. And finally, 'Except as provided in this section, the Senate shall have equal power with the House of Representatives in respect of all proposed laws'.

---

[67]There is no provision for the dissolution of the Senate elsewhere in the Constitution. (*Cf.* s.5 for a dissolution of the House of Representatives.) But note the inference in the Governor-General's statement that the Crown retains a reserve power to dissolve the Senate: (1975) 49 *Australian L. J.*, at p.648.

[68]Or if there is no majority, the judgment of those holding the balance of voting power.

[69]Maximum three years (s.28).

[70]Menzies argued this in a letter to Sir Philip Game on 3 November 1932, quoted in the *Australian* 16 October 1975.

[71]See Odgers, cited above n.56, Ch. XVI, for the application and interpretation of the restrictions in s.53 since Federation.

If interpreted literally, in isolation from the rest of the Constitution, s.53 appears to leave the Senate the power of absolute veto over all legislation. Such a power is not conferred in so many words. It is a literal consequence of the generality of the concluding paragraph. Nevertheless this interpretation of s.53 has been questioned. In a letter to the newspapers on 27 October 1975, Sir Richard Eggleston argued that the Senate has no power under s.53 either to reject supply or amend the motion for the second reading of appropriation Bills to provide that the Bills would not be passed until 'the Government agrees to submit itself to the judgment of the people'. The latter course of action had in fact been taken by the Senate on 16 October 1975.[72] Sir Richard based his argument on the express provision in s.53 that the Senate may not amend a Bill appropriating revenue for the ordinary annual services of government but may make suggestions for the omission or amendment of any item, which suggestions may be adopted by the House of Representatives 'if it thinks fit'. He argued that, if backed by such a sanction as the possibility of absolute veto of the Bill, the power of the Senate to make suggestions becomes in effect a power to make amendments, which is inconsistent with the prohibition in s.53. Similarly, the procedural steps by which the Senate deferred a vote on the appropriation Bills are equivalent to attaching an amendment to the Bills themselves, and therefore unconstitutional.

The argument involved the further proposition that if the power to veto appropriation Bills was withdrawn from the Senate by necessary inference from the first three paragraphs of s.53, the apparently plenary phrase 'all proposed laws' in the last paragraph must be restricted to Bills other than those imposing taxation or appropriating revenue for the ordinary annual services of government. Whatever its inherent merits, the present indications are that this understanding of s.53 is unlikely to be looked upon with favour by the present High Court.[73]

In a second letter to the newspapers on 1 December 1975, Sir Richard advanced a further argument to prove that the Senate does not have the power to reject supply under s.53. He pointed out that earlier drafts of the Constitution in 1891 and 1897 expressly conferred upon the Senate a power to reject appropriation Bills[74] whereas the final draft did not. He argued from this that s.53 was not intended to confer a power of rejection on the Senate. He justified the use of earlier drafts on the basis that as long ago as 1904 the High Court had approved the use of such material as evidence for the purposes of constitutional interpretation in *Tasmania v. Commonwealth and Victoria.*[75]

While not disputing the proposition that earlier drafts may be referred to for this purpose while the Convention debates may not, this provides an excellent example of how legal criteria of construction can produce historical error. The Convention debates show that no peculiar significance can be attached to the change in the wording of s.53. The compromise over the power of the Senate

[72]Senate, *Debates,* 16 October 1975, no. 20, p.1241.
[73]*Victoria* v. *Commonwealth (P.M.A. Case)* (1975) 7 A.L.R. 1, at pp. 13 (Barwick CJ), 31 (Gibbs J), 50 (Stephen J), 64 (Mason J).
[74]The relevant portion of cl.55, the equivalent of the present s.53, provided as follows:
The Senate shall have equal power with the House of Representatives in respect of all proposed laws, except laws imposing taxation and laws appropriating the necessary supplies for the ordinary annual services of the Government, which the Senate may affirm or reject, but may not amend.
[75](1904) 1 C.L.R. 329. The passage upon which he relies is from the judgment of Barton J, at p.351.

was reached in Sydney in 1891 and affirmed in Adelaide in 1897. The dispute had been almost entirely over the power of the Senate to amend or to veto in detail money Bills; it was accepted without question that the Senate would have a power of absolute veto, although some had qualms as to the manner in which it would be exercised. There is nothing in the debates to suggest that such a fundamental plank in the compromise of 1891 had been removed. On the contrary: in the closing debate on the draft Bill during the last session of the Convention in Melbourne in 1898, Sir Richard Baker, a staunch advocate of Senate powers[76] enumerated changes made to the 1891 draft Bill which had 'greatly decreased' the 'power, the dignity, and the importance of the Senate, so far as those Money Bills which must originate in the House of Representatives are concerned'.[77] The two changes he mentioned were first, the widening of the definition of 'Bills for imposing taxation', and secondly, the requirement that members of the executive be members of Parliament, which he regarded as inevitably weakening the position of the Senate.[78] It is inconceivable that he would have omitted to mention here the removal of the Senate's power of absolute veto.

It is likely that the alteration to the wording of the clause was a drafting alteration which attracted no attention in the committee of the Convention, and therefore does not appear in the debates.[79] The reason for the change may be inferred from a reply given by Barton to an objection of Isaacs to another part of cl. 53:[80] 'The object of that amendment is to make it clear that the first three paragraphs in cl.53 are intended as limitations on the power of the Senate, while the fourth paragraph is the power of suggestion which has been to some extent, a compensatory power granted under the Constitution'.[81] It appears from this that changes to the wording of cl. 53 may have been intended simply to re-arrange it in a more logical order, with the restrictions on Senate power at the beginning, the 'compensatory power' of suggestion in the fourth paragraph and the bestowal of a plenary power co-equal with the House of Representatives in all other respects at the end.

The most powerful argument against an interpretation of s.53 which enables the Senate to reject Bills appropriating revenue for the ordinary annual services of government is the fact that the only deadlock procedure provided by the Constitution, s.57, is in practice inappropriate to deal with a deadlock of this nature. This is so even if the double dissolution is granted on condition that 'provision be made for the carrying on of the services of Government', as was

[76]Later the first President of the Senate. He was described by Deakin as a 'technical constitutional lawyer': *Federated Australia*, ed. J.A. La Nauze (Melbourne, 1968), p.193.

[77]*Official Record of Debates*, 1898, p.2483.

[78]Sir Richard Eggleston's legal argument may be strengthened by this change. Not only does an examination of the drafts of 1891, 1897 and 1898 show that the express power of the Senate to reject money Bills was deleted between 1891 and 1898, but it also shows that the requirement for responsible government was inserted between 1891 and 1897.

[79]For example, the Committee made 'some four hundred' drafting amendments to the Bill towards the end of the Melbourne session of the Convention in 1898, many of which were approved by the Convention without debate: La Nauze, cited above n. 10, pp. 236-7. La Nauze adds this observation at p.236: 'it may one day interest a curious lawyer to inquire whether judicial review has lingered with significant consequences upon new words approved on trust, and intended, said Downer, merely "to put the wishes of the Convention in more concise and complete form" '.

[80]Isaacs objected the removal of the words 'as it thinks fit' from the paragraph empowering the Senate to make suggestions. The words were restored. *Official Record of Debates*, 1898, p.2450.

[81]*ibid.*

the case in the 1974 double dissolution.[82] The requirement that three months elapse between the first impasse in the Senate and the second passage of the Bill by the House of Representatives poses a unique problem in the case of major appropriation Bills: the money for the services of government will have run out long before the three month period has expired. This difficulty was acknowledged by the Governor-General in his statement of reasons for the dismissal of the Government in 1975.[83] It became a practical problem in both 1974 and 1975 when the Senate failed to pass supply.[84] The influence of practical problems on the correct interpretations of ss.53 and 57 is taken up later in connection with the relation of the Governor-General's intervention to s.57.

The meaning of a Constitution cannot however be determined simply by reference to its written provisions.[85] The literal terms necessarily must be supplemented by assumptions. Such assumptions, or implications, may have been made at the time the Constitution was framed or may have developed since in response to altered circumstances. An example of the former in the Australian Constitution is provided by ss.61-67, which provide a bare outline of the principles of responsible government[86] but fail to mention such fundamental components of that system as the Prime Minister or Cabinet, still less the Leader of Her Majesty's Opposition. An example of the latter is the express provision in s.59 that 'The Queen may disallow any law within one year from the Governor-General's assent'. Justified in 1901 by Quick and Garran as necessary for 'the existence and maintenance of that supreme supervision over all the affairs of the Empire, which is exercised by the Queen through her Imperial Ministers',[87] it is unthinkable that it would be exercised now. It follows that a literal construction of the terms of s.53 may not provide a complete answer to the question whether the Senate has the constitutional right to reject supply. Implications may be read into s.53 on a number of bases.

Even if a strictly legal power to reject supply exists under s.53, there is at least room for an implication that it should be exercised consistently with other provisions of the Constitution. In particular, one would expect an implication, in light of ss.61-67, that it should be exercised so as not to interfere with the operation of responsible government, which includes the proposition that the government holds office by virtue of its possession of the confidence of the

---

[82]'Your agreement to exercise this power was subject to the condition that the Houses would make provision for the carrying on of the services of government until the new Parliament assembles. I am able to give this assurance . . .' Letter from the Prime Minister to the Governor-General, 11 April 1974. *Documents Relating to the Simultaneous Dissolution of the Senate and the House of Representatives by His Excellency the Governor-General on 11 April 1974* (Tabled in Parliament, 29 October 1975), p.37. On the previous day the Senate had refused to pass Appropriation Bill (No. 3) 1973-4, Appropriation Bill (No. 4) 1973-4, and Appropriation Bill (No. 5) 1973-4. It is not hard to imagine circumstances in which such an assurance would be difficult to carry out.

[83]'Section 57 of the Constitution provides a means', perhaps the usual means, of resolving a disagreement between the Houses with respect to a proposed law. But the machinery which it provides necessarily entails a considerable time lag which is quite inappropriate to a speedy resolution of the fundamental problems posed by the refusal of supply': (1975) 49 *Australian L.J.*, at p.648.

[84]Letter from the Prime Minister to the Governor-General, 10 April 1974, requesting a double dissolution: 'funds for the payment of salaries . . . will be exhausted by the end of this month and . . . funds for certain capital works . . . will begin to run short as early as the end of this month', *Documents*, cited above n. 82, p.5.

[85]G. Marshall and G.C. Moodie, *Some Problems of the Constitution*, (rev. ed., London, 1961) p.47, draw the distinction between the legal and the constitutional position.

[86]*Amalgamated Society of Engineers* v. *Adelaide Steamship Co.* (1920) 28 C.L.R. 129, at pp. 146-7.

[87]Quick and Garran, cited above n. 10, p.693. Note the implication that although the section refers to disallowance by the Queen, it is to be exercised 'through her Imperial Ministers'.

lower House. Moreover it is apparent from the Constitution itself that the Senate was intended to operate both as a States House[88] and as a House of review.[89] This would justify an implication that the power in s.53 is intended to be exercised only for those purposes. Neither function would support the existence of a power under s.53 to reject a Bill to which the Senate had no specific objection in order to force the government from office.

Finally, it is possible that an implication has developed that the power of veto is no longer exercisable because the Senate no longer fulfils the function which originally justified its possession of such a power. There is precedent under s.15 of the Constitution for the modification in practice of the express terms of a provision because of the changed role of the Senate. Despite recent aberrations which have been almost universally deplored, it is accepted that the power to fill casual Senate vacancies, which was originally given to the States under s.15 in order to ensure the maintenance of State voting strength in the Senate, is to be exercised now in such a manner as to ensure the maintenance of the relative voting strength of political parties.

As the framers of the Constitution were aware, the Australian Senate is without parallel elsewhere in the world. No other system of government has attempted to combine federalism with responsible government by including a powerful upper House charged with the task of protecting State interests, and constituted accordingly, in a bicameral legislature which is expected to function in accordance with the principles of responsible government in the British sense.[90] The United States Senate is a powerful chamber[91] designed as a States House, but the executive arm of government is both separate from the legislature and elected, in the person of the President, for a fixed term. It therefore cannot be forced from office by a hostile Senate majority. Canada has both responsible government and a Senate with theoretical powers of substantial proportions, but the superficial similarity with Australia ends there. The Canadian Senate was primarily intended as a House of review, not a federal body;[92] accordingly, its members are appointed for life by the Canadian government. Nor does the Canadian Senate attempt to exercise its powers. Kunz cites the Senate's rejection of the Old Age Pensions Bill in 1926 as 'the only instance in its modern history where it failed to observe the delicately drawn line between what is legally permissible and constitutionally proper'.[93]

It follows that other systems of government do not furnish precedents either to confirm or deny the constitutional power of the Australian Senate to reject appropriation Bills. On occasions when upper Houses have taken such action, the upper Houses themselves have been distinguishable in history, composition and function from the Senate. This is particularly so in the case of the upper Houses of the Australian States which have rejected supply or appropriation

---

[88]This follows from most of the provisions in Chapter I, Part II.

[89]Section 13.

[90]Such other systems as the West German and Swiss, whilst manifesting interesting federal variations on the relationship between executive and upper House, are too far removed from British tradition and practice to be useful as precedents in the present context. See Bayne, 'Upper Houses Outside Australia' [1975] *Australian Current Law Digest* 301, at pp. 304-8.

[91]The only restriction on the United States Senate in respect of money Bills is that 'All Bills for raising Revenue shall originate in the House of Representatives': Art. 1, s.7. The U.S. Senate has other powers (for example, the treaty power, Art. 2, s.2), which clearly distinguish it from the Australian Senate.

[92]F.A. Kunz, *Modern Senate of Canada 1925-1963* (Toronto, 1965), p.10.

[93]*ibid.*, at p.352.

Bills from time to time.[94] Quite apart from the distinction which may be drawn between the rejection of supply at State and national level, by virtue of the respective consequences, there is and should be no comparison between the function of the Senate and the functions of the Legislative Councils. Even the most ardent supporters of Senate powers during the 1890s Conventions were anxious to decry such a comparison.[95]

Nevertheless, it is relevant to look for precedents for the rejection of appropriation Bills by the Senate itself at an earlier stage in its history. No such precedent exists before the failure of the Senate to pass Appropriation Bills Nos. 3, 4 and 5 in April 1974. The dearth of precedent has occurred despite the fact that for eighteen of those seventy-three years[96] the government with a majority in the House of Representatives did not have a majority in the Senate, but nevertheless submitted a total of 122 major appropriation Bills to the Senate which were passed.[97]

It is undeniable that earlier restraint on the part of the Senate is more likely to have been attributable to political expediency than constitutional principle. It is undeniable also that during this period the Senate has asserted its powers in relation to money Bills in other ways which have fallen short of the actual rejection of supply. For example, as early as 1901 the Senate insisted successfully that supply was a grant of both Houses of the Commonwealth Parliament and that supply Bills should be worded accordingly.[98] More recently, in 1970, the Opposition in the Senate asserted the right of the Senate to 'refuse its concurrence to any financial measure, including a tax Bill'.[99] In the same year, the Senate in fact rejected minor measures.[100] Nevertheless, the precedent (or lack of it) remains: for a period of seventy-three years, during which its function as a States House was eroded to the point of invisibility, the Senate as a fact passed all major appropriation and supply Bills introduced by the government.

The question whether the Senate has the constitutional power to reject an appropriation Bill under s.53 has never been raised directly before the High Court, but it arose indirectly in 1975 in the *P.M.A. Case*.[101] Apparently in

[94]The Victorian Legislative Council rejected supply in 1947 with the object of forcing an election for the Legislative Assembly. Supply was refused again in Victoria in 1952. See generally Z. Cowen, 'A Historical Survey of the Victorian Constitution 1856-1956' (1957) 1 *Melbourne Univ. L.R.* 9. The Tasmanian Council took similar action in 1948. *Cf.* the statement of Sir Isaac Isaacs on the Victorian rejection in 1947 made in a letter to the *Age*, 7 October 1947:

The Council has overstepped established usage, and has in effect violated the Constitution of the State. If the Council's demand were conceded as the price of an Appropriation Bill, that would be surrendering the well-established right of the Assembly to control money bills, and it would be a severe blow at democracy in this State.

[95]'There is no analogy between a senate and an upper chamber!' Cockburn, *Official Record of Debates*, 1891, p.50. See also Odgers, cited above n. 56, p.364 in reply to the charge that under a system of responsible government, an upper House should not reject major money Bills: 'What that argument forgets is that the Senate . . . was given its great financial powers because the Senate has a different responsibility than an Upper House like the House of Lords.'

[96]The practical importance of the conclusion that an Opposition with a majority in the Senate may block supply at will, subject only to political constraints, may be gleaned from the fact that fifteen of these eighteen years have occurred since the introduction of proportional representation in the Senate in 1948.

[97]See the list tabled by Mr Whitlam in House of Representatives, *Debates*, 28 October 1975, no. 21, pp. 2519-20.

[98]Odgers, cited above n. 56, p.314.

[99]Senate, *Debates*, 1970, vol. 44, p.2647 (Murphy).

[100]States' Receipts Duties (Administration) Bill 1970, States' Receipts Duty Bills (Nos. 1, 2 and 3) 1970, States' Grants (Receipts Duty) Bill 1970.

[101]*Victoria* v. *Commonwealth*, (1975) 7 A.L.R. 1.

response to argument by counsel for the Commonwealth that the purpose of the procedure in s.57 was to enable the will of the House of Representatives to prevail, four judges commented on the position of the Senate in the federal Parliament, including in their remarks reference to the powers of the Senate with respect to money Bills. The general tenor of these remarks was in favour of the existence of the power of the Senate to reject such Bills under s.53.[102] Although these comments are a guide to the meaning which would be attributed to s.53 by the High Court as presently constituted, should the matter ever be directly raised before it, they remain dicta at this stage. Moreover the High Court is limited to the construction of the precise terms of the written Constitution, which do not always reflect the actual constitutional position accurately. Those who regard this as an unacceptable proposition might test it against potential judicial interpretation of the literal terms of either s.13 or s.15, without regard to the practices which are acknowledged to operate in respect of each of them.[103]

Political Realities.   The failure of the Senate to pass supply in 1974 and 1975 makes further discussion of the constitutional power of the Senate to do so in the future trivial. Such ambiguity as existed over the legal powers of the Senate under s.53 has for practical purposes been resolved in favour of wider Senate powers by the Senate's own successful assertion of those powers. Such uncertainty as existed over the constitutional right of the Senate to block supply under the terms of the Constitution coupled with convention has been disposed of similarly. Whatever the theoretical legal or constitutional position it now appears likely that the Senate will exercise the power to reject appropriation legislation unless it is politically inadvisable to do so.[104]

Future Action by the Senate.   Although the depressing conclusion just reached appears to be unavoidable after the events of 1974 and 1975, that is the beginning of the problem rather than the end. Even political expediency tends to produce its own principles of action. The development of the convention that casual Senate vacancies should not disturb the political balance within the Senate is an instance. It is therefore possible that some general principles will emerge, or may indeed already have emerged, to govern the circumstances under which the Senate may be expected to consider a rejection of supply if the voting balance in that House is capable of producing a majority against the Government.

Two incidental matters must be borne in mind. The first is that although it is customary and convenient for the purpose of discussion to refer to an adverse majority in the Senate, the fact is that if a negative motion will suffice for the purpose in hand,[105] a majority is unnecessary; for by s.23 of the Constitution any motion which fails to command a majority does not pass. So far as supply

[102] *Cf.* Barwick CJ at p.13: 'Section 53 of the Constitution makes it abundantly clear that the Senate is to have equal powers with the House of Representatives in respect of all laws other than those specifically excepted'. See also Gibbs J (p.31), Stephen J (p.50), Mason J (p.64).

[103] *Report from the Joint Committee on Constitutional Review* 1959, paras. 273, 290; Australian Constitutional Convention, Standing Committee B, *Report to Executive Committee*, 1 August 1974, pp. 9-14.

[104] See C. Howard, 'The Constitutional Crisis of 1975' *Australian Quarterly*, vol. 48, 1 (1976), pp. 5-25.

[105] As was strictly the case in both 1974 and 1975, although in both instances an affirmative deferral motion was in fact moved.

is concerned this means that it can be refused by half the Senate. Secondly, the purpose of refusing to pass an appropriation Bill is not because of an objection to the content of the Bill itself, although this may coincidentally be the case. The purpose is to force a government with a majority in the House of Representatives from office.

The significance of both these factors is that they gravely weaken any argument based upon the Senate's functions in so far as they are sought to be distinguished from the functions of the House of Representatives. Since in this part of the discussion we are concerned with political principles of action, it should be said unambiguously that much of the rhetoric of constitutional powers, rights, duties and so on is beside the point. The plain fact, and one may say the universally understood fact, is that the point at issue is the use of the Senate as an instrument of political coercion. The circumstances under which this instrument will be used acquire corresponding importance.

The only available text derives from some remarks made by the present Prime Minister, Mr Malcolm Fraser, in his first press conference after assuming leadership of the Liberal Party in March 1975. His belief was that if a government 'has the numbers and could maintain the numbers in the lower House it is entitled to expect that it will govern for the three-year term unless quite extraordinary events intervene'. Elsewhere in the same interview he referred to circumstances 'in which the Government is so reprehensible that an Opposition must use whatever power is available to it'.[106] These two observations have since been reduced in common usage to 'extraordinary and reprehensible circumstances'. It is not known to the authors whether Mr Fraser ever actually used the short form himself in some television or press interview, but it appears to express accurately enough the gist of what he was talking about in March 1975.

On this basis it follows that when the Opposition moved in the Senate to defer the Loan Bill 1975[107] and Appropriation Bills Nos. 1 and 2, 1975-1976,[108] they did so on the basis that the foregoing prerequisites, whether extraordinary events or reprehensible circumstances, were present. The amendment moved by the Opposition to the motion for a second reading gives further and better particulars, citing the overseas loans affair, lack of prime ministerial control over ministers and mismanagement of the economy as evidence of the existence of circumstances justifying the blocking of supply.

There is of course nothing to be gained by debating whether any of these circumstances can legitimately be described as an extraordinary event or reprehensible, although many may think that the overseas loans affair is the only one of the three which justifies the adjective 'extraordinary'. As events subsequently demonstrated, the third point, management or mismanagement of the economy, was probably the most important single factor in the minds of the general public. It is possible however to express some disquiet at the demonstration that the words 'extraordinary' and 'reprehensible' serve to conceal circumstances which, however undesirable, are hardly so far removed from the normal accidents of politics as to justify the employment of such an extreme measure as the refusal of supply.

It is reasonable to observe that the state of the economy and what steps are

---

[106] *Age*, 22 March 1975.
[107] Senate, *Debates*, 15 October 1975, no. 20, p.1156.
[108] Senate, *Debates*, 16 October 1975, no. 20, pp. 1240-1.

being taken in relation to it is a standard and constant bone of contention between government and Opposition at all times. Whether a charge of mismanagement is sufficiently serious to justify arbitrarily removing a government from office is a matter which can hardly be entrusted with equanimity to a hostile Opposition, whatever its political complexion. The relationship between any prime minister and his Cabinet might strike the impartial observer as an almost trivial ground for forcing a government from office. As to the overseas loans affair, it is very far from the intention of the present authors to advance any argument in justification of that regrettable episode. Nevertheless, in terms of the national well-being it was no more than an unsuccessful scandal which, after exhaustive investigation by the Opposition, proved to be quite ludicrous in its details, certainly yielding no substantial ground for the arbitrary removal of an entire government nearly a year later. One would have thought that the time for action was earlier, as soon as the sheer impropriety of the attempt to circumvent the Financial Agreement became apparent. Moreover, as a ground for removing the Government it suffers from the defect that the Governor-General was personally associated with the authorisation for raising the loan. One cannot but feel disquiet at the application of a doctrine which is distinctly selective in its operation.

The best conclusion at which one can arrive by way of projection for the future is that, although principles of action will no doubt continue to be developed for the application of the new doctrine, on the present evidence these principles will amount to no more than political expediency based on public unease about a substantial issue and public excitement about anything less substantial which happens to be prominent at the time. This is a distinctly tawdry outfit for a brand new doctrine to wear. It is to be observed that the total absence of any constitutional foundation for the doctrine of reprehensible circumstances, or any analogous formulation, is emphasised by both the Governor-General's statement of reasons and the opinion of the Chief Justice, for neither makes any reference to it.

III
THE DISMISSAL OF THE GOVERNMENT

But even if His Excellency exercised the extreme prerogative, and dismissed them—a thing never heard of in these colonies . . .

Reid, Adelaide 1897[109]

Introduction

On 11 November 1975, the Governor-General, Sir John Kerr, dismissed the Whitlam Government in purported exercise of his powers under s.64 of the Constitution.[110] He then commissioned a new Government under the leadership of Mr Malcolm Fraser, to 'act as a caretaker Government and . . . make no appointments or dismissals or initiate new policies before a general election is held'.[111] Before doing so he asked for assurances from Mr Fraser on two matters. The first was that Appropriation Bills Nos. 1 and 2, 1975-6 be passed by the Senate. The second was that the new Prime Minister would advise a

---

[109] *Official Record of Debates*, Adelaide, 1897, p.909.

[110] Letter to Mr Whitlam, 11 November 1975: quoted in (1975) 49 *Australian L.J.*, at p.646.

[111] Letter from Mr Fraser to the Governor-General, 11 November 1975. House of Representatives, *Debates*, 1975, no. 22, p.2928.

dissolution of both Houses of Parliament pursuant to s.57 of the Constitution. Both undertakings were fulfilled the same day. The Proclamation for the dissolution of the Parliament was based on twenty-one Bills which had fulfilled the procedural requirements of s.57,[112] and was signed by Malcolm Fraser, as Prime Minister.

The event which precipitated the dissolution of Parliament[113] was the refusal of the Senate to pass Appropriation Bills No. 1 and 2, 1975-6 until 'the Government agrees to submit itself to the judgment of the people'.[114] In political terms this action of the Senate was made possible by the fact that the Liberal-National Country Party Opposition were in a majority in the Senate.[115] This fact made it possible also for Mr Fraser to fulfil his assurance to the Governor-General that the Senate would pass supply.[116]

At the time when Mr Whitlam was dismissed by the Governor-General and Mr Fraser commissioned, the former possessed a majority in the House of Representatives and the latter did not. Accordingly, while Mr Fraser was able to ensure the passage of the Appropriation Bills through the Senate, he was unable to control the lower House. The practical significance of this was demonstrated when the newly commissioned Government lost five divisions in the House of Representatives within three quarters of an hour after its formation had been announced, including a decision on the following motion:

> That this House expresses its want of confidence in the Prime Minister and requests the Speaker to immediately advise His Excellency, the Governor-General, to call the honourable member for Werriwa to form a government.[117]

The Speaker made an appointment to wait on the Governor-General in order to advise him of the resolution of the House of Representatives; but the Parliament was prorogued just before the time set.[118]

It is likely that a great deal is still unknown about the events surrounding the dismissal of the Government on 11 November 1975. Rumours abound but this paper is concerned neither to evaluate nor discuss them. In particular we have no wish to give credence to the conspiracy theory. Nevertheless, the very existence of such a theory emphasizes the undesirability of vice-regal intervention in the government of a country in a way which may be construed as partisan.

Certain facts are sufficiently well substantiated to be accepted. Some are related above. Others follow here. It is known that before the dismissal of the Whitlam Government that Government had been engaged in attempting to raise temporary finance from the banks and other outside sources,[119] although

---

[112]*Australian Government Gazette*, 11 November 1975, no. S229.

[113]In his statement the Governor-General acknowledged the immediate cause of the dissolution to be 'the deadlock which developed over supply between the two Houses of Parliament and between the Government and the Opposition parties'. (1975) 49 *Australian L.J.*, at p.646.

[114]Senate, *Debates*, 16 October 1975, no. 20, pp. 1221, 1241.

[115]The numbers were Liberal/N.C.P. 30; A.L.P. 27; Liberal Movement 1, and Independent 1. The two last mentioned voted with the Government on this issue. Another Independent (Senator Field) was technically on leave as his right to sit was in dispute.

[116]Senate, *Debates*, 11 November 1975, p.1885.

[117]House of Representatives, *Debates*, 11 November 1975, no. 22, pp. 2930-2.

[118]Letter to the Queen from the Speaker (G.G.D. Scholes), 12 November 1975.

[119]These arrangements were referred to by the Governor-General in his statement, but dismissed on the basis that they 'do not amount to a satisfactory alternative to supply'. (1975) 49 *Australian L.J.*, at p.648.

the details of these proposed arrangements remain obscure. It is known also that Mr Whitlam had resolved to advise the Governor-General on 11 November to request the State Governors to issue writs for a half-Senate election in the hope that the deadlock might be broken thereby.[120] His commission was terminated before he was able to offer this advice. It is known that the Governor-General sought and received advice from the Chief Justice of the High Court, Sir Garfield Barwick, on his 'constitutional rights and duties'[121] and that he received unsolicited advice also from the Solicitor-General of the Commonwealth on whether a duty existed to dissolve the House of Representatives in these circumstances.[122] Both opinions have been made public. It appears that the Governor-General followed the advice of the former, rather than the latter.[123]

The following discussion of the constitutional issues raised by the dismissal of the Government in November 1975 will be divided into two parts. The first will deal with the existence of a discretion in the Governor-General to dismiss a government. The second will deal with the way in which that discretion was exercised.

Discretion to Dismiss a Government

In Principle.   Before dealing with the analysis of the constitutional issues it is worth considering whether a vice-regal discretion to dismiss a government should exist in principle, given the stage of development of our parliamentary democracy. In this context it is relevant that searchers for English precedent for the exercise of similar discretions are obliged to resort to such distant events as the resignation of Peel over Queen Victoria's 'bed-chamber question' in 1839,[124] the 'ambiguous exchanges' between William IV and Lord Melbourne in 1834[125] or the dismissal of Lord North by George III in 1783.[126] Since these events took place, parliamentary government has developed to a stage which makes the mere existence of these powers, quite apart from their exercise, inappropriate. The connection between the development of parliamentary democracy and the exercise (or non-exercise) of the reserve power of the Crown to dismiss a government was made by the Privy Council in *Adegbenro* v. *Akintola:*[127]

> Since the principles which are accepted today began to take shape with the passing of the Reform Bill of 1832 no British Sovereign has in fact dismissed or removed a Prime Minister.

---

[120]Governor-General's statement, 11 November 1975. (1975) 49 *Australian L.J.*, at p.648.

[121]Letter from the Chief Justice to the Governor-General, 10 November 1975. (1975) 49 *Australian L.J.*, at p.648.

[122]Opinion of the Solicitor-General, 4 November 1975, extracted in the *Financial Review*, 19 November 1975, p.1.

[123]The Chief Justice advised that the Governor-General had a 'constitutional authority and duty . . . to invite the Leader of the Opposition . . . to form a caretaker Government': (1975) 49 *Australian L.J.*, at p.649. The Solicitor-General denied the existence of a 'duty' to act.

[124]Marshall and Moodie, cited above n. 85, p.52. The authors mention this only as a dubious exception to their proposition that no Government in England had been dismissed 'since Queen Victoria came to the throne'.

[125]*Adegbenro* v. *Akintola* [1963] A.C. 614, at p.631.

[126]S.A. de Smith, *Constitutional and Administrative Law*, (2nd ed., London, 1973), p.104.

[127][1963] A.C. 614, at p.631.

There is no reason to suspect that this principle should be any less applicable in Australia.

The power of the Crown to exercise a discretion to dismiss a government is sometimes defended on the ground that it provides a necessary safety-valve, for use in extreme circumstances. De Smith cites circumstances in which the government is 'purporting to subvert the democratic basis of the Constitution'[128] as being appropriate for the exercise of the power of dismissal. He also describes the power as 'the most drastic form of royal initiative . . . a recourse of last resort, an ultimate weapon which is liable to destroy its user'.[129] The issue thus becomes one of the degree of reliance which may be placed in our parliamentary system. Can it be trusted to work out its own difficulties, or must the ultimate solution rest with a single, appointed, unrepresentative individual?

Constitutional Powers of the Governor-General. Many of the actions taken during the constitutional crisis in 1975 and the events which preceded it were justified by recourse to the literal terms of the Constitution. There must therefore be taken into account first the extent to which the actions of the Governor-General which resulted in the dismissal of the Government in 1975 can be supported on a literal construction of the Constitution.

Sections 61-67 are relevant for this purpose. Section 61 vests the executive power of the Commonwealth in the Queen but provides that it is 'exercisable' by the Governor-General. Executive power is defined as extending 'to the execution and maintenance of this Constitution and of the laws of the Commonwealth'. There is no written indication that the Governor-General must act otherwise than on his own discretion in exercising the executive power, unless it be inferred as a necessary consequence of the provision in s.62 for a 'Federal Executive Council to advise the Governor-General in the government of the Commonwealth'.

Section 64 empowers the Governor-General to appoint officers to administer such departments of state as may be established by the Governor-General in Council. It makes clear that these officers are expected both to be members of the Federal Executive Council (and therefore advisers to the Governor-General under s.62) and the 'Queen's Ministers of State for the Commonwealth'. In their latter capacity these officers must acquire seats in the Senate or the House of Representatives within three months after their appointment. On a literal construction of the provisions the discretion of the Governor-General to choose his advisers and appoint and retain ministers is unfettered. There is a potential inconsistency between the provision in s.64 empowering the Governor-General to 'appoint officers to administer . . . departments' who 'shall be . . . Ministers of State' and the provision in s.65 that 'Ministers of State . . . shall hold such offices as the Parliament prescribes, or, in the absence of provision, as the Governor-General directs'. It is an inconsistency which might be resolved either by confining the power to 'appoint' officers to performance of the formal act of appointment, or by distinguishing between the administration of departments under s.64 and the offices held by ministers under s.65. In any event it is an inconsistency of little relevance for present purposes.

It is relevant for present purposes however to note that there is no reference

---

[128]de Smith, cited above n. 126, p.104.
[129]*ibid.*

to the office of Prime Minister, to Cabinet, to the government, or to the
well-established principle that those who are chosen to 'administer . . . departments of State' and who thereby become 'the Queen's Ministers of State' (in
other words, form the government) owe their selection to their possession of the
confidence of the lower House. Thus, although the Constitution makes the
connection between ministers, members of the Executive Council and advisers
to the Governor-General in the exercise of executive power, it does not make
any such connection with the processes of Parliament by which a government
is formed except to provide that ministers must sit in Parliament.

It follows that the Governor-General has no power under the literal terms of
the Constitution to dismiss the government. He does have power however to
dismiss his advisers, and the Queen's Ministers of State,[130] under ss. 62 and 64.
Similarly he has power to commission new ones. As a consequence, although
the government owes its existence to the confidence of the House of
Representatives, rather than to the Governor-General, it loses its power to
execute the laws of the legislature if its link with the Federal Executive
Council and the Governor-General is broken. Although the Governor-General
has no legal power under the Constitution to dismiss a government, the
exercise of the power he does possess, to dismiss his advisers, achieves the same
result in practice.

It has been argued already that the literal words of the Constitution should
not be read in isolation from accepted constitutional practice and convention.
Indeed, were it not for recent events one would have thought the proposition
both self-evident and trite. This is particularly true for the sections of the
Constitution which deal with the powers of the Crown and its relation with the
responsible ministers, and with the relationship of those ministers to the
Parliament. The relevant sections are ss. 61-67, and other sections scattered
throughout the Constitution which confer power on the Governor-General
alone.[131]

If these sections are read in the light of constitutional convention, two major
consequences follow. The first is that the existence of the Prime Minister, the
Cabinet and the government must be assumed, and must be identified with the
Federal Executive Council mentioned in ss. 62 and 64. This completes the
necessary link between Parliament and the Executive. Its effect in the present
context is twofold. First, when the appointment of advisers to the Governor-
General is terminated under s.62 or s.64 they cease to form the government.
Secondly, as the ministry owes its existence to the possession of the confidence
of the lower House, and must by convention be identified with the Federal
Executive Council, the Governor-General's choice of advisers under s.62 must
be circumscribed accordingly. By this means is achieved 'the modern political
institution, known as responsible government, which shortly expressed means
that the discretionary powers of the Crown are exercised . . . according to the
advice of ministers, having the confidence of that branch of the legislature
which immediately represents the people'.[132]

The second major consequence is that although certain sections of the

[130]In his letter withdrawing Mr Whitlam's Commission the Governor-General referred to his
positions as 'chief adviser and head of the Government', neither of which are known to the
Constitution: (1975) 49 *Australian L.J.*, at p.646.

[131]*E.g.* ss.5, 57.

[132]Quick and Garran, cited above n.10, p. 703.

Constitution confer powers on the Governor-General in Council,[133] and others on the Governor-General apparently in the exercise of his unfettered discretion,[134] the latter class of powers must be exercised by the Governor-General on the advice of responsible ministers. The discrepancy between the two is, in the words of Quick and Garran 'historical and technical, rather than practical or substantial'.[135] It rested originally on the distinction between Crown prerogatives and those powers of the Crown which had been superseded by statute in England in the 1890s.[136] Under the Australian Constitution the former were formally vested in the Governor-General[137] and the latter in the Governor-General in Council.

The framers of the Constitution were in no doubt as to the obligation of the Governor-General to exercise his powers under the Constitution on the advice of his ministers. Barton explained this painstakingly:

> The prerogative is never in these days exercised as a personal act of the Crown as we understand it, but there are certain acts which have become, either by the gradual march of statute law or in any other way, nothing but ordinary executive acts and these are expressed to be exercisable only with the advice of the Executive Council. There are others again which have not been expressly affected by legislation, and while these remain nominally in the exercise of the Crown they are really held in trust for the people, although they are exercises of the prerogative. . . [I]t is understood that the Crown exercises the prerogative only upon ministerial advice, and it is exercised not personally by the Crown, but only with the advice of the Ministry or a Minister.[138]

Some delegates, particularly Reid, argued that the retention of the distinction between prerogative and statutory powers of the Crown was meaningless in a Constitution which was itself a statute and intended to embrace both. In discussion on cl. 58 of the 1897 draft Bill[139] Reid tentatively advanced the suggestion that

> it would be well in this clause, whilst providing that the Executive power and authority of the Commonwealth shall be vested in the Queen, and shall be exercised by the Governor-General as the Queen's representative, that we should add that which will in reality be the practice, that it is by and with the advice of the Executive Council.[140]

Barton disagreed, and won the day:

> We shall be told, if we alter the drafting of it in this particular . . . we shall be told how the distinction would be made every time. The words 'With the advice of the Federal Council' would be struck out and the words: 'The Queen' or 'The Governor-General' would be left. There will be this little further result: We shall be told that we did not know how to draft an Act of Parliament because we did not have sufficient constitutional knowledge.[141]

---

[133]*Cf.* ss. 32, 33, 64, 67, 72, 103.

[134]*Cf.* ss. 5, 28, 56, 57, 58, 64, 68.

[135]Quick and Garran, cited above n.10, p.707.

[136]*ibid.*

[137]Also pursuant to tradition, provisions vesting power in the Governor-General use the discretionary 'may'. This was not intended to have substantive significance either.

[138]*Official Record of Debates*, Adelaide, 1897, p.910.

[139]The forerunner of the present s.61, and in substantially similar terms for present purposes.

[140]*Official Record of Debates*, Adelaide, 1897, p. 908.

[141]*Official Record of Debates*, Adelaide, 1897, p.913. To which Carruthers replied: 'I should think we would be prepared to put up with a little bit of criticism. We are not supposed to understand the whole of the laws of the Empire . . .'

Reserve Powers of the Crown. It is a well-established constitutional principle that the Crown will act on the advice of responsible ministers. The question remains whether there are any circumstances in which the Crown may act otherwise than on ministerial advice, in exercise of 'ill-defined residuary discretionary powers'.[142]

For present purposes the first inquiry is whether the Crown may exercise such powers in relation to the dismissal of a government on the dissolution of Parliament.[143] The existence of a reserve power to dismiss a government is directly relevant because it was in purported exercise of such a power that the Governor-General dismissed the Whitlam Government in November 1975.[144] The reserve power of the Crown in relation to the dissolution of Parliament is relevant for two reasons. The first is that there are many more precedents for the exercise of vice-regal discretion in relation to the dissolution of Parliament (almost all of them exercised for the purpose of refusing a dissolution, rather than forcing one) than there are for the exercise of such discretion in relation to the dismissal of a government. The second is that although the Governor-General dissolved Parliament pursuant to s.57 on the advice of his newly commissioned chief adviser, there is an inference in his statement that he also retains a reserve power to do so owing to the inadequacy of s.57 as a solution to all deadlocks. It will be convenient to deal with this possibility in passing.

The extent and perhaps the very existence of the reserve powers of the Crown is uncertain. De Smith justifies this uncertainty on the ground that the powers may be used in 'novel or highly unusual circumstances' which 'one cannot readily envisage', and that therefore 'it is impracticable to state exhaustively the scope of the residual powers'.[145] Other writers have criticized the uncertainty on the ground that it forces the Crown to make decisions (either positively or negatively) which may be construed as political. This argument was advanced by Evatt in support of his general thesis that the reserve powers of the Crown should be 'authoritatively defined, preferably by Statute'.[146] It follows that the only guides to the existence or otherwise of a reserve power in particular circumstances are precedent and expressions of principle by learned commentators. As discussed above, precedent for the dismissal of a government or exercise or discretion in relation to the dissolution of Parliament is lacking entirely in England within a period of at least 150 years. Consequently the most recent precedents belong to a period when the structure of government was so dissimilar to the present that the precedent is worthless.

Pronouncements on the matter by commentators are more readily available, but inconclusive. The major division of opinion is discussed by Marshall and Moodie.[147] In particular they observe:

---

[142]de Smith, cited above n.126, p.103.

[143]The question may arise also in other contexts, such as the refusal of Royal assent to Bills: de Smith, cited above n. 126, p.108.

[144]See letter of the Governor-General to the Prime Minister, 11 November 1975. Also his statement: 'I should be surprised if the Law Officers expressed the view that there is no reserve power in the Governor-General to dismiss a Ministry which has been refused supply by the Parliament ... This is a matter on which my own mind is quite clear': (1975) 49 *Australian L.J.*, at p.648.

[145]de Smith, cited above n. 126, p.103.

[146]H.V. Evatt, *The King and His Dominion Governors* (2nd ed. Melbourne, 1967), p.7. See also Marshall and Moodie, cited above n. 85, pp. 54-6.

[147]Marshall and Moodie, cited above n.85, pp. 50-66.

There appears to be universal agreement that the Monarch may never use these powers arbitrarily and entirely on his own responsibility: some Ministers must be prepared to advise and then defend the Monarch's action. But whereas one view implies that a Monarch may actively seek Ministers who are prepared to give the desired advice,[148] the other [149] insists that a Monarch is restricted to accepting the advice of whichever Ministers are in office at the time (or, in other words, that these are not personal prerogatives at all)[150]

This passage is directed in particular to the power of the Crown to refuse a request for a dissolution. In a footnote,[151] the authors assert that no writers 'now argue that the Crown may *force* a dissolution'. Marshall and Moodie conclude that in England '[t]here appears to be no issue which could justify the exercise of the Royal Prerogative of dissolution. Similar arguments apply against the dismissal of a government'.[152]

Marshall and Moodie argue that the powers of the Governors-General may be greater than those of the Queen.[153] This argument is based on certain precedents for the exercise of vice-regal discretion, which they are concerned to distinguish, and on the fact that Governors-General are appointed for a limited term so that the appearance of partisanship will discredit the temporary incumbent of the office rather than the office itself. Whatever the validity of this argument in relation to other Commonwealth countries, it is unacceptable in view of the express words of the Australian Constitution. Section 61 of the Constitution vests the executive power in the Queen. It is merely exercisable by the Governor-General. Section 2 of the Constitution identifies the Governor-General as 'Her Majesty's representative' who 'shall have . . . such powers and functions of the Queen as Her Majesty may be pleased to assign to him'.[154] It would be clearly inconsistent with these sections for the Governor-General to exercise powers greater than those possessed by the Queen, although there is a tenable argument that his powers are less.[155]

This position is not changed by the alteration in the relationship between Britain and Australia since 1901. The Report of the Imperial Conference of 1926 affirmed

that the Governor-General of a Dominion is the representative of the Crown, holding in all essential respects the same position in relation to the administration of public affairs in the Dominion as is held by His Majesty the King in Great Britain, and that he is not the representative or agent of His Majesty's Government in Great Britain[156]

---

[148]Sir William Anson is cited as a supporter of this view.

[149]Represented by Bagehot and Lord Hugh Cecil. Marshall and Moodie appear more inclined to this view.

[150] Marshall and Moodie, cited above n.85, p.51.

[151]*ibid.*, p.54. Italics in original.

[152]*ibid.*, p. 56.

[153]*ibid.*, pp. 52-3.

[154]A relatively narrow range of functions was assigned by the Queen in Letters Patent in 1900. Further powers were assigned in 1954: J.I. Fajgenbaum and P. Hanks, *Australian Constitutional Law* (Melbourne, 1972) pp. 34, 38. *Cf.* the width of the Letters Patent issued to the Canadian Governor-General in 1947; *ibid.*, p.39.

[155]On this point, see Fajgenbaum and Hanks, cited above n.154, pp. 34-47. The argument revolves around the extent of the definition of 'executive power' in s.61: does it include Crown prerogatives? If not, the additional powers conferred on the Governor-General by the Queen become important. The Letters Patent contain no plenary grant of prerogative, nor an express grant of power to dismiss ministers.

[156]Quoted in R.M. Dawson (ed.), *Development of Dominion Status 1900-1936* (London, 1937), p.333. For a more comprehensive discussion of the effect of this statement, see Evatt, cited above n.146, Ch. XXI.

While this statement supports the inability of the Queen 'to intervene in person in matters which are so clearly placed within the jurisdiction of the Governor-General by the Constitution Act,[157] it lends no support to the proposition that the powers of the Governor-General are greater than those of the Queen.

Although there is support for the view that reserve powers to the extent of those claimed by the Governor-General no longer exist in England, and that those of the Governor-General must be limited accordingly, there are some precedents for the exercise of vice-regal discretion outside England which need to be examined briefly. A famous or notorious precedent for the dismissal of a government by the Crown was the dismissal of the Lang Ministry by the Governor of New South Wales, Sir Philip Game, in 1932. There is no other precedent for such an action by the Crown which is close enough in time and sufficiently similar in circumstance to the dismissal of the Government in 1975 to be useful. Nevertheless, it is clearly distinguishable on a number of grounds.

First, the dismissal was based on the opinion of the Governor that the Lang Government was acting illegally:

> The position as I see it is that Ministers are committing a breach of the law. . . If Ministers are not prepared to abide by the law, then I must state without any hesitation that it is their bounden duty under the law and practice of the Constitution to tender their resignations[158]

Even if this be accepted as a proper basis for the exercise of the prerogative power to dismiss a government, it is not the basis on which the Whitlam Government was dismissed. However, a similar proposition is supported by Lumb: [159]

> If a government were pursuing a policy based on a disregard for the fundamental principles on which our constitutional structure is founded (for instance, parliamentary supremacy or ministerial responsibility) and was, for example, attempting to rule without the support of Parliament or contrary to its laws then that would justify a refusal to act on the advice of the government and also its dismissal.

The only authority cited for this proposition is the dismissal of Lang. It would seem inapplicable to the circumstances surrounding the dismissal of the Whitlam Government unless a very extended view is taken of what constitutes the 'support of Parliament' or 'disregard for . . . our constitutional structure.'

Secondly, the position held by a Governor may be distinguishable from that of a Governor-General.[160] The Governor is still formally responsible to the Crown whereas it is clear that the Governor-General acts only on the advice of his Australian ministers. Thirdly, Sir Philip Game's decision in 1932 has been cogently criticized on substantial grounds.[161] The low regard in which his intervention has ever since been held, combined with the length of time which has since elapsed and the quite different circumstances, seriously weakens its usefulness as a precedent.

Lastly, and in our view more importantly than any of the preceding points,

---

[157]Letter to the Speaker of the House of Representatives, G.G.D. Scholes, dated 17 November 1975.

[158] *Sydney Morning Herald*, 14 May 1932. Quoted Evatt, cited above n.146, p.164.

[159]R.D. Lumb, *The Constitutions of the Australian States* (3rd ed., Brisbane, 1972), pp. 78-9.

[160]*ibid.*, p.77, '. . . precedents in recent years indicate that the State Governor may possess a wider degree of discretionary authority than resides in the Commonwealth Governor-General'. For argument to the contrary, see *ibid.*

[161]Evatt, cited above n.146, Ch. XIX, in particular the comments of Keith quoted at p.169.

there is simply no analogy between the dismissal of a government at the State level and the dismissal of a government at the national level, whatever the immediate context in other respects. If such an obvious proposition needs to be supported by reference to any more particular factors, we need mention only that the structure of the national legislature, in particular of the Senate, is quite different, and subject to quite different constitutional conditions and restrictions, from the legislature of any State. It is equally obvious that its powers, responsibilities and functions under the Constitution are different in both fundamentals and details from those of the government of any State.

Precedents for the exercise of discretion by a Governor or a Governor-General in relation to the dissolution of Parliament are more readily available.[162] Nevertheless, their usefulness in the present context is limited by two factors.

First, the discretion has been claimed or exercised in relation to the power of the Crown to grant a dissolution. Considerations which have been taken into account in determining whether to exercise the discretion or not have usually included the possibility of forming another government with a workable majority in the Parliament. The issue has arisen therefore in circumstances where there is such a degree of instability in the lower House that it is uncertain which party or parties should or could form a government. For example, the celebrated refusal of the Canadian Governor-General, Lord Byng, to grant a dissolution to Mr Mackenzie King in 1926 was based on the possibility that Mr Meighen, the Leader of the major Opposition Party, might have been able to form a government 'and that all reasonable expedients should be tried before resorting to another Election'.[163] The composition of the Canadian House of Commons was such at the time that neither leader was able to command an absolute majority.[164]

Secondly, although the existence of a discretion in the Crown to refuse a dissolution has been claimed, it has not been exercised in recent years. For example, in 1950, 1956 and 1959 in Tasmania, the Governor (in 1959 the Administrator) asserted that he was not bound to accept the advice of the Premier to grant a dissolution, but did so nevertheless.[165] More relevantly for present purposes, the Governor-General of Australia has never rejected the advice of the Prime Minister to grant a double dissolution of the Commonwealth Parliament, although on the first occasion,[166] in 1914, the Governor-General consulted the Chief Justice (with the concurrence of the Prime Minister). On the second occasion, in 1951,[167] the existence of such a discretion was neither confirmed nor denied.[168] Again, in 1974, although the grounds on which the double dissolution was requested were presented in great detail to

---

[162]See E. Campbell, 'The Prerogative Power of Dissolution: Some Recent Tasmanian Precedents', [1961] *Public Law* 165; Evatt, cited above n.146, Chs. IV, VII, VIII; E.A. Forsey, *Royal Power of Dissolution of Parliament in the British Commonwealth* (Toronto, 1968).

[163]Letter from Lord Byng to Mr King, 29 June 1926, quoted in *Historical Documents of Canada*, vol. 5, ed. C.P. Stacey (Toronto, 1972), p.4.

[164]The Conservatives (Meighen) had 116 seats, and the Liberals (Mackenzie King) 101. The balance was held by the Progressives (24) and Labour and Independents (4).

[165]W.H. Craig, 'The Governor's Reserve Powers in Relation to the Dissolution of the Tasmanian House of Assembly' (1960) 1 *Tasmanian Univ. L. R.* 488.

[166]Evatt, cited above n. 146, Ch. V; Odgers, cited above n.56, pp. 22-6.

[167]Evatt, cited above n. 146, Introduction by Z. Cowen, p.xxvii; Odgers, cited above n.56, pp. 26-33.

[168]But *cf.* Odgers, cited above n.56, p. 33.

the Governor-General, there is nothing to either confirm or deny that a discretion was exercised.

Neither the absence of any recent precedent for the exercise of the discretion of the Crown to refuse a dissolution nor the controversial reception which its exercise received on earlier occasions[169] assists the case for the exercise of a vice-regal discretion in the unique circumstances prevailing in November 1975.

The Governor-General and 11 November. If the reserve power to dismiss a government with the confidence of the popularly elected House of Parliament exists at all, it is for use only in the most extreme circumstances: in the words of de Smith, 'a recourse of last resort'.[170] The question remains to be asked whether the action of the Governor-General in dismissing the Government in November 1975 was such a last resort.

The deadlock which occurred between the two Houses of Parliament in 1975 was the result of a political struggle between the headstrong leaders of two political parties. Its genesis and character was such that it should have been solved by political means. It follows that intervention by the Governor-General inevitably would be construed as political intervention. On 11 November, there were some signs that a political solution was, if not imminent, at least approaching. It seems likely that the ultimate solution would have been a negotiated surrender of the Opposition parties and the passage of the Appropriation Bills through the Senate. This analysis derives from the mounting body of public opinion at the time that it was for the politicians to resolve a deadlock which they themselves had deliberately created; from the responsiveness of politicians to adverse public opinion; and from the fact known to one of the authors, and doubtless to many others, that the ranks of the Opposition in the Senate were not as united as they appeared.[171] Viewed purely as a political struggle, it strains credulity that the resolve of the Opposition would have proved greater than that of the Government in these circumstances.

Preference for a political and parliamentary solution rather than vice-regal intervention depends on the degree of faith placed in the processes of parliamentary democracy. In 1975 a great deal of faith was required. Funds for the maintenance of the ordinary services of government were becoming depleted rapidly. It was said that unless Parliament was dissolved on 11 November, an election could not be held in time to solve the deadlock before the money ran out. Nevertheless it was apparent to cool heads that the tightening time pressure was virtually dictating a political compromise. The knowledge that November 11 was the last day for solution by election inevitably increased the likelihood on and from 12 November that the solution would be otherwise, which meant the passage of supply by the Senate. It is impossible to credit that both leaders would have maintained their stand to the point where there was a total breakdown in civil order, still less that party discipline could have been maintained to that point.

Although it may be argued by some that the Governor-General should not

---

[169]See Marshall and Moodie, cited above n.85, p. 52 with respect to the Canadian precedent of 1926 and the South African precedent of 1939. *Cf.* Lord Byng's plaintive letter to a friend: 'Mr. King . . . told me (1) I was ruining the Constitution (2) Breaking up the Empire (3) Putting Canada back in a colonial status'. Quoted in Stacey, cited above n.163, p.8.

[170]de Smith, cited above n.126, p.104; see also Lumb, cited above n.159, pp. 78-9.

[171]This was widely offered as an explanation for the deferral rather than the outright rejection of the Appropriation Bills.

have intervened at all, there was in fact a legitimate function for him to perform. Throughout the crisis he should have been available to the leaders of both parties to act as negotiator between them. Furthermore, it would have been proper for him to assume a more positive role by intervening directly if asked to do so by the Government. This would not have left him open to a charge of partisanship. It would have been seen that he was taking the constitutionally proper course of acting on the advice of ministers who possessed throughout the confidence of the lower House. In the events which happened it is possible to argue that by his intervention the Governor-General, far from giving effect to the intention of the Constitution, positively frustrated its express provisions.

The starting point is the literal interpretation of the last paragraph of s.53 which was made in 1975 to support the proposition that the Senate has legal power to refuse supply. If this is the correct way to approach s.53, literal construction without regard to the consequences, it is presumably the correct way to approach other sections of the Constitution. The assertion of Senate power under s.53 produced a deadlock between the Houses which in all respects fulfilled the preliminary conditions of s.57, the express provision of the Constitution for the resolution of deadlocks. It follows that on a literal construction the correct course was to adhere to the further procedures of s.57 and that by intervening the Governor-General prevented this from happening.

The evident reason why this view of the matter was not taken by the Governor-General was that long before the cumbersome processes of s.57 had been worked through, the money for government services would have run out. But neither s.53 nor s.57 says anything about that. Although a good reason for not applying s.57 in a literal way, the failure of the money supply is an equally good reason for not applying s.53 in a literal way either. If the fault with s.57 is that it cannot apply effectively to the resolution of a supply crisis, the fault with s.53 is that it is capable of creating such a crisis in the first place. In truth, the technique whereby s.53 is read literally but s.57 is not is intellectually dishonest. It amounts to getting the best of both worlds, by way of maximising their respective powers, for both the Senate and the Governor-General at the expense of the House of Representatives. A less contentious procedure would have been to assume that ss. 53 and 57 were intended to work harmoniously together and to read the last paragraph of s.53 down accordingly.

As it is, we are left with two other methods of resolving a supply crisis neither of which has any but the most tenuous connection with anything actually written in the Constitution. One was advanced by the Governor-General in his statement of reasons. He argued that because s.57 was ineffective to solve deadlocks of this kind, 'Its presence in the Constitution does not cut down the reserve powers of the Governor-General'. The implications of this assertion are not clear. If it means that the Governor-General retains a reserve power to resolve such deadlocks by whatever means seem to him appropriate, including the dissolution of the Senate, it is hard to accept. The Senate is established by the Constitution in s.13 as a body with a continuing membership. It contrasts sharply in this respect with the House of Representatives, which under s.28 is to be wholly re-elected at least every three years and which under ss.5 and 28 the Governor-General is given express power to dissolve. It is a logical inference that the Senate is to be dissolved only in the extreme circumstances envisaged by s.57, and that to that extent the reserve powers of the Crown are cut down.

The second alternative was advanced by the Chief Justice, Sir Garfield Barwick, in his letter of advice to the Governor-General of 10 November 1975, and also by the Governor-General himself in his statement of reasons. They both adopt the proposition that a supply deadlock should be resolved by the resignation of the Prime Minister. If this is the correct position, it needs to be emphasized that it rests entirely on an unwritten convention which, so far as the present writers can discover, was invented for the purpose in hand in 1975. There is no precedent for it. The only way in which anything of the kind can be extracted by inference from the Constitution, which imposes no such obligation in express terms, is by combining a power in the Senate to reject supply under s.53 with the principles of responsible government obliquely incorporated in ss.61-67. This can hardly be accounted a cogent exercise because it ignores the relevance of s.57.

Lastly on s.57 and the Governor-General, it is to be observed that to the extent that, in addition to or in the alternative, the Governor-General was relying on the existence in 1975 of twenty-one other Bills which had fulfilled the conditions of s.57 for a double dissolution, his power to do so is dubious. It is an unanswered question whether as a matter of law s.57 can be used as a means of resolving a deadlock between the two Houses which does not concern any Bills which have already met the requirements of that section. Indeed, an impartial reading of s.57 suggests clearly that it was not intended to be used for the resolution of any deadlock which had not been evidenced and persisted in the manner prescribed by the section.

A possible solution to the deadlock over supply was to hold an election as soon as possible for half the Senate. Such an election was due in any event by June the following year.[172] The Prime Minister had decided to advise such an election on the morning of 11 November. It has been argued that the half-Senate election would not necessarily solve the deadlock over supply. The possibility that it would was based on the fact that although most of the newly-elected senators would not take their seats until the following June, the four new senators from the two Territories[173] and the replacements for the two casual vacancies[174] would take their seats immediately. The balance of the Senate might have been altered sufficiently thereby to enable the appropriation Bills to be passed. The result of the election might also have given a clear indication of the response of the electorate to the specific issue of the passage or rejection of supply.

On the other hand, as the Governor-General stressed in his statement, 'a half-Senate election held whilst supply continues to be denied does not guarantee a prompt or sufficiently clear prospect of the deadlock being resolved in accordance with proper principles'. The element of uncertainty sprang not only from the unpredictability of the election result[175] but also from the possibility that some State Governors might refuse to issue writs for the election under s.12. If this action had been taken by the Governors of New South Wales and Queensland, the two States in which casual Senate vacancies were to be filled, the chances of a resolution of the deadlock through a half-Senate election would have been diminished. Nevertheless, a half-Senate election offered

---

[172]There is nothing unconstitutional or even odd about a half-Senate election being held as early as this. See s.13 of the Constitution and *Report from the Joint Committee on Constitutional Review* 1959, paras. 253 and 254.

[173] *Senate (Representation of Territories) Act* 1974, s.6.

[174]Constitution, s.15.

[175]Even a full election for both Houses could not guarantee the long-term resolution of the deadlock, as is plain from the 1974 election results.

positive prospects of solving the deadlock by constitutional means. If the Governor-General had been advised by the leader of a government commanding a majority in the House of Representatives that the government wished to follow this course of action, his duty would have been to accept the advice, for it represented an attempt to resolve the crisis in a parliamentary way. In the event, the Prime Minister was dismissed before the advice was offered, which was a much more extreme course of action.

If, as he himself said in his statement,[176] the Governor-General was unwilling to accept the advice of the Prime Minister to hold a half-Senate election on the grounds that in his opinion it did not 'guarantee a prompt or sufficiently clear prospect of the deadlock being resolved', the determination of the Prime Minister's commission was not the only course of action available to him. The Governor-General was faced with a conflict between his personal belief that the interests of the nation would be better served by a course of action other than a half-Senate election, and the advice of his Prime Minister that a half-Senate election should be held. Adherence to his personal belief, and consequent rejection of the Prime Minister's advice, involved an unprecedented break with the well-established constitutional principle that the Crown acts on the advice of the representatives of the majority of the people (and has retained its nominal authority to act only because it habitually does so). There was at least some evidence on which an opinion could be based that the crisis had not yet been reached, that such a fundamental breach of constitutional convention was unjustified. If the Governor-General was unable to reconcile his opinion with the advice of his responsible ministers, it was open to him to resign or risk dismissal in the interest of the preservation of this convention.

This would not have been an empty gesture. On the contrary, it might well have been a very effective step to take, for there would have been nothing to prevent the Governor-General from publishing a statement of his reasons. His reasons could very well have included a firm expression of opinion that gentlemen who occupy the powerful and responsible positions of Prime Minister and Leader of the Opposition should not between them bring the operation of parliamentary government to the point where the Governor-General feels obliged to resign because of conflict between his conscience and the constitutional limitations within which he must act. Such an event and such an announcement, in the atmosphere of early November 1975, would very probably have had a marked effect on public opinion, and consequentially upon the political representatives of the people. It is ironical to reflect that if Sir John Kerr had taken this apparently negative step he might have emerged as something of a popular hero instead of the rather sad symbol of conflict which he has now become.

The Manner of the Dismissal

The Taking of Advice. In a matter so fraught with legal technicality and uncertain constitutional practices, and having consequences so serious for the country as a whole, it is unreasonable to expect a Governor-General to exercise any discretion which he may have, or to determine the limits of that discretion, solely on the basis of his own knowledge or expertise. Yet the source from

---

[176]'If such advice were given to me I should feel constrained to reject it . . .': (1975) 49 *Australian L.J.*, at p.648.

which he seeks advice will influence considerably his eventual decision. There is a question from whom such advice may legitimately be sought. If the principles of responsible government are accepted and adhered to, it follows that acceptable sources of advice are the Law Officers of the Crown: the Attorney-General and the Solicitor-General. As a matter of common sense, however, the advice of the Attorney-General may be unacceptable, or at least suspect, in such a case as 1975. This is so for two reasons. First, the Attorney-General is a member of the government and as such unlikely to give advice which is politically dispassionate. While this is irrelevant in the context of the duty of the Governor-General to act on the advice of his responsible ministers in the performance of his executive functions, it is highly relevant when the Governor-General is in search of an objective legal opinion which may influence his later actions. Secondly, the Attorney-General himself is not necessarily a lawyer, certainly not necessarily a good one, and may not be capable of furnishing adequate advice.

Neither of these objections applies to the Solicitor-General, who fills a statutory office, is independent and is a highly qualified lawyer. The Governor-General would not only have been justified in asking the Solicitor-General for advice but was at the very least under a moral duty to do so before embarking on such an extreme course of action. Under the provisions of the *Law Officers Act* 1964 the request would have to be submitted through the Attorney-General.[177] It does not follow, however, that the nature of the advice either sought or given need be revealed to the Government if the Governor-General does not so wish. It is known that Sir John Kerr did receive a copy of an opinion from the Solicitor-General, which he had not sought and which was not sent to him by the Solicitor-General, on the general question whether he had a *duty* to act. He neither sought nor received one on whether he had the *right* to act in the particular circumstances.

It follows from both the principles and the proprieties of responsible government that it would be proper for the Governor-General to seek advice from any other source with the agreement of the Prime Minister. However, for the reason referred to above in connection with the political affiliations of the Attorney-General, this may on occasion not be a course of action acceptable to the Governor-General.

Sir John Kerr sought and obtained the advice of the Chief Justice of the High Court of Australia. In all respects this advice corresponds closely to the actions taken subsequently by the Governor-General, and to the reasons he gave for those actions. It is unsound in principle for an approach to be made to the Chief Justice for advice in these circumstances. There is nothing in the office of Chief Justice which gives his opinion greater authority than that of any other judge on the High Court Bench,[178] but the general public is unlikely to know this. Nor could the Court as a whole be consulted, for the High Court does not give advisory opinions,[179] but the distinction between the Court and its chief judge is unlikely to be appreciated by the community at large.

---

[177]Section 12(c).

[178]Decisions in some recent constitutional cases have revealed the Chief Justice expressing opinions on matters of law which differ in substantial respects from those of the majority of the Court, e.g., *Cormack* v. *Cope* (1974) 131 C.L.R. 432; *Victoria* v. *Commonwealth (P.M.A. Case)* (1975) 7 A.L.R. 1; *Western Australia* v. *Commonwealth (Territory Senators Case)* (1975) 7 A.L.R. 159.

[179]*In re Judiciary Act 1903-20 and Navigation Act 1912-1920*; (1921) 29 C.L.R. 257.

Apart from public misapprehension there are fundamental reasons of principle why the opinion of the Chief Justice should not have been sought. Despite Sir Garfield Barwick's unargued assertion to the contrary,[180] it was far from inconceivable that the matters upon which his advice was given would be challenged before the High Court at some future time. As an instance, four judges of the High Court have found occasion already to express views on the power of the Senate to reject supply.[181] Furthermore, had the Australian Labor Party won the election and the twenty-one double dissolution Bills been passed at a joint sitting, it would have been perfectly possible for the procedural passage of any one of those twenty-one Bills to have been challenged before the High Court, directly raising some of the issues canvassed in the Chief Justice's opinion.[182] It should not have been the part either of the Chief Justice or of the Governor-General to make assumptions about the result of the election.

Surprise Tactics. When the Prime Minister arrived at the Governor-General's residence on 11 November 1975 to tender him the advice to call a half-Senate election he was handed a letter withdrawing his commission and a statement explaining the reasons for the withdrawal.[183] These tactics are understandable. If the Governor-General was determined to pursue this course of action, it was likely that it could be brought to a successful conclusion only by dismissing the Prime Minister before the Prime Minister, in turn, could advise the Queen to dismiss the Governor-General. Nevertheless the secrecy and lack of dignity entailed emphasize further the questionable wisdom of the whole affair, deriving as it does directly from the determination of the Governor-General to reject the advice of his responsible Ministers.

Caretaker Government. The new Government was commissioned by the Governor-General as a 'caretaker Government' which 'will make no appointments or dismissals or initiate new policies before a general election is held'.[184] Although these were necessary and desirable restrictions to place on a Government which was merely chosen by the Governor-General and lacked a majority in the popular House, they represented a major departure from previous constitutional practice. The Governor-General not only claimed and exercised a discretion to reject the advice of a government with a majority in the House of Representatives, and dismiss it on the basis of his own assessment of the likelihood of a political solution, and choose and commission another government, but he also devised and imposed on the latter restrictions within which it was instructed to operate. It is hard to see how such restrictions could have any legal force, but they certainly made a fitting culmination to a startling and deeply disquieting series of events.

---

[180]'. . . an existing situation which, of its nature, was unlikely to come before the Court'. Letter to the Governor-General from the Chief Justice, 10 November 1975, (1975) 49 *Australian L.J.*, at p. 648.

[181]*Victoria* v. *Commonwealth (P.M.A. Case)* (1975) 7 A.L.R. 1, at pp. 13 (Barwick CJ), 31 (Gibbs J), 50 (Stephen J), and 64 (Mason J).

[182]*Cf. Cormack* v. *Cope*, (1974) 131 C.L.R. 432; *Victoria* v. *Commonwealth (P.M.A. Case)* (1975) 7 A.L.R. 1; *Western Australia* v. *Commonwealth (Territory Senators Case)* (1975) 7 A.L.R. 159.

[183]It has been widely believed that before being handed the letter Mr Whitlam was asked by the Governor-General whether he would resign or advise an election of the House of Representatives or a double dissolution. This version of the facts derives support from the Governor-General's letter. On 8 August 1976, however, at the Melbourne University Federal Anniversary Seminar Mr Whitlam categorically denied that any such question had been put to him by the Governor-General.

[184]House of Representatives, *Debates*, 11 November 1975, no. 22, p.2928.

IV
CONCLUSION

The fundamental cause of the constitutional troubles which came upon Australia in 1975 lies in the self-contradictory character of our machinery of government. The framers of the Australian Constitution wished both to create a federal structure and to preserve parliamentary government of the British kind. These two aims were, and are, incompatible. The delegates to the constitutional Conventions attempted to make them compatible by creating the Senate as an expression of the federal idea and the House of Representatives as an expression of the parliamentary idea and combining the two in one institution.

It is clear from the examination of the Convention debates which we make in the first part of this essay that the delegates were well aware of the problem confronting them. In the end they accepted as inevitable the unsatisfactory nature of the compromise which was eventually reached. It could hardly be said that this compromise was agreed upon. It seems rather to have been the product of the impossibility of agreement. The most that those delegates who were best equipped to deal with the matter could hope for was that the compromise might survive better in practice than it seemed likely to do in the advance of the occasion. The hope proved not altogether unjustified, for it endured for nearly three quarters of a century.

Open conflict between federalism and popular democracy did not erupt until 1975. When it did, federalism won, but it is an illusion to suppose that it won in any decisive or permanent sense. The victory was dearly bought. At the time of writing there is much ground for arguing that the balance of power in the federal Parliament has shifted from the House of Representatives to the Senate, and that all that prevents this change from being a constantly obvious factor is the influence of party political discipline. It can be cogently argued further that the office of Governor-General has been suddenly transformed from a very minor manifestation of government to a highly significant one. But even if both these propositions are true, it does not follow that they will prove to be tolerable for any length of time.

The events of 1975, arising as they did out of nothing more dignified than a political brawl of unusual bitterness, were characterised to an exceptional degree by intellectual dishonesty. Most of what passed for interpretation of the Constitution by way of justifying the major events which occurred is a travesty of legal reasoning. Although it is not a matter for surprise that this should have happened, it is certainly a matter for abiding regret. The arguments which were advanced to justify a major disruption of our normal habits of political life may well be thought by many to have served their purpose and to be suitable for swift oblivion. Unfortunately this is unlikely to be the outcome. It is always more difficult to raise standards than to lower them. The standards of constitutional wisdom which were set in 1975 represented not only a sudden but also a very drastic fall in quality. It is hardly to be expected that those who suffered by the change will regard themselves as inhibited from using similar methods to their own advantage in future. Even if they were to do so, there would be others who, having seen that such a course of action cleared the path to power once, would be prepared to try it again.

The difficulty of extracting from the events of 1975 any principles of political action for the future which can be in any way welcomed has been commented on in the course of the essay. The conclusion is unavoidable that, however desirable the object of changing the government as soon as possible may have seemed to many people, the means adopted to attain that end have dealt a measure of destruction to our constitutional structure which may prove to be beyond adequate remedy. The process of adaptation to the new state of affairs may take many forms. It is always possible that the means will be found for a new set of political assumptions to arise which will modify the working of the written Constitution in directions sufficiently flexible to accommodate Australia's new governmental difficulties. It would however be unwise to rely on such a development. One of the many legacies of 1975 appears to be a strong reinforcement of literal and piecemeal modes of interpretation of the Constitution. Such a habit of mind does not produce flexibility. Secondly, any process of adaptation which has to deal with a rigid constitutional structure must depend to a great extent on accepted but unwritten rules of conduct. No one needs to be reminded of the blows dealt in 1975 to the idea that unwritten rules of conduct are at least as valuable to the community as written ones.

Not one of the public figures espousing the doctrines and tactics which prevailed in 1975 has offered comment on the problems which lie ahead as a result. Still less have their talents been made available to assist in the anticipation and solution of those problems. It has been said many times already that the losing side in 1975 has remained unduly preoccupied with its grievances ever since. Perhaps so. It can with equal justice be said that the winning side has with similar obsessiveness averted its gaze from the consequences of its own actions, except for an occasional shrill essay in self-justification. Neither attitude assists in any way towards the solution of fundamental problems whose confrontation cannot be postponed indefinitely.

COMMENTARIES

R.J. Ellicott

My comments on this lengthy essay must necessarily be selective. There are many propositions in it with which I would disagree and in the space at my disposal it would be impossible to deal with them all. Although the writers attempt a 'politically impartial examination' of the subject, the essay bears a distinct bias which I could not accept. There is also a curious intermingling and confusion of legal and political argument which, despite its obvious research, weakens considerably its value as a detached and profound analysis of the events to which it is directed.

The essay begins with a lament, which I share, that Sir Owen Dixon is no longer with us to give us the benefit of his views. Let me offer from his writings one taste of what he might have said:

> We, under our conception of democracy, so far from separating the executive and the legislature, insist on the dependence of Cabinet upon Parliament. We insist too that if a difficulty arises between the executive government and the Parliament, it shall be resolved by an appeal to the people, and we place on the representative of the Sovereign the responsibility of saying whether the case is one for the dissolution of Parliament and a general election. This we can do because we have proudly preserved the monarchy as the apex of our constitutional system.[1]

This is perhaps the most comprehensive statement he made. There are others which deal with the more limited circumstances of an executive losing the confidence of the lower House.

Considerable time is taken in the essay in an analysis of the Convention debates. This is apt for they contain a wealth of instruction on the principles underlying the Constitution and the reasoning behind sections relevant to the present debate. In the Convention records you can of course find a quotation to support almost any proposition. However in the speeches of those whose constitutional learning and political capacity stand high a number of basic and relevant propositions are expounded.

With respect to the relationship between the two Houses on money Bills, it was decided that the Constitution should make express provision and not leave it to practice to be derived from other countries. Sir Henry Parkes said at the first Convention:

> I contend that it will be absolutely necessary not to trust to derivations to be drawn from principles or practice in other countries, but to expressly provide that all money bills shall originate and undergo amendment only in the house of representatives.[2]

The framers of the Constitution did not leave the relationship between the two Houses to convention but expressly defined it in s.53.[3] The United Kingdom Parliament took a similar step in 1911. Thus, quite apart from the weakness of the argument that there has grown up a convention that the Senate will not

[1]Sir Owen Dixon, 'Government under the American Constitution' (1944) in *Jesting Pilate* (Melbourne, 1965), at p.107.

[2]Australian Constitutional Convention, *Official Record of Debates*, 1891, p.26.

[3]*Cf.* Sir Kenneth Bailey in his Introduction (1936) to H.V. Evatt, *The King and His Dominion Governors* (2nd ed., Melbourne, 1967), at pp. xxxvii-xxxviii: 'the relations between the two Houses ... have been defined and expressed in the form of law'.

exercise its intended power of rejection, there is the clear answer that s.53 itself was intended to settle the matter.

The Senate was clearly intended by the framers of the Constitution to have a power to reject money Bills. This is not really disputed by the essay and there is no need to dwell on it.

The Senate's power of rejection was intended to be a 'real living power', as Reid described it, not, as he said, 'an antiquated power never to be used'.[4] Sir Samuel Griffith described it as follows:

> But it must be remembered that it is not proposed to deny the senate the power of veto. Surely if the senate wanted to stop the machinery of government the way to do that would be to throw out the appropriation bill. That would effectively stop the machinery of government. I for my part am much inclined to think that the power of absolute rejection is a much more dangerous power than the power of amendment; yet it is a power that must be conceded. We all admit that; and in a federation there is much more likelihood of that power of rejection being used than there is of the power of amendment being used.[5]

Deakin said:

> Under this Constitution that right is given without qualification; and the special circumstances and certain special occasions are left to the Senate themselves to determine. This power of veto may be exercised absolutely.[6]

The framers of the Constitution were prepared to accept the power of rejection as consistent with responsible government. The power of amendment was not so seen and this is why the debate on it was so vital. It is expressed in a most telling way by Sir Edmund Barton:

> If the Second Chamber makes suggestions . . . and if the suggestions are not adopted, that House must face the responsibility of deciding whether it will veto the bill or not. If the procedure is to be by way of amendment and the amendments are disagreed with by the House of Representatives and are still insisted upon by the Second Chamber then it is upon the House of Representatives that the responsibility must rest of destroying its own measure . . . in the first case the responsibility rests where it should, with those who wish to negative the policy of finance upon which the entire policy of the Government hangs; because without money you cannot govern. If the policy of the Ministry according to their desires in the main is not carried out, there must be another Ministry, and those who lead to the formation of that Ministry should take the responsibility. If the procedure is by way of suggestion, which is insisted upon, the Senate must take the responsibility of the veto.[7]

There is implicit in these and other quotations two further basic constitutional propositions. First, the Senate's veto of a money Bill destroys the government's capacity to govern. Barton said:

> it is only when the fuel of the machine of government is withheld that the machine comes to a stop; and that fuel is money.[8]

Moore said:

> In this country Ministers are created and put out of office on the question of Money Bills . . . 'finance is government and government finance'.[9]

---

[4] *Official Record of Debates*, Adelaide, 1897, p.485.

[5] *Official Record of Debates*, 1891, p.429.

[6] *Official Record of Debates*, Adelaide, 1897, p.507.

[7] *ibid.*, p.557.

[8] *Official Record of Debates*, Sydney, 1897, p.620.

[9] *Official Record of Debates*, Adelaide, 1897, p.568.

Secondly, if a government's money Bills are vetoed by the Senate, there should be an election. As Deakin said:

> If the Senate decided to take the important step of rejecting the financial policy of the Executive, what would happen? It would thus challenge the policy of the Government and the Government would consult the electors.[10]

As the essay concedes, a number of the delegates conceived that party government would operate after Federation and that members and senators would divide into parties. Deakin makes this clear. It is difficult to accept that the framers of the Constitution did not have in contemplation the possibility in special circumstances of the exercise of the power even though the character of the House as a State House may have changed, for Deakin certainly did.

The application of s.57 to appropriation Bills was also well in mind. Higgins referred to it:'Keep an Appropriation Bill in your mind,' he said, 'because I am putting the most awkward case which may arise and it is quite possible that it may arise'.[11]For some delegates it was in relation to the stoppage of supply that a need for s.57 arose.[12]

I would therefore suggest that the Convention debates not only endorsed the view that the Senate was intended to have a power of rejection but it was contemplated that it would have it in circumstances with which we have recently been concerned, and that the result of refusal of supply by the Senate was that the government must go to the people.

A consideration of the Senate's present power over supply must commence with the constitutional provisions. The essay seems to concede that s. 53 construed literally and in isolation gives the Senate power to reject money Bills. For my own part I find the words of the section perfectly clear:

> Except as provided in this section, the Senate shall have equal power with the House of Representatives in respect of all proposed laws.

There is nothing else in the section which takes away the power of rejection. I have no need to dwell on the fact that this is a view which is supported by at least four of the justices of the High Court.[13] The description of it by the authors as a literal interpretation, and as a theoretical power to refuse supply, seems to me to be an attempt to use political arguments to determine what is basically a question of constitutional law.

Reference is made to other sections and particularly to s.57. There is no conflict between s.53 and s.57. As I have pointed out Barton saw s.57 as particularly necessary to resolve a deadlock arising over finance. Higgins thought it could apply. Clearly enough s.57 in its terms could apply to the rejection of a money Bill. There is nothing to prevent it given appropriate circumstances. Mr Byers agreed in his opinion.

We have followed the practice for many years of introducing a Budget in August. If it were introduced before the commencement of the financial year, as it could be, and supply was available under other measures until the end of November, s.57 could well operate to bring about a double dissolution on it.

The problem faced in October was due to the fact that the Government was

[10]*ibid.*, p.295.

[11]*Official Record of Debates*, 1898, p.2224.

[12]Barton, *Official Record of Debates*, Sydney, 1897, p.620.

[13]*Victoria* v. *Commonwealth (P.M.A. Case)* (1975) 7 A.L.R. 1, per Barwick CJ at p.13, Gibbs J at p.31, Stephen J at p.50 and Mason J at p.64.

running out of its interim supply. Had it sought and obtained interim supply, s.57 may well have operated with an election occurring in March instead of December. It never sought nor, I believe, would it have accepted it. I understand Mr Whitlam made this clear at the conference between Leaders on the morning of 11 November.

The essay also relies on implication mainly based on the alleged change in the function of the Senate. For those interested in the construction of the Constitution in accordance with the *Engineers Case*[14] this is a very curious argument. If it were to be applied to the external affairs power, Australia's external relations would still be under the aegis of Westminster. Clearly Deakin conceived of the Senate operating on party lines and exercising its power of veto. It was therefore within the contemplation of the Constitution when it was framed.

Sir Richard Eggleston has expressed the view that s.53, correctly construed, does not give power to reject supply. In my opinion this is contrary to the true construction of s.53 and appears to be a view not acceptable to a number of the Justices of the High Court. It reads words of limitation into s.53 which I think are inappropriate. Sir Richard relies on several arguments. The first is textual. He says, as I understand him, that the course for the Senate to take is specifically pointed out, i.e., to make suggestions, and that it is then for the House of Representatives to decide on those suggestions. A House considering a measure has many alternatives: it may pass, amend, defer or reject it. There is no suggestion in parliamentary practice or s.53 that one must precede the other. With respect, I think such a construction lacks an understanding of parliamentary practice. Sir Richard also relies on the fact that during the Convention debates the text of s.53 was changed to omit the words 'which the Senate may affirm or reject'. Would one argue that because the power of affirmation was expressly omitted, the Senate has no power to affirm a money Bill? I find no substance in the argument and there is no support for it in the Convention debates. He also says that the power to reject or a power to defer would confer a power to compel the acceptance of amendments. Both in logic and in political practice this is a non sequitur. There is a further argument against his view. It overlooks ss.1 and 58 of the Constitution. Section 1 vests the legislative power in the Queen, Senate and House of Representatives. Section 58 contemplates that a Bill will only be presented to the Governor-General after it has passed *both* Houses. Where a Bill is passed without the assent of both Houses under s.57 the provision expressly deems it to have been duly passed by both Houses.

Reliance is also placed on the non-use of the power by the Senate to support the existence of a convention. It will be apparent from the Convention debates that the power was regarded as one to be exercised on rare occasions. The fact that it was not exercised on a number of occasions when it might have been is only an indication of the fact that the Senate did not think it appropriate to do so. On no occasion has the Senate conceded the power to have fallen into desuetude. From the very beginning the Senate emphasised that it had a joint role with the House in the granting of supply. This occurred in 1901. It has constantly policed its rights in relation to money Bills in other respects. The true position is, as I have already emphasised, that the relationship between the two Houses in relation to money Bills has been committed to law in the

---

[14] *Amalgamated Society of Engineers v. Adelaide Steamship Co. Ltd* (1920) 28 C.L.R. 129.

Constitution. Indeed, the authors seem to concede that the earlier restraint was attributable to political factors rather than constitutional principle.

Nor can one overlook the Whitlam acceptances of the Senate's power to reject. They may be quickly summarised. First, his commitment to the report on the Constitution of 1959 which expressly acknowledges that the provision of finance by the Parliament is essential for the maintenance of responsible government and accepts the existence of the Senate's power of rejection or deferral; secondly, his two famous comments in 1970, in one of which he said of the Budget: 'we will vote against the bills here and in the Senate. Our purpose is to destroy this Budget and to destroy the Government which sponsored it';[15] thirdly, his acceptance of the existence of the power in acceding to the double dissolution of April 1974; and fourthly, his reported comments in March 1975 in relation to supply for Medibank:

> ... if there is again a refusal of a supply Bill there will certainly be an election but we see some marvellous issues to fight on, not the least Medibank.

> I don't seek a double dissolution. I am not working for one but if supply were refused there will be a double dissolution.

Early in September last I was told by a member of the Labor Party that 'Gough is not going to give in to you this time. He is going to tough it out'. From then on he proceeded to do so. May I be pardoned for thinking that Mr Whitlam's belated affection for the principle that the Senate should not reject supply smacks of political expediency.

Both the essay and the previous Government asserted that a power to reject supply is inconsistent with responsible government. I would repeat what I have already said, that it is clear that the framers of the Constitution did not so regard it. What they insisted on was that the House should have the power of determining financial policy. The Senate was to have the power of rejecting but if it exercised it, it must accept the responsibility. If this was a compromise on the British system it was a compromise written into the Constitution and it is still there.

When the Senate first deferred the Appropriation Bills on 16 October 1975 it is, I think, clear that it was exercising a power conferred on it under the Constitution. Mr Byers, in his opinion, although he referred to convention, accepts this. Indeed, by 4 November when he signed it, he concluded that the refusal of the Senate to entertain consideration of the Appropriation Bills may have amounted to a failure to pass them within the meaning of s.57. That is to say, a constitutional process was under way. It was a process which the Governor-General could not ignore for it was his duty to execute and maintain the Constitution and the laws of the Commonwealth. Even if, contrary to my view, there were a convention, the Senate was ignoring it. The law of the Constitution had to prevail as it had to in 1909 when Asquith went to the people.

Before dealing further with the dismissal of the Government, I should like to quote from the late Sir Kenneth Bailey:

> One of the distinctive features of the British constitution . . . is the combination of the democratic principle that all political authority comes from the people, and hence that

---

[15]House of Representatives, *Debates*, 25 August 1970, vol. 69, p.463. The other comment was made in respect of proposed receipt duty legislation in House of Representatives, *Debates*, 12 June 1970, vol. 68, pp. 3495-6: 'Any Government which is defeated by the Parliament on a major taxation Bill should resign . . . This Bill will be defeated in another place. The Government should then resign'.

the will of the people must prevail, with the maintenance of a monarchy armed with legal powers to dismiss ministers drawn from among the people's elected representative and even to dissolve the elected legislature itself. In normal times the very existence of those powers can simply be ignored. In times of crisis, however, it immediately becomes of vital importance to know what they are and how they will be exercised ... It is not too much to say that the whole future of the British constitutional system is likely to depend on the extent to which, in the next few years, it is demonstrated that the reserve powers of the Crown are not the antithesis but the corollary of the democratic principle that political authority is derived from the people.[16]

It is apparent from a reading of the Constitution that some powers are given to the Governor-General in Council and others simply to the Governor-General. It is, I think, significant that the powers of dissolution conferred by ss. 5 and 57 are given to the Governor-General. It is also significant that under ss. 63 and 64 Executive Councillors and Ministers of State are to hold office during the pleasure of the Governor-General. I believe the framers of the Constitution clearly had the question of reserve power well in mind. It was recognised that there were times when the Governor-General had to make a decision himself, even though the responsibility for it would be accepted by advisers. Just as Mr Fraser had to accept responsibility for the dismissal of Mr Whitlam.

There is no space to debate the existence of the reserve power either to refuse a dissolution or to dismiss ministers. Evatt and Forsey, both of whom were socialists, give many illustrations. A Governor-General could properly conclude from these works that these powers still existed. My own view is that these powers exist and under our Constitution as presently framed are necessary to deal with extreme cases. They are there to protect the people as Sir Kenneth suggests. Again note that Mr Byers in his opinion does not deny the existence of the reserve power. He was more concerned with whether there was a duty to exercise it.

Of course if it were not for the reserve powers the Governor-General would be a mere automaton to do the bidding of a Prime Minister. This was and is the Whitlam view. But as recently as October 1972 Sir Paul Hasluck had said:[17]

It is not that the Governor-General ... can over-rule elected representatives of the people but in the ultimate he can check the elected representatives in any extreme attempt by them to disregard the rule of law or the customary usages of Australian government and he could do so by forcing a crisis.

In relation to dissolution, he said:

It is open to the Governor-General to obtain advice on the constitutional question from other quarters—perhaps from the Chief Justice, the Attorney-General or eminent counsel—and then a solemn responsibility rests on him to make a judgment on whether a dissolution is needed to serve the purpose of good government by giving to the electorate the duty of resolving a situation which Parliament cannot resolve for itself. In crude terms the case for dissolving Parliament in mid-term is that Parliament has become unworkable.

---

[16]Bailey, cited above n.3, at p.xxxv.

[17]William Queale Memorial Lecture, delivered in Adelaide on 24 October 1972. An edited text is published in the *Australian*, 23 October 1975.

In February 1975, in India, Sir John Kerr also asserted the independence of the Governor-General. Both Governors-General would, of course, accept the proposition that he must act upon the advice of ministers. I have not space to develop it but this was implicit in every action Sir John Kerr took.

During October the Governor-General made clear to the Government his concern as to his powers and duties. He sought advice on a statement I had issued. At the same time he sought information from the Treasurer and the Attorney-General about the crisis. These actions were not consistent with the Governor-General accepting the role of an automaton. This should have been obvious to Mr Whitlam. However, he took the view and committed himself to it that the Governor-General must follow his advice and none other. We do not know what passed between him and the Governor-General except that the Governor-General in his letter said:

> You have previously told me that you would never resign or advise an election of the House of Representatives or a double dissolution . . .[18]

I could not believe that Sir John Kerr would have written that had it not been true.

When a Parliament moves into a crisis situation such as occurred in October 1975, there is a great need for statesmanship on the part of the Crown's chief adviser for this is the Crown's protection. He is under a special duty to give that advice which will resolve the crisis without involving the Crown's representative in it personally. When Asquith's Finance Bill was rejected by the House of Lords in 1909 he immediately went to the people. He knew what was the correct course of action. So did Deakin, Barton, Churchill and Attlee. But they were statesmen. Our country's chief lament about these events must be that Prime Minister Whitlam did not act like a statesman for that is what the occasion demanded.

The Governor-General has been accused of deceit and impropriety in the most contemptuous manner possible. Such words come easily to the mouth of a demagogue. But from lawyers a more objective analysis is required. Attempts are still being made to fan ill-will against him. If any lawyer lends himself to this he bears a heavy responsibility for what is involved is a person and his reputation and the office itself. The only way for a fair-minded lawyer to judge this charge is to sit for a moment himself in the Governor-General's chair and at the same time ask himself: what did Sir John have to gain from dismissing Whitlam? This is how I choose to answer this essay with which I am in basic disagreement.

Let me quickly outline a number of known and relevant facts and a number of propositions that a person in his position could reasonably adopt:

(a) the Senate had power under the Constitution to reject or defer supply;
(b) even if there was an argument to support the existence of a convention against deferral or rejection, he, the Governor-General, was bound by what the Constitution said;
(c) there was strong support for the view both on a reading of the Constitution and a consideration of Evatt and Forsey that he had reserve powers relating to dismissal and dissolution;

---

[18]Letter from Governor-General to Mr Whitlam, 11 November 1975: (1975) 49 *Australian L.J.,* at p.646.

(d) Mr Whitlam and Ministers were emphasising by word and action the seriousness of the lack of supply. Mr Whitlam was asserting that he would not have an election at least for a year, that he was going to smash the Senate, and making it clear that he would not resign. Mr Byers said: 'the Ministry has not resigned and will not do so';

(e) by early November the Government was making overtures to the banks to arrange by some method payment of public servants and public accounts. Some of the banks apparently received advice that these arrangements would not be within power. Written into the Constitution is the principle that a Government cannot spend money from the Treasury except under the authority of an Act of Parliament. The Constitution contemplates an executive responsible to the Parliament and obtaining its supply from the Parliament. The framers of the Constitution in passages I have quoted clearly thought that a government denied supply by the Senate must go to the people. An executive which seeks to stay in power with money obtained elsewhere or by devices to achieve the same end is clearly subverting this basic principle. In any event, the device suggested could only be temporary and could not cover all situations of government. There had to be a moment of truth;

(f) by early November it was apparent that the ordinary supply was to run out by late November;

(g) a request for an election for a half-Senate was delayed until November 11 and it was at least a reasonable view that such an election would not provide a clear solution to the problem;

(h) the Senate was strongly maintaining its attitude, and offers of compromise had been discussed and rejected between Leaders. The Solicitor-General suggested that the Senate had already failed to pass the Bills;

(i) it was clear that if an election was to be held before Christmas a decision to do so had to be made around November 11 to 13. If not then held it would be difficult to hold such an important election before late February;

(j) at no time had interim supply been sought by the Prime Minister as he could have had he accepted the view which his Solicitor-General expressed that s.57 could apply. Indeed, on the morning of 11 November I understand that he had made it clear that he would neither seek nor accept interim supply even during a half-Senate election;

(k) one previous Governor-General had sought advice from a Chief Justice and another had recently said it was proper. The Chief Justice in fact advised that the Senate and the Governor-General had the powers in question;

(l) on 11 November Mr Whitlam himself confronted the Governor-General with a decision on a half-Senate election. The fact that it was a day for a decision was confirmed.

In those circumstances, knowing that in a month the country would probably be facing financial chaos and what that could mean to its people, its economy and to civil order—what would any one in Sir John Kerr's shoes have done?

If you believed that the Constitution appeared to give the Senate this power (even though you might have thought its actions wrong), knew that a half-Senate election would in all probability not solve the problem, knew that you were after all choosing a course which in the circumstances the Constitution permitted of sending the whole Parliament to the people, would you have thought it unreasonable to take this course? Would you have felt condemned if you had?

These are considerations and questions which need to be carefully pondered before judgment is passed. If harsh judgment is passed and the demagogue is acclaimed, I believe this is not only unjustly condemning a man who to this time had had an unblemished record of public service: it is also to undermine the office he holds and to play into the hands of elements bent on undermining our basic fabric. The lawyers of Australia have a very heavy responsibility.

Sir Richard Eggleston

I have read with great interest the historical survey provided by the authors, but I remain in some doubt as to what their attitude to the question of construction is. Do they agree with me that on the true construction of s.53, the Senate has no power to reject supply? Or do they think that the final words of the section confer that power? If the second view is the one they espouse, do they arrive at that conclusion from an examination of the words of the section, using only traditionally accepted materials in aid; or do they think that it is permissible to look at the Convention debates with a view to finding out what was in the minds of the delegates?

My position is the traditional one. Whenever a written document is accepted as the embodiment of the intentions of the parties to it, what they agree to be bound by is the document as construed by whatever tribunal has jurisdiction to do so. It is not open to them to point to statements made by individual parties in the course of the negotiations for the purpose of proving that their intention was something different from what they have said in the document. Where the intention of the legislature is embodied in a statute, the debates in Parliament will not be looked at by the courts. But in the case of the Constitution, the position is much less favourable to the use of the Convention debates. What the delegates were doing was to produce a draft for submission to the people in a referendum. This draft in turn was to be submitted to the Imperial Parliament for enactment as a statute. In the event, it was altered still further before it was finally adopted. New South Wales refused to accept the deadlock provisions as settled in 1898 and insisted that they should be altered; they were so altered as a result of a Premiers' Conference in 1899.

In truth the delegates had no higher status than draftsmen, and moreover, draftsmen who, as the debates show, frequently misunderstood the significance of what they were doing. For example, the delegates refused to alter the words in s.56 from 'the House in which the proposal originated' to words referring only to the lower House, despite the fact that it was pointed out to them that because of the terms of s.53, such proposals could not originate in the Senate.

As the authors point out,[1] the delegates did not regard the rejection by the Senate of a Bill appropriating money for the ordinary annual services of government as a serious possibility. To the passages there referred to one may add this exchange, on 9 March 1898:

Mr McMillan (N.S.W.): . . . I can scarcely imagine the Senate rejecting a Bill which would put the finances into any difficulty—say, the usual Bill for the expenses of the country . . .

Mr Trenwith (Victoria): . . . It is admitted generally that the Executive will allow some reasonable time, probably not less than three months, but it is urged that there may be occasions when, if a Bill is not carried, the whole of the finances of the Commonwealth will be thrown into confusion. That could only happen on the rejection of an Appropriation Bill.

Mr McMillan: . . . Which would mean revolution?

Mr Trenwith: . . . Yes, and that is inconceivable.[2]

[1]Above, p.257.
[2]Australian Constitutional Convention, *Official Record of Debates*, 1898, p.2165.

In truth, as the authors have said, many changes were made in the federal scheme between 1891 and 1899, the principal ones being in the direction of greater power for the lower House. Indeed complaints that the powers of the Senate were being eroded were frequently voiced by delegates. In particular, the deadlock provisions were introduced and refined, attaining their final form (except for the alteration made by the Premiers) in 1898; and the provision for responsible government was introduced between 1891 and 1897. The significance of this latter change is brought out by a remark of Barton's in the final stages of the Convention:

> We might perhaps have made the two Houses of the Federal Legislature entirely co-ordinate, and that we could not do with responsible government.[3]

The argument against reliance on the omission of the word 'reject' from s.53 may be stated as follows: no one drew attention to the significance of the omission, therefore it should be inferred that the delegates did not intend to change the meaning from what it had been in the previous draft.

As I have pointed out, the intention of the delegates was not the significant thing, but in any case, when s.53 was before the Convention in the form recommended by the drafting committee, Mr Isaacs drew attention to the fact that the words 'if it thinks fit' had been omitted from the section. He said:

> I do not think that there would be any legal difference, so far as I can see at the moment, if they were omitted, but they were put in with a very distinct object, and I am sure the presence of the words had weight with some honourable members, as showing that to grant the power of suggestion was not as great as to grant the power of amendment. I think it will be better to leave in the words.[4]

After the comment by Mr Barton referred to by the authors,[5] Mr Isaacs moved that the words be restored, and this was done. In the light of this passage, it is difficult to imagine that no delegate observed the omission of the vital words 'affirm or reject' which had been dropped from the section, and to which the observation of Mr Isaacs applied with equal force.

If we abandon the search for the intention in the minds of the delegates, and construe the words according to the well-established rules of construction, what result do we get?

The conventional view of the section, which asserts the right of the Senate to reject all Bills, of whatever kind, is based on the view that the last sentence, 'Except as provided in this section, the Senate shall have equal power with the House of Representatives in respect of all proposed laws', was intended to confer a power of rejection in respect of those Bills which the Senate could not amend. But this is to assume the very thing that has to be established, namely, that the preceding words of the section do not by implication deny the power of the Senate to reject a Bill which it may not amend. For if the preceding words, properly construed, do deny that power, the words 'Except as provided in this section' preserve that denial intact.

Do the preceding words deny the Senate the power of rejection? In my opinion they do, for the following reasons. First, I have already referred to the omission from the earlier draft of the words 'affirm or reject'. In *Tasmania* v.

---

[3] *ibid.*, p.2470.
[4] *ibid.*, p.2450.
[5] Above, p.264.

Commonwealth and Victoria[6] the Court ruled that the successive drafts could be referred to as an aid to interpretation, and Barton J said:

> The successive alterations of the drafts seem rather to point to the view, not that the final provisions are to be interpreted in the same sense as those struck out of the draft, but that the first intentions were given up, and that entirely different intentions, to be gathered from the language of the Constitution, are those by which we are to abide.[7]

A similar view was expressed by Griffith CJ.[8] As I have pointed out, the attention of the delegates was drawn to the omission of the words 'if it thinks fit', so that even if we do have recourse to the debates, the force of the point is hardly diminished.

Secondly, the section expressly states that the Senate may send a message requesting the omission or amendment of any item or provisions in a money Bill. Not much significance would attach to this provision if there had been any doubt about the right of one House to send messages to the other, but the present practice of the Houses in Britain as to sending messages was established in 1855[9] and the inclusion of an express provision strongly suggests that it was intended to exclude other action by the Senate in respect of Bills which it could not amend. As the majority of the High Court said in the *Boilermakers' Case*[10]:

> The fact that affirmative words appointing or limiting an order or form of things may have also a negative force and forbid the doing of the thing otherwise was noted very early in the development of the principles of interpretation: 1 Plowden 113.[11]

Thirdly, the words 'if it thinks fit', insisted on by Mr Isaacs, make it clear that the final decision as to whether any omissions or amendments suggested by the Senate should be made rests with the lower House. It would clearly be anomalous if the lower House had the final say as to all omissions short of total rejection, but the Senate still had power to reject the whole.

Fourthly, the construction which allows the Senate power to reject money Bills, and to send messages requesting amendments or omissions, while denying power to amend, leads to an absurd result. In the ordinary course of the parliamentary process, if one House amends a Bill sent to it by the other, the originating House can either accept or reject the amendment. If it rejects it, the second House can either reject the Bill, or agree to pass it as it was originally. If the Senate has power to reject money Bills, the Senate's power in relation to such Bills is indistinguishable from its power in relation to Bills which do not fulfil that description. If one adds to that a power to defer the Bill upon conditions (an addition that is essential if the events of 11 November 1975 are to survive scrutiny) the position is even more absurd. The fact is that the drafts of 1891 and 1897 contained this absurdity, and the final version of the 1898 draft removed it.

Finally, the form of the deadlock provisions affords a powerful argument that it was not intended to allow the Senate to force an election by refusing the

---

[6](1904) 1 C.L.R. 329.

[7]*ibid.,* at p.351.

[8]*ibid.,* at p.335.

[9]*Erskine May's Parliamentary Practice,* ed. Sir Barnett Cocks (18th ed., London, 1971), pp. 589-90.

[10]*R. v. Kirby; Ex parte Boilermakers' Society of Australia* (1956) 94 C.L.R. 254; afd. [1957] A.C. 288.

[11](1956) 94 C.L.R.254, at p.270.

government an appropriation to cover the ordinary annual services. Section 57 provides that in the event of a deadlock, a procedure can be put into effect which requires a minimum of three months for the resolution of the crisis. If an election for the lower House is due in less than six months, the procedure cannot be operated at all. The logical outcome of consideration of the deadlock provisions would be a recognition of their unsuitability to resolve a crisis brought about by the refusal of ordinary supply. Two solutions would be open—either to produce a procedure that would enable such a crisis to be resolved, or to amend the draft, by omitting the provision giving the Senate power to reject such supply, so that such a deadlock could never arise. It is of course to be noted that the appropriation Bills which the Senate is forbidden to amend are confined to those for the ordinary annual services of the government.

As we have seen, the possibility of the Senate refusing to pass that kind of appropriation Bill was regarded by many of the delegates as quite remote. The possibility of rejection of a taxing Act presented other problems, which the Convention did not grapple with in any event.

It will be seen from what I have said that the argument against the view I have taken depends almost entirely on the absence of any comment by the delegates as to the omission of the words 'affirm or reject'. Since we do not know what went on in the drafting committee, the reasons for the change remain speculation. But the change was made, and if, as the High Court has so far continuously maintained, we are not to look at the debates, even this basis for the interpretation disappears.

When we turn to the question of deferral, the argument for the impropriety of what was done by the Senate is even stronger. Section 55 provides that laws imposing taxation shall deal only with the imposition of taxation, and any provision therein dealing with any other matter shall be of no effect. Section 54 provides that the proposed law which appropriates revenue or moneys for the ordinary annual services of the government shall deal only with such appropriation. Clearly, the intention was that money Bills should not be used by the lower House to attempt to compel the Senate to agree to something not connected with the financial matters specified. There did not appear to be any need to provide that the upper House was not to attempt tacking, since the upper House had no power to amend such a Bill. But the course adopted by the majority in the Senate on the motion for the second reading of the Appropriation Bill, on 16 October 1975, was an attempt to do indirectly what the Senate could not do directly, i.e. to use the Bill as a means of compelling the lower House to do something quite unrelated to the provisions of the Bill, without rejecting the Bill itself. The amendment proposed to change the motion for the second reading by substituting the words 'this Bill be not further proceeded with until the Government agrees to submit itself to the judgment of the people . . .' (then follow the statements of the reasons on which the motion was based).

The motion was in fact in conflict with the Senate Standing Orders which provide that no amendment to the motion for the second reading can be accepted unless it is relevant to the subject matter of the Bill, except one to defer consideration for six months, which, if accepted, 'shall finally dispose of the Bill'.[12] But no one took this point. Senator Cavanagh did take the point that

---

[12]Senate Standing Orders 194 and 195. See the comments of Barwick CJ in *Victoria* v. *Commonwealth* (*P.M.A. Case*) (1975) 7 A.L.R. 1, at p.13.

the Bill could not be amended, and Senator Melzer, who was in the Chair, ruled that the amendment was only to a procedural motion, and allowed the amendment to be voted on.

Whatever may be said about the rejection of supply, a possibility which the delegates, at least until 1898, were prepared to tolerate because it seemed so unlikely an event, I think the deferral was clearly improper. If the Senate can not only send messages requesting amendment, and reject the Bill if these requests are not complied with, but can also tack conditions to its willingness even to consider the ordinary annual appropriations, it is impossible to see the point of the elaborate provisions of s.53. It is also impossible to see what more the advocates of Senate power could possibly have gained. As the events of last year have demonstrated, that interpretation makes the Senate superior, not co-ordinate.

Two questions have to be asked. When the four members of the High Court in the *P.M.A. Case*[13] expressed the view that the Senate had power to reject supply, what material were they relying on, and if it included reference to the Convention debates, when was the rule of construction changed?

The second question is, if the action of the Senate on 16 October 1975 was unconstitutional, what should have been the consequence? To this question a variety of answers, which I have not space to discuss, could be given. One answer which clearly could not have been given was the dismissal of the Prime Minister and the installation of the Leader of the Opposition in his place.

---

[13](1975) 7 A.L.R. 1, per Barwick CJ at p.13, Gibbs J at p.31, Stephen J at p.50 and Mason J at p.64. The opinion of the Chief Justice was of course reiterated in his letter of 10 November 1975 to the Governor-General: (1975) 49 *Australian L.J.*, at p.648.

PART FOUR

A LABOR RETROSPECT

Mr Whitlam's account of his prime ministership ranges over the whole subject matter of this book: the evolution of a new pattern of relationships between federal, State and local government; the creative approach adopted toward the restructuring of government machinery and the utilization of the Commonwealth's own legislative and executive powers; the reaction of the courts to the Labor Government's various initiatives; and the role played by the Senate and the Governor-General — and the Chief Justice — in ensuring the Government's final demise. Of particularly compelling interest is the sustained critique, mounted in Part IV of the essay, of certain aspects of the High Court's procedure and decision-making performance, and Mr Whitlam's own perception of the events of 11 November and their implications for the future of Australian social democracy.

9 The Labor Government and the Constitution

E.G. Whitlam

I
THE RELEVANCE OF THE CONSTITUTION

The irrelevance of Australia's written Constitution was demonstrated more in the last three-quarters of 1975 than in the first three-quarters of this century. Its irrelevance was not seen in any impediments it placed in the way of contemporary legislation during my Government's term of office. In fact, as interpreted by the High Court, the Constitution allowed my Government a considerable degree of freedom compared with Labor administrations in the past. The great reforming Governments of Deakin and Chifley were much frustrated by decisions of the High Court; mine was not. Rather, the irrelevance of the Constitution was seen in its total failure to make provision for the realities of our political system and what ought to be the foundations of the democratic process. It was the machinery of government under the Constitution that was shown to be inadequate, not the Australian government's legislative power. It was this irrelevance which made possible the unprecedented actions of State governments, the Senate, the Chief Justice and the Governor-General during 1975. These actions were all unconstitutional in the English sense, in that they all were breaches of long established conventions. I am concerned to show that those actions must never be accepted as precedents—not by politicians, still less by lawyers.

The Labor Government was in power from 5 December 1972 to 11 November 1975. I shall deal with the constitutional issues during that period under four headings: the interlocking functions of federal, State and regional government; the fuller use of the Commonwealth's own legislative responsibilities; the interpretations and administration of the High Court; and the conduct of the Senate, the Crown and the Chief Justice.

II
FEDERAL, STATE AND LOCAL GOVERNMENT RELATIONS

In 1944 Curtin sponsored a referendum to give the federal Parliament the necessary powers for efficient regulation of a modern peacetime economy. The referendum failed, but Curtin's objectives are still important. I believed then, as I still do, that the distribution of powers between the Australian government and the States under the Constitution, appropriate enough for a transitional government of a group of former colonies, is wholly inadequate to the needs of a modern federal state.

My support for constitutional amendments to give the Australian government greater powers and my exploration of the limits of its existing powers have left

me with the reputation of a committed centralist. I don't object to the term—it
has far more abusive connotations for others than it has for me—but it conveys
only part of my attitude. Certainly I believe that the Constitution ought to be
amended to give the Australian government powers comparable to those of
other democracies, particularly in the area of economic regulation. Certainly I
believe that if the government of the post-war suburbs of our great cities, and
the running of our education, health and transport systems, are left to the
States, then our political machinery will be neither efficient, equitable nor
responsive. But it is a grotesque caricature to depict the philosophy of my
Government in purely centralist terms.[1] The whole thrust of the program of
the Labor Government was to provide a proper relationship between the tasks
discharged by all three tiers of our federal system.

In September 1971 I outlined the approach Labor would follow in government in the following terms:

> Each of our three levels of government has functions which it is best able to perform.
> The key to effective performance is not domination but consultation, not centralisa-
> tion but co-ordination.[2]

Far from centralising all power in the Australian government, the Labor
Government did more to achieve a meaningful devolution of power than any of
its predecessors. We did so by recognising that a real devolution of power
depended on a proper recognition of the role of local government and incentives
for local authorities to work together. Our policies made possible a *co-operative*
attack on the problems confronting State and local governments and the
day-to-day needs of the people.

Efficiency, equality, responsiveness—those were the hallmarks of Labor's
approach to federalism. Efficiency has never been the strong point of our federal
system, but in many respects we were able to make the system work better.
Where we saw the need for short-term, emergency action in the public sector—for example, in the underfinanced and historically neglected areas of
sewerage and urban transport—we allocated the necessary funds. Where we saw
the need for a continuing government responsibility we set up permanent
commissions to allocate resources and determine priorities. The Schools
Commission, for example, permitted co-operative planning for the needs of all
children, no matter where they lived or what type of school they attended. It
enabled a much more rational distribution of the increased funds we provided
for education and relieved the States of much of the burden on their budgets.
But we never regarded inadequate finance as the only cause of inefficiency
under the federal system. Lack of planning was another. The States, through
lack of planning, created a wholly inefficient conglomeration of transport
systems. Section 101 of the Constitution envisaged an Inter-State Commission
as a mechanism for co-ordinating and planning a national policy on trade and
commerce. Transport is obviously a key element in trade and commerce.
Australians who live in Tasmania, in the Riverina, in Western Australia, are
acutely aware of the inefficiencies of our State-based transport systems with
their different freight rates and limited services. It was a measure of how
irrational the centralism of the States can be that our legislation to restore the

---

[1] See E.G. Whitlam, 'The New Federalism: A Review of Labor's Programs and Policies' in
Making Federalism Work: Towards a More Efficient, Equitable and Responsive Federal System, ed.
R.L. Mathews (Canberra, 1976).

[2] E.G. Whitlam, 'A New Federalism' *Australian Quarterly*, vol. 43, 4 (1971), at p.17.

Inter-State Commission, a body designed to tackle a problem which can only be tackled nationally and envisaged as long ago as 1900 by the founding fathers, was resisted by some States as an attack on their rights.

The Inter-State Commission was designed to serve as well the second aim of Labor's federalism, greater equality. Inequalities between regions in transport costs have been a concern of mine for years, but they were not the only inequalities which concerned my Government. When Labor came to power we found, for example, inequalities within Australia in terms of access to education. The Pre-School Commission and the Children's Commission were designed to overcome these inequalities. The abolition of fees at tertiary institutions was designed to assure greater equality of access to higher education. We found great inequalities between regions in matters within the responsibility of local government. We therefore legislated to require the Grants Commission to promote equality between regions by means of direct grants to local authorities, just as it had formerly promoted equality between the States.

Efficiency and equality, then, were key aspects of Labor's approach to federalism. But the most novel, and perhaps the most interesting aspect, was the idea of responsiveness. In 1971 I said:

> We will not return power to the people simply by concentrating assistance on the existing States. A meaningful devolution of power will be effected in this country only when we provide local authorities with the means and incentives to associate freely on the basis of shared urban and regional interests. The new federalism will rest on a national framework for the establishment of investment priorities and a regional framework for participation in all those areas which most directly determine the quality of our lives.[3]

The key to our efforts was local government. It was essential to involve local government as a full partner in the federal system. When the Constitution was drawn up local government was rudimentary; it was not mentioned in the Constitution. Today local government is extensive and complex. If the Constitution were being drawn up today it could not fail to give prominence to local government. The States, however, have given local government many powers which it is too impoverished to discharge. The States have starved local government. Our legislation for the Australian Assistance Plan, upheld by the High Court, has shown that it is possible to make grants to local government, just as it is possible to make grants to the States under the Constitution. It is not necessary to amend the Constitution to enable grants to be made to local government, but there is still a need to amend it with regard to local government loans. The federal government lacks the power to take over local government debts. They remain a heavy burden on local authorities. Indeed, the financial position of local government in funding its debts is as serious as was that of the States in 1927, which led to the present Financial Agreement.

In 1973, to help involve local government as a full partner in the federal system, I made it a condition of Australian government participation in the Constitutional Convention that local government be directly represented. At the Convention's session in Melbourne in 1975 I supported resolutions designed to give constitutional recognition to direct financial relationships between the Australian government and local government—an issue which, at my initiative, was again to be considered at the October 1976 session of the

---

[3]E.G. Whitlam, 'A New Federalism' *Australian Quarterly*, vol. 43, 4 (1971), at p.17.

Convention in Hobart. We proposed an amendment of the Financial Agreement to give semi- and local government authorities a voice and a vote at the Loan Council. The Australian Assistance Plan and the Area Improvement Program were examples of programs designed to make our federal system responsive to the needs of the people by involving authorities at the local level in planning, decision-making and implementation.

I believe we left a permanent legacy of constitutional reform in local government. Not all our aims were achieved; we are still a considerable distance from proper constitutional recognition of the federal government's ability to deal directly with local government. Not all our gains for local government are being maintained; the Fraser Government has already announced that the Grants Commission will be replaced by seven separate bodies, putting local government once more at the mercy of State governments and preventing a national approach to regional inequalities. There have, however, already been gains of lasting significance. In the longer term the most important may prove to be the least tangible, namely, the changed expectations of local government about its right to help plan and implement government policy, and the changed expectations of citizens about their ability to influence and participate in the processes of government. Regardless of future government policy at the centre, there is now a growing demand for participation by the community in the decisions that affect people's lives. The success of our federal system will depend, at least in part, on its success in meeting that demand.

The main constitutional legacy of our federalism has been the precedent for wider use of the Australian government's financial powers. It was commonplace before the Labor Government came to office for tied grants under s.96 of the Constitution to be made to the States. What had never before been attempted was the use of those grants to achieve far-reaching reforms in education, medical services, hospitals, sewerage, transport and other urban and regional development programs. In virtually all these areas we set up expert independent inquiries whose reports were made public and became the basis of our legislative reforms. The extent of our concern and scale of our grants were more than justified by the problems faced by our cities and towns. The way the grants were made showed how a reform government can operate effectively within the Constitution. To ensure that the grants were used to meet the most pressing needs we increased greatly the percentage of tied grants—from about 30 per cent to over 50 per cent of the total of all grants. We did so not from any wish to dictate from the centre, but to ensure that the problems identified by expert inquiries were tackled promptly and effectively in accordance with the expressed wishes of the electorate.

My Government also employed for the first time on any scale direct money grants 'for the purposes of the Commonwealth' under s.81. For a number of reasons the making of grants through State governments unnecessarily complicates the machinery of government. In the case of the Australian Assistance Plan and the Australian Legal Aid Office, for example, several States had shown either their unwillingness or their inability to provide urgently needed services. In both cases my Government made direct grants of funds under s.81. Our grants in this form under the Australian Assistance Plan were upheld by the High Court—as indeed, were all our other constitutional innovations. In the case of the Australian Assistance Plan the High Court[4] made it clear that the Australian government could exercise its prerogative powers as the executive government on all matters of concern to Australia as a nation and not merely on those expressly within Commonwealth legislative power. As Jacobs J said:

> The Constitution envisages the exercise of the prerogative through the Governor-General in those matters appertaining to the Government of the Commonwealth in its provision by s.61 that the executive power of the Commonwealth extends to the execution and maintenance of the Constitution . . . The extent of its exercise . . . has throughout the years of federation been a growing extent. The area of its exercise on the advice of Australian Ministers is limited by the terms of the Constitution. Primarily its exercise is limited to those areas which are expressly made the subject matter of Commonwealth legislative power. But it cannot be strictly limited to those subject matters. The prerogative is now exercisable by the Queen through the Governor-General acting on the advice of the Executive Council on all matters which are the concern of Australia as a nation.[5]

I emphasise those words 'all matters which are the concern of Australia as a nation'. They are the key to the High Court's judgment. They are the key to effective Australian government in a modern society. The State of Victoria had contended that 'the purposes of the Commonwealth' in s.81 are restricted to those purposes for which the Australian Government is empowered to make laws. As Murphy J said:

> The chilling effect that such an interpretation would have on governmental and parliamentary initiatives is obvious. It is not a formula for operating a Constitution. It is one for stultifying government.[6]

Indeed, as Murphy J and some of his brothers point out, if the Victorian submission were correct, the general economic management of the economy—seen by most Australians as the most important task of the Australian government—would be beyond its power. The *A.A.P. Case* presents Australian governments with great opportunities to tackle national problems through the appropriation power. I doubt whether the present federal Government will be as anxious as we were to test the limits of that decision, but a future Labor government will certainly accept the opportunity offered by the Court and seek a proper financial relationship between the three tiers of our federal system.

I mention one further development in the federal system during Labor's term. In the *Offshore Sovereignty Case*[7] the High Court decided that the Commonwealth and not the States had sovereign rights to explore and exploit the natural resources of the continental shelf. By no means all the reasoning used by the High Court in reaching that conclusion will appeal to those of us who applaud its judgment, but we can all agree that in a federal system the only rational outcome to this case was the recognition of Commonwealth sovereignty. The way is now open for a reformist national government to involve itself in national problems too long ignored. The Court's decision also offers the prospect of a sensible resolution of the border problems in the Torres Strait—a problem which my Government was unable to resolve in the absence of a clear constitutional power to act. The way is now open for comprehensive legislation for the management of the marine environment and for the

[4] *Victoria* v. *Commonwealth (A.A.P. Case)* (1975) 7 A.L.R. 277.
[5] *ibid.*, at pp. 333-4.
[6] *ibid.*, at p.345.
[7] *New South Wales* v. *Commonwealth* (1975) 8 A.L.R. 1.

management of its resources. The way is also now open for a comprehensive offshore mining code.

In August 1975 I concluded a paper[8] on Labor's federalism with the following words:

> I believe the record of the past two and a half years justifies the assertion that the Australian Government has tried to inject a new life into the Australian federal system and a new meaning into Australian federalism. It has not been done through any mindless, centralist doctrine, but by a genuine effort to build more modern, efficient machinery at all levels of government. It has been a genuine, creative, constructive, co-operative effort to make Australian federalism more efficient, more equitable and, above all, more responsive to the people of Australia wherever they live.

I stand by those words.

III
THE COMMONWEALTH'S LEGISLATIVE RESPONSIBILITIES

Labor carried out its policies under a federal system largely by using the Australian government's spending powers in ways that had not previously been contemplated. But our attempts to expand the traditional limits of the Constitution were not limited to the spending powers. We sought to pursue our programs through use of the legislative powers specifically conferred on the Commonwealth by s.51. We were successful; and our success demonstrated that a reform government can achieve many of its aims within the Constitution as it stands.

I had not always been confident that Labor could achieve its legislative aims without extensive constitutional amendment. In 1957 I chose for the title of my Chifley Memorial Lecture 'The Constitution *versus* Labor', a title which indicated my own feelings of frustration at the limitations placed on reform by the Constitution as it was then interpreted. I concluded my address in the following terms:

> The way of the reformer is hard in Australia. Our parliaments work within a constitutional framework which enshrines Liberal policy and bans Labor policy. Labor has to persuade the electorate to take two steps before it can implement its reforms: first to elect a Labor Government, then, to alter the Constitution.[9]

In time, however, particularly after my experience on the Joint Committee on Constitutional Review from 1956 to 1959, I came to believe that much could be done within the strictures imposed by the Constitution as it stood. By 1961 I was able to conclude a similar speech in more optimistic terms. I said:

> The Australian Government has as much constitutional freedom as any other national government to plan the public sector in Australia and to make arrangements with other countries. Through its financial hegemony it can create better conditions in transport, housing, education and health; it can create new industries; it can create new communities. Through international arrangements it can share in the more orderly and equitable production, distribution and exchange of goods and skills. Socialists have to play the most dynamic role in the relatively skilled and affluent community inhabiting our remote, dependent and unevenly developed continent.[10]

---

[8]Cited above n. 1.

[9]E.G. Whitlam, 'The Constitution *versus* Labor' in *Labor and the Constitution* (Victorian Fabian Society Pamphlet 11, Melbourne, 1965), at p.32.

[10]'Socialism Within the Constitution' in *Labor and the Constitution*, cited above n.9, at p.56.

I foresaw at that time the use of Commonwealth powers with respect to taxation, interstate and overseas trade, State grants and external affairs being the main foundations of an expanded Commonwealth role in regulating private enterprise and planning the public sector. I could not foresee the added impetus to reform which the *Concrete Pipes Case*[11] would provide by revitalizing the power with respect to trading and financial corporations in s.51(20) of the Constitution.

In 1973, 1974 and 1975 the Labor Government demonstrated how reforms could be achieved using the corporations power as its constitutional base. It also used a number of other powers in ways not previously contemplated. I do not have space to canvass all of those powers here. Instead I propose to examine our use of the corporations power and the trade and commerce power and to review briefly some of the important reforms introduced under other heads of power.

There were three main reforms implemented on the basis of the corporations power; two others were planned but not completed when our term of office was cut short. Of these the *Trade Practices Act* 1974 was perhaps the most important. Although it was not based solely on the corporations power it drew its basic strength from it. It was, of course, far more than an amended version of earlier legislation. The approach to restrictive trade practices was completely changed, making practices illegal by force of the Act itself. The Act also included provisions not included in earlier legislation, most importantly those concerning consumer protection, exclusive dealing, price discrimination and restraints of trade by agreement or arrangement. These provisions were made possible by a series of decisions establishing that the Trade Practices Tribunal was not a judicial body[12], that competition could be enforced by federal regulation[13], and that legislation banning resale price maintenance did not offend the requirement in s.92 of the Constitution that interstate trade should be absolutely free.[14]

Taken together, these decisions made it clear that the High Court would permit vigorous Commonwealth action in the trade practices field based on the corporations power. Labor took up that challenge immediately and the Trade Practices Act is the result. Despite predictions of disruption by the business community, the Act has been widely accepted.

The second major initiative was the *Financial Corporations Act* 1974. Commonwealth powers with respect to banking and taxation have enabled direct Commonwealth regulation of the banking sector for many years. That regulation was a vital factor in monetary policy but its use increasingly had the effect of squeezing the banking sector at the expense of the fringe banking sector which could not similarly be regulated. The result was a proliferation of non-bank financial institutions, most of them foreign-owned. Soon after Labor came to office we announced that there were to be no new non-bank financial institutions established in Australia. We began a process of consultation with the finance industry concerning the appropriate form for regulating legislation. In the light of that consultation, and again relying on the corporations power, we enacted the Financial Corporations Act. The Act established machinery to

[11] *Strickland v. Rocla Concrete Pipes Pty Ltd* (1971) 124 C.L.R. 468.

[12] *R. v. Trade Practices Tribunal; Ex parte Tasmanian Breweries* (1970) 123 C.L.R. 361.

[13] *Concrete Pipes Case* (1971) 124 C.L.R. 468.

[14] *Mikasa (N.S.W.) Pty Ltd v. Festival Stores* (1972) 127 C.L.R. 617.

enable the Australian government to obtain information about the activities of different classes of financial corporations and then regulate their credit policies by setting financial ratios, much as is already done with banks. The High Court has not yet had the Financial Corporations Act before it. I am confident, however, that the Court would agree that this form of regulation is central to the legislative power with respect to financial corporations granted by s.51(20).

The third initiative of my Government in the area of the regulation of corporations was the Prices Justification Tribunal. The present Government's promise to abolish the tribunal became after the election, in Ronald Ziegler's immortal word, 'inoperative'. The decision to retain the Tribunal was one breach of promise by the Fraser Government we can applaud. If the price of labour must be justified then the price of goods and services must also be justified. The Labor Government sought direct constitutional power over prices and wages by referendum. To give the Australian government direct power over prices would have enabled it to guide the national economy with the same powers enjoyed and exercised by other national governments. In a campaign regrettably typical of referendum campaigns in Australia, emotional arguments prevailed over rational arguments and the referendum was lost. The Prices Justification Tribunal was the most that could be salvaged. Its authority has never been questioned; its rulings have never been defied; its achievements have exceeded expectations. It has now become an accepted part of the Government's regulatory machinery.

In the light of the *Concrete Pipes Case*[15] there can be no doubt that the Commonwealth has the power to regulate the trading activities of trading corporations; and the selling price is obviously central to trading activity. If, therefore, there is any doubt about the constitutional basis of the Prices Justification Tribunal it can only arise from the operation of s.92. I shall comment elsewhere about the dangers inherent in the recent tendency to base constitutional decisions on personal glosses and unstated assumptions. Nowhere is this tendency more evident than in s.92 cases. It would be absurd if the Australian government were to be denied, on the basis of a judicially created doctrine of practical burdens on interstate trade, even the limited regulatory power over prices which the Prices Justification Tribunal provides.

The two pieces of legislation under the corporations power which my Government developed but did not enact before our period in office was terminated were the Corporations and Securities Industry Bill and the National Companies Bill. No developed western country has such inadequate legislation in these fields. The Australian securities industry has been rocked by scandals, the most recent being the failure of Patrick Partners. Those events had undoubtedly weakened public confidence in the securities industry and seriously affected private enterprise capital formation. Every responsible body which has examined the question has recommended in favour of effective national regulation of the industry and of companies generally. All responsible sections of the business community want national regulation in these fields. So do consumers. Yet our attempts to legislate effectively were repeatedly blocked. The Australian government has the constitutional power to legislate for the control of companies and the securities industry. I believe that the Australian government has a responsibility to press ahead with strong legislation of its own.

---

[15](1971) 124 C.L.R. 468.

If the corporations power was for many years a neglected source of legislative power, the trade and commerce power remains, in my view, the most neglected of all. The Australian government's power over trade and commerce is worded in virtually the same terms as the American government's power, which has been the fountainhead of so much legislative activity in the field of regulating the private sector. Of course, the American Constitution does not contain a 's.92'. But despite that limitation on our powers in Australia, the possibilities of the trade and commerce power go far beyond the tentative legislative activity founded on that power to date.

The Labor Government sought to use the trade and commerce power in three main contexts—the environment, the mining industry and roads. The use of the Australian government's power over external trade to impose internal policy has long been familiar. An obvious example was the use of the control over imports to impose the two-airline policy. In 1961 I suggested that this precedent be expanded to channel overseas investment into certain industries or regions or to require extractive industries to build their own processing plants within a certain time. By 1972 there were three urgent priorities for Australian government intervention which could be tied to external trade. The first was the environment. Environmental problems had for too long, and with unfortunate results, been left to the States. There was a tendency to equate environmental problems with pollution and to limit legislation to licensing industries traditionally regarded as high polluters. Our aim was to implement a more far-reaching system of environmental management, but our tools for doing so were limited. We nevertheless passed some important measures—the *Environment Protection (Impact of Proposals) Act 1974*, the *States Grants (Nature Conservation) Act 1974*, the *National Parks and Wildlife Conservation Act 1975* and the *Great Barrier Reef Marine Park Act 1975*. The Environment Protection (Marine) Bill lapsed with the dissolution. Future governments will have even clearer power to regulate the environment. In the *Murphyores Case*[16] the High Court upheld the use of the trade and commerce power to ban exports on environmental grounds. As a result of that decision it is clear that the Australian government has considerable scope for environmental regulation.

Similarly, the Australian government has the power to control the mining and export of our natural resources through its control over export licences. Few Australians would now dispute that ownership of our resources ought to remain as far as possible in Australian hands and that their exploitation ought to be regulated by the government. I believe that the Australian government ought to go further and undertake exploration and mining activity itself in those areas where it can do so efficiently, or where only the government has the necessary resources, or where the risks are too great for private enterprise. To that end we legislated for the establishment of the Petroleum and Minerals Authority.[17] That Act was struck down, not because the substance of what we were seeking to do was beyond power, but because the High Court held that the conditions of s.57 of the Constitution concerning double dissolutions had not been satisfied with respect to that Bill.[18] I have argued for years that the aims of democratic socialism in Australia are best achieved through competitive

---

[16] *Murphyores Incorporated Pty Ltd v. Commonwealth* (1976) 9 A.L.R. 199.

[17] *Petroleum and Minerals Authority Act* 1973.

[18] *Victoria v. Commonwealth (P.M.A. Case)* (1975) 7 A.L.R. 1.

public enterprise rather than nationalisation, even if the latter were constitutionally possible. The Petroleum and Minerals Authority is a good example of the type of public enterprise which ought to be fostered.

The third field in which my Government drew on the trade and commerce power was roads. Again there was a precedent for reliance on the power in this context. The federal government since World War II had given the States hundreds of millions of dollars for roads but we still cannot enjoy day-in and day-out use of the Hume Highway. The road linking Australia's two largest cities, two of the largest cities in the world, is on some days every year impassable at one point or another. Responsibility for such roads is accepted in every other federal system by the federal government. The federal government must accept responsibility in Australia. My Government did so. Through the National Roads Act we mounted a systematic effort to upgrade our road system to acceptable national and international standards.

The trade and commerce power and the corporations power were by no means the only powers exploited by my Government. The *Family Law Act* 1975 gave new life to the marriage and matrimonial causes power. The Government Insurance Corporation, which would have saved millions of dollars in home insurance and would have provided cover for natural disasters, was to have been based on the insurance power. The national compensation and rehabilitation scheme, had it not foundered in the face of a combined attack from the insurance industry, the trade unions and the legal profession, would have been based, like Medibank, on the social welfare power. Our legislation for Aboriginal land rights and enterprises was based on the new power with respect to Aboriginals. The *Racial Discrimination Act* 1975 was a much amended and tentative step in the direction of human rights legislation based on the external affairs power. The Human Rights Bill did not get far, although the external affairs power can and ought to be used to fulfil Australia's international legal obligations in these important areas. These were some of the highlights of three years of vigorous reform government. The result was to demonstrate how much can be achieved despite the limitations of an aging Constitution.

An argument sometimes heard and widely exploited in the campaign within the legal profession to bring down the Australian Legal Aid Office is that it is somehow immoral to exploit constitutional power or to test its limits. That argument is nonsense. If there is a community need the government has a duty to use whatever power is available to meet it. It is the High Court's function, not the government's, to draw the line. If the High Court will allow the power with respect to posts and telegraphs to be used to control the sharemarket, and if there is a need to control the sharemarket, then that power ought to be so used. If any question of morality arises it does so when governments use constitutional excuses for failing to fulfil mandates given to them by the people.

IV
THE HIGH COURT AND THE CHIEF JUSTICE

Labor's period in government was a period of intense constitutional litigation, mainly sponsored by conservative State governments. Challenges to our legislation caused delays in much needed reforms, delays compounded by the High Court itself; but in the final analysis we won every major challenge to our exercise of power.[19] The decision in *McKinlay's Case*[20] could have done more to guarantee a democratic basis for our parliamentary institutions, but even in that case some gains were made. The *P.M.A. Case*[21] could have been based on a realistic understanding of Senate techniques of obstruction, but it should be emphasised that the High Court did not have before it the question of the legality of the Petroleum and Minerals Authority itself.

Subject to these two qualified exceptions, the record of my Government before the High Court on matters of constitutional significance is a highly successful one. So I hope I shall not be thought churlish if I complain about aspects of the High Court's decisions and procedures. By and large I have agreed with the thrust of the High Court's decisions as they affected the Labor program. I have, however, become increasingly concerned about some aspects of the approach of the Court and its implications for the future government of this country.

My first concern relates to the tendency, particularly of the present Chief Justice, to base decisions on constitutional glosses and unstated assumptions. His extra-judicial invention of the doctrine of caretaker governments in the Westminster system is only the most notorious manifestation of the Chief Justice's bent. Let me make it clear at the outset that I have long felt that the Australian Constitution would have been better interpreted over the years if the Court had based its decisions more on an understanding of the philosophical basis of our political system and of the realities of its operations in practice, and less on the precise words of a text written long ago for a different world. As early as 1957 I said:

> No method of interpretation will enable a court to overcome the uncertainties and anomalies inherent in the judicial interpretation of political questions under a Federal system. The present High Court under the powerful influence of the Chief Justice has striven resolutely to determine constitutional matters by the strict application of legal principles. It must be said, with respect, that this approach has led to as obnoxious a political result and as insoluble a legal result as any previous approach in the days when the court, as under Isaacs, was more empirical.[22]

I maintain that view; but I also believe that governments and litigants have a right to know what factors other than the words in the text will be taken into account. If they did they would be able to present arguments on them. I further believe that personal doctrines should not be elevated above the combined experience of many years of constitutional interpretation.

Let me illustrate the difficulties and inconsistencies which can arise from unstated assumptions. When the Chief Justice finds support for the proposition which he wishes to adopt in the express words of the Constitution he defers to no one as a strict textualist. Thus in *McKinlay's Case* the following passage appears in his judgment:

> The problem is not to be solved by resort to slogans or to political catch-cries or to vague and imprecise expressions of political philosophy ... The only true guide and the only course which can produce stability in constitutional law is to read the language of the Constitution itself, no doubt generously and not pedantically, but as a whole: and to find its meaning by legal reasoning. I respectfully agree with Sir Owen

---

[19]Some sections of the Family Law Act were of course struck down: *Russell* v. *Russell; Farrelly* v. *Farrelly (Family Law Case)* (1976) 9 A.L.R. 103.

[20]*A.-G. (Australia) (Ex rel. McKinlay)* v. *Commonwealth* (1975) 7 A.L.R. 593.

[21](1975) 7 A.L.R. 1.

[22]'The Constitution *versus* Labor', cited above n.9, at p.7.

Dixon's opinion that 'there is no other safe guide to judicial decision in great conflicts than a strict and complete legalism'.[23]

However, when the text is not so helpful the Chief Justice can find the most surprising interpretation by reliance on what he regards as having been the purpose of the provision. Thus in *Webster*[24] he begins with an examination of how unfortunate is the particular provision in the Constitution with which he is dealing and goes on to say:

> the provision is part of the Constitution and, however vestigial, must be enforced. But in its construction and application, the purpose it seeks to attain must always be kept in mind.[25]

That is a statement with which we could all agree. However, the Chief Justice uses it to reach an interpretation of the Constitution which even his most loyal supporters have found difficult to share and which, with respect, finds no foundation in the words of the Constitution itself.

There are a number of cases where the Chief Justice has sought to create a new constitutional doctrine to underpin his interpretation of the Constitution, often without the support of his brothers. This tendency first became obvious in cases relating to the freedom of interstate trade. There are two aspects to the Chief Justice's attitude to s.92 cases. The first is a strong restatement of the *laissez faire* premises he holds to be the basis of the section. There is, of course, nothing novel in that approach, however quaint and irrelevant it may be in 1976. What is novel is his refusal to accept the Dixon formula for the application of s.92 or to replace it with one of his own. Instead we are left with an ill-defined concept of burden in a free yet legally regulated society, and the Chief Justice's self-confident belief that he can recognise a breach of s.92 when he sees one. That recognition is presumably based on non-legal considerations of his own to which the rest of us are regrettably not privy. The result is an *ad hoc* approach to the application of s.92 and a new lease of life for it at a time when it has increasingly less relevance to the problems of regulating and planning a modern national economy. We should, however, be grateful that the Chief Justice has not allowed his doctrinal commitment to free enterprise to weaken his support for trade practices legislation, legislation which he had supported so strongly in the overt political phase of his career.

The attempt to create new doctrines is not, of course, limited to s.92 cases. In the Chief Justice's judgments in both the *McKinlay* and *P.M.A.* cases, great weight is given to his view of the proper role of the States in our federal system, the facts of political life notwithstanding. In the *P.M.A. Case* he expressed it in the following terms:

> It is evident from the terms of the Constitution that the Senate was intended to represent the States, parts of the Commonwealth, as distinct from the House of Representatives which represents the electors throughout Australia. It is often said that the Senate has, in this respect, failed in its purpose. This may be so, due partly to the party system and to the nature of the electoral system: but even if that assertion be true it does not detract from the Constitutional position that it was intended that proposed laws could be considered by the Senate from a point of view different from that which the House of Representatives may take. The Senate is not a mere house of

---

[23](1975) 7 A.L.R. 593, at p.600.
[24]*Re Senator Webster* (1975) 6 A.L.R. 65.
[25]*ibid.*, at p.70.

review: rather, it is a house which may examine a proposed law from a standpoint different from that which the House of Representatives may have taken.[26]

Again, we should be grateful that the Chief Justice did not follow a similar States rights approach in determining the validity of the Seas and Submerged Lands Act.

The point of these illustrations is that judges decide their attitude to any particular case in the light of a number of factors, not all of them legal. It adds nothing to the judicial process to attempt to construct artificial doctrines and then force decisions in some, but not all, cases into that framework. Equally, the judicial process is badly served if decisions are based on assumptions not made clear to the parties during argument and not consistently applied.

My second concern about the judiciary and the Constitution relates to procedural shortcomings of the High Court during our period in government. The constitutional litigation conducted during the last three years was characterised by inordinate delays between the completion of argument and the delivery of the judgment. To give one example among many, the argument in the *Offshore Sovereignty Case*[27] was completed on 16 April 1975. The judgment was delivered on 17 December 1975. The problem was not so novel nor the judgments so profound as to require eight months for the judgment to be prepared. Delays of this order cause needless uncertainty and concern about the state of the law. In this particular instance it had a major impact on the exploration activities of an important industry. In other instances delays in the Court caused delays in the delivery of services and benefits to the people and the implementation of social reforms. There can be a number of reasons for such delays, some of them justified. But when they are as frequent and as lengthy as they have been in recent years they expose the Court to allegations of improper practice. Indeed, some commentators have suggested that the High Court was deliberately delaying its judgments in constitutional cases until the next important constitutional case had begun so as to render changes in the membership of the Court difficult to effect. Whether this suggestion is justified or not is less important than the fact that the Court has exposed itself to such suspicions.

There is also a tendency in the present High Court for some judges to behave more like barristers than judges during the argument of cases. I do not think it is an exaggeration to say that after the first day of most of the important constitutional cases argued before the Court it was not only clear which way certain judges were leaning but what reasons they were intending to adduce in support of their judgment. The *P.M.A. Case*[28] was a good example. It may be that the issues in question were relatively clear-cut, although I doubt it. It may be that on such matters judges always have their own opinions and argument before them is unlikely to change their minds. However, I believe that in the interest of giving at least the appearance of justice being done, judges ought to endeavour to listen to the arguments put forward by counsel and consider them on their merits.

In the particular case of *Re Senator Webster*[29] I believe that the procedural decisions taken did nothing to enhance the reputation of the Court nor to

---

[26](1975) 7 A.L.R. 1, at pp. 13-14.

[27](1975) 8 A.L.R. 1.

[28](1975) 7 A.L.R. 1.

[29](1975) 6 A.L.R. 65.

ensure that Senator Webster was given the benefit of a clear decision one way or the other. That matter was referred to the Court by the Parliament. It did so because it believed that an important question of constitutional principle was involved and ought to be determined. Instead of referring the matter to the Full Court for the consideration and determination fitting a matter of such importance, the Chief Justice chose to determine the matter himself, sitting alone as a Court of Disputed Returns. I have already said that, regardless of the facts of the particular case, I do not believe that the general proposition of law advanced by the Chief Justice in that case can be supported. I believe that better consideration might have been given to the principles involved if the case had been heard in the appropriate manner.

I am concerned at the extent to which the High Court has been involved in political matters. The Chief Justice's decision to tender secret advice to the Governor-General last November—and to do so without first informing and consulting his colleagues—was, in my view, a breach of the duties and responsibilities of his office. The advice given by the Chief Justice was, in my opinion, at the very least inadequate and probably wrong. His decision to bring the High Court into the subsequent debate over the events of 11 November 1975 by giving a press conference demeaned his office in a manner none of his predecessors would have contemplated. These are serious charges and I do not make them lightly. People who know me know of my great respect—some would say too great respect—for judicial office. However, the decision to involve the Chief Justice in political events was his, not mine. He must now accept the fact that he has entered the political arena and his views must be canvassed in the terms appropriate to that arena.

Let me explain each of these charges in turn. I believe that the Chief Justice was wrong to give advice. Certainly in his judicial capacity the Chief Justice has no power to give advisory opinions. Moreover, to quote one of the Governor-General's most spirited defenders, Professor D. P. O'Connell:

> The dangers inherent in an obscuring of the separation of powers when the judiciary is partially recruited from politics can engender public disquiet and give excuse to those who stigmatise the events as an establishment plot.[30]

There is also the point that, despite the Chief Justice's protestations to the contrary, the subject matter of his advice could readily have come before the High Court. Say, for example, a Prime Minister decided to test the legality of bypassing the Senate altogether by putting appropriation Bills to the Governor-General for the royal assent before the Senate had passed them. As the High Court demonstrated in the *P.M.A. Case*[31], it would not have felt restrained from involving itself in questions concerning the legality of such an action. The Governor-General was profoundly concerned at the High Court repudiating his predecessor and probably sought the Chief Justice's opinion not because he thought that his own actions could not be reviewed by the Court but because he thought that they might. I believe that at the very least the Chief Justice ought to have consulted his brother judges on such an important question. The title of Chief Justice does not necessarily confer on the incumbent greater wisdom or independence than that enjoyed by his brother judges.

---

[30]D. P. O'Connell, 'The Dissolution of the Australian Parliament: 11 November 1975' *The Parliamentarian* vol. LVII, 1 (1976), at p.10.

[31](1975) 7 A.L.R. 1.

It has, of course, been argued that there was a precedent for the Governor-General consulting the Chief Justice. Professor Sawer dismisses that precedent effectively in the following terms:

> Resort to the Chief Justice for advice was barely tolerable in 1914, when done with the cordial agreement of the Prime Minister, and having regard to the unique historical position of Sir Samuel Griffith. Resort to Chief Justice Barwick in 1975 was thoroughly objectionable, even if (as seems unlikely) it was done with Prime Ministerial approval, since today it is impossible to be sure that a particular constitutional question will not come before the High Court; there were additional reasons arising from the Chief Justice's political past and the presence in the list of undecided cases before him of one to restrain the holding of a general election on existing electoral boundaries.[32]

Let me assure you that the consultation with the Chief Justice in 1975 was not done with Prime Ministerial approval; indeed, it took place without the knowledge and against the advice of the Prime Minister.

Not only do I believe that the Chief Justice was wrong to give advice; I believe that the advice he gave was wrong and inadequate. First, as already explained, the assertion in the advice that the matter was non-justiciable is certainly wrong. Secondly, the Chief Justice cannot simply dissociate himself, as he purports to do, from the political consequences of his advice. Indeed, those political consequences, given all the circumstances, ought to have been important considerations in formulating the advice tendered. Thirdly, the Chief Justice asserts, without any supporting argument, that a supply deadlock ought to be resolved by the resignation of the Prime Minister. There is no precedent for such a proposition in Westminster parliamentary democracies; there is no support for it in the express terms of the Constitution. Fourthly, and above all, the Chief Justice asserts as a secure proposition of constitutional law, and virtually without adducing any arguments in support, that the Senate has constitutional power to refuse to pass a money Bill or to refuse supply to the government. Given the controversy raging at the time, that assertion was, as Professor Howard has remarked, 'breathtaking in its audacity'.

The irony of the Chief Justice's intervention in the events of last November is that less than a month before he advised the Governor-General that he had the power to dismiss me he had himself delivered a judgment clearly establishing the illegality of the Governor-General's action in dissolving Parliament. In the *Territory Senators Case*,[33] the judgment in which was delivered on 17 October 1975, the day after supply had been first deferred, the Chief Justice said:

> Proposed laws which twice have not been passed by the Senate may not be stockpiled. They may not be laid aside against the possibility of a double dissolution founded on some event . . . unrelated to the situation in which the 'stockpiled' or stale bill was twice rejected by the Senate.[34]

When he was reminded of this statement at the National Press Club he said with proper modesty, 'I was in the minority in expressing that opinion, so I must have been wrong'.[35] It is true that he was in the minority in his reasons

---

[32] Geoffrey Sawer, 'The Governor-General of the Commonwealth of Australia' *Current Affairs Bulletin,* vol. 52, 10 (1976), at p.28.

[33] *W.A.* v. *Commonwealth* (1975) 7 A.L.R. 159 (decision 10 October; reasons 17 October).

[34] *ibid.*, at pp. 167-8.

[35] *Financial Review* 11 June 1976, p.2: part of an edited transcript of the Chief Justice's answers to questions at the National Press Club, Canberra, on 10 June 1976.

for the decision in that case. What he failed to point out was that the particular question, of stockpiling Bills and using them technically to found a dissolution really based on other circumstances, was not decided in the case.

Before I leave the judiciary's constitutional role during our period of government there are two reforms of my Government which deserve mention. The first concerns appeals to the Privy Council. The process of limiting appeals to the Privy Council beyond the limitation imposed by the Constitution itself was begun in 1968 by the present Chief Judge in Equity in the Supreme Court of New South Wales when he was Australian Attorney-General. I have always strongly believed that Australia's nationhood requires that its judicial system should be entirely free from the supervision of the Court of another country, sitting in another country, composed of judges appointed by the government of that other country and delivering its judgments in the form of advice to the Head of State of that other country. To that end I believe the High Court should be the ultimate court of appeal from all decisions made within the Australian legal system. The alternative not only diminishes our nationhood but creates the possibility of two streams of authority. Accordingly, my Government introduced the *Privy Council (Appeals from the High Court) Act 1975*, which had the effect of preventing appeals from the High Court on federal matters. We also attempted to abolish *all* appeals to the Privy Council, but the Opposition, which had previously protested its support for the High Court as the ultimate court of appeal, opposed the legislation in the Senate and it was not enacted. There may be argument as to whether the abolition of appeals is best carried out by State or Commonwealth or Imperial legislation. Surely there can be no argument with the proposition that the abolition of appeals to the Privy Council is a logical and reasonable development in our history as a nation.

Again because of Opposition obstruction we were unable to establish the Superior Court. It has been accepted for decades among the judiciary, the Law Officers of the Crown and the legal profession that the High Court of Australia ought to be relieved of much of its original jurisdiction and some of its appellate jurisdiction. Four successive Liberal Attorneys-General sponsored the proposal. Four successive Solicitors-General were involved in the development of the proposal. The present Solicitor-General and the present Attorney-General made major contributions to the work. Last July, in a speech to the Eighteenth Australian Legal Convention in Canberra, Mr Justice Mason summed up the problem faced by the High Court and the absurdity of shelving the Superior Court. He said:

> As the Prime Minister observed on the opening day of this Convention, in 1963 a proposal was initiated for a Federal Superior Court designed to relieve the High Court of most of its original jursidiction and part of its appellate jurisdiction. A reduction in the jurisdiction of the Court was then thought to be a necessary step. Notwithstanding that everyone is agreed that the High Court should be relieved of part of its existing original and appellate jurisdiction, that proposal has perished on the rock of State rights. Meantime, although we have been relieved of the taxation work at first instance the balance of the Court's jurisdiction remains. What is more important, it continues to grow in volume and, I should add, difficulty, with the marked upsurge in constitutional work. It is a matter of concern when changes in the Court's jurisdiction which should be made are not made because there is a question whether a Federal court or State courts should receive the jurisdiction. The choice to be made between these alternatives is much less important than the desirability, indeed the necessity, of

ensuring that the High Court's jurisdiction is appropriate to that of an ultimate Court of Appeal.[36]

At both the 1972 and 1974 elections my Government promised to proceed with the Superior Court Bill. We first introduced a Bill in the Senate in December 1973. It lapsed when Parliament was prorogued on the occasion of the Queen's visit. It was reintroduced in the Senate in March 1974 and defeated on 2 April. The Bill was introduced in the House of Representatives after the elections of May 1974 and passed on 24 July 1974. In the Senate, however, the Bill was defeated in a tied vote on 26 February 1975. The Bill was again passed by the House of Representatives on 3 June last but again defeated on 11 June in the Senate. The Bill was cited in the Proclamation dissolving both Houses on Remembrance Day 1975. I am glad to see now that the Attorney-General is to proceed with the legislation after all.

V
THE SENATE AND THE CROWN

Legal obstruction and judicial intervention were by no means the most drastic methods used to block the Labor Government's program. For that we must look to the parliamentary arena. The past three years were a time of extraordinary upheaval. The third and fourth double dissolutions since Federation occurred in that time. For the first time a joint sitting had to be held. More Bills were defeated in the Senate during those three years than in all the other years since Federation. Supply was deferred for the first time since Federation and then, within eighteen months, deferred for the second time. Government legislation was subjected to a degree of obstruction without precedent in our system. The Speaker of the House of Representatives was ignored by the Queen's representative in a manner never before seen in Australia or any other Westminster system. For the first time the Chief Justice tendered private advice to the Governor-General without the knowledge of the Prime Minister. For the first time in our history—and for the first time since responsible government came of age in any Westminster system—the Queen's representative dismissed a Prime Minister.

Any one of these events taken alone would have been a development of momentous constitutional importance. Taken together they constituted a fundamental threat to parliamentary democracy. Given the nature of that threat and the coalition of interests which brought it about, the Labor Party and its supporters acted with remarkable restraint after 11 November 1975. I stand amazed at our own moderation. In contrast to the behaviour of the Liberal Party and its supporters during the previous three years, we observed and enjoined the proprieties of the democratic system and eschewed counsels of violence to the Constitution and the statutory processes. We fought the election as we had fought elections for the previous seventy-five years. We lost the election; we accepted the loss. We cannot accept, and no Australian ought to accept, a situation in which the unprecedented actions of 1974 and 1975 are now accepted as precedents.

I wish to canvass three aspects of the machinery of government in the light of the last three years—electoral reform, techniques developed for obstructing government action, and the dismissal of the Labor Government itself.

---

[36]The Hon. Sir Anthony Mason, 'Where Now?' (1975) 49 *Australian L.J.* 570, at p.576.

Two of the most important initiatives of my Government in the area of electoral reform were the referendum proposals for simultaneous elections and for democratic elections. In the national Parliament, in the fourteen-year period from December 1961 to December 1975, there were ten national elections. They are too frequent by all tests—too frequent for the people, too frequent for the good working of the Parliament, and too costly. Apart from the two double dissolutions, only one of these elections, that in December 1961, was an election for the Senate and the House of Representatives simultaneously. As a general aim, elections for the national Parliament should be held every three years, for the Senate and the House of Representatives simultaneously. There is no derogation in this from the authority or responsibility of either House. But there are great benefits in public convenience and worthwhile savings of expenditure. Most of all, there is the benefit to the Parliament—the reflection in both Houses simultaneously of the people's will so that the Government and the Parliament may get on with the job. Unfortunately, that simple, rational proposition was not endorsed at the referendum in May 1974 and inexplicably the Governor-General did not exercise the explicit discretion given to him in s.128 of the Constitution to submit it to the electors in December 1975. I would hope that it will be endorsed at the next opportunity and that in the meantime governments adopt the practice of calling the elections simultaneously.

At the Constitutional Convention held in September 1973 in Sydney, I said on behalf of the Australian Government that we would propose to the Parliament, for decision by the people, an amendment of the Constitution which would write into it the principle of substantial equality of electoral divisions for all the Parliaments of Australia. There was not such equality then. Thanks to the defeat of our referendum for democratic elections there is still no such equality today. The Bill we proposed was a Bill for an Act 'to alter the Constitution so as to ensure that the members of the House of Representatives and of the Parliaments of the States are chosen directly and democratically by the people'. It provided that electoral divisions in both the federal Parliament and the State parliaments should have as nearly as practicable the same number of people. At the time of the last census for which statistics are available, 30 June 1971, the Division of Werriwa in the House of Representatives had a population of 142,568; Chifley 138,665; Kalgoorlie 135,790; Burke 135,547; and Melbourne 131,127. At the other extreme, and excluding Tasmanian divisions for which the Constitution makes specific provision, the Division of Wakefield had a population of 77,195; Wimmera 77,526; Lyne 80,475; Maranoa 81,500; and Hume 82,365.

A result similar to that which we sought by referendum could have been achieved if the High Court had chosen to read the Constitution in the light of the democratic principles on which it is supposed to be based. It was argued in *McKinlay's Case* that s.24 requires electoral districts to consist of equal or practically equal numbers of people or of electors. That argument rested on the words 'directly chosen by the people' in s.24 and the interpretation which similar words have received in the United States.

Mr Justice Murphy said:

> the Supreme Court of the United States held that the provision that the members shall be chosen 'by the people' expresses the most basic right of the people and commands that there shall be equal representation, an equal sharing of political power in the election in each State for the House of Representatives. It is a remarkable result if the same words carried into our Constitution and used for the same purpose of describing how the members shall be chosen are construed by our High Court as a vague

philosophic statement requiring a direct choice but permitting the choosing to be by a few of the people only, with exclusions on grounds of sex or property, or other arbitrary criteria, and allowing the voting to be debased by unequal divisions or other devices.[37]

Yet that is the remarkable result which the High Court reached in *McKinlay*. That result means that, failing a referendum, the most that can be achieved is to limit the degree of variation permitted in the number of electors using the fragile mechanism of the Electoral and Representation Acts. Accordingly my Government legislated to make that variation no greater than 10 per cent. *McKinlay's Case* requires the Government to redistribute electorates in time for the next election. The Court has decided that this need not wait upon the census. The Government has already acknowledged that the latest statistics of the Commonwealth entitle both Western Australia and Queensland to receive an additional member and New South Wales one fewer. That redistribution ought to be commenced forthwith.

In addition to changes in the Representation Act the Labor Government also legislated for expanded representation of the territories by providing for two senators from each of the Northern Territory and A.C.T. and two members for the A.C.T. in the House of Representatives. Despite its addiction to the concept of the Senate as a 'States House' in other contexts, the High Court upheld this legislation. It was a sensible recognition of the growing population and importance of the territories and the need for all citizens to be represented in the national Parliament.

I turn now to obstruction of the processes of Parliament. The Opposition abused the concept of the Senate as a House of review in order to delay, side-track and reject our legislation and it twice cut short our period of government. In 1973 alone, ten major Bills were rejected by the Senate. A further twenty-three Bills were deferred or side-tracked into committees and many more were amended in ways inconsistent with the policies which the people had endorsed at the election. This sort of obstruction continued throughout our term of office. It was not based on any concept of protecting State rights but purely on party political considerations.

I shall give two illustrations of the techniques used by the Senate other than outright rejection. The Corporations and Securities Industries Bill was sent to the Senate from the House on 6 March 1975 and the second reading speech was given in the Senate that day. The debate began on 9 April. On 10 April Senator Greenwood introduced an amendment to refer the Bill to a select committee, which was carried after twenty-five pages of debate in Hansard. The committee was due to report by 1 September 1975. It held ten desultory meetings between 10 April 1975 and 1 September. It did not report on 1 September. It met fitfully after 1 September but no report was ever made. A similar fate befell the National Compensation Bill. That Bill was introduced in the Senate on 30 October 1974. The second reading speech was made on that date but it was then referred immediately to the Senate Standing Committee on Legal and Constitutional Affairs without any second reading debate at all. This step was taken because the Opposition parties had stated that unless it was referred to a committee they would reject it outright. The standing committee did not report until 21 July 1975, nearly nine months later. The Senate in each case referred

[37](1975) 7 A.L.R. 593, at p.645.

the Bill to a committee before reaching the committee stage. It did not give the second reading which alone can lead to effective consideration in committee.

These two instances, and there are others, illustrate the obstruction my Government faced and the difficulties the Senate posed for orderly government. At the time of the fourth double dissolution a further twenty-one Bills had been twice rejected by the Senate. What will happen in future? Parity in numbers between the parties in the Senate or a government minority in the Senate have not been uncommon in the past. They are likely to be common in future. The precedents of the last three years condemn us to ineffective government, continually under the threat of an election. These precedents have been compounded by the High Court's decision in the *P.M.A. Case*[38].

Section 57 of the Constitution was designed to ensure that if the Senate obstructed legislation for an unreasonable period the government could advise the dissolution of both Houses. If the government was then re-elected in the House of Representatives but still unable to get its legislation through the Senate, it could pass that legislation at a Joint Sitting. The clear intent of the section was to give the Senate three months from the time when the House of Representatives passed the legislation to either pass it or reject it. If it did neither, then it had 'failed to pass' the legislation within the meaning of s.57. I have no doubt whatever that the great politicians who drafted the Constitution intended s.57 to be interpreted in this way. As Mr Justice Jacobs said in the *P.M.A. Case*:

> In the context of common English usage which we find in s.57 I likewise find the only practicable construction to be one where the interval of three months from a failure to pass is the interval during which the Senate does not pass the proposed law when it might have passed it. That interval is the three months after the House of Representatives passes the proposed law and sends the bill to the Senate.[39]

To hold otherwise, as the majority of the High Court did, has the effect that, as Jacobs J put it, 'no time limit on the consideration of the proposed law by the Senate is then provided.[40] It thus has the effect of grotesquely prolonging and complicating the machinery of government and defeating the whole purpose of s.57.

By the second half of 1975 Senate obstruction had built up to a point where any kind of reforming government was virtually impossible. It culminated in the dismissal of the Government. I want to examine the implications of the dismissal and the many abuses of the parliamentary process which led up to it. I do so from the standpoint of a lawyer, one long removed from the practice of his profession but not unfamiliar with either the Constitution or the events I describe.

One abuse concerned the filling of casual Senate vacancies. Senator Murphy's seat in the Senate became vacant on 9 February 1975. The convention observed in every State by both sides of politics since proportional representation was introduced in the Senate had been for casual vacancies to be filled by the State government with a member of the previous senator's party. On 27 February the New South Wales Government used its majority in the State Parliament to replace Senator Murphy with a non-Labor senator. Senator Bunton was sworn on 4 March. A worse example occurred in Queensland.

---

[38](1975) 7 A.L.R. 1.
[39]*ibid.*, at pp. 71-2.
[40]*ibid.*, at p.74.

Senator Milliner died on 30 June 1975. The Queensland Parliament on 3 September chose a non-Labor senator to replace him. Senator Field was sworn on 9 September. It is true that he took no part in subsequent divisions on the issue of supply. The significance of his appointment, however, is that had Senator Milliner been replaced by a Labor senator the Senate would have been evenly divided on these issues, and the Opposition would not have been able to carry a motion for deferment of the appropriation Bills. It would have had to vote on the Bills, with the risk that some Opposition senators might have refused to reject them.

The Senate chose the technique of deferment rather than attempting outright rejection for good reasons. It wanted to be sure that it would be able to pass supply in the event of the Government's dismissal without having to rely on the House of Representatives. It showed remarkable foresight, to say the least. It persisted in a process of debate and deferment for a period of nearly three months. The Budget papers were tabled in the Senate on 19 August. Debate began on 27 August. The actual Appropriation Bills were received from the House of Representatives on 14 October and the motion for deferment was first carried on 16 October. The House of Representatives requested reconsideration of the Bills on 21 October, 28 October and 6 November. Each time an amendment was carried to defer consideration.

Moreover, the Opposition parties did everything possible to prevent an election for the Senate. There was every justification, and every precedent, for an election for half the Senate at the end of 1975. Yet the Federal Council of the Liberal Party passed a resolution on 13 October calling on 'the Federal and State Parliamentary Parties and Liberals everywhere' to do 'all in their power' to prevent the Whitlam Government 'gaining control' of the Senate. This was an instruction to non-Labor Premiers to advise their State Governors not to issue writs for an election for half the Senate at the request of the Australian Government. The Governor-General was considerably agitated by this development and discussed it with the Governors of States with Liberal governments when they were assembled in Melbourne for the Melbourne Cup, the week before the coup.

From the time of the first Senate election State governments of every political complexion had automatically issued Senate writs as and when requested by the federal government. Prime Minister Menzies called separate elections for half the Senate in 1953 and 1964; Prime Minister Holt did so in 1967 and Prime Minister Gorton in 1970. These elections were held at a time chosen by the government of the day. Moreover, on each occasion the Prime Minister announced his intention to Parliament before advising the Governor-General to request the State Governors to issue the writs. It is interesting to reflect on what would have happened if I had announced to Parliament on 11 November my intention to have a half-Senate election before seeking to tender this advice—traditionally no more than a formality—to the Governor-General. The Opposition parties would have had to accept the situation. It is arguable that the Governor-General would have had to accept it. If I had not shown a degree of courtesy to the Governor-General which had never been shown by my Liberal predecessors events might have taken a different course.

I showed courtesy throughout these events, not only to the Governor-General but to the Opposition. I made it my business to observe the proprieties and conventions. When Sir John Kerr sought my permission on 21 October to confer with the Leader of the Opposition I readily agreed. When Sir John Kerr asked me what opinion the Law Officers of the Crown held about Mr Ellicott's advice on the reserve powers of the Governor-General I undertook to give it to him in writing. The Governor-General showed no courtesy to me and gross discourtesy to the Speaker of the House of Representatives. His treatment of Mr Speaker Scholes on 11 November was more than discourtesy; it displayed contempt for the Speaker's office and the rights of the Parliament. Just after 2 p.m. the Senate passed the Budget. At 3 p.m. the House passed a motion expressing want of confidence in the caretaker Government and instructing the Speaker to convey its views to the Governor-General. At 3.15 the Speaker sought an appointment. The Governor-General fixed the appointment for 4.45. Meantime he was able to have a Prime Minister who did not have the confidence of the House sign a Proclamation dissolving the Parliament.

If the events of last November go unchallenged it means that the party which wins a majority in the people's House at the election is not necessarily entitled to govern. It means that a Senate, of which no member may have faced the people for three years and some members may not have faced the people for six years, can deny the party with the majority in the lower House the right to govern and force it to an election without itself facing the people at that election. It means that elections for the House of Representatives can occur every six months. It means that no government without control in the Senate can afford to take unpopular measures which may be necessary for good government for fear of being forced to an election at a time when its popularity is low. It means that seventy-four years and literally hundreds of precedents in our own system alone, to the effect that a hostile Senate does not deny supply, are to be ignored. It means that a Governor-General need no longer act on the advice of his ministers and, indeed, may act contrary to that advice. It means that a Governor-General may keep his intention to so act secret from his ministers and not even give them a chance to dissuade him or propose alternative courses of action. It means that a Governor-General can ignore the advice of the Law Officers of the Crown and without the knowledge and even against the advice of the Prime Minister seek the advice of the Chief Justice in secret. It means that a Chief Justice of a court not entitled to give advisory legal opinions can give advisory political opinions to a Governor-General. It means that whenever the technical provisions of s.57 are satisfied a Governor-General can dissolve both Houses without, and even against, the advice of the government. It means that a Governor-General can dismiss a Prime Minister who has the confidence of the lower House and appoint and maintain in office one who does not. It means that a Governor-General, who cannot obtain the Prime Minister's signature on a Proclamation of dissolution to validate that Proclamation, can dismiss that Prime Minister and appoint one who will sign the Proclamation. It means that a Governor-General can impose political conditions on his appointment of a Prime Minister and lay down policies his appointed Prime Minister must follow. It means that in filling casual vacancies in the Senate, State governments need pay no regard whatsoever to the wishes the people expressed at the last election for the Senate. It means that whether or not a Senate election can occur will depend on the caprice of State governments in deciding whether or not to issue the writs for the election. It means that a Governor-General may ignore a request from the Speaker of the House of Representatives to attend him and may in the meantime act in a manner directly contrary to the request he knows the Speaker to be carrying from the House. It means that a Governor-General as delegate of the Queen enjoys powers which the Queen has never herself enjoyed and which her forbears have not enjoyed for centuries.

I know it is sometimes argued that practical considerations will prevent these precedents destabilizing our parliamentary system, that the precedents will only become relevant in the most extreme circumstances. But what *were* the extreme circumstances in 1975? No one has ever alleged any illegality on the part of my Government, nor could they do so. The elected government held a majority in the House. It was in no danger of defeat. It has acted with complete legality. All its legislation had been upheld by the Court. There were economic problems, but they were comparable to those of other countries. There was no threat to social order or cohesion. Like all Western democracies economic circumstances had weakened our popularity in the electorate, but we were at the mid-point of our term of office. The circumstances of November 1975 were no more 'extreme' than this: a reforming government was showing signs of managing the economy successfully enough to stand a chance of re-election when its term was up. That situation, I expect, will occur again. The constitutional *coup d'etat*, the *putsch*, must never occur again.

From the wreckage of conventions broken in November 1975 several issues of paramount constitutional importance emerge. The first is whether the Senate does, or should, have constitutional power to block supply to the elected government. Argument about the Senate's powers has concentrated on two questions. What was intended by the founding fathers? And what is the proper literal interpretation of ss. 53 and 57?

As far as the intentions of the founding fathers are concerned, a number of propositions are clear. First, they contemplated a power in the Senate to reject money Bills only when the Senate disagreed with the substance of the specific measure on which they were voting. Secondly, they envisaged the Senate disagreeing with the measure, not for party political reasons, but because of its impact on States' rights. Thirdly, they considered a formula which would have spelt out a general power to reject money Bills, but did not include it in the final draft. Finally, from the very earliest days of the Convention, it was never envisaged that the Senate would use its power in the circumstances and in the manner it was used in 1974 and 1975.

As far as the literal meaning of ss. 53 and 57 is concerned, I do not believe any satisfactory answer can be given. As we discovered as a government, and as the Governor-General discovered when he purported to dismiss the Government, ss. 53 and 57 are wholly unworkable as machinery for the resolution of differences between the Houses on questions of supply. Any possible literal interpretation of the sections only serves to underline that unworkability. To make the scheme of the Constitution sensible in this area, as in so many others, one must resort to the understandings, or conventions, on which the Constitution was based. One of those was clearly that the Senate ought not to reject supply for party political reasons.

The plain fact is that supply has now twice been blocked and the Opposition was rewarded for its action by being appointed a caretaker government. In these circumstances it is perhaps more relevant to concern ourselves with the need to alter the Constitution to put the question beyond doubt. The third session of the Australian Constitutional Convention will convene in Hobart in October 1976. Originally the agenda for that session contained no item raising the question of the Senate's powers, perhaps the greatest constitutional issue of our time. Despite the opposition of the conservative parties such an item has now been included on the agenda by the Executive Committee at the initiative of the Federal Parliamentary Labor Party. I shall propose to the Convention that it recommend that the Constitution be amended to make clear that the Senate has no power to reject, delay or otherwise block supply to a duly elected government.

I turn now to two other questions of overriding constitutional significance—the power of a Governor-General to dismiss a government and his power to dissolve the Parliament.

I do not believe that the Governor-General acting alone has the power to dismiss an elected government. Sections 61 to 67 of the Constitution are meaningless unless they are read in the context of responsible government and in the light of the existence of a Prime Minister, a Cabinet and a Government, none of which is mentioned in those sections. Since the Reform Bill of 1832 it has been axiomatic that the Sovereign acts only on the advice of ministers. After 1832 the prerogative power was not to be exercised as a personal act of the Crown. That was regarded as axiomatic by the founding fathers in 1900. It is regarded as axiomatic by the Queen of Britain in 1976. It ought to have been regarded as axiomatic by the delegate of the Queen of Australia in 1975.

Sections 2 and 61 of the Constitution make it clear that the Governor-General is the representative of the Queen, that it is her power that he exercises. Whatever reserve powers the Governor-General enjoys cannot be wider than the Queen's. Constitutional lawyers are unanimously of the opinion that she does not enjoy the power to dismiss a British Prime Minister in parallel circumstances to those which prevailed in Australia in 1975. The Queen of Australia is powerless once she has appointed her representative. Having appointed a Governor-General she is *functa officio* until she appoints his successor.

I deal next with the Governor-General's right to dissolve Parliament. A comparison has been drawn by some with the double dissolution granted to Prime Minister Menzies by Governor-General McKell in 1951. That was an entirely different situation. On that occasion a Governor-General was advised by a Prime Minister to dissolve the Parliament. In tendering that advice the Prime Minister suggested that the Governor-General had a discretion not to accept the advice given. In fact, the Governor-General did accept the advice. Whatever may be said about the Governor-General's discretion in that case, it is certainly not possible to turn the precedent on its head and argue that the Governor-General can act virtually on his own and dissolve Parliament against the wishes of the Prime Minister.

If the Governor-General indeed had the power to dismiss the Government and dissolve the Parliament because the Government had failed to obtain supply, why did he use the double dissolution provisions of s.57? I have already argued that the Chief Justice's letter of advice to the Governor-General was wrong and inadequate. But not even the Chief Justice suggested that the Governor-General should use s.57 to achieve his purpose. Indeed, only a matter of days before he gave his advice to the Governor-General, the Chief Justice had delivered an opinion to the effect that Bills could not be stockpiled under s.57 and then used as the basis for a double dissolution in circumstances unrelated to the rejection of the Bills themselves. Yet that is precisely what the Governor-General did. One result of this is that no Prime Minister can ever afford to allow a situation to develop in which a Bill satisfies the requirements of s.57 unless he wishes to advise a double dissolution immediately. In any other situation the Bill would become a sword of Damocles. It could be used to dissolve the Parliament at the whim of the Governor-General irrespective of the wishes of the elected government.

The effect of the Chief Justice's advice, as opposed to the actual steps which the Governor-General took, would be equally dangerous. If the Chief Justice is correct then a Governor-General has the power, to be exercised at his own discretion, to force the House of Representatives alone to the people whenever a hostile Senate uses its numbers to defer supply. The most basic tenet of our parliamentary democracy is that the party with the elected majority in the popular House, the House of Representatives, is entitled to govern. The Constitution recognises that tenet indirectly by providing in s.57 a mechanism for resolving conflicts between the two Houses. To hold, as the Chief Justice does, that conflicts can simply be resolved by dismissing the Prime Minister and dissolving the House of Representatives is to elevate to the pre-eminent position in our parliamentary system a Senate which is not representative of the people and half of which may not have faced the people for six years.

VI
A CONSTITUTION FOR SOCIAL DEMOCRATS

Looking back over three years of Labor Government, the social democrat has reason for considerable optimism and for considerable pessimism. His optimism flows from the significant achievements in developing and extending the legislative and executive powers of the national government, from the sanction given to those developments by the High Court and from the progress achieved in making our federal system more efficient, equitable and responsive. His pessimism flows from the damage done to the democratic system by its repeated abuse, the failure to democratise our electoral system and the examples which conservative forces have given of devices to dismiss a reformist government when it suits them. We must begin now to plan policies which will maximize the benefits of constitutional development and minimize the dangers of future abuse of the Constitution.

I believe that the basic aims of the social democrat in Australia can be achieved under the present Constitution and that we now have a clearer perception of what social democracy means. Social democracy in Australia means that a national government has a direct responsibility to intervene in the distribution of wealth and incomes and social benefits, in order to distribute them more equally and justly. A Labor government will have the constitutional power to achieve that redistribution through its social welfare policies, its policies on education, the status of women, ethnic groups and Aboriginals and its policies for the management of the Australian economy.

Social democracy means that a national government has a responsibility to intervene as a countervailing power on behalf of Australian citizens and consumers to regulate the impact of the private sector on the rights of the individual. A Labor government will have the constitutional power to exercise that influence through its policies with respect to consumer protection, the securities industry, trade practices, the environment and foreign investment. It will also have a responsibility to establish independent mechanisms capable of giving the citizen similar protection against the exercise of government power by the executive arm.

Social democracy means that a national government has a responsibility to intervene on a temporary basis in those areas which, for reasons of historical neglect by conservative State and federal governments, can only now be brought to an acceptable standard by national planning and finance. A Labor government will have the constitutional power to intervene in the great problems of the post-war suburbs of our cities, in sewerage, urban development and transport. Once the problems of neglect have been overcome, a Labor government will have the constitutional power to ensure that the responsibility for governing these areas is a co-operative endeavour of all three levels of our federal system.

Social democracy also means direct participation by the government in the production of goods and services where it can do so efficiently, where the government is an appropriate organisational base for the productive activity or where the government is a prime customer of the product in question. A Labor government will have the constitutional power to compete in our mixed economy in insurance, in pharmaceutical production, in the development of land.

I said in my Chifley Memorial Lecture in 1957 that Labor must first persuade the people to elect it to government and then persuade them to alter the Constitution. It is still necessary to convince the electorate to elect a Labor government and I am confident that they will do so in 1978. It is still desirable to alter the Constitution, but much can be done in implementing the policies of the Labor Party within the existing Constitution. Labor and the Constitution can co-exist. Australia can still have a vigorous, reforming government, but our constitutional traditions will need to be strengthened and defined, and much vigilance exercised by democrats of all kinds, and not least by lawyers, if such a government is to have a chance of surviving and putting its objectives into practice.

APPENDICES

Appendix A

The Constitution of the Commonwealth of Australia

COMMONWEALTH OF AUSTRALIA CONSTITUTION ACT

(63 & 64 VICTORIA, CHAPTER 12)

An Act to constitute the Commonwealth of Australia.

[9th July 1900]

WHEREAS the people of New South Wales, Victoria, South Australia, Queensland, and Tasmania, huzly relying on the blessing of Almighty God, have agreed to unite in one indissoluble Federal Commonwealth under the Crown of the United Kingdom of Great Britain and Ireland, and under the Constitution hereby established:

And whereas it is expedient to provide for the admission into the Commonwealth of other Australasian Colonies and possessions of the Queen:

Be it therefore enacted by the Queen's most Excellent Majesty, by and with the advice and consent of the Lords Spiritual and Temporal, and Commons, in this present Parliament assembled, and by the authority of the same, as follows:—

1. This Act may be cited as the Commonwealth of Australia Constitution Act.

2. The provisions of this Act referring to the Queen shall extend to Her Majesty's heirs and successors in the sovereignty of the United Kingdom.

3. It shall be lawful for the Queen, with the advice of the Privy Council, to declare by proclamation that, on and after a day therein appointed, not being later than one year after the passing of this Act, the people of New South Wales, Victoria, South Australia, Queensland, and Tasmania, and also, if Her Majesty is satisfied that the people of Western Australia have agreed thereto, of Western Australia, shall be united in a Federal Commonwealth under the name of the Commonwealth of Australia. But the Queen may, at any time after the proclamation, appoint a Governor-General for the Commonwealth.

4. The Commonwealth shall be established, and the Constitution of the Commonwealth shall take effect, on and after the day so appointed. But the Parliaments of the several colonies may at any time after the passing of this Act make any such laws, to come into operation on the day so appointed, as they might have made if the Constitution had taken effect at the passing of this Act.

5. This Act, and all laws made by the Parliament of the Commonwealth under the Constitution, shall be binding on the courts, judges, and people of every State and of every part of the Commonwealth, notwithstanding anything in the laws of any State; and the laws of the Commonwealth shall be in force on all British ships, the Queen's ships of war excepted, whose first port of clearance and whose port of destination are in the Commonwealth.

6. "The Commonwealth" shall mean the Commonwealth of Australia as established under this Act.

"The States" shall mean such of the colonies of New South Wales, New Zealand, Queensland, Tasmania, Victoria, Western Australia, and South Australia, including the northern territory of South Australia, as for the time being are parts of the Commonwealth, and such colonies or territories as may be admitted into or established by the Commonwealth as States; and each of such parts of the Commonwealth shall be called "a State."

"Original States" shall mean such States as are parts of the Commonwealth at its establishment.

7. The Federal Council of Australasia Act, 1885, is hereby repealed, but so as not to affect any laws passed by the Federal Council of Australasia and in force at the establishment of the Commonwealth.

Any such law may be repealed as to any State by the Parliament of the Commonwealth, or as to any colony not being a State by the Parliament thereof.

333

8. After the passing of this Act the Colonial Boundaries Act, 1895, shall not apply to any colony which becomes a State of the Commonwealth; but the Commonwealth shall be taken to be a self-governing colony for the purposes of that Act.

9. The Constitution of the Commonwealth shall be as follows:—

THE CONSTITUTION.

This Constitution is divided as follows:—

CHAPTER I.

THE PARLIAMENT.
PART I.—GENERAL.

1. The legislative power of the Commonwealth shall be vested in a Federal Parliament, which shall consist of the Queen, a Senate, and a House of Representatives, and which is herein-after called "The Parliament," or "The Parliament of the Commonwealth."

2. A Governor-General appointed by the Queen shall be Her Majesty's representative in the Commonwealth, and shall have and may exercise in the Commonwealth during the Queen's pleasure, but subject to this Constitution, such powers and functions of the Queen as Her Majesty may be pleased to assign to him.

3. There shall be payable to the Queen out of the Consolidated Revenue fund of the Commonwealth, for the salary of the Governor-General, an annual sum which, until the Parliament otherwise provides, shall be ten thousand pounds.

The salary of a Governor-General shall not be altered during his continuance in office.

4. The provisions of this Constitution relating to the Governor-General extend and apply to the Governor-General for the time being, or such person as the Queen may appoint to administer the government of the Commonwealth; but no such person shall be entitled to receive any salary from the Commonwealth in respect of any other office during his administration of the Government of the Commonwealth.

5. The Governor-General may appoint such times for holding the sessions of the Parliament as he thinks fit, and may also from time to time, by Proclamation or otherwise, prorogue the Parliament, and may in like manner dissolve the House of Representatives.

After any general election the Parliament shall be summoned to meet not later than thirty days after the day appointed for the return of the writs.

The Parliament shall be summoned to meet not later than six months after the establishment of the Commonwealth.

6. There shall be a session of the Parliament once at least in every year, so that twelve months shall not intervene between the last sitting of the Parliament in one session and its first sitting in the next session.

PART II.—THE SENATE.

7. The Senate shall be composed of senators for each State, directly chosen by the people of the State, voting, until the Parliament otherwise provides, as one electorate.

But until the Parliament of the Commonwealth otherwise provides, the Parliament of the State of Queensland, if that State be an Original State, may make laws dividing the State into divisions and determining the number of senators to be chosen for each division, and in the absence of such provision the State shall be one electorate.

Until the Parliament otherwise provides there shall be six senators for each original State. The Parliament may make laws increasing or diminishing the number of senators for each State, but so that equal representation of the several Original States shall be maintained and that no Original State shall have less than six senators.

The senators shall be chosen for a term of six years, and the names of the senators chosen for each State shall be certified by the Governor to the Governor-General.

8. The qualification of electors of senators shall be in each State that which is prescribed by this Constitution, or by the Parliament, as the qualification for electors of members of the House of Representatives; but in the choosing of senators each elector shall vote only once.

9. The Parliament of the Commonwealth may make laws prescribing the method of choosing senators, but so that the method shall be uniform for all the States. Subject to any such law, the Parliament of each State may make laws prescribing the method of choosing the senators for that State.

The Parliament of a State may make laws for determining the times and places of elections of senators for the State.

10. Until the Parliament otherwise provides, but subject to this Constitution, the laws in force in each State, for the time being, relating to elections for the more numerous House of the Parliament of the State shall, as nearly as practicable, apply to elections of senators for the State.

11. The Senate may proceed to the despatch of business, notwithstanding the failure of any State to provide for its representation in the Senate.

12. The Governor of any State may cause writs to be issued for elections of senators for the State. In case of the dissolution of the Senate the writs shall be issued within ten days from the proclamation of such dissolution.

13. As soon as may be after the Senate first meets, and after each first meeting of the Senate following a dissolution thereof, the Senate shall divide the senators chosen for each State into two classes, as nearly equal in number as practicable; and the places of the senators of the first class shall become vacant at the expiration of ~~the third year,~~ **three years,** and the places of those of the second class at the expiration of ~~the sixth year,~~ **six years,** from the beginning of their term of service; and afterwards the places of senators shall become vacant at the expiration of six years from the beginning of their term of service.

The election to fill vacant places shall be made ~~in the year at the expiration of which~~ **within one year before** the places are to become vacant.

For the purposes of this section the term of service of a senator shall be taken to begin on the first day of ~~January~~ **July** following the day of his election, except in the cases of the first election and of the election next after any dissolution of the Senate, when it shall be taken to begin on the first day of ~~January~~ **July** preceding the day of his election.

14. Whenever the number of senators for a State is increased or diminished, the Parliament of the Commonwealth may make such provision for the vacating of the places of senators for the State as it deems necessary to maintain regularity in the rotation.

15. If the place of a senator becomes vacant before the expiration of his term of service, the Houses of Parliament of the State for which he was chosen shall, sitting and voting together, choose a person to hold the place until the expiration of the term, or until the election of a successor as herein-after provided, whichever first happens. But if the Houses of Parliament of the State are not in session at the time when the vacancy is notified, the Governor of the State, with the advice of the Executive Council thereof, may appoint a person to hold the place until the expiration of fourteen days after the beginning of the next session of the Parliament of the State, or until the election of a successor, whichever first happens.

At the next general election of members of the House of Representatives, or at the next election of senators for the State, whichever first happens, a successor shall, if the term has not then expired, be chosen to hold the place from the date of his election until the expiration of the term.

The name of any senator so chosen or appointed shall be certified by the Governor of the State to the Governor-General.

16. The qualifications of a senator shall be the same as those of a member of the House of Representatives.

17. The Senate shall, before proceeding to the despatch of any other business, choose a senator to be the President of the Senate; and as often as the office of President becomes vacant the Senate shall again choose a senator to be the President.

The President shall cease to hold his office if he ceases to be a senator. He may be removed from office by a vote of the Senate, or he may resign his office or his seat by writing addressed to the Governor-General.

18. Before or during any absence of the President, the Senate may choose a senator to perform his duties in his absence.

19. A senator may, by writing addressed to the President, or to the Governor-General if there is no President or if the President is absent from the Commonwealth, resign his place, which thereupon shall become vacant.

20. The place of a senator shall become vacant if for two consecutive months of any session of the Parliament he, without the permission of the Senate, fails to attend the Senate.

21. Whenever a vacancy happens in the Senate, the President, or if there is no President or if the President is absent from the Commonwealth the Governor-General, shall notify the same to the Governor of the State in the representation of which the vacancy has happened.

22. Until the Parliament otherwise provides, the presence of at least one-third of the whole number of the senators shall be necessary to constitute a meeting of the Senate for the exercise of its powers.

23. Questions arising in the Senate shall be determined by a majority of votes, and each senator shall have one vote. The President shall in all cases be entitled to a vote; and when the votes are equal the question shall pass in the negative.

PART III.—THE HOUSE OF REPRESENTATIVES.

24. The House of Representatives shall be composed of members directly chosen by the people of the Commonwealth, and the number of such members shall be, as nearly as practicable, twice the number of the senators.

The number of members chosen in the several States shall be in proportion to the respective numbers of their people, and shall, until the Parliament otherwise provides, be determined, whenever necessary, in the following manner:—

      (i.) A quota shall be ascertained by dividing the number of the people of the Commonwealth, as shown by the latest statistics of the Commonwealth, by twice the number of the senators:

      (ii.) The number of members to be chosen in each State shall be determined by dividing the number of the people of the State, as shown by the latest statistics of the Commonwealth, by the quota; and if on such division there is a remainder greater than one-half of the quota, one more member shall be chosen in the State.

But notwithstanding anything in this section, five members at least shall be chosen in each Original State.

25. For the purposes of the last section, if by the law of any State all persons of any race are disqualified from voting at elections for the more numerous House of the Parliament of the State, then, in reckoning the number of the people of the State or of the Commonwealth, persons of that race resident in that State shall not be counted.

26. Notwithstanding anything in section twenty-four, the number of members to be chosen in each State at the first election shall be as follows:—

New South Wales ....twenty-three;
Victoria ....twenty;
Queensland ....eight;
South Australia ....six;
Tasmania ....five;

Provided that if Western Australia is an Original State, the numbers shall be as follows:—

New South Wales ....twenty-six;
Victoria ....twenty-three;
Queensland ....nine;
South Australia ....seven;

Western Australia ....five;

Tasmania ....five.

27. Subject to this Constitution, the Parliament may make laws for increasing or diminishing the number of the members of the House of Representatives.

28. Every House of Representatives shall continue for three years from the first meeting of the House, and no longer, but may be sooner dissolved by the Governor-General.

29. Until the Parliament of the Commonwealth otherwise provides, the Parliament of any State may make laws for determining the divisions in each State for which members of the House of Representatives may be chosen, and the number of members to be chosen for each division. A division shall not be formed out of parts of different States.

In the absence of other provision, each State shall be one electorate.

30. Until the Parliament otherwise provides, the qualification of electors of members of the House of Representatives shall be in each State that which is prescribed by the law of the State as the qualification of electors of the more numerous House of Parliament of the State; but in the choosing of members each elector shall vote only once.

31. Until the Parliament otherwise provides, but subject to this Constitution, the laws in force in each State for the time being relating to elections for the more numerous House of the Parliament of the State shall, as nearly as practicable, apply to elections in the State of members of the House of Representatives.

32. The Governor-General in Council may cause writs to be issued for general elections of members of the House of Representatives.

After the first general election, the writs shall be issued within ten days from the expiry of a House of Representatives or from the proclamation of a dissolution thereof.

33. Whenever a vacancy happens in the House of Representatives, the Speaker shall issue his writ for the election of a new member, or if there is no Speaker or if he is absent from the Commonwealth the Governor-General in Council may issue the writ.

34. Until the Parliament otherwise provides, the qualifications of a member of the House of Representatives shall be as follows:—

> (i.) He must be of the full age of twenty-one years, and must be an elector entitled to vote at the election of members of the House of Representatives, or a person qualified to become such elector, and must have been for three years at the least a resident within the limits of the Commonwealth as existing at the time when he is chosen:

> (ii.) He must be a subject of the Queen, either natural-born or for at least five years naturalized under a law of the United Kingdom, or of a Colony which has become or becomes a State, or of the Commonwealth, or of a State.

35. The House of Representatives shall, before proceeding to the despatch of any other business, choose a member to be the Speaker of the House, and as often as the office of Speaker becomes vacant the House shall again choose a member to be the Speaker.

The Speaker shall cease to hold his office if he ceases to be a member. He may be removed from office by a vote of the House, or he may resign his office or his seat by writing addressed to the Governor-General.

36. Before or during any absence of the Speaker, the House of Representatives may choose a member to perform his duties in his absence.

37. A member may by writing addressed to the Speaker, or to the Governor-General if there is no Speaker or if the Speaker is absent from the Commonwealth, resign his place, which thereupon shall become vacant.

38. The place of a member shall become vacant if for two consecutive months of any session of the Parliament he, without the permission of the House, fails to attend the House.

39. Until the Parliament otherwise provides, the presence of at least one-third of the whole number of the members of the House of Representatives shall be necessary to constitute a meeting of the House for the exercise of its powers.

40. Questions arising in the House of Representatives shall be determined by a majority of votes other than that of the Speaker. The Speaker shall not vote unless the numbers are equal, and then he shall have a casting vote.

PART IV.—BOTH HOUSES OF THE PARLIAMENT.

41. No adult person who has or acquires a right to vote at elections for the more numerous House of the Parliament of a State shall, while the right continues, be prevented by any law of the Commonwealth from voting at elections for either House of the Parliament of the Commonwealth.

42. Every senator and every member of the House of Representatives shall before taking his seat make and subscribe before the Governor-General, or some person authorised by him, an oath or affirmation of allegiance in the form set forth in the schedule to this Constitution.

43. A member of either House of the Parliament shall be incapable of being chosen or of sitting as a member of the other House.

44. Any person who—

 (i.) Is under any acknowledgment of allegiance, obedience, or adherence to a foreign power, or is a subject or a citizen or entitled to the rights or privileges of a subject or a citizen of a foreign power: or

 (ii.) Is attainted of treason, or has been convicted and is under sentence, or subject to be sentenced, for any offence punishable under the law of the Commonwealth or of a State by imprisonment for one year or longer: or

 (iii.) Is an undischarged bankrupt or insolvent: or

 (iv.) Holds any office of profit under the Crown, or any pension payable during the pleasure of the Crown out of any of the revenues of the Commonwealth: or

 (v.) Has any direct or indirect pecuniary interest in any agreement with the Public Service of the Commonwealth otherwise than as a member and in common with the other members of an incorporated company consisting of more than twenty-five persons:

shall be incapable of being chosen or of sitting as a senator or a member of the House of Representatives.

But sub-section iv does not apply to the office of any of the Queen's Ministers of State for the Commonwealth, or of any of the Queen's Ministers for a State, or to the receipt of pay, half pay, or a pension, by any person as an officer or member of the Queen's navy or army, or to the receipt of pay as an officer or member of the naval or military forces of the Commonwealth by any person whose services are not wholly employed by the Commonwealth.

45. If a senator or member of the House of Representatives—

 (i.) Becomes subject to any of the disabilities mentioned in the last preceding section: or

 (ii.) Takes the benefit, whether by assignment, composition, or otherwise, of any law relating to bankrupt or insolvent debtors; or

 (iii.) Directly or indirectly takes or agrees to take any fee or honorarium for services rendered to the Commonwealth, or for services rendered in the Parliament to any person or State:

his place shall thereupon become vacant.

46. Until the Parliament otherwise provides, any person declared by this Constitution to be incapable of sitting as a senator or as a member of the House of Representatives shall, for every day on which he so sits, be liable to pay the sum of one hundred pounds to any person who sues for it in any court of competent jurisdiction.

47. Until the Parliament otherwise provides, any question respecting the qualification of a senator or of a member of the House of Representatives, or respecting a vacancy in either House of the Parliament, and any question of a disputed election to either House, shall be determined by the House in which the question arises.

48. Until the Parliament otherwise provides, each senator and each member of the House of Representatives shall receive an allowance of four hundred pounds a year, to be reckoned from the day on which he takes his seat.

49. The powers, privileges, and immunities of the Senate and of the House of Representatives, and of the members and the committees of each House, shall be such as are declared by the Parliament, and until declared shall be those of the Commons House of Parliament of the United Kingdom, and of its members and committees, at the establishment of the Commonwealth.

50. Each House of the Parliament may make rules and orders with respect to—

 (i.) The mode in which its powers, privileges, and immunities may be exercised and upheld:

 (ii.) The order and conduct of its business and proceedings either separately or jointly with the other House.

PART V.—POWERS OF THE PARLIAMENT.

51. The Parliament shall, subject to this Constitution, have power to make laws for the peace, order, and good government of the Commonwealth with respect to:—

    (i.) Trade and commerce with other countries, and among the States:

    (ii.) Taxation; but so as not to discriminate between States or parts of States:

    (iii.) Bounties on the production or export of goods, but so that such bounties shall be uniform throughout the Commonwealth:

    (iv.) Borrowing money on the public credit of the Commonwealth:

    (v.) Postal, telegraphic, telephonic, and other like services:

    (vi.) The naval and military defence of the Commonwealth and of the several States, and the control of the forces to execute and maintain the laws of the Commonwealth:

    (vii.) Lighthouses, lightships, beacons and buoys:

    (viii.) Astronomical and meteorological observations:

    (ix.) Quarantine:

    (x.) Fisheries in Australian waters beyond territorial limits:

    (xi.) Census and statistics:

    (xii.) Currency, coinage, and legal tender:

    (xiii.) Banking, other than State banking; also State banking extending beyond the limits of the State concerned, the incorporation of banks, and the issue of paper money:

    (xiv.) Insurance, other than State insurance; also State insurance extending beyond the limits of the State concerned:

    (xv.) Weights and measures:

    (xvi.) Bills of exchange and promissory notes:

    (xvii.) Bankruptcy and insolvency:

    (xviii.) Copyrights, patents of inventions and designs, and trade marks:

    (xix.) Naturalization and aliens:

    (xx.) Foreign corporations, and trading or financial corporations formed within the limits of the Commonwealth:

    (xxi.) Marriage:

    (xxii.) Divorce and matrimonial causes; and in relation thereto, parental rights, and the custody and guardianship of infants:

    (xxiii.) Invalid and old-age pensions:

    (xxiiiA.) The provision of maternity allowances, widows' pensions, child endowment, unemployment, pharmaceutical, sickness and hospital benefits, medical and dental services (but not so as to authorize any form of civil conscription), benefits to students and family allowances:

    (xxiv.) The service and execution throughout the Commonwealth of the civil and criminal process and the judgments of the courts of the States:

    (xxv.) The recognition throughout the Commonwealth of the laws, the public Acts and records, and the judicial proceedings of the States:

    (xxvi.) The people of any race, ~~other than the aboriginal race in any State,~~ for whom it is deemed necessary to make special laws:

    (xxvii.) Immigration and emigration:

    (xxviii.) The influx of criminals:

(xxix.) External affairs:

(xxx.) The relations of the Commonwealth with the islands of the Pacific:

(xxxi.) The acquisition of property on just terms from any State or person for any purpose in respect of which the Parliament has power to make laws:

(xxxii.) The control of railways with respect to transport for the naval and military purposes of the Commonwealth:

(xxxiii.) The acquisition, with the consent of a State, of any railways of the State on terms arranged between the Commonwealth and the State:

(xxxiv.) Railway construction and extension in any State with the consent of that State:

(xxxv.) Conciliation and arbitration for the prevention and settlement of industrial disputes extending beyond the limits of any one State:

(xxxvi.) Matters in respect of which this Constitution makes provision until the Parliament otherwise provides:

(xxxvii.) Matters referred to the Parliament of the Commonwealth by the Parliament or Parliaments of any State or States, but so that the law shall extend only to States by whose Parliaments the matter is referred, or which afterwards adopt the law:

(xxxviii.) The exercise within the Commonwealth, at the request or with the concurrence of the Parliaments of all the States directly concerned, of any power which can at the establishment of this Constitution be exercised only by the Parliament of the United Kingdom or by the Federal Council of Australasia:

(xxxix.) Matters incidental to the execution of any power vested by this Constitution in the Parliament or in either House thereof, or in the government of the Commonwealth, or in the Federal Judicature, or in any department or officer of the Commonwealth.

52. The Parliament shall, subject to this Constitution, have exclusive power to make laws for the peace, order, and good government of the Commonwealth with respect to—

(i.) The seat of government of the Commonwealth, and all places acquired by the Commonwealth for public purposes:

(ii.) Matters relating to any department of the public service the control of which is by this Constitution transferred to the Executive Government of the Commonwealth:

(iii.) Other matters declared by this Constitution to be within the exclusive power of the Parliament.

53. Proposed laws appropriating revenue or moneys, or imposing taxation, shall not originate in the Senate. But a proposed law shall not be taken to appropriate revenue or moneys, or to impose taxation, by reason only of its containing provisions for the imposition or appropriation of fines or other pecuniary penalties, or for the demand or payment or appropriation of fees for licences, or fees for services under the proposed law.

The Senate may not amend proposed laws imposing taxation, or proposed laws appropriating revenue or moneys for the ordinary annual services of the Government.

The Senate may not amend any proposed law so as to increase any proposed charge or burden on the people.

The Senate may at any stage return to the House of Representatives any proposed law which the Senate may not amend, requesting, by message, the omission or amendment of any items or provisions therein. And the House of Representatives may, if it thinks fit, make any of such omissions or amendments, with or without modifications.

Except as provided in this section, the Senate shall have equal power with the House of Representatives in respect of all proposed laws.

54. The proposed law which appropriates revenue or moneys for the ordinary annual services of the Government shall deal only with such appropriation.

55. Laws imposing taxation shall deal only with the imposition of taxation, and any provision therein dealing with any other matter shall be of no effect.

Laws imposing taxation, except laws imposing duties of customs or of excise, shall deal with one subject of taxation only; but laws imposing duties of customs shall deal with duties of customs only, and laws imposing duties of excise shall deal with duties of excise only.

56. A vote, resolution, or proposed law for the appropriation of revenue or moneys shall not be passed unless the purpose of the appropriation has in the same session been recommended by message of the Governor-General to the House in which the proposal originated.

57. If the House of Representatives passes any proposed law, and the Senate rejects or fails to pass it, or passes it with amendments to which the House of Representatives will not agree, and if after an interval of three months the House of Representatives, in the same or the next session, again passes the proposed law with or without any amendments which have been made, suggested, or agreed to by the Senate, and the Senate rejects or fails to pass it, or passes it with amendments to which the House of Representatives will not agree, the Governor-General may dissolve the Senate and the House of Representatives simultaneously. But such dissolution shall not take place within six months before the date of the expiry of the House of Representatives by effluxion of time.

If after such dissolution the House of Representatives again passes the proposed law, with or without any amendments which have been made, suggested, or agreed to by the Senate, and the Senate rejects or fails to pass it, or passes it with amendments to which the House of Representatives will not agree, the Governor-General may convene a joint sitting of the members of the Senate and of the House of Representatives.

The members present at the joint sitting may deliberate and shall vote together upon the proposed law as last proposed by the House of Representatives, and upon amendments, if any, which have been made therein by one House and not agreed to by the other, and any such amendments which are affirmed by an absolute majority of the total number of the members of the Senate and House of Representatives shall be taken to have been carried, and if the proposed law, with the amendments, if any, so carried is affirmed by an absolute majority of the total number of the members of the Senate and House of Representatives, it shall be taken to have been duly passed by both Houses of the Parliament, and shall be presented to the Governor-General for the Queen's assent.

58. When a proposed law passed by both Houses of the Parliament is presented to the Governor-General for the Queen's assent, he shall declare, according to his discretion, but subject to this Constitution, that he assents in the Queen's name, or that he withholds assent, or that he reserves the law for the Queen's pleasure.

The Governor-General may return to the House in which it originated any proposed law so presented to him, and may transmit therewith any amendments which he may recommend, and the Houses may deal with the recommendation.

59. The Queen may disallow any law within one year from the Governor-General's assent, and such disallowance on being made known by the Governor-General by speech or message to each of the Houses of the Parliament, or by Proclamation, shall annul the law from the day when the disallowance is so made known.

60. A proposed law reserved for the Queen's pleasure shall not have any force unless and until within two years from the day on which it was presented to the Governor-General for the Queen's assent the Governor-General makes known, by speech or message to each of the Houses of the Parliament, or by Proclamation, that it has received the Queen's assent.

CHAPTER II.

THE EXECUTIVE GOVERNMENT.

61. The executive power of the Commonwealth is vested in the Queen and is exerciseable by the Governor-General as the Queen's representative, and extends to the execution and maintenance of this Constitution, and of the laws of the Commonwealth.

62. There shall be a Federal Executive Council to advise the Governor-General in the government of the Commonwealth, and the members of the Council shall be chosen and summoned by the Governor-General and sworn as Executive Councillors, and shall hold office during his pleasure.

63. The provisions of this Constitution referring to the Governor-General in Council shall be construed as referring to the Governor-General acting with the advice of the Federal Executive Council.

64. The Governor-General may appoint officers to administer such departments of State of the Commonwealth as the Governor-General in Council may establish.

Such officers shall hold office during the pleasure of the Governor-General. They shall be members of the Federal Executive Council, and shall be the Queen's Ministers of State for the Commonwealth.

After the first general election no Minister of State shall hold office for a longer period than three months unless he is or becomes a senator or a member of the House of Representatives.

65. Until the Parliament otherwise provides, the Ministers of State shall not exceed seven in number, and shall hold such offices as the Parliament prescribes, or, in the absence of provision, as the Governor-General directs.

66. There shall be payable to the Queen, out of the Consolidated Revenue Fund of the Commonwealth, for the salaries of the Ministers of State, an annual sum which, until the Parliament otherwise provides, shall not exceed twelve thousand pounds a year.

67. Until the Parliament otherwise provides, the appointment and removal of all other officers of the Executive Government of the Commonwealth shall be vested in the Governor-General in Council, unless the appointment is delegated by the Governor-General in Council or by a law of the Commonwealth to some other authority.

68. The command in chief of the naval and military forces of the Commonwealth is vested in the Governor-General as the Queen's representative.

69. On a date or dates to be proclaimed by the Governor-General after the establishment of the Commonwealth the following departments of the public service in each State shall become transferred to the Commonwealth:—

Posts, telegraphs, and telephones:
Naval and military defence:
Lighthouses, lightships, beacons, and buoys:
Quarantine.

But the departments of customs and of excise in each State shall become transferred to the Commonwealth on its establishment.

70. In respect of matters which, under this Constitution, pass to the Executive Government of the Commonwealth, all powers and functions which at the establishment of the Commonwealth are vested in the Governor of a Colony, or in the Governor of a Colony with the advice of his Executive Council, or in any authority of a Colony, shall vest in the Governor-General, or in the Governor-General in Council, or in the authority exercising similar powers under the Commonwealth, as the case requires.

CHAPTER III.

THE JUDICATURE.

71. The judicial power of the Commonwealth shall be vested in a Federal Supreme Court, to be called the High Court of Australia, and in such other federal courts as the Parliament creates, and in such other courts as it invests with federal jurisdiction. The High Court shall consist of a Chief Justice, and so many other Justices, not less than two, as the Parliament prescribes.

72. The Justices of the High Court and of the other courts created by the Parliament—
(i.) Shall be appointed by the Governor-General in Council:
(ii.) Shall not be removed except by the Governor-General in Council, on an address from both Houses of the Parliament in the same session, praying for such removal on the ground of proved misbehaviour or incapacity:
(iii.) Shall receive such remuneration as the Parliament may fix; but the remuneration shall not be diminished during their continuance in office.

73. The High Court shall have jurisdiction, with such exceptions and subject to such regulations as the Parliament prescribes, to hear and determine appeals from all judgments, decrees, orders, and sentences—
(i.) Of any Justice or Justices exercising the original jurisdiction of the High Court:
(ii.) Of any other federal court, or court exercising federal jurisdiction; or of the Supreme Court of any State, or of any other court of any State from which at the establishment of the Commonwealth an appeal lies to the Queen in Council:
(iii.) Of the Inter-State Commission, but as to questions of law only:
and the judgment of the High Court in all such cases shall be final and conclusive.

But no exception or regulation prescribed by the Parliament shall prevent the High Court from hearing and determining any appeal from the Supreme Court of a State in any matter in which at the establishment of the Commonwealth an appeal lies from such Supreme Court to the Queen in Council.

Until the Parliament otherwise provides, the conditions of and restrictions on appeals to the Queen in Council from the Supreme Courts of the several States shall be applicable to appeals from them to the High Court.

74. No appeal shall be permitted to the Queen in Council from a decision of the High Court upon any question, howsoever arising, as to the limits inter se of the Constitutional powers of the Commonwealth and those of any State or States, or as to the limits inter se of the Constitutional powers of any two or more States, unless the High Court shall certify that the question is one which ought to be determined by Her Majesty in Council.

The High Court may so certify if satisfied that for any special reason the certificate should be granted, and thereupon an appeal shall lie to Her Majesty in·Council on the question without further leave.

Except as provided in this section, this Constitution shall not impair any right which the Queen may be pleased to exercise by virtue of her Royal prerogative to grant special leave of appeal from the High Court to Her Majesty in Council. The Parliament may make laws limiting the matters in which such leave may be asked, but proposed laws containing any such limitation shall be reserved by the Governor-General for Her Majesty's pleasure.

75. In all matters—

    (i.) Arising under any treaty:

    (ii.) Affecting consuls or other representatives of other countries:

    (iii.) In which the Commonwealth, or a person suing or being sued on behalf of the Commonwealth, is a party:

    (iv.) Between States, or between residents of different States, or between a State and a resident of another State:

    (v.) In which a writ of Mandamus or prohibition or an injunction is sought against an officer of the Commonwealth:

the High Court shall have original jurisdiction.

76. The Parliament may make laws conferring original jurisdiction on the High Court in any matter—

    (i.) Arising under this Constitution, or involving its interpretation:

    (ii.) Arising under any laws made by the Parliament:

    (iii.) Of Admiralty and maritime jurisdiction:

    (iv.) Relating to the same subject-matter claimed under the laws of different States.

77. With respect to any of the matters mentioned in the last two sections the Parliament may make laws—

    (i.) Defining the jurisdiction of any federal court other than the High Court:

    (ii.) Defining the extent to which the jurisdiction of any federal court shall be exclusive of that which belongs to or is invested in the courts of the States:

    (iii.) Investing any court of a State with federal jurisdiction.

78. The Parliament may make laws conferring rights to proceed against the Commonwealth or a State in respect of matters within the limits of the judicial power.

79. The federal jurisdiction of any court may be exercised by such number of judges as the Parliament prescribes.

80. The trial on indictment of any offence against any law of the Commonwealth shall be by jury, and every such trial shall be held in the State where the offence was committed, and if the offence was not committed within any State the trial shall be held at such place or places as the Parliament prescribes.

CHAPTER IV.

Finance and Trade.

81. All revenues or moneys raised or received by the Executive Government of the Commonwealth shall form one Consolidated Revenue Fund, to be appropriated for the purposes of the Commonwealth in the manner and subject to the charges and liabilities imposed by this Constitution.

82. The costs, charges, and expenses incident to the collection, management, and receipt of the Consolidated Revenue Fund shall form the first charge thereon; and the revenue of the Commonwealth shall in the first instance be applied to the payment of the expenditure of the Commonwealth.

83. No money shall be drawn from the Treasury of the Commonwealth except under appropriation made by law.

But until the expiration of one month after the first meeting of the Parliament the Governor-General in Council may draw from the Treasury and expend such moneys as may be necessary for the maintenance of any department transferred to the Commonwealth and for the holding of the first elections for the Parliament.

84. When any department of the public service of a State becomes transferred to the Commonwealth, all officers of the department shall become subject to the control of the Executive Government of the Commonwealth.

Any such officer who is not retained in the service of the Commonwealth shall, unless he is appointed to some other office of equal emolument in the public service of the State, be entitled to receive from the State any pension, gratuity, or other compensation, payable under the law of the State on the abolition of his office.

Any such officer who is retained in the service of the Commonwealth shall preserve all his existing and accruing rights, and shall be entitled to retire from office at the time, and on the pension or retiring allowance, which would be permitted by the law of the State if his service with the Commonwealth were a continuation of his service with the State. Such pension or retiring allowance shall be paid to him by the Commonwealth; but the State shall pay to the Commonwealth a part thereof, to be calculated on the proportion which his term of service with the State bears to his whole term of service, and for the purpose of the calculation his salary shall be taken to be that paid to him by the State at the time of the transfer.

Any officer who is, at the establishment of the Commonwealth, in the public service of a State, and who is, by consent of the Governor of the State with the advice of the Executive Council thereof, transferred to the public service of the Commonwealth, shall have the same rights as if he had been an officer of a department transferred to the Commonwealth and were retained in the service of the Commonwealth.

85. When any department of the public service of a State is transferred to the Commonwealth—

    (i.) All property of the State of any kind, used exclusively in connexion with the department, shall become vested in the Commonwealth; but, in the case of the departments controlling customs and excise and bounties, for such time only as the Governor-General in Council may declare to be necessary:

    (ii.) The Commonwealth may acquire any property of the State, of any kind used, but not exclusively used in connexion with the department; the value thereof shall, if no agreement can be made, be ascertained in, as nearly as may be, the manner in which the value of land, or of an interest in land, taken by the State for public purposes is ascertained under the law of the State in force at the establishment of the Commonwealth:

    (iii.) The Commonwealth shall compensate the State for the value of any property passing to the Commonwealth under this section; if no agreement can be made as to the mode of compensation, it shall be determined under laws to be made by the Parliament:

    (iv.) The Commonwealth shall, at the date of the transfer, assume the current obligations of the State in respect of the department transferred.

86. On the establishment of the Commonwealth, the collection and control of duties of customs and of excise, and the control of the payment of bounties, shall pass to the executive Government of the Commonwealth.

87. During a period of ten years after the establishment of the Commonwealth and thereafter until the Parliament otherwise provides, of the net revenue of the Commonwealth from duties of customs and of excise not more than one-fourth shall be applied annually by the Commonwealth towards its expenditure.

The balance shall, in accordance with this Constitution, be paid to the several States, or applied towards the payment of interest on debts of the several States taken over by the Commonwealth.

88. Uniform duties of customs shall be imposed within two years after the establishment of the Commonwealth.

89. Until the imposition of uniform duties of customs—

    (i.) The Commonwealth shall credit to each State the revenues collected therein by the Commonwealth.

    (ii.) The Commonwealth shall debit to each State—

        (*a*) The expenditure therein of the Commonwealth incurred solely for the maintenance or continuance, as at the time of transfer, of any department transferred from the State to the Commonwealth;

        (*b*) The proportion of the State, according to the number of its people, in the other expenditure of the Commonwealth.

    (iii.) The Commonwealth shall pay to each State month by month the balance (if any) in favour of the State.

90. On the imposition of uniform duties of customs the power of the Parliament to impose duties of customs and of excise, and to grant bounties on the production or export of goods, shall become exclusive.

On the imposition of uniform duties of customs all laws of the several States imposing duties of customs or of excise, or offering bounties on the production or export of goods, shall cease to have effect, but any grant of or agreement for any such bounty lawfully made by or under the authority of the Government of any State shall be taken to be good if made before the thirtieth day of June, one thousand eight hundred and ninety-eight, and not otherwise.

91. Nothing in this Constitution prohibits a State from granting any aid to or bounty on mining for gold, silver, or other metals, nor from granting, with the consent of both Houses of the Parliament of the Commonwealth expressed by resolution, any aid to or bounty on the production or export of goods.

92. On the imposition of uniform duties of customs, trade, commerce, and intercourse among the States, whether by means of internal carriage or ocean navigation, shall be absolutely free.

But notwithstanding anything in this Constitution, goods imported before the imposition of uniform duties of customs into any State, or into any Colony which, whilst the goods remain therein, becomes a State, shall, on thence passing into another State within two years after the imposition of such duties, be liable to any duty chargeable on the importation of such goods into the Commonwealth, less any duty paid in respect of the goods on their importation.

93. During the first five years after the imposition of uniform duties of customs, and thereafter until the Parliament otherwise provides—

> (i.) The duties of customs chargeable on goods imported into a State and afterwards passing into another State for consumption, and the duties of excise paid on goods produced or manufactured in a State and afterwards passing into another State for consumption, shall be taken to have been collected not in the former but in the latter State:
>
> (ii.) Subject to the last subsection, the Commonwealth shall credit revenue, debit expenditure, and pay balances to the several States as prescribed for the period preceding the imposition of uniform duties of customs.

94. After five years from the imposition of uniform duties of customs, the Parliament may provide, on such basis as it deems fair, for the monthly payment to the several States of all surplus revenue of the Commonwealth.

95. Notwithstanding anything in this Constitution, the Parliament of the State of Western Australia, if that State be an Original State, may, during the first five years after the imposition of uniform duties of customs, impose duties of customs on goods passing into that State and not originally imported from beyond the limits of the Commonwealth; and such duties shall be collected by the Commonwealth.

But any duty so imposed on any goods shall not exceed during the first of such years the duty chargeable on the goods under the law of Western Australia in force at the imposition of uniform duties, and shall not exceed during the second, third, fourth, and fifth of such years respectively, four-fifths, three-fifths, two-fifths, and one-fifth of such latter duty, and all duties imposed under this section shall cease at the expiration of the fifth year after the imposition of uniform duties.

If at any time during the five years the duty on any goods under this section is higher than the duty imposed by the Commonwealth on the importation of the like goods, then such higher duty shall be collected on the goods when imported into Western Australia from beyond the limits of the Commonwealth.

96. During a period of ten years after the establishment of the Commonwealth and thereafter until the Parliament otherwise provides, the Parliament may grant financial assistance to any State on such terms and conditions as the Parliament thinks fit.

97. Until the Parliament otherwise provides, the laws in force in any Colony which has become or becomes a State with respect to the receipt of revenue and the expenditure of money on account of the Government of the Colony, and the review and audit of such receipt and expenditure, shall apply to the receipt of revenue and the expenditure of money on account of the Commonwealth in the State in the same manner as if the Commonwealth, or the Government or an officer of the Commonwealth, were mentioned whenever the Colony, or the Government or an officer of the Colony, is mentioned.

98. The power of the Parliament to make laws with respect to trade and commerce extends to navigation and shipping, and to railways the property of any State.

99. The Commonwealth shall not, by any law or regulation of trade, commerce, or revenue, give preference to one State or any part thereof over another State or any part thereof.

100. The Commonwealth shall not, by any law or regulation of trade or commerce, abridge the right of a State or of the residents therein to the reasonable use of the waters of rivers for conservation or irrigation.

101. There shall be an Inter-State Commission, with such powers of adjudication and administration as the Parliament deems necessary for the execution and maintenance, within the Commonwealth, of the provisions of this Constitution relating to trade and commerce, and of all laws made thereunder.

102. The Parliament may by any law with respect to trade or commerce forbid, as to railways, any preference or discrimination by any State, or by any authority constituted under a State, if such preference or discrimination is undue and unreasonable, or unjust to any State; due regard being had to the financial responsibilities incurred by any State in connexion with the construction and maintenance of its railways. But no preference or discrimination shall, within the meaning of this section, be taken to be undue and unreasonable, or unjust to any State, unless so adjudged by the Inter-State Commission.

103. The members of the Inter-State Commission—
> (i.) Shall be appointed by the Governor-General in Council:
> (ii.) Shall hold office for seven years, but may be removed within that time by the Governor-General in Council, on an address from both Houses of the Parliament in the same session praying for such removal on the ground of proved misbehaviour or incapacity:
> (iii.) Shall receive such remuneration as the Parliament may fix; but such remuneration shall not be diminished during their continuance in office.

104. Nothing in this Constitution shall render unlawful any rate for the carriage of goods upon a railway, the property of a State, if the rate is deemed by the Inter-State Commission to be necessary for the development of the territory of the State, and if the rate applies equally to goods within the State and to goods passing into the State from other States.

105. The Parliament may take over from the States their public debts ~~as existing at the establishment of the Commonwealth,~~ or a proportion thereof according to the respective numbers of their people as shown by the latest statistics of the Commonwealth, and may convert, renew, or consolidate such debts, or any part thereof; and the States shall indemnify the Commonwealth in respect of the debts taken over, and thereafter the interest payable in respect of the debts shall be deducted and retained from the portions of the surplus revenue of the Commonwealth payable to the several States, or if such surplus is insufficient, or if there is no surplus, then the deficiency or the whole amount shall be paid by the several States.

105A.—(1.) The Commonwealth may make agreements with the States with respect to the public debts of the States, including—
> (*a*) the taking over of such debts by the Commonwealth;
> (*b*) the management of such debts;
> (*c*) the payment of interest and the provision and management of sinking funds in respect of such debts;
> (*d*) the consolidation, renewal, conversion, and redemption of such debts;
> (*e*) the indemnification of the Commonwealth by the States in respect of debts taken over by the Commonwealth; and
> (*f*) the borrowing of money by the States or by the Commonwealth, or by the Commonwealth for the States.

(2.) The Parliament may make laws for validating any such agreement made before the commencement of this section.

(3.) The Parliament may make laws for the carrying out by the parties thereto of any such agreement.

(4.) Any such agreement may be varied or rescinded by the parties thereto.

(5.) Every such agreement and any such variation thereof shall be binding upon the Commonwealth and the States parties thereto notwithstanding anything contained in this Constitution or the Constitution of the several States or in any law of the Parliament of the Commonwealth or of any State.

(6.) The powers conferred by this section shall not be construed as being limited in any way by the provisions of section one hundred and five of this Constitution.

———

CHAPTER V.

THE STATES.

106. The Constitution of each State of the Commonwealth shall, subject to this Constitution, continue as at the establishment of the Commonwealth, or as at the admission or establishment of the State, as the case may be, until altered in accordance with the Constitution of the State.

107. Every power of the Parliament of a Colony which has become or becomes a State, shall, unless it is by this Constitution exclusively vested in the Parliament of the Commonwealth or withdrawn from the Parliament of the State, continue as at the establishment of the Commonwealth, or as at the admission or establishment of the State, as the case may be.

108. Every law in force in a Colony which has become or becomes a State, and relating to any matter within the powers of the Parliament of the Commonwealth, shall, subject to this Constitution, continue in force in the State; and, until provision is made in that behalf by the Parliament of the Commonwealth, the Parliament of the State shall have such powers of alteration and of repeal in respect of any such law as the Parliament of the Colony had until the Colony became a State.

109. When a law of a State is inconsistent with a law of the Commonwealth, the latter shall prevail, and the former shall, to the extent of the inconsistency, be invalid.

110. The provisions of this Constitution relating to the Governor of a State extend and apply to the Governor for the time being of the State, or other chief executive officer or administrator of the government of the State.

111. The Parliament of a State may surrender any part of the State to the Commonwealth; and upon such surrender, and the acceptance thereof by the Commonwealth, such part of the State shall become subject to the exclusive jurisdiction of the Commonwealth.

112. After uniform duties of customs have been imposed, a State may levy on imports or exports, or on goods passing into or out of the State, such charges as may be necessary for executing the inspection laws of the State; but the net produce of all charges so levied shall be for the use of the Commonwealth; and any such inspection laws may be annulled by the Parliament of the Commonwealth.

113. All fermented, distilled, or other intoxicating liquids passing into any State or remaining therein for use, consumption, sale, or storage, shall be subject to the laws of the State as if such liquids had been produced in the State.

114. A State shall not, without the consent of the Parliament of the Commonwealth, raise or maintain any naval or military force, or impose any tax on property of any kind belonging to the Commonwealth, nor shall the Commonwealth impose any tax on property of any kind belonging to a State.

115. A State shall not coin money, nor make anything but gold and silver coin a legal tender in payment of debts.

116. The Commonwealth shall not make any law for establishing any religion, or for imposing any religious observance, or for prohibiting the free exercise of any religion, and no religious test shall be required as a qualification for any office or public trust under the Commonwealth.

117. A subject of the Queen, resident in any State, shall not be subject in any other State to any disability or discrimination which would not be equally applicable to him if he were a subject of the Queen resident in such other State.

118. Full faith and credit shall be given, throughout the Commonwealth to the laws, the public Acts and records, and the judicial proceedings of every State.

119. The Commonwealth shall protect every State against invasion and, on the application of the Executive Government of the State, against domestic violence.

120. Every State shall make provision for the detention in its prisons of persons accused or convicted of offences against the laws of the Commonwealth, and for the punishment of persons convicted of such offences, and the Parliament of the Commonwealth may make laws to give effect to this provision.

CHAPTER VI.

NEW STATES.

121. The Parliament may admit to the Commonwealth or establish new States, and may upon such admission or establishment make or impose such terms and conditions, including the extent of representation in either House of the Parliament, as it thinks fit.

122. The Parliament may make laws for the government of any territory surrendered by any State to and accepted by the Commonwealth, or of any territory placed by the Queen under the authority of and accepted by the Commonwealth, or otherwise acquired by the Commonwealth, and may allow the representation of such territory in either House of the Parliament to the extent and on the terms which it thinks fit.

123. The Parliament of the Commonwealth may, with the consent of the Parliament of a State, and the approval of the majority of the electors of the State voting upon the question, increase, diminish, or otherwise alter the limits of the State, upon such terms and conditions as may be agreed on, and may, with the like consent, make provision respecting the effect and operation of any increase or diminution or alteration of territory in relation to any State affected.

124. A new State may be formed by separation of territory from a State, but only with the consent of the Parliament thereof, and a new State may be formed by the union of two or more States or parts of States, but only with the consent of the Parliaments of the States affected.

CHAPTER VII.

MISCELLANEOUS.

125. The seat of Government of the Commonwealth shall be determined by the Parliament, and shall be within territory which shall have been granted to or acquired by the Commonwealth, and shall be vested in and belong to the Commonwealth, and shall be in the State of New South Wales, and be distant not less than one hundred miles from Sydney.

Such territory shall contain an area of not less than one hundred square miles, and such portion thereof as shall consist of Crown lands shall be granted to the Commonwealth without any payment therefor.

The Parliament shall sit at Melbourne until it meet at the seat of Government.

126. The Queen may authorise the Governor-General to appoint any person, or any persons jointly or severally, to be his deputy or deputies within any part of the Commonwealth, and in that capacity to exercise during the pleasure of the Governor-General such powers and functions of the Governor-General as he thinks fit to assign to such deputy or deputies, subject to any limitations expressed or directions given by the Queen; but the appointment of such deputy or deputies shall not affect the exercise by the Governor-General himself of any power or function.

~~**127.** In reckoning the numbers of the people of the Commonwealth, or of a State or other part of the Commonwealth, aboriginal natives shall not be counted.~~

CHAPTER VIII.

ALTERATION OF THE CONSTITUTION.

128. This Constitution shall not be altered except in the following manner:—

The proposed law for the alteration thereof must be passed by an absolute majority of each House of the Parliament, and not less than two nor more than six months after its passage through both Houses the proposed law shall be submitted in each State to the electors qualified to vote for the election of members of the House of Representatives.

But if either House passes any such proposed law by an absolute majority, and the other House rejects or fails to pass it, or passes it with any amendment to which the first-mentioned House will not agree, and if after an interval of three months the first-mentioned House in the same or the next session again passes the proposed law by an absolute majority with or without any amendment which has been made or agreed to by the other House, and such other House rejects or fails to pass it or passes it with any amendment to which the first-mentioned House will not agree, the Governor-General may submit the proposed law as last proposed by the first-mentioned House, and either with or without any amendments subsequently agreed to by both Houses, to the electors in each State qualified to vote for the election of the House of Representatives.

When a proposed law is submitted to the electors the vote shall be taken in such manner as the

Parliament prescribes. But until the qualification of electors of members of the House of Representatives becomes uniform throughout the Commonwealth, only one-half the electors voting for and against the proposed law shall be counted in any State in which adult suffrage prevails.

And if in a majority of the States a majority of the electors voting approve the proposed law, and if a majority of all the electors voting also approve the proposed law, it shall be presented to the Governor-General for the Queen's assent.

No alteration diminishing the proportionate representation of any State in either House of the Parliament, or the minimum number of representatives of a State in the House of Representatives, or increasing, diminishing, or otherwise altering the limits of the State, or in any manner affecting the provisions of the Constitution in relation thereto, shall become law unless the majority of the electors voting in that State approve the proposed law.

SCHEDULE.

OATH.

I, *A.B.*, do swear that I will be faithful and bear true allegiance to Her Majesty Queen Victoria, Her heirs and successors according to law. SO HELP ME GOD!

AFFIRMATION.

I, *A.B.*, do solemnly and sincerely affirm and declare that I will be faithful and bear true allegiance to Her Majesty Queen Victoria, Her heirs and successors according to law.

(NOTE.— *The name of the King or Queen of the United Kingdom of Great Britain and Ireland for the time being is to be substituted from time to time.*)

Appendix B
Chronology of Constitutionally
Significant Events 1972-1975

1972

Dec. 2   Labor wins General Election.
          House of Representatives: A.L.P. 67, L.-C.P. 58.
          Senate: A.L.P. 26, L.-C.P. 26, D.L.P. 5, Ind. 3.

     5   Whitlam-Barnard 'Duumvirate' Ministry sworn in.

    19   First full Whitlam Ministry sworn in: major reorganization of depart-
          ments of state.

1973

Feb. 17   *Black Mountain Tower Case* decided.

June 1   *Prices Justification Act* assented to.

    18   *Grants Commission Act* assented to.

Sept. 3-7 Australian Constitutional Convention, First Session, Sydney.

    10   *Rhodesia Information Centre Case* decided.

Nov. 21   Human Rights Bill introduced.

Dec. 4   *Seas and Submerged Lands Act* assented to.

     8   Prices and Incomes referendums defeated.

    12   House of Representatives first passes P.M.A. Bill.

    13   P.M.A. Bill introduced into Senate: consideration adjourned until next
          sitting.
          Senate adjourned until February.

1974

Feb. 8   Mr Justice Jacobs appointed to High Court.

    14   Parliament prorogued.

    28   Parliament re-opened by Queen.

Mar. 14   Governor-General approves, on recommendation of Prime Minister,
          appointment of Senator Vincent Gair as Ambassador to Ireland.

    21   Executive Council approves Gair appointment.

Apr. 2   Queensland Governor issues writs for half-Senate election in
          Queensland.
          P.M.A. Bill defeated in Senate.

     4   Mr Snedden announces intention to oppose Supply Bills.

     8   Senate resolves that Gair still a senator as at 3 April.
          P.M.A Bill passed for second time by House of Representatives.

    10   Senate defers P.M.A. Bill for six months.
          Opposition moves to defer Supply Bills in Senate.
          Governor-General accepts Prime Minister's advice to dissolve both
          Houses (based upon blockage of six Bills, including the P.M.A. Bill).

    11   Double dissolution proclaimed.

May 18   Labor Government re-elected.
          House of Representatives: A.L.P. 66, L.-C.P. 61.
          Senate: A.L.P. 29, L.-C.P. 29, Ind. (Hall, Townley) 2.

          Four referendum proposals defeated: Simultaneous Elections, Mode of
          Altering Constitution, Democratic Elections and Local Government.

June 12   Reconstituted Ministry sworn in.

1974

July 11   Sir John Kerr succeeds Sir Paul Hasluck as Governor-General.

     30   Proclamation of Governor-General convening Joint Sitting.

Aug. 5   *Cormack* v. *Cope* decided.

     6-7   Joint Sitting of Parliament (Passage of *Commonwealth Electoral Act (No. 2) 1973, Senate (Representation of Territories) Act 1973, Representation Act 1973, Health Insurance Commission Act 1973, Health Insurance Act 1973*, and *P.M.A. Act 1973*).

     7   *Financial Corporations Act* assented to.

     24   *Trade Practices Act* assented to.

Oct. 3   National Compensation Bill introduced.

Dec. 17   *Albury-Wodonga Development Act* assented to.

     5   Corporations and Securities Industry Bill introduced.

     13   Executive Council approves US$4,000 million overseas borrowing.

     17   *Environment Protection (Impact of Proposals) Act* assented to.

1975

Jan. 28   Overseas borrowing authority reduced to US$2,000 million.

Feb. 3-7   A.L.P. National Conference, Terrigal, N.S.W.

     9   Mr Justice Murphy appointed to High Court.

     10   N.S.W. Premier Lewis announces that Murphy will be replaced by a non-Labor senator.

     13   Senate passes motion affirming principle of replacement of casual vacancies from the same party.

     27   N.S.W. Parliament appoints Cleaver Bunton to fill Murphy casual vacancy.
Resignation of Speaker Cope.

     28   Sir John Kerr addresses Indian Law Institute in New Delhi on Governor-General's role.

Mar. 4   Senator Bunton sworn in.

     21   Malcolm Fraser replaces Mr Snedden as Leader of the Opposition. Mr Fraser acknowledges limits, subject to 'extraordinary' and 'reprehensible' circumstances, on Senate's right to block supply.

Apr. 22   Senate refers Senator Webster's qualifications to Court of Disputed Returns.
Common Informers (Parliamentary Disqualifications) Act passes all stages in both Houses.

     30   *Privy Council (Appeals from the High Court) Act* assented to.

May 6   Treasury seeks advice from Attorney-General's Department, without Treasurer's consent, as to legality of loan authority letter written by Treasurer.

     20   US$2,000 million overseas borrowing authority revoked.

June 11   *Racial Discrimination Act* assented to.

     12   *Family Law Act* assented to.

     24   *P.M.A. Case* decided.
Senator Webster Case decided.

     30   Death of Senator Milliner.

July 2   Dismissal from Ministry of Dr Cairns, for misleading Parliament re loans negotiations.

     15-16   Solicitor-General and Senior Departmental officers called before Bar of Senate to answer questions on overseas loan negotiations: privilege claimed.

     22   Mr G. Karidis called before Bar of Senate re overseas loan negotiations.

1975

Aug. 19   Treasurer, Mr Hayden, introduces Budget Appropriation Bills.

28   *Administrative Appeals Tribunal Act* assented to.

Sept. 3   Queensland Parliament appoints Albert Patrick Field to fill Milliner casual vacancy.

9   Senator Field sworn in.
Senate composition now: A.L.P. 27, L.-C.P. (incl. Townley) 30, Ind. (Hall, Bunton, Field) 3.

24-26   Australian Constitutional Convention, Second Session, Melbourne.

Oct. 1   Senator Field granted leave of absence from Senate to defend court challenge to his qualifications.

10   *Territory Senators Case* decided.
Queen of Queensland Case decided.

13   Federal Council of Liberal Party calls on Party to do 'all in their power' to prevent the Whitlam Government 'gaining control' of the Senate.

14   Resignation of Minister for Minerals and Energy, Mr Connor, on grounds of misleading Parliament re loans negotiations.

15   Mr Fraser announces that Appropriation Bills will be blocked in Senate until Government agrees to election.

16   Senate defers Appropriation Bills. Mr Whitlam states that Government will not resign.

17   *A.A.P. Case* decided.

26   Queensland Governor, Sir Colin Hannah, on advice of Prime Minister, stripped of right to act as stand-in Governor-General.

27   *Inter-State Commission Act* assented to.

Nov. 6   Solicitor-General's opinion as to Governor-General's role tendered to Sir John Kerr by Attorney-General, Mr Enderby.

10   Chief Justice Sir Garfield Barwick advises Governor-General as to his 'constitutional rights and duties'.

11   9.15   Mr Whitlam and Mr Fraser meet and fail to reach agreement.

10.00   Mr Whitlam informally notifies Governor-General that he will advise half-Senate election.

10.10   Mr Whitlam tells Labor Caucus he will advise half-Senate election.

1.10   Mr Whitlam calls upon Governor-General to advise half-Senate election, and is dismissed from office.

1.30   Governor-General appoints Mr Fraser 'caretaker' Prime Minister.

2.20   Senate passes Appropriation Bills.

2.35   Mr Fraser announces in House of Representatives that he has been commissioned as Prime Minister.

3.15   House of Representatives votes no confidence in Fraser Government.
Speaker seeks audience with Governor-General to advise of no confidence resolution: appointment made for 4.45.

4.45   Double dissolution proclaimed (in reliance on twenty-one Senate-blocked Bills, including seven Electoral Bills, Privy Council Appeals Abolition Bill, and Superior Court of Australia Bill).

Dec. 1   *McKinlay's Case* decided.

13   Liberal and Country Parties win Election.
House of Representatives: L.-C.P. 91, A.L.P. 36.
Senate: L.-C.P. (incl. Hall) 36, A.L.P. 26, Ind. (Harradine) 1.

17   *Offshore Sovereignty Case* decided.

Appendix C

Letter and Statement by the Governor-General 11 November 1975

Government House,
Canberra. 2600.
11 November 1975

Dear Mr Whitlam,

In accordance with section 64 of the Constitution I hereby determine your appointment as my Chief Adviser and Head of the Government. It follows that I also hereby determine the appointments of all of the Ministers in your Government.

You have previously told me that you would never resign or advise an election of the House of Representatives or a double dissolution and that the only way in which such an election could be obtained would be by my dismissal of you and your ministerial colleagues. As it appeared likely that you would today persist in this attitude I decided that, if you did, I would determine your commission and state my reasons for doing so. You have persisted in your attitude and I have accordingly acted as indicated. I attach a statement of my reasons which I intend to publish immediately.

It is with a great deal of regret that I have taken this step both in respect of yourself and your colleagues.

I propose to send for the Leader of the Opposition and to commission him to form a new caretaker Government until an election can be held.

Yours sincerely,

(signed) John R. Kerr

STATEMENT BY THE GOVERNOR-GENERAL

I have given careful consideration to the constitutional crisis and have made some decisions which I wish to explain.

Summary

It has been necessary for me to find a democratic and constitutional solution to the current crisis which will permit the people of Australia to decide as soon as possible what should be the outcome of the deadlock which developed over supply between the two Houses of Parliament and between the Government and the Opposition parties. The only solution consistent with the Constitution and with my oath of office and my responsibilities, authority and duty as Governor-General is to terminate the commission as Prime Minister of Mr Whitlam and to arrange for a caretaker government able to secure supply and willing to let the issue go to the people.

I shall summarise the elements of the problem and the reasons for my decision which places the matter before the people of Australia for prompt determination.

Because of the federal nature of our Constitution and because of its provisions the Senate undoubtedly has constitutional power to refuse or defer supply to the Government. Because of the principles of responsible government a Prime Minister who cannot obtain supply, including money for carrying on the ordinary services of government, must either advise a general election or resign. If he refuses to do this I have the authority and indeed the duty under the Constitution to withdraw his Commission as Prime Minister. The position in Australia is quite different from the position in the United Kingdom. Here the confidence of both Houses on supply is necessary to ensure its provision. In the United Kingdom the confidence of the House of Commons alone is necessary. But both here and in the United Kingdom the duty of the Prime Minister is the same in a most important respect—if he cannot get supply he must resign or advise an election.

If a Prime Minister refuses to resign or to advise an election, and this is the case with Mr Whitlam, my constitutional authority and duty require me to do what I have now done—to withdraw his commission—and to invite the Leader of the Opposition to form a caretaker government—that is one that makes no appointments or dismissals and initiates no policies, until a general election is held. It is most desirable that he should guarantee supply. Mr Fraser will be asked to give the necessary undertakings and advise whether he is prepared to recommend a double dissolution. He will also be asked to guarantee supply.

The decisions I have made were made after I was satisfied that Mr Whitlam could not obtain supply. No other decision open to me would enable the Australian people to decide for themselves what should be done.

Once I had made up my mind, for my own part, what I must do if Mr Whitlam persisted in his stated intentions I consulted the Chief Justice of Australia, Sir Garfield Barwick. I have his permission to say that I consulted him in this way.

The result is that there will be an early general election for both Houses and the people can do what, in a democracy such as ours, is their responsibility and duty and theirs alone. It is for the people now to decide the issue which the two leaders have failed to settle.

Detailed Statement of Decisions

On 16 October the Senate deferred consideration of Appropriation Bills (Nos. 1 and 2) 1975-1976. In the time which elapsed since then events made it clear that the Senate was determined to refuse to grant supply to the Government. In that time the Senate on no less than two occasions resolved to proceed no further with fresh Appropriation Bills, in identical terms, which had been passed by the House of Representatives. The determination of the Senate to maintain its refusal to grant supply was confirmed by the public statements made by the Leader of the Opposition, the Opposition having control of the Senate.

By virtue of what has in fact happened there therefore came into existence a deadlock between the House of Representatives and the Senate on the central issue of supply without which all the ordinary services of the government cannot be maintained. I had the benefit of discussions with the Prime Minister and, with his approval, with the Leader of the Opposition and with the Treasurer and the Attorney-General. As a result of those discussions and having regard to the public statements of the Prime Minister and the Leader of the Opposition I have come regretfully to the conclusion that there is no likelihood of a compromise between the House of Representatives and the Senate nor for that matter between the Government and the Opposition.

The deadlock which arose was one which, in the interests of the nation, had to be resolved as promptly as possible and by means which are appropriate in our democratic system. In all the circumstances which have occurred the appropriate means is a dissolution of the Parliament and an election for both Houses. No other course offers a sufficient assurance of resolving the deadlock and resolving it promptly.

Parliamentary control of appropriation and accordingly of expenditure is a fundamental feature of our system of responsible government. In consequence it has been generally accepted that a government which has been denied supply by the Parliament cannot govern. So much at least is clear in cases where a ministry is refused supply by a popularly elected Lower House. In other systems where an Upper House is denied the right to reject a money bill denial of supply can occur only at the instance of the Lower House. When, however, an Upper House possesses the power to reject a money bill including an appropriation bill, and exercises the power by denying supply, the principle that a government which has been denied supply by the Parliament should resign or go to an election must still apply—it is a necessary consequence of Parliamentary control of appropriation and expenditure and of the expectation that the ordinary and necessary services of government will continue to be provided.

The Constitution combines the two elements of responsible government and federalism. The Senate is, like the House, a popularly elected chamber. It was designed to provide representation by States, not by electorates, and was given by Sec. 53, equal powers with the House with respect to proposed laws, except in the respects mentioned in the section. It was denied power to originate or amend appropriation bills but was left with power to reject them or defer consideration of them. The Senate accordingly has the power and has exercised the power to refuse to grant supply to the Government. The Government stands in the position that it has been denied supply by the Parliament with all the consequences which flow from that fact.

There have been public discussions about whether there is a convention deriving from the principles of responsible government that the Senate must never under any circumstances exercise the power to reject an appropriation bill. The Constitution must prevail over any convention because, in determining the question how far the conventions of responsible government have been grafted on to the federal compact, the Constitution itself must in the end control the situation.

Sec. 57 of the Constitution provides a means, perhaps the usual means, of resolving a disagreement between the Houses with respect to a proposed law. But the machinery which it provides necessarily entails a considerable time lag which is quite inappropriate to a speedy resolution of the fundamental problems posed by the refusal of supply. Its presence in the Constitution does not cut down the reserve powers of the Governor-General.

I should be surprised if the Law Officers expressed the view that there is no reserve power in the Governor-General to dismiss a Ministry which has been refused supply by the Parliament and to commission a Ministry, as a caretaker ministry which will secure supply and recommend a dissolution, including where appropriate a double dissolution. This is a matter on which my own mind is quite clear and I am acting in accordance with my own clear view of the principles laid down by the Constitution and of the nature, powers and responsibility of my office.

There is one other point. There has been discussion of the possibility that a half-Senate election might be held under circumstances in which the Government had not obtained supply. If such advice were given to me I should feel constrained to reject it because a half-Senate election held whilst supply continues to be denied does not guarantee a prompt or sufficiently clear prospect of the deadlock being resolved in accordance with proper principles. When I refer to rejection of such advice I mean that, as I would find it necessary in the circumstances I have envisaged to determine Mr Whitlam's commission and, as things have turned out have done so, he would not be Prime Minister and not able to give or persist with such advice.

The announced proposals about financing public servants, suppliers, contractors and others do not amount to a satisfactory alternative to supply.

Government House,
Canberra. 2600.
11 November 1975

Table of Cases

ABBREVIATIONS

A

B

Table of Legislation

COMMONWEALTH OF AUSTRALIA
CONSTITUTION ACT 1900

NEW SOUTH WALES

VICTORIA

QUEENSLAND

UNITED KINGDOM

Index

Abbott, P.P., 86
Aboriginal Land (Northern Territory) Bill, 46
Aboriginal Legal Aid Services, 46
Aboriginals
  judicial appointments of, 116
  land rights and enterprises, 314
  provisions in Racial Discrimination Act, 48
  referendum, 1967: 76-7
  social welfare programmes,
    constitutional basis of, 39
Academic lawyers, bleatings of, 214, 243-5 *passim*
Academic Salaries Tribunal, 130
Administration, relationship to policy and politics, 157, 161
Administrative Appeals Tribunal, 112, 140, 155-6
Administrative Arrangement Orders, 137, 138
Albury-Wodonga, 11-12, 62, 139
Ames, F., 205
Anson, W.R., 185, 277
Appropriation Bills
  1972-3: 138
  1973-4: 218, 265
  1975-6: 235, 238, 269-71, 325
Arbitration Commission
  appointments to, 117
  Government intervention before, 26
Area Improvement Program, 308
Aristotelian politics, and judicial bias, 120
Ashworth, T.R., 86
Asquith, H., 292, 294
Assistant Ministers
  constitutionality, 146-7
  desirability, 146-7, 160-1
Attlee, C., 294
Attorney-General, grant of fiat by, 206-7
'Australia', *cf.* 'Commonwealth', 72
Australia Council, 139
Australian Aluminium Production Commission, 52
Australian Assistance Plan (A.A.P.)
  and co-operative federalism, 9
  and direct grants to local government, 307-8
  and regional organization, 11-12, 98
  constitutional challenge to, 41-5, 308-9
  grants power preferred as basis, 73
  significance of litigation on, 74
Australian Atomic Energy Commission, 54, 55
Australian Broadcasting Commission, 142

Australian Constitutional Convention: *see* Constitutional Conventions
Australian Government Insurance Corporation, 35, 314
Australian Heritage Commission, 64, 142
Australian Housing Corporation, 35, 72, 139, 142
Australian Industry Development Corporation (A.I.D.C.), 11, 35, 54, 55, 142
Australian Labor Party
  federalism platform, 3-8, 14
  socialist objective
    and achievements in office, 8, 313-4
    and platform modernization, 4, 66
    Blackburn amendment, 10
    constitution as obstacle to, 17
    federalism as obstacle to, 14
    Whitlam attitude to, 10-11
Australian Law Journal, editorial views
  on casual vacancies convention, 213-4
  on conventions of the constitution, 184-5, 189
  on effect of invalid electoral provisions, 212
Australian Legal Aid Office (A.L.A.O.)
  constitutional challenge to, 41, 47, 314
  establishment of, 46, 308
  position of employee lawyers, 138
Australian Legal Convention
  Tenth, 132
  Thirteenth, 133
  Eighteenth, 230, 320
Australian National Line, 35
Australia Police Bill, 46, 131
Australian Security Intelligence Organization (A.S.I.O.), 8, 131, 140-1
Australian Wheat Board, 13

Bagehot, W., on reserve powers, 277
Bailey, Sir K., 142, 241-2, 288, 292-3
Baker, Sir R., 258, 264
Barton, Sir Edmund
  and self-appointment to High Court, 118
  as statesman, 294
  on federalism and responsible government, 298
  on money Bills, 256, 264, 289, 290
  on reserve powers of Governor-General, 275
  on State rights, 255
  on Swiss Constitution, 258
  See Table of Cases for other judgment references.

366